2002

Operating Systems

A Modern Perspective

Second Edition

Gary J. Nutt

University of Colorado

▲ ADDISON-WESLEY
An imprint of Addison Wesley Longman, Inc.

Reading, Massachusetts • Menlo Park, California
New York • Harlow, England
Don Mills, Ontario • Sydney • Mexico City
Madrid • Amsterdam

Acquisitions Editor: *Maite Suarez-Rivas*
Assistant Editor: *Jason Miranda*
Project Manager: *Trillium Project Management*
Production Assistant: *Tracy Treeful*
Composition: *Michael and Sigrid Wile*
Text Design: *Delgado Design, Inc.*
Cover Illustration: *Susan Cyr*
Cover Design: *Lynne Reed*
Copyeditor: *Stephanie Argeros-Magean*
Proofreader: *Trillium Project Management*

Access the latest information about Addison-Wesley titles from our World Wide Web site: www.awlonline.com

This book was typeset in Quark 3.3 on a Macintosh G3. The font families used were Times, ITC Officina, and Prestige Elite. It was printed on New Era Matte.

LIBRARY OF CONGRESS CATALOG CARD NUMBER 99-073717
ISBN 0-201-61251-8

To my wife and best friend, Mary, and my
grandson and best buddy, Scott

Preface

To the Student

Operating systems is an exciting software area because the design of an operating system (OS) exerts a major influence on the overall function and performance of the entire computer. When studying operating systems for the first time, I believe that it is important to understand the *principles* behind the designs of all operating systems, and also to see how those principles are put into *practice* in real operating systems. The goal of this book is to provide a complete discussion of OS principles, supplemented with code, algorithms, implementation issues, and lab exercises to provide you with an understanding of contemporary OS practice. I have attempted to differentiate the conceptual material from the applied material by discussing the principles in the main flow of the text, and placing much of the practice material in supplemental discussions and lab exercises.

The heart of the matter is the conceptual material. Many OS principles can be described in formal (mathematical) terms or in informal discussion. Informal descriptions are relatively easy to read, but formal descriptions are more precise. For example, an informal discussion of a dictionary might explain that it is "a list of terms with their definitions," whereas a formal description might indicate that a dictionary is "a mechanism, f, to map a term, x, to its definition, $f(x)$." The first explanation is intuitive, the second focuses on the

Features at a Glance

This book provides a comprehensive description of OS principles, supplemented with the following:

- *Analytic exercises* to stimulate thinking about OS principles.
- *In the Hangar* sections to show how the principles are applied in practice in the UNIX family and Windows NT operating systems.
- *Performance Tuning* sections to explain how system designers have exploited the basic principles to achieve higher performance than could otherwise be achieved.
- *Laboratory exercises* to allow students to gain hands-on experience with the details of how to use Linux/ UNIX. Each lab exercise begins with a problem statement, followed by a Background section, and an Attacking the Problem section. The Background section is a detailed discussion of information needed to gain comprehensive understanding of the problem and to create a design for the solution. The Attacking the Problem section provides specific guidance for solving the problem. In early lab exercises, the background and solution design discussions are more comprehensive than they are in later exercises. This allows students to get a significant amount of help in solving the early exercises but requires them to develop their design skills with each subsequent exercise.

logical intent of the dictionary. The first description suggests a list or table implementation, the second admits implementations ranging from tables, to lists, to associative memories, to databases, to network servers, and so on. The informal definition connotes word dictionaries, but the formal definition applies just as well to compiler symbol tables. My goal is to explain general OS principles so you will have a deep understanding of how an OS is designed. This goal is best supported using formal descriptions because they focus on the logical intent of the concept rather than on an example of how the concept is implemented. This has motivated me to describe OS concepts using informal or specific descriptions in the early chapters, but with increasing amounts of formal discussion as you progress through the book. In Chapter 7 you will see some formal discussion about scheduling coupled with the informal discussion, then more formal discussion about deadlock in Chapter 10, and even more in the discussion of virtual memory in Chapter 12. The formal discussion of concepts is always accompanied by informal discussion and examples.

Operating systems are designed around performance issues. However, detailed discussions of performance tend to obscure the concepts. In this case I decided to forgo extensive coverage of analysis and performance theory in favor of a generally informal explanation of performance issues. This will encourage you to develop your intuition on performance issues so that you can study them formally later. If the comments about performance fit naturally into the description of the concept, I have included them with the discussion of the concept. However, in those cases where the performance issues add a level of complication to understanding the principle, I have separated that discussion from the conceptual material by placing it in a distinct *Performance Tuning* section.

As I mentioned earlier, experimentation with real OS code provides you

---

PERFORMANCE TUNING

Predicting Wait Times for FCFS

I t is not difficult to predict analytically a process's wait time under FCFS scheduling. Suppose we know the service rate, μ. Let L be the length of the queue at the time process p arrives. We can then estimate the time that the new process, p, will have to wait before it begins to receive service:

$$W(p) = L(1/\mu) + 1/2(1/\mu).$$
$$= L/\mu + 1/(2\mu).$$

Here is the rationale for this expression: If each job in the queue uses an average of $1/\mu$ time units for service, $L(1/\mu)$ will be the amount of time for

all L of them to be processed. The average time for the process that is already using the CPU is half of its service time, or $1/2(1/\mu)$. According to the FCFS policy, only the load that is present when process p arrives is relevant, since any subsequent processes will be served after process p.

In the example, we could estimate $W(p_4)$, which is 1200 in the Gantt chart, by computing the average service time ($1/\lambda$ or τ) of the first four processes:

$$\tau = (350 + 125 + 475 + 250)/4$$
$$= 1200/4$$
$$= 300 \text{ time units.}$$

When p_4 arrives, $L = 3$; the estimated waiting time for p_4 is thus

$$W(p_4) = L/\mu + 1/(2\mu)$$
$$= 3(1/300) + 150$$
$$= 1050.$$

Notice that the estimate assumes half of a job has already executed. (We did not assume this in the Gantt chart.)

---

times will never be served. This total starvation of large processes may be a serious liability of the scheduling algorithm.

Again suppose the ready list contains the processes shown in Table 7.1. The arrival order is irrelevant here, provided all of the processes are already in the queue at the time it is analyzed. In this example, assume no other jobs (processes) arrive during the ser-

---

with an understanding of how OS concepts are implemented in real systems. I have also provided two other types of material to help you learn about current OS practice: In the Hangar examples and Laboratory Exercises.

- *In the Hangar* examples explain how concepts are used or implemented in UNIX, Linux, Windows NT, or other operating systems. Many of the In the Hangar sections are code examples. The intent of including code examples is to provide you with insight into how an OS can implement the theory. A few of these code examples are complete programs that have been compiled and executed. Most examples, however, are simply descriptions of algorithms or techniques using the C programming language. These abbreviated descriptions deliberately omit fine detail that would be necessary in an actual implementation but that do not contribute to the understanding of the algorithm. The context in which the code appears should make clear when the code is an actual implementation; otherwise it should always be assumed to be a description of an algorithm or technique. I have experimented with using pseudocode languages for these descriptions, but students and reviewers have consistently preferred the use of C. Be careful not to interpret the descriptions in C as complete implementations.

- The book also includes several *Laboratory Exercises*; each exercise poses a problem then provides you with comprehensive background information needed to solve the problem, and a section to help you plan your solution. These exercises will give you valuable practice with Linux systems (most of the exercises can be done using any version of UNIX). Because of the growing importance of Windows NT, your instructor may have chosen to take lab exercises from a companion book on Windows NT [Nutt, 1999a].

13.2 ■ LOW-LEVEL FILE IMPLEMENTATIONS   379

⟩ IN THE HANGAR

UNIX File Structure

The UNIX file structure uses a variant of the indexed allocation scheme. The storage device detail part of the inode contains pointers to 15 different storage blocks of 4KB each (see Figure 13.13). The first 12 blocks of the file are indexed directly from the first 12 of 15 pointers in the inode. The last three pointers are used for indirect pointers through *index blocks*. If the file manager is configured with 4KB blocks, the 12 direct pointers in the inode accommodate files up to 48KB. Experience indicates this is an efficient mechanism for addressing the blocks (see [Ousterhout et al. 1985]). If a file requires more than 12 blocks, the file system

LABORATORY EXERCISE: OBSERVING OS BEHAVIOR   147

**Laboratory Exercise:
Observing OS Behavior**

In this chapter you have learned that the OS is a program that uses various data structures. Like all programs in execution, you can determine the performance and other behavior of the OS by inspecting its state—the values stored in its data structures. The goal of this exercise is to study some aspects of the organization and behavior of a Linux system by observing values in kernel data structures.

Write a program to report the behavior of the Linux kernel. Your program should have three different options: The default version should print the following values on stdout:

- CPU type and model
- Kernel version
- Amount of time since the system was last booted

A second version of the program should print the same information as the first version plus:

- The amount of time the CPU has spent in user mode, system mode, and the amount of time the system was idle
- The number of disk requests made on the system
- The number of context switches the kernel has performed
- The time at which the system was last booted
- The number of processes that have been created since the system was booted

The last version of the program should print the same information as the second version, plus (be sure to look at the relevant man pages for /proc to get more context for the requested information):

- The amount of memory configured into this computer
- The amount of memory currently available
- A list of load averages (each averaged over the last minute). This information would allow another program to plot these values against time so that a user could see how the load average varied over some time interval. For this version of

The study of operating systems has traditionally been one of the most challenging and exciting software disciplines in computer science. I hope this book makes complex aspects of operating systems easy to understand and avoids making simple aspects boring. Good luck in your study of operating systems; I hope you enjoy it as much as I do!

Topic Order

The order of presentation is based on the response to the first edition of the book, my experience teaching OS, and the input from many other instructors. This organization thus reflects the combined knowledge and practice of many different teachers and I believe the result is logical, conducive to learning, and generally accepted by most OS instructors.

Each chapter begins with a transition from the previous chapter and a preview of what is covered in the current chapter. You can look at this material as well as the summary at the end of the chapter to get a quick idea of what a chapter is about.

Chapters 1 through 4 consist of important introductory material that provides a solid foundation for the study of operating systems. Teachers may decide to go over this material rather quickly, perhaps assigning it as outside reading material, especially if this was covered in prerequisite courses. However, understanding this material is critical before you dive into the further study of the meat of operating systems, starting in Chapter 5.

- Chapter 1 shows how operating systems fit into software technology. In earlier drafts, a historical perspective had been included; instructors tend to like a little history and context, but many students think it is boring, so I have dispensed with a separate discussion of history.

- Chapter 2 is unique among operating system books in that it considers how to use an operating system, particularly how to use multiple processes. This chapter was added because my experience with computer science juniors and seniors is that they may have written considerable single-threaded code but

Changes in the Second Edition

This edition is based on the constructive criticism I have received from people who used and/or reviewed the first edition. The goal in the previous edition was to separate the hands-on material from the principles; the comments I received indicated that instructors preferred better integration of simple examples. I have dropped the In the Cockpit examples that were used in the first edition, and greatly reduced the number of In the Hangar and Performance Tuning examples. Most of the material that appeared in the omitted examples has now been incorporated into the main text. Since the frequent examples in the first edition often made the mainline text difficult to follow, the book has been redesigned so that the remaining In the Hangar examples and Performance Tuning discussions are more easily distinguished from the main text.

Chapters 2 and 6 were reorganized and revised. The intent of Chapter 2 is for students to focus on *using* processes and resources, especially for concurrent applications. Chapter 6 is the cornerstone of the process management design discussion. The rewritten chapters now have better focus than they did in the first edition.

The most significant content change in the second edition is the addition of the laboratory exercises. A shortcoming of the first edition (and other conceptual OS textbooks) is the lack of material to support experimental lab exercises. This often forces students to purchase a second book to use with the laboratory component of the OS course. The second edition is a self-contained book including material for lectures on OS concepts and for recitations on OS practice.

are far less likely to have written or studied multithreaded software. This chapter offers an immediate opportunity to learn this new material.

- Chapter 3 describes the fundamental organization of operating systems, including implementation strategies.
- Chapter 4 finishes the preliminaries for studying operating systems—computer organization. For students who have already taken a computer organization class, the first half of Chapter 4 will be review. The second half describes interrupts, emphasizing the aspects that are critical to operating systems.

Chapter 5 describes device management, specifically general techniques, buffering, and device drivers. It is tempting to become completely immersed in Linux device drivers. However, in the main part of the chapter I have resisted this temptation to focus instead on a macrolevel view of the purpose and general organization of interrupt-driven I/O. Included are extensive discussions of device drivers, but these stop short of providing an actual Linux driver. The chapter examines devices before considering processes because devices provide an elementary case in which physical concurrency exists in the computer and the software must be carefully designed to control that concurrency. This provides a natural introduction to process management.

Chapters 6 through 10 are devoted to process management. They start from the basic tasks and organization of process and resource managers (Chapter 6) and move to scheduling (Chapter 7), synchronization (Chapters 8 and 9), and deadlock (Chapter 10).

Chapter 11 deals with traditional issues in memory management, while Chapter 12 covers the contemporary approach to memory managers using virtual memory. Because of the popularity of paging, most of the discussion is directed at this technology. However, with the current trends in memory technology, it would be a mistake to ignore segmentation. Thus part of this discussion deals with segmentation. Unfortunately, the best example of a robust segmentation system is still the (now obsolete) Multics system.

Chapter 13 describes file management. Less space is devoted to file management than is customary in operating systems books because it is not as difficult to understand as process management and memory management. The laboratory exercise provides a means for taking a closer look at the details of file management. This discussion is augmented in Chapter 16, which deals with remote files.

Chapter 14 provides a general discussion of protection mechanisms and security policies. It might be argued that this section belongs in the process management discussion, although much of the technology is just as closely related to files, memory, and other resources. It is much easier for someone to appreciate the need for protection and security after they have seen the process, memory, and file managers.

Chapters 15 through 17 introduce OS technology to support distributed computing. Distributed computing is a dominant aspect of modern operating systems and I feel strongly that coverage of this important issue belongs in all introductory texts on operating systems.

To the Instructor

Operating systems continues to be an essential computer science course, yet as I have taught it over many years, I became increasingly dissatisfied with the OS texts that were available. I sought a book that had more content on principles than the existing ones. At the same time, I felt that if my students were not exposed to extensive lab practices, the principles would be difficult to absorb. The first edition described OS principles at a level I felt was necessary, and now this edition adds material to explicitly support the practice component that is so important to understanding operating systems.

The main thread of this book concentrates on OS concepts, usually illustrated with brief examples. The In the Hangar and Performance Tuning sections are more extensive examples or explanations of concepts, usually providing a practical perspective on the conceptual material that they follow. If you want your students to get an applied perspective of the OS, you should explicitly assign these supplementary sections as reading. The new Laboratory Exercises are accompanied by the applied material a student needs to solve the problem in a Linux environment (most can be solved in any UNIX environment). The intent of including these exercises is to provide you with a single book that can be used to teach conceptual material as well as basic lab materials.

Many books begin with materials on process management. In my classes, I have found that it is necessary to provide background information of the type in Chapters 1 through 4. Specifically, my experience shows that it is really worth the time to lecture on the material in Chapter 2, since very few students have used `fork` and `exec` (or their analogs in non-UNIX systems) before they take an OS course. The Laboratory Exercise in Chapter 2 allows students to learn about basic concurrency concepts by writing a simple shell program.

I start the detailed discussion of operating systems with device management. At first, you may find this approach unusual, although it follows the traditional evolution of operating systems. A natural segue exists from the discussion of interrupts in Chapter 4 to the discussion of device management in Chapter 5. This approach provides a sound foundation for introducing independent threads of execution (in the hardware and the software), concurrency, and synchronization. After you have finished the device material, it is natural to generalize these ideas into process and resource management, scheduling, synchronization, and deadlock.

Memory management is also important and another topic instructors usually want to address as soon as possible. I choose to phase it in after process management and then move to file management. Then I finish the essential material with a discussion of protection and security, which is deferred until the student has had a chance to absorb the notions of process and various kinds of resources (generic resources, memory, and files).

Any contemporary OS must be built to operate in (or be evolved to) distributed systems. All current research on operating systems is deeply influenced by distributed operating systems. Chapters 15 through 17 introduce distributed operating systems after all the discussion of traditional topics has been covered. Because of the nature of commercial systems and networks, an instructor would be remiss to completely ignore these topics in an OS course. In a one-semester course, I spend two to three weeks on this material.

Finally, in spite of all logical intentions it is impossible to organize this material so that it meets every instructor's desires. The organization I use in my course is reflected in the book. However, there is no particular harm caused by shuffling the material to suit individual desires.

Today, there is a wealth of information on operating systems available on the Internet through ftp sites and on the World Wide Web. I would encourage you to point your students toward them. Because such sites change so frequently, I maintain a Web page at `http://www.cs.colorado.edu/~nutt/osamp.html` where I keep a current set of links to relevant operating systems information. If you have some material that should be shared with our readers, let me know (email me at `osamp@cs.colorado.edu`) and I will add it to the page. I also welcome your questions, comments, suggestions, and advice (and I will even try to accept your criticism in good humor :–)).

About the Laboratory Environment

There are only a handful of widely used commercial operating systems. While studying these systems is valuable, there are practical barriers to experimenting with any of them in the classroom. First, commercial operating systems are by definition very complex since they must offer full support to commercial applications. It is impractical to experiment with such complex software because it is sometimes difficult to see how specific issues are addressed within the software. Small changes to the code may have unpredictable effects on the behavior of the overall operating system. Second, the OS software sometimes has distinct proprietary value to the company that implemented it. As a consequence, the company may be reluctant to provide OS source code to anyone wishing to study and learn how the implementation was done.

I have experimented with two approaches to this problem in the classroom [Nutt, 1999b]:

- Base the course on an *external view* of real operating systems; this is essentially the approach in the ACM/IEEE 1991 curriculum recommendation.
- Base the course on an *internal view* of some "manageable" OS.

I have also discussed this problem with numerous OS instructors (including participants at a Birds of a Feather session at the Operating Systems Design and Implementation meeting in New Orleans in February 1999). There is general confusion about choosing the right laboratory component for the undergraduate OS course. However, at the OSDI session, those in attendance unanimously agreed that the external view of an OS should be used in the first OS course.

This book provides materials to study the external view of Linux. If you want to use Windows NT to teach the external view, the companion lab manual [Nutt, 1999a] provides more than enough exercises for a one-semester course. All of the lab exercises have students write user space code that allows them to get specific insight into the way the kernel works. The dependence on "crashable" lab facilities was my primary consideration in deciding not to include a device driver lab exercise.

While there is general consensus that teaching OS internals in the first course is too difficult, there is nevertheless a strong desire to offer an OS internals course as early as possible in the curriculum. If you decide to teach an internals course—as the first or second course—your choices are limited: Linux or FreeBSD if you want to study a real OS, or one of the pedagogical systems otherwise. My future plan is to write lab manuals that are compatible with this book, and which provide enough details to study OS internals for the best real systems for which source code is available.

Acknowledgments

Many people have helped to edit and refine this book. First there are the students at the University of Colorado: Jason Casmira, Don Lindsay, Ann Root, and Sam Siewert were great teaching assistants who created laboratory exercises and solutions, and generally helped make the book better. Scott Brandt provided comments and insight into how the material should be presented. Adam Griff spent many hours helping me with my Linux system. Scott Morris set up my Windows NT machine and offered insider tips about how it worked.

Addison-Wesley arranged to have additional students from other institutions look at the manuscript: Eric F. Stuckey, Shawn Lauzon, Dan Dartman, and Nick Tkach at Montana State University, and Jeffrey Ramin now at Berbee Information Networks Corporation. There were many people who spent hours looking at drafts or otherwise suggesting ways to organize and improve the material: Divy Agrawal (University of California at Santa Barbara); Vladamir Akis (California State University at Los Angeles); Kasi Anantha (San Diego State University); Charles J. Antonelli (University of Michigan); Lewis Barnett (University of Richmond); Lubomir F. Bic (University of California, Irvine); Paosheng Chang (Lucent Technologies); Randy Chow (University of Florida); Wesley J. Chun; Carolyn J. Crouch (University of Minnesota, Duluth); Peter G. Drexel (Plymouth State College); Joseph Faletti, Gary Harkin (Montana State University); Dr. Sallie Henry (Virginia Tech); Mark A. Holliday (Western Carolina University); Marty Humphrey (University of Virginia); Kevin Jeffay (University of North Carolina at Chapel Hill); Phil Kearns (The College of William and Mary); Qiang Li (University of Santa Clara); Darrell Long (University of California at Santa Cruz); Junsheng Long, Michael Lutz (Rochester Institute of Technology); Carol McNamee (Sacremento State University); Donald Miller (Arizona State University); Jim Mooney (West Virginia University); Ethan V. Munson (University of Wisconsin – Milwaukee); Deborah Nutt, Douglas Salane (John Jay College); Henning Schulzrinne (Columbia University); C. S. (James) Wong (San Francisco State University); and Salih Yurttas (Texas A&M University). The second edition was reviewed by Toby Berk (Florida International University); David Binger (Centre College); Richard Guy (UCLA); Zhiyuan Li (Purdue University); John Noll (University of Colorado, Denver); Kenneth A. Reek (Rochester Institutes of Technology); Joseph J. Pfeiffer, Jr. (New Mexico State University); and Irene Tseng (Gallaudet University).

Thank you all for sharing your experience, insight, and suggestions.

Finally, the editorial staff at Addison-Wesley and several freelance consultants have been invaluable in helping me produce this book. In the first edition, Christine Kulke, Angela Buenning, Rebecca Johnson, Dusty Bernard, Laura Michaels, Pat Unubun, Dan Joraanstad, and Nate McFadden provided invaluable help and direction. Carter Shanklin, acquistion editor for the first edition, had a vision for how the book should be written, and I am indebted to him for his considerable effort in getting the correct organization and content for the first edition. Maité Suarez-Rivas, acquisition editor for the second edition, pushed for the inclusion of laboratory exercises and a tighter integration of applied and conceptual materials that appears in this edition. Maité and her assistants Molly Taylor and Jason Miranda worked tirelessly to find out how the first edition could be improved, then they provided extraordinary support in producing the new edition. The second edition production staff, especially Karen Wernholm, Amy Rose, and Tracy Treeful, worked hard to transform the ideas into the finished product.

The book has benefited immensely by these collective efforts, but of course any remaining errors are solely my responsibility.

Gary Nutt
Boulder, Colorado

Contents

Chapter 3   Operating System Organization   55

Chapter 8   Basic Synchronization Principles   183

Chapter 9   High-level Synchronization   215

Chapter 14   Protection and Security   405

Chapter 17 Distributed Computing   509

1

Introduction

T he time has come," the walrus said,

"To talk of many things...."

—Lewis Carroll, *The Walrus
and the Carpenter* ■

CHAPTER OBJECTIVES

Operating systems have earned the reputation for being the most critical software in a computer system. Hence, only the most skilled and experienced programmers are allowed to design and modify a computer's operating system.

Performance and functionality are key to the usefulness of an operating system (OS). The OS's performance sets the stage for the performance of all software on a computer. Perhaps one of the most important reasons for studying operating systems is to learn how to extract the best performance from them. In addition, the OS provides a wide range of functions to assist in processing a program. A high-performance OS that provides little functionality forces more work onto its application programs. As a programmer, you need to understand how to use the system's functionality most effectively. Specifically, you must understand its design so that you will be able to exploit that design during program execution.

This book explores the issues that arise during the design of operating systems, as well as the different approaches used to analyze and resolve those issues. All operating systems are designed under various constraints and circumstances. Design decisions are often reflected in the interface for the system's application programs. These may take the form of apparent discontinuities, anomalies, or other logical inconsistencies. You can better use an OS if you understand the rationale behind some of these. This book will enable you to learn how to work around design flaws. Or it may show you how to refine your own model of how a system was designed—that is, how a perceived inconsistency may be a flaw in that model. By gaining an understanding of the design issues and decisions, as well as the tradeoffs involved, you will be better able to write software that takes advantage of the design of an OS.

This chapter covers what operating systems are and how they have arrived at their current state of development. First, it touches on the overall software environment so that you can see how an OS fits in. Next, it deals with the demands on modern operating systems—abstraction and sharing—and how they came about. Finally, it examines the popular OS strategies and how they have influenced the services of modern operating systems.

1.1 ▪ Computers and Software

Computer systems consist of software and hardware that are combined to provide a tool to solve specific problems. Software is differentiated according to its purpose. *Application software* is designed to solve a specific problem. For example, inventory control application software uses the computer to track and report a company's inventory. *System software* provides a general programming environment in which programmers can create specific applications to suit their needs. This environment provides new functions that are not available at the hardware level and performs tasks related to executing the application program. The OS is a subset of the system software.

The original motivation for system software in general and operating systems in particular was to provide functions that a programmer could use to implement application software. Over time, another important purpose of operating systems evolved: enabling application software to *share* the hardware in an orderly fashion. This sharing increases overall system performance by allowing different programs to use different parts of the computer simultaneously, thereby decreasing the time needed to execute a collection of programs and increasing the system's performance. To ensure that this sharing is done most safely and efficiently, the OS is the software that is implemented "closest to the hardware." Other system software and all application software use the OS as an interface to the hardware and as a means to support sharing among executing programs.

Before focusing on system software and operating systems, it is important to stress the overall importance of the application software. Ultimately, the cost of any computer is justified by the value of its application software. That is, a person or a company buys a computer to solve problems in one or more application domains; anything other than the application software is part of the overhead cost of solving the problem. In particular, system software is usually no more important to the computer purchaser than, say, the power supply in the hardware. System software and hardware exist to support the creation and effective use of application software.

1.1.1 ▪ General System Software

From the application programmer's perspective, system software is meant to simplify the programming environment and to enable efficient use of the hardware. System software covers a broad spectrum of functionality. An important class of system software is the runtime system for a programming language. In the UNIX system software, important parts of this runtime functionality are implemented in C libraries (accessed using various .h files); for example:

- The standard input/output (I/O) library provides procedures to perform buffered input/output on a stream of data.
- The math library provides functions to compute trigonometric and other mathematical functions.
- Graphics libraries provide functions to render images on a bitmapped display.

Other examples of system software are a window system and database management system. A window system is system software that provides a virtual terminal to an application program. The window is termed "virtual" because the programmer constructs the application software using functions to read and write the window as if it were a terminal device, even though there is no physical terminal uniquely associated with the window. The system software maps these virtual terminal operations so that they apply to a specific physical region on a screen. It then translates the software's operations on the virtual terminal to appropriate operations on the physical terminal. One physical terminal can support several virtual terminals.

A database management system is a full system that can be used to store information on the computer's permanent storage devices such as magnetic tapes and disks. The database system provides abstract data types (called *schema*) and creates new application-specific software optimized for efficient queries/updates on the data according to the schema definition.

Not all system software applies equally to all application domains. Some system software, such as a graphics library, is specific to a particular application domain and may not be useful in others. Other system software, like a relational database, is intended to be very general. It can support programs written for many different application domains. In the case of databases, different kinds of database management systems can be designed for different domains. Once a database technology is chosen to support the domain, it may be further specialized to better support a subdomain such as image processing or an artificial intelligence expert system. And even within the image processing database system software, further specialization of the system software may be appropriate so that it supports specific applications. For example, the image database may be designed to support only monochrome topographic images.

An OS interacts directly with the hardware to provide an interface to other system software and with application software whenever it wants to use system resources. It is largely domain-independent. This means that the same OS can be used to support a broad range of application domains, such as inventory management software and software for computing fluid flow over an airplane wing. The application program uses the resource abstraction provided by the OS to determine its detailed interaction with the hardware components. The OS allows different applications to share the hardware resources through its resource management policies. Resource abstraction and sharing are two key aspects of the operating system.

1.1.2 ■ Resource Abstraction

System software hides the details of how the hardware operates, thereby making computer hardware relatively easy for an application programmer to use. It does this by providing an abstract model of the operation of hardware components. While the abstraction simplifies the way the application programmer controls the hardware, it also limits the flexibility by which specific hardware can be manipulated. Generality has its price in specificity. That is, while certain operations become easy to perform, other hardware control may be impossible to achieve using the abstraction. As an analogy, an automated bank teller machine may provide an abstract operation that allows a user to withdraw $40 from a checking account by pushing a single button. However, users who want to withdraw $30 must push several different buttons: To indicate that they want to make a withdrawal, that the withdrawal should be from the checking account, and that the amount should be $30.

There are many different kinds of hardware components—referred to as *resources*—that an application program might use. Any particular resource, such as a disk drive, has a generic interface that defines how the programmer can make the resource perform a desired operation. An abstraction, however, can be made to be much simpler than the actual resource interface, as in the case with virtual terminals. Abstractions are implemented within the system software. With abstractions, the programmer doesn't have to learn each specific resource's interface in order to use the resource; instead the abstract interface (that ignores the fine detail of how the device is operated) is used. Thus the programmer can then focus on higher-level issues.

Furthermore, similar resources can be abstracted to a *common* abstract resource interface. For example, the system software may abstract floppy disk and hard disk operation into a single abstract disk interface. While an application programmer must be aware of the general behavior of drives, learning the details of disk input/output is not desirable or even necessary. The programmer needs to know about and use only the disk abstraction.

As a specific example, suppose a programmer is writing an application to analyze stock market trends. The effort to design and debug code to read and write information to/from a disk drive would represent a significant fraction of the overall effort. The skill and experience required to write the software to control the disk drive are not the same as that to design the stock analysis portion of the program. While an application programmer must be aware of the general behavior of a disk drive, it is generally preferable to avoid learning the details of disk input/output. Abstraction is the perfect approach, since the application programmer uses a previously implemented abstraction to read and write the disk drive. A disk software package is an example of system software. Programmers can focus their attention on the application programming problem rather than diverting it to tasks not specific to the application domain. In other words, system software is generally transparent to the end user but is of major significance to the programmer.

In designing system software, you must first define a set of abstractions that will be general across resources, yet intuitive for a programmer and suited to the target application domain. A good abstraction will be easy for the programmer to understand and use and will allow the programmer to easily perform every kind of operation on the resources required in the domain.

The In the Hangar section on the next page illustrates that abstraction can be used at more than one level. Once a hardware component has been simplified with an interface, higher-level system software may then be defined to abstract that resource into an even higher-level interface. The raw disk block model of operation was abstracted to provide a track-sector write operation, which was generalized again to use integer block addresses. Next the integer-addressed blocks were abstracted into a list of related blocks that contain a logical stream of bytes. Note that a reason for referring to "resources" rather than "hardware components" is to allow the abstraction to apply to computer components—physical resources—or to software artifacts implemented in the lower-level system software art—abstract resources.

➣ IN THE HANGAR

A Disk Device Abstraction

The idea behind resource abstraction can be examined in more detail by considering the operation of a disk device. The device is controlled with software operations for copying a block of information from the computer's main memory into the device's buffer memory:

```
load(block, length, device);
```

for moving the read/write head to specified areas on the disk surface:

```
seek(device, track);
```

and other operations such as to writing a block of data from the buffer to the device:

```
out(device, sector);
```

Thus a series of commands is required to write information from a primary memory block onto a disk, such as

```
load(block, length, device);
seek(device, 236);
out(device, 9);
```

A simple abstraction would be to package these commands (with any other necessary supplementary commands) into a procedure such as

```
void write(char *block, int len, int device, int track,
int sector)
{
. . .
load(block, len, device);
seek(device, 236);
out(device, 9);
. . .
}
```

(continued)

A higher-level abstraction might translate every block specification so that a non-negative integer address is used instead of a track and sector number. This would enable the programmer to ignore physical positioning in favor of logical addresses when specifying a part of the disk to be written. Now an output operation such as

```
write(block, 100, device, 236, 9);
```

can be written as

```
write(block, 100, device, 3788);
```

An even higher-level abstraction would provide system software with a way to treat the disk as file storage. Suppose the system software provides a file identification, fileID, as the abstraction of the disk. Then a library, such as the C stdio library, can provide a function to write an integer variable, datum (stored in a small memory block), onto the device at an implicit offset from the beginning of the file. The programmer then uses operations such as

```
fprintf(fileID,"%d", datum);
```

to write information to the disk. Such an abstraction also could be used for tape device input/output operations by having a different part of the system software implement the same abstraction for the tape device. Such abstractions will be considered in detail throughout the book.

1.1.3 ■ Resource Sharing

Abstract and physical resources may be shared among a set of concurrently executing programs. There are two types of sharing: space-multiplexed and time-multiplexed. *Space-multiplexed sharing* means that the resource can be divided into two or more distinct units of the resource. Different executing programs—*processes*—can be allocated exclusive control of different units of a resource at the same time. Memory and disks are examples of space-multiplexed resources.

Time-multiplexed sharing means that a resource is not divided into units. Instead, a process is allocated exclusive control of the entire resource for a short period of time. After that time has elapsed, the resource is deallocated from the process and allocated to another. Time-multiplexing is used with the processor resource. The processor is switched among processes holding other resources, such as memory space and network access. There is only one processor in the machine, but the computer user gets an illusion of simultaneous execution of different programs. This approach permeates OS design so much that such sharing is called concurrent execution or simply *concurrency* among the executing programs. Even though the execution is strictly sequential in a system with only one processor, much of the rest of the system is designed as if the concurrently executing processes were really executing simultaneously. Hence, reference to concurrent execution means either that the execution may actually be simultaneous or that the processor is time-multiplexed across a set of processes holding space-multiplexed resources.

There are two important aspects to resource sharing. First, the system must be able to isolate resource access according to an allocation policy, and second, the system must be able to cooperatively share resources when that is desired. Resource sharing can be authorized or not; the operating system must prevent unauthorized sharing, while still providing for authorized sharing. *Resource isolation* refers to the obligation of the operating system to prevent unauthorized access of resources by one process when they are currently allocated to another process. For example, a memory isolation mechanism allows two programs to be loaded in different parts of memory at the same time. The processor isolation mechanism forces the processes to sequentially share the system's processor. Neither program will be able to change or reference the memory contents being used by the other program.

The system software also must explicitly enable two or more executing applications to *share resource access* when that is desired. Solving the isolation requirement typically introduces a new problem. Suppose the programmer intends for two executing programs to share resources explicitly (in addition to the processor). The OS must ensure that the isolation mechanism does not preclude this intended resource sharing.

There can be no guarantees of resource isolation without a guarantee that the system software correctly implements the isolation mechanism. In turn, part of the system software must be trusted to implement resource isolation in a way that cannot be violated by other programs. This trusted part of the software is encapsulated in the operating system. Even the OS software must depend on the hardware to implement key parts of the mechanism to ensure resource isolation. While all system software is concerned with some form of resource abstraction, operating systems implement the software part of the trusted mechanisms that manage sharing.

Abstract resource-sharing mechanisms are often implemented in higher-level system software, but they rely on the safe operation of the OS. This distinction between system software and the OS is emphasized Figure 1.1. First, all system software implements an abstraction of resources used by application programmers, but the OS implements the abstraction directly from the physical resources. Second, the OS provides the fundamental trusted mechanisms to manage resource sharing. The figure also shows several important interfaces between these components of the overall system. The application software uses the application programming interface to the system software, the generic system software uses the OS interface, and the operating system uses the software-hardware interface to interact with the hardware. (The hierarchy shown in the figure is not strictly adhered to, since, for example, application programs execute some instructions directly on the hardware.)

1.1.4 ■ Computers Without System Software

If application software can be constructed without a need for resource abstraction or sharing, there is probably no need for system software. This was the case with early personal computers. Devices were deemed to be so simple as to not require resource

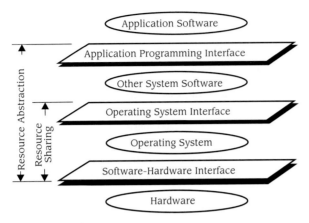

Figure 1.1
System Software and the Operating System

abstraction, and there was no requirement to support concurrency through processor multiplexing. The application program was responsible for all I/O operations on, for example, the keyboard, display, and disk. The complexities of device I/O and the popularity of the mouse pointing device soon signaled the end of this era because the software to control these devices became far too complex for most application programmers to manage. Personal computer manufacturers began to include resource abstraction mechanisms built into ROM (read-only memory). The BIOS (Basic Input/Output System) routines in IBM personal computers are one example of this.

Since then, personal computers have become so powerful that there is a growing need to support concurrent execution through processor multiplexing. As a consequence, contemporary personal computer system software now includes a resource-sharing mechanism. For IBM-compatible personal computers, this movement led to the creation of newer operating systems such as Microsoft Windows NT to replace the earlier DOS operating system.

1.2 ▪ Operating System Strategies

Today's operating systems build on several basic strategies for providing different kinds of services: batch, timesharing, personal computing, dedicated, and network strategies. The "favored" strategy for any given computer depends on how the computer is to be used, the cost-effectiveness of the strategy implementation in the application environment, and the general state of the technology at the time the OS is developed.

The earliest computers were dedicated to a single program-in-execution at a time. Then, as now, applications had to justify the cost of the entire system, so they were generally used in critical tasks such as national defense. Programmers were given exclusive access to the entire machine in order to develop and debug their single program. When the program was ready for production use, the machine was allocated to the end user to execute the program. The only purpose of the OS was to simplify device programming through resource abstraction.

In the late 1950s, economic pressures and software technology evolved to a point where users came to expect concurrent execution of multiple programs on a single computer. Operating systems were extended from mechanisms that provided simple device abstraction functions to ones that incorporated *multiprogramming*—the technique of loading multiple programs into space-multiplexed memory while time-multiplexing the processor. Today, multiprogramming remains the basic technology for sharing used by most OS strategies. In a multiprogramming environment, the OS provides solutions to the resource isolation and sharing problems described in Section 1.1.

To establish a perspective on OS strategies, the rest of this chapter briefly discusses the following:

- *Batch processing systems,* which service a collection of jobs, called a *batch.* They do this by sequentially reading the jobs into the machine and then executing the programs for each job in the batch. A *job* is a predefined sequence of commands, programs, and data that are combined into a single unit—the job—and submitted to the system. The user does not interact with programs while they operate. Batch processing systems stimulated development of resource isolation technology. These systems are considered in detail in Section 1.2.1.

- *Timesharing systems,* which support multiple interactive users. Rather than the user preparing a job for execution ahead of time, the user establishes an interactive session with the computer and then provides commands, programs, and data as they are needed during the session. Timesharing stimulated multiprogramming development, especially for support of multiple executing programs under the control of a single interactive user. It drove the need for the OS to provide timely response for users and sharpened the focus on resource management and protection mechanisms. Timesharing systems are considered in detail in Section 1.2.2.

- *Personal computers and workstations,* which established a trend away from multi-user sharing of a single computer toward an environment in which interactive response times are more predictable than in timesharing systems. This technology substantially changed the way any particular user used the machine's resources and the way resource-allocation mechanisms were designed. However, even these single-user machines are multiprogrammed so that the computer can be performing several different tasks concurrently on behalf of the user. PC and workstation systems are considered in detail in Section 1.2.3.

- *Process control and real-time computers,* which were originally used to control "autonomous systems" such as hydroelectric dams, satellites, and robots. The multiprogramming OS is required to guarantee response times for particular computing tasks. If the system cannot provide the desired service prior to a deadline, the application is deemed to have failed. Today, the technology is rapidly elevating in importance due to the desire to support multimedia computing (with more flexible deadline strategies than in traditional real-time systems). Process control and real-time systems are considered briefly in Section 1.2.4.

- *Network technology,* which has evolved rapidly since 1980. Modern computer configurations use high-speed networks to interconnect groups of personal computers, workstations, batch systems, timesharing systems, and sometimes even real-time

PERFORMANCE TUNING

Multiprogramming Systems

H ow can multiprogramming improve the performance of a computer? In single-user systems, users quickly became aware that for much of the time that a computer was allocated to a single user, the processor was idle while the user entered information, debugged programs, or was otherwise involved in human-computer interaction. Computer scientists observed that overall performance of the machine could be improved by letting a different program use the processor whenever one program was waiting for input/output. In a uniprogrammed system, if N users were to execute programs with individual execution times of $t_1, t_2, \ldots, t_N$, then the total time to service all N users would be

$$t_1 + t_2 + \ldots + t_N$$

However, the time each program actually uses the processor is a very small fraction of the total execution time. In fact, usually the sum of all the processor time used by N jobs rarely exceeds a small fraction of the time to run any one of the jobs. However, with multiprogramming the processor can switch from one program, X, to another, Y, whenever X is involved in the input/output phase of the execution. Since the processing time is much less than a single job's runtime, the total time to service all N users with a multiprogramming system can be reduced to approximately

$$\text{maximum}(t_1, t_2, \ldots, t_N)$$

This is an example of performance enhancement through the use of parallel operation: X's use of the I/O hardware occurs in parallel with Y's use of the processor. This is a recurring strategy for improving performance that permeates operating system designs. It also hints at the rationale for distinguishing between the time where one user's program is executing versus the time when another user's program is executing—the rationale for defining processes to be programs in execution.

systems. Another shift in OS strategy arose due to the need for resource and information sharing across the network. The presence of powerful workstations and high-speed networks drives contemporary OS development. Network systems are considered in detail in Section 1.2.5.

1.2.1 ■ Batch Systems

A batch processing system services individual jobs from a queue. A batch *job* is a predefined collection of commands that are executed without the users interacting with the program while it is in execution. In the 1960s, batch jobs were entered into the machine as a deck of keypunched cards. Today batch execution specifications use files to represent the parts of a job. Each job includes a control record or file specifying the processing steps for the job. The OS reads the entire job description and then stages it for execution. When the resources required by the job become available, the OS executes it.

1.2.1.1 ■ The User's Perspective

From the user's perspective, the job control specification provides all the information the OS needs to run the programs in the job. For example, if the job is intended to produce a corporation's monthly invoices, the OS may have to execute several different programs to produce the invoices. However, these programs process information contained in files rather than information supplied by an interactive user. There is no need for human interaction with the job when it runs, since all the information required to complete the job is kept in files.

Modern operating systems do not use the pure batch strategy in which jobs are copied from an input device into a system queue for processing. Instead, the user's perspective of batch processing is preserved by allowing the user to define a complex set of OS commands to be defined as a control file. The batch capability then will execute the commands in the control file.

Many applications are well-suited to batch processing, since they do not require any human interaction as they are executed. Thus all modern operating systems incorporate facilities to support batch-style processing. A user can define a job control specification by constructing a file with a sequence of commands. Although these commands could also be typed at the keyboard in an interactive session, the batch facility executes them without user intervention.

1.2.1.2 ■ Batch Processing Technology

In early batch processing systems, a computer operator collected decks of key-punched cards that represented jobs and then read them into a job queue for the system (see Figure 1.2a). The memory allocator (also called the *medium-term scheduler*) managed the primary memory space. When space was available in the main memory, a job was selected from the job queue and loaded into memory. Loading a job into memory meant the space was allocated to the job. Various job steps could then be executed by loading the designated program into the memory space and executing it.

Once a job was loaded into primary memory, it could compete for the processor. When the processor became available, the processor scheduler (also called the *short-term scheduler*) selected a job that was currently loaded in the memory and allocated the processor to it. In some cases, the OS might deallocate the memory allocated to the job if the memory allocation policy called for that action. Such systems are called *swapping systems*. For example, the memory allocation policy might be to release the job's memory and move it back to disk if it had been a particularly heavy or particularly light user of the processor. A heavy processor user might be penalized by being swapped out so that other programs would have more available processor cycles. A light processor user might be swapped out based on the rationale that it is not using the processor very much, so it should not tie up the memory resource while it is idle. While a job was loaded in memory, it could share the processor. When a job completed execution, its memory was released and the output for the job was copied onto an output spool for later printing.

Figure 1.2(b) illustrates how the traditional batch strategy is incorporated into modern operating systems to provide a batch file processing capability. Although there is no job queue, a batch file can be submitted for processing in an interactive session,

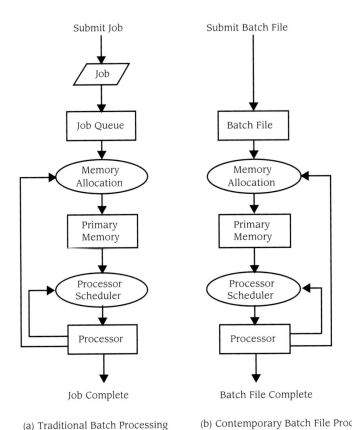

Figure 1.2
Two Types of a Batch System

thus causing the commands in the batch file to be executed in the same way the traditional batch system processed jobs were.

In multiprogrammed batch systems, jobs compete for resources, first for memory and later for other resources. This competition is managed by the various resource handlers. The process and resource management facilities for batch systems are distributed across the memory allocator and processor scheduler. Multiprogramming batch systems forced the evolution of memory management, memory protection, and scheduling in operating systems.

When batch processing was the dominant strategy, computers were increasingly used to manage bulk information. Business data processing became a viable computer application domain, thus encouraging the development of file technology. File management was a critical issue in early multiprogramming batch systems. This was because the technology enabled many more application programmers to write programs, and the problem of training them to use the disk directly was very difficult. The major contribution from batch processing, then, was in the development and refinement of multiprogramming, and in the refinement of resource abstraction.

Batch systems provided a major step forward in allowing multiple users to share a machine. However, multiprogrammed batch systems discouraged real-time interaction between the user and the computer—the user was represented by the job. In the systems predating batch systems, the user was able to sit at the system console and debug a program. In batch systems, programs could be debugged only by preparing a job, submitting it to the job queue, and waiting for the job to be executed and returned. To aggravate the problem, batch system users were typically not allowed to enter their own jobs into the system or to remove the output from the line printer. In fact, the batch system might be located at some geographically distant point. It was not unusual for a professional programmer to have only two opportunities a day to enter a job into the batch stream. Contrast that mode of software development with today's environment in which you can recompile and execute a program in seconds!

➤ *IN THE HANGAR*

Batch Files

Most operating systems support batch file processing, including DOS, UNIX, IBM MVS, DEC VMS, Windows 95/98, and Windows NT. Even though all of these operating systems are interactive timesharing systems, a user can prepare a batch file with a set of commands that the OS should execute without interacting with the user. The simplest example of batch files in DOS are the `config.sys` and `autoexec.bat` files. These define a set of commands to be executed when the computer begins operation. An elementary programming language can be used in the batch file to define the flow of control among the commands, although sequential execution is the norm. Figure 1.3 shows an example `autoexec.bat` file from a DOS computer. The file establishes a set of paths to search for executables, a location for a set of libraries, and a location for a set of header files.

```
PATH=C:\BIN;C:\TC\BIN;C:\WINDOSs;C:\WINDOWS\COMMAND
LIB=C:\TC\LIB
INCLUDE=C:\TC\INCLUDE
```

Figure 1.3
A DOS `autoexec.bat` Batch File

Figure 1.4 shows a batch file for a UNIX system. As in DOS, the batch file can be executed by a shell, causing each line in the file to be treated as a command to the OS. In the example, the first step is to compile a file named `menu.c`, thus producing a relocatable file named `menu.o`. The second line in the command file compiles a file named `driver.c` and link edits its relocatable object file with `menu.o` and the C library. The third line executes the file driver produced by the link edit execution by reading the input file named `test_data` and writing the output file named `test_out`. The fourth line prints the `test_out` file to a printer named thePrinter. The fifth line produces a tar file named `driver_test.tar` that contains the source code and test output. The last line in the command file encodes the tar file and writes the result into a file named `driver_test.encode`.

```
1 cc -g -c menu.c
2 cc -g -o driver driver.c menu.o
3 driver < test_data > test_out
4 lpr -PthePrinter test_out
5 tar cvf driver_test.tar menu.c driver.c test_data test_out
6 uuencode driver_test.tar driver_test.tar >driver_test.encode
```

Figure 1.4
A Shell Script Batch File for a UNIX System

1.2.2 ■ Timesharing Systems

Timesharing systems became popular in the 1970s. They were designed to enable many users to interact with the computer system at the same time by using a terminal keyboard and display device. This strategy was the first step in making the computer available to many people who were involved in many different types of information processing tasks.

There were four early systems that essentially defined timesharing OS strategy:

■ **CTSS, the Compatible Time Sharing System.** CTSS was developed for the IBM 7090 in the mid–1960s at M.I.T. [Corbato, et al., 1962]. It was the vehicle that supported the initial research on radical scheduling algorithms (radical when compared to those in existence at that time) and modern memory-management techniques.

■ **Multics** [Organick, 1972]. Multics replaced CTSS early on. It was intended to be more like a utility than a timesharing computer. It was designed to be extremely capable and reliable, whereas its contemporaries were often unreliable. Multics was the OS used to develop fundamental knowledge about virtual memory, protection, and security.

■ **Cal.** The Cal timesharing system was designed and implemented about the same time as CTSS and Multics [Sturgis, 1973]. The research results attributable to Cal generally concern generic timesharing technology, protection, and security.

■ **UNIX.** AT&T Bell Labs UNIX designers had been associated with Multics but wished to have a far less complex OS to manage a minicomputer. Hence, they developed UNIX in 1970. Note that "minicomputer" meant something different then than it does now. In 1970, a minicomputer was a machine that had about 4KB of RAM, a few serial ports, and a small disk drive. The PDP 11/45 described in the original UNIX paper by Ritchie and Thompson [1974] was much larger than the typical minicomputer of the time and was a precursor to the type of machine that came to be associated with the term minicomputer (such as DEC VAX machines).

1.2.2.1 ■ The User's Perspective

Batch systems forced the user to carefully plan how a job was to be executed before the job was ever submitted to the computer. Timesharing systems follow a philosophy whereby the user can establish a session with the system—called "logging onto/into" the system—and then decide which command to process immediately before it is executed. During execution, the user interacts directly with the program, supplying information to the program's read statements and seeing the direct result of the program's write statements.

Multiple interactive sessions are implemented by a set of *virtual* (or *abstract*) *machine*s, one for each user (see Figure 1.5). Each virtual machine (VM) is actually a simulation of real hardware implemented by the OS. Each user interacts with the computer by typing commands to the VM on a virtual system console and receiving results back from the machine as soon as they are computed. Each user directs the virtual machine to perform different commands. These commands are then executed on the physical machine in a multiprogramming environment.

Timesharing systems focus on policies to implement equitable processor sharing. This allows users to treat the machine as if they have exclusive control of a "comparatively slow" computer—the virtual machine. As long as the timesharing system does not become overloaded, the relative response time is usually so small that no user ever perceives any "comparative slowness" in the computer's performance.

1.2.2.2 ■ Timesharing Technology

The OS that implements timesharing uses multiprogramming—short-term scheduling and memory sharing—to support multiple virtual machines. The scheduling and memory allocation strategies of timesharing systems differ significantly from those used for batch systems. Whereas batch systems attempted to optimize the number of jobs that could be processed in an hour, a timesharing system attempts to provide equitable amounts of processor and memory resources to each virtual machine.

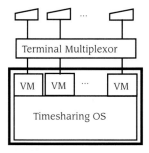

Figure 1.5
A Timesharing System

As timesharing environments evolved, they caused designers to distinguish between the notion of a job and that of a program in execution, since the user might implicitly or explicitly execute two different programs at the same time. This thinking led directly to the notion of a *process* as any "program in execution." A timesharing job might run two or more processes at any given time, while a batch job would execute only one program at a time on behalf of the job. For example, a user logged into a machine may want a program to continue to run even after the user has ended the session. Thus the single user has initiated two or more programs in execution, each competing with the others. This is much like any set of programs that compete for resources if it were attempting to execute simultaneously with others. As timesharing evolved, processes were sometimes called *tasks*. A timesharing multiprogramming system that supports multiple processes per user is sometimes called a *multitasking system.*

While all multiprogrammed machines support multiple users, timesharing systems highlight the importance of establishing barriers and safeguards among the users and their processes. Without such barriers, one process might inadvertently damage the memory image of another process. The barriers put into place to ensure memory protection also make information sharing between two jobs more difficult to support, since the two jobs must override the memory protection scheme. The protection barriers also extend into the file system shared by the users. In many cases, it is desirable for a user to create files that are not to be written to by other users and sometimes not even to be read by other users. Protection and security became major issues in the early days of timesharing, even though these issues apply equally to batch systems. Because they are also crucial issues in today's systems, they are discussed in Chapter 14.

1.2.3 ■ Personal Computers and Workstations

In the 1980s and early 1990s, personal computer system software was designed to allow one user to execute one program at a time. The earliest personal computer systems had no system software because there was no requirement for isolation or sharing. Also the amount of commercial software (and device sophistication) did not justify the development of resource abstraction software.

1.2.3.1 ■ The User's Perspective

Personal computers and workstations gave users new freedom in computing and changed the way they perceived the computer. Rather than viewing it as an ominous corporate resource, they began to think of it as a tool for accomplishing work, similar to a telephone, typewriter, or photocopier. As personal productivity tools such as word processors, desktop publishing systems, spreadsheets, and databases were developed, the single-user computer became deeply entrenched in corporations.

1.2.3.2 ■ OS Technology

The trend toward single-user computers began with the development of small computers, or minicomputers, that could be placed directly in the office rather than in a special computer room. The first minicomputers included the DEC PDP 8 and the Data General Nova. These were relatively inexpensive and easy to install in any location.

Minicomputers quickly grew in computational power to become the basic hardware platform for timesharing machines.

As minicomputers became larger, new, smaller machines—*microcomputers*—were built. The fundamental element of a microcomputer is a single integrated-circuit implementation of a processor. Early microcomputers were built with 8-bit processor chips with clock rates of around 1 million cycles per second (1 MHz). In comparison, contemporary microcomputers employ 32-bit microprocessors with typical clock rates exceeding 400 MHz.

The first personal computers incorporated the barest essentials of an operating system, which was usually encoded into ROM. These "operating systems" typically served the same function as the device interface aids did on the earliest systems. That is, they provided a few routines to control the personal computer's devices. Soon, ROM-based systems were enhanced by additional random access memory (RAM) resident software to manage files. The most popular of the early personal computer operating systems was CP/M, which was ultimately displaced by MS DOS (or the IBM version, PC DOS).

In the original personal computer market, personal computers with MS DOS eventually dominated other operating system products. Today many of these machines use Microsoft's follow-on operating systems, Windows 95/98 and Windows NT. DOS was not a true multiprogramming operating system, although it provided a file system similar to the one offered by UNIX. Its major contributions to operating system technology was that it popularized computing and it offered flexibility in configuring parts of the operating system when the machine was initialized.

Personal computers are traditionally single-user systems. In general, they do not support multiple users and often do not support multitasking or multiprogramming. Just as minicomputers replaced existing large machines, microcomputers have grown into more sophisticated systems, often called *workstations.*

Workstation hardware was generally more flexible and faster than personal computer hardware. Workstations typically incorporated considerably more resources than did personal computers, including more memory, a faster, more powerful processor, larger disk storage, and higher-resolution graphics monitors for the console. Workstations were also explicitly designed to operate in a network environment with other workstations and larger shared machines that had faster processors and more memory. These workstations generally required a more-complex operating system to manage the resources. Today, however, there is no real distinction between personal computers and workstation hardware.

Traditionally, workstations relied heavily on UNIX. Although UNIX was designed as a timesharing system, its multiprogramming support as well as the extensibility of function fit naturally into the workstation environment, particularly when the workstation was used for software development. UNIX grew with the workstation market. As the market called, for example, for graphics support, UNIX incorporated means to support high-resolution graphics. Similarly, as network protocols became important to workstation technology, UNIX began to accommodate network protocols. Meanwhile personal computers evolved into the same class of machines with multiprogrammed systems. Many of these machines use Microsoft Windows 95/98, or the more sophisticated Windows NT—an operating system of the same class as modern implementations of UNIX.

1.2.3.3 ■ Contributions to Modern OS Technology

Along with the increasing numbers of single-user machines is an increasing need for the machines to communicate with each other. In the simplest case, this means individual machines need to be able to exchange files or electronic mail. In a more complex case, the individual machines might be used as a team to work on a single problem. This need for communication fits naturally with the rapid evolution of networking (see Section 1.2.5).

Personal computers and workstations stimulated tremendous growth in system software to support personal computing tools. This demand in turn caused the interests of OS developers and human-computer interface developers to converge—for example, in creating effective point-and-select interfaces. The Sun OpenWindows/NeWS window systems and the X/Motif window systems are deeply rooted in system software technology (and implementation). Similarly, Windows NT Version 4 differs from earlier versions in that substantial amounts of the windows and graphic software were implemented as OS code. Interest in this class of machines also stimulated new OS developments to support multiple sessions and virtual terminals.

1.2.4 ■ Process Control and Real-time Systems

A process control computer is dedicated to a single application. Examples of such applications include controlling the floodgates of a dam, controlling the cooling process of a nuclear reactor, guiding a missile, controlling a point-of-sale terminal, and controlling a residential sprinkler system. Process control computers have been commercially successful for many years, but they reached new levels of popularity with the introduction of large-scale integrated circuits in the 1970s and 1980s. The process may be very complex or very simple, but because there is only one application, the OS need not manage isolation and sharing among concurrent application programs. Instead, its main purpose is to provide hardware resource abstractions.

Because only one program ever uses the abstractions, the designer may decide to collapse the resource management into the application. This would be done to avoid performance penalties associated with interactions between the application program and the OS. The result is that the system is designed with only one program devoted to the application, and the system contains no identifiable operating system.

Real-time computer applications are often associated with process control applications. Real-time computing is based on the idea that the "user" (a piece of equipment or a human user) is required to receive a guaranteed response time for any request to perform work. This poses two challenging problems: how to guarantee a maximum response time and how to achieve a minimum response time. Real-time systems technology is driven by response-time guarantees. If the machine is multiprogrammed, the OS must ensure that requests will be met before a hard deadline for the request has occurred. Many real-time applications specify a soft deadline rather than a hard one. That is, the OS should make its "best effort" to meet the deadline, but if it fails to meet the deadline, it should continue to provide service rather than simply abandon the service request.

Today, real-time computing has extended beyond deadline scheduling to address various other quality of service (QoS) issues. For example, application processes may require that information be delivered over a network in a prescribed amount of time or with a minimized deviation in its delivery rate (minimized "jitter"). The solutions to these requirements are difficult, and they are the subject of considerable effort in contemporary operating system designs.

Real-time system techniques tend to trade off generality of operation for efficiency in order to ensure that deadlines can be met. Designers of other classes of operating systems commonly use techniques employed in real-time systems when raw performance is the goal.

1.2.5 ∎ Networks

The popularity of personal computers and workstations led to a high demand for systems that can perform nontrivial local computing and yet use information stored at another computer accessible via a high-speed network. Today, system software is highly focused on providing functionality to support the use of individual computers interconnected via local area networks and wide area networks. Resource isolation, sharing, and abstraction for local and remote resources provide a new challenge for system software designers and essentially define the leading edge of contemporary research in the area.

Until the 1980s, computers were generally interconnected with point-to-point, bit-serial communication media that operated at speeds of less than 10 kilobits per second (Kbps). If one needed to interconnect more than two machines, then either a fully connected network of point-to-point connections was used or machines were interconnected with a routing network. (In a routing network, a "path" exists between any pair of machines. Each machine must be able to forward information to other machines so that all machines collectively implement a logical network that behaves as if it were fully connected. Routing networks are described in more detail in Chapter 15.)

Local area networks (LANs) became a cost-effective communication technology at about the same time personal computers and workstations began to evolve. Ethernet and Token Ring LAN technology each provide a fully connected network operating at 10 to 16 megabits per second (Mbps)—three orders of magnitude faster than point-to-point forwarding networks. These LANs enabled small machines to be interconnected both amongst themselves and to large machines, with relatively high-speed connections and at relatively low costs. The result was a revolution in computer hardware configurations and in the way computing was accomplished in all organizations.

Software technology, stimulated by the presence of inexpensive computer hardware and network bandwidth, rapidly evolved to large-grained, loosely coupled distributed computation, primarily in the form of client-server computing. Today, network disk servers, file servers, print servers, database servers, communications servers, and others are commonplace in 10–100Mbps LAN installations. Soon, these components will be interconnected with 500Mbps or faster networks. The evolution of client-server computing also forced operating systems to evolve from timesharing and multiprogramming systems to those supporting network communication, client and server resource management strategies, new interprocess communication strategies, and new memory management strategies. These configurations are dominated by network operating systems that evolved from timesharing technology to handle the LAN computing environment.

1.2.6 ■ The Genesis of Modern Operating Systems

Modern operating systems evolved from all of the systems discussed in the previous sections: batch, timesharing, personal computer and workstation, real-time, and early network operating systems (see Figure 1.6). They inherited multiprogramming technology from batch and timesharing systems. While protection and security first appeared in batch systems, both developed rapidly in timesharing environments. Human-computer interaction technology became an issue with timesharing systems. The trend was accelerated with the dedicated memory and processors offered with personal computers and workstations. Users began to demand windows and other visually oriented technologies. The client-server network programming model (file servers, print servers, database servers, and so on; discussed in Chapter 15) evolved from systems that supported network communications. Real-time and process control computing have influenced synchronization approaches, scheduling, and data movement in modern operating systems.

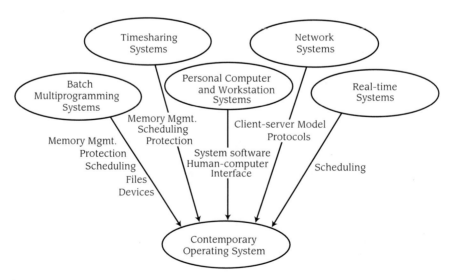

Figure 1.6
The Evolution of Modern Operating Systems

1.3 ■ Summary

Computer purchases are justified by the functionality provided by application software. If the application software is not effective, the entire computer system is not effective. The system software and hardware are transparent to the end user—the person using the application software to process information—so they provide no direct value to that end user. Rather, they are intended to support the programmer.

Application software programmers depend on system software to abstract the interface to various resources provided by the hardware and lower-level system software. System software enables the application programmer to use system resources with relatively little effort and to share otherwise isolated resources when required. The OS part of the system software manages system resources so that they can be shared among a set of concurrently executing application programs. The OS ensures that private resources are protected from unauthorized access and that shared resources are accessible to all relevant processes.

Operating systems have evolved from single-user computers, to batch multiprogramming systems, to timesharing systems, to personal computers and workstations interconnected with networks. Batch multiprogramming systems introduced technology to support concurrency among jobs. Timesharing operating systems extended multiprogramming so that each job could have multiple processes executing on behalf of the user at any one time. Because of the proliferation of processes in timesharing systems, protection and security among processes and users became critical. Today, protection and security have continued to grow in importance due to the ubiquity of computers.

This book focuses on issues in general OS design and implementation, although many explanations and exercises are cast in a variant of UNIX. You will be best served in understanding the various issues if you have a personal computer and a copy of a pedagogic OS available for experimenting with concepts and doing exercises.

As a continuation of the introduction to operating systems, the next chapter considers the programmer's model of the abstract resources provided by system software in general, and the operating system in particular.

1.4 ■ Exercises

1. For a UNIX system, characterize each of the following as application software, general system software, or OS software:

   a. The `grep` program
   b. A program to compute homework score averages
   c. The X Window library (`Xlib`)
   d. The `ls` program
   e. The `fprintf` function
   f. A spreadsheet program

2. Differentiate between an abstract resource and a physical resource. Give two examples of each.

3. An IBM personal computer provides an interface to its devices in the Basic Input/Output System (BIOS) routines. What abstractions do the IBM PC BIOS routines provide to the Intel 8088 abstract machine that are not available by using the hardware directly? (*Hint:* In general terms, what is the difference between the commands you would have to execute to write a character to the display if you did not have BIOS?)

4. Virtual terminals were briefly described in Section 1.1.1. Explain how software could be designed so that a program would print output to a virtual terminal, but the user would control the shape and size of the virtual terminal instance (window) on the physical screen. You need not provide code, just an explanation of how this could be accomplished.

5. Describe the kinds of abstractions you think the designers may have been trying to provide when they created each of the following systems software packages. Your answer should briefly describe the intent and provide a few examples to characterize how the abstraction is achieved.

   a. UNIX `termcap` or `printcap` facility
   b. UNIX `curses` facility
   c. X Window `Xlib` library
   d. The Motif application programming interface
   e. The Apple Macintosh Quickdraw toolbox
   f. Microsoft Windows
   g. The Borland C/C++ graphics library
   h. The CORBA standard

6. The *degree of multiprogramming* is the maximum number of processes that may be supported by a uniprocessor at any given time. Discuss some factors that must be considered in determining the degree of multiprogramming for a particular system. You may assume a batch system with the same number of processes as jobs. (Several of these factors will be discussed in detail in later chapters.)

7. Describe the time a batch processing system requires to respond to a request to perform work (called the *response time*). Describe the response time in a timesharing system. Which type of system is likely to have a faster response time? Why?

8. When is batch processing the preferred strategy for work to be done by the computer? When is timesharing the preferred strategy?

9. How might a timesharing processor scheduler's policy differ from a policy used in a batch system?

10. How is the UNIX `makefile` similar to a batch file? How is it different from the control file described in the chapter?

2

Using the Operating System

E verything should be made as simple as possible, but not simpler.

—Albert Einstein ■

CHAPTER OBJECTIVES

Chapter 1 explained why operating systems exist. This chapter examines the environment programmers expect when they use the OS. If you are an experienced programmer, you will have learned this material when you studied your programming environment. Otherwise, it will provide a unifying view of several concepts you must know before you can make the most effective use of the computer.

This chapter considers the essential elements of the programming environment provided by an operating system from the application programmer's perspective. The rest of the book focuses on the OS from the system designer/programmer's point of view. The explanation of operating systems issues and concepts uses an extended example of the UNIX programming environment throughout this chapter to illustrate how these ideas are realized in at least one real system. First the computational model used in modern operating systems is described, including a description of resources and the specialized file resource. Next, process creation is described, including examples in UNIX and Windows NT. Finally the chapter considers two new, alternative models: threads and objects.

2.1 ■ The Abstract Model of Computing

The application programmer views a computer as a mechanism that can access, transform, and store information. The OS provides an environment in which the programmer can define specific information management tasks. This environment must provide some abstractions of the hardware that will enable the programmer to conceptualize units of program execution and the components of the system used in the computation. In modern OS environments, the fundamental unit of computation is the process, and the fundamental unit of information storage is the file. Other system components are resources used to conduct one type of computation or another, more specialized in their functions than files. The programmer implements applications by specifying programs to perform the information management task. Programs define the behavior of a set of one or more processes by defining how they read information from files, transform the information using system resources, and store the information into other files. The resources implementing storage facilities are usually viewed as files of information, so the program interacts with the information using the file interface. Other resources have their own interfaces defined according to how the operating system designer has decided to represent the resource abstraction. For example, a bitmapped display device may have an interface built around the block of display memory. Application programs copy information into this special block of information, where it is displayed by the system.

Extended system software provides additional resource abstractions such as indexed files, databases, and object storage for files. It also provides windows for terminal displays and variations on processes for computational units. In most cases, the OS will provide the abstractions of processes and files supplemented by various other resource interfaces as the primitives of its computational environment. Since files and other resources must be used to fully describe processes, files and general resources are described before discussing processes.

2.2 ■ Resources

The OS treats any entity as a resource if it satisfies these characteristics:

- A process must request it from the OS.
- The process must suspend its operation until the entity is allocated to it.

Traditionally, the most common resource is a file. A process must request a file before it can read it or write it. Further, if the file is unavailable, the process must wait until it becomes available. This abstract description of a resource is crucial to the way various entities (such as files, memory, and devices) are managed. In Chapter 10, this description is crucial to understanding the theory behind deadlock in a computer system.

2.2.1 ■ Files

A sequential *file* is a named, linear stream of bytes of memory. You can store information by opening a file—creating an abstract file resource description and assigning a name to it—and then writing a block of bytes into the file. Similarly, you can access information stored in a file by opening the file and reading the block of bytes stored in the file. The operating system is responsible for implementing the basic file abstraction using storage devices such as magnetic/optical disks or tapes. It implements the abstraction by mapping bytes in the stream to blocks of information stored on the device. Files are distinguished from other resources for two reasons:

- They are the prevalent form by which information is stored in a computer.
- Operating systems often take the file as a primitive and then model other resource abstractions after it.

Like other resources, files have descriptors that enable the OS to record how the file is being used, its availability, and so on. In the case of files, the descriptor will also be used to store information that the operating system can use to map bytes in the file stream to their locations on storage devices.

➤ IN THE HANGAR

POSIX Files

A POSIX file is a named sequential collection of bytes, or a byte stream. BSD UNIX has a slightly different interface. The POSIX file system interface provides only a few basic operations for manipulating a file. You can learn more about these system calls and commands on your local Linux (or other POSIX compliant) system by reading the online documentation using the man command. (For example, to read the documentation on the open command, type man open to the shell; it will display the documentation on the login screen. The man man command describes the on-line documentation for the man command itself.) The file commands are shown in Table 2.1. See your local system's description for details of these system calls, particularly fcntl (or ioctl on some systems).

The complete program shown in Figure 2.1 illustrates how files are used with the POSIX interface. A process executing the program copies the contents of the file named in_test, character-by-character, to another file named out_test. A process using this program will open an input file for reading and an output file for writing. Then it will copy each byte in the input file to the output file.

Figure 2.1
A Linux File Manipulation Program

```
#include <stdio.h>
#include <fcntl.h>
  int main() {
  int inFile, outFile;
  char *inFileName = "in_test";
  char *outFileName = "out_test";
```

(continued)

```
  int len;
  char c;

  inFile = open(inFileName, O_RDONLY);
  outFile = open(outFileName, O_WRONLY);
/* Loop through the input file */
  while((len = read((inFile, &c, 1)) > 0)
    write(outFile, &c, 1);
/* close files and quit */
  close(inFile);
  close(outFile);
}
```

TABLE 2.1 POSIX File Operations

Command	Description
open	The open call specifies the path name of a target file to be pre-pared for reading or writing. Parameters to the call enable one to lock the file, thus providing exclusive reading or writing as long as the file is open. When the file is opened, a system pointer addresses the first byte in the stream (or, if the file is empty, the location where the first byte will be written). The call returns an unsigned integer file reference when it is successful; this value is used to identify the open file.
close	The close call closes the file, thereby releasing locks and system resources used to represent the status of the open file.
read	The read call specifies a file descriptor (returned by open), a buffer address, and a buffer length. Normally, this call causes the process to block until the read has completed. However, the seman-tics can be changed with an appropriate call to the fcntl com-mand, explained shortly.
write	The write call is similar to read, except it transmits information to the file.
lseek	The lseek call explicitly moves the read/write pointer in the byte stream, since the file is construed as a linear byte stream. This movement affects subsequent read and write commands.
fcntl	The fcntl call (it stands for file control) provides a means for sending arbitrary control requests to the operating system. For example, normal file read operations block the calling process if it performs a read on an empty file; using fcntl, it is possible to have the read operation return to the caller if an attempt to read the file would block the calling process. (The details of this are explained in the Laboratory Exercise in Chapter 15.)

➤ IN THE HANGAR

Windows NT Files

Windows NT also defines a file as a named byte stream. In the Win32 API (application programming interface) when Windows NT opens the file it creates an OS data structure, and the OS call returns a typed *handle* (reference) to the OS data structure. All file operations use the handle to reference the file. There are many file commands in Windows NT, but Table 2.2 describes the basic commands, and Figure 2.2 presents a complete program to copy a file (block-by-block) from a file named in_test to one called out_test.

TABLE 2.2 Windows NT Basic File Commands

Command	Description
CreateFile	The CreateFile (or OpenFile) call is used to create an open file object in the OS, to prepare the file for reading or writing, and to initialize the OS data structure. When the file is opened, a system pointer addresses the first byte in the stream (or, if the file is empty, the location where the first byte will be written).
CloseHandle	The CloseHandle call closes the file, thereby closing the system resources used to represent the status of the open file.
ReadFile	The ReadFile call reads a block of information from the file and advances the file pointer.
WriteFile	The WriteFile call writes a block of information to the file and advances the file pointer.
SetFilePointer	The SetFilePointer call moves the file pointer to a new position.

Figure 2.2
A Windows NT File Manipulation Program

```
#include <windows.h>
#include <stdio.h>

#define BUFFER_LEN ... // # of bytes to read/write

/* The producer process reads information from the file name
   in_test then writes it to the file named out_test.
*/
```

(continued)

```c
int main(int argc, char *argv[]) {
// Local variables
   char buffer[BUFFER_LEN+1];

// CreateFile parameters
   DWORD dwShareMode = 0; // share mode
   LPSECURITY_ATTRIBUTES lpFileSecurityAttributes = NULL;
                // pointer to security attributes
   HANDLE hTemplateFile = NULL;
                // handle to file with attributes to copy

// ReadFile parameters
   HANDLE sourceFile; // Source of pipeline
   DWORD numberOfBytesRead; // number of bytes read
   LPOVERLAPPED lpOverlapped = NULL; // Not used here

// WriteFile parameters
   HANDLE sinkFile; // Source of pipeline
   DWORD numberOfBytesWritten; // # bytes written

// Open the source file
   sourceFile = CreateFile (
        "in_test",
        GENERIC_READ,
        dwShareMode,
        lpFileSecurityAttributes,
        OPEN_ALWAYS,
        FILE_ATTRIBUTE_READONLY,
        hTemplateFile
   );
   if(sourceFile == INVALID_HANDLE_VALUE) {
        fprintf(stderr, "File open operation failed\n");
        ExitProcess(1);
   }

// Open the sink file
   sinkFile = CreateFile (
        "out_test",
        GENERIC_WRITE,
        dwShareMode,
        lpSecurityAttributes,
        CREATE_ALWAYS,
        FILE_ATTRIBUTE_NORMAL,
        hTemplateFile
   );
   if(sinkFile == INVALID_HANDLE_VALUE) {
        fprintf(stderr, "File open operation failed\n");
        ExitProcess(1);
   }
```

```
// Main loop to copy the file
   while
   (
        ReadFile(
                 sourceFile, buffer,
                 BUFFER_LEN, &numberOfBytesRead,
                 lpOverlapped
                 )
                 &&
                 numberOfBytesRead > 0
   ) {
        WriteFile(sinkFile, buffer, BUFFER_LEN,
                 &numberOfBytesWritten, lpOverlapped);
   }

// Terminating
   CloseHandle(sourceFile);
   CloseHandle(sinkFile);
   ExitProcess(0);
}
```

2.2.2 ■ Other Resources

A *resource* is any abstract machine component, including a file, that a program must have explicitly allocated before it can execute the program. If the process requests a resource that is unavailable, the process normally discontinues execution and remains *blocked* until the resource becomes available. The processor is the most obvious resource the process requires. The reference to the processor resource is implicit, but necessary for the process to proceed. The system must allocate the processor to the process as part of the operating paradigm.

Memory is another resource. The program may request and reference all needed memory at the time the process comes into existence, or it may be permitted to request that memory be dynamically allocated and freed as needed. Another resource is a tape drive. If the programmer wishes to read information from a magnetic tape, then the drive must be allocated to the process prior to the tape's being mounted and read. How process management is designed is discussed in Chapters 6 through 10. There, you will see that the notion of resource can be generalized to include intangible components, such as signals or information.

Every operating system provides access to a number of resources in addition to files, including the processor, memory, keyboards, and displays. If the interface to all resources is the same, then it is easier for the programmer to know how to use all of these resources than if the interface differs from resource type to resource type. UNIX illustrates this approach: While there is an attempt to make most resource interfaces similar to file interfaces, in some cases, the interface has no similarity to a file at all. As in other timesharing systems, the processor resource management is explicitly handled by the processor scheduler. A process implicitly requests the use of the processor whenever it is ready to execute.

Like other timesharing systems, UNIX incorporates a memory allocator to provide memory to a process based on the requirements of the text/data/stack segments of the program being executed. There are many schemes for handling the memory: Some versions of UNIX employ swapping. This means that when the processor and/or memory are subject to heavy demand, the operating system may deallocate a process's primary memory (the process's state and memory image are saved on the secondary storage) as well as the processor. These allocation/deallocation activities are transparent to the process but sometimes painfully obvious (through delayed response) to the interactive user of the process.

In UNIX the file abstraction is used for pipes and devices. Devices, such as keyboards and displays, are described in more detail in Chapter 5. For now, it suffices to say that a device has `open`, `close`, `read`, `write`, `seek`, and `ioctl` commands implemented in the driver, just as in the file interface. The `read` and `write` operations operate on byte streams, so a device `read` operation appears much like a file `read` operation. Pipes are an abstract resource used to enable two different processes to communicate with one another. They are described in Chapter 9.

2.3 ■ Processes

A *process* is a sequential program in execution. The components of a process are the following (see Figure 2.3):

- The *object program* (or *code*) to be executed.
- The *data* on which the program will execute (obtained from a file or interactively from the user of the process).
- *Resources* required by the program (for example, files containing requisite information).
- The *status* of the process's execution.

For the process to execute, it must have a suitable *abstract machine environment* to manage the sharing and isolation of resources among the community of processes. The process status is used to map that environment's state to the physical machine state. For

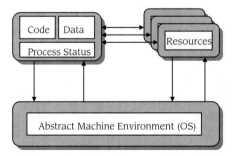

Figure 2.3
A Process

example, part of the status information of the process is the location of the current instruction in the program text for the process. As indicated in Figure 2.3, the abstract machine environment manages the processes and resources, allocating resources to processes when they are needed.

There is an explicit distinction between a program and a process. A program is a static entity made up of program statements that define process behavior when executed on some set of data. A process is a dynamic entity that executes a program on a particular set of data using resources supplied by the system. Two or more processes could be executing the same program, each using their own data and resources. Figure 2.4 shows three processes sharing one copy of a program, yet each has its own data and resources. In particular, each process has its own status record indicating information such as which part of the program is being executed and the identity of resources currently allocated to the process.

A process can run to completion only when all requested resources have been allocated to the process. In particular, a process can be described by a formal model of its operation; throughout this book various models are provided to study different aspects of operating systems. The basic representation of a process is intended to be intuitive and descriptive, so it is described in terms of running programs on traditional computers. The operation of the processor on a program is a process.

The OS keeps an internal data structure to describe each process it manages, just as it does for files and other resources. When it creates the process, it creates this process descriptor. When the process is terminated, the descriptor data structure is released. The exact contents of the descriptor varies from OS to OS, though it may contain the identification number of the process and the identity of resources allocated to it, and the contents of various processor registers if it is not currently using the processor. When one process needs to reference another process, it does so by referencing the OS descriptor data structure.

A process defines the fundamental unit of computation for the computer, since these units are used for processor sharing among executing programs. Even though the classic unit of computation is the process, some modern operating systems may use one

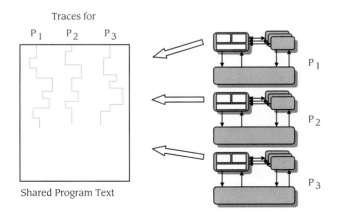

Figure 2.4
Sequential Operation

or both of two additional specialized units of computation: threads and objects. There is no explicit relationship between threads and objects, although some researchers have used threads to implement objects. While most operating systems use the process as the basis of the thread or object, a few experimental systems implement these alternatives in the operating system rather than in higher-level system software.

2.3.1 ■ Creating Processes

When a computer is started, it must begin executing instructions stored in memory. This *initial process* will first perform the bootstrap loading task described in detail in Section 4.2. This loads the OS into memory. Then the computer will begin to execute the OS. How do subsequent processes come into existence? The conventional means for creating a process is to execute a *spawn* system call to create another process. The generalized spawn operation is often specialized as a *clone* or *fork* instruction that creates another process to execute the same program the creating process is executing.

In 1963, Conway postulated three operating system functions named FORK, JOIN, and QUIT [Conway, 1963]. Dennis and Van Horne described a variant of them in 1966 [Dennis and Van Horne, 1966]. These primitives are used to create and execute a family of processes. Unlike modern operating systems, the processes created using the classic FORK command execute within the same address space, meaning they are sharing one copy of a program and all information. As they execute, they reference the same variables rather than having their own copies of the variables. The behavior of the commands is defined as follows:

■ FORK(label) results in the creation of a second process (defined by the procedure currently being executed). This process begins execution in the same address space as the original process at the statement with the specified label. The process executing FORK continues execution at the next instruction. Once the new process has been created, the original process and the new process coexist and proceed concurrently.

■ QUIT() is used by the process to terminate itself. The process is destroyed and its process descriptor is released.

■ JOIN(count) is used to merge two or more processes into a single process. When a process executes this statement, it executes code equivalent to

```
/* Decrement a shared variable */
count = count - 1;
/* QUIT unless this the last process */
if (count!= 0) QUIT();
```

on a shared variable named count. Only one process can execute the JOIN statement at any given time. Once a process executing begins to execute the JOIN system call, no other process can get control of the CPU until the process finishes executing it. This code segment implements a *mutual exclusion* concurrency strategy (which is considered in much more detail in Chapter 8), since an execution of JOIN cannot be interrupted.

FORK, JOIN, and QUIT can be used to describe computations made up of cooperating sequential processes executing in a single address space. Again note that the processes explicitly share data as well as the program.

In contrast to the original FORK/JOIN/QUIT commands, a modern system's spawn command (called fork, CreateProcess, or other similar names) creates a child process that executes in its own address space. While the shared address space approach used in the original commands allows a child process to share code and data with its parent and siblings, the approach also essentially prevents the memory manager from isolating one process's memory contents from the others. Providing a separate address space for each new process enables every process to have a private, isolated address space.

More important, the child process ought to be able to execute a different program than the parent does. Otherwise, every spawned child would have to run the same program as the initial process (since *every* process is spawned directly or indirectly from the initial process). As a result, every modern operating system incorporates a mechanism for enabling the child to redefine the contents of its address space.

➤ **IN THE HANGAR**

Using FORK, JOIN, and QUIT

Consider the program segments shown in Figure 2.5. Process A is executing proc_A that will compute some value (in the code segment designated by <compute section A1>) and then update the information into a shared variable, x. Meanwhile, a process B begins to execute proc_B, although it should not be allowed to execute the retrieve(x) statement until after process A has performed its update operation. Similarly, process A should not perform the retrieve(y) operation on the shared variable, y, until after process B has completed the update(y) instruction. This particular code segment is especially complex because the two processes execute loops and one process may be able to iterate through its loop much faster than

```
procA() {                          procB() {
   while(TRUE) {                       while(TRUE) {
      <compute section A1>;               retrieve(x);
      update(x);                          <compute section B1>;
      <compute section A2>;               update(y);
      retrieve(y);                        <compute section B2>;
   }                                   }
}                                   }
```

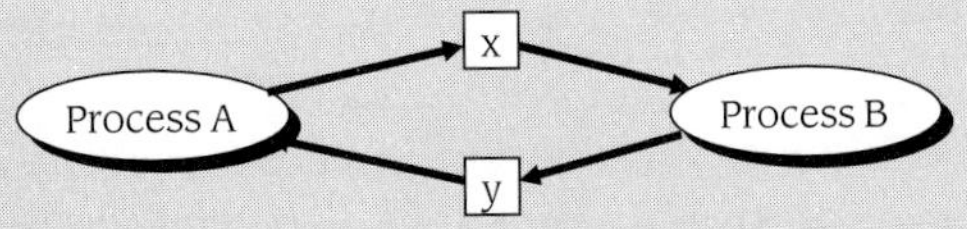

Figure 2.5
Cooperating Processes

the other. This implies that the values passed back and forth via x and y may be lost because the faster process overwrites a value before the slower one can read it.

Perhaps counter to one's intuition, the process primitives allow two processes, A and B, to execute concurrently and to coordinate their execution to prevent shared values from being overwritten before they are read. To force an ordering throughout the execution of some of the statement, one could rewrite the procedures as shown in Figure 2.6. The encoding of the two procedures into a single body of code is the result of the JOIN instruction's address space being within a single procedure. Also, since the FORK construct uses a label to specify the point at which the newly spawned process will begin execution, these language constructs require the use of labels in high-level source code.

Figure 2.6
FORK, JOIN, QUIT Example

```
L0: count = 2;
    <compute A1>;
    update(x);
    FORK(L2);
    <compute A2>;
L1: JOIN(count);
    retrieve(y);
    QUIT();
L2: retrieve(x);
    <compute B1>;
    update(y);
    FORK(L3);
    goto L1;
L3: <compute B2>;
    goto L0;
```

➢ *IN THE HANGAR*

Creating Processes in UNIX

The behavior of a UNIX process is defined by its text segment, data segment, and stack segment. The *text segment* contains the compiled object instructions, the *data segment* contains static variables, and the *stack segment* holds the runtime stack used to store temporary variables. A set of source files that is translated—compiled and linked—into an executable form is stored in a file with the default name of a.out (of course, the file can be explicitly given any name by the programmer). This executable file defines the three parts of the executable program (see Figure 2.7). In the text segment program branch and procedure call addresses refer to locations within the text segment. If the program references statically defined data, such as C static variables, a template for the data segment is defined in the executable file. The data segment will be created and initialized to contain values and space for variables when the executable file is loaded and executed. The stack segment is used to allocate storage for dynamic elements of the program, such as automatic C variables that are created when they come into scope and are destroyed when they pass out of scope.

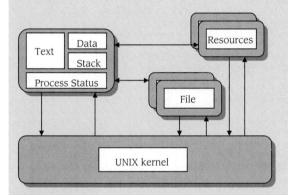

Figure 2.7
UNIX Processes

The executable file is created by the compiler, linker, and loader. These do not define a process; they define only the program text and a template for the data component that the process uses when it executes the program. When a process loads a program into the computer's memory, the system creates appropriate data and stack segments.

A process has a unique process identifier, a PID, that is essentially a pointer—an integer—into a table of process descriptors used by the UNIX OS kernel to reference the process's descriptor. Whenever one process references another process in a system call, it provides the PID of the target process. The UNIX `ps` command lists each process associated with the user executing the command. The PID of each process appears as a field in the descriptor of each process. The next time you are using UNIX, try the `ps -aux` command to observe the PID value identifying each process in the system.

The UNIX command for creating a new process is the `fork` system call. Whenever a (parent) process calls `fork`, a child process is created with its own descriptor, including its own copies of the parent's program text, data, and stack segments, and access to all open file descriptors (in the kernel). The child and parent processes execute in their own separate address spaces. This means that even though they have access to the same information, when the child is created, both the child and its parent each reference its own *copy* of the information. No part of the address space of either process is shared; hence, the parent and child cannot communicate by referencing variables stored at the same address in their respective address spaces. In UNIX, the only thing the two processes can reference in common is open files. UNIX process creation is considered later in the section.

UNIX systems also provide several forms of the `execve` system call to enable a process to reload its address space with a different program:

```
execve(char *path, char *argv[], char *envp[]);
```

This system call causes the load module stored in the file at `path` to replace the program currently being executed by the process. After `execve` has completed executing, the program that called it is no longer loaded. Hence, there is no notion of returning from an `execve` call, since the calling program is no longer loaded in memory. When the new program is started, it is passed the argument list, `argv`, and the process uses a new set of environment variables, `envp`.

UNIX also provides a system call, `wait` (and a frequently used variant, `waitpid`), to enable a parent process to detect when one of its child processes terminates. Details of the terminating child's status may be either returned to the parent via a value parameter passed to `wait` or ignored by the parent. The `waitpid` variant allows the parent to wait for a particular child process (based on its PID) to terminate, while the `wait` command does not discriminate among child processes. When a process exits, its resources, including the kernel process descriptor, are released. The operating system signals the parent that the child has died, but it will not release the process descriptor until the parent has received the signal. The parent executes the `wait` call to acknowledge the termination of a child process.

The parent program shown in Figure 2.8 illustrates how `execve` and `wait` can be used. In this complete example, the parent process creates a child using the `fork` command and then simulates execution with the `printf` and `sleep` function calls. In a more practical application, the parent would execute from its own address space in place of the `printf` and `sleep` calls. After the `fork`, the child performs an `execve` to replace the program shown in Figure 2.8 by the program shown in Figure 2.9. After the child finishes executing the `execve` in Figure 2.8, the next instruction it executes is the first one in the program in Figure 2.9. You may wish to experiment with this program schema by typing it into your lab machine and running it. Put the code in each figure in a separate file. Then compile the two files separately to produce an absolute module for the parent and one for the child named child. Run the parent code in a process, which will `fork` and `execve` the child.

Figure 2.8
A Simple Parent Program

```
#include <sys/wait.h>
#define NULL 0

int main (void){
    if (fork() = = 0){ /* This is the child process */
        execve("child", NULL, NULL);
        exit(0); /* Should never get here, terminate */
    }
/* Parent code here */
    printf("Process[%d]: Parent in execution ... \n",
                    getpid());
    sleep(2);
    if(wait(NULL) > 0) /* Child terminating */
        printf("Process[%d]: Parent detects terminating child \n",
                    getpid());
    printf("Process[%d]: Parent terminating ... \n", getpid());
}
```

Figure 2.9
A Simple Child Program

```
int main (void){
/* The child process's new program
   This program replaces the parent's program */

    printf("Process[%d]: child in execution ... \n", getpid());
    sleep(1);
    printf("Process[%d]: child terminating ... \n", getpid());
}
```

➤ *IN THE HANGAR*

Creating Processes in Windows NT

In Windows NT one process creates another process at the Win32 API with the CreateProcess function (which in turn calls the Windows NT kernel functions NtCreateProcess and NtCreateThread). Whenever a process is created, the calling process is telling the NT OS to perform a large amount of work—to set up a new address space and allocate resources to the process, and to create a new base thread (see the next section for more information about threads). Once the new process has been created, the old process will continue using its old address space while the new one operates in a new address space with a new base thread. This means that there can be many different options for creating the process, so the CreateProcess function has many parameters, and some of these parameters can be quite complex. Contrast this with the UNIX `fork()` call, where there are *no* parameters—the child's behavior is completely defined by parent's profile and default behavior. After the Windows NT OS has created the new process, it will return a handle for the child process and a handle for the base thread in the process.

Below is a copy of the function prototype for `CreateProcess` (taken from the Win32 API reference manual). The function prototype does not use any standard C types; instead, it uses a set of types defined in the `windows.h` file, many of which are just aliases for standard C types. This level of indirection in name types creates an abstract interface that NT implementers can use as they wish.

```
BOOL CreateProcess(
    LPCTSTR lpApplicationName,
            // pointer to name of executable module
    LPTSTR lpCommandLine,
            // pointer to command line string
    LPSECURITY_ATTRIBUTES lpProcessAttributes,
            // pointer to process security attributes
    LPSECURITY_ATTRIBUTES lpThreadAttributes,
            // pointer to thread security attributes
    BOOL bInheritHandles, // handle inheritance flag
    DWORD dwCreationFlags, // creation flags
    LPVOID lpEnvironment,
            // pointer to new environment block
    LPCTSTR lpCurrentDirectory,
            // pointer to current directory name
    LPSTARTUPINFO lpStartupInfo,
            // pointer to STARTUPINFO
    LPPROCESS_INFORMATION lpProcessInformation
            // pointer to PROCESS_INFORMATION
);
```

The ten parameters in `CreateProcess` provide great flexibility to the programmer, but for the simple case, a default value can be used for many of them. For example, the following code shows how to create a child process using the Win32 API to Windows NT:

```
#include <windows.h>
#include <stdio.h>
#include <string.h>
...
STARTUPINFO startInfo;
PROCESS_INFORMATION processInfo;
...
strcpy(lpCommandLine,
       "C:\\WINNT\\SYSTEM32\\NOTEPAD.EXE temp.txt");
ZeroMemory(&startInfo, sizeof(startInfo));
startInfo.cb = sizeof(startInfo);
if(!CreateProcess(NULL, lpCommandLine, NULL, NULL, FALSE,
       HIGH_PRIORITY_CLASS  CREATE_NEW_CONSOLE,
```

```
            NULL, NULL, &startInfo, &processInfo)) {
        fprintf(stderr, "CreateProcess failed on error %d\n",
                        GetLastError());
        ExitProcess(1);
    };
    ...
    CloseHandle(&processInfo.hThread);
    CloseHandle(&processInfo.hProcess);
```

2.4 ■ Threads

The motivation for the thread model is to create a simple OS abstraction where there can be multiple entries that execute the same program, using the same files and devices. A thread is an alternative form of schedulable unit of computation to the traditional notion of process. In the thread model of computation, the process is an OS abstraction that can be allocated various resources, yet which has no component that can execute programs. A *thread* (sometimes called a *lightweight process*) is an entity that executes using the program and other resources of its associated process. There can be several threads associated with a single process. Sibling threads—threads associated with the same process—share the program and resources of the process. The thread must have a minimum of its own allocated resources so that its internal state is not confused with the internal state of other threads associated with the same process. As a practical matter, these minimum resources are a stack, a portion of the traditional process's status information, and some OS table entries (see Figure 2.10). In a thread model the normal notion of process corresponds to a passive resource with a single active thread to carry out program execution.

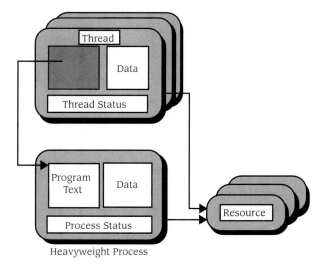

Figure 2.10
A Process and Its Associated Threads

A thread scheduler, analogous to the process scheduler in the more traditional model, switches the processor among a set of competing threads. In some systems, the thread scheduler is a user program and in others it is part of the OS. Since threads have little state, the thread scheduler has less work to do when actually switching from one thread to another than is required for switching processes. Hence, an important motivation for using threads is to minimize context switching time. This allows the processor to switch from one unit of computation (a thread) to another unit of computation with minimal overhead. Even so, the thread manager requires a descriptor to save each thread's register and stack contents.

Since all related threads share a common procedural description, they all use the same program to define their behavior. Often, two threads coordinate their actions with one another using exactly the same code. This symmetry among processes allows the programmer to (relatively) easily construct a program in which a community of threads interacts to manage shared resources allocated to the heavyweight parent process.

Threads are an especially useful programming model when several different units of computation need to utilize shared but logically distinct facilities (for example, see [Bershad, et al., 1988; Hauser, et al., 1993]). The shared facility is managed by a community of threads that is defined by a common process. Threads have become very popular for certain classes of distributed applications. Contemporary window systems often use the thread paradigm for managing virtual terminal sessions in the context of a physical terminal. Suppose a window system is built with a heavyweight physical screen manager, with several related virtual screen threads (see Figure 2.11). All threads run the same code, and all share the physical screen, yet each thread manages just one window in the collection of windows. Response time is very important in this type of system, so context switching among individual virtual screen managers is important. Threads are an ideal mechanism for implementing such a system and are widely used in commercial windowing systems.

Today, threads are an important tool in the repertoire of the concurrent programmer. A thread executes within the address space of a process but as an independent unit of computation. In this sense, a thread is like a process managed by the FORK/JOIN/QUIT

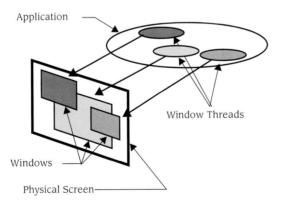

Figure 2.11
Using Threads

primitives described earlier in the chapter. This means that a scheduler can control the progress of each thread in a community of threads. However, threads share the resources allocated to the "mother ship" process—threads always exist within the context of a process. Furthermore, a set of threads associated with a process use the same address space as the process, so the thread siblings execute the same programs using the same resources and data. Threads are a way to refine and divide the work normally associated with a process.

➤ IN THE HANGAR

C Threads

Today some operating systems support threads internally, while others support them as library routines. The C threads package was developed as part of the Mach operating systems design effort as a library thread package (see the Mach literature for information about the package [Accetta et al., 1986]). The POSIX threads library package is a similar package gaining in popularity, since it is part of the POSIX open systems standards. Both packages have a programming interface similar to the UNIX process package, although threads are not always supported by a UNIX kernel. (Both Sun Solaris and Linux do support threads via the POSIX interface.)

Figure 2.12 shows how a thread can be created in a program using the C threads library. The heavyweight process is viewed as one thread (with resources), and each child thread is created with a call to cthread_fork. Once a child thread has been created, it shares static variables with its parent and with other children of the parent. The child can defer execution to the parent—or the parent to the child—using the cthread_yield library call.

Figure 2.12
A C Thread Skeleton

```
#include <cthreads.h>
    . . .
int main(int argc, char *argv[]) {
  t_handle = cthread_fork(tchild, I);
/* A child thread is now executing the tChild function */
  cthread_yield(); /* Yield to another thread */
}

void tChild(int me) {
/* This function is executed by the child */
  . . .
  cthread_yield(); /* Yield to another thread */
  . . .
}
```

⤴ IN THE HANGAR

Windows NT Threads

When a process is created, a kernel "base thread" is created to execute on behalf of the process. One can also create additional threads in the current process using the `CreateThread` Win32 API function (which uses the `NtCreateThread` Native API call). Since each thread represents an independent computation of a shared program on shared data, all within the context of an existing process address space, creating a thread requires that the programmer supply information relating to the execution environment for this thread while presuming all of the process-specific information. The best way to discuss the procedure for creating a thread is to first look at the function prototype.

```
HANDLE CreateThread(
    LPSECURITY_ATTRIBUTES lpThreadAttributes,
                // pointer to thread security attributes
    DWORD dwStackSize,
                // initial thread stack size, in bytes
    LPTHREAD_START_ROUTINE lpStartAddress,
                // pointer to thread function
    LPVOID lpParameter,    // argument for new thread
    DWORD dwCreationFlags, // creation flags
    LPDWORD lpThreadId
                // pointer to returned thread identifier
);
```

This prototype uses six parameters to describe the characteristics of the new thread. In this case, the function will create only one handle (the one for the thread) and return it as the result of the call. Again, this means that a system resource is implicitly allocated on a successful call to `CreateThread`, so the programmer is obliged to explicitly close the handle when it is no longer being used.

With a process, it was necessary to provide the name of an executable file. However, for a thread, it is only necessary to provide the OS with an address in the current address space where the new thread should begin to execute. The `lpStartAddress` parameter is such an address. In conventional programming languages (such as C), it is generally not possible for a computation to simply start off in the middle of some procedure. A branch to a new logical context is handled by bundling the new code in a procedure and then calling the procedure at its entry point. The `lpStartAddress` is the address of an entry point for a function that has a prototype of the form

```
DWORD WINAPI ThreadFunc(LPVOID)
```

That is, in a language that checks the type of a called entry point compared to the function call (as is done in C++ and ANSI C), there must be a function prototype before an entry point address can be used as a parameter. Of course, this means that there must also be a function to implement the prototype, the function that the new thread will begin executing after it is created.

One other complication in this scenario relates to passing parameters to the function that will be executed by the new thread. Since there is a function call and prototype, if a parameter is to be passed, then either its type must be known and declared or a `void *` type must be used (to tell the compiler that the type of the parameter to the thread's function is unknown at compile time). `CreateThread` uses the latter approach; this is why the function prototype uses `LPVOID` (which is defined as a `void *`). The `lpParameter` value will be passed to the function when the new thread starts to execute it.

For example, one might define a function with the prototype

```
DWORD WINAPI myFunc(LPVOID);
```

that the new thread is to begin executing. Further, assume that the "parent thread" intends to pass an integer argument to the new "child thread." Now the example call will take the following form:

```
DWORD WINAPI myFunc(LPVOID);
DWORD targetThreadID;
int theArg;
...
CreateThread(NULL, 0, myFunc, &theArg, 0,
    &targetThreadID);
```

2.5 ▪ Objects

Objects were originally derived in simulation languages. An object was a model of an autonomous entity to represent the operation of those units in the simulated system. A simulation program can be thought of as a program that manages a large number of individual units of computation, each of which performs small amounts of computation at a time and each of which is closely correlated with sibling units of computation. The Simula 67 simulation language created the idea of *classes* to define the behavior of a simulation unit of computation, just as a program defines the behavior of a process. The definition of the class includes facilities that allow an object to declare its own data that are private to the class computation. Thus a class is similar to an abstract data type that maintains its own state in its private variables and can be executed as an autonomous unit of computation. The simulation then is defined by specifying a set of class instances—objects—that interact with one another only by passing messages.

Contemporary object-oriented systems have continued to use this class model to define the behavior of a unit of computation. Thus a "model of a process" is used to define objects as an alternative schedulable unit of computation. Objects react only to messages. Once an object is created, other objects send it messages. It responds by performing computation on its internal data and by sending other messages back to the original sender or to other objects. Since an object's behavior is defined by its class definition, the object-oriented programmer designs a system by defining a set of classes and describing when objects should be instantiated from the class definitions.

Objects were first widely used in user interface systems. The InterViews systems [Linton, Vlissides, and Calder, 1989] is representative of many of these systems; every item that appears on a screen—even a character in a document editor—is represented by an object. When objects interact with one another, such as when they are formatted for display, they do so exclusively by sending messages back and forth, rather than by sharing common variables. InterViews and related systems have clearly illustrated the power of object-oriented programming in building document editors, graphics editors, and other visually oriented interfaces. Today, the object approach is also used in almost all application domains.

Object-oriented languages have established a new computing paradigm for application programming. Because of the growing popularity of the model, some operating systems are now implemented by using objects (for example, see the Spring operating system [Hamilton and Kougiouris, 1993; Khalidi and Nelson, 1993]). They also provide specialized support for the object model. This support assists traditional sequential programmers in achieving a strong intuition about distributed computing. This enables them to take advantage of contemporary multiprocessors and networks of computers.

Objects are significant in the context of operating systems because they define another mechanism for specifying the behavior of a distributed system of computational units. This is done by specifying the behavior of individual units of serial computation and the model by which they are coordinated when they execute. The operating system may use this approach for its implementation, as well as being required to provide efficient support for objects.

2.6 ■ Summary

Application programmers using modern operating systems use a computing environment made up of processes, files, and other resources. Processes are the fundamental schedulable unit of computation representing the execution of a program. Files are persistent information containers used to save information from one session to the next. All operating systems provide sequential byte stream file organizations, though some may support more-complex file types. Other resources include the processor, memory, devices, and anything else a process can request from the operating system. Resources, particularly files, are system-controlled items that the process needs before it can execute. A process has a program to define its behavior, resources that are used to carry out the execution, and data on which to operate. Contemporary system software sometimes abstracts the notion of a process to a thread or an object. In UNIX, the fundamental unit of computation managed by the operating system is the process and the fundamental unit of secondary memory is the file.

With an understanding of how operating systems are used, you are now ready to begin studying the operating system design. In the next chapter, the discussion begins by considering the overall organization.

2.7 ■ Exercises

1. Consult application programmer documentation for writing a program to merge two sorted files into a single file in Linux/UNIX. Using pseudo C code, describe the application program for each operating system.

2. In the early 1990s, the IEEE POSIX committee described an operating system interface based on the AT&T System V UNIX interface definition. Several vendors stated they would comply with the POSIX.1 standard using their own proprietary operating system. Explain how a vendor with a proprietary operating system might be able to comply with a standard based on such a variant of UNIX.

3. Describe how a shell script (or any other file containing a reference to a program) could "automatically" be executed once every hour in a UNIX system. (*Hint:* See the UNIX `cron` facility.)

4. POSIX defines a standard thread package in the context of the C programming language. Several manufacturers provide a POSIX thread package as a user library along with their C programming facilities. If you have a system available to you that supports threads, then design and implement a thread program so that one thread reads a file, while a second thread writes the data to another file.

5. Consider the program shown in Figure 2.1. The C `stdio` library provides a similar set of file operations using the `FILE` data structure for a file description. Rewrite the simple file copy example in the figure using the C `stdio` library routines rather than the UNIX kernel routines.

6. Write a shell script to interrogate the operating system to determine the number of processes considered by the short-term scheduler for processor allocation (processes currently "ready to run") at any given time. Then append the result, along with a time-stamp, on a log file. Be sure to say which operating system and shell version you are using. (*Hint:* See the Linux/UNIX man pages for the `ps` and `wc` commands. Consider all processes that are in the machine.)

7. Write a C/C++/UNIX procedure, `getTime`, that returns the execution time of code segments by calling it before the code segment is executed and again after the code segment is executed; for example:

```
double getTime(int);
start = getTime(-3);
<code segment>;
stop = getTime(-3);
elapsedTime = stop - start; // in milliseconds
```

Use the UNIX kernel `gettimeofday` call to read the clock on your host system. The parameter specifies the resolution of the time. If the parameter is i, then the length of time for one time unit is 10^i. (i = -3 means return the time in milliseconds and i = -6 means return the time in microseconds.) State the smallest clock resolution for which your routine operates properly on your host machine.

Lab Exercise:
A Shell Program

Write a C/C++ program that will act as a *command line interpreter* (or *shell*) for the Linux kernel. Your shell program should use the same style for running programs as the UNIX sh command. In particular, when the user types a line such as

```
identifier [identifier [identifier]]
```

your shell should parse the command line to build the argv data structure in the form expected in any C/UNIX main program. It should then search the directory system in the order specified by the PATH environment variable for a file with the same name as the first identifier (which may be a file name or a full pathname for a file). When the file is found, execute it with the optional parameter list specified by the other identifiers, just as sh does. Use the execv form of execve (that is, you are required to search the PATH variable to find the directory in which the command appears).

BACKGROUND

A *command line interpreter*, or *shell*, program is a mechanism with which each interactive user can issue commands to the OS and by which the OS can respond directly to the user. Whenever a user has successfully logged into the computer (a process will have been assigned to the user when they begin the login procedure), the OS causes the user process to execute a shell. The OS does not ordinarily have a built-in window interface—instead the OS assumes a simple character-oriented interface in which the user types a string of characters (terminated with the "enter" or "return" key), and in which the OS responds by typing lines of characters back to the screen. If the human-computer interface is to be a graphic window interface, then the software that implements the window manager subsumes the shell tasks on which we focus in this exercise. Thus the character-oriented shell assumes a screen display with a fixed number of lines (usually 25) and a fixed number of characters (usually 80) per line.

Shell Behavior

In an interactive system, a shell program is executed by the login process after it has authenticated the user. Once the shell has initialized its data structures and is ready to start work, it clears the 25-line display, then prints a prompt in the first few character positions on the first line. Linux systems are usually configured to include the machine name as part of the prompt. My Linux machine is named kiowa.cs.colorado.edu, so the shell that I use prints

```
kiowa$
```

as its prompt string. (My BSD workstation uses the C shell, so its prompt is "pawnee%".) The shell then waits for the user to type a command line in response to the prompt. The command line could be a string such as

```
kiowa$ ls -al
```

terminated with an enter or return character (in Linux, the character is represented internally by the NEWLINE character, '\n'). When the user enters a command line, the shell's job is to cause the OS to execute the command embedded in the command line.

Every shell has its own language syntax and semantics. In the standard Linux shell, bash, a command line has the form

```
command argument_1 argument_2 ...
```

where the command to be executed is the first word in the command line and the remaining words are arguments expected by that command. The number of arguments depends on which command is being executed. For example, the directory listing command can be used with no arguments—simply by typing "ls", or it may have arguments prefaced by the "-" character, as in "ls -al" where "a" and "l" are arguments. Other commands use their own syntax for accepting an argument; for example, a C compiler command might look like

```
kiowa$ cc -g -o deviation -S main.c inout.c -lmath
```

where the arguments "g", "o", "deviation", "S", "main.c", "inout.c", and "lmath" are all being passed as parameters to the C compiler , "cc". That is, the command determines which of the arguments may be grouped (like the "a" and "l" in the ls command), which arguments must be preceded by a "-" symbol, whether or not the position of the argument is important, and so on.

The shell relies on an important convention to accomplish its task: The command for the command line is usually the name of a file that contains an executable program. For example, ls and cc are the names of files (stored in /bin on most UNIX-style machines). In a few cases, the command is not a file name, but is actually a command that is implemented within the shell; for example cd ("change directory") is usually implemented within the shell rather than in a file. Since the vast majority of the commands are implemented in files, think of the command as actually being a file name in some directory on the machine. This means that the shell's job is to find the file, to prepare the list of parameters for the command, then to cause the command to be executed using the parameters.

There is a long line of shell programs used with UNIX variants, including the original Bourne shell (sh), the C shell (csh) with its additional features over sh, the Korn shell, and so on, to the standard Linux shell (bash—meaning Bourne-Again shell). All these shells have followed a similar set of rules for command line syntax, though each has its own special features. The cmd.exe shell for Windows NT uses its own similar, but distinct, command language.

Basic UNIX-style Shell Design

A shell could use many different strategies to execute a user's computation. The basic approach used in modern shells is to create a new process (or thread) to execute any new computation. For example, if a user decides to compile a program, the process interacting with the user creates a new child process. The first process then directs the new child process to execute the compiler program. This same technique can be used by the initial process (the OS) when it decides to service a new interactive user in a timesharing environment. That is, when the user attempts to establish an interactive session, the OS treats this as a new computation. It awakens a previously created process for the login port or creates a new process to handle the interaction with the user.

This idea of creating a new process to execute a computation may seem like overkill, but it has a very important characteristic. When the original process decides to execute a new computation, it protects itself from any fatal errors that might arise during that execution. If it did not use a child process to execute the command, a chain of fatal errors could cause the initial process to fail, thus crashing the entire machine.

The UNIX paradigm for executing commands is illustrated in Figure 2.13. Here, the shell has prompted the user with the % character and the user has typed "grep first f3". This command means the shell should create a child process and cause it to execute the grep string search program with parameters first and f3. (The semantics of grep are that the first string is to be interpreted as a search pattern and the second string is a filename.)

The Bourne shell is described in Ritchie and Thompson's original UNIX paper [Ritchie and Thompson, 1973]. The Bourne shell and others accept a command line from the user, parse the command line, then invoke the OS to run the specified command with the specified arguments. When a user passes a command line to the shell, it is interpreted as a request to execute a program in the specified file—even if the file contains a program that the user wrote. That is, a programmer can write an ordinary C program, compile it, then have the shell execute it just like it was a normal

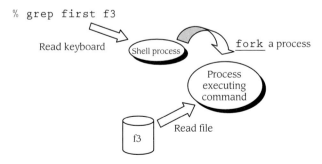

Figure 2.13
The Shell Command Line Interpreter

UNIX command. For example, you could write a C program in a file named main.c, then compile and execute it with shell commands like

```
kiowa$ cc main.c
kiowa$ a.out
```

The shell finds the `cc` command (the C compiler) in the /bin directory, then passes it the string "`main.c`" when it creates a child process to execute the `cc` program. The C compiler, by default, translates the C program that is stored in `main.c`, then writes the resulting executable program into a file named `a.out` in the current directory. In the second command, the command line is just the name of the file to be executed, `a.out` (without any parameters). The shell finds the `a.out` file in the current directory, then executes it.

Consider the detailed steps that a shell must take to accomplish its job:

- Printing a prompt. There is a default prompt string, sometimes hardcoded into the shell, e.g., the single character string "%", "#", ">" or other. When the shell is started, it can look up the name of the machine on which it is running, and prepend this string name to the standard prompt character, for example giving a prompt string such as "`kiowa$`". The shell can also be designed to print the current directory as part of the prompt, meaning that each time the user employs `cd` to change to a different directory, the prompt string is redefined. Once the prompt string is determined, the shell prints it to `stdout` whenever it is ready to accept a command line.

- Getting the command line. To get a command line, the shell performs a blocking read operation so that the process that executes the shell will be blocked until the user types a command line in response to the prompt. When the command has been provided by the user (and terminated with a NEWLINE character), the command line string is returned to the shell.

- Parsing the command. The syntax for the command line is trivial. The parser begins at the left side of the command line and scans until it sees a white space character (such as space, tab, or the end of the line). The first such word is treated as the command name, and subsequent words are treated as parameter strings.

- Finding the file. The shell provides a set of *environment variables* for each user— this variable is first defined in the user's `.login` file, though it can be modified at any time with the `set` command. The PATH environment variable is an ordered list of absolute pathnames that specifies where the shell should search for command files. If the `.login` file has a line such as

```
set path=(.:/bin:/usr/bin)
```

the shell will first look in the current directory (since the first pathname is "." for the current directory), then in /bin, and finally in /usr/bin. If there is no file with the same name as the command (from the command line) in any of the specified directories, the shell responds to the user that it is unable to find the command.

- Preparing the parameters. The shell simply passes the string parameters to the command as the `argv` array of pointers to strings.
- Executing the command. Finally the shell must execute the binary object program in the specified file. UNIX shells have always been designed to protect the original process from crashing when it executes a program. That is, since a command can be *any* executable file, the process that is executing the shell must protect itself in case the executable file has a fatal error in it. Somehow, the shell wants to "launch" the executable so that even if the executable contains a fatal error (which destroys the process executing it), the shell will remain unharmed. The Bourne shell uses multiple processes to accomplish what the UNIX-style system calls `fork`, `execve`, and `wait`.

  - `fork`. This system call *creates* a new process which is a copy of the calling process except that it has its own process identification (with the correct relationships to other processes) and its own pointers to shared kernel entities such as file descriptors. After `fork()` has been called, *two* processes will execute the next statement after the `fork` in their own address spaces—the parent and the child. If the call succeeds in the parent process, `fork()` returns the process identification of the newly created child process, and in the child process, `fork()` returns a zero value.

  - `execve`. This system call is used to *change* the program that the process is currently executing. It has the form

    `execve(char *path, char *argv[], char *envp[])`

    The `path` argument is the pathname of a file that contains the new program to be executed. The `argv` array is a list of parameter strings, and the `envp` array is a list of environment variable strings and values that should be used when the process begins executing the new program. When a process encounters the `execve` system call, the next instruction it executes will be the one at the entry point of the new executable file. This means that the kernel performs a considerable amount of work in this system call: It must find the new executable file, load it into the address space currently being used by the calling process (overwriting and discarding the previous program), set the `argv` array and environment variables for the new program execution, then start the process executing at the new program's entry point. There are various versions of `execve` available at the system call interface; they differ in the way parameters are specified (for example, some use a full pathname for the executable file, others do not).

  - `wait`. This system call is used by a process to block itself until the kernel signals the process to execute again—for example, because one of its child processes has terminated. When the `wait` call returns as a result of a child process terminating, the status of the terminated child is returned as a parameter to the calling process.

This discussion provides the bare minimum functionality for a shell. A production shell must also keep track of the current directory, implement several commands, handle background processes (invoked by terminating the command line with a "&"

character rather than a NEWLINE), handling redirection of stdin and stdout, supporting the pipe operation (""), providing a scripting language, and so on.

Attacking the Problem

There are several aspects of this lab exercise that might require more discussion. The following sections describe:

- How command names and parameter lists should be managed by the shell.
- How you should go about finding the location of the file that contains the command.
- How to execute the program for the command.
- How to organize your shell program.

Determining the Command Name and the Parameter List

You should recognize the argv name in the execve call from writing C programs in your introductory programming classes. That is, if you write a C program and you want the shell to pass parameters (from the command line) to your program, you declare the function prototype for your main program with a line like

```
int main(int argc, char *argv[]);
```

The convention is that when your executable program (a.out) is executed, the shell will build an array of strings, argv, with argc entries in it. argv [0] points to a string with the command name ("a.out"), argv [1] points to a string specifying the first parameter, argv [2] points to a string specifying the second parameter, and so on. When your program is executed, it reads the argv array to get the strings, then applies whatever semantics it wants to interpret the strings. For example your program might be run with a command line of the form

```
a.out foo 100
```

so that when your program begins execution it will have argc set to 3, argv [0] will point to the string "a.out", argv [1] will point to "foo", and argv [2] will point to the string "100". Your program can then interpret the first parameter (argv [1]) as, say, a file name, and the second parameter (argv [2]) as, say, an integer record count. The shell would simply treat the first word on the command line as a file name and the remaining words as strings.

Refer to the Code Skeleton section for the following discussion. After you have read the command line into a string, commandLine, you will need to parse it to populate the command_t fields (name, argc, and argv). The explanation in the Background section should be sufficient for you to design and implement code to parse the command line so that you have the name of the file containing the command in command->name, and (a pointer to) the array of pointers to parameter strings in command->argv.

Finding the Full Pathname

The user may have provided a full pathname as the command name word, or only have provided a relative pathname that is to be bound according to the value of the PATH environment variable. If the name begins with a "/", then it is an absolute pathname that can be used to launch the execution. Otherwise, you will have to search each directory in the list specified by the PATH environment variable to find the relative pathname.

Launching the Command

The final step in executing the command is to fork a child process to execute the specified command and to cause the child to execute it. The following code skeleton will accomplish that:

```
if(fork() == 0) {
   // This is the child
   // Execute in same environment as parent
    execvp(full_pathname, command->argv, 0);

} else {
   // This is the parent - wait for child to terminate
      wait(status);
}
```

Code Skeleton

The Background section provides a general, verbal description of how a shell behaves. That description can be refined into the skeleton of a specific software solution with the following pseudocode

```
struct command_t {
  char *name;
  int argc;
  char *argv[];
  ...
};

int main () {
  ...
  struct command_t *command;
  ...
// Shell initialization
  ...

// Main loop
  while(TRUE) {
  // Print the prompt string
    ...
```

```
    // Read the command line and parse it
      . . .
    // Find the full pathname for the file
      . . .
    // Create a process to execute the command
      . . .
    // Parent waits until child finishes executing command
    }

  // Shell termination
    . . .
  }
```

■ First, implement the basic parts to print the prompt and read the command line. In this first-cut version, just print the command that is to be executed instead of trying to execute it. After you are able to determine the command name, complete the code to parse the command line and build the `argv` array, again just printing the results to `stdout`.

■ Next, implement the command execution functionality. This means you will implement the `fork/exec/wait` code. Initially use `execvp` instead of `execv` (it is easier to use since you do not have to search the PATH directories).

■ After you get the program working with `execvp`, implement the PATH search capability and switch from using `execvp` to `execv`.

Operating System Organization

One of our problems is trying to figure out which way is up and which way is down.

—John Young, *Apollo X* astronaut ■

CHAPTER OBJECTIVES

Chapter 2 featured the application programmer's view of the operating system. In the rest of the book, you will study operating systems from the system programmer's perspective. This chapter discusses the general characteristics of the overall organization of an OS. In subsequent chapters, the focus will be on specific design issues.

The chapter first covers the factors that influence the design of multiprogramming operating systems and expands on the fundamental requirements to support hardware abstraction and sharing. Then it introduces the basic functions required of any OS: device management, process and resource management, memory management, file management, and functional organization. It finishes by introducing techniques that have been used to implement those functions.

3.1 ▪ Factors in OS Design

The OS provides an abstraction of the computer's resources to simplify the programmer's job of creating application programs. As discussed from the application programmer's perspective in Chapter 2, processes are the abstraction of the operation of the processor and primary memory, file resources are the classic abstraction of storage devices, and other resources are the abstraction of all other components of the system for which a process competes to accomplish its computation. During computation, processes are the active agents of the computation and resources are the passive elements used by processes. The OS provides mechanisms to enable a process to create and destroy other processes, to request and release resources, to use resources, and to coordinate its own operation with the operations of related processes. It also includes facilities to manage resources so that they can be allocated upon request, be time-multiplexed (shared across time) or space-multiplexed (divided into parts that can be shared at the same time), and be used exclusively or shared in a way such that their use does not cause improper or unintended behavior. In addition to these basic requirements for management facilities, a number of other factors have significantly influenced the evolution and design of operating systems:

- Performance
- Protection and security
- Correctness
- Maintainability
- Commercial factors
- Standards and open systems

The influence of each of these is explained in the rest of this section.

3.1.1 ▪ Performance

People use computers because the potential for very rapid information processing is vastly greater than what can be accomplished using manual techniques. Using computers, they attack problems they would never consider if the related computation were to be carried out manually. For example, for basic number crunching, the benefit of rapid automatic electronic computation is obvious.

At the basic requirements level, operating systems have also been justified by their ability to provide simplified programming interfaces and a mechanism to manage resource sharing. Both of these functions are management functions in the sense that they do not contribute directly to problem solutions but instead provide an *environment* in which these solutions can be produced by application programmers in a cost-effective manner. Even if one accepts that this management function is justified by the overall effectiveness of the computer, there remains the issue of the cost of the service to individual processes. For example, even if an abstraction makes it easier to write a program to solve a particular problem, how much does the use of the abstraction slow down the execution of the program? What is the performance cost of using files rather than commands that manipulate storage devices directly?

Every design issue in an OS must be evaluated with respect to its contribution to the functionality of the system *and* its impact on the computer's performance. Such performance considerations have often prevented an otherwise excellent function from being incorporated into an OS. In many of these cases, increases in performance at the hardware level eventually led designers to use the functionality in spite of its inefficiencies. Traditional examples of this are high-level programming languages, objects, various virtual memory functions, graphics functions, and network functions.

There is no clear way to determine when a costly function should be implemented in the operating system. This is resolved on a case-by-case basis with careful engineering work and a careful analysis of the trade-offs of functionality versus its performance. The study of operating systems is deeply intertwined with the study of computer performance. Throughout this book, performance issues permeate the discussions of designs. In many cases, particular performance issues are isolated in special sections labeled as *Performance Tuning*.

3.1.2 ■ Protection and Security

Multiprogrammed computer systems support multiple processes at the same time. This establishes a computational environment in which processes share resources. It also quickly leads to the requirement for the OS to provide a mechanism by which one process does not interfere with others currently using the machine. A process should not be allowed to use a resource unless it is explicitly authorized to do so. A process must be able to determine either that it has exclusive control of a resource before accessing it or that the access occurs in an environment in which all participating processes are explicitly designed to accommodate resource sharing. Consequently, the OS must be able to create a configuration in which specific resources are isolated to one process or shared among a specific set of processes. At the same time, it must have the flexibility to change that configuration according to the changing needs and desires of all the processes. This flexibility, in turn, implies that the system must incorporate software-controlled mechanisms that ensure isolation yet still allow sharing.

Protection *mechanisms* are tools that the operating system provides to implement a particular security policy chosen by the system's administrator(s). A security *policy* defines the strategy for managing access to a resource. For example, a policy may specify that only one process can have a particular file open for writing at a time but that many processes may open the file simultaneously for reading. A file protection mechanism to implement this policy would provide read and write locks on files to implement the policy.

Protection mechanisms must be enforced by the OS software. This requirement creates an interesting challenge to operating system designers. That is, if OS software sets up a policy, how can application software be prevented from changing that policy? This is a fundamental challenge of modern OS design. Protection and security are a specific subarea of study in OS technology (see Chapter 14). However, like performance, they are so important to the operating system functionality that their consideration permeates every design decision for every function in the OS. As shown in Section 3.3.1, the practical solution to this problem is for the hardware to distinguish between operating system software and application software.

3.1.3 ■ Correctness

Software *correctness* is a critical factor in the acceptance of application programming technology. With regard to protection, some parts of the software can be described as being "trusted" and others as "untrusted" (Section 1.1.3). Ultimately, the system's protection strategy depends on the correct operation of the trusted OS software. Correctness can be determined only if there are specific requirements for each OS function. This enables the designer to argue that the module under scrutiny meets those requirements. For example, it would not be possible to determine if a scheduler were correct unless we knew exactly what the scheduler was required to do. Detailed requirements for operating systems are difficult to construct. This problem has led to the development of one branch of operating system research explicitly devoted to selecting designs for which requirements could be derived and for which implementations could be developed to meet those requirements. Other OS designers may use only informal requirements and arguments to demonstrate that the trusted part of the software system is correct. Correctness is another basic requirement that must be considered when designing and evaluating any function to be added to the OS.

3.1.4 ■ Maintainability

In the 1960s, it became clear that the complexity of operating systems was beginning to exceed any single person's ability to understand every line of code used in the implementation (for example, see Brooks's discussion of the design of the OS/360 software [1975]). In addition to the obvious concern about correctness in such software designs, a new issue arose. How could one change the operating system software and have any assurance the result could be trusted, was correct, and did not introduce new bugs? One branch of designers chose to ensure that their implementations could be easily maintained, perhaps at some cost in generality or performance, by choosing techniques that favored maintainability rather than performance. This maintainability issue has usually driven tactical decisions in an operating system's design.

3.1.5 ■ Commercial Influence on Operating Systems

Most contemporary commercial operating systems are based on multiprogrammed timesharing operating systems extended to handle network interactions. UNIX was designed as a timesharing OS, and its evolutionary systems, the BSD and AT&T versions, continue to be basically timesharing systems. UNIX's commercial acceptance in multiprogramming environments, such as those provided by minicomputers and workstations, is generally attributed to the fact that it is a portable timesharing OS developed at Bell Laboratories by a group having no connection to commercial hardware. (AT&T was legally restricted from manufacturing computer hardware at the time UNIX was derived.) On the other hand, personal computer software environments have been dominated, first by Microsoft DOS and now by Microsoft Windows, probably due to its designer's relationship with the dominant hardware, the IBM PC. Now, the evolution of personal computer hardware has converged on workstation technology, and there is a growing need for multiprogramming on personal computers. The dilemma is that while UNIX supports multiprogramming, Windows operating systems are more widely used.

As of this writing, programmers and users must choose among either multiprogramming systems compatible with DOS, such as Windows 95 and Windows NT, or a commercial variant of UNIX. Ultimately, commercial operating systems may converge on a single approach or the marketplace may continue to support two or more alternatives. In either case, marketing and other commercial concerns, rather than technology, are likely to be the dominant factor.

The success of the UNIX and Windows OS interfaces has resulted in severe constraints on continued growth of operating system technology. For a new OS to be successful, it must have language processors (compilers, linkers, and loaders), text editors, and a runtime library. The existing environments provide all of those tools and applications, all based on the commercial systems. So new OS implementations can contain as much innovation as desired, provided they can be used by other application and system software as if they were a UNIX or Windows implementation. The most radical commercial approach to this problem is the Open Systems Foundation OSF–1 approach. Their operating system implementation is based on the Mach operating system produced at Carnegie Mellon University in the late 1980s [Accetta et al., 1986]. Originally designed to be a multiprocessor operating system, Mach uses messages for interconnecting different parts of the operating system. This approach was intended to enable different parts of the OS to potentially be implemented on different processors.

Today, research operating systems still follow the general trend of implementing some variant of a UNIX interface. However, the trend is now clearly toward microkernel implementations (described in Section 18.2.1). For example, the original Mach kernel has been redesigned to use the microkernel approach, as do most experimental operating systems introduced in research literature.

3.1.6 ■ Standards and Open Systems

Since the late 1980s, a revolution has occurred in the way computers are used in a business organization. Prior to then, an organization purchased all its computing equipment from the same manufacturer. As organizations grew more dependent on information technologies, it became clear it was in the best interests of the end purchaser to acquire computing equipment in an open, competitive market. The desire for a mixture of vendors provides the motivation for *open systems* technology—that is, technology that enables an organization to use diverse computers, operating systems, and applications, while enabling its employees to work together using their different types of machines.

Open systems is essentially a business area in which computer technology has a tremendous influence on the success of the information processing facilities in business [Nutt, 1992b]. Today's organizations must be able to make good business decisions based on their understanding of computer systems technology. The goal of an open systems architecture is to enable end users to employ a heterogeneous network of computers (a network containing more than one kind of computer) to accomplish information-processing tasks within an organization. The fundamental problem is to implement a distributed system such that information is distributed across heterogeneous machines, yet all information is available to each end user (within a specific security policy).

There are at least three complementary strategies for achieving the goals of open systems:

■ **Application integration.** All application programs could be built so that they present a common interface to users, they can exchange data effectively, and their functions interlock. This approach suggests there should be a consistent set of abstract machine facilities that manage devices and information. It argues for a standardized operating system.

■ **Portability.** Application programs could be built so that they can be moved easily from one type of hardware to another. This approach argues for a stringent application programming interface and, implicitly, for a standardized set of facilities at the operating system level.

■ **Interoperability.** Facilities could be provided in a network environment to standardize access to remote facilities. This feature would allow the building of a common set of applications using proprietary services offered on the network. Doing this would require relying on distributed programming and operating system support for distributed computation.

The POSIX standard effort attempts to address most aspects of open systems technology. Particularly, POSIX.1 attempted to broaden the base of OS implementations beyond pure UNIX. It did this by standardizing the interface to the OS rather than the implementation organization. This standardization encouraged various vendors with proprietary operating systems to announce an implementation of POSIX.1. However, most available POSIX.1-compliant operating systems are UNIX-based operating systems. The move toward standardization also imposes an additional design constraint on the software, including on the operating system.

3.2 ■ Basic Functions

The operating system provides mechanisms for supporting an abstraction for computation for the process and for managing resources used by the community of processes. It also addresses the various practical considerations relating to performance, protection, correctness, maintainability, commercial factors, and open systems. There is no complete agreement about the set of functions required for an OS, so for this book, the most widely accepted general framework was chosen for considering more detailed requirements, design issues, architectures, and implementation. OS functions can be classified roughly into four categories:

■ Device management
■ Process and resource management
■ Memory management
■ File management

3.2.1 ■ Device Management

Most operating systems treat all devices such as disks, tapes, terminals, and printers in the same general manner, with special management for the processor and memory. Device management refers to the way these generic devices are handled. Generally, the OS must manage the allocation, isolation, and sharing of the devices according to desired policies. Even operating systems that do not support multiple processes incorporate device management. Normally, the source code for an OS is provided with the computer hardware. If an end user organization adds a physical device to the computer, it must also add a device driver to the OS. If it does not have access to source code, it cannot recompile the OS to include the new driver.

This limitation has led to the development of reconfigurable device drivers in modern operating systems. The device driver can be written (or acquired) by the end user, compiled, and added to the OS without the user's having to recompile the OS.

Device management is an important but relatively simple part of the overall OS design. A general discussion of devices is in Chapter 4 as part of the computer organization discussion. Because device management is essentially defined by the hardware design, it is addressed in detail in Chapter 5, immediately following the discussion of computer organization and before that on the more general, process management function.

3.2.2 ■ Process and Resource Management

Processes are the basic unit of computation defined by programmers, and resources are the elements of the computing environment needed by a process so that it can execute. Process management and resource management could be separated into their own modules, but most operating systems combine them into a single module, since together they define the program execution environment.

In Chapter 2, the UNIX process model was described as one example of how an OS can define a computational environment. A UNIX-style OS provides a set of process management facilities for creating, destroying, blocking, and running a process. Similarly, a thread-based or object-based OS such as Windows NT provides an environment for its respective alternative units of computation with a set of operations for managing that unit of computation. The resource manager part of this module allocates resources to processes when they are requested and available.

The single module allows multiple users (or processes) to share the machine by providing multiple "console devices" and by scheduling the processor so that each process receives an equitable fraction of the available time. A primary consideration of the process and resource manager is how it will enforce isolation of resource access among the processes (according to some policy) and how it will allow the processes to circumvent the isolation mechanism when the policy calls for the processes to share a resource. Resource allocation mechanisms are also generally incorporated into the process and resource management facilities. These mechanisms include those for representing the resource for the process to use and those for managing the resource allocation and use according to the desired policy. Chapters 6 through 10 focus on process and resource management issues.

3.2.3 ■ Memory Management

The memory manager administers the allocation and use of the primary memory resource. Every process requests and uses memory according to its program definition. The memory manager allocates memory to competing processes according to a specified policy and enforces sharing restrictions. A strategy that allows sharing is more complex to design than one with no sharing. Hence, the memory manager incorporates specific isolation mechanisms to support policies for keeping processes from accessing one another's allocated primary memory space and sharing mechanisms for sharing blocks.

Modern memory managers provide *virtual memory* extensions so that the computer's primary memory appears to be larger than it really is. This is accomplished by integrating the computer's main memory and the memory from its storage devices, thus allowing processes to reference memory stored on a storage device as if it were stored in the main memory. Virtual memory requirements differ from conventional memory management requirements. That is, the system is managing an abstract resource—the virtual memory space—which must be managed in conjunction with the physical memory space policies for both primary and secondary memory. In *segmented virtual memory*—memory in which processes reference information by using a block number and an offset—the memory manager also implements mechanisms and policies as part of a file manager. Segmented virtual memory systems tend to draw memory and file management closer together than do operating systems that use another memory management strategy, since the segmented virtual memory approach uses the file manager.

Modern memory managers now also provide a means for a process on one machine to access and share physical memory on another machine. It does this by using an interconnecting network to transmit and receive messages in order to provide a distributed shared memory abstraction. In this case, the memory manager is combining its "native" functionality with network device functionality. Chapters 11 and 12 discuss memory management approaches, issues, and designs, and Chapter 17 extends the discussion to distributed shared memory.

3.2.4 ■ File Management

Files are an abstract resource of storage devices. Information stored in the main memory will be overwritten as soon as the memory is deallocated from a process. Information to be saved must be copied to a storage device, such as a magnetic tape or a disk. As pointed out in Chapter 2, the need to produce abstractions of the details of I/O operations for storage devices was one of the first pushes toward operating systems, and files are the classic abstract resource in operating systems.

The trend has continued in that operating systems all provide a file abstraction for storage device use. Different file managers provide different abstractions, with the requirements ranging from those that model the storage system as a simple byte stream to those that treat it as a logical repository for indexed records. In modern operating systems, the file system is distributed so that a process on one machine can read and write files stored on its local system, as well as those stored in the storage devices of other machines accessible using a network. In Chapter 13, the discussion is expanded to explain how local file systems are defined and implemented to simplify application programming. Chapter 16 generalizes the discussion to remote file systems implemented in a network environment.

3.2.5 ■ Functional Organization

This section explains how the basic functions are combined to satisfy the requirements for an OS. Figure 3.1 shows the general organization for the basic OS modules (the lines between modules indicate interactions). The process and resource manager creates the process definition and execution environment on top of the hardware processor. It uses the abstractions produced by the other managers for resource management. The memory manager is typically distinct from the mechanism that manages the other resources. Thus it is classically a separate part of the OS. As virtual memory has become commonplace, the responsibility of the memory manager has increased to handle the implementation of this virtual memory. The file manager is the part of the OS that abstracts device I/O operations into a relatively simple operation. The device manager handles the details of reading and writing the physical storage devices and is implemented within device drivers.

Resource allocation is handled in the process and resource manager. The file manager makes heavy use of the facilities for reading and writing devices provided by the device manager. Because of the widespread use of device managers that read and write the main memory directly, the file manager is typically required to interact heavily with the memory manager, particularly in virtual memory systems. Thus, even though the goal was to use these four modules to isolate function, they all interact heavily. This interaction is the basic rationale for a monolithic kernel OS design.

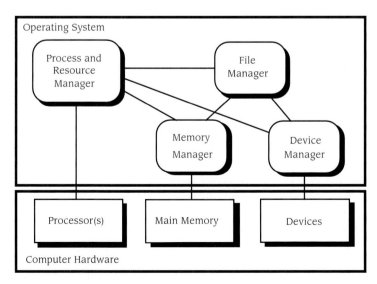

Figure 3.1
Basic Operating System Organization

3.3 ▪ Basic Implementation Considerations

Three basic implementation mechanisms are used in every contemporary operating system design:

- **Processor modes.** The mode bit is used to distinguish between execution on behalf of an OS and execution on behalf of a user.
- **Kernels.** The most critical part of the OS is encapsulated in a kernel. The kernel is designed as a trusted software module that supports the correct operation of all other software.
- **Method of requesting system service.** This issue is concerned with the way user processes request services from the operating system: by calling a system function or by sending a message to a system process.

3.3.1 ▪ Processor Modes

Contemporary processors incorporate a mode bit to define the execution capability of a program on the processor. This bit can be set to *supervisor* mode or *user* mode. In supervisor mode, the processor can execute every instruction in its hardware repertoire, whereas in user mode it can execute only a subset of the instructions. Instructions that can be executed only in supervisor mode are called *supervisor, privileged,* or *protected* instructions to distinguish them from the user mode instructions.

I/O instructions are protected instructions, so if an application program executes in user mode, it cannot perform its own I/O. Instead, it has the OS perform I/O in its behalf. When an application program makes a system request, a special hardware instruction is invoked that switches the processor to supervisor mode and begins to execute the device driver (which invokes the I/O instructions).

The mode bit is also used to address the software protection and security dilemma mentioned in Section 3.1. Instructions that can change the current protection state of the system are privileged instructions. For example, a protection mechanism may rely on the validity of a processor register or certain blocks of memory to store a process's authorization status, pointers to resources, and so on. To protect these registers and memory, privileged load and store instructions must be used to change the contents.

Older computers, such as the Intel 8088/8086 processor, do not include a mode bit. Hence, they do not distinguish between supervisor and user instructions. As a result, it is difficult to provide robust memory isolation in such computers, since any user program can load the segment base registers with any value at any time. Any process can reference any part of the primary memory if the process sets a base register to address a 64KB block of memory.

Subsequent microprocessors in the Intel chip family incorporate a mode bit, so these base registers can be changed only with protected instructions. Newer Intel microprocessors are upward compatible with the 8088/8086 to accommodate software written for the older microprocessors. This compatibility is accomplished by including another processor flag that instructs, say, a 80486 or Pentium to emulate an 8086 by ignoring the mode bit, thereby effectively executing all instructions in supervisor mode.

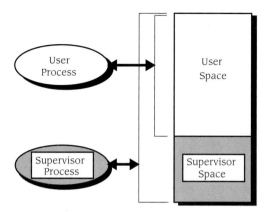

Figure 3.2
Supervisor and User Memory

The system may logically extend the mode bit to define areas of memory to be used when the processor is in supervisor mode versus when it is in user mode (see Figure 3.2). If the mode bit is set to supervisor mode, the process executing on the processor can access either the supervisor or user partition of the memory. If user mode is set, the program can reference only the user memory space. Operating system discussions frequently call the two classes of memory *user space* and *system* (or *supervisor, kernel,* or *protected*) space.

In general, the mode bit extends the operating system's *protection rights.* The mode bit is set by the user mode *trap* instruction, also called a *supervisor call instruction.* This instruction sets the mode bit and branches to a fixed location in the system space. It is similar to a hardware interrupt, so detailed discussion of the instruction operation is left until Section 4.7, after interrupts have been described. The presumption is that only the operating system routines will be loaded in the system space, which is explicitly protected because no user program can load its own code into it. Since only system code is loaded in the system space, only system code can be invoked via a trap. When the operating system has completed the supervisor call, it resets the mode bit to user mode prior to the return.

3.3.2 ■ Kernels

The parts of the OS critical to its correct operation execute in supervisor mode, while other software (such as generic system software) and all application programs execute in user mode. This fundamental distinction is usually the irrefutable distinction between the operating system and other system software. In the abstract machine organization used by an OS, the part of the system software executing in supervisor state is called the *kernel,* or *nucleus,* of the operating system. The kernel operates as trusted software, meaning that when it was designed and implemented, it was intended to implement protection mechanisms that could not be covertly changed through the actions of untrusted software executing in user space. Extensions to the OS execute in user mode, so the operating system does not rely on the correctness of those parts of the system software for correct operation of the OS. Thus a fundamental design decision for any function to be incorporated into the OS is whether it needs to be implemented in the kernel. If it is implemented in the kernel, it will execute in supervisor space and have access to other parts of the kernel. It will also be trusted software by the other parts of the kernel. If the function is implemented to execute in user mode, it has no access to kernel data structures, yet it normally requires very limited effort to invoke the function. While kernel-implemented functions may be easy to implement, the trap mechanism and authentication at the time of the call are usually relatively expensive. The code runs fast, but there is large performance overhead in the actual call.

3.3.3 ■ Requesting Services from the Operating Systems

There are two techniques by which a program executing in user mode can request the kernel's services:

- System call
- Message passing

Figure 3.3 summarizes the differences between the system call and message passing techniques. First, assume that a user process wishes to invoke a particular target system function (represented as an annotated shaded rectangle in the figure). For the *system call* approach, the user process uses the trap instruction (see Section 3.3.1). The idea is that the system call should appear to be an ordinary procedure call to the application program; the OS provides a library of user functions with names corresponding to each actual system call. Each of these "stub functions" contains a trap to the OS function. When the application program calls the stub, it executes the trap instruction, which switches the CPU to supervisor mode, then branches indirectly through an OS table to

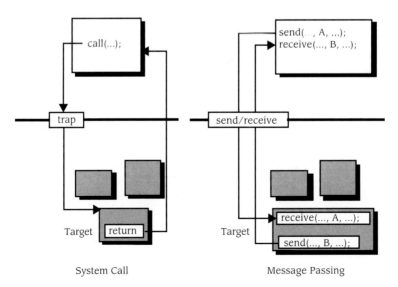

Figure 3.3
Procedure Call and Message Passing Operating Systems

the entry point of the function that is to be invoked. When the function completes, it switches the processor to user mode and then returns control to the user process (thus simulating a normal procedure return).

In the *message passing approach,* the user process constructs a message, A, that describes the desired service. Then it uses a trusted `send` function to pass the message to a trusted OS process. The `send` function serves the same purpose as the trap; it carefully checks the message, switches the processor to supervisory mode, and then delivers the message to a process that implements the target function. Meanwhile, the user process waits for the result of the service request with a message `receive` operation. When the OS process completes the operation, it `sends` a message (B in the figure) back to the user process.

The distinction between the two approaches has important consequences regarding the relative independence of the OS behavior from the application process behaviors and the resulting performance. As a rule-of-thumb, operating systems based on a system call interface can be made more efficient than those requiring messages to be exchanged between distinct processes, even though the system call must be implemented with a trap instruction. This efficiency follows from the cost of process multiplexing, message formation, and message copying versus the cost of a trap instruction execution.

The system call approach has the interesting property that there is not necessarily any OS process. Instead, a process executing in user mode changes to supervisor mode when it is executing kernel code and back to user mode when it returns from the OS call. If the OS is designed as a set of separate processes, it is usually easier to design it so that it gets control of the machine in special situations than if the kernel is simply a collection of functions executed by user processes in supervisor mode. (Even procedure-based operating systems usually find it necessary to include at least a few "system processes"—called daemons in UNIX—to handle situations whereby the machine is otherwise idle, scheduling, handling the network, and so on.)

3.4 ■ Summary

Operating systems define a computational environment to support applications. The environment implements processes, resources, and facilities to manage the use of resources by processes. Resources include processors, memory, and various abstractions of hardware and software facilities. In addition to these fundamental requirements on the OS, several other more detailed requirements must be satisfied. All facilities implemented in the software introduce performance overhead to the basic computation, so the value of the facility must justify the performance cost. All facility designs and implementations must be scrutinized carefully to ensure high performance. The facilities must provide a safe sharing environment in which one process cannot interfere with another process or its resources. The OS software is large and complex, but it also must be correct and maintainable. Commercial factors also have had a strong influence on operating systems technology regarding compatibility and ultimately the adherence to standards to support open system philosophies.

Modern operating systems incorporate managers for processes and resources, including specialized managers for memory, files, and devices. This modularization of basic functions has come from historical perspective rather than sound software modularization principles. It is well-entrenched, so it is not likely that the basic modules will change much in operating systems for some time.

Implementation techniques for modern operating systems rely on a few fundamental technologies. Contemporary processors incorporate a mode bit to allow the processor to execute in supervisor or user mode. If the processor is in user mode and wishes to set the mode bit to supervisor mode, it must execute a special trap instruction to set the bit and then branch to OS code. If the processor is in supervisor mode, the bit can be set to user mode with no special action. The part of the OS that executes in supervisor mode is called the kernel. Some modern operating systems use system call interfaces so that the application process executes OS software in supervisor mode. Others are designed as separate processes that interact with application processes by using message-passing mechanisms.

Operating systems provide various abstractions of the computer hardware. In the next chapter, the detailed study of operating systems begins with a discussion of the fundamental operation of contemporary computer organization.

3.5 ■ Exercises

1. Suppose you are asked to develop an OS for a personal computer with an expected market life of 5 years. What might be the relative importance of the various requirements described in Section 3.1? Which of these requirements would be different for an operating system for a large mainframe with a market life of 20 years?

2. Which of the four basic OS modules might be required on a computer system where there is no multiprogramming?

3. State some factors that might differentiate between the time to do a normal procedure call from an application program to one of its own procedures compared to the time it might take to perform a system call to an OS procedure. (Several of these factors are discussed in the chapters that follow.)

4. Assume the OS for a set of workstations provides a message-passing mechanism. Explain how one might implement a shared memory environment on top of the mechanism. Think of arguments for why this implementation might be a good idea.

5. The original IBM PC and its clones employed the Intel 8088/8086 microprocessor. This machine did not incorporate a mode bit for supervisor and user modes. Hence, any application program (written in assembly language) could load the segment registers any time it wanted to. Suppose an assembly language procedure is called from a C program and the procedure writes a new value into the stack segment register. What will happen when the procedure returns to the C program? Suppose a procedure writes a new value into the code segment register. What will be the effect?

4

Computer Organization

It is evident that the machine must be capable of storing in some manner not only the digital information needed in a given computation ..., but also the instructions which govern the actual routines to be performed on the numerical data.

—Arthur W. Burks, Herman H.
Goldstine, and John von Neumann,
*Preliminary Discussion of an Electronic
Computing Instrument* (1946) ■

CHAPTER OBJECTIVES

An OS provides a layer of abstraction to simplify the model of operation of the hardware. The detailed discussion of operating systems begins in this chapter with background information on computer hardware and its organization that is usually covered in a prerequisite course to operating systems. The material is included in this book for completeness and to highlight some of the hardware issues that are especially critical to the design of operating systems.

Processes are an abstraction of the operation of von Neumann computers. You can understand the intuition behind processes if you understand how a von Neumann computer executes a program. A deep understanding of operating systems depends on this basic knowledge about how computer hardware is organized, especially the control unit and device operation. Device management is introduced in this chapter and refined in Chapter 5. Collectively, the information in Chapters 4 and 5 provide the classic example of the interaction between OS and hardware design and introduces the recurring situation in which the OS must manage two or more distinct mechanisms. Although the focus in this chapter is on the hardware, the point of view of the computer continues to be from the system programmer's perspective.

4.1 ■ The von Neumann Architecture

Unlike other electronic devices, computers are based on the idea that the machine has a fixed set of electronic parts controlled by a program that can be varied according to the problem requirements (see Figure 4.1). Since the program can be changed, different functions can be implemented by acquiring a single hardware system and then constructing different programs to perform sequences of operations to achieve different behavior from the hardware. This characteristic is the crucial difference between these *stored program computers* and other electronic devices.

Stored program computers are often referred to as "general-purpose computers," meaning they can be adapted to do many types of computational and information storage tasks independent of the hardware details. Charles Babbage designed a device during the nineteenth century that essentially incorporated the notion of the stored program computer. The idea was independently invented and implemented using electronic elements in the 1930s. In the 1940s, a group of scientists, including John von Neumann, designed a specific organization for stored program computers—the *von Neumann computer architecture*. This architecture is the basis of modern computers and the basis of the intuitive notion of a "process." That is, the notion of process corresponds to the sequential execution of a program on some set of data using a von Neumann computer.

The von Neumann computer architecture defines a family of stored program machines that form the basis for almost all contemporary computer systems. (Computers designed for specialized processing tasks like signal processing may diverge from the von Neumann architecture; there are no widely known commercial computers that are not von Neumann computers.) As shown in Figure 4.2, the hardware in a von Neumann computer has the following components:

■ A central processing unit (CPU) made up of an arithmetical-logical unit (ALU) and a control unit

■ A primary (or executable) memory unit

■ I/O devices

Programs and data are brought into the machine from the external world using the device controllers and devices. Some of the devices are *storage devices*. Information can be read in from the external world and then stored for an indefinite period of time

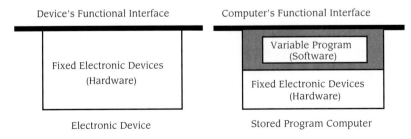

Figure 4.1
Stored Program Computers and Electronic Devices

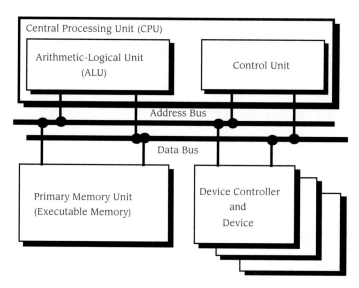

Figure 4.2
The von Neumann Architecture

on a storage device. When the program and data are ready to be used, they are copied into the primary memory unit from either the external environment or a storage device. Once the program has been loaded into the primary memory, the control unit reads each instruction in the program, decodes the instruction, and causes it to be executed by the component responsible for executing that particular instruction. The ALU performs all arithmetic operations such as adding, subtracting, multiplying, and dividing numbers. It also performs logical operations such as comparing two numbers, detecting if a number is zero, and so on.

All units are connected using a *bus* to carry electronic signals from one unit to the other. In Figure 4.2, the bus is divided into an *address bus* and a *data bus* that interconnect various units. In some cases, this pair of buses may be replicated to provide more available bandwidth among units. For example, an input/output bus (consisting of an address part and a data part) might be attached only to devices and memory but not be used by the processor. Such an organization assumes a device can be made to read and write information from/to predetermined memory locations without the direct attention of the processor. Each bus consists of many individual signal carriers ("wires"). Some of the wires are used to arbitrate access to the bus (for example, to allocate the bus to a device when it wants to transfer data between itself and memory). Others are used to carry information—addresses or data. Still others are used for various control functions. It is common for a bus incorporating 16 individual wires for moving data from one unit to another to have twice as many control lines. Thus a bus can be an expensive and complex part of the computer.

All von Neumann computers have a CPU with an ALU and control unit, a primary memory unit, and a set of devices. (Non–von Neumann computers might diverge from the basic architecture—for example, by using alternative units in the machine, coalescing two or more of the units into a single unit, or having a single control unit and multiple ALUs.) The hardware is controlled by loading software into the primary memory and then executing it. Next, the units in a von Neumann computer are discussed in more detail.

4.2 ■ The Central Processing Unit

As shown in Figure 4.2, the CPU is made up of an ALU and a control unit. The ALU performs computations, and the control unit directs the hardware operations according to the program definition. That is, the control unit, as the logical brain of the computer, decodes a stored program and the ALU executes it.

4.2.1 ■ The Arithmetical-Logical Unit

The ALU contains a *function unit* to perform the arithmetic and logical operations and various *registers*—such as general registers and status registers—to hold information being processed by the CPU (see Figure 4.3). General registers are loaded from a specified primary memory location and can have their contents stored into a primary memory location. Contemporary CPUs have 32 to 64 general registers, each typically able to hold a 32-bit value. (This number continues to grow with each wave of new CPUs— some new machines have 64-bit values.) The general registers provide the operands to the function unit and accept the result of an operation by the function unit. Status registers are used by various parts of the CPU to store the status of operations. Throughout this book, all new uses for status registers are explained as the need for them is justified. For now, think of a status register as a place where the CPU stores information regarding the computations currently being carried out in the unit, such as "the result of the last function unit operation was equal to 0."

The function unit can perform various operations (such as add, multiply, shift, or logical AND) on binary representations of integer and floating-point (real) numbers. Computations are accomplished by loading values into general registers, performing

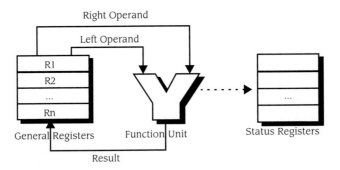

Figure 4.3
A General Arithmetical-Logical Unit

operations on the registers, and then saving the results back into memory. For example, if a C source program contains the code segment

```
a = b + c;
d = a - 100;
```

then the following assembly language instructions can be executed by the CPU to accomplish these two statements:

```
// Code for a = b + c;
load       R3,b // Copy the value of b from memory to R3
load       R4,c // Copy the value of c from memory to R4
add        R3,R4 // Sum placed in R3
store      R3, a // Store the sum into memory cell a
// Code for d = a - 100
load       R4,=100 // Load the value 100 into R4
subtract   R3,R4 // Difference placed in R3
store      R3,d // Store the difference in memory cell d
```

Floating-point operations are usually far more complex than are integer operations, so some function units may not incorporate the extra logic required to perform floating-point arithmetic. Instead, either an auxiliary processor performs those operations or those operations are implemented as a software library routine.

In more complex CPUs, there may be multiple specialized functional units that can execute operations at a very high speed. An ALU that contains such units is designed so that the units can execute at the same time (but ensuring that they execute instructions as if there were only one unit). For example, suppose the ALU diverges from the traditional von Neumann architecture by including two adder units and a multiplier unit. If the program called for the evaluation of the expression

```
a + (b * c) + d + e
```

then one of the adders can be computing "d + e " at the same time the multiplier is computing "b * c ". The other adder would remain idle, waiting for the sum and product to be computed and then combine their results.

4.2.2 ■ The Control Unit

In a stored program computer—all modern computers—the control unit is responsible for causing a sequence of instructions stored in the executable memory to be retrieved and executed. As shown in Figure 4.4, the control unit includes a component to fetch an instruction word from memory, one to decode the instruction, and one to signal the other parts of the computer to execute the instruction. The *program counter* (*PC*) register contains the memory address of the instruction the control unit is currently processing. The *instruction register* (*IR*) contains a copy of the current instruction once it has been fetched from the primary memory. In Figure 4.4, the IR contains the image of the

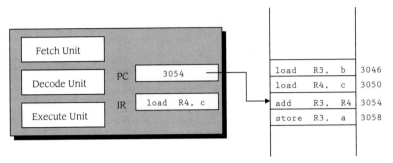

Figure 4.4
The PC, IR, and Memory

load instruction from location 3050 and the PC contains 3054 (the address of the next instruction to be fetched for execution).

The operation of the control unit is better understood by looking at its *fetch-execute algorithm* (see Figure 4.5). When the machine is initially started, the PC is loaded with the address of the first instruction to be executed. This is normally done by a hardware bootup sequence. That is, the machine executes its first instruction from a primary memory address hardwired into the machine. The control unit fetches the first instruction, loads the instruction from the primary memory that is stored at the designated location, and then begins normal operation. In the algorithm description, a haltFlag is included that is tested each time through the loop to determine when the control unit is to be stopped (there are many variants as to how this part of the algorithm is defined for any particular von Neumann computer). When the control unit is halted, the computer is halted. When the system software wishes to execute a program—this system software is being executed by the control unit—it loads the program into the primary memory and then stores the program's entry point in the PC.

Since the CPU always begins operation by reading an instruction from the same memory location (as determined by the hardwired startup sequence), machines must be designed to allow system programmers to define how the hardware begins to execute the operating system. Today, essentially all computers employ a read-only memory (ROM) to define the basic instructions for the machine to use when it starts. When the control unit is started, it branches to a fixed memory location; the ROM is configured so that it is at the address for that fixed memory location. That is, the hardwired

Figure 4.5
The Hardware Fetch-Execute Cycle

```
PC = <machine start address>;
IR = memory[PC];
haltFlag = CLEAR;
while (haltFlag not SET during execution) {
    PC = PC + 1;
    execute(IR);
    IR = memory[PC];
};
```

Figure 4.6
A Bootstrap Loader Program

```
FIXED_LOC:                // Bootstrap loader entry point
      load    R1, =0
      load    R2, =LENGTH_OF_TARGET
loop: read    R3, FIXED_DISK_ADDRESS
      store   R3, [FIXED_DEST, R1]
      incr    R1
      bleq    R1, R2, loop
      br      FIXED_DEST
```

address initially loaded in the PC points to the ROM. This ROM contains a small *boot-strap loader,* a program to begin loading the operating system. This bootstrap loader may be comprehensive enough to store the nucleus of the operating system in memory. Or it may first store a more comprehensive loader that in turn installs the nucleus in memory.

Figure 4.6 is an example ROM bootstrap loader. The power-up sequence causes the hardware to execute an instruction corresponding to

```
load PC, FIXED_LOC
```

where FIXED_LOC is the ROM address at which the bootstrap loader is stored. This bootstrap loader is stored in ROM so that it is always present whenever the computer is powered on. The bootstrap loader is a simple program that will read LENGTH_OF_TARGET words from a fixed disk location, FIXED_DISK_ADDRESS, and store them consecutively in FIXED_DEST. In this representation of the machine language, you can assume that an address and register enclosed in square brackets causes the machine to compute a new address by adding the address in the instruction to the contents of the corresponding register. The bootstrap process loads the program from the fixed location on the disk and then unconditionally branches to it to begin executing.

Once the machine has completed the bootstrap phase and is operating normally under software control, this software can set the PC to start any program executing that has been loaded into memory (by setting the PC to the address of the entry point of the desired program).

4.3 ■ Memory

The primary memory unit stores both programs and data while they are being operated on by the CPU. As shown in Figure 4.7, the memory has an interface composed of three relevant registers: the *memory address register (MAR)*, the *memory data register (MDR)*, and the *command register (Cmd)* For information to be written into the memory, a datum is placed in the MDR, the desired memory address is placed in the MAR, and a `write` command is placed in the command register. Figure 4.7 illustrates the register and memory contents after a `write` command is placed in the command register. The memory unit stored the contents of the MDR (98765) into the memory location loaded in the MAR (1234). A `read` operation is accomplished by placing an

Speeding up the Machine

Computers use synchronous digital logic, meaning there is a basic clock cycle that defines when operations are performed in the lowest–level circuitry. Thus a computer's clock cycle frequency is one factor in determining how fast the computer performs computations; of course, the amount of work done in each cycle is equally important. For contemporary machines, simple machine instructions can be executed in a single clock cycle, although even memory access instructions require multiple clock cycles.

Basic clock cycle times are often used to provide a first-order approximation of the speed of the machine. For example, the IBM PC AT, introduced in the early 1980s, had a basic clock cycle time of 6 MHz [Messmer, 1995]. Thus, a lower bound on instruction execution time on this machine was the amount of elapsed time in one basic cycle, or 0.167×10^{-6} seconds. This is equivalent to 0.167 microseconds (abbreviated μs, one millionth of a second) and 167 nanoseconds (abbreviated ns, a billionth of a second). In contrast, a contemporary Intel Pentium processor might have a basic cycle time of 500 MHz or more, meaning that fastest instructions can be executed in 0.002 μs, or 2 ns.

Another approach to increasing the speed of the computer is to design the control unit so that different parts of the control unit run concurrently. Computer architects realized a machine could be made to run almost twice as fast as normal by overlapping the fetch of the next instruction with the execution of the current instruction. For example, by overlapping the fetch and execute work, the fetch component of the control unit could be obtaining a copy of the instruction in location 3054, while the other parts of the control unit were decoding and executing the instruction in 3050. However, this overlap does cause the control unit to be more complex than the strictly sequential version already described, since, for example, the PC will contain 3054, while the instruction in 3050 is being executed.

address in the MAR and placing a `read` command into the command register. After a *memory cycle,* the memory unit copies the contents of the designated memory cell into the MDR.

The number of cells and the width of each cell in the primary memory is determined by the technology used to construct the memory and by hardware design considerations. For example, if the memory were based on decimal technology, then a word (cell) might be capable of representing any three-digit number between 000 and 999. Each of the three digits could take on a value between 0 and 9. Since there are 10 such values, the numbers would be referred to as decimal (base 10) numbers.

With decimal technology, numbers are stored internally using base 10 arithmetic. In contemporary computers, *binary* technology (base 2 arithmetic) is used to represent information stored in words. Binary technology is used because it is much easier to represent an individual subcell within a cell by an electronic component that is either

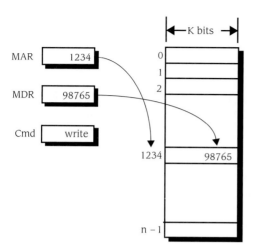

Figure 4.7
The Memory Organization

off (equivalent to the value 0) or on (equivalent to the value 1) than it is to represent decimal numbers. A subcell within a word can store a single *binary integer,* or *bit.* Again, each cell contains a fixed number of subcells, so an 8-bit cell, a *byte,* is composed of 8 binary values. A byte can contain any binary number between 00000000 and 11111111. (In the decimal system, 00000000 base 2 = 0 base 10 and 11111111 base 2 = 255 base 10.)

Suppose the memory contains n words, each with K bits (see again Figure 4.7). The addresses of the n cells are the integers 0 through n − 1. The $i + 1^{st}$ memory cell has address i. In the figure, the memory cell with address 1234 contains the value of 98765 (stored in a binary memory as a 32-bit binary number 0 … 011000010110110101). Notice that the addresses themselves can also be represented in base 2 notation, so 1234_{10} is represented by the 12-bit number 010011010010_2. If n is an integer power of 2, say n = 4,294,967,296 = 2^{32}, then a 32-bit cell can be used to store addresses. Now, if the memory word width K is greater than or equal to 32, one memory cell can be used to store addresses of other memory cells (these addresses can be used, for example, as indirect addresses). If K is less than 32, it is still possible to store an address in the memory by breaking the address into parts and storing the parts in consecutive cells.

In modern computers, a memory cell is 8 bits wide. Even in cases in which each memory cell is an 8-bit byte, groups of 2 or 4 bytes may be operated on as one unit in the CPU called a *word*—different computers define the word size according to the design of their CPU and machine instructions. Even though the CPU often operates on words, the computer hardware is usually organized so that the memory is byte-address-able—that is, each cell is a byte. The CPU can then be designed to perform numeric operations on words and character operations on bytes. This will be so even though the data bus connecting the CPU and the memory transfers words, so memory is read/written using 8-bit byte operations or 32-bit word operations.

Parallel Processors

P arallel processors have been studied for several decades, but the 1980s saw them mature into a viable commercial computing environment. It is useful to consider a few of the approaches used in parallel machines to achieve higher performance than that possible with the basic single-processor von Neumann computer.

The first successful parallel machines incorporated pipelining processors that could execute several instructions—each at a different *stage* of execution—at the same time. Overlapping the fetch and execute cycles can be thought of as a two-stage pipeline—fetching an instruction is the first stage and executing the instruction is the second. These machines proved to be especially effective at computations in which the data types are vectors. The technique is widely used in supercomputers such as the Cray Research machines.

The *single-instruction, multiple-data* (*SIMD*) machines are designed to execute a single program as if it were a serial process. However, each instruction is simultaneously executed on different data streams by the independent processing of elements in the array. The Illiac IV and the Connection Machine CM–2 are examples of this class of machines. Operating systems have not evolved as rapidly as the hardware technology for these machines. Consequently, the SIMD machines tend to incorporate a von Neumann front-end machine that uses a conventional sequential OS and computing environment to control the SIMD machine. The SIMD machine itself is treated as a device by the front-end machine. For example, a typical machine of this type might incorporate 2,000 processing elements in the SIMD architecture but be controlled by a workstation.

Shared-memory multiprocessors employ a collection of off-the-shelf processors such as an Intel Pentium, Sun SPARC, or HP PA-RISC—"killer micros." The processors are interconnected with one another and/or with primary memory using specialized hardware to interconnect processors and memory. In the 1980s, the first wave of such processors used a conventional bus as the interconnection network. This interconnection required that the processors incorporate various buffering techniques to reduce the contention for the common interconnection bus. Even so, no manufacturer was able to construct a viable machine with more than about 20 state-of-the-art processors. If the number exceeded 20, then the contention on the bus became a severe performance bottleneck, thus eliminating the possibility of adding more processors. Such machines are said to not be *scalable*. Shared-memory machines quickly became popular with programmers because the software tools used to develop software for a single process could easily be used with the shared-memory architecture. Doing this required the application to be partitioned into two or more sequentially executed units (each implemented by a process) that could communicate with one another using common memory locations. It has been said that these machines are scalable in the software but not in the hardware. This was because in this machine environment, it is easy to write software that

Parallel Processors *(continued)*

grows with the size of the problem, but difficult to build components that allow the machine to do the same.

Although shared-memory systems are fundamentally distinct from von Neumann machines, they have had little impact on OS technology. Commercial shared-memory multiprocessors typically employ a UNIX timesharing OS with extensions to support various explicit network operations—for example, file management and explicitly shared memory.

Distributed memory multiprocessors are composed of a collection of processors with their memory interconnected with a high-speed network. In some cases, the network is specialized and implemented internally to one physical multicomputer. In others, it is a relatively standard local area network or high-speed fiber optic network. Processes on different computers communicate with one another exclusively through messages, since there is no common memory. Distributed memory machines do not ordinarily support sequential programming languages "transparently," like shared-memory machines do. The software is based on a paradigm that calls for processes to interact with one another by exchanging messages rather than sharing a common memory area. While it is sometimes possible to construct a compiler so that it converts shared-memory references into an appropriate set of message sends and receives, this approach has been only a qualified success. In these machines, the highest levels of performance can be obtained only by writing programs with explicit message passing. Thus the software does not tend to be scalable.

Parallel processing has resulted in new requirements for operating systems to facilitate message management. Much contemporary OS research is focused on effective management of parallel processing environments. This focus suggests there is exciting research to be done in this area. However, it has not reached a point at which technologists have agreed on the best way to manage the environments. The impact of parallel, message-passing systems will be evident in a detailed discussion of OS issues in Chapters 9 and 17.

4.4 ■ Devices

The I/O-devices of the von Neumann machine are used to place data into the primary memory and to store its contents on a more permanent medium. Each I/O device is made up of logic to control detailed operation and the physical device itself. The device may be a storage device such as a magnetic disk or tape; a character device such as a terminal display, a mouse, or a keyboard; or a communication device such as a serial port connected to a modem or a network interface. There are many types of devices of each class, ranging from slow and inexpensive ones to fast and expensive ones. As a result, there is a wide range of interfaces to the devices used by software.

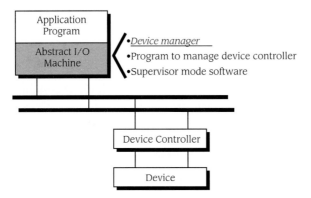

Figure 4.8
The Device-Controller-Software Relationship

Every device uses a *device controller* to connect it to the computer's address and data bus. The controller provides a set of physical components that CPU instructions can manipulate in order to perform I/O operations. While the details of the interface differ among controllers, each controller provides the same basic interface (described in the next subsection). The OS is required to hide the differences among controllers behind an interface common to all types of devices. Then, even though the speeds, capacities, and operation details differ among controllers, the programmer need not know the details about each device in order to use the device effectively. Commonality is achieved by abstracting the operational characteristics of device controllers into a common high-level definition in the OS (see Figure 4.8, and an earlier discussion in In the Hangar: POSIX Files in Chapter 2). Programmers use an abstract I/O paradigm implemented by the high-level definition to write I/O code for a broad spectrum of devices without knowing the details for any of the devices. The high-level machine provides operations to `open`/`close` the device (`allocate`/`deallocate` the device) and to `read`/`write` information. It also provides a general-purpose operation by which the programmer can invoke device-specific operations. In turn, the high-level machine software implementation encapsulates device-specific aspects of each type of controller behind the common interface.

4.4.1 ■ General Device Characteristics

Devices can be characterized as *block-oriented* or *character-oriented,* depending on the number of bytes transferred on an individual operation (many or one, respectively). They can be further characterized as *storage* devices or *communications* devices, depending on whether they are used for permanently storing information or for interconnecting computers and/or terminals. Storage devices are used to store data while the computer is off. Hence, they can be used to keep archival information and to transfer bulk information from one machine to another. Communications devices introduce data into the machine and pass data from one machine to another.

Specific characteristics of storage and communication devices are discussed in Chapter 5.

4.4.2 ■ Device Controllers

A device may require constant attention during its operation. If software were to control the device directly, it would need to continuously monitor the device's detailed operating status during the operation. Much of this attention is simply to observe status, provide detailed commands, and correct for minor errors. It is easy to incorporate into hardware algorithms to manage some of this mundane housekeeping. This is done as a *device controller*. The interface between devices and controllers is important to the industry that manufactures devices but not to software designers. This device-controller interface is concerned with the means by which devices manufactured by one vendor can be connected to a controller manufactured by another. The SCSI (small computer serial interface) is an example of such an interface. The interface between the bus and the controller is important to anyone wishing to attach a device to a computer so that the device can interoperate with other facilities in the machine. However, like the device-controller interface, this interface is conceptually transparent to software.

A higher-level interface defines the interaction between software and the controller via the controller's registers. This interface defines how software manipulates the controller to cause the device to perform I/O operations.

Figure 4.9 shows a software interface to a hardware controller. Devices effectively incorporate two flags as part of their `status` register interface: `busy` and `done`. If both flags are set to 0 (or `FALSE`), the software can place a command in the

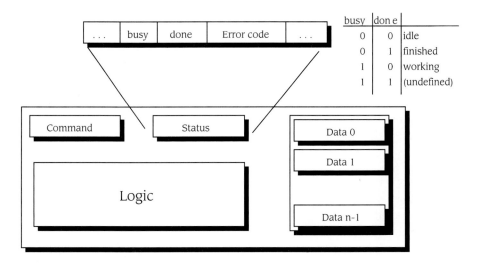

Figure 4.9
The Device Controller Interface

`command` register to activate the device. After software has put data in one or more of the `data` registers for an output operation, the device is available for use. The presence of a new I/O command causes the controller to set the `busy` flag to `TRUE` and to begin the operation. An output operation causes the data in the `data` register to be written to the device, and an input operation causes a read operation to be sent to the device. The process can detect the status of the operation by checking the `status` register. When the I/O operation has completed (successfully or unsuccessfully), the controller clears the `busy` flag and sets the `done` flag. On completion of the read operation, data will have been copied into the `data` register from the device. On completion of a write operation, data will have been copied from the controller `data` register to the device. If the device flags have both been set to `FALSE` after a write operation, it is safe to write new data to the controller `data` register. When the software reads the data from the controller, the controller clears the `done` register to indicate the device is again ready for use. If the controller encountered an unrecoverable error, then when it terminated, it would set the error code field in the `status` register. Controllers must incorporate a small amount of memory to temporarily hold data after it is read from the device but before it is retrieved by the program in the CPU. Conversely, the memory must hold data waiting to be written to the device. This memory is called a (hardware) *buffer* and is sometimes used to increase the chances of overlapping the operation of the device and the CPU (see Chapter 5).

➤ IN THE HANGAR

Asynchronous Serial Devices

An asynchronous terminal is a character-oriented device that exchanges characters with the computer, using explicit signals to control the transfer of each character. Other than IBM 3270-style terminals, nearly all conventional terminals use the asynchronous technique. While an asynchronous terminal is really a communications device, it is distinguished from many other communications devices in that it is character-oriented. Data is transferred between the terminal and the computer in single-byte quantities. Each terminal is really two devices: a keyboard input device and a display output device. An input operation transfers a byte from the device's keyboard controller to a processor register or memory location. An output operation transfers a character from a register or a memory location to the display controller.

The RS–232 standard defines the interface between an asynchronous terminal (keyboard and display) and the controller for exchanging 8-bit bytes of information. The first part of the standard specifies the type of the physical connection (a 9-pin or 25-pin connector), and the second part specifies the meaning of the signal on each connected pin (only four wires are required on the RS–232 interface). The controller accomplishes an output operation by putting a sequence of electronic signals on the wires at prescribed time intervals. The device reacts to the signals and constructs a byte based on them. The byte may be a control byte to the display (for example, to reverse the video colors—black-to-white and white-to-black) or a character to be displayed. The control bytes recognized by the display are device-dependent and typically differ among terminals. (The UNIX `termcap/terminfo` database is used to standardize and abstract these control functions.) Serial terminal devices and controllers can exchange information at speeds in the range of 110 to 57,600 signals per second. This rate of exchange is called the *baud rate* of the terminal. In the RS–232 standard, 11 signals are transmitted for each 8-bit byte transmitted. Three of the eleven signal times are used for synchronizing the operation of the device and the controller for every byte transmitted.

Asynchronous serial device controllers are typically implemented on a single chip having the computational power of a small microprocessor. This chip is designed to provide signals to the device at one of various baud rates, with one of various parity options (odd, even, none), different numbers of overhead bits (2 or 3, depending on what the device is expecting), and so on. The chip has most of its detailed operation specified by a program stored in a ROM with the device. However, the software must choose appropriate parameters to specify the desired operations when the chip performs I/O. This selection can be done directly by either application software or a device driver. The chip itself typically costs less than a dollar, but it must be incorporated into a controller board with other logic, fasteners, and so on. The resulting serial controller still costs much less than $100.

Almost every computer incorporates one or more serial device controllers as part of the basic system. The system console is usually connected to the machine via a serial device controller. The serial device's software/hardware behavior is defined by the small microprocessor and the controller's registers. When such a device is added to a system, it can be used only if software initializes the device by passing commands to the controller to select desired parameters, such as transmission speed and start/stop bits. After the controller has been initialized, it can be directed via write and read commands to transmit or receive information.

4.4.3 ■ Device Drivers

The device controller provides an interface to be used by the high-level machine software shown in Figure 4.10. This software implements the device management part of the OS as a collection of *device drivers*. The device driver to controller interface may be relatively complex in the sense that there can be many parameters to set prior to starting the controller and many aspects of the status to check when each operation has completed. However, because of the "standardized" device driver to application software interface, application software can deal uniformly with different kinds of devices. Drivers for different devices implement a similar interface, so a higher-level machine need not be especially concerned with the details of the particular device (see Figure 4.10). The goal is to simplify the software interface to devices as much as possible, the reason being that differences between controllers produced by different manufacturers will be transparent to application software and even differences between different types of devices will be as transparent as possible.

The presence of devices, controllers, and drivers enables two parts of a program to operate at the same time—one part using the CPU and the other part using the devices.

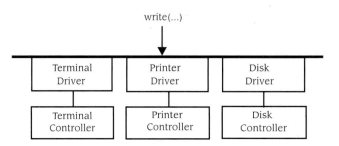

Figure 4.10
The Device Driver Interface

One goal of an OS is to provide facilities that enable application programmers to take advantage of the physically separate devices so as to execute logically separate operations simultaneously. Unfortunately, most programming languages discourage such overlap through the semantics of high-level I/O instructions. Nevertheless, the OS can manage the processes so that CPU utilization by one process overlaps the I/O operation of another. While this overlap does not increase the performance of either process, it makes the use of the hardware more effective, since two or more parts are used simultaneously rather than sitting idle.

The device driver is the OS entity that controls CPU-I/O parallelism. A device can be started by the device driver, and the application program can continue operation in parallel with the device operation. A problem arises in providing some OS mechanism to notify the part of the program that is executing on the CPU that the I/O operation has completed. Contemporary computer systems use interrupts, discussed next, to accomplish this notification.

4.5 ▪ Interrupts

The busy-done flags must be tested by the driver software that determines when the device has completed its operation. When a process is using the CPU but is repeatedly testing the flags, a *busy-wait* situation occurs. The process uses the CPU but is logically waiting for the device to complete its operation. A busy-wait wastes processor cycles that might be better used by other processes.

If the process does not use the processor to check the controller status continually, there will be a time period after which the device has completed operation but before the process checks and detects the completion. This period adds to the time the process is blocked waiting for the I/O operation to conclude.

Clearly, the most efficient overlap between the device and the CPU could be obtained if the device would signal the processor as soon as it has completed the I/O operation. This would eliminate the need for busy-waits and minimize the idle time. The von Neumann architecture can be modified to implement this approach by incorporating *device interrupts* through which a device notifies the processor when it has completed an I/O operation. First, an *interrupt request flag* is incorporated into the hardware and the control unit is modified so that it checks the flag during each instruction fetch-

Figure 4.11
The Fetch-Execute Cycle with an Interrupt

```
while (haltFlag not set during execution) {
  IR = memory[PC];
  PC = PC + 1;
  execute(IR);
  if (InterruptRequest) {/* Interrupt the current process */
    memory[0] = PC; /* Save the current PC in address 0 */
    PC = memory[1]; /* Branch indirect through address 1 */
}
```

execute cycle (see Figure 4.11). Conceptually, the hardware connects all device done flags to the interrupt request flag in the control unit using inclusive-OR logic, as shown in Figure 4.12. Whenever the done flag is set on any controller, the interrupt request flag, InterruptRequest, is set. The control unit will be aware of a device completion within the time it takes to execute a single instruction—microseconds or even nanoseconds, depending on the time taken to finish executing the current instruction.

The signal from the hardware to the software—the *interrupt*—causes the processor to cease executing the sequence of instructions addressed by the PC and to branch to a new instruction sequence whose address is stored in, for example, memory location 1 (denoted memory[1]). When the branch occurs, the hardware saves the old PC location (address of the next instruction to be executed) of the interrupted process. The address of the *interrupt handler* is stored as an indirect address in memory[1] when the machine is started. The interrupt handler is a part of the operating system that will be executed when any device completes its operation. So the application software need not continuously poll the device to detect when it has completed.

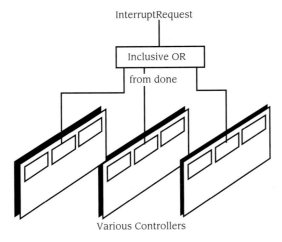

Figure 4.12
Detecting an Interrupt

When the interrupt handler begins execution, the CPU registers will contain values being used by the interrupted process (excluding the PC). The interrupt handler must immediately perform a *context switch* to save all the general and status registers of the interrupted process and to install its own values for every CPU register so that it can handle the completion of the I/O operation. As shown in Figure 4.13, the interrupt handler inspects the various device done flags to determine which device completed and caused the interrupt.

The InterruptRequest flag shown in Figure 4.12 and the interrupt handler code schema shown in Figure 4.13 provide a means for a device to interrupt the CPU and handle the device I/O completion within one machine instruction. Modern computers extend the mechanism so that the source of the interrupt can be detected more rapidly than this simple mechanism allows. The idea is for the hardware to incorporate an *interrupt vector* rather than just a single flag. The single inclusive OR gate in Figure 4.12 is replaced by a vector of interrupt requests. If the system contains N devices and the vector has K coordinates, then N/K device done flags are connected to each vector coordinate. Further, a table containing the entry point for K different interrupt handlers is kept in memory. If coordinate i in the interrupt vector is set to TRUE, the normal instruction sequence is interrupted, as shown in Figure 4.11, and the ith interrupt handler from the table of interrupt handlers is started.

If two or more devices finish during the same instruction cycle, then the code schema shown in Figure 4.13 will detect only the first one that finished. Once the cause of the interrupt has been determined, the interrupt handler branches to the *device handler code* for the device. This action will cause the done flag to be cleared and the I/O operation to be completed. Completion of the processing includes signaling and subsequent resumption of the process that was blocked waiting for the I/O to complete.

Another problem must be dealt with if an interrupt occurs while the interrupt handler is in the midst of execution. That is, before the processor can finish handling the first interrupt, it will restart due to the occurrence of a second interrupt. Depending on exactly which part of the interrupt or device handler is currently being executed for the first interrupt, the processor state may be lost or the completion processing for a device operation may never be completed. Of course, some parts of the device handler can be interrupted and then resumed later without harm. When the interrupt handler begins to execute, it begins saving the state of the interrupted process and determining the cause of the interrupt. If another interrupt occurs while the interrupt handler is performing these operations, it is difficult to ensure that the proper values will be saved for the

Figure 4.13
The Interrupt Handler

```
Interrupt_Handler{
    saveProcessorState();
    for (i=0; i<Number_of_devices; i++)
      if (device[i].done == 1) goto device_handler(i);
/* Something wrong if we get here */
}
```

Figure 4.14
Disabling Interrupts

```
if(InterruptRequest && InterruptEnabled) {
/* Interrupt current process */
    disableInterrupts();
    memory[0] = PC;
    PC = memory[1];
}
```

process that was originally interrupted and that the cause of the original interrupt will be detected. If the second interrupt causes an error in the interrupt handler, one of the two I/O operations may fail. This *race condition* between the execution of the interrupt handler code and the occurrence of another interrupt must be avoided if the machine is to perform I/O operations reliably.

The race condition can be handled by incorporating another mechanism to prevent interrupts from interrupting the handler. Suppose the machine was designed to include an interrupt-enabled flag, `InterruptEnabled`, a `disableInterrupt` instruction to set the flag to `FALSE`, and an `enableInterrupt` instruction to set the flag to `TRUE`. The instructions are implemented by again modifying the control unit so that the part of its operation that checks for an interrupt occurrence behaves as described in Figure 4.14. If `disableInterrupt` has been executed prior to the interrupt occurrence, thereby causing the `InterruptRequest` flag to be set to `TRUE`, then the `InterruptEnabled` flag is `FALSE` and the control unit ignores the interrupt occurrence.

Interrupts do not alter the control flow of the process executing on the processor. Once the enable instruction has been executed, the `InterruptEnabled` flag is set to `TRUE`. Any pending interrupt is then "caught" by the interrupt handler and dispatched to the appropriate device handler as before. The first interrupt occurring after the interrupts have been disabled will be saved by virtue of the corresponding `done` flag, which remains `TRUE` until the device handler executes. If two or more interrupts occur while the interrupt handler is handling an interrupt, the hardware may not save subsequent interrupts for processing—that is, the late interrupts may be lost.

4.6 ■ The Mode Bit Revisited: The Trap Instruction

Section 3.3.1 introduced the CPU mode bit for differentiating between privileged and user instructions. Any instruction that sets the `haltFlag` in the control unit should be a privileged instruction, since `haltFlag` causes the computer to cease executing any more instructions.

If the CPU is running in user mode and a process wishes to begin executing in supervisor mode, the environment must ensure that when the mode bit is switched from user mode to supervisor mode, the processor will then begin executing kernel code. Otherwise, a user mode program could switch modes, execute its own privileged instructions, and then return to user mode. There would be no mechanism to prevent any process from executing an arbitrary set of privileged instructions.

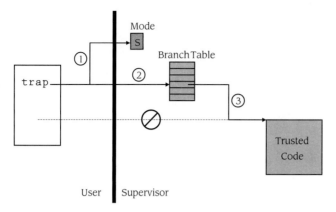

Figure 4.15
The Trap Instruction Operation

As mentioned in Section 3.3.1, the supervisor mode is set by a `trap` instruction. Suppose the assembly language representation for a trap is

```
trap argument
```

Figure 4.15 pictorially represents the indirect behavior of a trap instruction (to accomplish the effect of the dotted line branch); it switches the CPU to supervisor mode and then branches to an operating system *trap handler* (see Figure 4.16). That is, a trap produces the same action as a vectored interrupt, where the trap handler table is loaded at location 1000. This simple mechanism provides a safe way for a user-mode process to execute only pre-defined software when the mode bit is set to supervisor mode.

4.7 ■ Summary

Stored program computers provide a means by which fixed-function hardware can be controlled through variable software specifications. This flexibility is unique among electronic and mechanical devices, and it is the aspect of electronic devices that defines them as computers. For over 50 years, the von Neumann architecture has been the dom-

Figure 4.16
Trap Handler

```
executeTrap(argument) {
    setMode(supervisor);
    switch(argument) {
    case 1: PC = Memory[1001];
    case 2: PC = Memory[1002];
    . . .
    case n: PC = Memory[1000+n];
}
```

inant approach to computer design. A von Neumann computer is based on a processor that has an ALU and a control unit, a primary memory that can store the program and data, and devices to store programs and data when the computer is turned off, to introduce data into the computer, and to write the results computed by processes.

CPU design operates on a basic fetch-execute cycle in which a machine instruction is retrieved from the executable memory, decoded by the control unit, and then executed by some part of the CPU and/or devices. The ALU is the workhorse for arithmetical and logical operations. The control unit is responsible for determining the sequence of instructions to be executed. The memory is organized as a set of cells with contiguous addresses. A memory cell is used to store information for use by the processor.

Devices introduce information into the memory and record the results of computations performed by the machine. Many kinds of devices can be added to a machine, ranging from sensors for process control applications to networks capable of transferring enormous amounts of information from one machine to another in mere seconds. Communications devices are used to transmit and receive information, and storage devices are used to save information.

Each device has a controller to abstract the physical device into a higher-level interface shared by different device producers. This abstraction allows manufacturers to build a family of devices with different performance and size characteristics that provide a common hardware interface to software. It even allows competing manufacturers to provide "plug compatible" devices.

Device drivers constitute another layer of abstraction in which a standardized software interface is defined so that a programmer can interact with devices while knowing few details of the device itself. The interface is biased toward software I/O operations rather than toward device behavior.

The problem of detecting when an I/O operation has been completed has led to the development of interrupts. An interrupt enables a process that is blocked on an I/O operation to simply "sleep" until the operation has completed. It also creates situations in which race conditions can occur. If an interrupt should occur just after another interrupt has occurred and is being processed, the operating system may lose track of the correct processing and erroneously handle the I/O operation. (In Chapter 8, you will discover that the problem is actually much worse than described in this chapter!)

In the next chapter, the simplest software extension—device management—is discussed.

4.8 ■ Exercises

1. The machine instruction

```
br FIXED_DEST
```

causes the computer to execute its next instruction from memory location FIXED_DEST. What are the detailed steps of the ALU and/or control unit to execute this instruction? Provide the same steps for the conditional branch instruction

```
bleq R1, R2, loop
```

which branches to the instruction labeled "loop" if the contents of R1 are less than or equal to the contents of R2.

2. Figure 4.5 describes the fetch-execute algorithm for a sequential control unit. The discussion of the control unit informally describes how a machine can be made to run much faster by overlapping the fetch and execute operations. List the steps necessary to accomplish this overlap by explaining any new registers that might be needed, indicating which control unit components operate at the same time, and by rewriting the fetch-execute algorithm.

3. Suppose a workstation has a clock rate of 25 MHz, which means that the machine is capable of performing 25 million basic operations per second. For example, a register test instruction might take just 1 clock cycle, but an arithmetic instruction might require 10 clock cycles, while an I/O instruction might require hundreds.

   a. What is the time duration of one basic operation?
   b. Assuming the average instruction takes 2.5 clock cycles, how many instructions can be executed in 100 microseconds?

4. High-level programming languages can be thought of as abstract machines for machine language instruction sets. Given the C assignment statement

   ```
   a = b + c;
   ```

   do the following:

   a. Describe an implementation of the abstract machine by using a pseudo assembly language as the machine language generated by a compiler if the statement is preceded by a declaration of the form

   ```
   int a, b, c;
   ```

   b. Describe an implementation of the abstract machine if the statement is preceded by a declaration of the form

   ```
   float a, b, c;
   ```

   Show how the machine language for this code segment differs from the code in part a.

   c. Describe an implementation of the abstract machine if the statement is preceded by a declaration of the form

   ```
   int a;
   float b, c;
   ```

   Show how the assembly language for this code segment differs from the code in parts a and b.

5. Microprocessor chips often do not include floating-point operations in their hardware instruction set. Floating-point instructions must then be implemented either by using software functions or via the inclusion of a supplementary floating-point chip to be used with the microprocessor chip.

    a. Using pseudocode, describe the algorithm for summing two floating-point numbers.

    b. Describe the algorithm for multiplying two floating-point numbers together.

    c. What might be the performance difference between a floating-point multiplication in a microprocessor having the algorithm implemented in a floating-point chip rather than in a software algorithm? (Answer this question by indicating which method would be faster. Then estimate the difference in speeds by a expressing a factor such as 3, 10, 100, and 1000).

6. Assume it takes an average of 2.5 clock cycles to execute an instruction in a one-address machine language (that is, each individual instruction can reference at most one memory location). Estimate the number of clock cycles it would take to execute the C loop that follows if the code is compiled without optimization. Explain your answer.

```
for(i=0; i<100; i++) a[i] = 0;
```

7. Maintaining a system clock that can be read by any user program requires only that the operating system read a physical device (keeping physical time) and then write the time into a globally readable variable. Suppose the time to read the physical clock and to update the variable is 100 microseconds. What percentage of the total CPU time is spent maintaining a clock that is accurate to the millisecond resolution (that is, the clock always reflects the correct time to the closest millisecond)? The 100 microsecond resolution? The 10 microsecond resolution? Explain your rationale.

8. C++ type hierarchies could be used to define device drivers by encoding standard operations for all devices in a base class and then refining the behavior for various devices with derived classes. Describe a type hierarchy, including member functions and data, for a keyboard, display, mouse, serial line printer, floppy disk, and hard disk. Do not include details of the functions.

9. Using C-like pseudocode, describe a device driver, interrupt handler, and device status table to implement the following:

    a. `open(device)`

    b. `close(device)`

    c. `get_block(device, buffer)`

    d. `put_block(device, buffer)`

Because this specification of the problem ignores many details of a real system, you will need to make some assumptions about the hardware and operating systems environment. You may use any system as a guideline for your assumptions. However, be sure to specify all assumptions you make in your solution.

10. Conventional high-level programming languages rely on sequential semantics for their operation. In particular, when programmers write a code segment such as

```
. . .
read(io_port, &buffer, length);
x = f(buffer[i]);
. . .
```

they expect the assignment statement will not be executed until the read statement has retrieved input data and written it into memory at address `buffer`. Write a pseudocode description of how these semantics could be implemented with a "read" library routine and a corresponding program to use the routine.

11. Describe a new read function, "xRead," along with other functions that could enable one to write programs in a high-level language such that the application can continue processing after the "xRead" call but can block itself before using data in the process of being read.

12. Serial asynchronous communication ports are widely used in contemporary computers to connect a terminal (keyboard and display) or a printer to the computer. The signaling protocol typically employs 1 or 2 start bits and a single stop bit to encapsulate each byte. A transmitter sends start bits to the receiver to indicate that a byte is about to be transmitted. The 8 bits in the byte are then transmitted, followed by a single stop bit. How many bytes per second can be transmitted over a 9,600-baud serial line using this protocol? What is the percentage of time spent on transmitting overhead bits?

13. Read the documentation for programming a personal computer serial port. Then write a pseudocode description of the steps to handle a serial port.

14. Personal computers (executing in 8086 emulation mode) incorporate simple devices for accomplishing I/O with the keyboard and display and for accomplishing asynchronous serial I/O, with more complex interfaces to disks and networks. Consult a personal computer hardware technical reference manual to determine how the bitmap display can be programmed. Then write a C/C++ program to draw rectangles on the display without using the BIOS routines, graphics library, and so on.

5

Device Management

It seems that most designers of computing machines agree that the time required for the input of one number should be of the same order of magnitude as the time required for an arithmetic operation, or perhaps longer by one order of magnitude.

—Franz L. Alt on the Bell Laboratories
Computing Machine (1948) ■

CHAPTER OBJECTIVES

Contrary to the goals of I/O systems of half a century ago, today the speed ratio of CPU to I/O operations is now several orders of magnitude. As a result, today's systems go to great efforts to overlap the I/O operations with the CPU to reduce the overall effect on the speed at which a computation can be completed. This chapter extends the discussion of devices in Chapter 4 by considering the software to manage devices—in particular, device drivers and the interrupt handler, the part of the OS that provides device management.

The chapter begins with a summary of basic device management approaches: direct I/O with polling, interrupt-driven direct I/O, memory-mapped I/O, and direct memory access. Next, it considers how buffering can be used to increase I/O performance. In buffering, the device manager reads data from the device before it is requested by the process and stages information to be written when a busy device becomes idle. It is important to see how buffering works and why it can decrease the amount of time required to execute a process. The chapter then considers several generic details of device driver organization, although ultimately, each driver's function and organization depends on the controller it manages. Finally, some device-specific aspects of the management of common classes of devices in a modern computer are discussed.

5.1 ▪ Device Management Approaches

Device management is that part of the operating system responsible for directly manipulating the hardware devices. It provides the first-level abstraction of these resources that will be used by applications to perform I/O. In this section, various approaches by which device management can abstract I/O operation are discussed.

The simplest scenario is to use direct I/O. This involves requiring the CPU software to explicitly transfer data to and from the controller's data registers. In one variant of direct I/O—direct I/O with polling—the device management software polls the device controller status register to detect completion of the operation. Another variant of direct I/O is interrupt-driven direct I/O. Recall from Chapter 4 that interrupts simplify the software's responsibility for detecting operation completion.

Another aspect of the problem is to use memory-mapped I/O. Here, device addressing simplifies the interface, resulting in widespread use in contemporary systems. Memory-mapped I/O can be used with the polling or interrupt strategy.

A final aspect is to use direct memory access. This indirect I/O approach involves designing device hardware to avoid having the CPU perform the transfer of information between the memory and the controller's data register.

5.1.1 ▪ I/O System Organization

In modern operating systems, device management is implemented either through the interaction of a *device driver* and interrupt routine (called interrupt-driven I/O) or wholly within a device driver if interrupts are not used (called direct I/O with polling). Figure 5.1 summarizes the units involved in I/O operations for both approaches.

An application process uses a device by issuing commands and exchanging data with the device management device driver. The device driver has two major responsibilities:

▪ Implement an abstract application programming interface (API) to the application process.
▪ Provide device-dependent operations to issue appropriate commands to implement functions defined on the API.

The APIs among different device drivers should be as much alike as possible. This will reduce the amount of device-specific information the application programmer needs to know in order to use the device. That is, the abstractions implemented by various device drivers should be as much alike as possible for all drivers. However, since each device controller is unique to the particular device, the driver implementation must be device-specific so that it can provide the correct commands to the controller, interpret the controller status register contents correctly, and transfer data to and from the controller data registers as required for correct device operation. The first requirement of device management is to provide software that meets these two responsibilities.

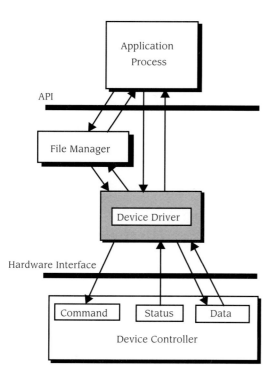

Figure 5.1
Device Management Organization

5.1.2 ■ Direct I/O with Polling

Direct I/O refers to the method of accomplishing I/O whereby the CPU is responsible for transferring the data between the machine's primary memory and the device controller data registers. While managing the I/O, the device manager may poll the device `busy-done` flags or use interrupts to detect the operation's completion. This section concentrates on the most basic technique; that is, the CPU starts the device and then polls the status register to determine when the operation has completed.

Here are the specific steps required to accomplish an input operation using polling (see Figure 5.2):

1. The application process requests a read operation.

2. The device driver queries the status register to determine if the device is idle. If the device is busy, the driver waits for it to become idle.

3. The driver stores an input command into the controller's command register, thereby starting the device.

4. The driver repeatedly reads the status register while waiting for the device to complete its operation.

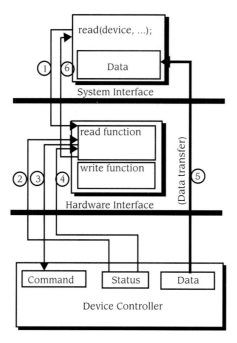

Figure 5.2
Polling I/O Read Operation

5. The driver copies the contents of the controller's data register(s) into the user process's space.

The steps to perform an output operation are as follows:

1. The application process requests a write operation.
2. The device driver queries the status register to determine if the device is idle. If the device is busy, the driver waits for it to become idle.
3. The driver copies data from user space memory to the controller's data register(s).
4. The driver stores an output command into the command register, thereby starting the device.
5. The driver repeatedly reads the status register while waiting for the device to complete its operation.

Each I/O operation requires that the software and hardware coordinate their operations to accomplish the desired effect. In direct I/O with polling, this coordination is accomplished by encapsulating the software part of the interactions with the device controller hardware wholly within the device driver. However, with this approach it is generally difficult to achieve highly effective CPU utilization, since the CPU must constantly check the controller status. As a result, CPU cycles are used to repeatedly test the controller interface while the device is busy. As discussed in Chapter 4, in a multi-programmed system these wasted CPU cycles could be used by another process. Because the CPU is used by other processes in addition to the one waiting for the I/O to complete, multiprogramming may result in sporadic detection of I/O completion. This can be remedied through the use of interrupts.

5.1.3 ■ Interrupt-driven I/O

The motivation for incorporating interrupts into the computer hardware is to eliminate the need for the device driver to constantly poll the controller status register. Instead, the device controller "automatically" notifies the device driver when the operation has completed. In the scenario using interrupts, the device management functionality is partitioned into four different parts:

- "Top half" (a name coined in BSD UNIX) of the driver that initiates the operation
- Device status table
- Interrupt handler
- Device handle

The following are the steps for performing an input instruction in a system by using interrupts (see Figure 5.3):

1. The application process requests a read operation.
2. The top half of the device driver queries the status register to determine if the device is idle. If the device is busy, the driver waits for the device to become idle.
3. The driver stores an input command into the controller's command register, thereby starting the device.
4. When the top half of the device driver completes its work, it saves information regarding the operation that it began in the *device status table*. This table contains an entry for each device in the system. The top half of the driver writes information into the entry for the device it is using such as the return address of the original call and any special parameters for the I/O operation. The CPU then can be used by another program, so the device manager invokes the scheduler part of the process manager. It then terminates.
5. Eventually the device completes the operation and interrupts the CPU, thereby causing the *interrupt handler* to run.
6. The interrupt handler determines which device caused the interrupt. It then branches to the *device handler* for that device.
7. The device handler retrieves the pending I/O status information from the device status table.
8. The device handler copies the contents of the controller's data register(s) into the user process's space.

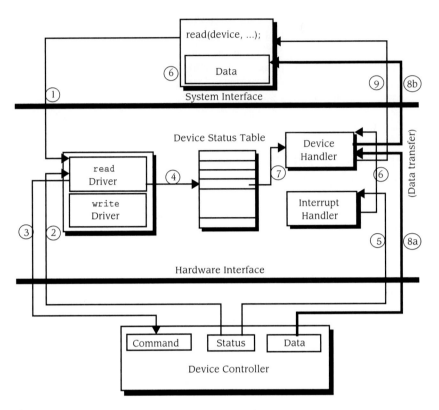

Figure 5.3
Interrupt-driven I/O Operation

9. The device handler—behaving as the "bottom half" of the device driver invoked by the application process—returns control to the application process.

The output operation behaves similarly. From the viewpoint of the application process, the activity has the same semantics as an ordinary procedure call. However, the time to execute the program may be considerably shorter than it is for a polling system, depending on the time ratio of computing, the I/O, and the timeliness with which the software processes poll the device. This added delay in a polling system stems from the accumulation of delays between the time that the device finishes the operation and the time that the executing program observes this event and continues its normal execution.

The software interface to an I/O device usually enables the OS to execute alternative processes when any specific process is waiting for I/O to complete, while preserving *serial execution semantics* for an individual process. This means serial programs have simple I/O semantics that allow the programmer to treat read and write operations as sequential operations. When programmers use a read statement in a program, they know the read instruction has completed before the next instruction is executed.

For example suppose a process executes code such as

```
. . .
read(deviceX, "%d", x);
y = f(x);
. . .
```

Figure 5.4 shows the situation after the read system call has started the deviceX device but before the operation has completed. If the CPU were to execute the assignment statement, y = f(x), after the device driver had started the device but before it had completed the I/O operation, then the f function would be executed using an old value of x, not the one being read from the device. To prevent this situation, the operating system explicitly blocks the process that is executing the sample code after it issues the read call. The operating system then waits for the process to complete the operation before it executes the assignment statement.

More complex semantics could allow the programmer to initiate the read operation—that is, to start the device and then to continue processing. This would require that the programmer have some way to determine that the read operation had completed before referencing the variables that are receiving the result of that operation. In the conventional approach, the device driver interface implements a standard procedure call mechanism for accomplishing I/O (from the application program). The application program calls a procedure to request the I/O operation. When the procedure returns, the operation will have been completed. Operation of an individual process and its I/O is serialized.

Even though an individual process may not be able to take advantage of the overlap of CPU and I/O operation, the OS can switch the CPU to another process whenever one process invokes an I/O operation. Thus the overall system performance can be improved due to the resulting overlap, although the individual process will still execute sequentially across the processor and the I/O device. This requirement for serialization

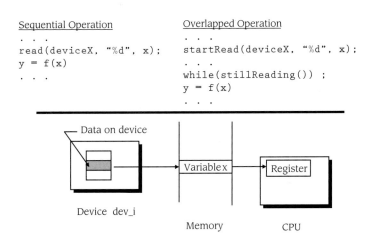

Figure 5.4
Overlapping the Operation of a Device and the CPU

within a process means that the process management part of the OS must become involved in I/O operations. This ensures that an I/O call will result in the calling process yielding control of the CPU to another application process. When the I/O completes, the original process can be rescheduled.

PERFORMANCE TUNING

Interrupts Versus Polling

I n general, the time to execute a process can be broken down into the time spent on computation, $time_{compute}$, the time spent on I/O operations, $time_{device}$, and the time the process spends determining when each I/O operation is complete, $time_{overhead}$, as follows:

$$time_{total} = time_{compute} + time_{device} + time_{overhead}$$

In an I/O device manager using polling, $time_{overhead}$ is the accumulated amount of time after a device completes an operation but before the polling loop has determined that the completion has occurred ($time_{polling}$). This is generally only a few instruction execution times.

In a system with interrupts, $time_{overhead}$ is calculated as follows:

$$time_{overhead} = time_{handler} + time_{ready}$$

where $time_{handler}$ is the accumulated time required to execute the interrupt handler

and device handler routines, and $time_{ready}$ is the accumulated time the process waits to use the CPU after it has completed its I/O but another process is using the CPU.

Polling is normally superior from the viewpoint of the individual process, since normally

$$time_{polling} < time_{handler} + time_{ready}$$

However, consider the effect of both approaches on the overall performance of the system, rather than this turnaround time for one process. Suppose three processes are to be executed on a system. Process 1 requires $time_{total1}$ to complete, process 2 requires $time_{total2}$ to complete, and process 3 requires $time_{total3}$ to complete. In a polling system, process 1 might run to completion before process 2 is started, and process 2 would run to completion before process 3 is started. The total time to execute all

three processes with polling would be

$$time_{TOTAL-P} = time_{total1} + time_{total2} + time_{total3}$$

In a system with interrupts, multiprogramming can make good use of the CPU by processes 2 and 3 when process 1 is conducting I/O. Ideally,

$$time_{device1} \le time_{compute2}$$
$$time_{device2} \le time_{compute3}, and$$
$$time_{device3} \le time_{compute1},$$

meaning the total time to execute the three processes in a system with interrupts is

$$time_{TOTAL-I} = time_{compute1} + time_{compute2} + time_{compute3} + time_{overhead}$$

where the overhead is the sum of the overhead times of the individual processes. The average time to finish a process is $time_{TOTAL-I}$ divided by 3. Hence, the average time to execute a process is much less with interrupts than it is with polling.

5.1.4 ■ Memory-mapped I/O

An I/O device is managed by having software read/write information from/to the controller's registers. The computer designer must decide what instructions will be included in the machine repertoire to manipulate each controller's registers.

Traditionally, the machine instruction set includes special I/O instructions to accomplish this task. For example, to perform the I/O operations an instruction set might include instructions such as the following:

```
input     device_address
output    device_address
copy_in   CPU_register, device_address, controller_register
copy_out  CPU_register, device_address, controller_register
test      CPU_register, device_address
```

Here, each I/O instruction refers to the device's address by a unique hardware identifier for a particular controller board. The `input` instruction causes the read operation to be placed in the command register of the designated device. The `output` instruction places the write operation in the command register. (The controller will likely ignore an attempt to execute an `input` or `output` instruction if the device is busy. The exact effect will depend on the controller design.) The `copy_in` and `copy_out` instructions copy information into or out of a CPU register from/to the designated controller's data register. The `test` instruction copies the contents of the designated CSR to a CPU register.

Figure 5.5 describes the memory-mapped I/O approach, contrasted with the traditional approach. With separate device addresses (see Figure 5.5a), each component in a

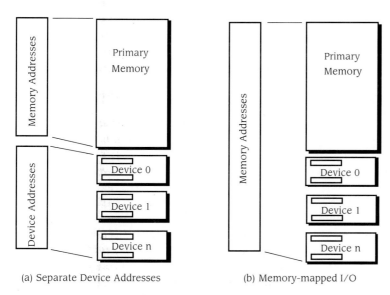

(a) Separate Device Addresses   (b) Memory-mapped I/O

Figure 5.5
Addressing Devices

device has a two-component address such as (i, j), where i is the device address and j is the address of the command, status, or data registers within device i. For example, an assembly language statement such as

```
copy_in R3, 0x012, 4
```

will cause the machine to copy the contents of data register 4 in the controller with device address 0x012 into CPU register R3.

In the memory-mapped approach shown in Figure 5.5(b), devices are associated with logical primary memory addresses (*memory-mapped I/O*) rather than having a specialized device address. Each component of the device that is referenced using software is assigned a normal memory address. For example, device 0x0012 might have a block of addresses from 0xFFFF0120 to 0xFFFF012F to reference the device's command, status, and 14 data registers. A memory-mapped I/O instruction to accomplish the same task as the `copy_in` instruction might be

```
load     R3, 0xFFFF0124
```

Memory-mapped I/O reduces the number of instruction types in the processor. This happens because memory load/store instructions can be used to interact with the device's registers in a memory-mapped I/O system. In the traditional approach, the computer must incorporate additional I/O instructions to read and write the device's registers.

5.1.5 ■ Direct Memory Access

In the direct I/O with polling approach, the CPU is used to transfer data between the controller data registers and the primary memory (see Figure 5.8a). The device driver copies the data from the application process data area to the controller for each output operation and vice versa for input operations. In the interrupt-driven I/O approach, the device handler is responsible for the transfer task. To transfer a block of data from primary memory to the controller's data registers, a code segment such as the following is used:

```
        load  R2, =LENGTH_OF_BLOCK // R2 is index reg
loop: load  R1, [data_area, R2]  // Load the block[i]
        store R1, 0xFFFF0124       // Put in ctlr data reg
        incr  R2                   // Increment index
        bge   loop                 // Test for loop termination
```

Direct memory access (DMA) controllers are able to read and write information directly from/to primary memory addresses with no CPU intervention after a driver has initiated the I/O operation (see Figure 5.8b). DMA can be used with either polling or interrupt software. The DMA controller includes logic that allows it to perform the same operations that the software uses to transfer data between the memory and the controller, but to do so using only the controller hardware. DMA hardware enables the

I/O-Processor Overlap

I/O controllers enable a system to overlap device I/O operation with processor operation. This results in more effective use of computing facilities and less real time needed for a process to have its computational needs met. The Gantt chart shown in Figure 5.6 illustrates how device I/O operations might be overlapped. It features the execution of two different application programs in an interrupt-driven system. Prior to time t_1, Application 1 is executing on the CPU, and at time t_1, it initiates a device operation. After the controller begins the operation for Application 1, the CPU is multiplexed to Application 2. At time t_2, Application 2 gives up the processor. However, it begins using it again immediately because Application 1 is still waiting for the I/O operation to complete. At time t_3, the controller completes the operation requested by Application 1. To minimize the response time of Application 1, the application must begin executing as soon after t_3 as possible. In the Gantt chart, Application 2 initiates I/O activity at t_4, releasing the CPU so that Application 1 can resume operation while Application 2 waits for the I/O operation to complete.

Figure 5.7 provides a different scheme for CPU-controller overlap (illustrated again using a Gantt chart). In this case, suppose the application program has been constructed to explicitly execute a program on the CPU in parallel with its *own* I/O operations. Assume that the I/O approach uses polling. At time t_1, the processor starts the controller on a read operation but then continues using the CPU. As long as the application does not need the result of the read operation, it can execute the program on the CPU at the same time the I/O operation is taking place. When the process needs the result of the pending read operation, the program execution must pause until the I/O has completed; the process yields the CPU to other processes (as in Figure 5.6) until the I/O operation has concluded. In the figure, the application yields the CPU at t_2, since the device is busy and the application needs the results of the read operation before it can proceed. At time t_3, the process is reassigned the CPU and polls the device until time t_4, when it again yields the CPU. At time t_5, the process resumes checking the device,

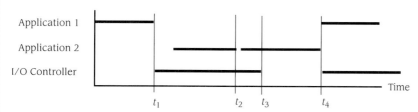

Figure 5.6
Overlapping Processing and I/O

I/O-Processor Overlap *(continued)*

finding it busy until t_6. The process then begins performing work on data obtained by the read. At time t_7, the process again starts the device and executes other instructions until it needs the results of the I/O at time t_8, and so on.

The overlapped CPU-device operation results in an overall reduction in the amount of time it takes to execute the program and its I/O serially. From time t_1 to t_2 and from t_7 to t_8, the CPU and controller are operating in parallel, thus reducing the overall runtime from the sum of the two time intervals to the maximum of their time intervals. From t_3 to t_4 and from t_5 to t_6, the process is in a busy-wait state, so from the viewpoint of achieving effective computation, those time periods are wasted, since there is no overlapped operation.

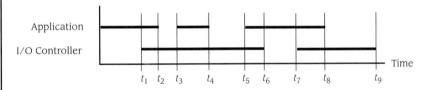

Figure 5.7
Overlapping CPU-Controller Operations in a Process

data transfer to be accomplished without using the CPU at all. (However, the controller and the CPU may compete for the bus if the CPU happens to need the bus at the same time that a device is performing a direct memory transfer.) DMA can markedly increase the machine's I/O performance. With DMA, the controller logically need not even contain data registers, since the controller can read and write directly between the device and memory. However, the DMA controller must include an address register loaded by the driver with a pointer to the relevant memory block. This pointer is used by the controller to locate the target block in primary memory.

5.2 ■ Buffering

Buffering is a technique by which the device manager can keep slower I/O devices busy during times when a process is not requiring I/O operations. *Input buffering* is the technique of having the input device read information into the primary memory before the process requests it. *Output buffering* is the technique of saving information in memory and then writing it to the device while the process continues execution. Buffering is intended to explicitly overlap a process's use of the CPU and its devices.

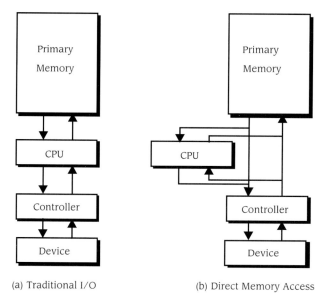

(a) Traditional I/O   (b) Direct Memory Access

Figure 5.8
Direct Memory Access

To help you understand how buffering can enhance performance, consider some characteristics of processes. Some processes are *I/O-bound,* meaning that their overall time to execute is dominated by the time to perform the cumulative I/O operations. A process that copies one file to another is an example of an I/O-bound process. Other processes are *compute-bound,* meaning that the time they spend in I/O operations is small compared to the amount of time spent using the CPU. A process that computes prime numbers is compute-bound. Many processes have phases in which they are I/O-bound and other phases in which they are compute-bound. The device manager can sometimes use memory management techniques to decrease the effective time to perform I/O for sequential streams of data.

Consider a simple character device controller that reads a single byte from a modem for each input operation, as shown in Figure 5.9(a). The normal mode of operation for the controller is for the one-byte data register to contain the last character read following the driver's read operation. When the next read is to occur, the driver passes another command to the controller. The controller, in turn, instructs the device to input the next byte and place it in the data register. The process calling for the byte waits for the operation to complete and then retrieves the character from the data register.

In parts (b) and (c) of Figure 5.9, we see how a *hardware buffer* can be added to the controller to substantially decrease the amount of time the process has to wait for a character if the controller buffers it ahead of time. In Figure 5.9(b), the next character to be read by the process has already been placed into data register B by the controller. The device is currently reading the next character from the device and placing it in data register A, even though the program has not yet called for the read operation. In Figure 5.9(c), the process requests the character previously read into controller data register A,

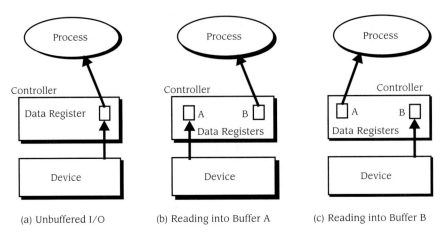

Figure 5.9
Hardware Buffering

so the device is started on a read operation to fill buffer B. The device read for character $i + 1$ will be overlapped with the CPU execution that uses character i. The overlap will be "well-matched" if the time to read the next character is the same as the time the process needs before it requests the next character.

The hardware buffering technique can also be applied at the controller-driver level (see Figure 5.10). This is generally called *double buffering,* since there are two buffers in the system. One buffer is for the driver or controller to store data while waiting for it to be retrieved by higher levels of the hierarchy. The other buffer is to store data from the lower-level module. The example in Figure 5.10 illustrates software and hardware double buffering for bytes. The technique also can be used with block-oriented devices such as magnetic tape drives. In this case, each buffer in the controller and in the driver must be large enough to store an entire block.

In Figure 5.11, the number of buffers is extended from 2 to n. The data *producer* (the controller in read operations; the CPU in write operations) is writing into buffer i while the data *consumer* (the controller in write operations; the CPU in read operations) is reading from buffer j. In this configuration, buffer elements j to $n - 1$ and 0 to $i - 1$ are full. The consumer can read buffers j, j + 1, j + 2, ... $n - 1$, and 0, 1,... i − 1 while the producer is filling buffer i. Alternatively, the producer could fill buffers i, i + 1, i + 2,... j − 1 while the consumer is reading buffer j. In this *circular buffering* technique, the producer cannot "pass" the consumer because it would overwrite buffers before they had been consumed. The producer can only fill up to buffer j − 1 while data in buffer j is waiting to be consumed. Similarly, the consumer cannot "pass" the producer because it would be reading information before it was placed into the buffer by the producer.

Can performance be increased by adding more buffers? The effect of buffering on performance depends heavily on the process's characteristics. A process that is consistently I/O-bound will tend to read every buffer as quickly as it is filled by the controller and to fill all available buffers with output before the controller has time to write them to the device. A process that is compute-bound will produce the opposite situation; that

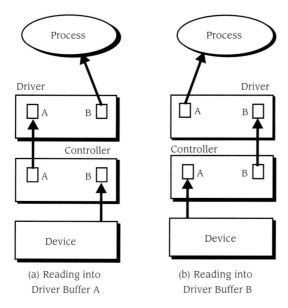

(a) Reading into
Driver Buffer A

(b) Reading into
Driver Buffer B

Figure 5.10
Double Buffering in the Driver

is, the input buffers will tend to be full and the output buffers empty. Simple processes are often purely I/O bound. More-complex ones tend to have phases in which they are I/O-bound and other phases in which they are compute-bound. Figure 5.12 illustrates the changing phases of a hypothetical program over time. Initially, the program is I/O bound. At time t_1, it becomes compute-bound. Then it switches back to being I/O bound at time t_2, and so on. This process profile takes good advantage of buffering, since during compute-bound phases the controllers will be filling "input-full" buffers and emptying "output-full" buffers at a rate higher than they will be consumed. When the process become I/O-bound, it will have buffers available from the compute-bound phase. It will gradually use all of these buffers, ideally just when the process swings back to a compute-bound phase.

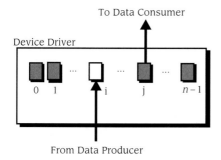

Figure 5.11
Using Multiple Buffers

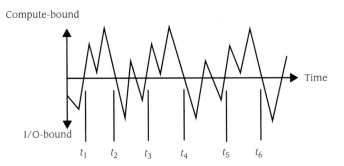

Figure 5.12
Phases of a Program

5.3 ■ Device Drivers

Now that you've seen the general approaches for designing device managers and the buffering techniques, you can consider specific characteristics of device driver design. Device drivers are the part of the device manager used by an application process to call for an I/O operation. When the process makes a request of the device driver, the driver translates that controller-independent request into controller-dependent actions for interacting with the device. As described in Section 5.1, after the device is put into operation, the driver either polls the controller to detect the completion of the operation or places information into a device status table entry to prepare for the device interrupt.

The difficulty in designing the device manager is to invoke controller-specific I/O operations while satisfying three constraints:

■ Create an API that implements the I/O functions available on the device, yet which complies with the interface implemented by the other drivers.

■ Achieve correct coordination among the application processes, drivers, and device controllers.

■ Optimize the overall machine performance with correct driver strategies.

5.3.1 ■ The Device Driver Interface

Each OS defines an architecture for its device management system. These designs vary among systems; thus there is no universal organization. Each of these systems has two important interfaces to the device manager: the API and the interface between a driver and the OS kernel.

5.3.1.1 ■ The Application Programming Interface

The application programming interface (API) provides a set of functions that an application programmer can call to manage a device. A device is generally used for communications or storage. All input devices produce information, either from an arbitrary unit, in the case of communications devices, or from a storage medium, in the case of storage devices. A process writes information to output devices, either to be "consumed" by a communications device or to be stored for later retrieval. The device manager must track the state of the device, including when the device is idle, when it is being used, and which process is using it. The device manager may maintain, in addition to the information kept in the device status table, a device descriptor to specify other properties of the device as determined by the software design. Therefore most driver interfaces include an open and a close function to allow the device manager to initiate/terminate the device's use by a process. The open command allocates the device and initializes the tables and the device for use. The close command releases dynamic table entries and otherwise makes the descriptor states reflect the fact that the device is not being used.

Each device driver provides a function to allow the programmer to read from and/or write to the device. While the goal is to make the semantics of the operations consistent among devices, this is not completely possible. A typical concession to differences among devices is to define different *classes* of devices, such as character devices and block devices. All character devices behave roughly the same, and all block devices have similar semantics. However, character devices such as keyboards are not expected to have the same read semantics as block-oriented devices such as optical disks.

Another distinction between classes of storage devices is whether the information can be read from or written to any arbitrary location. *Sequentially accessed devices* are designed so that an operation can be applied only to the "next" location after the last operation. For example, a magnetic tape is a sequentially accessed device, since normally it must be read block-by-block from the first to the last block. If the tape is positioned in the tape drive so that it can read block i, then the next read is expected to be block i (followed by a read of block $i + 1$). It is not necessary to provide the address of the information to be read or written in these devices, since the address is implicitly defined by the previous operation. A seek command can be used with a sequentially accessed device to move the point of the next interaction with the device. Buffering is heavily used in sequentially accessed devices.

Randomly accessed devices have no physical limitation to encourage reading or writing the information from/to the device in any particular order. For example, a floppy disk is a randomly accessed device. This is because after block i is read, the next block to be read can be any block j, since the disk read/write head can be moved directly to another block without its having to read intervening blocks. Because there is no assumption of sequential access, each read/write operation includes an address on the device to specify the point of interaction.

The OS design needs to provide other functions on the API to allow the process, for example, to allocate/deallocate a device, rewind a tape drive, power up/down a disk drive, and invert the video image on a display. In some designs, this requirement broadens the API considerably. In UNIX, however, most of the functions are passed to the device driver as arguments in an I/O control (`ioctl`) command. (A UNIX interface is discussed in an example in Section 5.4.2.)

5.3.1.2 ■ The Kernel Interface

The device driver must execute privileged instructions when it interacts with the device controller. This means the driver must be executed as part of the OS rather than as part of a user program. The driver must also be able to read and write information from/to the address spaces of different processes, since the same device can be used by different processes.

In older systems, a driver was incorporated into the OS by changing the OS source code and then recompiling. Hence, the organization that was installing the driver had to have a copy of the OS source code and considerable prerequisite knowledge to accomplish the task. This scenario was acceptable when all computers and devices in the user's organization were acquired from the same vendor, since the vendor's service organization would install the driver when it installed the device. Economic pressures for open systems, however, resulted in organizations buying a device and driver from a third party and then having to install the OS source code.

Modern operating systems simplify driver installation by using *reconfigurable device drivers.* Such a system allows one to add a device driver to the OS without recompiling the OS (although the system will generally have to be reconfigured by some set of operations). This reconfiguration is accomplished by designing the OS so that it dynamically binds the OS code to the driver functions. For example, in Figure 5.13, an indirect table for device *i* points at driver modules for open, read, and other functions on the interface. A reconfigurable device driver is standardized to have a fixed API. Because the device driver is added to the kernel after the kernel has been compiled, the kernel also provides an interface to allow the device driver to allocate space for buffers, to manipulate tables in the kernel, and so on.

The OS uses an indirect reference table to access the different driver entry points based on the device and function name. That is, the kernel provides an API as part of the OS interface. When a process performs a system call, the kernel passes the call onto the device driver via the indirect reference table. When the driver is installed, information

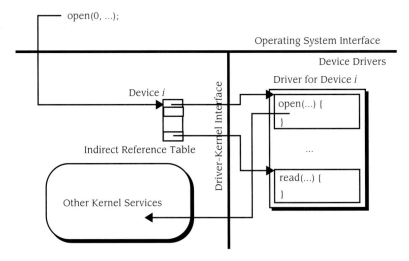

Figure 5.13
Reconfigurable Device Drivers

for the indirect reference table is provided to the OS so that it can read the information at runtime.

5.3.2 ■ CPU-device Interactions

The CPU and each device are physically distinct components capable of operating independently. The device manager must provide a means by which a process executing on the CPU can coordinate its behavior with the devices performing I/O on its behalf. Figure 5.14 shows the three units involved in an I/O operation and how they coordinate their operations with one another. In the figure, the controller hardware, driver software, and application software operations are described by C code segments. Since the controller is a hardware component, it is always in operation (so it is represented in C code as an infinite `for`-loop). First, the device "asks for work" by waiting for a command to be placed in its command register (or, equivalently, for the controller busy flag to be set by the driver). Then, when the device controller receives a command, it processes the command and returns a signal that it has completed (using the `done` flag in the controller status register). The device driver is a part of the OS that is invoked by a user action. Conceptually, each function implemented by the device driver is a procedure, which is called by the application process. When the driver function is called, it performs a "hardware call" on the controller interface by setting the controller's registers. In a polling system (as in Figure 5.14), the driver waits for the device to complete its operation, via a busy-wait on the `done` flag. In an interrupt system, the "return" from the device is accepted by the device handler. In either case, control is then returned to the calling process using the procedure return paradigm.

The details of how to handle the interaction among the application process, the device manager, and the device hardware is a fundamental design problem in operating systems, particularly the process management aspect. The basic techniques used in process synchronization described in Chapter 8 evolved from the technology for coordinating actions among processes, drivers, and devices.

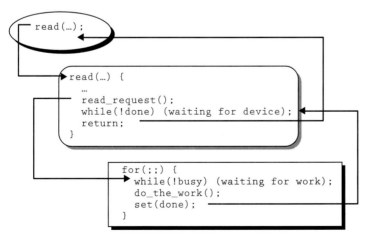

Figure 5.14
Coordinating the I/O Operation

5.3.3 ▪ I/O Optimization

The recurring theme in OS design is "how to provide function at high performance." Performance is a critical aspect of device management. There are few general techniques for optimizing performance; hence, device driver engineering can be difficult. However, although general optimizations are difficult to come by, it is possible to take advantage of various classes of devices to perform optimizations. For example, communications devices and sequentially accessed storage devices almost always take advantage of buffering (see Section 5.2). Buffering is carried to an extreme in the case of device management for printers (which are sequentially accessed devices), where entire print files are buffered on the disk system to be printed when the printer is available.

Randomly accessed storage devices provide another opportunity for optimization, described in detail in Section 5.4. Briefly, the idea is that multiprogramming systems often provide many different disk I/O requests, thereby causing the disk device to be a performance bottleneck. The driver attempts to minimize overall service time by processing device requests in an order that minimizes certain expensive device operations.

5.4 ▪ Some Device Management Scenarios

Until now, the discussion regarding device management has been general, applying to all types of devices. In this section, a few aspects of the most popular devices used on contemporary general-purpose computers are discussed.

5.4.1 ▪ Serial Communications

Serial communications devices were introduced in the examples in Chapter 4. These devices are used to transmit information from a computer to a device using a bit-serial medium such as coaxial cable or telephone wires. Serial communications technology is the predecessor of contemporary network technology (discussed in Chapter 15). While networks dominate in large-scale computer-computer installations, serial communications devices are still heavily used for connecting terminals, printers, scanners, pointing devices, and modems to computers.

Communications devices are character devices used to transfer bytes of information between a computer and a remote device (see Figure 5.15). To use the device, the driver must manipulate the communications controller, which in turn manipulates the device using a controller-device protocol. The RS–232 protocol is an example of a communications controller-device protocol. As mentioned in Chapter 4, this protocol specifies the physical nature of the cabling that connects the controller and device and the way that signals are exchanged between the controller and device. For a device to be connected to a serial communications port, the device and port must agree on the interface as well as the protocol for using that interface. Thus, to connect a modem to a computer, the computer must include a serial communications controller that can be

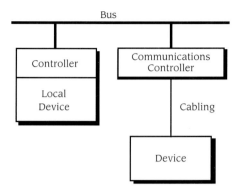

Figure 5.15
A Generic Communications Device

attached to the modem using an external cable. Once the connection is made, the controller must implement the protocol that the modem is expecting.

From a device driver perspective, the critical interface is the one between the communications controller and the driver. Part of this interface specifies the parameters of the protocol used between the controller and the device (for example, the modem may be expecting a protocol to use two synchronizing bits before any data bits are transmitted). These parameter values are specified to the controller by the driver.

Today, serial communications controllers are implemented using a specialized microprocessor, called a Universal Asynchronous Receiver Transmitter (UART), that has onboard ROM and RAM. Because the operation has been standardized to support RS–232 controller-device interactions, the UART needs to have only a few parameters defined by the driver in order to fully specify the controller-device protocol used for read/write operations. Once the UART has been initialized (at the time the device is opened), the driver needs only to provide a character buffer plus a command in order to accomplish a read or write operation. These drivers are among the simplest of all drivers.

➤ IN THE HANGAR

UNIX Device Drivers

UNIX explicitly attempts to simplify the application programming model for files and devices by making files and devices as similar as possible. The UNIX device driver API uses operation names similar to the file interface (described in Chapter 2), although they apply to physical devices rather than to storage abstractions. Device drivers are intended to be accessed by user space code. If an application accesses a driver, it uses one of two standardized interfaces: the block device interface or the character device interface. Both interfaces define a fixed set of functions. (See Table 5.1 for the most common BSD UNIX functions.) Any driver can implement a subset of the functions that makes sense for the particular device (according to the device characteristics and the design requirements for the driver). When a user program calls the driver, it performs a system call. The kernel looks up the entry point for the device in the block or character indirect reference table (the *jump table*) and then calls the entry point. The exact semantics of each function depends on the nature of the device and the intent of the driver design. Hence, the function names suggest only a purpose for each. In the UNIX family of systems, the logical contents of the jump table are kept in the file system in the /dev directory.

TABLE 5.1 BSD UNIX Driver Entry Points

Function	Block	Character
close	A routine to indicate the application no longer intends to use the device.	A routine to indicate that the application no longer intends to use the device.
ioctl	Not in the interface.	Passes driver-specific information to the driver.
open	Prepares the device for operation by the calling application.	Prepares the device for operation by the calling application.
read	(See strategy.)	Requests an input operation from the device and then copies it into memory.
select	Not in the interface.	Checks the device to see if a read or write operation will succeed.
strategy	Starts a block read/write operation.	Not in the interface.
stop	Not in the interface.	Discontinues a stream output operation.
write	(See strategy.)	Requests an output operation to the device from memory.

Source: This information is taken from McKusick et al. [1998]. Chapter 6 of their book provides a comprehensive discussion of device drivers for 4.3 BSD UNIX.

A UNIX driver has three parts:

■ System initialization code

■ Code to initiate device operations

■ Device interrupt handlers

The initialization code is run when the system is bootstrapped. It tests for the physical presence of devices and then initializes them. The API implements functions for a subset of the entry points shown in Table 5.1. This part of the code also provides information to the kernel as to which functions are implemented. The device interrupt handler is called by the system interrupt handler that corresponds to the physical device causing the interrupt.

Notice that there are no `read/write` entry points for block devices; instead, there is a `strategy` entry point that defines those points. This approach allows buffering routines to be written in the kernel that can be bound to the I/O command at runtime.

System administrators are responsible for installing devices and drivers (see Nemeth et al. [1995, ch. 6] for details about how this is accomplished). The information necessary to install a driver can be incorporated into a configuration file by the administrator and then processed by the configuration builder tool, `/etc/config`, to build a `makefile` capable of building the kernel.

5.4.2 ■ Sequentially Accessed Storage Devices

Storage devices implement *persistent* storage in a computer system, meaning that information placed in a storage device can be preserved after the computer is turned off and until it is turned back on again. Storage devices are either sequentially accessed or randomly accessed devices. Both types of storage device are usually block-oriented, which means that data are read from and written to the device as a block of bytes. The size of a block depends on the characteristics of the device and its controller.

Sequentially accessed, or sequential, storage devices physically store the blocks on a recording medium in a linear sequence. Bytes may or may not be stored linearly within the block. The read/write interface to the device precludes programmers from ever really knowing exactly how bits and bytes are physically stored within a block. A read operation returns a block of bytes from the device, and a write operation copies a block of bytes to the device.

Magnetic tape is the prevalent sequential storage medium for today's systems. Traditional magnetic tape is 0.5-inch plastic tape with a ferrite coating, although smaller cassette tapes prevail today. As with audiotape, information is stored on the tape by magnetizing geographical areas on the tape's surface. Tapes may be any length, although common lengths range from 600 to 2,400 feet. Special applications such as the magnetic tape on the back of a credit card may be very short—for example, 3 inches long.

Traditional 0.5-inch tapes are formatted with 9 logical tracks, each running the full length of the tape. When the tape is placed under a read/write head, the head can sense one segment—an 8-bit byte with a parity bit—crossing the 9 tracks. (The parity bit is the sum of the other 8 bits taken modulo 2. It is used as a simple way to detect if a bit is incorrectly read from or written to the medium.) A collection of bytes is packed densely on the tape to form a *physical record* containing one block of data. Physical records are separated by an inter-record gap. When the driver issues an I/O operation, the tape drive must accelerate the tape across the read/write head so that it can read or write the tracks. It is impractical to place an inter-record gap between each byte, so the block operation is the only plausible approach for reading and writing the information. The density of the bytes on a tape is a physical characteristic of the design of the read/write mechanism. The density refers to the number of bytes to be placed in some fixed length of tape; for example, 6,250-bpi tape has 6,250 bytes stored on one inch of the tape. Today's compact cartridge tapes can hold gigabytes of information.

The information stored on a tape must be physically accessed by moving the tape forward and backward across the read/write head. Thus data can be accessed only at reasonable rates if the process reading the tape intends to read all of the information in the order it is stored on the tape. Positioning the tape in the drive causes the significant delays in such an operation. If the process desires only certain information on the tape, it must cause the tape drive to position the tape so that the correct information is under the read/write heads before it can be processed. This movement is called *seeking* the correct block address on the tape. Seeking can be a very slow operation, measured in tens of seconds. Thus it prohibits the use of tapes for almost anything but sequential access.

Many of these cartridge tape drives have a search feature that assigns an index to each physical record. A seek operation can be performed more rapidly using the index than it can if the tape drive has to read each physical record on the tape. Such drives, however, are relatively slow compared to the access speeds possible with randomly accessed devices.

5.4.3 ■ Randomly Accessed Devices

Randomly accessed storage devices allow a driver to access the blocks on the device in an arbitrary order. This capability exacts a small, but measurable, performance penalty for accessing blocks stored at physically distant locations on the recording surface. Rotating disks are the most prevalent form of randomly accessed storage device. These disks employ a block read/write interface between the controller and the device. The block orientation is propagated to the driver/controller interface. However, disks do not ordinarily directly support sequential access, since contiguous blocks on the device do not necessarily hold logically contiguous blocks of information. Thus software intending to access information stored on a randomly accessed storage device is responsible for determining the order in which blocks should be read and written on the device. File abstraction fits in naturally with this assumption. The file manager (discussed in Chapter 13) implements a strategy for storing logically contiguous information in non-contiguous physical blocks on the random device interface.

The storage technology used by disks includes magnetic and optical approaches. Magnetic disks use the same technique for storing a bit on a surface as do magnetic tapes, although the "patch" of recording surface is positioned under the read/write head in a different manner than with tapes. Optical disks (such as CD-ROMs) use light to detect physical storage patterns on the disk surface. The alignment of areas of the disk under a read head is accomplished in the same manner used with magnetic disks. Optical disk readers are much less expensive than are devices that read and write the medium. Hence, most machines using optical disks include only the read capability. Both types of device are called rotating media devices.

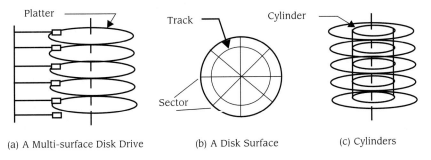

(a) A Multi-surface Disk Drive   (b) A Disk Surface   (c) Cylinders

Figure 5.16
Rotating Media

Rotating media are organized as one or more disk platters, each having one or two storage *surfaces* (see Figure 5.16a). Each surface is logically divided into several *sectors* defined as an angular portion of the disk circle, like slices of a pie. The surface of each disk is also organized into several concentric *tracks* passing through each sector. Figure 5.16(b) shows one track passing through 8 sectors. If a disk has 500 tracks and 32 sectors on a surface, then each sector contains 1/32nd of each of the 500 tracks. The track is used to radially align the read/write head over a physical portion of the disk. The sector is used to determine the angular location of the track used to store a physical block of information. In informal usage, a track segment lying within a sector, or a block of data, is often called a disk sector, although technically the sector crosses all tracks. A physical disk record is stored on one track in one sector on one surface on the rotating medium. The number of blocks stored on the disk is determined by the number of tracks, the number of sectors, and the number of surfaces. Because of engineering economics for devices, read/write heads are ordinarily attached to a single arm to be positioned over a particular track while the media rotates under the head. This approach means the read/write heads for each surface are positioned over the track at the same radial distance from the center of all surfaces at the same time. The set of tracks on the different surfaces is called a *cylinder* of the disk (Figure 5.16c).

The read/write head is positioned at some radial distance from the center of the rotating disk in order to read information on a particular track. Head movement across tracks is the most time-consuming operation in rotating media operations, since it is difficult to design physical mechanisms to move the arm accurately enough at high speed to fit precisely over a track. This track seek time dominates all other aspects of the time taken to access a block of information. Less expensive disk drives employ a mechanism to move the head one track at a time. If the driver has just read a block from track 20 and next needs to read a block from track 50, it must step the head 30 times, once across each intervening track. More expensive disks can move a head directly from track 20 to 50 with a single hardware operation. This operation is much faster than the single-track stepping mechanisms, although the time involved is still a function of the number of tracks crossed.

When the head has been positioned over the appropriate track (or in the appropriate cylinder on a multiple-surface disk), the device generally has to wait for the proper sector to rotate under the head before it can access the information. This rotational delay is called *disk latency time,* and it depends on the speed at which the disk rotates. Rotation speeds vary by at least an order of magnitude among different disk types. Floppy disks rotate at about 360 rpm, while fixed hard disks rotate at 7,200 rpm or more.

Multiple-surface disks can be designed so that the controller provides an interface that makes data stored within a cylinder appear to be on a single track with many sectors. Suppose a disk has S surfaces and R sectors. The disk could provide an interface to map the block at sector r $(0 \leq r < R)$ on surface s $(0 \leq s < S)$, denoted (s, r), to logical sector t $(0 \leq t < RS)$. The obvious mapping is to correlate the block at $(0, 0)$ with logical block 0, $(0, 1)$ with logical block 1, ... $(0, R-1)$ to logical block $R-1$, $(1, 0)$ with logical block R, and so on. Now the driver (or file system), once it seeks to the given cylinder, can access any of the RS blocks in the cylinder without seek delays. Depending on the controller design, sectors on different surfaces may be mapped so that logically contiguous sectors are on different surfaces, rather than being physically adjacent to one another. For example, logical sector 0 might be on $(0, 0)$, logical sector 1 on $(1, 1)$, and so on.

Rotating device design continues to improve. Magnetic disk technology miniaturizes the physical dimensions of the disk while decreasing seek time and increasing the transfer rate of data from the disk surface to the machine's memory. Average disk seek times depend on the number of tracks and the head movement time. One can expect contemporary magnetic disks to have an average seek time in the 5 to 25 millisecond range. Data transfer rates depend on the density at which bits are stored within a sector and the rotational speed of the disk. At the time of this writing, these rates can be expected to be on the order of 1 to 5Mbps within a block. Optical disk read performance is slightly slower.

PERFORMANCE TUNING

Optimizing Access on Rotating Devices

In a multiprogramming system, many different processes may attempt to access the disk at the same time. At any given moment, the disk driver may have several I/O requests it needs to service. In general, successive requests arriving at the driver will reference disk blocks physically remote from one another. As a result, the disk could spend considerable time seeking different tracks to service its requests.

For example, suppose a disk request queue receives six requests for blocks on tracks 12, 123, 50, 13, 124, and 49 in the order listed.

One would expect the disk to first seek to track 12 and service the first request; seek to track 123 and service the second request; seek to track 50 and service the third request; and so on. Suppose the disk can seek to an adjacent track in X milliseconds, but it requires $X + YK$ milliseconds

Optimizing Access on Rotating Devices *(continued)*

to seek to a track Y tracks away. If K were 3, then the disk could seek from track 12 to track 13 in $X + 3$ milliseconds but would require $X + 333$ milliseconds to seek to track 123 from track 12. For the example queue of disk requests, the driver would spend

$$(X + 3*(123 - 12)) + (X + 3*(123 - 50))$$

$$+ (X + 3*(50 - 13))$$

$$+ (X + 3*(124 - 13))$$

$$+ (X + 3*(124 - 49))$$

or $5X + 921$ milliseconds seeking to the tracks in the order they are requested.

Since the seek time dominates the I/O time, all requests could be satisfied faster if the disk first serviced the requests for track 12, then 13, then 49, then 50, then 123, and finally for 124. The total seek time would be reduced to

$$(X + (X + 3*(49 - 13)) + X + (X + 3*(123 - 50)) + X)$$

or $5X + 327$ milliseconds.

Obviously the amount of savings depends on the characteristics of the seek mechanism on the disk and the mix of pending application operations. Some disks have very

sophisticated seek mechanisms that allow them to seek to a track without stopping at intermediate tracks. However, even these drives will have a fixed amount of time to start a seek (the X factor) and some amount of time that is proportional to the number of tracks moved (the YK factor). The savings from optimizing the order in which requests are satisfied can have a substantial effect on all disks incurring seek time as part of the access time.

This faster approach serviced the requests according to a "scanning" algorithm where the driver makes a sweep across the disk, servicing pending requests at the next higher-numbered track. Realistically, more requests will arrive while the driver is in the process of satisfying some set of requests in the queue. Thus this approach could cause some requests to wait for a relatively long time. Suppose that immediately after the driver finished accessing the blocks on track 50, a request arrived for a block on track 45. Should the algorithm continue its sweep toward higher-numbered tracks, or should it return to service the request for data on track 45? In the 1970s, there

was an intensive effort to study disk seek optimization algorithms, but there has been little new insight in the research since then. Here are a few of the most important strategies evolving from that research, some of which are now implemented directly in disk controller hardware rather than in the driver.

First-Come-First-Served (FCFS)

In FCFS, requests are serviced in the order in which they arrive at the driver. This approach is essentially a baseline approach in the sense that it takes no special action to minimize the overall seek time. Suppose the disk request queue contains a set of references for blocks on tracks 76, 124, 17, 269, 201, 29, 137, and 12. FCFS would begin at track 76, move 48 tracks to 124, and so on as described in Figure 5.17. The head will move across 880 tracks as it services the requests.

Shortest-Seek-Time-First (SSTF)

Suppose the driver selected the next request as the one requiring the minimum seek time from the current position. SSTF may tend to move

Optimizing Access on Rotating Devices *(continued)*

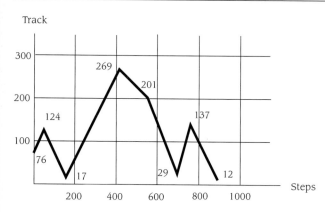

Figure 5.17
FCFS Disk Optimization

the head away from some requests during its local minimization. Under heavy load, SSTF can prevent distant requests from ever being serviced; this phenomenon is known as *starvation*. When the driver catches up with the load, it will ultimately have to move to the requests not serviced, thus resulting in a large performance cost for the head movement to a new part of the disk.

In contrast, SSTF responds to the disk request load used to describe the FCFS example by moving the head from track 76 to 29, 17, 12, 124, 137, 201, and 269,

crossing 331 tracks, as shown in Figure 5.18.

Scan/Look

The Scan algorithm has the head start at track 0 and move toward the highest-numbered track, servicing all requests for a track as it passes the track. When it reaches the highest-numbered track, it reverses the direction of the scan, servicing newly arrived requests as it moves toward track 0. Look is a variant of Scan that ceases the scan in the high-numbered track direction after it has serviced the request with the highest number, and then it reverses

the direction of the scan. For example, if the highest-numbered sector is 299, but the highest-numbered request is 269, Look will service the request for track 269 and then reverse the direction of its scan toward track 0, rather than continuing on to track 299 as Scan would.

Given the disk request load used in the FCFS example with the head currently at track 76 and moving toward higher-numbered tracks, Scan and Look would move the head from track 76 to 124, 137, 201, 269, 29, 17, and 12. Look would cross 450 tracks, and Scan would cross an

Optimizing Access on Rotating Devices *(continued)*

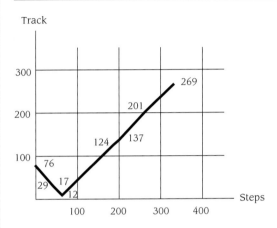

Figure 5.18
SSTF Disk Optimization

extra 60 tracks, as shown in Figure 5.19. Both Scan and Look are guaranteed to service every request in one complete pass through the disk; thus neither are susceptible to starvation.

Circular Scan/Look

As Scan or Look move from high-to-low or low-to-high numbered tracks, new requests will continue to arrive. For example, suppose Scan has just served requests for track 15 in a scan toward the high-numbered track and a request arrives for track 13. The new request will not be serviced for almost two full scans of the disk—from 15 to the highest-numbered track

and back to track 13. Circular Scan always scans the disk in the same direction—for example, from low-numbered tracks to high-numbered tracks. If the request for track 13 were to arrive right after the request for track 15 had been serviced, the request would have to wait for at most a single scan of the disk. Circular Look is related to Circular Scan in the same way Look is related to Scan. Circular Scan and Circular Look both rely on the existence of a special homing command that moves the head to track 0 in a short amount of time, relative to movement to any other track. Disks with inexpensive step-

ping motors (such as a floppy disk drive) do not incorporate this ability to quickly home to track 0.

Given the disk request load used in the FCFS example with the head currently at track 76 and moving toward higher-numbered tracks, Circular Scan and Circular Look would move the head from track 76 to 124, 137, 201, 269, 12, 17, and 29, as shown in Figure 5.20. In this example, assume that the drive requires the equivalent of 100 steps to move the head from 269 or 299 to 0. This is possible in some disk drives that incorporate a homing command to return the head to track 0.

Optimizing Access on Rotating Devices *(continued)*

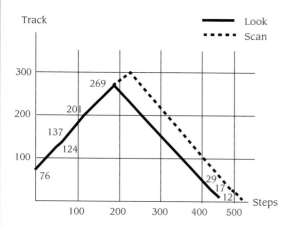

Figure 5.19
Scan and Look Disk Optimization

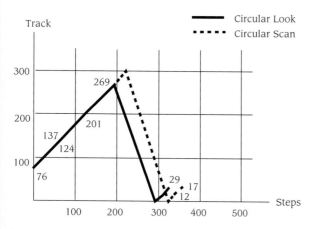

Figure 5.20
Circular Scan and Look Disk Optimizations

5.5 ■ Summary

Device management is implemented across resource managers, device drivers, and device interrupt handlers. Devices vary widely in their characteristics. The computer designer determines how the device will be referenced, either as part of the memory address space or with a separate space and instructions. Some incorporate direct memory access so that the controller can read and write information directly into/from memory without processor intervention.

The trend toward open systems has encouraged OS designers to make it easy for a systems administrator to add a device and driver to the system without having to change the OS source code. UNIX and Windows NT employ this technique by providing tools to the administrator to assist in configuring new devices as they are added.

Device I/O is the bottleneck for I/O-bound processes. Because many processes are I/O-bound or have large phases in which they are I/O bound, substantial effort has been invested in increasing the performance of the I/O subsystem. Buffering is a traditional technique used to increase performance through the overlap of execution. If the execution and I/O of an individual process can be overlapped, the process can have decreased response time. If the overlap can be achieved by overlapping the I/O operation for one process with the execution of another, the system's throughput rate will be increased, meaning service to any particular process will be improved. In rotating storage devices, head movement can be optimized based on the queue of I/O requests from various processes in a multiprogramming system. These optimizations increase device throughput and, on the average, reduce an individual process's waiting time for I/O.

Storage devices are a fundamental part of contemporary computer systems. As computers are applied to larger and larger information processing problems, the emphasis on processor performance is becoming more balanced with the need for performance of the storage system. Storage technology continues to rapidly improve with the development of higher-density disks, new storage media, and faster access times.

5.6 ■ Exercises

1. Provide the detailed steps involved in performing an output operation in a system that uses interrupts. Use the explanation of the input instruction in Section 5.1 as a pattern for your answer.

2. For a system using direct I/O with interrupts, explain how a device handler can "return" from a function call to a device driver.

3. Suppose three processes, $p_1, p_2,$ and p_3, are attempting to use a machine with direct I/O and interrupts concurrently. Suppose p_1 has $t_{compute} = 20$ and $t_{device} = 50$, p_2 has $t_{compute} = 30$ and $t_{device} = 10$, and p_3 has $t_{compute} = 15$ and $t_{device} = 35$. What is the minimum amount of time required to execute the three processes?

4. Section 5.1.4 provides examples of instructions used to perform I/O with and without memory-mapped I/O. Write pseudocode segments to write a single byte to a hypothetical device using instructions for device-specific addresses and for memory-mapped I/O machines.

5. Refer to hardware double buffering (Figure 5.9) and explain the effect of buffering on the runtime of the process if the process is I/O-bound and requests characters at a much higher rate than the device can provide them. What is the effect if the process is compute-bound and rarely requests characters from the device?

6. Should magnetic disk controllers include hardware buffers? Explain your answer.

7. System designers distinguish between the physical blocks read by the driver and the logical blocks presented to the application process. Explain how this distinction might be useful on a system that has floppy and hard disk drives.

8. Is it necessary for an operating system to have a driver-kernel interface in a system that does not use reconfigurable device drivers? Explain your answer.

9. Explain why a serial communications port that manages a terminal keyboard does not normally use the same optimization techniques as a serial communications port that manages a printer.

10. Identify some optimization techniques you would consider for a device driver for a magnetic tape drive. Justify each technique.

11. Suppose the read/write head is at track 97, moving toward track 199 (the highest-numbered track on the disk) and the disk request queue contains read/write requests for sectors on tracks 84, 155, 103, 96, and 197, respectively.

    a. What is the total number of head movements to satisfy the requests in the queue using the FCFS optimization strategy?
    b. What is the total number of head movements to satisfy the requests in the queue using the Scan optimization strategy?
    c. What is the total number of head movements to satisfy the requests in the queue using the Look optimization strategy?

12. Construct a scenario in which a disk optimization algorithm other than SSTF requires fewer steps to satisfy all requests for disk I/O. Use a 300-track disk with a maximum 100-track traversal time for any seek operation.

13. This exercise is a programming practice that requires additional information regarding the details of Linux. You can find additional information on the Internet from *The Linux Kernel Hacker's Guide* [Johnson, 1995a] and "Writing Linux Device Drivers" [Johnson, 1995b]. You can also look at reference books on Linux, such as Beck et al. [1996].

    Write C code for a loadable module character clock device. This device should be accessible through a device special file `/dev/clock`. A read of this device should return the equivalent of the `gettimeofday` system call "packed" into the read buffer. A write to this device, with a `timevalue` and `timezone` structure packed into the buffer, should work like the system call `settimeofday`. Your device must also support open and close system calls (the release file operation is needed to support close). You will need to write "pack" and "unpack" functions for the `timevalue` and `timezone` structures that can be used in your device driver code as well as by a user of your clock device. Here are some additional notes on the problem:

- Linux source code in `/usr/src/linux/kernel/time.c` for the `gettime-ofday` and `settimeofday` system calls may be reused in your code. This greatly simplifies this problem.

- You are not required to compile, install nor test this device. However, the code must be valid compilable C code. If you want to compile and/or test your device, additional instructions dependent on your local installation need to be provided by your instructor.

- When writing device code: You cannot rely on libraries. Safety checks must be made when writing to user buffers. You must ensure correct interrupt disabling/enabling.

- Be sure to use the most current Linux source code such as that found on your local distribution.

6

Process Management

Look into the pewter pot,

To see the world as the world's not.

—A. E. Housman, *Terence,*
This Is Stupid Stuff ■

CHAPTER OBJECTIVES

A process is the basic computational element in a modern computer system, and process management refers to the full spectrum of OS services to support the orderly administration of a collection of processes. A detailed consideration of process management is the natural place to begin the study of OS details.

The complete discussion of process management is provided in this chapter and the subsequent four chapters. This chapter describes the responsibilities and organization of the process manager. Subsequent chapters focus on more detailed aspects of specific tasks. The first section of this chapter provides the system programmer's perspective of processes and resources, as contrasted with the application programmer's perspective described in Chapter 2. Next, it describes how an OS is started when the computer is started. The address space of the process defines the mapping between the symbols used in a source program and the locations in the executable memory used by the CPU when the process executes. The introduction continues with a discussion of how an address space is created for a process. The chapter concludes with remarks about the process and resource abstractions, and how process hierarchies influence OS policies.

6.1 ▪ The System View of Processes and Resources

Chapter 2 explained a process from the application programmer's view. Now we look at processes and resources from the OS designer's perspective. A process is a schedulable unit of computation that requires certain entities (resources) be allocated to it in order for it to execute. The process specifies its resource needs to the process manager part of the OS, and the process manager then causes resources to be allocated and the process to be executed in conjunction with the execution of other processes. In other words, the process manager creates the process abstraction by implementing a software environment in which one program in execution can be distinguished from other programs in execution, and in which processes are able to gain exclusive control of resources or selectively share them with one another.

The process manager is one of the four major parts of the OS. It provides software that creates models for each resource and for the way the process uses the CPU and any other system resources (see Figure 6.1). As discussed in Chapter 1, much of the complexity of the OS stems from the need for multiple processes to share the hardware at the same time. Different OS designs implement process and resource management using different software strategies. However, every process manager provides the basic algorithms and data structures to implement the process and resource abstractions, CPU sharing (called *scheduling,* see Chapter 7), process *synchronization* (discussed in Chapters 8 and 9), and a *deadlock* strategy (discussed in Chapter 10). In addition, the process manager implements fundamental parts of the

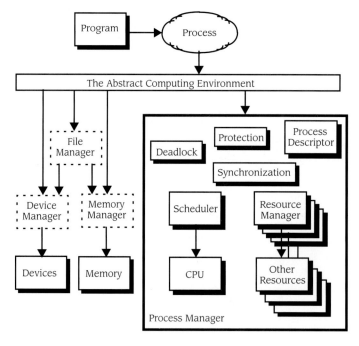

Figure 6.1
Process Management

operating system's protection strategy (*protection* and *security* are discussed in general in Chapter 14).

6.1.1 ■ Implementing the Process Model

When a von Neumann computer is powered up, the control unit begins fetching and executing instructions. This "initial process" is described in detail in Section 6.2, but for now observe that when the machine starts there is at least one program in execution— the initial process. The initial process creates the OS, which can then create other processes as needed. Once the OS is in operation, one process can create another process with a system request (such as a system call to `fork` in UNIX). The process manager creates a new instance of the process by creating its own new internal representation for the process abstraction. Practically speaking, this means that the process manager has a set of algorithms and data structures it uses to implement process abstractions; process creation means that the process manager creates a new instance of the process data structure that the algorithms can then manipulate. The *process descriptor* (also called the process control block, or other names in various systems) is the data structure used by the process manager algorithms to record the status of a process while the process manager algorithms monitor and control the process. Process descriptors will be described in detail in Section 6.4. The process descriptor is the tangible representation of the process; as a consequence, most systems create a *process identifier* that (directly or indirectly) references the process descriptor when the process is created. If a process is to be referenced, then it is identified by its process identifier. In UNIX, the process identifier is returned to the parent process as a result from the `fork` system call.

A process is composed of the following tangible elements:

■ A *program* to define the behavior of the process.

■ The *data* operated on by the process and the results it produces.

■ A set of *resources* to provide an environment for the execution.

■ The *process descriptor* to keep track of the progress of the process during its execution. (The process descriptor will identify the process's program, data, and resources.)

Once the process descriptor has been created, the process manager can allocate the set of resources required by the process when it is initialized—for example, the process will need some memory in which it keeps its program, stack, and data. The child process may also inherit resources (or inherit access to shared resources such as open files), so the process manager must ensure that the process descriptor (as well as other OS data structures) reflect that these allocations are setup correctly. Eventually, the process manager will finish initializing the process—meaning initializing the OS data structures for the process and initializing resources if that is required. The new process is then ready to begin executing its own program.

After a process has been made ready for execution, it begins to compete with the other processes (that are also ready for execution) for the use of the CPU. That is, in a multiprogrammed OS there are usually several processes that are ready to execute their programs, but only one CPU. The process that is currently using the CPU may voluntarily yield the CPU to other processes—for example, by requesting an I/O operation. Alternatively, the process manager may decide to preempt the CPU from the running process by interrupting its execution, saving the context in which it was executing (in the interrupted process's descriptor), and allocating the CPU to a different process. The process manager includes a set of algorithms and data structures to manage CPU multiplexing (we return to the discussion of scheduling in Chapter 7).

In the case that two or more processes intend to share some of their resources (such as primary memory or files), the process manager will set the resource status to allow sharing and also provide synchronization tools that the community of processes can use to accomplish orderly sharing among themselves. Part of the job is to ensure that if a process does *not* want to share its resources, then no other process will be able to access the resource—this is part of the system protection mechanism. There will be more discussion of basic process management in Section 6.4.

6.1.2 ■ Implementing the Resource Model

Resource management refers to the task of allocating "requested entities" to processes according to their needs and within a system-wide allocation policy. Because of the diversity of resource types, the OS provides several different types of resource managers. Each resource manager defines the resource model, accepts requests for the use of the resource, and then allocates units of the resource according to the cumulative requests and the allocation policy.

Each process uses resources to execute programs on data. The CPU is the hardware resource that executes the program, provided the program and data have been stored in the (allocated) executable memory resource. During execution, the process may request other resources according to the particular behavior defined by the program. As mentioned in the previous subsection, multiprogramming systems allow multiple processes to exist at any given time, where only one can use the CPU at any given moment. While one process is using the CPU, the remaining processes are using the I/O resources, are waiting for resources to become available, or are waiting for the CPU. The resource management part of the process manager—the scheduler—is responsible for implementing the algorithms and data structures used to control these resources. Just as there is a process descriptor for each process, there is a *resource descriptor* data structure for each resource. This data structure is used to store all the information the OS algorithms need to manage that resource.

Resource management comes into play whenever a process requests a resource, is allocated a resource (in case the resource was not available at the time it was requested), and whenever a process releases a resource. A resource request causes the resource manager to decide if the requested resources should be allocated to the process, and to block the process if its request cannot be honored at the moment of the request. Whenever a request can be honored, the resource manager assigns the resources to the process. When the process releases resources, the resource manager resumes control of the resources, and potentially allocates them to some other process that is blocked waiting for them. Section 6.5 elaborates on resource managers.

6.2 ▪ Initializing the Operating System

When the computer is powered up, it begins to execute the fetch-execute cycle for the program that is stored in the memory at the bootstrap entry point (see Section 4.2.2). This first program defines the most primitive operation of the system. It must ultimately create the OS environment to support its computation model—processes, threads, objects, files, and other resources. Once the OS has been loaded and started, it takes control of all hardware resources and initializes various data structures and all the device states (thereby creating resource abstractions). The OS remains in control of the machine and all the resources until the machine is turned off. After the OS has initialized itself, it starts executing a command line interface (the "shell") at the system console. The computer operator can then direct the OS to begin running other processes to perform desired work.

When the bootstrap code is executed, an *initial process* is defined. That is, since a process is a program in execution on a von Neumann computer, the moment the hardware begins the fetch-execute cycle on the bootstrap loader code, one can say that exactly one process exists in the system. Even though the OS has not yet begun to run (so it cannot have created its process abstraction), there is the notion of the initial process running. Hence the initial process is really just a name to characterize the program execution before the OS gains control of the machine.

The computer's operator uses the console shell to direct the OS to execute other programs. In a batch system, the directives used to control the machine are completely different from those used in a timesharing machine or personal computer. In a timesharing machine, the operator executes a program that enables other terminals and users to run their programs on the machine. Each terminal or user uses its own surrogate system process created during this initialization phase. Once the initialization code has completed, the system is ready to use in multiuser mode with one surrogate system process per potential user.

When a machine is booted with UNIX, the OS begins operation in single-user (but multiple process) mode. The OS and machine are assumed to be under the control of a user who has administrative knowledge and authority—the *superuser*. The single-user system bypasses the standard protection mechanisms intended to support isolation.

Part of the UNIX initialization process is to execute an `rc` (for "run control") file that defines configuration information. For example, each physical serial port on the machine is initialized so that it can be connected to a printer or be used as a login port. Furthermore, a process executing an appropriate program is started on each port. Each serial port supporting logins runs the `getty` program (see Figure 6.2).

The `getty` process initializes itself, then waits for a user to begin using the port. When the port begins to be used, `getty` runs the `login` program; it expects a user identification on the first line and a password on the second line. After the port's `login` program obtains the identification and the password, it verifies the user's identity by looking up the given identification and password in the system's `/etc/passwd` file. Each entry has the form

```
jblow:eNcrYPt123:3448:35:Joe Blow:/home/kiowa/jblow:/bin/bash
```

Each line in this file is a record to describe a different user, with fields in the record separated by the ":" character. In the example record, the user login is "jblow",

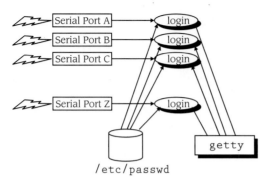

Figure 6.2
The getty Program

"eNcrYPt123" is an encrypted copy of the password, the next two numbers are the user ID and group ID, the fifth field is the user's real name, "/home/kiowa/jblow" is the user's home directory, and "/bin/bash" is the path to the shell command line interpreter preferred by the user. If this authentication is successful, the login process changes to the user's home directory, then executes the specified shell program so that the user can interact directly with the login process using the shell.

A user who logs into a UNIX machine simply begins using a process that was created when the machine was started. (There are actually many more details to starting a shell, but conceptually, this description is accurate.) Thus the user's process is executing a shell program (for example, the Bourne shell, the C shell, or the Korn shell) with a unique copy of the data and stack segments for the shell execution. The unique data includes the user's environment variables such as the PATH variable. When the user logs off the machine, the login process returns from executing the shell and waits for the next user to login.

6.3 ■ Process Address Spaces

The behavior of a process is defined by the program it executes. A program is specified by an application programmer as a set of source code modules that reference a collection of library object modules. The executable program is prepared by combining the modules so that when the process is executing in a module derived from one source file, it can reference a specific part of another module defined in a source program from a different file. These references may be jumps in the instruction execution sequence, an instruction reading/writing data when it executes, or references to other resources. The procedure for combining the modules for cross-referencing defines a linear address space in which the process refers to all the aspects of the computation—the program, variables, and so on. That is, the *address space* is a set of locations used by the process to reference, for example, primary memory locations, OS services, and resources (see Figure 6.3).

The largest part of the address space maps to primary memory locations. This section focuses on how this part of the address space is defined for a process. The other

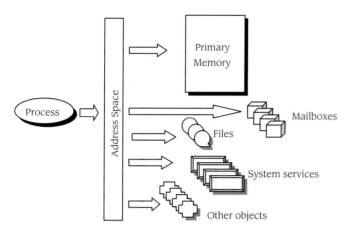

Figure 6.3
The Address Space

objects referenced by the program must either be configured at some address in the address space (as is done with the memory-mapped I/O technique discussed in Chapter 5) or be passed into the process from an external source and then temporarily stored in the address space. A process can reference only memory and other entities that have been mapped into the address space. The address space defines all the logical entities used by a process and specifies an address by which they are referenced.

A program can be thought of as an operational specification of the work to be accomplished by a process. It prescribes the precise set of instructions to be executed. The specification also defines the set of variables the program will use. When a process's program is made ready for execution, a load map is prepared to define where individual procedures and data will be placed in the address space when the program is loaded into primary memory. Thus the program image defines the set of all primary memory addresses a process uses.

6.3.1 ■ Creating the Address Space

The memory part of the address space is created by the source program translation system. As shown in Figure 6.4, a programmer directs the language translator to create an *executable program* using a series of system software tools. First, specific language translators (such as assemblers and compilers) translate the source modules into a set of *relocatable object modules,* one for each source code file. Next, the *link editor* (also called the *linkage editor*) combines the relocatable object modules with library modules to form an *absolute program*—a data structure that includes the translated program, the addresses in which each instruction will be stored, and a description of how variables should be set up when the program runs. In UNIX systems, the absolute program is called the *load module* (and may also be referred to by its default name of a.out). A UNIX load module consists of a program segment that contains the translated instructions and a data segment that defines the space for static variables. The link editor writes the absolute program to a file in the secondary memory until it is needed. When

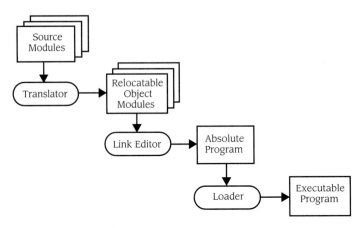

Figure 6.4
Creating an Executable Program

the absolute program is to be executed, the loader reads the absolute program from the secondary memory and places it into the primary memory, where the CPU can decode and execute each instruction. More is said about translation in the discussion of memory management in Chapter 11.

6.3.2 ■ Loading the Program

Before a program can be executed, primary memory must be allocated to the process. Once the system knows which primary memory locations are going to be used to execute the program, it can then map the allocated primary memory addresses into the address space. The executable program is then translated into its final executable form—the form expected by the hardware control unit—and loaded into the primary memory at the proper location. When the PC (program counter) is set to the primary memory address of the first executable instruction—the *main entry point*—for the program, the hardware begins to execute the program. The link editor will have identified the entry point when it created the absolute program.

6.3.3 ■ Maintaining Consistency in the Address Space

The loader produces the executable program when it loads the absolute program into primary memory. In some operating systems, the memory manager may choose to remove the executable program from primary memory, save it in secondary memory and then deallocate the memory so that the memory resource manager can allocate it to another process. Thus, even after an absolute program has been converted into executable form, it may be stored back into secondary memory until it is needed. If the program is copied to secondary memory, then when it is copied back into primary memory, there is one copy of the executable program in secondary memory and another copy in primary memory. The complete program image exists in both memories. However, as the process executes, it changes parts of primary memory image without updating the secondary memory image. For example, each time the program computes a new value for a variable, it writes the value into the location in primary memory that corresponds to the variable. However, the corresponding copy of the data in secondary memory will be updated only if the process explicitly executes output instructions to update the secondary memory version of the variable or if the memory manager periodically rewrites the image from primary to secondary memory.

In von Neumann computers, data are copied from the primary memory into registers before they are used as operands, and then written back to the primary memory after new values have been computed for the operands. Instructions are fetched into the control unit instruction register for decoding and execution but are not rewritten to the memory, since they do not change. The von Neumann architecture employs a *memory hierarchy* in which data and instructions are kept in secondary memory, M_s, primary memory, M_p, and processor registers, M_R, as shown in Figure 6.5. The memory hierarchy in that figure is the one used in the original von Neumann architecture. In modern machines, the hierarchy has several additional layers including a cache memory between the primary memory and CPU registers. Cache memories and the rest of the hierarchy are discussed in Chapter 11 rather than here because including these other layers unnecessarily complicates the discussion of the address space.

Data and instructions cannot be loaded directly into CPU registers from secondary memory (except by I/O instructions) because the hardware does not support such operations. Instead, they are copied from secondary memory, M_s, into the primary memory, M_p, before being loaded into a register. Hence, the primary memory contains a redundant copy of the secondary memory image and some of the CPU registers contain a redundant copy of information in the primary memory. Specifically, for every data register R_i (denoted M_{Ri}), there is usually a corresponding location j in the primary memory (denoted M_{pj}) and a corresponding location k in the secondary memory (denoted M_{sk}), where at some point in time $M_{Ri} \neq M_{pj} \neq M_{sk}$ even though they represent the same variable.

Instructions are not changed in the primary memory, so $M_{pj} = M_{sk}$ for the corresponding locations at each level of the hierarchy, provided it contains an instruction. The memory hierarchy is considered *consistent* for locations that contain instructions, since corresponding memory locations in the three parts of the memory hierarchy

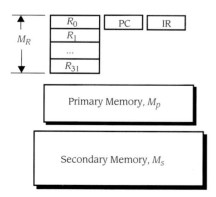

Figure 6.5
The Basic Memory Hierarchy

always contain the same value. The data, however, may change at each level of the hierarchy as the program executes, so it is not consistent unless the application programmer explicitly makes it be consistent. Whenever the process changes M_{Ri}, it contains a different value than its corresponding location in primary memory, so $M_{Ri} \neq M_{pj}$ until the process executes the appropriate store instruction. Similarly, once the primary memory location has been updated, then $M_{pj} \neq M_{sk}$ until the process executes an appropriate output instruction to the storage device. The program image describes the behavior of a process and instructs the OS and hardware in how to execute instructions to achieve the desired behavior. The data image (throughout the hierarchy) describes the process's state while it is executing the program. The process manager must maintain each process's complete state even though the state may be inconsistent due to updates of parts of the memory in different parts of the memory hierarchy. In particular, the OS must be designed so that when the scheduler switches the CPU from one process to another, it saves the processor registers for the first process independent of inconsistencies resulting from cases in which $M_{Ri} \neq M_{pj}$. It saves M_{Ri} as if it were different from M_{pj}. Similarly, if the memory manager deallocates primary memory, the primary and secondary memory image differences must be tracked and made to be consistent. The process manager ordinarily chooses to simply write the complete primary memory image back into secondary memory to make the two consistent before deallocating the primary memory. It does this rather than keeping track of what has changed. In some systems, the memory manager is charged with the task of maintaining the consistency of the primary and secondary memories while the programmer is responsible for maintaining CPU register consistency with respect to primary memory contents.

6.4 ■ The Process Abstraction

A resource is any entity that may be required by a process, which will be blocked from executing if one or more resources are unavailable when needed. Thus coexisting processes will compete for resources if they need the resources at the same time. One process will win the competition and be allocated the resource, while the second must wait until the first process releases the resource. The OS must keep track of how each resource is allocated, which processes are waiting for which resources, and so on. This tracking is accomplished by recording detailed information regarding the processes and resources stated in their resource and process descriptors.

6.4.1 ■ Process Descriptors

The OS keeps track of each process's complete status. The *process descriptor* is the basic data structure used to represent the specific state for each process. This includes the following:

- Its processor registers contents at the time the process was last suspended
- Its processor state (for example, if it is blocked or ready)
- The address space mapping details
- Its memory state
- A pointer to its stack

- The resources that have been allocated to it
- The resources that it needs

A fundamental part of the detailed design strategy for the process manager is reflected in the design of the process descriptor data structure.

When an OS is configured, it usually has a fixed number of process descriptors that represent the maximum number of processes it can support at any one time. A process descriptor is allocated when the process is created; it is released when the process dies. Even though the process descriptor is ultimately managed by the process manager, various other parts of the OS query change individual fields in the process's descriptor.

Table 6.1 shows the various fields that might be included in a process descriptor. Which fields are incorporated in any particular operating system's process descriptor depends on the OS algorithm and data structure design.

TABLE 6.1 Process Descriptor

Field	Description
Internal process name	An internal name of the process, such as an integer or table index, used in the operating system code.
State	The process's current state.
Owner	A process has an owner (identified by the owner's internal identification such as the login name). The descriptor contains a field for storing the owner identification.
Parent process	A pointer to the process descriptor of this process's parent.
List of child processes	A pointer to a list of the child processes of this process.
List of reusable resources	A pointer to a list of reusable resource types held by the process. Each resource type will be a descriptor of the number of units of the resource.
List of consumable resources	Similar to the reusable resource list (see Section 6.5).
List of file descriptors	A special case of the reusable resource list.
Message queue	A special case of the consumable resource list.
Protection domain	A description of the access rights currently held by the process (see Chapter 14).
CPU status register content	A copy of each of the CPU status registers at the last time the process exited the running state.
CPU general register content	A copy of each of the CPU general registers at the last time the process exited the running state.

6.4.2 ■ Process State Diagram

The process manager algorithms change the state of various processes, depending on the current activity, the state of each process, and the state of the system. State diagrams are a useful tool to represent the action, based on a process's current state, that the process manager takes. A *state diagram* is composed of a set of states and transitions between states. A state represents the operating system's characterization of a process in terms of how it is managed. For example, if the process manager can schedule the process, it is said to be in a state of readiness. A transition from one state to another is caused by a process activity or by the application of a control function to the process.

Figure 6.6 is a simple example of a state diagram for processes in a hypothetical system. (The state diagram is purposely simplified so that you can see how diagrams can be used to design the process manager; the diagram is refined later in the chapter.) In this state diagram, a process may be in any one of three states—running, ready, or blocked. The process state can change if it is involved in some action, as indicated by the labels in Figure 6.6. When a process, p_i, has been allocated memory and is created, the *start* transition occurs, placing p_i in the ready state. This means that p_i is waiting for the CPU scheduler to allocate a processor to it.

The process manager uses the state diagram to determine the type of service to provide to the process. If the process is in the ready state, it is competing for the CPU. There is no other transition out of the ready state. If the process is in the running state, it can complete execution, in which case the process manager will release resources and remove the process. Alternatively, the process may request a resource when it is in the running state—for example, by requesting an I/O operation. In most operating systems, if a running process requests an immediately available resource, the process is allowed to continue in the running state. Otherwise, the process manager removes the process from the CPU and notifies the appropriate resource manager that the process requires units of its resource. The scheduler is then invoked to allocate the processor to the next selected process in the ready state. From the blocked state, the process can move to the ready state only by being allocated the requested resource. It is then once again competing for the processor.

A good first step in designing a process manager is to design the state diagram for each process. The next section deals with how the resource manager interacts with the process manager.

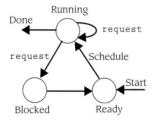

Figure 6.6
Process States

6.5 ■ The Resource Abstraction

The resource manager is logically a part of the OS process manager, although any given OS may treat it as a separate entity. The resource manager is responsible for allocating resources to processes when they are needed and returning released resources to a pool of available resources when the process has finished with them.

In this introduction to resource management, a formal model of OS components begins to evolve. The model will be continuously enhanced in the next four chapters. The first part of the model identifies the different resource types in the system and the number of units of each resource type that are available. Suppose the system has m different types of resources. Then

$$R = \{R_j \mid 0 \leq j < m\}$$

represents the different resource types. For example, a tape drive is one resource type, a disk is another resource type, and a mouse is a third. The model should explicitly represent the number of units of each type of resource currently available to be used by processes. Each resource type, R_j, has an associated count, c_j, to represent this number of units of R_j that are available:

$$C = \{c_j \geq 0 \mid \text{for each resource type } R_j \in R \ (0 \leq j < m)\}.$$

For example, if R_3 is the floppy disk type and the system has two floppy disk drives, then c_3 is 2. If there are m different resource types, then the operating system will be configured with m different resource managers and each manager will have a descriptor for each resource to hold the count of currently available units.

Recall that a resource is *anything* that can potentially block a process from executing. If a process requests a block of memory and none is available, then the memory resource manager blocks the process from subsequent execution until the memory becomes available. This notion of a resource can be extended to abstract entities such as messages or input data. Since a process can be blocked while waiting for input data from a device, it has, in effect, requested data (using a read operation), and it must suspend execution until the data is "allocated" to the process by becoming available from the device.

Resources (such as memory) that can be allocated and must be returned to the system after the process has finished using them are called *reusable resources*. A more abstract resource, such as input data, that can cause a process to be blocked on request but that is never subsequently released by that process, is called as a *consumable resource*. The system always has a fixed, finite number of units of a reusable resource—that is, c_j is a fixed integer for a reusable resource type. However, the number of units of a consumable resource is unbounded, since there are one or more producer processes for the consumable resource and there is no way to know the number of units of the resource that this set of processes might produce in the future.

A process in the running state may request c_i units of R_j at any time (of course c_i must be less than or equal to c_j if R_j is a reusable resource). If the units are unavailable, the process manager deallocates the processor from the process (and automatically schedules another process to run). It then changes the process's state to blocked and

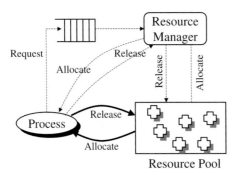

Figure 6.7
A Resource Manager

queues the process on the *resource queue* for R_j (see Figure 6.7). The resource manager for R_j accepts release commands from other processes to add units of available resources to the available resource pool and assigns available units to processes waiting for the resource. Once all requested units are allocated, the process is moved to the ready state to begin competing for the processor again.

A process creates a consumable resource by releasing one or more units of the resource. For example, if a message is a resource, a receiver process will be queued on the message resource type. (If there are no pending messages, the unit count is 0 and the process is blocked on the resource.) When another process sends a message, the message-handling code releases a unit of the resource type to the resource manager. The resource manager then can allocate the unit of resource to the requesting process so that it can proceed.

Because the pattern of resource requests among the processes is unpredictable, there is dynamic competition for the resources. A requesting process may be blocked for an arbitrary interval. The amount of time is generally not predictable at the time the request is made, since the resource may already be allocated to another process, or, in the case of consumable resources, may not yet have been produced. It is generally impossible to predict the amount of time such a process may hold a reusable resource. Eventually, the process releases resources or it terminates by executing an exit system call. Process termination causes the OS to deallocate the resources currently allocated to the process, starting with the processor and memory, but ultimately including all reusable resources allocated to the process. The consumable resources held by the terminating process are assumed to have been consumed by the process, so they are not recovered.

The resource descriptor is used to save the state of any resource, R_j. It includes the information described previously and summarized in Table 6.2.

6.6 ■ Process Hierarchy

Multiple process software environments implicitly define a hierarchy among the set of processes implementing the environment. This hierarchy allows the community of processes to agree on basic tasks such as which processes can control which other

TABLE 6.2 Parts of a Resource Descriptor

Field	Description
Internal resource name	An internal name for the resource used by the operating system code.
Total units	The number of units of this resource type configured into the system.
Available units	The number of units currently available.
List of available units	The set of available units of this resource type that are available for use by processes.
List of blocked processes	The list of processes that have a pending request for units of this resource type.

processes and how resources should be allocated to processes. The basis of the hierarchy evolves from the process-creation mechanism.

The spawn operation naturally implies a hierarchical parent-child relationship. A parent can have many child processes, but each child process has exactly one parent process (see Figure 6.8). The initial process is the root of the tree of all processes. Whenever a process spawns a child, a leaf node is added to the tree.

Some operating systems use this hierarchical relationship, while others simply ignore it. For example, the OS may be designed so that a parent process has the right to block a child process, thus preventing it from executing. The parent may also be able to activate a blocked child process, to destroy a child process, or to allocate resources to the child process. Suppose the OS attaches all of these semantics to the spawn relationship. Then, because all processes are created by the initial process, each child is ultimately under the full control of the initial process. The initial process can allocate resources to each child, block/activate the process, destroy each child, and so on.

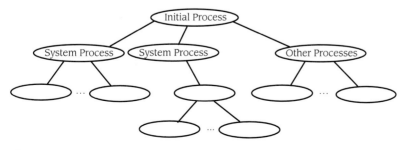

Figure 6.8
A Process Hierarchy

6.6.1 ■ Refining the Process Manager

If control semantics are added to the parent-child relation, therefore enabling, for example, a parent to control a child, process management becomes more complex. This can be shown by considering how the state diagram for a process becomes more complex. Figure 6.6 provided a state diagram for process management that focused only on resource management and processor multiplexing; Figure 6.9 enhances the original state diagram to show how the process is to be managed when a parent process is allowed to suspend and activate a child process through requests to the process manager. If a parent suspends a child, then the child is not allowed to use the CPU; when a parent activates a child, the child can compete for the CPU, provided it is not blocked. A parent may decide to suspend a child process for any of a number of reasons, including temporarily removing the primary memory from a process (called "swapping the process out").

During the derivation of a new state diagram, the blocked state from the original diagram is partitioned into `blockedActive` and `blockedSuspended` states. Similarly, the ready state is divided into `readyActive` and `readySuspended` states. After an initial set of resources, including memory, has been allocated to a process, the process comes into existence in the `readySuspended` state. This means that internally, the new process is ready to compete for the CPU, but its controlling process has not activated it. It can be moved to the `readyActive` state once its controlling process decides to activate it. When the process becomes `readyActive`, it is placed in the CPU ready list, meaning it is blocked, waiting for the scheduler to allocate the CPU to it. Based on the strategy used by the controlling process, it may choose to suspend a child process in the `readyActive` state or the scheduler may allocate the CPU to the process. In the former case, the process returns to the `readySuspended` state, and in the latter, it becomes a running process on the CPU.

A process in the running state may be involuntarily removed from the CPU if the scheduler chooses to do so (or if the parent, running on a different processor, chooses to block the child). The process may also voluntarily move itself to the `readyActive`

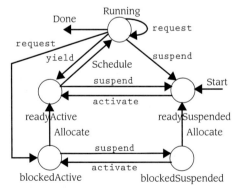

Figure 6.9
A Process State Diagram Reflecting Control

state (by executing a `yield` command) if, for example, it is involved in a busy-wait. It may also move to the `blockedActive` state by requesting an unavailable resource. A process is ready if it needs the CPU in order to proceed, and it is blocked if it needs a different resource to proceed.

A `blockedActive` process can become `readyActive` if the requested resource is allocated to it. It can become `blockedSuspended` if a controlling process chooses to suspend it while it is blocked. A resource allocation operation is required for the process to be moved from either of the blocked states to the corresponding ready states. An `activate` operation is required to move the process from a suspended state to the corresponding active state.

6.6.2 ■ Specializing Resource Allocation Strategies

The responsibility for resource management can be delegated to each child process when it is created. This implies that the child must provide its own algorithms and data structures to manage the resources of child processes it creates. The OS for the RC 4000 carries this approach to its extreme [Brinch Hansen, 1970]. This system was designed so that the *nucleus* provided fundamental process management mechanisms but deferred resource allocation policies to its clients and their children. Child processes were created from the nucleus process, and each of these children comprised a special-purpose OS, implementing its own resource policy in its own resource manager. This approach enabled the nucleus to support a real-time extension to the nucleus, a timesharing extension to the nucleus, and a batch extension to the nucleus, all at the same time, since the specialized resource managers were implemented in each child of the nucleus rather than in the nucleus itself. The real-time extension could allocate resources according to service priorities, the timesharing extension according to response time, and the batch extension according to turnaround time. This strategy can be (and was, in the RC 4000) propagated throughout the process hierarchy, so resources are always allocated by a process's parent rather than by the "operating system."

Obviously, this approach greatly complicates the definition of child processes when compared with other systems—in UNIX, for example—since the parent program has considerably more responsibility than in environments in which the OS manages resources. But in the RC 4000 system, it is also possible to design and build much more flexible process hierarchies than can be built in UNIX.

The thread scheduling mentioned in Section 2.4 is an example of this philosophy. User threads are implemented by library code that executes in user space. The OS is unaware that threads exist in such an environment; it treats all its clients as processes. A process can support multiple threads of execution by using the thread library to create, schedule, synchronize, and destroy threads operating within the process. A thread is scheduled by the process to use a portion of the process's timeslice (which has been allocated by the OS scheduler).

Variants of the process management strategy employed by the RC 4000 have been used in many other operating systems. In the 1970s and 1980s, several commercial machines incorporated a virtual machine operating system to implement fundamental resource management tasks such as address space allocation and CPU multiplexing mechanisms. The IBM VM was probably the most well-known of these virtual machine operating systems. Each such system nucleus essentially provided a simulated hardware environment to conventional, special-purpose operating systems to handle time-sharing applications, batch users, and so on.

In the 1980s, this same technology was widely used in workstations to preserve application software investments. For example, UNIX suppliers created Intel 80386 emulator applications that enabled users to execute a DOS environment within a UNIX process.

The movement to microkernel OS architectures essentially corresponds to the same strategy. The microkernel implements a virtual machine that provides address space and protection mechanisms with as much of the policy as possible implemented in its client software. One difference between contemporary microkernel architectures and older virtual machine architectures is that microkernels use a client-server organization (see Chapter 15) to separate the resource managers from the scheduler.

6.7 ■ Summary

Sequential processes are the basis of modern computational models; the behavior of a sequential process is defined by the program the process executes. The process manager is responsible for creating the environment in which the sequential process executes, including implementing resource management.

The community of processes that exists in the OS at any given time is derived from the initial process that is created when the computer begins operation. The initial process boots up the OS, which can create other processes to service interactive users, printers, network connections, and so on.

A program image is created from a set of source modules and previously compiled library modules in relocatable form. The link editor combines the various relocatable object modules to create an absolute program in secondary memory. The loader places the absolute program into the primary memory when the program is executed by a process. The program image, along with other entities that the process can reference, constitutes the process's address space.

The address space can be stored in different parts of the machine's memory hierarchy during execution. Programs and data may move up and down the memory hierarchy from the secondary memory to the primary memory to CPU registers. Redundant copies of information in different parts of the hierarchy allow for inconsistencies to exist among corresponding locations. Some of the inconsistencies must be handled by the programmer (for example, inconsistencies between CPU register values of variables and their values in primary memory). The OS attempts to maintain consistency between the primary and secondary memory versions of the program and data.

Resource management in the OS controls the allocation of units of a resource to processes in the blocked state (after they have requested resources) and retrieves and reallocates units of a resource released by other processes. The resource manager resolves competition among processes needing units of resources.

Process creation is a fundamental part of process management in that it defines the means by which one process can spawn another and how the parent process can control child processes by suspending or destroying them.

This chapter described the general organization of the process and resource manager. The next chapter focuses on the CPU resource manager known as the short-term scheduler.

6.8 ▪ Exercises

1. Redraw Figure 6.4 using the names of the Linux/UNIX system tools used to prepare a set of C program modules—`file1.c`, `file2.c`, and `file3.c`—for execution. Explicitly label `stdio` and the C library, `libc.a`, in the diagram. Use the default names for relocatable object modules and absolute programs.

2. In Linux/UNIX, is it possible for the link editor to combine relocatable object modules created from compilers for different programming languages? Explain why or why not.

3. Give an example process execution scenario in which $M_{Ri} \neq M_{pj} \neq M_{sk}$ until the programmer or system takes action to ensure consistency.

4. When a new process moves from the ready state to the running state (in Figure 6.6), each register in the CPU must be set either to initial values or to the values the process had when it was last interrupted. Explain why the PC register is typically the last register loaded for the new process. Show a pseudo assembly language code segment to load a new process onto a CPU (that is, to change the PC after restoring other registers) for a processor that contains arithmetic-logical registers R0-R3, processor status register PSR, condition code register CC, program counter PC, and instruction register IR.

5. If the source code for your lab OS is available, inspect the source listing to find the fields in the system's process descriptor. (*Hint:* In Linux, for example, you would start by looking at the code that implements the `fork` system call. Then look for a `C struct` that seems appropriate.) How many entries are in a descriptor? In what form does the owner's name appear in the descriptor? What is the name of the state field in the descriptor?

6. Read the operating system source code and then construct a state diagram to represent the relevant states that a process may be in at any given time.

7. Suppose a process is defined to behave as described in Figure 6.6. Design and implement a resource manager for reusable resources. When multiple processes are blocked on a resource and one or more units become available, call a policy function to select the process to receive resources. Implement any simple policy you like. Test your resource manager by creating a testbed with N different processes (N is a testbed parameter), M different resources (M is a testbed parameter), where R_i initially has c_i units of the resource (c_i is a testbed parameter). Only one process can be running at one time, so you will also need a simple scheduler to allocate the processor to processes in the order they become ready. A running process should

execute for a small random amount of time and then request one of the units of resource, transitioning to the blocked state. When the resource is allocated to the process, it should be moved to the ready state. Later, the testbed should release each resource it acquired. Your testbed processes need only simulate real work by real processes. For example, your testbed might have a code schema similar to this:

```
#define N 50
   . . .
scanf("%d", M); // Define a value for M
for(i=0; i<M; i++) { . . . }          // Define values for c[i]
   . . .
for(i=0; i<N; i++) {
    waitTime = rand();
    for(j=0; j<waitTime; j++) { }; // Simulate running
                                   // process
    request(r[i%M], . . .); // Ask for k < c[i%M] units
    waitTime = rand();
    for(j=0; j<waitTime; j++) { }; // Simulate running
                                   // process
    release(r[i%M], . . .);          // Release resource
}
   . . .
```

A more comprehensive test procedure would cause processes to hold more than one resource type at a time. If you have time, make your test driver check some of these more complex situations.

Experiment with various small values of $N < 8$, $M < 10$, and c_i. The random amount of time a process runs should be kept as small as possible so that your tests do not take an inordinate amount of time. Be sure your test cases cause processes to block for unavailable resources. Hand in a listing of your resource manager and testbed along with a trace (fewer than five pages) of state transitions in a test session.

Laboratory Exercise: Observing OS Behavior

In this chapter you have learned that the OS is a program that uses various data structures. Like all programs in execution, you can determine the performance and other behavior of the OS by inspecting its state—the values stored in its data structures. The goal of this exercise is to study some aspects of the organization and behavior of a Linux system by observing values in kernel data structures.

Write a program to report the behavior of the Linux kernel. Your program should have three different options: The default version should print the following values on stdout:

- CPU type and model
- Kernel version
- Amount of time since the system was last booted

A second version of the program should print the same information as the first version plus:

- The amount of time the CPU has spent in user mode, system mode, and the amount of time the system was idle
- The number of disk requests made on the system
- The number of context switches the kernel has performed
- The time at which the system was last booted
- The number of processes that have been created since the system was booted

The last version of the program should print the same information as the second version, plus (be sure to look at the relevant man pages for /proc to get more context for the requested information):

- The amount of memory configured into this computer
- The amount of memory currently available
- A list of load averages (each averaged over the last minute). This information would allow another program to plot these values against time so that a user could see how the load average varied over some time interval. For this version of the program you will need to provide two additional parameters to indicate (1) how often the load average should be read from the kernel and (2) the time interval over which the load average should be read.

For example, the first version of your program might be called by ksamp, the second version with ksamp -s, and the third version with ksamp -1 2 60 (which would cause the load average observation to run for 60 seconds, sampling the kernel table about once every 2 seconds). In solving this part of the exercise, you will probably find it useful to read about the sleep systems call.

BACKGROUND

In 1991, Linus Torvalds began creating the first version of Linux.[1] The UNIX kernel was introduced to the world as a minimal OS that implemented the bare necessities, leaving the software to provide the desired bells and whistles to libraries and other user mode software. The early UNIX kernel followed the principle of "small is beautiful," though over the years it has grown large and complex; Linux returns to the original principle.

In general, much of process and resource management is implemented in the kernel. There are many versions of the kernel interface, one differing from another in the details (file name characteristics, error codes, parameter settings on system calls, and so on). Linux supports the POSIX.1 system call interface. Since POSIX.1 is a UNIX-style API, the general definition of the process and resource abstractions are already defined by UNIX.

Kernel Organization

The Linux kernel uses the same organizational strategy as other UNIX kernels, though Linux reflects current technology in the detailed design; this organization is known as a *monolithic* kernel (see Section 18.2). This means that almost all of the kernel functions—process and resource management, memory management, and file management—are implemented within a single module. In traditional UNIX systems, device management functions are implemented in device drivers that can be added to the kernel at a later time. The premise of this approach is that the only functionality that one should add to the kernel (after it has been designed) is code to manage new devices that a user might add to the computer. By allowing device drivers to be added to the kernel, new devices can be accommodated. By limiting the additions to being device drivers, the kernel designers are assured that the main part of the kernel will not be disturbed when new supervisor mode code for device support is added. Linux provides an additional mechanism for adding functionality called a *module*. Whereas device drivers are statically configured into a kernel configuration, modules can be dynamically added and deleted as the OS executes. Modules can be used to implement dynamically loadable device drivers or other desired kernel functions.

User programs view the kernel as a large abstract data type (similar to an object) that maintains state, and which has a number of functions on its public interface—the POSIX.1 API. This OS "object" provides service to a user program whenever the program calls a function on its public interface;[2] the exact nature of the service depends on the parameters used in the function call as well as the state of the OS when the

---

[1] The `comp.os.minix` newsgroup had a few postings from Torvalds in early 1991 in which he let the world know that he was working on a public implementation of POSIX.

[2] There is no claim here that the kernel is an object in the strict sense; this is an analogy to help you understand how the kernel is designed and implemented. While it has a public interface and a private implementation, it has few other properties of, say, a C++ object.

function is called. Hence, the public interface specification for the kernel is the main description of the OS functionality. As mentioned above, the POSIX.1 interface is the nominal specification of Linux's public interface. It is only nominal, since any particular version of Linux may not implement all of the fine details of the specification, and because some parts of the specification do not completely specify the semantics of the interface. However the POSIX.1 specification is sufficiently complete that programmers are generally willing to accept it as a basic OS interface specification.

The private implementation of the OS defines the way any particular kernel is implemented. Figure 6.10 illustrates the relationship among user programs (the solid arrows mean system calls), the monolithic kernel, device drivers, and modules used in Linux implementations. In theory—and generally in practice—the boundaries between device drivers or modules and the kernel are not discernible to the user program. These are characteristics of the internal design, not of the public interface. Thus the POSIX system call interface defines functions that may be implemented in the kernel, device drivers, or modules. If the function is implemented in a device driver or module, when a user program invokes the function, the kernel accepts the call, then passes it through an internal interface to the appropriate device driver or module.

Continuing with the object analogy, the kernel "object" is passive. That is, the kernel object does not have any internal thread of execution or process—it is simply a collection of functions and data that maintain state. Any process that uses the kernel services makes a kernel request by making a call on a function in the system call interface (using a trap instruction—see Section 4.6). In this model, then, a process that is executing in user mode begins to execute inside the kernel when it makes the system call. During a system call, the same process that was executing an application program in user mode will then be executing a kernel function in supervisor mode. In Linux (and other UNIX implementations) there is no "kernel process" (but see the discussion of daemons in the next section). Just as in the object model, when the process is executing kernel code, it can reference data stored in the kernel's address

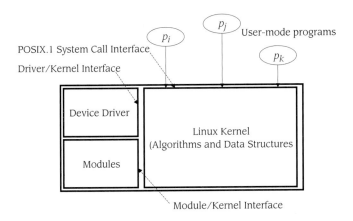

Figure 6.10
The Linux Kernel, Device Drivers, and Modules

space (but which is not accessible to the process when it is executing outside the kernel in user mode). Processes are allowed to switch back and forth between user and supervisory mode, but they can execute privileged instructions and reference the kernel's data structures only while they are executing kernel software.

Linux is a multiprogramming kernel; however kernel functions are normally executed without interruption. That is, once a process calls a function, the function normally runs to completion and returns before the CPU will be allocated to a different process. This is called a *single-threaded kernel,* since only one thread of execution is allowed to execute in the kernel at any one time; one thread of execution cannot start a function call and become interrupted by the scheduler to let another process run (and possibly make a kernel call). There are at least two important implications of this approach:

- A kernel function can update various kernel data structures without being concerned that another process will interrupt its execution and change related parts of the same data structures. (This problem will be discussed in detail in Chapter 8.)
- If you are writing a new kernel function, you must always keep in mind that you cannot write code that will block, waiting for a message or other resource that can only be released by some other process. This might cause the kernel to be permanently blocked waiting for a resource that will never be made available. (These deadlock situations are discussed more in Chapters 8 and 10.)

Daemons

In the previous section, we explained how processes execute kernel code—that is, that there is no "kernel process" that executes kernel code. While this is accurate, there are several user transparent processes called *daemons* that are started when a Linux machine is activated, and which must exist for correct operation of the OS. For example, if the machine is connected to a network, there must be a process to respond to incoming network packets; another daemon process logs system messages and errors, and so on. The particular daemons that are running on any Linux installation vary according to the way the system administrator set up the machine. By convention, daemon processes execute programs whose names end with the character "d"—for example, the network daemon is usually called inetd and the system logging daemon is called syslogd. You can make a good guess as to what daemons are running on your Linux machine by typing "ps -aux | more" to your shell. The ps command reports the process status, and the -aux parameters indicate that you want a report in user format (the u parameter) for all processes (the a parameter) including those without a controlling terminal (the x parameter). As you scan the list, look for commands that end with the character "d" and which have a TTY field of "?" (no controlling terminal). You will normally see syslogd, klogd, crond, and lpd running on your system. You can find out what each of these daemons is doing by looking at the manual page (for example, use "man syslogd" to read the manual page for syslogd) for the program that the daemon is running.

Some Process Management Details

PROCESSES AND TASKS

Linux uses a different low-level view for how the OS is designed than the process model that appears at the system call interface [Beck et al., 1998]. Recall from Section 6.2 that when the hardware is started, the initial process begins to run. After it completes the bootup procedure, the Linux kernel will have been loaded and the initial process begins executing the kernel code. The kernel's view of multiprogramming is that the initial process never really spawns any children processes; a `fork` command simply defines a new kernel *task,* and as the initial process executes kernel code, it simply executes different task programs in a different address space as it sees fit. At the system call interface, this behavior has the appropriate UNIX process semantics.

A `fork` system call requires that the kernel do the following:

1. Create a process descriptor entry (an instance of the `struct task_struct` data structure—if you have the source code for Linux you can take a look at the `struct task_struct` by looking at `/src/linux/include/linux/sched.h`).

2. Assign a process ID to the task.

3. Define the address space that the task will use.

4. Load the desired program into the address space. (This is the purpose of `exec`.)

5. Initialize the data segment, stack segment, and file descriptors.

6. If the task is ready to run, then link the task structure instance into a list of tasks that the initial process should execute.

The action of the initial process can then be viewed as shown in Figure 6.11. When a UNIX process is created, this causes the kernel to create a task. If the process is in the running state, then the kernel links the corresponding task descriptor into its list of runnable tasks. The initial process executes the basic kernel algorithm; when the

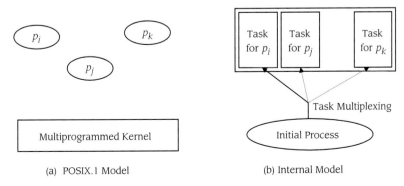

(a) POSIX.1 Model

(b) Internal Model

Figure 6.11
Kernel-level Multitasking

algorithm calls for a user process to be executed, the initial process switches the CPU to user mode, sets register contents appropriately, then "calls" one of the tasks corresponding to a user process.

PROCESS STATES

The kernel algorithms make decisions about the nature of service they provide to a process based in part on the current state of the process (see Section 6.4.2). The UNIX model defines a set of external states for the process (see the online manual page for the ps command):

- Runnability aspects of the state

    Runnable
    Stopped
    Waiting for a page to be loaded
    Waiting, but not to be interrupted (for example, because a disk I/O is in progress).
    In a short-term (less than 20 second) sleep.
    In a long-term (longer than 20 second) sleep.
    Zombie, meaning that the process has terminated, but the parent has not acknowledged the termination.

- Swapped or not
- Priority changes (has the process used the nice command)
- Whether or not the process requires special treatment by the virtual memory manager

When a process is executing in supervisory mode, it may be in any one of six states:

- *Running:* The task is using the CPU in user mode and can transition to the interrupt routine state if an interrupt occurs, or to the system call state if it traps to the kernel.
- *Interrupt routine:* An interrupt is being processed for the task; it can transition to the waiting state, or to the return from system call state, depending on the outcome of the interrupt processing.
- *System call:* As soon as the system call has been completed, the task is switched to the return from system call state.
- *Return from system call:* When the task is in this state, the kernel checks to be sure that the system call was completed, and whether or not the task needs to be scheduled. The task can either be switched to running or ready states.
- *Waiting:* The task is waiting for an external event to occur. When the event occurs, the task will be switched back to the interrupt routine state or the system call state, depending on which it was in when it began waiting.
- *Ready:* The task is waiting for the initial process to execute its code.

THREADS

Contemporary operating systems have refined the notion of a process so that one can think of two different components: (1) the set of resources used when the process executes and (2) the representation of the actual execution (such as the stack, registers, and other context) used by the process. OS designers still refer to the first component as a "process," but have begun to refer to the second component—the one representing the dynamic execution of a program within an address space—as a *thread*. Some operating systems (such as Mach [Tanenbaum, 1995] and Windows NT [Solomon, 1998]) have been designed from the beginning with the thread idea in mind. In Linux, thread support was added after the original kernel had been implemented.

The traditional UNIX interface includes the `fork` call to request that the kernel create a new process. However, since the thread notion became popular long after UNIX had been designed, there were no system calls for thread management. The POSIX.1 interface defines a series of function calls for creating and managing threads. These functions are usually implemented as user `Pthread` library code, but the Linux kernel includes a special `clone` system call to support kernel threads. The `clone` call performs the same action as the `fork` call, except that it uses an existing address space rather than defining its own. According to Beck et al. [1998], "LINUX supports threads by making available the (LINUX-specific) system call `clone`, which provides the necessary kernel support to implement threads. ... Up to now, however, there does not appear to be any implementation of the POSIX thread interface based on `clone`." However, things are changing rapidly in Linux.

Attacking the Problem

The Linux kernel is implemented as a monolithic block of code loaded in supervisor space. Because it is monolithic, the data structures may be manipulated by widely disparate parts of the kernel. As a consequence it is sometimes difficult to locate specific data structures, and, hence, to determine the OS state. Linux, Solaris, and some other versions of UNIX provide the `/proc` file system, a very useful mechanism for inspecting the kernel state. This will be the key mechanism you can use to solve this lab exercise.

The `/proc` File System

McKusick et al. [1996, p. 113] mentions that the `/proc` file system comes from UNIX Eighth Edition and that it has been used with 4.4 BSD: "In the `/proc` system, the address space of another process can be accessed with `read` and `write` system calls, which allows a debugger to access a process being debugged with much greater efficiency. The page (or pages) of interest in the child process is mapped into the kernel address space. The requested data can then be copied directly from the kernel to the parent address space." They also mention (p. 239) that `/proc` can be used to collect information about processes in the system.

Linux uses the `/proc` file system to collect information from kernel data structures. The `/proc` implementation provided with Linux can read many different kernel data structures. If you `cd` to `/proc` on your local Linux system, then list the files and directories at that location, you will see several directories and several files. The files in this directory subtree each read some kernel tables; the subdirectories with numeric names contain pseudo files to read information about the process whose process ID is the same as the directory name. The directory named `self` contains process-specific information for the process that is using `/proc`.

Files in `/proc` are read just like ordinary ASCII files. That is, you must open the file, then you can use `stdio` library routines such as `fgets` or `fscanf` to read the file. The exact files (and tables) read depend on the specific version of Linux that you are using. You must read the `proc (5)` manual page on the system before you will know exactly which file interfaces are available to you through `/proc`. For example, the Redhat Linux 2.0.36 distribution provides a file named `/proc/sys/kernel/osrelease`. If you open this file and read it, you will see the ASCII string "2.0.36". You can also simply use the shell `cat` command to experiment with the files in `/proc` and its subdirectories.

Before you begin using the `/proc` filesystem, note that the various read functions may behave differently. For example, some of the routines may read the kernel tables only when the pseudo file is opened, and others may read the tables each time the file is read.

Designing the Report Program

Your program is required to have three different options, so you will need to parse the command line with which it is called to determine the shell parameters being passed to it via the `argv` array. Identify a file—say, `/proc/sys/kernel/foo`—that contains the information you want. Open the file with a call such as

```
fid = fopen("/proc/sys/kernel/foo", "r");
fscanf(fid, " ...", ...);
```

After you have read the data from the appropriate pseudo file, parse the string to extract the information you need, then print your report on `stdout` using `stdio` functions.

Scheduling

No good times, no bad times,

There's no times at all,

Just the New York Times.

—Paul Simon, *Overs* ∎

CHAPTER OBJECTIVES

CPU resource management is commonly known as *scheduling*. The scheduling policy is determined by the way the computer will be used, although most policies can use a common scheduling mechanism. This mechanism determines how the CPU will be allocated to processes and the policy determines the order in which ready processes will receive service.

This chapter first discusses mechanisms and then considers two classes of policies: nonpreemptive and preemptive algorithms. Nonpreemptive algorithms allow a process to run to completion once it obtains the processor, while preemptive algorithms use the interval timer and scheduler to interrupt a running process to reallocate the CPU to a higher-priority ready process. The objectives are to describe the mechanisms that are used in modern operating systems, to consider the framework for implementing different strategies, and then to study examples of both classes of algorithms.

7.1 ■ Scheduling Mechanisms

As mentioned in Chapter 1, a multiprogramming operating system allows more than one process to be loaded into the executable memory at a time and for the loaded processes to share the CPU using time-multiplexing. Part of the reason for using multiprogramming is that the OS itself is implemented as one or more processes, so there must be a way for the OS and the application processes to share the CPU. Another major reason is the need for processes to perform I/O operations in the normal course of computation. Since I/O operations ordinarily require orders of magnitude more time to complete than do CPU instructions, multiprogramming systems allocate the CPU to another process whenever a process invokes an I/O operation.

The *scheduling mechanism* is the part of the process manager that handles the removal of the running process from the CPU and the selection of another process on the basis of a particular strategy. The first section focuses on how to design and implement the scheduling mechanism. It first considers the general organization of the scheduler, including a discussion of how the scheduler can be invoked. The rest of the chapter addresses strategies for the design and implementation of scheduling policy algorithms.

7.1.1 ■ The Process Scheduler Organization

The scheduler is responsible for multiplexing processes on the CPU. When it is time for the running process to be removed from the CPU (and moved to a ready or blocked state), a different process is selected from the set of the processes in the ready state. Then the selected process is allocated the CPU (its state is changed from ready to running). The scheduling *policy* determines when it is time for a process to be removed from the CPU and which ready process should be allocated the CPU next. The scheduling *mechanism* determines how the process manager knows it is time to multiplex the CPU, and how a process is allocated to and deallocated from the CPU. The focus is first on the mechanism for how to multiplex the CPU. The discussion of how the process manager is able to use a policy to determine when to multiplex the CPU is deferred to Sections 7.1.3 and 7.1.4.

The scheduling mechanism is composed of several different parts, depending on exactly how it is implemented in any particular OS. Figure 7.1 shows three conceptually distinct parts incorporated into every scheduler: the enqueuer, the dispatcher, and the context switcher. When a process is changed to the ready state, the process descriptor is updated and the *enqueuer* places a pointer to the process descriptor into a list of processes that desire the CPU (called the *ready list*). The ready list is a process manager data structure that is a queue of pointers to the process descriptors, where each pointer represents a ready process. The enqueuer may compute the priority for allocating the CPU to the process when it is inserted into the ready list, or the priority may be determined when the process is considered for removal from the ready list.

When the scheduler switches the CPU from executing one process to executing another, the *context switcher* saves the contents of all processor registers (PC, IR, condition status, processor status, and ALU status) for the process being removed from the CPU in its process descriptor. The part of the scheduler that performs the context switch is specific to the technique used for determining when to multiplex the CPU—volun-

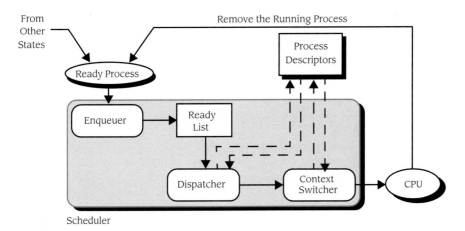

Figure 7.1
The Scheduler

tary or involuntary multiplexing. In voluntary techniques (Section 7.1.3), the context switcher is invoked by the running process that intends to release the CPU. In involuntary techniques, an interrupt causes the running process to be removed from the CPU, so it is the interrupt handler code that performs the context switch.

With both the voluntary and involuntary techniques, the *dispatcher* is invoked after the application process has been removed from the CPU. (This, of course, requires that the dispatcher's context be loaded on the CPU in order for it to run. The CPU context is switched from the application process to the dispatcher part of the scheduler.) The dispatcher selects one of the ready processes enqueued in the ready list and then allocates the CPU to the process by performing another context switch from itself to the selected process.

Figure 7.2 shows another view of how a process flows through a system that has one CPU. The process releases the CPU when it voluntarily makes a resource request (passing control through to the appropriate resource manager/scheduler). The process

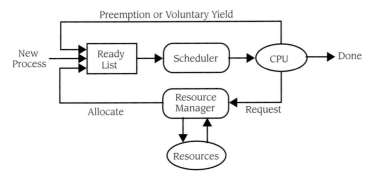

Figure 7.2
Process Scheduling

voluntarily gives up the CPU so that other processes can use it, or it may be involuntarily *preempted* from using the processor. The process is immediately returned to its ready state in the case of voluntary/involuntary release of the CPU. If the process gave up the CPU due to a request for an unavailable resource, it will be blocked from further use of the CPU until the corresponding resource manager allocates the resource. Then it will be placed in the ready state and returned to the ready list.

7.1.2 ■ Saving the Process Context

Whenever the CPU is multiplexed, two pairs (four total) of context switches occur. In the first, the original running process has its context saved by the OS and the dispatcher's context is then loaded. The second pair is for the dispatcher to be removed and the selected application process to be loaded onto the CPU. Context switching can significantly affect performance, since modern computers have a lot of general and status registers to be saved. A modern CPU, for example, incorporates 32 or more 32- or 64-bit registers, plus status registers. The context switching part of the scheduler ordinarily uses normal software load and store operations to save the register contents. Here, a context switch requires $(n + m)b \times K$ time units to save the state of a processor with n general registers and m status registers, assuming b store operations are required to save a single register and each store instruction requires K time units.

A processor might require 50 nanoseconds (10^{-9} seconds) to store 1 unit of information in a contemporary memory. Suppose there is a 16-bit path between the processor and the memory and each register is 32 bits wide. Each register then requires 2×50 nanoseconds to store its contents. Now, if there are 32 general-purpose registers and 8 status registers, the total time to save registers is $40 \times 2 \times 50$ nanoseconds, or 4 microseconds. Another 4 microseconds are required to restore the registers for another process to execute (ignoring the time for the dispatcher to select another process). Of course, when the dispatcher must run between application processes, the context switch time is greater than 8 microseconds due to dispatcher context switch time and the time taken to select the next process. A 200 MHz processor can execute a register instruction in about 10 nanoseconds; this means that during the 8 microseconds required for a context switch, the processor could have executed 800 instructions doing useful work (as opposed to performing the overhead of a context switch). The cost of context switching is a significant factor in considering processor multiplexing (scheduling) operations.

Some hardware systems employ two or more sets of processor registers to reduce the amount of context switching time. One set is used when the processor is in supervisor mode and the other set is used for applications. A context switch then can be reduced to the time to change a pointer to the current register set when moving back and forth between the OS and application code.

7.1.3 ■ Voluntary CPU Sharing

A key part of the scheduler's mechanism is the way the scheduler is invoked. The simplest approach is for the scheduler to assume that each process will explicitly invoke the scheduler periodically, voluntarily sharing the CPU. Some hardware is designed to include a special `yield` machine instruction to allow a process to release the CPU. The `yield` instruction is similar to a procedure call instruction in that it saves the address of the next instruction to be executed and then branches to an arbitrary address. It differs from a procedure call instruction in that the address of the next instruction is not saved on the process's stack but in a designated memory location. There is also a similarity between the function of yield and the hardware action resulting from an interrupt (see Chapter 4).

In Figure 7.3, when process p_1 executes yield(r, s), the parameter r is an address that is determined as a function of p_1's process identifier, usually an address in p_1's process descriptor. Address r can be determined by knowing which process is currently running in the CPU—for example, by incorporating a process status register in the CPU. When a process is loaded, the content of the internal identifier field from the process descriptor is placed in the process status register. The value of r is computed as a function of the register content—for example, by a table lookup operation. Hence,

```
r = f(p₁.identifier)
```

It is convenient to abbreviate the computation of this parameter by writing yield(*, s), where the first parameter is associated with the process identifier of the process executing the instruction.

The s parameter is similarly related to a process that will begin to run after the yield instruction has been executed. While p_1 is executing, but prior to the execution of yield, the contents of memory[r] are irrelevant. After yield has completed execution, memory[r] contains the address of the instruction following the yield and the PC has been set to resume execution of the process p_2, where

```
s = f(p₂.identifier)
```

The CPU is switched from running the program that executes the yield to running another program whose last active PC value is stored at memory[s]. For example, suppose memory[s] contains the last PC value for p_2. When process p_1 executes the yield instruction, it yields control of the CPU to process p_2, which could then cooperate by executing yield(*, r) to restart p_1.

If more than two processes were ready to use the CPU, p_2 could act as a scheduler by choosing some memory location, scheduler, that contains the entry point for p_2's program. Then it could have every process execute yield(*, scheduler) when it releases the CPU (see Figure 7.4). When the scheduler runs as p_2, it would select some ready process, p_i, where

```
s = f(pᵢ.identifier)
```

and then execute yield(*, s).

Figure 7.3
The yield Instruction

```
yield(r, s) {
    memory[r] = PC;
    PC = memory[s]
}
```

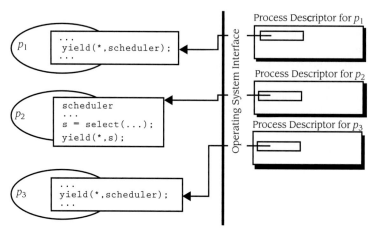

Figure 7.4
Scheduling with the `yield` Instruction

This cooperative form of multiprogramming was employed in the Xerox Alto personal computer [Thacker et al., 1981]. Many of the Xerox developers went to work at Apple prior to the introduction of the Macintosh. The cooperating technique for scheduling was incorporated into earlier versions of the Macintosh operating systems.

Building a system that relies on the `yield` instruction poses a problem: The processes may not voluntarily cooperate with one another. The failure of a process to periodically execute a `yield` instruction blocks all other processes from using the processor until that process exits or requests a resource. This problem is especially serious if the running process happens to be executing an infinite loop containing no resource requests. The process will never give up the processor, so all ready processes will wait forever. This problem could be avoided entirely if the system itself could interrupt the running process periodically—that is, engage in involuntary sharing.

7.1.4 ■ Involuntary CPU Sharing

The interrupt system can enforce periodic involuntary interruption of any process's execution; that is, it can force a process to effectively execute a `yield` instruction. This is done by incorporating an *interval timer device,* which produces an interrupt whenever the timer expires. An interval timer behaves like an egg timer. To use the timer, the system programmer chooses an interval of time, sets the device, and then proceeds with other processing. When the specified time interval has passed, the timer raises an alarm in the form of an interrupt. The basic operation of the interval timer is summarized by the `IntervalTimer` procedure given in Figure 7.5. The interval timer hardware completes an operation each time a real-time clock ticks—for example, for all T oscillations of a crystal. Setting the `InterruptRequest` variable represents the timer hardware's setting the interrupt request flag. The effect is that every $K \times T$ time units, the interrupt request flag will be set. The interval (K = number of ticks) can be specified by the `SetInterval` call shown in the figure, and it is thus called a *programmable interval timer.*

Figure 7.5
The Interval Timer

```
IntervalTimer(){
  InterruptCount = InterruptCount - 1;
  if(InterruptCount <= 0) {
    InterruptRequest = TRUE;
    InterruptCount = K}
  }
}
SetInterval(<programmableValue>) {
  K = <programmableValue>;
  InterruptCount = K;
}
```

An interrupt will occur every K clock ticks, thus causing the hardware clock's controller to execute the logical equivalent of the `yield` instruction to invoke the interrupt handler. The device handler for the interrupt timer device calls the scheduler to reschedule the processor without any action on the part of the running process. The scheduler is guaranteed to be invoked once every K clock ticks. A scheduler that uses involuntary CPU sharing is called a *preemptive scheduler.* Even if a particular process is executing an infinite loop, it cannot block other processes from running. This is because the interrupt timer will periodically invoke the scheduler, which, in turn, will run other processes. In principle, the scheduler could be implemented in this clock device handler, although in practice the clock device routine causes the scheduler to execute in a separate process.

7.1.5 ■ Performance

The scheduler can have a dramatic effect on the performance of a multiprogrammed computer, since it is in complete control of when a process is to be allocated the CPU. If the scheduler consistently selects a process whenever it becomes ready, the process will spend relatively little time in the ready list and tend to use the CPU whenever it needs it. The computer performance will vary directly with the hardware speed. On the other hand, if the process tends to be neglected by the dispatcher, the amount of time it spends in the ready list waiting for the CPU to be allocated to it may be very large compared with the amount of CPU time it needs to complete its execution. As a result, the perceived performance will be very low, independent of the speed of the computer hardware.

As already noted, the performance is influenced by the time to perform context switching. This performance overhead tends to be determined by the hardware design. The aspect of performance related to how long a process has to wait once it becomes ready is determined by the scheduling policy, a decision that tends to have much more impact on performance than does the time to do context switching.

Schedulers have been heavily studied over the last three decades for several reasons:

■ Designers of multiprogramming operating systems knew the scheduler's behavior was critical to the performance of the individual process's perspective.

■ Those designers believed the scheduler's behavior might be critical to the overall behavior of the system.

■ The methodologies used to study schedulers were well-entrenched in operations research.

■ Schedulers were a nice theoretical computer science problem.

This discussion of scheduling is built around its influence on the overall machine performance. In general, whenever a process becomes ready there will be other processes in the ready list. When the dispatcher selects a process to run on the processor, what criteria should it use to select from among the ready processes? If a process is continually ignored by the dispatcher, it will effectively never receive the CPU time it needs to run to completion, a phenomenon called *starvation*. If the process is selected almost immediately each time it is placed in the ready list, its real execution time will approach hardware speeds. The scheduling policy/strategy must define the criteria for choosing which process should be executed. The mechanisms discussed here are used to implement a policy chosen by the system administrator or system designer based on the way the computer is to be used. Some strategies favor predictable performance, others favor equitable sharing, and still others attempt to optimize performance for some particular class of processes. Performance determines the choice of strategy in each case.

7.2 ■ Strategy Selection

How can the scheduler be designed to allocate the processor to competing processes to meet external goals? Should it allocate on the basis of an external priority? Should it attempt to allocate as equitably as possible? Should it attempt to give priority to processes having very short (or very long) execution times? These classic policies (or strategies) for scheduling have been studied for many years. This has happened in particular because they resemble problems arising in operations research regarding the scheduling policy for, say, how loans should be processed in a mortgage company or how customers should be served in a bank.

For example, if the system is a real-time system, processes must be scheduled so that they meet very specific deadlines. If the OS is for a timesharing system, the criteria may focus on providing an equitable share of the processor per unit time to each user or process or to minimize users' response times. The criteria for selecting a scheduling strategy will depend in part on the goals of the OS. It also will depend on priorities of processes, fairness, overall resource utilization, maximized throughput, average or maximum turnaround time, average or maximum response time, maximized system availability, and deadlines.

Scheduling algorithms for modern operating systems ultimately use internal priorities. The *internal priority* (or simply *priority*) for a process determines the rank order the dispatcher will use to select a process to execute when the CPU is available. It is possible to assign a priority to each process so that it implements any of the general strategies mentioned in the previous paragraph. For example, in an external priority scheme, each user is assigned a priority number. When a process is created on behalf of the user, the process uses an internal priority that is the same as the external priority assigned to the user. As another example, priorities can be determined by dynamic circumstances. If the goal is to share the CPU equitably, then for every K time units in which n different processes are ready, each process should be allocated the CPU for K/n time units. This can be accomplished by having a process's priority increase the longer it waits but decrease while it is using the CPU. Other ways to adjust the priority to reflect a strategy are discussed later in the chapter.

In systems that use interrupts to force involuntary CPU sharing, there is an additional degree of freedom in the strategy design. If the process manager uses an interval timer to control when multiplexing occurs, there is a known *time quantum,* or maximum—also called the *time slice length.* The time quantum is the amount of time between timer interrupts (ignoring the scheduler overhead time), so it is closely related to the size of the timer interval setting. The time slice length may be less than the maximum if the process requests a resource during its time quantum and releases the CPU so that it can be rescheduled prior to the time at which the interval timer will interrupt. If this situation occurs, then the newly dispatched process will normally be allocated a full-time quantum, so it must be possible for the scheduler to reset the interrupt timer. Notice that there is no way to bound the amount of time any one process may continuously use the CPU if the hardware supports only voluntary multiplexing. Hence, these systems cannot use the idea of a time quantum as part of the scheduling strategy.

It is interesting to note that, given a particular set of processes (with known amounts of processor time) in the ready queue, a preemptive scheduler, and a specific goal for scheduling, one can compute the *optimal schedule,* provided no new processes enter the ready list while those in the ready list are being served. The optimal algorithm computes the number of time quanta—the number of times the CPU will be allocated to each process—and then enumerates all possible orders for scheduling the processor. The optimal strategy then can be selected, based on the optimality criteria, by systematically considering every ordering.

There are several flaws in this approach:

- New processes *do* arrive while the current processes are being serviced, meaning the schedule has to be recomputed each time a new process arrives.
- The actual running time of a process must be known before the process runs, although this is seldom possible.
- The known algorithms for enumerating the schedule with n processes in the ready list are no better than $O(n^2)$ algorithms, meaning the scheduler might use more time computing the optimal schedule than it does for actually servicing processes.

Before describing some representative scheduling algorithms, let's extend our working process model so that we can use it to describe scheduling policies. Let

$$P = \{p_i \mid 0 \leq i < n\}$$

be a set of *processes*. $S(p_i)$ is the *state* of process p_i, where $S(p_i) \in \{$running, ready, blocked$\}$.

Service time, $\tau(p_i)$	The amount of time a process needs to be in the running state before it is completed.
Wait time, $W(p_i)$	The time the process spends waiting in the ready state before its first transition to the running state.
Turnaround time for process p_i, $T_{TRnd}(p_i)$	The amount of time between the moment a process first enters the ready state and the moment the process exits the running state for the last time.

In other words, the service time represents the amount of time the process will use the CPU to accomplish useful work. The wait time is the time the process waits to receive its *first* unit of service from the processor. The turnaround time is the total time to complete a process's execution after it has been made ready to execute.

The process model and its time measurements are used to compare the performance characteristics of each algorithm. The general model must be adjusted to fit each specific class of OS environments. In a classic batch multiprogrammed system, the turnaround time is the most critical performance metric, since that time reflects the amount of time a user waits to get results from the computer. Here, the system's average turnaround time specifies the average time to handle a process (or job); the inverse of the average turnaround time is the system's *throughput rate* in jobs per minute. In batch systems, the *job* turnaround time is technically distinguished from the *process* turnaround time by the time to do spooling, memory allocation, and scheduling. Since batch systems focus on jobs more than they do processes, the job turnaround time is the performance metric of interest.

In timesharing systems, it is usually more meaningful to focus on a single phase of a process's execution—such as the time to process a command once a user requests that it be performed. For example, the time to execute a command can be broken down into its wait time (due to processor competition) and service time. An interactive user is most concerned with the amount of time required for the machine to give some kind of feedback, so the wait time—also called the *response time* in a timesharing system—is the performance metric of most interest.

Note that the process model does not address the resource manager's behavior except to identify the blocked state. It is possible to use a more complex model based on the complete process flow shown in Figure 7.2 that specifies the resource use pattern, but (as is traditional in considering scheduling strategies) that approach is not taken here.

A process may require its service time in a continuous block, or it may request different amounts of service time at different times in its execution, with interspersed resource allocation requests. The process scheduling model can be simplified to completely ignore all effects of resource competition except that for the CPU (see Figure 7.6). In this model, a process can be only in the running or ready state. The performance metrics are defined as previously, but the turnaround time metric now ignores the time that the process might have spent in the blocked state. This model can be justified as follows. A process can be said to come into existence when it enters the ready state with a specific processor service time request and to end when that service time has been satisfied by the processor. Realistically, this method might mean that these modeled

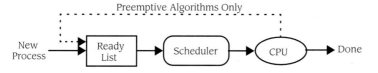

Figure 7.6
A Simpler Processor Scheduling Model

processes are created when a resource has been allocated to the process (it is made ready to run) and destroyed once they request another resource. The true process discussed earlier in the chapter can then have its behavior modeled by a series of "small," uninterrupted processes that are created and destroyed for small computations.

Scheduling algorithms are partitioned into two major classes: nonpreemptive and preemptive. Nonpreemptive algorithms are designed so that once a process enters the running state (is allocated a processor), it is not removed from the processor until it has completed its service time (or it explicitly yields the processor). Preemptive algorithms are driven by the notion of prioritized computation: The process with the highest priority should always be the one currently using the processor. If a process is currently using the processor and a new process with a higher priority enters the ready list, the process on the processor should be removed and returned to the ready list until it is once again the highest-priority process in the system. Preemptive algorithms are normally associated with systems that use interrupts to force involuntary CPU sharing, while nonpreemptive algorithms are consistent with voluntary CPU sharing.

7.2.1 ■ Partitioning a Process into Small Processes

Suppose a process intersperses computation and I/O requests so that it has k different times that it needs the processor and k different times that it needs to have I/O performed on its behalf. Then, the total service time can be written as

$$\tau(p_i) = \tau_1 + \tau_2 + \ldots + \tau_k$$

Suppose p_i is decomposed into k smaller process, $p_{i1}, p_{i2}, \ldots P_{ik}$, where τ_{ij} is the service time for p_{ij}. Each p_{ij} is intended to be executed as uninterrupted processing by the original process p_i, even though a preemptive scheduler will divide each τ_{ij} into time quanta when it schedules p_{ij}.

Recall the discussion of compute-bound and I/O-bound processes in Chapter 5. Here is a more precise discussion of that characterization. If a process requests k different I/O operations, the result is k service time requests, τ_i, interspersed with $d_1, d_2, \ldots,$ d_k times to represent the time to accomplish device I/O. Thus the total amount of time that the process requests CPU service plus I/O service is

$$\tau_1 + d_1 + \tau_2 + d_2 + \ldots + \tau_k + d_k$$

A compute-bound process has relatively large values of τ_i compared to the values for the d_j, although each τ_i can be expected to have a different value than the other τ_i values. In an I/O-bound process, the τ_i values are small compared to the d_j values.

7.3 ■ Nonpreemptive Strategies

Nonpreemptive scheduling algorithms allow any process to run to completion once it has been allocated the processor. In systems using a nonpreemptive scheduling algorithm, there is no path from the CPU back to the ready list (see Figure 7.6). Once a process is allocated the CPU, it uses it until it has completed the logical task and then releases it to the scheduler. Nonpreemptive algorithms are borrowed from classic operations research that studies how to schedule work in human-oriented systems. The concern in these systems is to determine how people should be scheduled for service in a bank, airport, or supermarket. Once humans begin receiving service in these systems, the full task is completed without switching to another person's task. This approach is natural to use in process management because it is intuitive. It also applies to systems that do not use interrupts to invoke the scheduler. Each time a process is allocated the CPU, it will retain it until it has completed the logical task and it decides to release the CPU to another process.

7.3.1 ■ First-Come-First-Served

The *first-come-first-served* (*FCFS*) scheduling strategy assigns priority to processes in the order in which they request the processor. The priority of a process is computed by the enqueuer by timestamping all incoming processes and then having the dispatcher select the process that has the oldest timestamp. Alternatively, the ready list can be organized as a simple FIFO data structure (where each entry points to a process descriptor). The enqueuer adds processes to the tail of the queue, and the dispatcher removes processes from the head of the queue.

   While the FCFS algorithm is easy to implement, it ignores the service time request and all other criteria that may influence the performance with respect to turnaround or waiting time. FCFS generally does not perform well under any specific set of system requirements, so it is not often used.

   Let's consider a practical example of FCFS scheduling and then examine the performance metrics. Suppose there are five processes in the ready list, as shown in Table 7.1.

   Further assume they entered the ready list in the order p_0, p_1, p_2, p_3, and finally p_4. FCFS will schedule the processes as shown in Figure 7.7.

TABLE 7.1 An Example Load

i	$\tau(p_i)$
0	350
1	125
2	475
3	250
4	75

Approximating System Load

Scheduling algorithms may use different criteria for selecting a process from the ready list, depending on the performance goals of the system. To assess the likely effects of these criteria, one is faced with two choices: (1) analyze a given algorithm and a hypothetical service load and predict the performance of each algorithm, or (2) consider a specific real load and simply report the behavior of the algorithm under that load. The primary goal in this book is to consider various strategies for scheduling rather than to engage in an intensive study of performance prediction. Even so, performance must be considered when comparing different algorithms. The consideration of algorithms here is intended to give you an intuitive feeling for how algorithms perform under various loads.

Observed performance represents actual values for performance metrics, so they are often represented as average values and as histogram plots of individual metrics for each process. Predictive analysis attempts to capture an algorithm's behavior under an arbitrary service load from an arbitrary pattern of process arrivals.

The model of systems operation shown in Figure 7.6 can be used to predict one aspect of performance. The system load can be characterized by the arrival rate of new processes into the ready list and the nature of the service times, $\tau(p_i)$. Let λ represent the *mean arrival rate* of new processes into the ready list (the rate in processes per time unit at which processes enter the ready list, where $1/\lambda$ is the *mean time between arrivals*). Let μ represent the *mean service rate* (where $1/\mu$ is the *mean service time of the processes*). If we ignore context switching time and assume that the CPU has sufficient capacity to service the load, the fraction of time the CPU is busy can be expressed by

$$\rho = \lambda \times 1/\mu = \lambda/\mu.$$

If the arrival rate, λ, is greater than the service rate, μ ($\rho > 1$), the CPU will be saturated (it will always have more work than it is able to do) independent of the scheduling algorithm employed in the system. In time, any finite-length ready list will overflow, since processes arrive at a higher rate than they can be serviced. Systems can reach a steady state only if $\lambda < \mu$ ($\rho < 1$). Systems operating under conditions where $\rho \to 1$ require arbitrarily large ready lists, so such conditions are also going to be problematic for long-term operation of the system.

For example, suppose processes arrive in a system at a rate of 10 processes per minute (meaning $\lambda = 10$ processes per minute) and the average service time for each job is 3 seconds (meaning that $1/\mu = 3/30 = 1/20$ minutes per process, or $\mu = 20$ processes per minute). The system load will be

$$\rho = \lambda/\mu$$

= 10 processes per minute/20 processes per minute

= 0.5

= 50%.

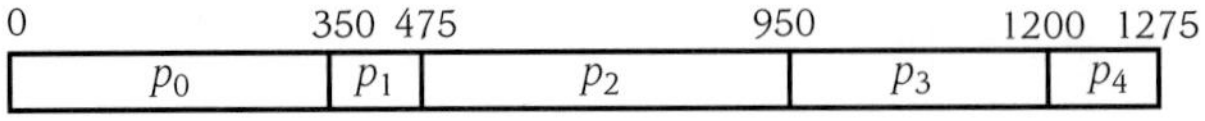

```
0              350 475          950        1200  1275
┌──────────────┬────┬──────────┬──────────┬──────┐
│      p0      │ p1 │    p2    │    p3    │  p4  │
└──────────────┴────┴──────────┴──────────┴──────┘
```

Figure 7.7
FCFS Schedule

We can determine each process's turnaround time by observing the FCFS schedule in the Gantt chart shown in Figure 7.7:

$$T_{TRnd}(p_0) = \tau(p_0) = 350$$
$$T_{TRnd}(p_1) = (\tau(p_1) + T_{TRnd}(p_0)) = 125 + 350 = 475$$
$$T_{TRnd}(p_2) = (\tau(p_2) + T_{TRnd}(p_1)) = 475 + 475 = 950$$
$$T_{TRnd}(p_3) = (\tau(p_3) + T_{TRnd}(p_2)) = 250 + 950 = 1200$$
$$T_{TRnd}(p_4) = (\tau(p_4) + T_{TRnd}(p_3)) = 75 + 1200 = 1275$$

Therefore the average turnaround time is

$$\overline{T}_{TRnd} = (350 + 475 + 950 + 1200 + 1275)/5 = 4250/5 = 850.$$

From the Gantt chart, we determine the waiting times to be

$$W(p_0) = 0$$
$$W(p_1) = T_{TRnd}(p_0) = 350$$
$$W(p_2) = T_{TRnd}(p_1) = 475$$
$$W(p_3) = T_{TRnd}(p_2) = 950$$
$$W(p_4) = T_{TRnd}(p_3) = 1200$$

So the average wait time is

$$\overline{W} = (0 + 350 + 475 + 950 + 1200)/5 = 2975/5 = 595.$$

7.3.2 ■ Shortest Job Next

Suppose the service time of all processes is known a priori—an unusual situation. The *shortest job next* (SJN) (also known as "shortest job first" or "SJF") scheduling algorithm chooses the process requiring minimum service time as its next one. The turnaround time for p_i is the sum of all of the service times of processes in the ready list that have lower service times than does p_i.

SJN minimizes the average wait time because it services small processes before it services large ones. While it minimizes average wait time, it may penalize processes with high service time requests. If the ready list is saturated, then processes with large service times tend to be left in the ready list while small processes receive service. In the extreme case, where the system has little idle time, processes with large service

PERFORMANCE TUNING

Predicting Wait Times for FCFS

It is not difficult to predict analytically a process's wait time under FCFS scheduling. Suppose we know the service rate, μ. Let L be the length of the queue at the time process p arrives. We can then estimate the time that the new process, p, will have to wait before it begins to receive service:

$$\begin{aligned}\overline{W}(p) &= L(1/\mu) + 1/2(1/\mu)\\ &= L/\mu + 1/(2\mu).\end{aligned}$$

Here is the rationale for this expression: If each job in the queue uses an average of $1/\mu$ time units for service, $L(1/\mu)$ will be the amount of time for all L of them to be processed. The average time for the process that is already using the CPU is half of its service time, or $1/2(1/\mu)$. According to the FCFS policy, only the load that is present when process p arrives is relevant, since any subsequent processes will be served after process p.

In the example, we could estimate $\overline{W}(p_4)$, which is 1200 in the Gantt chart, by computing the average service time ($1/\lambda$ or $\bar{\tau}$) of the first four processes:

$$\begin{aligned}\bar{\tau} &= (350 + 125 + 475 + 250)/4\\ &= 1200/4\\ &= 300 \text{ time units.}\end{aligned}$$

When p_4 arrives, $L = 3$; the estimated waiting time for p_4 is thus

$$\begin{aligned}\overline{W}(p_4) &= L/\mu + 1/(2\mu)\\ &= 3/(1/300) + 150\\ &= 1050.\end{aligned}$$

Notice that the estimate assumes half of a job has already executed. (We did not assume this in the Gantt chart.)

times will never be served. This total starvation of large processes may be a serious liability of the scheduling algorithm.

Again suppose the ready list contains the processes shown in Table 7.1. The arrival order is irrelevant here, provided all of the processes are already in the queue at the time it is analyzed. In this example, assume no other jobs (processes) arrive during the servicing of all the jobs in the ready list. SJN will produce the schedule shown in Figure 7.8. Since $\tau(p_4) = 75$ is the smallest service time, p_4 is scheduled first; since $\tau(p_1) = 125$, p_1 is next to be scheduled; and so on.

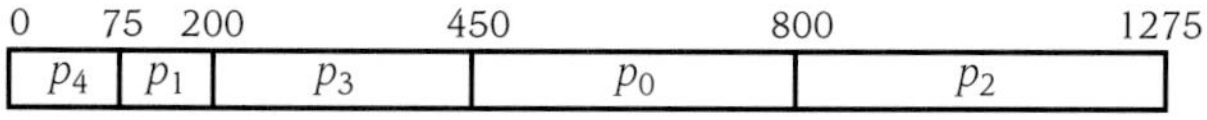
0
75
200
450
800
1275
p4
p1
p3
p0
p2

Figure 7.8
SJN Schedule

From the Gantt chart, we compute the following:

$T_{TRnd}(p_0) = \tau(p_0) + \tau(p_3) + \tau(p_1) + \tau(p_4) = 350 + 250 + 125 + 75 = 800$
$T_{TRnd}(p_1) = \tau(p_1) + \tau(p_4) = 125 + 75 = 200$
$T_{TRnd}(p_2) = \tau(p_2) + \tau(p_0) + \tau(p_3) + \tau(p_1) + \tau(p_4) = 475 + 350 + 250 + 125 + 75 = 1275$
$T_{TRnd}(p_3) = \tau(p_3) + \tau(p_1) + \tau(p_4) = 250 + 125 + 75 = 450$
$T_{TRnd}(p_4) = \tau(p_4) = 75$

Therefore the average turnaround time is

$$\overline{T}_{TRnd} = (800 + 200 + 1275 + 450 + 75)/5 = 2800/5 = 560.$$

We determine the wait times to be

$$W(p_0) = 450$$
$$W(p_1) = 75$$
$$W(p_2) = 800$$
$$W(p_3) = 200$$
$$W(p_4) = 0.$$

So the average wait time is

$$\overline{W} = (450 + 75 + 800 + 200 + 0)/5 = 1525/5 = 305.$$

Suppose an SJN scheduling policy controls CPU allocation, where $\rho = 1 - \epsilon$ for some very small value ϵ. As new processes arrive that have service times near the mean service time, $1/\mu$, those few processes with very large service times (much larger than the mean) will tend to have a lower priority than the average incoming process. Since the CPU utilization is very high, there will tend to be two or more processes in the ready list all the time. As a result, the processes with very large service time requests will starve, even though $\rho = \lambda/\mu < 1$.

7.3.3 ■ Priority Scheduling

In *priority scheduling,* processes are allocated to the CPU on the basis of an externally assigned priority. (In this explanation, lower numbers have higher priority. Some schedulers use the opposite ordering.) Internal priorities are derived from the process's operation within the computing environment, such as the priority determined by the service time request length used in SJN. External priorities reflect the importance of a task that the process is to perform based on factors that the process manager can only accept as input from the users. A process's external priority might be inferred from the user identification ("important people have high priorities"), the nature of the task ("a process turns on a heater when the temperature falls below a threshold value"), or any other arbitrary criteria.

TABLE 7.2 An Example Load with Priority

i	$\tau(p_i)$	Priority
0	350	5
1	125	2
2	475	3
3	250	1
4	75	4

The key to the performance of priority scheduling is in choosing priorities for the processes. Again, priority scheduling may cause low-priority processes to starve. This starvation can be compensated for if the priorities are internally computed. Suppose one parameter in the priority assignment function is the amount of time the process has been waiting. The longer a process waits, the higher its priority (the lower its priority number) becomes. This strategy tends to eliminate the starvation problem.

Table 7.2 describes a process load (the same as the load in Table 7.1, but with external priorities added to each process). Priority scheduling will produce the schedule shown in Figure 7.9.

We compute

$$T_{TRnd}(p_0) = \tau(p_0) + \tau(p_4) + \tau(p_2) + \tau(p_1) + \tau(p_3) = 350 + 75 + 475 + 125 + 250 = 1275$$
$$T_{TRnd}(p_1) = \tau(p_1) + \tau(p_3) = 125 + 250 = 375$$
$$T_{TRnd}(p_2) = \tau(p_2) + \tau(p_1) + \tau(p_3) = 475 + 12 + 250 = 850$$
$$T_{TRnd}(p_3) = \tau(p_3) = 250$$
$$T_{TRnd}(p_4) = \tau(p_4) + \tau(p_2) + \tau(p_1) + \tau(p_3) = 75 + 475 + 125 + 250 = 925.$$

Therefore the average turnaround time is

$$\overline{T}_{TRnd} = (1275 + 375 + 850 + 250 + 925)/5 = 3675/5 = 735.$$

We determine the waiting times to be

$$W(p_0) = 925$$
$$W(p_1) = 250$$
$$W(p_2) = 375$$
$$W(p_3) = 0$$
$$W(p_4) = 850.$$

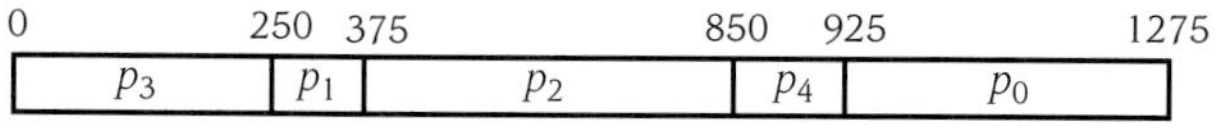

Figure 7.9
Priority Scheduling

TABLE 7.3 An Example Load with Deadlines

i	$\tau(p_i)$	Deadline
0	350	575
1	125	550
2	475	1050
3	250	(none)
4	75	200

So the average wait time is

$$\overline{W} = (925 + 250 + 375 + 0 + 850)/5 = 2400/5 = 480.$$

7.3.4 ▪ Deadline Scheduling

Hard real-time systems are often characterized as systems that have certain processes that *must* complete execution prior to some time deadline. The critical performance measure is whether the system was able to meet all such processes' scheduling deadlines; measures of turnaround and wait time are generally irrelevant. As a result, these schedulers must have very complete knowledge regarding how much time is required to execute each process (or part of a process). A process can be *admitted* to the ready list only if the scheduler can guarantee that it will be able to meet each deadline imposed by the process.

In continuous media systems, the deadline may be required in order to prevent jitter (irregular delivery of information) and latency (delay) in the audio or video processing. In process control systems, the deadline may be established by an external sensor reading.

Suppose our sample set of processes contained deadlines such as those shown in Table 7.3. There may be several different schedules satisfying the deadline. See Figure 7.10 for three such schedules. The middle schedule is an example of a strategy known as the *earliest deadline first scheduling*.

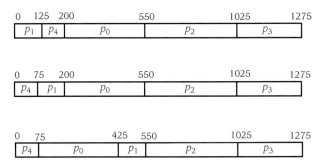

Figure 7.10
Possible Schedules Using Deadline Scheduling

7.4 ■ Preemptive Strategies

In *preemptive algorithms,* the highest-priority process among all ready processes is allocated the CPU. All lower-priority processes are made to yield to the highest-priority process whenever it requests the CPU. Whenever a process becomes ready, it can immediately interrupt the process currently using the CPU if it has higher priority than the one using the CPU. That is, the scheduler is called each time a process enters the ready state. It is also started each time the interval timer expires and a time quantum has elapsed.

Preemptive strategies are sometimes used to ensure quick response to high-priority processes or to ensure fair sharing of the CPU among all processes. Nonpreemptive SJN and priority scheduling have already been described. There are also preemptive versions of these algorithms. These versions differ from the nonpreemptive versions by keeping the highest-priority job in the running state at all times.

In SJN, the process with the smallest service time request is allocated the CPU. If p_i is executing and is preempted by the arrival of another process, p_j, then SJN need only compare $\tau(p_i)$ and $\tau(p_j)$. This is because p_i is guaranteed to have the smallest service time request of any ready process when p_j arrives. For example, suppose the processor is using preemptive SJN and is operating on process p_1 (after having processed p_4) in the process load shown in Table 7.1. If a new process arrives with a service time of 35 and p_1 has more than 35 time units remaining on its service time request, it will be preempted and the new process will be dispatched.

Similarly, assume a processor is operating with preemptive priority scheduling on the load shown in Table 7.2. If it is currently executing p_2 (after having executed p_3 and p_1) and a process arrives with a priority of 2, it will cause p_2 to be returned to the ready list while the new process uses the processor.

The discussion of nonpreemptive algorithms ignored the cost of context switching among processes, since the assumption is that a process completes a unit of work without being interrupted. In purely preemptive algorithms, whenever an interrupt occurs the previously running process may be replaced by a new, higher priority process. In preemptive scheduling systems, the cost of context switching can become a significant cost to computing optimal schedules.

The next two sections describes a few preemptive scheduling algorithms developed especially for preemptive environments.

7.4.1 ■ Round Robin

Round-robin (RR) scheduling is perhaps the most widely used of all of the scheduling algorithms. Basically, RR calls for the distribution of the processing time equitably among all processes requesting the processor. This distribution will tend to fit in with the general interactive multiprogramming philosophy in which each of n processes receives approximately $1/n$ time units of processing time for every real-time unit. (This is an approximation, since the cost of scheduling and context switching must also be factored into the real-time unit.) More precisely, suppose the CPU is idle and n arbitrary processes $\{p_i \mid 0 \leq i < n\}$ are all ready to run. Also (for notational convenience) the processes appear in the ready list in the same order as their index—that is, p_i appears before p_j if $i < j$. The processor will be allocated to p_0, then p_1, then $p_2, \ldots$ to p_{K-1}, then back to p_0, and so on.

There are a few options in implementing RR scheduling. If the processor finishes serving a process prior to the expiration of the time quantum, the scheduler is immediately invoked with a new time quantum to start a different process using the processor. When a new process arrives, it is placed in the ready list. However, its exact location in the list depends on another implementation option. That is, if the ready list is implemented as a ring-linked list, the new process is placed in the ring immediately behind the last process being executed so that the other $n-1$ processes receive service before the new process does. Still another option is to implement the ready list as a queue and then have the dispatcher process enqueue entries in order. The new process is placed at the end of the queue independent of which process is being executed at the time the new process arrives. The new process will wait an average of $n/2$ time slices before it is allocated the CPU.

Consider the effect of context switching time on RR scheduling. Let C be the time to perform a context switch between user processes (often one assumes C is small enough that it can be ignored). Each of the n processes will receive q units of time on the CPU for every $n(q+C)$ units of real time.

A system with a timer interrupt naturally fits with RR scheduling, since the interrupt interval can be set to the desired time quantum. The timer interrupt handler calls the scheduler whenever it is invoked. When a process completes, it is deleted from the ready list, and when a new process starts, it is entered into the ready list using the implementation option described in the previous paragraph.

Blocked processes can become ready processes any time a (different) executing process releases resources. When the resource manager is called with a release operation, it allocates newly available resources to one or more blocked processes, changes the state of those processes to ready, and places them in the ready list. The original process continues executing for the duration of its time slice.

When the timer interrupt occurs, the executing process's time quantum has completed. Therefore the scheduler removes the running process from the CPU. The scheduler then adjusts the ready list according to the implementation, resets the timer, and dispatches the process at the head of the ready list to the CPU.

Suppose the ready list contained the processes shown in Table 7.1 and the time quantum is 50 with a negligible amount of time for context switching. The Gantt chart describing the resulting schedule is shown in Figure 7.11.

The turnaround times (derived from the Gantt chart) are

$$T_{TRnd}(p_0) = 1100$$
$$T_{TRnd}(p_1) = 550$$
$$T_{TRnd}(p_2) = 1275$$
$$T_{TRnd}(p_3) = 950$$
$$T_{TRnd}(p_4) = 475$$

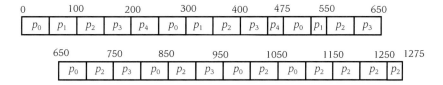

Figure 7.11
RR Schedule with a Time Quantum of 50

Therefore the average turnaround time is

$$\overline{T}_{TRnd} = (1100 + 550 + 1275 + 950 + 475)/5 = 4350/5 = 870.$$

From the Gantt chart, we determine the wait times (the time until the process first acquires the processor) to be

$$W(p_0) = 0$$
$$W(p_1) = 50$$
$$W(p_2) = 100$$
$$W(p_3) = 150$$
$$W(p_4) = 200.$$

So the average wait time is

$$\overline{W} = (0 + 50 + 100 + 150 + 200)/5 = 500/5 = 100.$$

The wait times illustrate the obvious benefit of RR (and other algorithms based on time quanta) in terms of how quickly a process begins to receive service. However, the average turnaround time does not differ significantly from that produced by the nonpreemptive algorithms.

Now reconsider the example in which the context switching time is included. Suppose each context switch requires 10 units of time (see Figure 7.12). The turnaround times (derived from the Gantt chart) are

$$T_{TRnd}(p_0) = 1320$$
$$T_{TRnd}(p_1) = 660$$
$$T_{TRnd}(p_2) = 1535$$
$$T_{TRnd}(p_3) = 1140$$
$$T_{TRnd}(p_4) = 565.$$

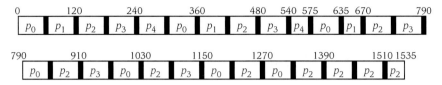

Figure 7.12
RR Schedule with Context Switching

Therefore the average turnaround time is

$$\overline{T}_{TRnd} = (1320 + 660 + 1535 + 1140 + 565)/5 = 5220/5 = 1044.$$

From the Gantt chart, we determine the waiting times to be

$$W(p_0) = 0$$
$$W(p_1) = 60$$
$$W(p_2) = 120$$
$$W(p_3) = 180$$
$$W(p_4) = 240.$$

So the average wait time is

$$\overline{W} = (0 + 60 + 120 + 180 + 240)/5 = 600/5 = 120.$$

7.4.2 ■ Multiple-level Queues

Multiple-level queues are an extension of priority scheduling whereby all processes of the same priority are placed in a single queue. The scheduler allocates the CPU across processes in these priority queues using one strategy and allocates the CPU to processes in the same queue according to a second strategy. In the simplest case, suppose that the ready list is partitioned into J smaller ready sublists, where all processes have some priority between 1 and J. Process p_i is in ready sublist k if it has a priority of k. If we assume preemptive priority scheduling for the cross-queue strategy, then all processes in ready sublist 1 will be completed before any process is run from ready sublists 2 through J, and so on. Within sublist k, the CPU may be allocated using any strategy.

A variant of the strategy for distributing the CPU utilization across queues is to favor higher-priority sublists over time. For example, the strategy may give the fraction $2 - j$ of the time to processes in the sublist j (saving a fraction of the time for various overhead functions). In this case, during 100 seconds of real time (ignoring overhead), 50 seconds are distributed to the processes in sublist 1, 25 seconds to the processes in sublist 2, 12.5 seconds to the processes in sublist 3, and so on.

Each of these more sophisticated scheduling algorithms increases the context switching time, so the most often-used scheduling algorithms for timesharing systems are simple forms of multiple-level queues, perhaps incorporating RR schedulers within a level.

7.4.2.1 ■ Foreground and Background Processes

Timesharing systems often support the idea of *foreground* and *background* processes. Foreground processes service an interactive user, while background processes are intended to run whenever no foreground process requires the CPU. There is a high-priority foreground ready sublist and a low-priority background ready sublist. Any foreground job takes precedence over all background jobs.

It is easy to imagine a number of different strategies that follow the foreground/background rationale. For example, interrupt handler processes might run at priority 1, device drivers at priority 2, interactive processing jobs at priority 3, interactive editing jobs at priority 4, normal batch jobs at priority 5, and "long" batch jobs at priority 6. Of course, such a choice suggests processes might change priority levels during execution, depending on the phase of computation they are currently executing. For example, if an interactive editing process became a compute-intensive process, its priority might be dropped to a lower level, since it is attempting to use an extra share of the CPU. The dual strategy is to increase the priority to a higher level during compute-intensive phases, with the rationale that the user needs a larger share of the CPU to sustain acceptable service. A system that allows processes to change ready sublists is called a *multiple-level feedback queue.*

7.4.2.2 ■ BSD UNIX Scheduling

BSD UNIX uses a multiple-level feedback queue approach, with 32 run queues. System processes use run queues 0 through 7, and processes executing in user space are placed in run queues 8 through 31. The dispatcher selects a process from the high-priority run queue whenever it allocates the CPU. Within a queue, BSD UNIX uses RR scheduling; thus only processes in the highest-priority run queue can execute. Time quanta vary among implementations, but all are less than 100 microseconds.

Every process has an external `nice` priority used to influence, but not solely determine, the run queue in which the process will be placed when it is ready. The `nice` priority has a default value of 0, but it can be changed with the `nice` system call. The `nice` priority can vary between −20 and 20; where −20 is the highest-priority user priority and 20 is the lowest. Approximately once per time quantum, the scheduler recomputes each process's current priority as a function of the `nice` priority and the recent demand on the CPU by the process (more utilization means a lower priority).

The `sleep` routine causes the same effect as that from executing a `yield` instruction (along with the context-saving task). When a process calls `sleep`, the scheduler is called to dispatch a new process. Otherwise, the scheduler is called as a result of a trap instruction execution or the occurrence of an interrupt.

7.4.2.3 ■ Windows NT Thread Scheduling

The NT thread scheduler is also a multiple-level feedback scheduler that also attempts to provide very high levels of service to threads that need very rapid response. A time quantum is computed as a multiple of the number of clock interrupts (for example, a time quantum might be three ticks of the host system's clock). On most NT machines, the time quantum ranges between about 20 to 200 milliseconds (ms). Servers are configured to have time quanta that are six times longer than for a workstation with the same processor type.

The scheduler supports 32 different scheduling levels. The 16 highest priority queues are called *real-time level queues,* the next 15 higher priority queues are called *variable level queues,* and the lowest priority queue is called the *system level queue.* The scheduler attempts to limit the number of threads that are entered into the real-time queues, increasing the probability that there will be little competition among threads that execute at these high priority levels. However, NT is not a real-time system and cannot *guarantee* that threads running at high priority will receive the processor before any fixed deadline. The highest level queue processing continues through the variable level queues, down to the system level queue. The system level queue contains a single "zero page thread" to represent an idle system. That is, when there are no runnable threads in the entire system, it executes the zero page thread until an interrupt occurs and another thread becomes runnable. The zero page thread is the single lowest priority thread in the system, so it runs whenever there are no other runnable threads.

The scheduler is *fully preemptive,* meaning that whenever a thread becomes ready to run, it is placed in a run queue at a level corresponding to its current priority. If there is another thread in execution at that time and that thread has a lower priority, then the lower priority thread is interrupted (it is not allowed to finish its time quantum) and the new higher priority thread is assigned the processor. In a single processor system, this would mean that a thread could cause itself to be removed from the processor by enabling a higher priority thread. In a multiple processor system the situation can be more subtle: Suppose that in a two-processor system, one processor is running a thread at level 10 and the other is running a thread at level 4. If the level 10 thread performs some action that causes a previously blocked thread to suddenly become runnable at level 6, then the level 4 thread will be halted and the new level 6 thread will begin to use the processor that the level 4 thread was using.

7.5 ■ Summary

The scheduler is responsible for multiplexing the CPU among a set of ready processes. It is invoked periodically by a timer interrupt or any time that a running process voluntarily releases the processor through a `yield` or resource request. The scheduler selects from among a ready list of processes waiting to use the processor and then allocates the processor to the selected process.

Scheduling strategies can be divided into nonpreemptive and preemptive strategies. Nonpreemptive strategies allow a process to run to completion once it obtains the processor, while preemptive strategies use the interval timer and scheduler to periodically reallocate the CPU. FCFS, SJN, priority, and deadline algorithms are well-known nonpreemptive algorithms, while RR and multiple-level queue algorithms (along with preemptive variants of priority and SJN) are often used to implement preemptive approaches.

Scheduling algorithms have been implemented in many different ways. The more sophisticated algorithms, including the BSD UNIX and Windows NT schedulers, are multiple-level feedback queue variants.

Scheduling is the heart of the CPU resource manager. It implements CPU sharing among a set of processes. Once the computing environment provides concurrent processes through scheduling, the process manager must add additional mechanisms to allow these concurrent processes to coordinate their operation. Process coordination is discussed in the next two chapters.

7.6 ■ Exercises

1. Regarding processor multiplexing using interrupts and the interval timer, the processor receives a timer interrupt when the interrupt request flag (InterruptRequest) is set to TRUE by the clock device. In the discussion, it is assumed that the interrupt software will reset InterruptRequest to FALSE when it processes the interrupt. What would happen if the clock interrupt software reset the flag but another interrupt occurred before the clock interrupt routine and scheduler completed their work?

2. Suppose you were considering different CPU scheduling strategies for RC 4000 operating systems extensions.

   a. What strategy would you incorporate into a real-time extension? Why?
   b. What strategy would you incorporate into a timesharing extension? Why?

3. Suppose a new process in a system arrives at an average of four processes per minute and each such process requires an average of 12 seconds of service time. Estimate the fraction of time the CPU is busy in a system with a single processor.

4. Assume you have the following jobs to execute with one processor, with the jobs arriving in the order listed here:

i	$\tau(p_i)$
0	80
1	20
2	10
3	20
4	50

   a. Suppose a system uses FCFS scheduling. Create a Gantt chart illustrating the execution of these processes.
   b. What is the turnaround time for process p_3?
   c. What is the average wait time for the processes?

5. Using the process load in the previous problem, suppose a system uses SJN scheduling.

   a. Create a Gantt chart illustrating the execution of these processes.
   b. What is the turnaround time for process p_4?
   c. What is the average wait time for the processes?

6. Suppose a system uses priority scheduling (under the following process load), where a small integer means a high priority.

i	$\tau(p_i)$	Priority
0	80	3
1	20	1
2	10	4
3	20	5
4	50	2

a. Create a Gantt chart illustrating the execution of these processes.
b. What is the turnaround time for process p_2 under priority scheduling?
c. What is the average wait time for the processes?

7. Assume you have the following jobs to execute with one processor:

i	$\tau(p_i)$	Arrival time
0	75	0
1	40	10
2	25	10
3	20	80
4	45	85

Suppose a system uses RR scheduling with a quantum of 15.

a. Create a Gantt chart illustrating the execution of these processes.
b. What is the turnaround time for process p_3?
c. What is the average wait time for the processes?

8. Assume the context switch time is five time units with RR scheduling.

a. Create a Gantt chart illustrating the execution of these processes.
b. What is the turnaround time for process p_3?
c. What is the average wait time for the processes?

9. Assume you have the following jobs to execute with one processor:

i	$\tau(p_i)$	Priority
0	80	2
1	25	4
2	15	3
3	20	4
4	45	1

The jobs are assumed to arrive at the same time. Using priority scheduling, do the following:

a. Create a Gantt chart illustrating the execution of these processes.

b. What is the turnaround time for process p_1?

c. What is the average wait time for the processes?

10. What is the effect of increasing the time quantum to an arbitrarily large number for RR scheduling?

11. The BSD UNIX priority values actually range from 0 through 127, rather than from 0 through 31 (corresponding to the run queue number). Speculate why the designers decided not to incorporate 128 run queues in the scheduler.

12. Inspect the Linux source code for the scheduler to determine the scheduling strategy used in Linux. What alternate strategies are easily enabled? Describe the algorithm for choosing the next process to run.

13. In this exercise, you will study the effect of several parameters used with RR scheduling (see Section 7.4.1). You must write a discrete simulation to study the performance of this strategy under different time slice lengths and different context switching times. Do this by writing a simulation program to imitate the behavior of a single-CPU system that has a preemptive RR scheduler.

Create an input file to represent process arrival and service times, where each line represents a process arriving into your simulated system. The first number is the arrival time (in integer seconds), and the second number is the amount of time the process requires to complete (in floating-point seconds). For example, the first several lines of the file might look like

```
30  0.783560
54  17.282004
97  32.814522
133 39.986730
163 42.805902
181 28.249353
204 45.561030
249 26.369485
287 48.582049
325 37.274777
365 37.144992
399 22.059136
424 47.168534
455 20.090157
488 56.053016
531 39.640908
572 0.717403
610 34.732701
637 21.593761
658 48.477451
685 21.472914
729 44.603773
```

This means the first process arrives at time 30 and requests 0.783560 seconds of CPU time; the second at time 54; and so on. Run simulation experiments using context switching times of 0, 5, 10, 15, 20, and 25 milliseconds and time quanta of 50, 100, 250, and 500 milliseconds.

In your simulation, assume the model shown in Figure 7.6. Using at least the data given previously, determine the average wait time and the average turnaround time for all processes. Plot your findings in two graphs. In the first graph, the *Y*-axis should be the average wait time and the *X*-axis should be the context switching time. You will have one curve on the graph for each time quantum you test. The second graph is the same as the first except that you should plot the average turn-around time for the processes. Report the fraction of time the processor is busy for each simulation run.

8

Basic Synchronization Principles

There were moments when we were functioning as a single unit with two oars, two fly rods and three heads. The mood was broken only occasionally when, for instance, some klutz dropped his rod.

—John Gierach, *Even Brook Trout Get the Blues* ∎

CHAPTER OBJECTIVES

Multiprogramming, timesharing, and parallel processing have made the notion of cooperating groups of sequential processes possible. Concurrent operation among a related group of processes allows a single application to take advantage of parallelism between the CPU and the I/O devices on a uniprocessor and among CPUs on a multiprocessor. However, multiple cooperating processes introduce the potential for new problems in software implementations, including deadlock, the existence of critical sections, and the possibility of nondeterminacy in the computations. These issues arise when two or more processes intend to compete for, or to cooperatively share, resources (including information). It is important to understand the potential subtlety of interactions among processes before attempting to design mechanisms to support those interactions. Therefore the first part of this chapter discusses the general nature of these interactions. The rest focuses on the classic tool the OS provides to address synchronization, the semaphore, including implementation techniques.

Synchronization is required in uniprocessors, multiprocessors, and networks. However, the problem is sufficiently complex that it is traditionally first studied in a uniprocessor environment. In this discussion, the results are generalized for multiprocessors (at the end of the chapter) and for networks (in Chapter 17). Synchronization issues are addressed in the order in which they were derived. Doing this helps explain why there is a certain oddity to some aspects of the solutions. In classic exposition, sometimes a false solution is explained first before a correct solution is given so that one can better understand why obvious techniques prove to be inadequate. In Chapter 9, the discussion of synchronization is extended to higher-level mechanisms.

8.1 ▪ Interacting Processes

Computer programs are realizations of *serial algorithms*—step-by-step procedures for accomplishing some information processing task. The use of serial algorithms to specify serial computations has dominated programming for over half a century; thus computing environments have focused on supporting serial computation. While popular programming languages such as C and C++ have generally neglected to address concurrency, the underlying hardware technology has systematically moved toward it, using distributed and parallel computing machines. Economic pressures have driven application requirements toward the use of parallel and distributed hardware. This trend is apparent in, for example, contemporary management information systems, office computing environments, and numerical applications. To understand how this approach works, see the In the Hangar section (p. 185).

The main barriers to effective use of concurrency for applications arise from the following issues:

- There are no widely accepted parallel programming languages in use by application programmers. Ada provides support for concurrency, but C and C++ do not.

- System software technologies have not converged on a widely used programming paradigm for concurrent programs. The approach used in the In the Hangar example is unique to that example.

- Operating systems typically provide only the minimum mechanism to address concurrency, since there are so many different ways to implement concurrency and none of them dominate the area (for example, see [Jamieson et al., 1987]).

Acceptable techniques for characterizing concurrent algorithms have proved to be a serious impediment to concurrent programming technology. What makes it so difficult to abstract concurrency to form a useful application model?

- Designing a set of processes so that they cooperatively implement an application is surprisingly complex. One reason is the variety of paradigms for implementing concurrency. Another is the difficulty in handling subtle interactions and dependencies.

- It is especially difficult to design software to efficiently handle the intricacies of these interactions in networks of workstations and parallel processors.

- Even with high-level mechanisms available, it is difficult to construct programs without creating new synchronization problems.

A parallel computation is made up of multiple, independent parts that are able to execute simultaneously using one part per process or thread. In some cases, the different parts are defined by one program, but in general they are defined by multiple programs. Cooperation is achieved through logically shared memory that is used to share information and to synchronize the operation of the constituent processes. The OS must provide at least a base-level mechanism to support sharing and synchronization among a set of processes.

In batch multiprogramming systems, files within the file system are shared. One process can share information with another by writing the information to a file so that the other process can open the file and read the information. Many styles of simultaneous operation of the two processes are nearly impossible to achieve with this granularity of shared information. The processes need to be able to synchronize using a simpler mechanism than sharing an entire file.

Timesharing systems further stimulate the need for finer-grained sharing, since a single user should be able to create two processes and have the output of the first process be routed to the input of the second process. UNIX pipes implement this type of sharing. This finer-grained capability for sharing assumes the simultaneous existence of two different communicating processes.

Concurrent programs need to be constructed so that processes can share information, yet not interfere with one another during certain critical parts of their respective execution. This requirement introduces a synchronization problem called the critical section problem. A second new problem is the possibility of deadlock among cooperating processes. That is, two or more processes can get themselves into a situation in which each holds resources the other needs and neither can proceed without the other's giving up its resources. The critical section and deadlock problems are discussed after considering a concurrent solution to an application problem.

➤ IN THE HANGAR

Solving a System of Linear Equations

Linear systems of equations are often used to model problems from business, economics, operations research, physics, engineering, and other disciplines. If we represent a problem in terms of three unknowns, x_1, x_2, and x_3, we can determine values for x_1, x_2, and x_3 by deriving three independent linear equations that explain relationships among the three variables, as follows:

$$a_{11}x_1 + a_{12}x_2 + a_{13}x_3 = b_1$$
$$a_{21}x_1 + a_{22}x_2 + a_{23}x_3 = b_2$$
$$a_{31}x_1 + a_{32}x_2 + a_{33}x_3 = b_3$$

Given the three equations, we can use any of several numerical methods to find the roots of x_1, x_2, and x_3. Since our objective is to illustrate how concurrency can be applied to such problems, we can rewrite the three equations as

$$x_1 = (b_1 - a_{12}x_2 - a_{13}x_3)/a_{11}$$
$$x_2 = (b_2 - a_{21}x_1 - a_{23}x_3)/a_{22}$$
$$x_3 = (b_3 - a_{31}x_1 - a_{32}x_2)/a_{33}$$

Next, we use some initial estimate of $x_1^{[1]}$, $x_2^{[1]}$, and $x_3^{[1]}$ to compute a second estimate of the three values, $x_1^{[2]}$, $x_2^{[2]}$, and $x_3^{[2]}$. We do this by solving the three equations *concurrently* using the initial estimates for x_1, x_2, and x_3. (The term "concurrently" has the same technical meaning adopted in Chapter 1. Namely, we design our software as if the three *x*-values were being solved simultaneously, although the scheduler may actually execute the different parts either simultaneously on different CPUs or sequentially on a single CPU.) This can be accomplished by spawning three equation-solver processes and starting each of them, concurrently solving one of the three derived equations. After all three processes have completed their computations using $x_1^{[i-1]}$, $x_2^{[i-1]}$, and $x_3^{[i-1]}$ to produce the new values $x_1^{[i]}$, $x_2^{[i]}$, and $x_3^{[i]}$, they must *synchronize* their operation with one another to see if the results of the computation have converged to an acceptable estimate. After the synchronization point, one process can plug the values back into the original system of equations to check if the left-hand side of the equation is sufficiently close in value to the right-hand side. If the estimate is close enough, the computation is complete; otherwise, the three processes are started on the *i*+1st iteration.

This algorithm is based on the classic Gaussian elimination method using a parallel-oriented technique known as *successive overrelaxation* (*SOR*) [Jamieson et al., 1987]. It is a natural concurrent algorithm for solving a linear system of *N* equations in *N* unknowns, since the computation is easily partitioned into streams of work to be performed by *N* different processes. The *N* processes must coordinate their operation at the end of each iteration so that they can exchange *x*-values and test for convergence.

8.1.1 ■ Critical Sections

Suppose an application is written so that two processes, p_1 and p_2, execute concurrently to access a common integer variable, *x*. For example, process p_1 might handle credits to an account, while p_2 handles the debits. The following code schema shows how the processes reference the shared balance:

```
shared double balance; /* shared variable */
```

Code schema for p_1

```
    . . .
    balance = balance+amount;
    . . .
```

Code schema for p_2

```
    . . .
    balance = balance-amount;
    . . .
```

These high-level language statements will be compiled into a few machine instructions, such as the following:

Code schema for p_1

```
load   R1, balance
load   R2, amount
add    R1, R2
store  R1, balance
```

Code schema for p_2

```
load   R1, balance
load   R2, amount
sub    R1, R2
store  R1, balance
```

The critical section problem can occur when the code segments are executing. Suppose p_1 is running on a uniprocessor when the interval timer expires. In particular, suppose process p_1 is executing the

```
load R2, amount
```

instruction. If the scheduler next selects process p_2 to run and it executes its machine language code segment for the "balance = balance − amount;" instruction before p_1 regains control of the processor, then a *race condition* exists between p_1 and p_2. If p_1 wins the race, the values it had read into its version of $R1$ and $R2$ will be added together and written back to the shared variable in the memory with no harm. If p_2 wins the race, it will read the original value of balance, compute the difference between balance and amount, and then store the difference at the memory location containing balance; p_1 will eventually resume using the old value of balance it had previously loaded into $R1$; the old value was saved when p_1 was removed from the processor. Process p_1 will compute the sum of balance and amount, and then generate a different value of balance from the one p_2 had written when p_1 was blocked. The update of balance by p_2 will be lost!

The programs defining p_1 and p_2 each have a *critical section* with respect to their use of the shared variable balance. For p_1, the critical section is computing the sum of the balance and amount, but for p_2 the critical section is computing the difference of balance and amount. The concurrent execution of the two processes is not guaranteed to be *determinate,* since different executions of the same programs on the same data may not produce the same result. In one execution, p_1 may win the race, and in the next execution, p_2 may win the race, thus resulting in a different final value in any shared variables. It is not possible to detect a problem by considering only p_1's program or only p_2's program. The problem occurs because of sharing, not because of any error in the sequential code. The critical section problem can be avoided by having either process enter its corresponding critical section any time it needs to do so *except when the other process is currently in its critical section.*

How can the two processes cooperate to enter their critical sections? In a multiprogrammed uniprocessor, an interrupt causes the problem, since it could cause the scheduler to run. Because of the register state save operation implicit with context switching, a process may resume execution using inconsistent data loaded in its registers. If the programmer realized the occurrence of an interrupt could lead to erroneous results, he or she could have the program disable interrupts while it was executing a critical part of its processing.

Figure 8.1 illustrates how, for the example, critical sections can be coded using the enableInterrupt and disableInterrupt instructions to avoid both processes's

Figure 8.1
Disabling Interrupts to Implement the Critical Section

```
shared double amount, balance; /* Shared variables */
```

Program for p₁

```
disableInterrupts();
balance = balance + amount;
enableInterrupts();
```

Program for p₂

```
disableInterrupts();
balance = balance - amount;
enableInterrupts();
```

being in their critical sections at the same time. Interrupts are disabled when a process enters its critical section and then enabled when the process exits its critical section. Of course, this technique may affect the behavior of the I/O system since interrupts may be disabled for an arbitrarily long time as determined by an application program. In particular, suppose a program contained an infinite loop in its critical section. The interrupts would be permanently disabled. For this reason, user made programs cannot generally invoke enableInterrupts and disableInterrupts.

An alternative to the solution in Figure 8.1 does not require interrupts to be disabled; thus the problems of long/infinite compute intervals are avoided. The idea is to make the two processes explicitly coordinate their actions through the use of another shared variable to synchronize their progress. (That is, the solution depends on the ability of the OS to provide shared variables.) Figure 8.2 uses a shared flag, lock, so that p_1 and p_2 can coordinate their accesses to balance. (The statement NULL is used to emphasize the use of a null statement in the body of the while loop. In subsequent examples, it will be dropped by simply omitting all statements from the body of the loop.) When p_1 enters its critical section, it sets the shared lock variable, so p_2 will be

Figure 8.2
Critical Sections Using a Lock

```
shared boolean lock = FALSE;    /* Shared variables */
shared double amount, balance; /* Shared variables */
```

Program for p_1

```
    . . .
/* Acquire lock */
  while(lock) {NULL;};
  lock = TRUE;
/* Execute crit section */
  balance = balance + amount;
/* Release lock */
  lock = FALSE;
  . . .
```

Program for p_2

```
    . . .
/* Acquire lock */
  while(lock) {NULL;};
  lock = TRUE;
/* Execute crit section */
  balance = balance - amount;
/* Release lock */
  lock = FALSE;
  . . .
```

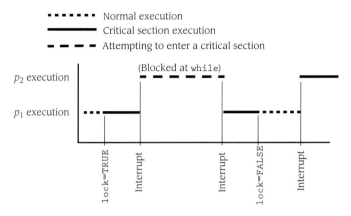

Figure 8.3
The Execution Pattern

prevented from entering its critical section. Similarly, p_2 uses the lock to prevent p_1 from entering its critical section at the wrong time.

Figure 8.3 illustrates an execution pattern for the two processes. Suppose p_1 is interrupted during the execution of the statement

```
balance = balance + amount;
```

after having set lock to TRUE and p_2 begins to execute. Blocked on the lock, p_2 will wait to obtain its critical section at its while statement. Eventually, the clock interrupt will interrupt p_2 and resume p_1, which can complete its critical section. When p_1 executes

```
lock = FALSE;
```

p_1 will have indicated it has completed its critical section. Eventually, p_1 will again be interrupted by the clock, and then p_2 can finally enter its critical section and continue with its work.

While locking on a shared variable is conceptually a good solution, it introduces a new critical section related to testing and setting the lock variable. If a process is interrupted after testing lock but before it sets it (for example, after the while statement but before the assignment statement), the solution fails. This new, smaller critical section for manipulating lock can be handled by using enter and exit system calls, as shown in Figure 8.4. In this case, interrupts are disabled in OS code only while lock is being manipulated, thus allowing them to be enabled while the main critical section is being executed. Hence, the amount of time the interrupts are disabled is very short.

Figure 8.4
Lock Manipulation as a Critical Section

```
enter(lock) {                          exit(lock) {
  disableInterrupts();                   disableInterrupts();
/* Wait for lock */                      lock = FALSE;
  while(lock) {                           enableInterrupts();
  /* Let interrupt occur */            }
    enableInterrupts();
    disableInterrupts();
  }
  lock = TRUE;
  enableInterrupts();
}
```

8.1.2 ■ Deadlock

In a deadlock situation, two or more processes get into a state whereby each is holding a resource the other is requesting. Since a request operation blocks the caller until the resource becomes allocated, neither process will ever have the desired resource allocated to it and both will remain in the blocked state forever. In process synchronization, we focus on the case in which the resource is a lock or critical section. Chapter 10 considers the general problem whereby a resource can be any resource in the system.

Consider a case in which two processes, p_1 and p_2, manipulate a common list. One task in list manipulation is for the process to add or delete an entry; another is to update a list descriptor with the length of the list. When a delete operation occurs, the length must be updated, or, if the length of the list is increased by one, an entry must be added to the list. To ensure consistency between the list and its descriptor, we could first try the approach shown in Figure 8.5. This, however, will turn out to be an insufficient solution.

If processes p_1 and p_2 are executed concurrently on a multiprogramming system, a clock interrupt may occur after p_1 deletes an element but before it updates the length in the list descriptor. If p_2 adds an element to the list and updates the length before p_1 resumes, then the contents of the list and its length in the descriptor will not be consistent with one another. A process should update both the list and the descriptor or neither. So we try a different solution in order to place modifications to the list and the descriptor within a more complex critical section scheme, as shown in Figure 8.6.

When p_1 enters its critical section to manipulate the list, it sets lock1. Thus p_2 will be prevented from entering its critical section to manipulate the list when it tests lock1. The same also holds for p_2 when it enters its list manipulation critical section and for both p_1 and p_2 to update the length. Suppose p_1 is interrupted during the <intermediate computation> (after having set lock1 to TRUE) and p_2 begins to execute; p_2 will set lock2 and then wait for lock1 at the while statement. Eventually, the clock interrupt will resume p_1, and p_1 can then complete the <intermediate computation> then block at its while statement test on lock2 (prior to updating the descriptor). However, now there is a new problem: Neither process can ever proceed, since each

Figure 8.5
Multiple Shared Variables with Disabled Interrupts

```
shared boolean lock1 = FALSE; /* Shared variables */
shared boolean lock2 = FALSE;
shared list L;
```

Program for p_1

```
. . .
/* Enter crit section to
   delete elt from list */
   enter(lock1);
   <delete element>;
/* Exit critical section */
   exit(lock1);
   <intermediate computation>;
/* Enter crit section to
   update length */
   enter(lock2);
   <update length>;
/* Exit critical section */
   exit(lock2);
   . . .
```

Program for p_2

```
. . .
/* Enter crit section to
   update length */
   enter(lock2);
   <update length>;
/* Exit critical section */
   exit(lock2);
   <intermediate computation>;
/* Enter crit section to
   add elt to list */
   enter(lock1);
   <add element>;
/* Exit critical section */
   exit(lock1);
   . . .
```

Figure 8.6
Ensuring Consistency in Related Values

```
shared boolean lock1 = FALSE; /* Shared variables */
shared boolean lock2 = FALSE;
shared list L;
```

Program for p_1

```
. . .
/* Enter crit section to
   delete elt from list */
   enter(lock1);
   <delete element>;
   <intermediate computation>;
/* Enter crit section to
   update length */
   enter(lock2);
   <update length>;
/* Exit both crit sections */
   exit(lock1);
   exit(lock2);
   . . .
```

Program for p_2

```
. . .
/* Enter crit section to
   update length */
   enter(lock2);
   <update length>;
   <intermediate computation>;
/* Enter crit section to
   add elt to list */
   enter(lock1);
   <add element>;
/* Exit both crit sections */
   exit(lock2);
   exit(lock1);
   . . .
```

holds the lock that the other needs. This forms a *deadlock* between p_1 and p_2, where the resource is an abstract "resource"—a lock. In our exploration of synchronization approaches, we must guard against the possibility of a deadlock.

8.2 ▪ Coordinating Processes

The need for interactions among processes leads to the need for synchronization, and synchronization introduces the critical section and deadlock problems. FORK, JOIN, and QUIT were introduced in Chapter 2 as mechanisms for creating and destroying processes. They can also be used to synchronize parts of a concurrent computation. In Figure 8.7(a), the schematic diagram represents how a computation uses FORK, JOIN, and QUIT to achieve concurrency. The initial process (or one of its descendants) creates a user process, A, by performing a FORK operation. Process A then executes FORK to create process B. A and B then JOIN, leaving only one process running, say B. Next, process B executes a FORK to create process C. Processes B and C execute concurrently and then JOIN, leaving only one process, again say B. Finally, process B performs a QUIT operation to compete the computation. In this example, there are three distinct processes in the application schema (ignoring the initial process).

Figure 8.7(b) represents an alternative approach using a *synchronization* operator similar to the lock mechanism introduced in the previous section. Again, process A is created, either directly or indirectly, by the initial process. Process A creates process B using a FORK command. At some of the points where FORK and JOIN would have been used to create and destroy processes, the two processes explicitly synchronize their operation, meaning neither will proceed beyond a certain point in the computation until both have reached their respective synchronization points. Neither process is destroyed through a JOIN or QUIT; they merely block until both have reached their

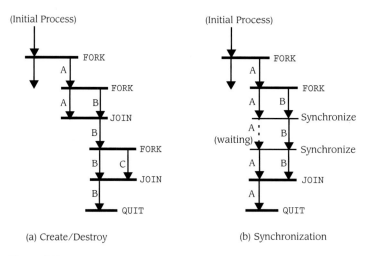

(a) Create/Destroy   (b) Synchronization

Figure 8.7
Synchronization using FORK, JOIN, and QUIT

respective synchronization points. Process A then waits while B performs sequential processing. The processes then synchronize again and continue concurrent execution. After all the work is done, the two processes JOIN. In Figure 8.7(b), process A is assumed to be the last to execute JOIN, so it continues and finally performs a QUIT to finish the computation.

The two approaches in Figure 8.7 also can be made to perform the same computation with the same amount of overlapped operation. Which approach is preferable? Since the introduction of FORK, JOIN, and QUIT, OS designers have observed that process creation and destruction tend to be very costly operations because they require considerable manipulation of process descriptors, protection mechanisms, and memory management mechanisms. However, the synchronization operation could be thought of as a resource request on a consumable resource, such as a pair of shared Boolean variables, and can be implemented far more efficiently. Because the number of machine cycles for creation/destruction is three or more orders of magnitude larger than for synchronization, the trend in contemporary operating systems is to incorporate synchronization mechanisms to complement the process creation/destruction operations.

In Section 8.1 some basic ideas have been covered, showing how the synchronization might be accomplished using locks on a shared variable, but the example solution relied on the semantics of the particular problem. In a generalized mechanism, a process should be able to block until some previously defined *event* has occurred in another process. Consider the example introduced in Figure 2.6 and repeated in Figure 8.8. The intent of these code segments is probably that proc_B should not execute its first read statement until proc_A completes the write for the variable *x*. Further, this synchronization should take place each time through the loop. When proc_B starts, it should suspend operation until the write event occurs in proc_A. This is a variant of the critical section problem in that the synchronization is to ensure cooperation between the processes executing proc_A and proc_B, rather than to resolve competition for access to a critical section.

Figure 8.8
Example Concurrent Processes

```
shared double x, y; /* Shared variables */

proc_A() {                          proc_B() {
  while(TRUE) {                       while(TRUE) {
    <compute A1>;                       read(x); /* Consume x */
    write(x); /* Produce x */           <compute B1>;
    <compute A2>;                       write(y); /* Produce y */
    read(y); /* Consume y */            <compute B2>;
  }                                   }
}                                   }
```

There are three basic approaches to implementing synchronization strategies:

- Use only user made software algorithms and shared variables, as suggested by the code solutions given so far in this book.

- Disable and enable interrupts around critical sections as indicated in Figure 8.1 although as already pointed out, such solutions potentially have a dramatic effect on the I/O system.

- Incorporate specialized mechanisms in the hardware and/or operating system to support synchronization. This approach was first proposed by Edsger Dijkstra [Dijkstra, 1968] and remains the basis of the standard solution. It relies on the use of the semaphore abstract data type implemented by the operating system.

Two of the three approaches involve explicit OS support. The semaphore approach (and its extensions) is much preferred to the software and interrupt-based solutions.

8.3 ■ Semaphores

A *semaphore* is an OS abstract data type that performs operations similar to the `enter` and `exit` functions described in Figure 8.4. Before discussing the principles of operation of semaphores, this section describes the assumptions that constrain semaphore behavior.

As already discussed, a process cannot enter its critical section if another process is already in its corresponding critical section. When a process is about to enter its critical section, it first determines if another process is in its critical section. If there is, the second process synchronizes its operation by blocking until the first process exits its critical section. An acceptable solution to the critical section problem is required to meet the following constraints:

- Only one process at a time should be allowed to be in its critical section (*mutual exclusion*).

- If a critical section is free and a set of processes indicates a need to enter into the critical section, then only those processes competing for the critical section participate in the selection of the process to enter the critical section.

- Once a process attempts to enter its critical section, it cannot be postponed indefinitely even if no other process is in its critical section.

- After a process requests entry into its critical section, only a bounded number of other processes may be allowed to enter their related critical sections before the original process enters its critical section.

The critical section problem is a software problem in its traditional formulation. For purposes of discussion, this section highlights other important aspects of the problem by considering the two process skeletons shown in Figure 8.9. In this and subsequent figures, the statement

```
fork(proc, N, arg1, arg2, ..., argN)
```

Figure 8.9
Cooperating Processes

```
proc_0() {                          proc_1() {
  while(TRUE) {                       while(TRUE) {
    <compute section>;                  <compute section>;
    <critical section>;                 <critical section>;
  }                                   }
}                                   }
<shared global declarations>;
<initial processing>;
fork(proc_0, 0);
fork(proc_1, 0);
```

is used to mean a process is created and begins executing `proc()` in its own address space using the *N* arguments provided. `<shared global declarations>` are intended to be the shared variables accessible in the address space of all the processes.

The following assumptions are made about the execution of the software schema in the figure:

- Writing and reading a memory cell common to the two processes is an indivisible operation. Any attempt by the two processors to execute simultaneous memory read or write operations will result in some unknown serial ordering of the two operations, but the two operations will not happen at the same time.

- The processes are not assumed to have any priority, where one or the other would take precedence in the case of simultaneous attempts to enter a critical section.

- The relative speeds of the processes are unknown, so one cannot rely on speed differentials (or equivalence) in arriving at a solution.

- As indicated in Figure 8.9, the processes are assumed to be sequential and cyclic.

8.3.1 ■ Principles of Operation

Edsger Dijkstra is well-known as the inventor of the semaphore as the first software-oriented primitive to accomplish process synchronization [Dijkstra, 1968]. In this classic paper, he introduced the idea of "cooperating sequential processes," illustrated the difficulty in accomplishing synchronization using only conventional (at that time) machine instructions, postulated the primitives, proved that they worked, and then provided a number of examples (many of which are used in examples and exercises in this book). In Dijkstra's original paper, the P operation was an abbreviation for the Dutch word *proberen,* meaning "to test," and the V operation was an abbreviation for *verhogen,* meaning "to increment." Dijkstra's work on semaphores established over 30 years ago the foundation of modern techniques for accomplishing synchronization, yet it is still a viable approach to managing communities of cooperating processes.

A semaphore, s, is a nonnegative integer variable changed or tested only by one of two indivisible access routines:

```
V(s):  [s = s + 1]
P(s):  [while(s == 0) {wait}; s = s - 1]
```

The square braces surrounding the statements in the access routines indicate that the operations are *indivisible,* or *atomic,* operations. In the V operation, the process executing the routine cannot be interrupted until it has completed the routine. The P operation is more complex. If s is greater than 0, it is tested and decremented as an indivisible operation. However, if s is equal to 0, the process executing the P operation *can* be interrupted when it executes the `wait` command in the range of the `while` loop. The indivisible operation applies only to the test and control flow after the test, not to the time the process waits due to s's being equal to zero.

The P operation is intended to indivisibly test an integer variable and to block the calling process if the variable is not positive. The V operation indivisibly signals a blocked process to allow it to resume operation. Given the semaphore with the P and V operations, we can solve the general critical section problem described in Figure 8.9 as shown in Figure 8.10. The initial value of the semaphore named `mutex` is 1. When a process gets ready to enter its critical section, it applies the P operation to `mutex` (a classic name from Dijkstra's original paper meaning "mutual exclusion"). The first process to invoke P on `mutex` passes and the second blocks. When the first invokes the V operation on `mutex`, it continues to execute, thus enabling the second to proceed when it gets control of the CPU.

Next, we'll explore how semaphores are used by considering a series of examples that employ semaphores to solve the critical section problem and to synchronize the operation of two processes. We start with some simple examples using *binary semaphores,* where the value of the semaphore takes on only the values 0 and 1. Usually, but

Figure 8.10
Using Semaphores for Critical Sections

```
proc_0() {                            proc_1() {
  while(TRUE) {                          while(TRUE) {
    <compute section>;                     <compute section>;
    P(mutex);                              P(mutex);
      <critical section>;                    <critical section>;
    V(mutex);                              V(mutex);
  }                                      }
}                                      }
semaphore mutex = 1;
fork(proc_0, 0);
fork(proc_1, 0);
```

not always (see the example in the In the Hangar section below), the semaphore is initialized to have the value 1.

➤ IN THE HANGAR

Examples Using Semaphore

There are various classic synchronization problems that were introduced in Dijkstra's original paper, or that appeared in later papers and textbooks. This section reviews several of the more common ones.

The Basic Critical Section Problem

Section 8.1 introduced a simple problem where two processes are allowed to update a common account balance. This problem is really just a special case of the problem solved in Figure 8.10 (see Figure 8.11).

Figure 8.11
Semaphores on the Shared Balance Problem

```
proc_0() {                        proc_1() {
  ...                               ...
/* Enter critical section */      /* Enter critical section */
  P(mutex);                         P(mutex);
    balance = balance + amount;       balance = balance - amount;
/* Exit critical section */       /* Exit critical section */
  V(mutex);                         V(mutex);
  ...                               ...
}                                 }
semaphore mutex = 1;
fork(proc_0, 0);
fork(proc_1, 0);
```

The Basic Synchronizing Problem

Figure 8.12 is a solution to the problem shown in Figure 8.8. Note that we cannot simply substitute enable/disable calls for P and V in this example to return to the original solution (as we could for the previous example), because more than one semaphore is used to accomplish synchronization. In this case, the semaphore is used to exchange synchronization signals among processes, as opposed to solving the strict critical section problem. This example illustrates that semaphores can have extremely general use, so we consider more examples to illustrate their utility.

Figure 8.12
Using Semaphores to Synchronize Two Processes

```
proc_A() {                        proc_B() {
  while(TRUE) {                     while(TRUE) {
    <compute A1>;                     /* Wait for proc_A signal */
    write(x); /* Produce x */         P(s1);
    V(s1); /* Signal proc_B */        read(x); /* Consume x */
    <compute A2>;                     <compute B1>;
  /* Wait for proc_B signal */        write(y); /* Produce y */
    P(s2);                            V(s2); /* Signal proc_A */
    read(y); /* Consume y */          <compute B2>;
  }                                 }
}                                 }
semaphore s1 = 0;
semaphore s2 = 0;
fork(proc_0, 0);
fork(proc_1, 0);
```

Software/Hardware Device Interaction

Chapter 4 explained the software/hardware interface between a device driver and controller. The busy and done flags in the status register can be viewed as hardware implementations of semaphores, since they are used to synchronize the operation of the software driver and the hardware controller. Figure 8.13 is a code skeleton representing the interaction.

Figure 8.13
The Driver-Controller Interface Behavior

```
/* Map the hardware flags to shared semaphores */
semaphore busy = 0, done = 0;
driver() { /* Synchronization behavior of the driver */
  <preparation for device operation>;
  V(busy); /* Start the device */
  P(done); /* Wait for the device to complete */
  <complete the operation>;
}

controller() { /* Controller's hardware loop */
  while(TRUE) {
    P(busy); /* Wait for a start signal */
    <perform the operation>;
    V(done); /* Tell driver that hardware has completed */
  }
}
```

The figure models the algorithmic behavior of the device driver software and the hardware controller. It is not intended to be a software implementation. For example, if this solution were the basis of an implementation, it would block the calling process. In the model, busy and done are initialized to 0, so when the device controller is started it enters an endless loop in which it synchronizes its operation with the software process by testing the busy flag. If busy is 0—the initialization condition—the controller blocks are waiting for a signal from the driver. The driver is called by an application program whenever it wants to perform an I/O operation. After preparing for the operation (for example, by setting controller registers, device status table entries, and so on), it signals the hardware process by a V operation on the busy semaphore. The V operation unblocks the controller and then blocks the driver on the done semaphore. When the device has completed the operation, it signals the driver by a V operation on the done flag.

The Bounded Buffer (Producer-Consumer) Problem

Suppose a system incorporates two processes, one of which produces information (the *producer* process) and another process that uses the information (the *consumer* process) [Dijkstra, 1968]. The two processes communicate by having the producer obtain an empty buffer from an empty buffer pool, fill it with information, and place it in a pool of full buffers. The consumer obtains information by picking up a buffer from the full buffer pool, copying the information out of the buffer, and placing it in the empty buffer pool for recycling. The producer and consumer use a fixed, finite number, N, of buffers to pass an arbitrary amount of information between them. This solution bounds the amount of memory used by the processes. It also uses the buffers to keep the producer and consumer roughly synchronized.

Figure 8.14 is a program schema for the producer and consumer processes. The empty and full semaphores illustrate a new type of semaphores, called *general,* or *counting,* semaphores. Whereas a binary semaphore takes on only the values 0 and 1, the counting semaphore takes on values from 0 to N for the N-buffer problem. In the solution, the counting semaphores serve a dual purpose. They keep a count of the number of empty and full buffers. They also are used to synchronize the operation of the processes by blocking the producer when there are no empty buffers and blocking the consumer when there are no full buffers.

The buffers are a contiguous block of memory logically split into N parts. Each buffer must contain space for links to associate the buffer with other empty or full buffers and space for the data itself. Since the producer and consumer each manipulate these links, the code for buffer pool manipulation must be treated as a critical section. The mutex semaphore protects access to the two buffer pools so that only one process takes or puts a buffer at a time.

Even with semaphores, subtleties can exist in the way the processes are defined. Consider the ordering of the first two P operations in the producer and the consumer. Suppose the P(full) and the P(mutex) instructions were reversed in the consumer. Then, if all the buffers were to become empty at one time, the consumer would obtain the mutex semaphore and block on the full semaphore, while hold-

Figure 8.14
The Bounded Buffer Problem

```
producer() {                        consumer() {
  bufType *next, *here;               bufType *next, *here;
  while(TRUE) {                       while(TRUE) {
    produceItem(next);                  /* Claim a full buffer */
  /*Claim an empty buffer */            P(full);
    P(empty);                         /* Manipulate the pool */
    /* Manipulate the pool */           P(mutex);
      P(mutex);                           here = obtain(full);
        here = obtain(empty);           V(mutex);
      V(mutex);                         copyBuffer(here, next);
      copyBuffer(next, here);          /* Manipulate the pool */
    /* Manipulate the pool */           P(mutex);
      P(mutex);                           release(here, emptyPool);
        release(here, fullPool);        V(mutex);
      V(mutex);                         /* Signal an empty buffer */
    /* Signal a full buffer */          V(empty);
      V(full);                          consumeItem(next);
  }                                   }
}                                   }


semaphore mutex = 1;
semaphore full = 0;
semaphore empty = N;
bufType buffer[N];
fork(producer, 0);
fork(consumer, 0);
```

ing the `mutex` semaphore. This is a deadlock situation because the consumer holds all the empty buffers and requests a full one, but the producer cannot create a full buffer without first obtaining an empty buffer. The order of appearance of the P operations is significant.

The Readers-Writers Problem

Courtois, Heymans, and Parnas [1971] posed another interesting synchronization problem called the readers-writers problem. Suppose a resource is to be shared among a community of processes of two distinct types: readers and writers. A *reader* process can share the resource with any other reader process but not with any writer process. A *writer* process requires exclusive access to the resource whenever it acquires any access to the resource.

This scenario is similar to one in which a file is to be shared among a set of processes. If a process wants only to read the file, then it may share the file with any other process that also only wants to read the file. If a writer wants to modify the file, then no other process should have access to the file when the writer has access to it.

Several different policies could be implemented for managing the shared resource. For example, as long as a reader holds the resource and there are new readers arriving, any writer must wait for the resource to become available. This policy is implemented by the algorithm shown in Figure 8.15. In this policy, the first reader accessing the shared resource must compete with any writers, but any succeeding readers can pass directly into the critical section, provided a reader is still in the critical section. The readers keep a count of the number in the critical section, with the readCount variable, which is updated and tested inside its own critical section. Only the first reader executes the P(writeBlock) operation, while every writer does so, since every writer must compete with the first reader. Similarly, the last reader to yield the critical section must perform the V operation on behalf of all readers that accessed the shared resource.

While this solution implements the stated policy, it is easy to see that the policy may not produce the desired result. Readers can dominate the resource so that no writer ever gets a chance to access it. In real systems, this situation is analogous to the case in which a pending update of a file must wait until all reads have completed.

Figure 8.15
First Policy for Coordinating Readers and Writers

```
reader() {                          writer()( {
  while(TRUE) {                       while(TRUE) {
    <other computing>;                  <other computing>;
    P(mutex);                           P(writeBlock);
      readCount = readCount+1;         /* Critical section */
      if (readCount == 1)               access(resource);
        P(writeBlock);                  V(writeBlock);
    V(mutex);                         }
    /* Critical section */          }
    access(resource);
    P(mutex);
      readCount = readCount-1;
      if(readCount == 0)
        V(writeBlock);
    V(mutex);
  }
}
resourceType *resource;
int readCount = 0;
semaphore mutex = 1;
semaphore writeBlock = 1;
/* Start the readers and writers */
fork(reader, 0); /* Could be many */
fork(writer, 0); /* Could be many */
```

In most cases, one would like the updates to take place as soon as possible. This desire leads to an alternative policy that favors writers. That is, when a writer process requests access to the shared resource, any subsequent reader process must wait for the writer to gain access to the shared resource and then release it.

An algorithm to implement the second policy is shown in Figure 8.16. This implementation still allows a stream of readers to enter the critical section until a writer arrives. The writer then takes priority over all subsequent readers, except those already accessing the shared resource. When the first writer arrives, it will obtain the `readBlock` semaphore. Then it blocks on the `writeBlock` semaphore, waiting for all readers to clear the critical section. The next reader to arrive will obtain the `writePending` semaphore and then block on the `readBlock` semaphore. Suppose another writer arrives at this time. It will block on the `writeBlock` semaphore,

Figure 8.16
Second Policy for Coordinating Readers and Writers

```
reader() {                              writer() {
  while (TRUE) {                          while(TRUE) {
    <other computing>;                      <other computing>;
    P(writePending);                        P(mutex2);
      P(readBlock);                            writeCount=writeCount+1;
        P(mutex1);                            if(writeCount==1)
          readCount = readCount+1;              P(readBlock);
          if(readCount == 1)                  V(mutex2);
            P(writeBlock);                    P(writeBlock);
          V(mutex1);                            access(resource);
        V(readBlock);                       V(writeBlock);
      V(writePending);                      P(mutex2);
      access(resource);                       writeCount=writeCount-1;
    P(mutex1);                              if(writeCount==0)
      readCount = readCount-1;               V(readBlock);
      if(readCount == 0)                    V(mutex2);
        V(writeBlock);                    }
    V(mutex1);                           }
  }
}
resourceType *resource;
int readCount = 0, writeCount = 0;
semaphore mutex1 = 1, mutex2 = 1;
semaphore readBlock = 1;
semaphore writePending = 1;
semaphore writeBlock = 1
/* Start the readers and writers */
fork(reader, 0); /* Could be many */
fork(writer, 0); /* Could be many */
```

assuming the first writer has progressed to the critical section. If a second reader arrives, it will block at the `writePending` semaphore. Now when the first writer leaves the critical section, any subsequent writer is required to have priority over all readers. The second and subsequent writers are blocked at `writeBlock`, and no reader is blocked on the semaphore, so the writers will dominate the resource. When all writers have completed, the readers are allowed to use the resource.

This example highlights a new problem. Semaphores provide an abstraction of hardware-level synchronization into a software mechanism used to solve simple problems, but problems of the complexity of the readers-writers problem are more difficult. How do we know a solution such as the second readers-writers solution is correct? We are left with two choices:

■ Create a higher-level abstraction (as in Chapter 9).

■ Prove our use of the low-level mechanisms is correct with respect to the synchronization primitives. Semaphores have not eliminated the need for proofs, but they enable us to write more complex scenarios than we could without them.

8.3.2 ■ Practical Considerations

There are a few practical considerations related to semaphore implementations. The rest of this section deals with how to implement semaphores, to avoid busy-waiting on semaphores, and to view semaphores as resources. We also consider an important detail related to the implementation of the V operation: active versus passive behavior.

8.3.2.1 ■ Implementing Semaphores

Figure 8.4 showed how interrupts can be disabled to manipulate a lock variable. The same technique can be used to implement the P and V operations. The description uses C++ to represent a semaphore class to emphasize that the semaphore is an abstract data type with a private implementation and a public interface. Since P and V are implemented as operating system functions, the model of a solution assumes that user processes can have a pointer to the semaphore, but the pointer is to an object in the OS. The syntax glosses this over, since a full implementation requires a fixed memory management organization as described in Chapter 11.

An implementation following this model disables interrupts, but only for very small periods of time (see Figure 8.17). When a process blocks on a semaphore, the interrupts are enabled; they are disabled only while the semaphore's value is manipulated. This has two important effects:

■ There is minimal effect on the I/O system.

■ While a process holds a semaphore, it prevents only other processes competing for a relevant critical section from running. All other processes are unaffected by the fact that one process is in its critical section.

Figure 8.17
Implementing Semaphores Using Interrupts

```
class semaphore {
   int value;
public:
   semaphore(int v = 1) {
   // allocate space for the semaphore object in the OS
      value = v
   };
   P() {
      disableInterrupts();
   // Loop until value is positive
      while (value == 0) {
         enableInterrupts();   // Let interrupts occur
         disableInterrupts(); // Disable them again
      }
      value--;
      enableInterrupts();
   };
   V() {
      disableInterrupts();
      value++;
      enableInterrupts();
   };
}
```

Semaphores can be implemented without disabling interrupts if the hardware makes a few special provisions. A direct implementation of the P and V instructions is reasonably difficult because of the need to accommodate the waiting loop in the P operation. Instead, a uniprocessor implementation will generally want to interact with the scheduler for the implementation of P, so part of the instruction will be implemented in hardware and part in software. The OS can create an abstract resource for each semaphore. Then it uses resource managers to block processes when they perform a P operation just as if they had performed a request operation on a conventional resource. The issue becomes how the semaphore resource manager can correctly implement simultaneous access to the semaphore without using interrupts.

The *test-and-set* (TS) instruction is the dominant way to accomplish the effects of P and V. TS is a simple instruction that can be included in a machine's repertoire without much effort, but it can make semaphore implementation relatively simple. TS of memory location, *m*, or TS(m), causes the contents of memory location *m* to be loaded into a CPU register (with the condition code register contents set to reflect the value of the data) and the memory to be written with a value of TRUE.

Assume TS is in the instruction repertoire of a machine and it is called by TS(m) on memory cell *m*. The critical section problem can be solved as shown in Figure 8.18(a).

Figure 8.18
Implementing the Binary Semaphore with TS

```
boolean s = FALSE;                   semaphore s = 1;
   . . .                                . . .
   while(TS(s)) ;                       P(s);
     <critical section>;                  <critical section>;
   s = FALSE;                           V(s);
   . . .                                . . .

          (a)                                  (b)
```

(Part (b) is the corresponding code using P and V, for comparison.) The solution takes advantage of TS being able to set m to TRUE and the original result being loaded into a testable register without interruption. After the original value from location m has been loaded, the interrupting process will detect the value stored in m as being TRUE and so will block at the while loop. This occurs even if an interrupt occurs before the process actually begins processing critical section code. The assignment statement's resetting of s is assumed to be atomic, since it would normally be atomic in any computer's instruction set.

One apparent shortcoming of TS is that it replaces only the P operation for binary semaphores—the ones taking on only the values of 0 and 1. However, counting semaphores take on any nonnegative value. This shortcoming can be overcome by finding an algorithm in which TS is used to implement the general (counting) semaphore. Figure 8.19 provides such an algorithm.

Figure 8.19
Implementing the General Semaphore with TS

```
struct semaphore {
   int value = <initial value>;
   boolean mutex = FALSE;
   boolean hold = TRUE;
};

shared struct semaphore s;

P(struct semaphore s) {          V(struct semaphore s) {
   while(TS(s.mutex)) ;              while(TS(s.mutex)) ;
   s.value = s.value - 1;           s.value = s.value + 1;
   if(s.value < 0) {                if(s.value <= 0) {
     s.mutex = FALSE;                 while(!s.hold) ;
     while(TS(s.hold)) ;              s.hold = FALSE;
   }                                }
   else                             s.mutex = FALSE;
     s.mutex = FALSE;            }
}
```

In the figure, s.mutex is used to implement mutual exclusion, while a process manipulates s.value to represent the value of the general semaphore. The s.hold Boolean is used to stage processes blocked by the semaphore. Thus any process waiting for the semaphore will be waiting at the statement

```
while (TS(s.hold));
```

in the P procedure. When s.hold returns a value of FALSE (the V operation will have set the value FALSE in those cases when it detected processes queued on semaphore s), the process invoking P will block at the TS in the outer while loop. Also, note that a process executing the P operation will release the critical section related to manipulating the s.value entry before it begins waiting on the s.hold variable.

One other statement in the solution merits careful consideration. In the V operation, the

```
while (!s.hold);
```

is required. This requirement follows because a race condition can occur in which a process believes it is blocked in the P procedure, yet the V procedure encounters s.hold as being TRUE. This situation can occur when consecutive V operations occur before any process executes a P operation. Without the while statement, the result of one of the V operations could be lost.

8.3.2.2 ■ Busy-Waiting

The solution to the general semaphore problem using the TS instruction may exhibit one unpleasant property under certain circumstances. Suppose this implementation were used in a multiprogrammed system that has a single processor. Then, whenever a process is scheduled to run and it blocks on a semaphore, it will repeatedly execute the

```
while(TS(s.hold));
```

instruction until the timer interrupt invokes the scheduler to multiplex the process off of the processor and another process onto the processor. When the blocked process obtains its next time slice, it will resume this busy-wait if s.hold is still TRUE. The result is that the blocked process is effectively slowing down some other process that would eventually execute a V operation and allow the first to proceed. The blocked process needs to indicate to the operating system that it cannot do anything useful at the moment. This can be done by executing the equivalent of the yield instruction (from Chapter 7). Each time the process detects it is blocked, it might simply yield to another process that can perform useful work. This method would suggest that the busy-waiting statement should be changed to

```
while (TS(s.hold))
  yield (*, scheduler);
```

to eliminate wasting the unused portion of the time slice by a blocked process.

8.3.2.3 ■ Active and Passive Semaphore Implementations

A semaphore can be thought of as a consumable resource. A process blocks if it requests a semaphore value and none is available. A process moves from the running state to the blocked state by executing a P operation on a zero-valued semaphore. A process moves from blocked to running when it detects a positive value of the semaphore; it decrements the semaphore at the same time it changes state. When another process releases a resource, in this case by performing a V operation, the resource allocator moves the first process from blocked to ready. Being in the ready state does not mean the process is physically executing on the CPU, but it is at least on the ready list. This style of operation creates the possibility for another complexity. That is, if one process performs a V operation, should the OS "guarantee" that a waiting process will immediately perceive the action?

Figure 8.10 described a pair of processes synchronizing on a semaphore, `mutex`. Suppose process 0 obtains the semaphore and enters the critical section, and process 1 subsequently blocks on its `P(mutex)` operation. Suppose further that process 0 exits the critical section and then executes `V(mutex)`, the `<compute section>`, and its own `P(mutex)`—all prior to process 1 actually having an opportunity to detect that the semaphore took on a positive value. Then process 1 could be prevented from entering its critical section even though the semaphore took on positive values. This scenario is most likely to occur on a multiprogrammed uniprocessor if process 0 does not give up the CPU immediately after incrementing the semaphore. In implementing the V operation, one is advised to add a `yield` to the procedure definition immediately after incrementing the semaphore. This form of implementation is called the *active V* operation. This contrasts with the *passive V* operation, where the implementation increments the semaphore with no opportunity for a context switch.

There is another aspect to semaphores that is highlighted with active and passive semaphores. Programmers sometimes treat the P operation as a "wait-for-event-occurrence" operation and the V operation as a "signal" to the waiting process. If the waiting process (the process blocked on a P operation) is not allowed to run at the time the signal is raised, is the event signaled by the V operation still TRUE at the time the P operation finally sees the signal? We will revisit this issue in Chapter 9, where monitors are discussed.

8.4 ■ Shared Memory Multiprocessors

Sections 8.1 and 8.3 described a technique for implementing semaphores by disabling interrupts. In a shared-memory multiprocessor, this is insufficient, since disabling the interrupts on one CPU does not affect the interrupts on other CPUs. Therefore commercial shared-memory multiprocessors all use specialized instructions such as TS to implement semaphores.

In shared-memory multiprocessors, the memory can be designed to support TS. When a process uses the busy-wait technique (without using `yield`), the only CPU unable to process other work is the one on which the blocked process executes. Another process capable of executing the V operation can be running on a different CPU. Therefore the busy-wait is a mechanism for very fast recognition of the instant at which a process becomes unblocked. In some cases, it is worth using one of N processors to *poll* the s.hold variable in order to detect the earliest possible moment the blocked process becomes unblocked.

Operating systems for shared-memory multiprocessor systems typically support this scenario by including *spin locks* in the operating system call interface. A spin lock is a procedure that repeatedly performs the TS instruction to test a specified lock variable. To complete the abstract machine interface to the lock, there will be calls to create the lock, to lock and unlock it, and to block the lock, and often a nonblocking call on the lock. This latter call is used so that if a process detects it is locked out of a critical section, it can do other operations.

8.5 ■ Summary

The basic synchronization techniques discussed in this chapter are the foundation of concurrent processing. Semaphores are the basic mechanism underlying synchronization. From a pragmatic viewpoint, semaphores can be implemented in the OS if the hardware provides a few simple enhancements, such as the TS instruction. The straightforward implementation of a semaphore (using the TS instruction) leads to busy-waiting. This waiting can be addressed by constructing the semaphore implementation so that it interacts with the scheduler. When a process enters a phase of busy-waiting, it should yield to the scheduler.

This chapter set the foundation of synchronization and discussed the complexity of dealing with synchronization using semaphores. The next chapter looks at synchronization abstractions.

8.6 ■ Exercises

1. Suppose processes p_0 and p_1 share variable V_2, processes p_1 and p_2 share variable V_0, and processes p_2 and p_3 share variable V_1.

   a. Show how the processes can use enableInterrupt and disableInterrupt to coordinate access to V_0, V_1, and V_2 so that the critical section problem does not occur.

   b. Show how the processes can use semaphores to coordinate access to V_0, V_1, and V_2 so that the critical section problem does not occur.

2. Enabling and disabling interrupts to prevent timer interrupts from invoking the scheduler is one way to implement semaphores. This technique can influence I/O because it makes the interrupt handler wait until the interrupts become enabled before the handler can complete an I/O operation. Explain how this could affect the accuracy of the system clock.

3. The following solution is alleged to be a solution to the critical section problem. Argue for its correctness or show a case in which it fails.

```
shared int turn;
shared boolean flag[2];
proc(int i) {
   while (TRUE) {
      compute;
  /* Attempt to enter the critical section */
      try: flag[i] = TRUE; /* An atomic operation */
      while (flag[(i+1) mod 2]){ /* An atomic operation */
         if (turn == i) continue;
         flag[i] = FALSE;
         while (turn != i);
         goto try;
      }
   /* Okay to enter the critical section */
      <critical section>;
   /* Leaving critical section */
      turn = (i+1) mod 2;
      flag[i] = FALSE;
   }
}
turn = 0; /* Process 0 wins a tie for the first turn */
flag[0] = flag[1] = FALSE; /* Initialize flags before
starting */
fork(proc, 1, 0); /* Create a process to run proc(0) */
fork(proc, 1, 1); /* Create a process to run proc(1) */
```

4. Dijkstra posed each of the following solutions as a potential software solution to the critical section problem and then explained why they failed [Dijkstra, 1968]. Provide your explanation about why they failed.

   a.

```
int turn;
  proc(int i) {
    while (TRUE) {
       compute;
       while (turn != i);
       critical_section;
       turn = (i+1) mod 2;
    }
  }
turn = 1;
fork(proc, 1, 0);
fork(proc, 1, 1);
```

b.

```
boolean flag[2];
proc(int i) {
  while (TRUE) {
    compute;
    while (flag[(i+1) mod 2]);
    flag[i] = TRUE;
    critical_section;
    flag[i] = FALSE;
  }
}
flag[0] = flag[1] = FALSE;
fork(proc, 1, 0);
fork(proc, 1, 1);
```

c.

```
boolean flag[2];
proc(int i) {
  while (TRUE) {
    compute;
    flag[i] = TRUE;
    while (flag[(i+1) mod 2]);
    critical_section;
    flag[i] = FALSE;
  }
}
flag[0] = flag[1] = FALSE;
fork(proc, 1, 0);
fork(proc, 1, 1);
```

5. In the solution to the bounded buffer problem provided in Figure 8.14, it was argued that the order of the P(full) and the P(mutex) instructions was important. Does the same argument hold for the order of the V(mutex) and the V(full) instructions at the end of the loop?

6. Assume the writePending semaphore was omitted from Figure 8.16. Describe a simple sequence of reader and writer activity that causes the solution to fail for the second readers-writers policy.

7. Two processes, p_1 and p_2, have been designed so that p_2 prints a byte stream produced by p_1. Write a skeleton for the procedures executed by p_1 and p_2 to illustrate how they synchronize with one another using P and V.

8. The following is alleged to be a solution to the critical section problem. Argue for its correctness or show a case in which it fails.

```
shared int turn;  /* shared variable to synchronize
                     operation */
boolean flag[2]; /* shared variable to synchronize
                     operation */
proc(int i){
  while (TRUE) {
    <compute>;
    flag[i] = TRUE; /* Attempt to enter the critical
                       section */
    turn = (i+1) mod 2;
    while ((flag[(i+1) mod 2]) && (turn == (i+1) mod 2));
  /* Now authorized to enter the critical section
    <critical_section>;
  /* Exiting the critical section */
    flag[i] = FALSE;
  }
}
turn = 0;
flag[0] = flag[1] = FALSE;
fork(proc, 1, 0); /* Start a process on proc(0) */
fork(proc, 1, 1); /* Start a process on proc(1) */
```

9. *The Sleepy Barber Problem* [Dijkstra, 1968]. A barbershop is designed so that there is a private room that contains the barber chair and an adjoining waiting room with a sliding door that contains N chairs. If the barber is busy, the door to the private room is closed and arriving customers sit in one of the available chairs. If a customer enters the shop and all chairs are occupied, the customer leaves the shop without a haircut. If there are no customers to be served, the barber goes to sleep in the barber chair with the door to the waiting room open. If the barber is asleep, the customer wakes the barber and obtains a haircut. Write code fragments to define synchronization schemes for the customers and the barber.

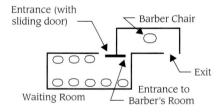

10. *The Dining Philosophers Problem.* Suppose five philosophers are seated around a table on which are placed five plates of pasta and five forks [Dijkstra, 1968]. While the philosophers think, they ignore the pasta and do not require a fork. When a philosopher decides to eat, he or she must obtain two forks, one from the left of the plate and one from the right of the plate. To make the analogy fit the behavior of sequential processes, assume a philosopher can pick up only a single fork at one time. After consuming food, the philosopher replaces the forks and resumes think-

ing. A philosopher to the left or right of a dining philosopher cannot eat while the dining philosopher is eating, since forks are a shared resource. The following code segment was posed as a scheme for synchronizing the actions of the philosophers. Argue for its correctness or provide a scenario in which it fails.

```
semaphore fork[5];
philosopher(int i){
    while (TRUE) {
    // Think
    // Eat
        P(fork[i]);
          P(fork[(i+1) mod 5]);
            eat();
          V(fork[(i+1) mod 5]);
        V(fork[i]);
    }
}
fork[0] = fork[1] = fork[2] = fork[3] = fork[4] = 1;
fork(philosopher, 1, 0);
fork(philosopher, 1, 1);
fork(philosopher, 1, 2);
fork(philosopher, 1, 3);
fork(philosopher, 1, 4);
```

11. Suppose a two-way (two-lane) north-south road contains a one-lane tunnel. A southbound (or northbound) car can use the tunnel only if there are no oncoming cars when the car arrives at the entrance to the tunnel. Because of accidents, a signaling system has been installed at the entrances to the tunnel. When a car approaches the tunnel, a sensor notifies the controller computer by calling a function named `arrive` and passes it a parameter indicating the car's direction of travel. When a car exits the tunnel, the sensor again notifies the tunnel controller computer by calling a function named `depart` (again, with the direction of travel passed as a parameter). The traffic controller computer sets signal lights: Green means proceed and red means stop. Construct a software skeleton for controlling the lights so that they operate correctly even when most cars approach the tunnel from one direction.

12. Provide a scenario in which a process executing the V procedure in Figure 8.19 will detect when `s.value` is less than or equal to 0 and then `s.hold` is TRUE.

13. Suppose a machine's instruction set includes an instruction named `swap` that operates as follows (as an indivisible instruction):

```
swap(boolean *a, boolean *b)
{
    boolean t;
    t = *a;
    *a = *b;
    *b = t;
}
```

Show how `swap` can be used to implement the `P` and `V` operations.

14. Semaphores are not implemented in older versions of UNIX, but processes with `stdout` of one process directed into `stdin` must synchronize their operation in a manner similar to that required in Problem 7. Write a program, `Source`, that copies a file to `stdout` and another program, `Sink`, that reads `stdin` and counts the number of bytes in the stream. Run `Source` and `Sink` with the output from `Source` piped into the input of `Sink`. How are the processes synchronized in your software?

9

High-level Synchronization

At the highest level, the description is greatly chunked, and takes
on a completely different feel, despite the fact that many of the
same concepts appear on the lowest and highest levels.

—Douglas R. Hofstadter, *Gödel, Escher,*
Bach: An Eternal Golden Band ■

CHAPTER OBJECTIVES

Semaphores capture the essence of process synchronization, but there are many
popular alternatives and abstractions of semaphores. This chapter considers alternative synchronization primitives, including UNIX signals, which are simple
abstractions of semaphores. At the most abstract level, it considers the monitor
mechanism for sharing and synchronization. Finally, it addresses generalized interprocess communication mechanisms that implement information transmission in
conjunction with synchronization. All modern operating systems provide semaphores or (more likely) at least one of the synchronization mechanisms described
in this chapter.

9.1 ■ Alternative Synchronization Primitives

Semaphores are invaluable in the study of the fundamental concepts of synchronization. However, as demonstrated in examples such as the readers-writers problems, they can sometimes be difficult to use as parallel applications increase in sophistication. The distinction between active and passive V implementations introduces another level of subtlety to synchronization scenarios. A number of alternatives and generalizations to semaphores have been described in the literature. Before you begin studying a few of these alternatives, it is useful to observe that they generally provide a more convenient mechanism for accomplishing various types of synchronization. However, they do *not* allow programmers to solve problems that are impossible to solve using only semaphores. This section discusses two simple alternatives to semaphores to achieve synchronization: (1) AND synchronization and (2) events.

9.1.1 ■ AND Synchronization

In many parallel programs, processes need to synchronize on some *set* of conditions rather than on a single condition. For example, suppose that two shared resources, R_1 and R_2, can be accessed by a community of processes, $\{p_i\}$. Some of the processes need only R_1 and others need only R_2. However, some processes require exclusive access to R_1 and R_2 at the same time. Using semaphores, we can write a code segment such as

```
P(mutex_j);
   <access R_j>
V(mutex_j);
```

each time a process wants to access R_j (j is either 1 or 2).

However, suppose a process, p_r, needs to access both resources. Suppose further that p_r simply nests P operations on both semaphores, as shown in Figure 9.1(a), while p_s arbitrarily nests P operations on the same two semaphores in the opposite order, as shown in Figure 9.1(b). The result can be a deadlock. Suppose p_r obtains `mutex_1` at the same time p_s obtains `mutex_2`. In this special case, p_r holds `mutex_1` and blocks waiting for `mutex_2`, while p_s holds `mutex_2` and blocks waiting for `mutex_1`. The problem arises because sometimes only one of the semaphores should be used, sometimes the other

Figure 9.1
Nesting Semaphore Operations

p_r **P Operation Order**

```
P(mutex_1);
   P(mutex_2);
      <access R_1>;
      <access R_2>;
   V(mutex_2);
V(mutex_1);
```

(a)

p_s **P Operation Order**

```
P(mutex_2);
   P(mutex_1);
      <access R_1>;
      <access R_2>;
   V(mutex_1);
V(mutex_2);
```

(b)

Figure 9.2
Simultaneous Semaphores

```
semaphore mutex = 1; /* Shared variables */
semaphore block = 0;

P.sim(int S, int R) {          V.sim(int S, int R) {
  P(mutex);                      P(mutex);
    S = S - 1;                     S = S + 1;
    R = R - 1;                     R = R + 1;
    if((S<0) || (R<0)) {          if(((S>=0) &&
      V(mutex);                         R>=0)) &&
      P(block);                       ((S==0) || (R==0))
    }                             )
    else                            V(block);
      V(mutex);                   V(mutex);
}                              }
```

semaphore should be used, and sometimes both should be used. Unfortunately, different programs can be written by different programmers to obtain the semaphores in an arbitrary pattern.

Suppose a single P operation could be used to obtain all required semaphores at once or none of them at all. The call would block the calling process whenever any of the semaphores could not be obtained. This *simultaneous P,* or *AND synchronization,* has the form

$$P_{simultaneous}(S_1, \ldots, S_n)$$

Figure 9.2 illustrates one possible implementation of $P_{simultaneous}(S_1, \ldots, S_n)$ for $n = 2$ semaphores. Notice that the simultaneous semaphore is a simple abstraction of the basic semaphore—it is a procedure implemented in terms of the basic semaphore. Also, the basic semaphore can be thought of as an abstraction of software solution to the basic synchronization problem—it simplifies the problem through the use of an abstract tool. Similarly, the simultaneous semaphore is merely a programming convenience to allow the concurrent programmer to solve a recurring synchronization problem using a single concept.

The simultaneous semaphore is an abstraction of the basic semaphore. Like the other mechanisms described in this chapter, whether a simultaneous semaphore mechanism is considered to be "primitive" depends on how it is implemented. If it is implemented using a technique similar to the one explained in Figure 9.2, then it is an abstraction that can be implemented in a library routine. If it is implemented in the operating system—for example, by using a code segment with TS instructions—it can be construed as a synchronization primitive.

9.1.2 ■ Events

Some operating systems use *events* as abstractions of semaphore operations, particularly to address the coordination applications for semaphores (as opposed to the critical section problems). An event represents the occurrence of some condition in the software. If one process needs to synchronize its operation on the occurrence of an event, it can block itself until the event occurs. When the event occurs, another process can have the OS inform the blocked process of the occurrence. Thus an event is analogous to a semaphore, waiting for an event is analogous to the P operation, and noting the occurrence of an event is analogous to the V operation.

This is an area of operating systems in which different OS designers have used the same name to implement slightly different variations of the same basic notion. All of these operating systems represent an event that uses a system data structure called an *event descriptor* (or *event control block* or other similar name). The exact semantics of event behavior vary among implementations. The most prevalent event implementations strongly resemble an implementation of semaphores with an active V implementation. If two or more processes synchronize on an event, then they both have a way of referencing the same event descriptor. The event `wait` operation blocks the calling process until another process performs a `signal` operation. The `signal` operation resumes exactly one waiting process if any are suspended on the event by a `wait` call. If no processes are waiting when the `signal` is issued, it is ignored. Hence, a major distinction between events and semaphores is that if no process is waiting, the result of the `signal` operation is not saved and its occurrence will have no effect. It is convenient to add a third function to the event management set, `queue`, to return the number of processes currently waiting for an event.

The rationale for these semantics is that a signal should represent the situation that an event has just occurred, not that it occurred some time in the past. If another process detects this occurrence at an arbitrary time later (as is the case with the passive semaphore operations) the causal relationships among calls to the `signal` and `wait` functions are lost. These semantics are reconsidered in the discussion of monitors in Section 9.2.

➤ IN THE HANGAR

Using Events

Suppose an event, `topOfHour`, has been declared. Then

```
topOfHour.signal();
```

means that a process calls the signal procedure for the `topOfHour` event. Another process using the `topOfHour` event can block on the event with a call such as

```
topOfHour.wait();
```

Now suppose several processes wish to suspend themselves until a certain time (say an exact hour such as 1:00:00 or 2:00:00). Each process calls `topOfHour.wait()` sometime after the last time the event has occurred (after the last hour) but before the next occurrence. This causes all such processes to be enqueued on the `topOfHour` event. Meanwhile, another process, written in the form shown in Figure 9.3, reads the system clock to determine when the time reaches the predefined time (the top of the hour in the example). When the clock-reading process detects that the time is right, it signals all the enqueued processes to occur concurrently. (Of course, the scheduling strategy will influence the accuracy of this solution, although the intent is that they run as soon as possible after the event has occurred.)

Figure 9.3
Code Skeleton for Signaling Process

```
/* Clock reader process */
...
while(TRUE) {
  if(isTopOfHour())
    while(topOfHour.queue() >0)
      topOfHour.signal();
}
...
```

➤ *IN THE HANGAR*

UNIX Signals

A UNIX *signal* is a mechanism by which the OS can inform user-space code of the occurrence of some event. A signal can be "raised" by one process, thus causing another process to be interrupted and to (optionally) "catch" the signal by executing prespecified code for the signal. Hence, signal implementations are likely to use a trap instruction if the host hardware supports it. A signal is most often used by an OS process to notify an application process that some event has occurred. It frequently represents the occurrence of a hardware event, such as a user's pressing the delete key or the CPU's detecting an attempt to divide by zero. Signals also may be used to notify a process of the existence of a software condition. For example, an OS daemon may notify a user process that its write on a pipe cannot succeed, since the reader of the pipe had been deleted.

Signals also can be used among application-level processes. Each signal has a type (called a "name") associated with it. There are 31 different types built into contemporary UNIX systems (including Linux), although the signal types differ in BSD UNIX (FreeBSD), AT&T System V Release 4 (SVR4), POSIX, and ANSI C. In each version, the system include file, signal.h, defines a number of symbolic names for the signal types. For example, all versions of UNIX define the SIGINT signal type, which is raised by the terminal driver when the user has pressed the terminal interrupt character, usually DELETE or control-C. Application programmers are not allowed to create new signals. But most versions of UNIX include SIGUSR1 and SIGUSR2, which can be used for application-to-application signaling.

A signal is raised by calling the `kill` function and identifying the process to receive the signal and the signal type. Essentially, a receiving application process can cause a signal to be handled in the default way, to be ignored, or to be caught by user-defined code. The UNIX `signal` function is called to identify the signal number and the way the signal is to be treated. For example, to ignore the `SIGALRM` signal, the process must execute the system call

```
signal(SIGALRM, SIG_IGN);
```

The default handling can be reinvoked by calling `signal` again with the `SIG_DFL` value. The application can process the alarm signal with its own code by supplying a function (that takes an integer argument and returns a void) as the second argument to `signal`.

Figure 9.4 is a complete C program illustrating how a signal handler is registered with the `signal` function call, the form of the signal handler routine itself, and how the whole mechanism operates. This code segment is pedagogic in that it illustrates how signals are raised and caught but does not implement any useful function. In the example code, we create a single signal handler, `sig_handler`, that is used by a parent and child process with the two calls to signal. Next, the example code determines its own process identifier using the `getpid` system call. It then creates a child so that the parent knows both the parent and child process identifiers, but the child knows only the parent's identifier. The child process sends a `SIGUSR1` to the parent and then enters a busy-wait that so it will still exist when the parent sends signals to the child. The parent sends a `SIGUSR2` to the child, followed by a termination signal (`SIGTERM`), and calls `wait` to obtain the report that the child has been terminated. The child and parent use the same signal handler definition, although the child will never see the `SIGUSR1`; nor will the parent see a signal for `SIGUSR2`.

Figure 9.4
UNIX Signal Handler

```
#include <signal.h>
static void sig_handler(int);
int main (void){
   int i, parent_pid, child_pid, status;
/* Prepare the sig_handler routine to catch SIGUSR1 and
   SIGUSR2 */
   if (signal(SIGUSR1, sig_handler)==SIG_ERR)
      printf("Parent: Unable to create handler for
            SIGUSR1\n");
   if (signal(SIGUSR2, sig_handler)==SIG_ERR)
      printf("Parent: Unable to create handler for
            SIGUSR2\n");
   parent_pid = getpid();
```

```
    if ((child_pid = fork())==0) {
      kill(parent_pid, SIGUSR1); /* Raise the SIGUSR1 signal */
      for (;;) pause(); /* Child process busy waiting for a
                           signal */
    } else {
      kill(child_pid, SIGUSR2); /* Parent raising SIGUSR2
                                   signal */
      printf("Parent: Terminating child ...");
      kill(child_pid, SIGTERM); /* Parent raising SIGTERM
                                   signal */
      wait(&status); /* Parent waiting for the child
                        termination */
      printf("done\n");
    }
}

static void sig_handler(int signo){
    switch (signo) {
    case SIGUSR1: /* Incoming SIGUSR1 signal */
        printf("Parent: Received SIGUSR1\n");
        break;
    case SIGUSR2: /* Incoming SIGUSR2 signal */
        printf("Child: Received SIGUSR2\n");
        break;
    default: break; /* Should never get this case */
    }
    return;
}
```

➤ IN THE HANGAR

Windows NT Dispatcher Objects

Every Windows NT OS object that is built using a class of objects called *dispatcher objects* contains a state variable that allows the object to be in either a *signaled* or *nonsignaled* state. For example, when a process or thread is running, the object is in the nonsignaled state, but when it terminates its dispatcher object component transitions to a signaled state. Various other operations can also cause the object state to transition. Software can synchronize its behavior by testing the state of the object using one of the Win32 API *wait* functions (the `WaitForSingle-Object` and the `WaitForMultipleObjects`). The wait functions use a handle to access an OS object and to test its state. If the target object is in the signaled state, the wait function returns to the caller. If the target object is in the nonsignaled state, the wait function blocks the calling thread until one of a set of conditions is met (for example, the object transitions to the signaled state, or a time-out interval for the call expires). On return from the function call, the calling thread is once again made runnable.

What causes an object to transition from one state to the other? In some cases the transition is caused as a side effect of other activity by the object, and sometimes the transition is accomplished through explicit actions. Objects whose primary purpose is something other than synchronization (for example, process, thread, and file objects) have implicit state transitions. Objects intended explicitly for synchronization have a spectrum of ways to cause state changes (which is why Windows NT provides more than one type of synchronization object). A typical sequence for controlling a child thread might appear as follows:

```
childThreadHandle = CreateThread( ...);
/* The child and parent threads continue concurrently */
...
/* The parent needs to wait for the child to terminate */
WaitForSingleHandle(childThreadHandle, INFINITE);
CloseHandle(childThreadHandle);
```

The `WaitForSingleHandle` call provides a parameter to say which OS object it is waiting to become signaled (`childThreadHandle`), and a second (`INFINITE`) that indicates that the wait operation is not subject to a timeout (that is, the call waits for an infinite amount of time if the object does not transition to a signaled state).

9.2 ■ Monitors

Semaphore-level synchronization primitives are difficult to use for complex synchronization situations. Monitors were derived to simplify the complexity of synchronization problems by abstracting away details. However, every synchronization problem that can be solved with monitors can also be solved with semaphores, and vice versa. Monitors simply provide a simplified paradigm for synchronization that is easier to use than semaphores for many synchronization problems.

9.2.1 ■ Principles of Operation

Monitors are based on *abstract data types*—modules that encapsulate storage, private procedures for manipulating the storage, and a public interface, including procedures and type declarations, that can be used to manipulate the information in the storage. Abstract data types hide the implementation of the information manipulation. A *monitor* is an abstract data type for which only one process may be executing a procedure at any given time. Monitors are generally credited to Hoare [1974] and Brinch Hansen [1977].

Abstract data types, objects, and monitors all encourage modularization of data structures so that the implementation of the data structure is private, with a well-defined public interface. The benefits of this approach include the following:

- Other software cannot take advantage of the implementation but instead must rely on the interface.

- The implementation can evolve without the users of the data structure having to change the way they use the structure.

- Detailed manipulation of the data structure is centralized in one software module, thereby making it possible to prove properties about the behavior of the data structure.

- There is an opportunity to control how a process or thread uses the data type, since it has a specific interface.

In a multiple-process environment, it is natural to want to share abstract data types. Each of two processes may wish to call interface procedures to manipulate the abstract data type. Since the internal implementation of the abstract data type is unknown to its users, if two processes simultaneously invoke distinct public interface procedures, then any particular operation at the interface may cause inconsistent computations to occur within the abstract data type. For example, suppose an abstract data type has been defined to manage a shared variable, `balance`, and there are interface routines to "credit" values to `balance` and to "debit" values from `balance`. For the abstract data type, its `credit(J)` function will result in J's being added to the current value of the `balance` variable inside the abstract data type and `debit(K)` will result in K's being subtracted from the `balance`. No two processes should execute `credit` and `debit` concurrently, since this may result in one of the operations being lost. Monitors explicitly eliminate the concurrent access problem.

A monitor inherently incorporates a critical section into a standard abstract data type template. Figure 9.5 illustrates how a monitor might be described as a standard abstract data type (syntactically the same as a C++ class in our notation) with the private `mutex` semaphore to ensure only one process is in the monitor at a time.

Figure 9.5
Critical Section Within a Monitor

```
monitor anADT {
  semaphore mutex = 1;
  <ADT data structures>
  . . .
public:
  proc_i(...) {
    P(mutex);
      <processing for proc_i>
    V(mutex);
  };
  . . .
};
```

Figure 9.6
A Shared Variable Monitor

```
monitor sharedBalance{
   int balance;
public:
   credit(int amount) {balance = balance + amount;};
   debit(int amount)  {balance = balance-amount;};
 }
```

Now consider how a monitor can be used to manage the shared variable, `balance`. Some processes will increment the shared variable; others will want to decrement it. The monitor shown in Figure 9.6 provides `credit` and `debit` functions to change the value but protects the access to the shared variable as a critical section. Even though the assignment statements may generate a sequence of machine code, a process is guaranteed to be able to complete the full sequence of statements as a critical section, since the statements appear inside the `sharedBalance` monitor.

9.2.2 ■ Condition Variables

In many cases, as a process is executing in a monitor it will discover that it cannot proceed until some other process takes some particular action on the information protected by the monitor. For example, suppose we were to attempt to solve the second readers-writers problem using monitors, as they have been defined so far. The readers and writers have the general forms shown in Figure 9.6. Figure 9.7 shows the monitor public

Figure 9.7
Reader and Writer Schema

```
reader() {                        writer() {
  while(TRUE) {                     while(TRUE) {
    . . .                             . . .
    startRead();                      startWrite();
      <read the resource>               <write the resource>
    finishRead();                     finishWrite();
    . . .                             . . .
  }                                 }
}                                 }

fork(reader, 0);
. . .
fork(reader, 0);
fork(writer, 0);
```

Figure 9.8
A Failed Attempt to Solve a Readers-Writers Problem Using a Monitor

```
monitor readerWriter_1{
  int numberOfReaders = 0;
  int numberOfWriters = 0;
  boolean busy = FALSE;
public:
  startRead () {
    while (numberOfWriters !=0);
    numberOfReaders = numberOfReaders+1;
  };
  finishRead () {
    numberOfReaders = numberOfReaders-1;
  };
  startWrite {
    numberOfWriters = numberOfWriters+1;
    while (busy || (numberOfReaders > 0));
    busy = TRUE;
  };
  finishWrite {
    numberOfWriters = numberOfWriters-1;
    busy = FALSE;
  };
};
```

procedures—startRead, startWrite, finishRead, and finishWrite—to be executed when a reader or a writer enters and leaves the critical section.

The solution shown in Figure 9.8 fails for this reason. In the start procedures, a process will obtain exclusive access to the monitor and not relinquish it again if the critical section is currently in use, since the process will perform a busy-wait at the while loop in either procedure. As long as a process holds the monitor while waiting, it maintains exclusive control of the monitor, even to the exclusion of a process that is attempting to perform a finish operation. It is necessary to allow the waiting process to temporarily relinquish the monitor, while maintaining its intent to detect a state change in the monitor at a later time. To accommodate this type of situation, monitors incorporate condition variables.

A *condition variable* is a structure that may appear within a monitor. It is global to all procedures within the monitor and may have its value manipulated by three operations:

■ wait: Suspends the invoking process until another process performs a signal on the condition variable.

■ signal: Resumes exactly one other process if any process is currently suspended due to a wait operation on the condition variable. If no process is waiting, then the signal is not saved (and will have no effect).

■ queue: Returns a value of TRUE if there is at least one process suspended on the condition variable, and FALSE otherwise.

The behavior of the signal operation distinguishes Hoare's version of monitors from Brinch Hansen's. With Hoare's monitor semantics, if a process p_1 is waiting for the signal at the time p_0 executes it from within the monitor, p_0 is suspended while p_1 immediately begins execution within the monitor. When p_1 finishes executing in the monitor, p_0 resumes its execution in the monitor. The rationale for Hoare's approach is that a condition is true at a particular instant in time when the signal occurs, but it may not be true later—for example, when p_0 finishes with the monitor. In his original paper, Hoare uses these semantics to simplify proofs of the correct behavior of monitors.

The semantics for Brinch Hansen's monitors incorporate the "passive" approach. (These semantics are also known as Mesa monitor semantics because of their implementation in the Xerox Mesa programming language.) When p_0 executes a signal, the condition is saved while p_0 continues to execute. When p_0 leaves the monitor, p_1 will attempt to continue its execution in the monitor by rechecking the condition. This occurs because even though signal indicates an event has occurred, the situation may have changed between the time p_0 performed signal and p_1 is allocated the CPU. The argument favoring Brinch Hansen semantics is that there will be fewer context switches than with the Hoare approach. Thus overall system performance will tend to be better using the Brinch Hansen semantics.

With Hoare semantics, a situation leading to a wait operation might appear as

```
. . .
if(resourceNotAvailable) resourceCondition.wait;
/* Now available — continue ... */
. . .
```

When another process executes a resourceCondition.signal, a context switch occurs in which the blocked process gains control of the monitor and continues executing at the statement following the if statement. The signaling process is then delayed until the waiting process finishes with the monitor.

With Brinch Hansen semantics, the same situation would be encoded as

```
. . .
while(resourceNotAvailable) resourceCondition.wait;
/* Now available — continue ... */
. . .
```

This code fragment ensures that the condition (in this case, resource-NotAvailable) is retested before the process executing resourceCondition.wait precedes. No context switch occurs until the signaling process voluntarily vacates the monitor.

> *IN THE HANGAR*

We next consider a few examples using monitors that have condition variables. In these examples, we write `condition.op` to indicate that `op` is applied to the condition variable named `condition`.

A Correct Readers-Writers Solution

The readers-writers solution shown in Figure 9.8 can be modified to use condition variables so that it performs correctly, as shown in Figure 9.9. This example is taken from Hoare's paper; the strategy differs slightly from either of the Courtois-Heymans-Parnas readers-writers solutions. A reader process invokes `startRead`

Figure 9.9
Monitor for Readers-Writers Solution

```
monitor reader_writer_2{
  int numberOfReaders = 0;
  boolean busy = FALSE;
  condition okToRead, okToWrite;
public:
  startRead {
    if (busy || (okToWrite.queue)) okToRead.wait;
    numberOfReaders = numberOfReaders+1;
    okToRead.signal;
  };
  finishRead {
    numberOfReaders = numberOfReaders-1;
    if (numberOfReaders = 0) okToWrite.signal;
  };
  startWrite {
    if ((numberOfReaders != 0) || busy)
okToWrite.wait;
    busy = TRUE;
  };
  finishWrite {
    busy = FALSE;
    if (okToWrite.queue)
      okToWrite.signal
    else
      okToRead.signal;
  };
};
```

whenever it attempts to use the shared resource and `finishRead` when it has finished. Similarly, a writer uses `startWrite` and `finishWrite` to bracket its access of the shared resource. The `startRead` monitor routine waits if the critical section contains a writer (indicated by `busy`'s being `TRUE`) or if there is a writer queued on the monitor. If the reader proceeds, it increments the number of readers in the shared resource and signals other readers to proceed. When a reader finishes, it signals the writers if there are no other readers waiting. When a writer attempts to enter the critical section, it waits if there are any readers or another writer in the critical section. When a writer finishes, it signals other writers if any are waiting or else it signals the waiting readers. (In Hoare's original paper [1974], the `if` test in the `finishWrite` function is written to test the `okToRead.queue`; in compilers with lazy evaluation, this would give preference to waiting readers over waiting writers.)

Synchronizing Automobile Traffic

The exercises for Chapter 8 introduced a problem involving the synchronization of automobile traffic through a one-way tunnel. Suppose a two-way (two-lane) north-south road contains a one-lane tunnel. A southbound (or northbound) car can use the tunnel only if, when it arrives at the entrance to the tunnel, there are no oncoming cars in the tunnel. When a car approaches the tunnel, a sensor notifies the controller computer by calling a function named `northboundArrival` or `southboundArrival` depending on the direction of travel of the car. When a car exits the tunnel, the sensor again notifies the tunnel controller computer by calling a function named `depart` (this time with the direction of travel passed as a parameter). The traffic controller computer sets signal lights: Green means proceed and red means stop. Figure 9.10 is a solution to the problem using monitors.

The monitor provides three functions: `northboundArrival`, `southboundArrival`, and `depart`. When a northbound automobile arrives at the tunnel, it calls the `northboundArrival` monitor function. The function checks to see if there are any southbound automobiles in the tunnel; if so, each northbound automobile waits on the `busy` condition. Similarly, southbound automobiles wait for northbound traffic. The `depart` monitor function checks to see if the tunnel is clear. If there are waiting cars from the opposite direction, it signals all of them to proceed.

The Dining Philosophers Problem

Introduced in the exercises for Chapter 8, the dining philosophers problem represents a situation that can occur in large communities of processes that share a large pool of resources. Dijkstra [1968] originally introduced the problem as an analogy in which five philosophers spend their lives alternately thinking and eating spaghetti. Suppose the philosophers are seated around a table on which is placed five plates of pasta and five forks. While philosophers think, they ignore the pasta and do not require forks. When a philosopher decides to eat, then he or she must obtain two

Figure 9.10
Traffic Synchronization

```
monitor tunnel{
  int northbound = 0, southbound = 0;
  traffic_signal northbound_signal = RED,
                                    southbound_signal = RED;
  condition busy;
public:
  northboundArrival() { // Northbound car wants to enter the
                        // tunnel
    if(southbound > 0) busy.wait; // Southbound cars in the
                                  // tunnel
    northbound = northbound+1; // OK to proceed
    northbound_signal = GREEN;
    southbound_signal = RED;
};
  southboundArrival() { // southbound car wants to enter the
                        // tunnel
    if(northbound > 0) busy.wait; // Northbound cars in the
                                  // tunnel
    southbound = southbound+1; // OK to proceed
    southbound_signal = GREEN;
    northbound_signal = RED;
};
  depart(Direction exit) { // A car exited the tunnel
   if(exit==north) {
    northbound = northbound-1;
    if(northbound==0) while(busy.queue) busy.signal;
    else if(exit==south) {
      southbound = southbound-1;
      if(southbound==0) while(busy.queue) busy.signal;
    }
  };
};
```

forks by first picking up the right fork and then picking up the left fork. (The "two fork" style of eating spaghetti comes from Dijkstra's original presentation of the problem. Sometimes the problem is described in an analogy with noodles and chopsticks.) A philosopher can pick up only a single fork at one time. After consuming food, the philosopher replaces the forks and resumes thinking. A philosopher to the left or right of a dining philosopher cannot eat while the dining philosopher is eating, since forks are a shared resource.

Simple solutions to the problem are fraught with difficulties relating to deadlock or unsafe conditions. Monitors can be used to provide a simple solution to the dining philosophers problem (see Figure 9.11). All philosophers are initially thinking, represented by the state[i] being set to the value thinking. When philosopher *i* wishes to eat, the pickUpForks(i) monitor function is called. This function allows the process to proceed only if both adjacent forks are available; see the private function test in the monitor. The philosopher moves to the eating state only if his or her two neighbors are not in the eating state. Otherwise, the philosopher waits for a signal. Suppose the philosopher had been blocked. He or she needs to be signaled when either neighbor calls putDownForks. However, the signal should not be issued until both neighbors have left the eating state. Whenever any philosopher is hungry, he or she tests the forks of both neighbors. If both neighbors are eating and the philosopher attempts to eat, then both will have to call putDownForks before the philosopher can move from the hungry state to the eating state. This solution allows a situation in which the philosopher never obtains both forks at once, since either the left or right neighbor might always have a fork.

Figure 9.11
Monitor for the Dining Philosophers

```
#define N
enum status {eating, hungry, thinking};
monitor diningPhilosophers{
  status state[N];
  condition self[N];
  int j;
// This procedure can only be called from within the monitor
  test(int i) {
    if ((state[i-1 mod N] !=eating) &&
        (state[i]==hungry) &&
        (state[(i+1) mod N] !=eating)) {
          state[i] = eating;
          self[i].signal;
    }
  };
public:
  pickUpForks(int i) {
    state[i] = hungry;
    test(i);
  if (state[i] !=eating) self[i].wait;
};
putDownForks(int i) {
  state[i] = thinking;
  test((i-1) mod N);
  test((i+1) mod N);
};
  diningPhilosophers() { // Monitor initialization code
    for(int i=0; i<N; i++) state[i] = thinking;
  };
};
```

9.2.3 ■ Some Practical Aspects of Using Monitors

Monitors can easily be misused. Suppose we encapsulated a monitor call within a monitor—that is, we have *nested monitor calls*. There is a danger one process could hold the outer monitor while it waited for the inner monitor to become available. Of course, another process might hold an outer monitor that is the same as the inner monitor requested by the first process, while it requests an inner monitor that is the same as the outer monitor held by the first process. The result is a deadlock.

A monitor is a powerful high-level mechanism for dealing with complex synchronization problems. In general, monitors have not been widely supported by commercial operating systems. For example, UNIX does not support general monitors (though some versions support mechanisms patterned after monitors). However, monitors are a high-level language construct that are useful for solving many difficult problems and are incorporated into languages such as Ada. We expect to see high-level tools like monitors be supported in newer operating systems. Perhaps the best insight into monitors comes from the implementation of a monitor in the Xerox Mesa programming language [Lampson and Redell, 1980]. The implementation experience reported in the paper highlights the difficulty of handling the myriad of details:

> When monitors are used in real systems of any size, however, a number of problems arise which have not been adequately dealt with: the semantics of nested monitor calls; the various ways of defining the meaning of wait; priority scheduling; handling of timeouts, aborts and other exceptional conditions; interactions with process creation and destruction; monitoring large numbers of small objects. [p. 105]

OS developers have tended to avoid the complexity of implementing monitors, leaving the programmer with tools such as locks, semaphores, events, and interprocess communication to solve synchronization problems.

The popularity of implementing concurrent applications using threads running within an address space has changed the nature of the general problem. While synchronization across threads running in different address spaces is the same problem as the interprocess synchronization described previously, it is possible to capture many of the characteristics of a monitor using programmer-scheduled threads within an address space. The resulting solutions are easier to derive than semaphore-based synchronization and are easier to implement than full monitors, since the threads share a common address space and only one thread will execute in the space at a time. Basically, the approach is to allow the program controlling the address space to schedule thread executions so that a thread runs only when it cannot violate a critical section. Whereas a generic solution cannot make assumptions about the presence or absence of critical sections, thread scheduling is performed by the programmer writing the application.

9.3 ■ Interprocess Communication

Monitors allow processes to share information by using shared memory within the monitor. Semaphores and events can be used to synchronize the operation of two processes but not to convey information between them (other than the synchronization signal). Up

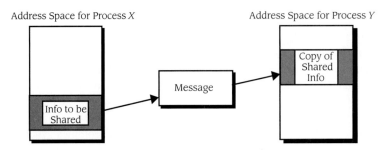

Figure 9.12
Using Messages to Share Information

to now, all the examples in which information sharing is required have assumed the existence of shared memory to accomplish the sharing. This section covers message-based *interprocess communication* (*IPC*) mechanisms as a way for one process to share information with others. A *message* is a block of information formatted by a sending process so that its syntax conveys meaning to the receiving process. A communication mechanism is explicitly intended to copy information from one address space into another process's address space using messages but without using shared memory.

Modern systems incorporate memory protection mechanisms to prevent one process from accidentally or maliciously accessing another's address space. Unfortunately, these mechanisms also disallow intentional sharing of variables between application processes. In computations in which concurrent computation is designed to operate within an address space, threads can be used to avoid the barrier between address spaces. However, if the concurrency is to be implemented across address spaces, the OS must include an additional mechanism by which it can copy information from one application's address space to another's. Applications can then use the OS as an intermediary to share information (by copying it) in these systems.

IPC abstractions are such a mechanism for enabling a process to copy information from its own address space into a message. The IPC mechanism then copies the information from the message into the receiving process's address space (see Figure 9.12). The act of copying information out of one space into a message and from the message into another address space requires that a *trusted* OS mechanism be used to violate the memory protection schemes of both processes. Sending or receiving a message involves OS intervention so that privileged instructions can be used to bypass the memory protection mechanism.

9.3.1 ■ Mailboxes

Figure 9.12 suggests that a message send operation could spontaneously change the contents of the receiving process's address space without the receiver being aware of the change. This paradigm is avoided by not actually copying the information into the receiver's space until the receiver performs an explicit message receive operation. The operating system buffers incoming messages in a mailbox prior to copying them into the

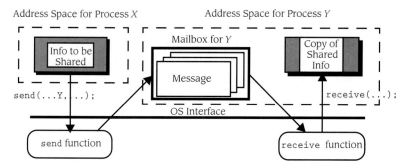

Figure 9.13
Message Passing with Mailboxes

receiver's address space. Figure 9.13 shows a more detailed view of message passing in which the operating system's role is explicit and the receiver's mailbox is identified.

Figure 9.13 shows the mailbox for process *Y*, which is located in the user space. Putting the mailbox there is a design decision for the OS designer. That is, should the mailbox be in an unused part of process *Y*'s address space, or should it be kept in the operating system's space until it is needed by process *Y*? If the mailbox is kept in the user space, then the receive call can be a library routine, since the information is being copied from one part of *Y*'s address space to another. However, the translation system (compiler and loader) will have to allocate space in each process for the mailbox. It is also possible the receiving process may inadvertently overwrite parts of the mailbox, thereby destroying links and losing messages.

The alternative is to keep *Y*'s mailbox in the system space and defer the copy operation until *Y* makes the receive call (see Figure 9.14). This option places the bur-

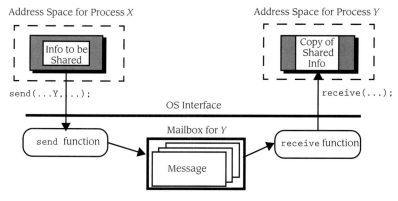

Figure 9.14
Mailboxes in System Space

den of mailbox space management on the OS. However, it also prevents inadvertent destruction of messages or headers, since the mailbox is not directly accessible to any application process. But this option requires the OS to allocate memory space for mailboxes for all processes. Thus there is a system-wide bound on the number of messages awaiting delivery at any given time. In the rest of this discussion, assume that mailboxes are implemented in the operating system, since this is the more common approach.

9.3.2 ■ Message Protocols

For a message to have meaning to the receiving process, it is formatted by a sending process. Furthermore, there must be a *protocol* between the sender and the receiver by which both agree on this message format. For example, the message may contain an instance of a C structure with the understanding that both processes have access to a common header file defining the structure. The message could also be a string of ASCII characters to be decoded by the receiver using a library routine such as scanf.

Most message-passing facilities employ a header for the message. This header, which is understood by all processes in the system, identifies various pieces of information relating to the message, including the sending process's identification, the receiving process's identification, and the number of bytes of information being transmitted in the body of the message. In robust message-passing systems, the message may even have a type, which can be used to identify messages containing specialized information such as synchronization information and error reporting. At the other end of the spectrum are IPC mechanisms (such as UNIX) in which no header or other structuring information is provided by the OS. Instead the cooperating processes choose and implement their own protocol.

9.3.3 ■ Using the send and receive Operations

There are two general options for using the send and receive operations:

- The send operation may use synchronous or asynchronous semantics.
- The receive operation may use blocking or nonblocking semantics.

9.3.3.1 ■ The send Operation

The send call may be synchronous or asynchronous, depending on whether the sender wishes to synchronize its own operation with the receipt of the message. The *asynchronous* send operation delivers the message to the receiver's mailbox and then allows the sending process to continue operation without waiting for the receiver to read the message. A sender that performs an asynchronous send operation is not concerned with *when* the receiver actually received the message. In fact, the sender will not even know whether the receiver ever retrieves the message from its mailbox.

The *synchronous* `send` operation incorporates a built-in synchronization strategy. It blocks the sending process until the message has been successfully received by the destination process. If the message is enqueued in a mailbox, the process transmitting the message using a synchronous `send` operation will be blocked until the receiving process actually retrieves the message from the mailbox. Message transmission uses the same basic cooperation paradigm as all other producer-consumer computations. The sender is a producer, and the receiver is a consumer. Think of a semaphore, `messageReceived` (initially 0), being used to coordinate the sender and receiver. The synchronous send operation acts as if the transmission were immediately followed by a `P(messageReceived)`. The corresponding `V(messageReceived)` implicitly occurs when the receiver accepts the message.

Either the synchronous or asynchronous `send` operation can fail in various situations. If the sender attempts to transmit a message to a nonexistent process, the OS will not be able to identify a mailbox in which to buffer the message. How should this situation be handled? In the case of a synchronous `send` operation, an error is returned to the sender so that it synchronizes with the occurrence of the error condition rather than with the completion of message transmission. In the case of an asynchronous `send` operation, the sender continues after "transmitting" the message and does not expect any return value. Without a mechanism such as UNIX signals, there is no way for the OS to inform the sending process that its operation failed. Therefore some systems block on an asynchronous `send` operation until the message is actually placed in the receiver's mailbox. However, there is no implied synchronization between the sending and receiving processes, since the receiver may read the mailbox at any arbitrary time after the message has been delivered.

9.3.3.2 ■ The `receive` Operation

A `receive` operation can be blocking or nonblocking. A *blocking* `receive` operation behaves like a normal file read operation in UNIX or Windows NT. That is, when a process calls `receive`, if there is no message in the mailbox, the process suspends operation until a message is placed in the mailbox. If the mailbox contains one or more messages, the blocking `receive` operation returns immediately with a message. Thus when the mailbox is empty, the blocking `receive` operation synchronizes the receiver's operation with that of the sending process. According to the synchronization paradigm, it is as if the receiver executes a `P(messageTransmitted)` on a semaphore with initial value of 0 before receiving the message. The synchronization is completed when the sender implicitly executes a `V(messageTransmitted)` when the message is sent. Observe that the `receive` operation is also analogous to a resource request in the sense that it causes the calling process to suspend until the resource, an incoming message, is available.

A *nonblocking* `receive` operation queries the mailbox and then returns control to the calling process immediately, either with a message if there is one in the mailbox or with an indicator that no message is available. This method allows a receiving process to poll the mailbox, but, if there is no pending message, to continue with other work. The receiver can still synchronize with a message from the sender, but it is not required to do so.

➤ IN THE HANGAR

Synchronized IPC

Two processes, p_1 and p_2, can copy information back and forth and synchronize their operation using synchronous `send` and blocking `receive` operations. In Figure 9.15, process p_1 sends $message_1$ to p_2 in an attempt to signal its intent to synchronize. If p_2 has already performed the `blockReceive` (blocking receive) operation, it is asleep, awaiting a message. If there were other messages in the mailbox, it will have done its side of the synchronization with the senders of those messages. Assuming p_2's mailbox was empty at the time p_1 sent $message_1$, process p_2 will be awakened by the incoming message and p_1 will resume as a result of the message having been received. At this point, p_1 and p_2 are synchronized. After the message has been received by p_2, the two processes proceed independently. When they wish to synchronize again, they follow the protocol by which the processes have been constructed: p_2 takes the initiative to transmit the synchronizing signal by sending $message_2$ to p_1, then p_1 cooperates in the synchronization by performing a `blockReceive` operation to wait for p_2's signal.

Figure 9.15
Synchronizing Using Messages

Process p_1

```
. . .
/* Signal p₂ for sync*/
syncSend(message₁, p₂);
. . .
/* Wait for p₂ signal */
blockReceive(msgBuffer,from);
. . .
```

Process p_2

```
. . .
/* Wait for p₁ signal */
blockReceive(msgBuffer, from)
. . .
/* Sync with p₁ */
syncSend(message₂, p₁);
. . .
```

9.3.4 ■ Deferred Message Copying

Message copying can become a major performance bottleneck, since the information must be copied from the sender's address space, first into a message and then into the receiver's address space. In concurrent applications in which processes pass messages almost as often as they call functions, the OS spends a significant fraction of its service time copying messages from user space to the message and copying the message contents into the receiver's address space.

In contemporary systems that have a single physical memory (independent of the number of CPUs), the *copy-on-write* optimization is often incorporated into the system. In many instances, information sent from one address space to another will be read by the receiver but never modified by either the sender or receiver. If the OS can override the memory protection mechanism, it can use copy-on-write message semantics to reduce the number of times a message is copied. When the sender identifies a block of memory in its address space as the source of the message, rather than copying the buffered information into a message, the OS constructs a pointer from the mailbox area to the buffered information. When the message is received, the OS copies the pointer, rather than the whole message, into the receiver's address space so that it can directly reference the information in the sender's buffer area. As long as the buffered information is not changed, both processes can read the information without either interfering with the other. However, if either attempts to *write* the information, the OS intervenes. It copies the information from the sender's buffer area into the private part of the receiver's address space so that each has its own copy and so that the effect of the write (by either process) will not be perceived by the other one.

9.4 ■ Explicitly Ordering Event Execution

Section 8.2 briefly considered using process creation/destruction as a mechanism for achieving synchronization. It was ignored for several years, however, because of the relatively high cost of creation/deletion compared with the use of semaphores. In the late 1970s, researchers began to note that synchronization can also be achieved by placing *precedence* on the occurrence of the set of all "important" events occurring in the collective processes. This is not as expensive as full creation/destruction, but it uses a philosophy to achieve coordination that is closer to creation/destruction than to semaphores. It has an added benefit of not requiring that synchronization be implemented using shared memory (for example, to store a semaphore, event control block, or monitor). The basic idea behind this technique is to determine ahead of time what the synchronization points should be for the execution of the processes to map these points into recognizable events, and then to specify the order of occurrence of the events according to the desired synchronization plan. Even though we coordinate the processes's activity according to event occurrence, we do not use event control blocks to record the occurrences.

For example, if event x in p_i cannot be allowed to occur until event y has occurred in p_j, then one could require that

$$(\text{occurrence of } y \text{ in } p_j) < (\text{occurrence of } x \text{ in } p_i)$$

be a constraint on the operation of p_i and p_j (the "$<$" symbol means y occurs in p_j before x occurs in p_i). Notice that many processes, p_k, are unconcerned about the occurrence of x and y. Thus proper operation of p_i could then be defined by specifying a *partial order* on all events in all the processes. For example, this technique involves *eventcounts*—integer variables, initially with a value of 0, that take on a strictly increasing set of nonnegative values [Reed and Kanodia, 1979]. An eventcount can be manipulated only by the following functions:

- `advance`: The `advance(evnt)` function announces the occurrence of an event related to the eventcount event, thus causing it to be incremented by 1.
- `await`: The `await(evnt, v)` causes the calling process to block as long as evnt $<$ v.

An eventcount can be thought of as a global clock ticking at each occurrence of the event through the explicit execution of an `advance` call. A process synchronizes with the global clock using the `await` call by blocking until the global clock reaches a predefined time—that is, until there have been "v" advance calls.

It is interesting to note that `advance` and `await` are not required to be implemented as indivisible operations, as is the case with semaphore functions. If a process is interrupted during the execution of `advance`, it is important only that the function ultimately runs to completion and increments the appropriate eventcount. Similarly, `await` does not prescribe exactly when a calling event is to be blocked but, rather, stipulates a lower bound; interruption does not make the function fail.

Another interesting characteristic of eventcounts is that they can be implemented by replicating the eventcount in different machines on a network, thereby eliminating the need for shared memory. The exact technique to do this is an advanced OS topic inspired by theoretical work on global clocks by Lamport [1978].

With the eventcount primitive, many synchronization problems can be solved. However, the primitive is not complete enough to solve all such problems. The generalization requires a read primitive as well as a companion primitive abstract data type called a *sequencer.* The sequencer is an advanced operating systems topic derived by Reed and Kanodia [1979] in their extension of eventcounts (see their paper for an explanation of sequencers).

Figure 9.16 demonstrates how eventcounts can be used to solve the bounded buffer problem (ignoring the critical section to manipulate buffers in the semaphore solution). The producer and consumer each maintain a private integer counter, *i*, used to select an eventcount value for synchronization. When the processes are initiated, the

Figure 9.16
Producer-Consumer Solution Using Precedence

```
producer() {                              consumer() {
/* i establishes local order */           /* i establishes local order */
  int i = 1;                                int i = 1;
  while(TRUE) {                             while(TRUE) {
  /* Stay N-1 ahead of consumer */         /* Stay N-1 behind producer */
    await(out, i-N);                         await(in, i);
    produce(buffer[(i-1) mod N]);            consume(buffer[(I-1) mod N];
  /* Signal a full buffer */               /* Signal an empty buffer */
    advance(in);                             advance(out);
    i = i+1;                                 i = i+1;
  }                                         }
}                                         }

eventcount in=0, out=0;
struct buffer[N];

fork(producer, 0);
fork(consumer, 0);
```

producer has N empty buffers and the consumer has no full buffers. The value $i - N$ in the producer initially takes on the value $-(N-1)$, thus causing the `await` call in the producer to block only when `out` (initially 0) is less than $-(N-1)$, a nonpositive number initially. Thus for $N \geq 1$, the producer passes through the `await` call, produces a buffer, and then advances the `in` eventcount. Meanwhile, the consumer will have encountered `await` with `in` initially set to 0 and `I` initially set to 1. It will have blocked until `in` is advanced. Just as the processes use `in` to establish a total order on the events related to the manipulation of the full buffers, they use `out` to establish a total order on the events related to the manipulation of the empty buffers. However, there is no specific ordering on the individual events within the two sets. The producer may periodically have many full buffers waiting for the consumer and at other times be blocking the consumer.

9.5 ■ Summary

Semaphores provide the fundamental mechanism to achieve synchronization, although they may be difficult to use to solve complex synchronization problems. Alternative primitives for semaphores include UNIX signals, the simultaneous P operation, and eventcounts. These mechanisms are simple abstractions of semaphores and thus invite many of the same criticisms. Monitors are a high-level language primitive for accomplishing information sharing and synchronization. They have a strong camp of followers but do not appear in many contemporary operating systems due to implementation complexities.

Interprocess communication abstracts synchronization to a level where the synchronization mechanism can also carry information among cooperating processes. IPC mechanisms enable processes to transmit messages among themselves. A message is a block of information copied from one process's address space indirectly into another. The sender and the receiver agree on the format of the message. Send operations may be synchronous or asynchronous, with the former enabling the sender to synchronize its operation with the receiver. Receive operations can be blocking or nonblocking. A blocking receive causes the receiver process to synchronize with a sending process in the case that the receive is executed prior to the corresponding send. Pipes are the analog of mailboxes in UNIX systems.

Eventcounts are based on events and the precedence that must occur on event occurrences for proper operation among a community of processes. Neither IPC nor eventcounts rely on shared memory, unlike the other synchronization mechanisms.

This chapter completes the discussion of synchronization. The next chapter looks at the fundamental aspects of deadlock, particularly at the level of abstraction used by a resource manager.

9.6 ■ Exercises

1. Suppose processes p_0 and p_1 share variable V_2, processes p_1 and p_2 share variable V_0, and processes p_2 and p_3 share variable V_1. In addition, p_0, p_1, and p_2 run concurrently. Write a code fragment (similar to those in the figures in this chapter) to

illustrate how the processes can use monitors to coordinate access to V_0, V_1, and V_2 so that the critical section problem does not occur.

2. Suppose process p_0 uses variables V_0 and V_1 at the same time, process p_1 uses variables V_1 and V_2 at the same time, and process p_2 uses variables V_2 and V_0 at the same time. Further, p_0, p_1, and p_2 run concurrently. Write a code fragment using the simultaneous semaphore operations to coordinate access to V_0, V_1, and V_2 so that the critical section problem does not occur.

3. Construct a monitor that implements semaphores. This will demonstrate that a monitor can be used any place a semaphore can be used.

4. *The Sleepy Barber Problem.* A barbershop is designed so that there is a private room that contains the barber chair and an adjoining waiting room with a sliding door that contains N chairs (see the diagram in Exercise 9 in Chapter 8). If the barber is busy, the door to the private room is closed and arriving customers sit in one of the available chairs. If a customer enters the barbershop and all chairs are occupied, the customer leaves the shop without a haircut. If there are no customers to be served, the barber goes to sleep in the barber chair with the door to the waiting room open. If the barber is asleep, the customer wakes the barber and obtains a haircut. Write a monitor to coordinate the barber and the customers.

5. Give an example of a concurrent application in which a sender process could use an asynchronous rather than a synchronous `send` operation. Provide another scenario in which the sender should use a synchronous `send` operation in order for the application to operate properly.

6. Explain why a concurrent application written using nonblocking message receive operations could require less real time to execute than if it were written using blocking receive operations. Also explain why the approach requiring less real time may be complex to construct.

7. Programmer-scheduled thread packages allow the programmer to control when each thread is executed and when it must wait. Calls to the thread package (executed by a thread) allow the programmer to schedule other threads. Explain how this type of control mechanism can be used to approximate the behavior of condition variables in a monitor for thread synchronization.

8. The Mach C threads and POSIX C threads libraries incorporate thread spawn operations to create a new thread within a process's address space (example C thread code appears in Chapter 2). Read the documentation on either package and compare the spawn operation with the UNIX `fork` operation. Explain how threads synchronize when a child thread exits.

9. Construct a C/C++ program for a UNIX environment to use the *trapezoidal rule* to approximate the integral of

$$f(x) = 1/(x+1)$$

for the interval [0, 2]. This approximation to an integral is called *numerical quadrature*. Construct your solution so that you compute the areas of n small trapezoids by N individual worker processes. The controller process should spawn N worker processes using the `fork` and `exec` UNIX system calls. There should be one pipe with which all N worker processes send results to the controller and N pipes the controller uses to assign a trapezoid to a worker process. Whenever a worker process is ready to compute the area for another trapezoid, it sends the controller a result on the shared "input" pipe. When the controller process receives all the sums from the worker processes, it sums them and prints the answer, along with the amount of time required to obtain the solution, and ignoring the time to set up the processes and the pipes. Experiment with various values of N between 1 and 8 for $n = 64$ trapezoids. Use a `getTime()` routine (see the exercises in Chapter 1) to instrument your program so that you can measure the amount of time spent processing your code. Include a suitably large `for` loop in your procedure to evaluate the area of a trapezoid so that you can measure the time to accomplish the computation. Plot the amount of time versus the value of N used in the approximation.

10. Solve the quadrature problem in the previous exercise using your local (C or POSIX) threads library. Example C thread code appears in Chapter 2.

11. *Successive overrelaxation* (SOR) is a method to solve linear $n \times n$ systems of equations, $Ax = b$ (see the example in Section 8.1). Given the coefficient matrix A, the right-side vector b, and an initial estimated solution vector x, the algorithm recomputes each x_i based on the x_j $(i \neq j)$, A, and b. First, write the n equations as

$$a_{11}x_1 + a_{12}x_2 + \ldots + a_{1n}x_n = b_1$$
$$a_{21}x_1 + a_{22}x_2 + \ldots + a_{2n}x_n = b_2$$
$$\ldots$$
$$a_{n1}x_1 + a_{n2}x_2 + \ldots + a_{nn}x_n = b_n$$

Arbitrarily use the ith equation to solve for x_i, yielding

$$x_i = (b_i - a_{i1}x - a_{i2}x_2 - \ldots - a_{in}x_n)/a_{ii}.$$

Now one can implement SOR on an n process system by having the ith process compute x_i. Implement an SOR solution using UNIX pipes calls.

12. Write a C/C++ program, `vt`, that will enable a user to simultaneously execute two interactive sessions. The `vt` program should support the two sessions by "filtering" all keyboard input before passing it to the subject programs and by keeping a virtual screen for each program to be written to the physical screen whenever the user is interacting with a particular program. You will have to implement a time-multiplexed display of the virtual screens on the physical screen. Thus the user will always have one or the other virtual screen visible at any given time, but never both. The visible screen represents the active program, and the invisible screen represents a dormant program. If the user types input, your keyboard routine should route the input to the active program. When the user types "ESCAPE" followed by "C," your

program should make the active program dormant and the dormant program active. This toggle should change the physical screen so that it shows the virtual screen for the newly activated program. You also will need the sequence "ESCAPE followed by Q" to terminate your program. You may assume that you do not have to pass "ESCAPE sequence" to any shell. When vt starts executing, run a shell on each virtual terminal. If you have solved the laboratory exercise in Chapter 2, the shell from that program will be easier to use than production-level shells such as sh.

Laboratory Exercise: Refining the Shell

Starting with your shell program from the Laboratory Exercise in Chapter 2, refine it to provide additional functionality to manage pipes and concurrency. As before, your shell program should use the same style for running programs as that used in the UNIX `sh` command.

When the user types a line such as

```
identifier [identifier [identifier]]
```

your shell should search the UNIX directory tree in the order identified by the PATH variable for a file with the same name as the first identifier, which may be a filename or a full path name. Then your shell should execute that file.

For this lab exercise, add the following functionality to your shell program:

- Implement the "&" modifier so that if the last character on the command line is "&", the program is executed in parallel with the shell, rather than the shell's having to wait for it to complete.
- Allow the standard input or output file to be redirected using the "<" and ">" symbols.
- The standard output from one program may be redirected into the standard input of another program using the "|" symbol.

Note, it is more difficult to implement the shell so that it simultaneously supports redirection, pipes, and putting a process in the background. It is not necessary for you to handle more than one of these cases on a single command line.

BACKGROUND

This exercise will give you substantial insight into how UNIX systems handle file identifiers and will hone your skills in concurrent programming.

Concurrent Processes

The normal paradigm for executing a command is for the parent process to create a child process, to start it executing the command, then to wait until the child process terminates (see the Laboratory Exercise in Chapter 2). If the "&" operator is used to terminate the command line, then the shell will create the child process, start it executing on the designated command, but not have the parent wait for the child to terminate. That is, the parent and the child are executing concurrently. While the child executes the command, the parent prints another prompt to `stdout` and waits for the user to enter another command line. If the user starts several commands, each terminated by "&", and if each of them takes a relatively long time to execute, then there can be many processes running at the same time.

When a child process is created and started executing on its own program, both the child and the parent expect their `stdin` stream to come from the user via the keyboard, and for their `stdout` stream to be written to the character terminal display. Notice that the user may not know which of the child processes will receive data on its `stdin` if data is typed to the keyboard while multiple child processes are running concurrently and all expect the keyboard to define their `stdin` stream. Similarly, if any of the concurrent processes write characters to `stdout`, they will be written to the terminal display wherever the cursor happens to be positioned. The kernel makes no provision for giving each of these child processes their own keyboard or terminal (unlike a window system, which controls the multiplexing and demultiplexing through explicit user actions).

I/O Redirection

When a process is created, it has three default file identifiers: `stdin`, `stdout`, and `stderr`. If the process reads from `stdin`, then the data it receives will be directed from the keyboard to the `stdin` file descriptor. Similarly, `stdout` and `stderr` are mapped to the terminal display.

The user can redefine `stdin` or `stdout` whenever a command is entered. By providing a file name argument to the command, and by preceding the file name with a "<" character, the shell will substitute the designated file for `stdin`; this is called "redirecting the input from the designated file." The output can be redirected (for the execution of a single command) by preceding a file name with the ">" character. For example a command such as

```
wc < main.c > program.stats
```

will create a child process to execute the `wc` command, but before it launches the command, it will redirect `stdin` so that it reads the input stream from the file named `main.c`, and it will redirect `stdout` so that it writes the output stream to a file named `program.stats`.

The shell can redirect I/O by manipulating the child processes file descriptors. When a child process is created, it inherits the open file descriptors of its parent. Specifically, it inherits the same keyboard for `stdin`, the terminal display for `stdout` and `stderr` (this explains more about why concurrent processes read and write the same keyboard and display). After the child has been created, the shell can change the file descriptors used by the child so that it reads and writes streams to files rather than to the keyboard and display.

Each process has its own file descriptor table (called `fileDescriptor` in this discussion, but not in the source code) in the kernel; the file descriptor will be explained further in the Laboratory Exercise in Chapter 13. When the process is created, the first entry in this table refers by convention to the keyboard, and the second two refer to the terminal display. Next, the C runtime environment and the kernel treat the symbol "`stdin`" so that it is always bound to `fileDescriptor[0]` in the kernel table, "stdout" is associated with `fileDescriptor[1]`, and "stderr" to `fileDescriptor[2]`.

The `close` system call can be used to close any open file, including `stdin`, `stdout`, and `stderr`. By convention, the `dup` and `open` commands always use the entry in the file descriptor table that was last closed. Therefore, a code fragment such as

```
fid = open(foo, O_WRONLY | O_CREAT);
close(1);
dup(fid);
close(fid);
```

is guaranteed to create a file descriptor, `fid`, to duplicate the entry, and to place the duplicate in `fileDescriptor[1]` (the normal `stdout` entry in the process's file descriptor table). The result is that when the process writes characters to `stdout`, they will be written to the file named `foo`. This is the key to redirecting both `stdin` and `stdout`.

UNIX Pipes

Pipes are the main IPC mechanism in uniprocessor UNIX (complemented by sockets in multiprocessor and network BSD UNIX; see Chapter 15). By default, a pipe employs asynchronous `send` and blocking `receive` operations. Optionally, the blocking `receive` operation can be changed to be a nonblocking `receive` (see the details for invoking nonblocking read operations in Section 15.9). Pipes are FIFO buffers designed with an API that is as similar as possible to the file I/O interface. A pipe can contain a system-defined maximum number of bytes at any given time—usually 4KB. As indicated in Figure 9.17, a process can send information by writing it into

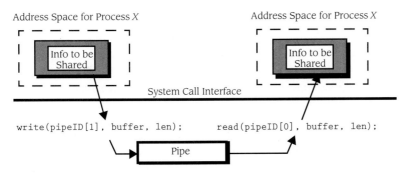

Figure 9.17
Information Flow Through UNIX Pipes

one end of the pipe and another can receive the information by reading the other end of the pipe.

A pipe is represented in the kernel by a file descriptor. When a process wants to create a pipe, it calls the kernel with a call of the form

```
int pipeID[2];
. . .
pipe(pipeID);
```

The kernel creates the pipe as a kernel FIFO data structure with two file identifiers. In this example code, `pipeID[0]` is a file pointer (an index into the process's open file table) to the read end of the pipe and `pipeID[1]` is file pointer to the write end of the pipe.

For two or more processes to use pipes for IPC, a common ancestor of the processes must create the pipe prior to creating the processes. Because the UNIX `fork` command creates a child that has a copy of the open file table (that is, the child has access to all files that the parent has already opened), each child inherits pipes that the parent created. To use a pipe, it need only read and write the proper file descriptors.

For example, suppose a parent creates a pipe; then it can create a child and communicate with it using a code fragment such as

```
. . .
pipe(pipeID);
if(fork() = = 0) { /* The child process */
    . . .
    read(pipeID[0], childBuf, len);
    /* process the message in childBuf */
    . . .
} else { /* The parent process */
    . . .
    /* Send a message to the child */
    write(pipeID[1], msgToChild, len);
    . . .
}
```

A pipe is used in place of a mailbox, where the asynchronous `send` operation is a normal `write` system call on the "write end" of the pipe (pipe descriptor `pipe_id[1]`) and the `read` operation is a blocking read on the "read end" of the pipe (pipe descriptor `pipe_id[0]`).

Pipes enable processes to copy information from one address space to another using the UNIX file model. The pipe read and write ends can be used in most system calls in the same way that a file descriptor can be used. Furthermore, the information written to and read from the pipe is a byte stream. UNIX pipes do not explicitly support messages, although two processes can establish their own protocol to provide

Figure 9.18
UNIX Pipes

```
int A_to_B[2], B_to_A[2];
main(){
    pipe(A_to_B);
    pipe(B_to_A);
    if (fork()==0) { /* This is the first child process */
        execve("prog_A.out", ...);
        exit(1); /* Error-terminate the child */
    }
    if (fork()==0) { /* This is the second child process */
        execve("prog_B.out", ...);
        exit(1); /* Error-terminate the child */
    }
/* This is the parent process code */
    wait( ...);
    wait( ...);
}

proc_A(){
    while (TRUE) {
        <compute A1>;
        write(A_to_B[1], x, sizeof(int)); /* Use this pipe to send info */
        <compute A2>;
        read(B_to_A[0], y, sizeof(int)); /* Use this pipe to get info */
    }
}

proc_B(){
    while (TRUE) {
        read(A_to_B[0], x, sizeof(int)); /* Use this pipe to get info */
        <compute B1>;
        write(B_to_A[1], y, sizeof(int)); /* Use this pipe to send info */
        <compute B2>;
    }
}
```

structured messages. There are also library routines that can be used with a pipe to communicate using messages.

Figure 9.18 illustrates how pipes can be used in UNIX to implement the concurrent processing example used in Figure 2.5.

Named pipes can be used to allow unrelated processes to communicate with one another. In normal pipes, the pipe ends are inherited as open file descriptors by the children. In named pipes, a process obtains a pipe end by using a string that is analogous to a file name but which is associated with a pipe. This allows any set of processes to exchange information using a "public pipe" whose end names are file names. When a process uses a named pipe, the pipe is a system-wide resource, potentially accessible by any process. Just as files have to be managed so that they are not inadvertently shared among many processes at one time, named pipes must also be managed (using the file system commands).

ATTACKING THE PROBLEM

The modifications to your shell program from the exercise in Chapter 2 involve considerable detail, but they use the concepts explained in the Background section of this exercise. You will have to design a way to parse the command line so that you recognize the special symbols, then to force your shell into the corresponding action. Because it is difficult to get general code where more than one of the special symbols is used in one command line, focus only solving the exercise when it uses "&", "<", ">", or "|", but not more than one of these.

10

Deadlock

I still don't know what I was waiting for,

And my time was running wild.

A million deadend streets.

Every time I thought I'd got it made,

It seemed the taste was not so sweet.

—David Bowie, *Changes* ∎

CHAPTER OBJECTIVES

Deadlock is a significant problem that can arise in a community of cooperating or competing processes. Deadlock was introduced in Chapter 8 in the context of synchronization, where many different examples of deadlock were considered in the various synchronization discussions. This chapter generalizes the discussion to apply to resources managed by the resource manager. The problem is especially interesting because, in general, its occurrence depends on the characteristics of two or more different programs and of processes executing the different programs at the same time. The programs might be executed repeatedly by several different processes without encountering deadlock and then become deadlocked because of some intricate resource usage pattern. There are three automated strategies for addressing deadlock: (1) prevention, (2) avoidance, and (3) detection and recovery, as well as manual handling. This chapter provides background for studying the problem using simple, but formal, models of processes and resources. It then considers the approach used in each of these strategies.

10.1 ■ Background

Dijkstra [1968] describes a *deadly embrace* that can occur among a group of two or more processes whereby each process holds at least one resource while making a request on another. The request can never be satisfied because the requested resource is being held by another process that is blocked, waiting for the resource that the first process is holding. Figure 10.1 illustrates a deadly embrace, or deadlock, among three processes on three resources. The three processes might have put the system in the state shown in the figure by executing as follows:

Process 1	Process 2	Process 3
. . .	. . .	. . .
request(resource1);	request(resource2);	request(resource3);
/*Holding res 1*/	/*Holding res 2*/	/*Holding res 3*/
. . .	. . .	. . .
request(resource2);	request(resource3);	request(resource1);

Process 1 is holding Resource 1 and requesting Resource 2; Process 2 is holding Resource 2 and requesting Resource 3; Process 3 is holding Resource 3 and requesting Resource 1. None of the processes can proceed because all are waiting for a resource held by another blocked process. Unless one of the processes detects the situation and is able to withdraw its request for a resource and release the one resource allocated to it, none of the processes will ever be able to run.

Resource managers and other OS processes can be involved in a deadlock situation. Suppose a very large application process wishes to acquire a disk block through a request to a disk resource allocator. When the application process was activated, it was allocated almost all of primary memory by the memory manager. Now suppose the disk block allocation manager is a process swapped out of the primary memory. It requires memory so that it can be loaded to satisfy the disk block request, but the application process has not left enough free memory for the disk block allocator to be loaded! As shown in Figure 10.2, the application process and the disk block allocation process are deadlocked.

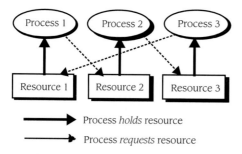

Process *holds* resource
Process *requests* resource

Figure 10.1
Three Deadlocked Processes

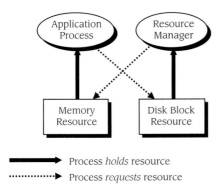

Process *holds* resource
Process *requests* resource

Figure 10.2
Deadlock Between an Application and the OS

Deadlock also occurs in many guises in the real world. Probably the most well-known example is *gridlock* among automobiles in heavy traffic. Gridlock occurs when the four one-way streets around a block have heavy traffic on them and automobiles enter the intersections in an attempt to progress (see Figure 10.3). In the example, a stream of automobiles traveling along a one-way street corresponds to a process and each intersection is a shared resource. The northbound automobiles hold the intersection resource at the southwest corner of the block and require control of the northwest intersection to proceed. However, the eastbound traffic stream holds the northwest intersection and requests the northeast intersection, and the southbound traffic holds the northeast intersection and requests the southeast intersection. The westbound traffic completes the deadlock because it holds the southeast intersection and requires the southwest intersection held by the northbound stream.

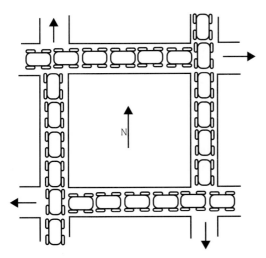

Figure 10.3
Automobile Gridlock

In Chapter 8, deadlock was introduced as a side effect of synchronization strategies. Because two processes wished to update a pair of shared variables in a consistent manner, they used a lock flag to ensure that when the value of one variable was changed, the other's value would be updated. Similar situations recur frequently in communities of processes that are sharing any kind of resources. In fact, that is why a resource is defined as being anything that a process needs—consumable or reusable—in order to proceed. Memory, a tape drive, a message, a positive semaphore value, a particular tape to be mounted on a tape drive—are all resources. A process can block when it requests any of these entities; thus any of them can contribute to a deadlock.

Deadlock is a global condition rather than a local one. If we analyzed a program for any process involved in a deadlock, we would find no discernible error. The problem lies not in any single process but in the collective action of the group of processes. How, then, can a programmer be expected to deal with a deadlock? An individual program cannot generally detect a deadlock, since it is blocked and unable to use the processor to do any work. Deadlock detection must be handled by the OS. How can operating systems be constructed to ensure that a deadlock is handled properly? There are three general approaches plus one ad hoc approach:

- Prevention

- Avoidance

- Detection and recovery

- Manual deadlock management

10.1.1 ■ Prevention

Suppose the following conditions hold regarding the way a process uses resources:

- *Mutual exclusion:* Once a process has been allocated a particular resource, it has exclusive use of the resource. No other process can use a resource while it is allocated to a process.

- *Hold and wait:* A process may hold a resource at the same time it requests another one.

- *Circular waiting:* A situation can arise in which process p_1 holds resource R_1 while it requests resource R_2, and process p_2 holds R_2 while it requests resource R_1. There may be more than two processes involved in the circular wait.

- *No preemption:* Resources can be released only by the explicit action of the process, rather than by the action of an external authority. This assumption includes the case in which a process places a request for a resource and the resource is not available. Then the process cannot withdraw its request.

These conditions occur in almost all resource allocation strategies in almost all modern operating systems. A deadlock is possible only if all four of these conditions simultaneously hold in the community of processes. That is, these conditions are *necessary* for a deadlock to exist (although their presence is not *sufficient* to ensure that a deadlock does exist, since they may hold but there is no deadlock in the system). Deadlock prevention strategies attack these conditions by designing the collective resource managers so that they are guaranteed to violate at least one of the conditions at all times. For example, Windows NT assures that there will be no circular wait on mutex objects (Nagar [1997]). Prevention strategies are easy to implement within certain systems, such as batch systems, but essentially impossible to design in other systems such as timesharing systems. The prevention strategies are described in Section 10.3.

10.1.2 ■ Avoidance

Avoidance strategies rely on a resource manager's ability to predict the effect of satisfying individual allocation requests. If a request can lead to a situation in which a deadlock could occur, avoidance strategies will refuse the request. Since avoidance is a predictive approach, it relies on information about the resource activity that will be occurring for the process. For example, if a process announces in advance the maximum number of resources it would ever request—its *maximum claim*—it is possible to avoid a deadlock when specific resource requests are made. This strategy is discussed in Section 10.4. Avoidance is a conservative strategy. It tends to underutilize resources by refusing to allocate them if there is the potential for a deadlock. Consequently, it is rarely used in modern operating systems.

10.1.3 ■ Detection and Recovery

Some systems are designed to allow resource allocation to proceed with no particular intervention. Instead, the system checks to see if deadlock exists, either periodically or whenever certain events occur. A difficult aspect of this approach is to determine when the detection algorithm should be executed. If it is executed too often, it merely wastes system resources. But if it is not run frequently enough, deadlocked processes and system resources will be tied up in a nonproductive fashion until the system is recovered. This problem occurs because the presence of deadlock results in the nonoccurrence of events rather than the occurrence of some exceptional event that might trigger the execution of the detection algorithm.

When a detection algorithm runs, there are two phases to the strategy. The first is the *detection* phase, during which the system is checked to see if a deadlock currently exists. If a deadlock is detected, the system goes through the second phase, *recovery,* by preempting resources from processes. This recovery means the nonpreemption condition has been violated and selected processes will be destroyed. Any work they may have accomplished prior to becoming deadlocked may be lost. The detection and recovery strategy is the most widely used deadlock strategy. The conditions under which it is invoked are often determined manually—that is, the computer's operator manually invokes the detection algorithm when the system appears to be inactive.

10.1.4 ■ Manual Deadlock Management

Many commercial systems do not take the possibility of deadlock into account. Their manufacturers do not think that it occurs frequently enough to justify designing the OS so that it addresses the issue. When deadlock becomes sufficiently costly to the system users, and hence to the manufacturer, deadlock strategies will gain more importance commercially. Meanwhile, when a deadlock does occur in these systems, it is up to the users or operator of the system to detect it (for example, by comparing the real response time in the system with expected response time).

10.2 ▪ A System Deadlock Model

System deadlock can be studied by using a model to represent the resource allocation status of the system's components. This can be done by modeling every state the system might be in at any given moment and then identifying which are deadlock states. Of course, one would probably never construct the full model of each state a priori, but the idea of the system state model can be used to address deadlock. Given the existence of such a conceptual model, one can then define the precise characteristics that cause a deadlock to occur and then use the model to determine policies for implementing avoidance, prevention, and detection strategies.

This section informally describes a model of processes and resources that can be formalized into a precise mathematical model. While the model is in sufficient detail to understand how it works, its full exposition and proofs are left to a more advanced treatment of deadlock (for example, the formal approach is used in [Nutt, 1992a]).

Let P be a set of n different processes and R be a set of m different resource types, where c_j is the number of units of resource type R_j in the system. Next, how the resources can be allocated to the various processes must be defined. Since the allocation of resources to processes changes as the process executes, the model will have to reflect each of these changes. A useful way to show this type of behavior is to use a state diagram. So let a state in the model represent the pattern of resource requests and allocations that exist in the system at any particular moment—the model state represents the system state. In the system, the state changes when resources are requested, allocated, or deallocated, and in this model, state transitions occur to represent request, allocation, and deallocation operations.

Let S be a set of states in the model that represents corresponding states in the system. The *initial state* is s_0; this represents the situation in which all resources are unallocated. All other states, s_i, represent possible system states, so each model state represents whichever units of every resource are being requested or held by each process. The details of how a specific state can be represented are considered when we examine individual deadlock strategies in Sections 10.4 and 10.5 (prevention strategies do not use state definitions to deal with a deadlock). For now, the focus is on the state transitions. The pattern in which resources are requested, acquired, and deallocated determines whether the system is deadlocked. This pattern corresponds to the list of transitions occurring in the state-transition model. All other activities of the process are not relevant to the study of deadlock, so they are ignored in this model.

In a set of processes, P, any process, $p_i \in P$, might cause a state transition depending on whether p_i

- requests a resource (designated by a transition with the label r_i),
- is allocated a resource (designated by a transition with the label a_i), or
- deallocates a resource (designated by a transition with the label d_i).

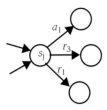

Figure 10.4
A State in Which p_2 is blocked

Whenever the system is in state $s_j \in S$, and an event x_i (x_i is one of r_i, a_i, or d_i) occurs, then the system's state changes to a new state, $s_k \in S$, due to the occurrence of the event x_i.

Since we are deriving a model to represent system state changes, we are interested in the effect of a series of transitions that take the system from one state to another. Process p_i is *blocked* in s_j if p_i cannot cause a state transition out of s_j. In other words, a blocked process is incapable of changing the state of the system, since it cannot cause any transition out of the current state. In Figure 10.4, p_2 is blocked in state s_j because all the transitions out of state s_j are caused by other processes; none are caused by p_2. Any state transition is due to actions by p_1 or p_3 but not by p_2.

Even if p_i is blocked in s_j, some process other than p_i might change the state of the system from s_j to a new state s_k, where p_i could proceed. If we can determine that there is no series of state transitions leading from the current state to one in which process p_i is unblocked, then the process can never execute again—p_i is *deadlocked* in s_j. In other words, process p_i is deadlocked in s_j if for every s_k that can be reached through some series of transitions from s_j, p_i is still blocked in s_k. If there is any process deadlocked in a state s_k, then s_k is called a *deadlock state*.

➤ IN THE HANGAR

Single Resource Type

Consider a very simple system in which one process may request up to two units of a single resource type. For example, the system supports one process in a configuration with two floppy disk drives. (Of course, deadlock is not possible in a system that has only one process, although the scenario allows us to develop a simple example of the state-transition model.) Assume that the process is allowed to request only a single unit of the resource at a time (and cannot ask for a cumulative total of more than 2 units, since there are only 2 units in the system). Figure 10.5 is a state diagram for the system. State s_0 represents the case in which the process neither holds nor requests any unit of the resource. The only possible state transition from s_0 is by a request, r, on the resource. This request will cause the system to move to state s_1, representing the case in which the process still holds no resources but now needs 1 unit. The system can transition to s_2 if the process acquires a unit of the resource. From s_2, two transitions are possible. Either the process may release the resource, thus changing the state to s_0 (the initial state), or the process may request a second unit of the resource, thus causing the new state to be s_3, where the process holds 1 unit of the resource and needs another.

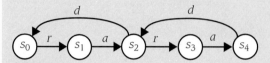

Figure 10.5
State Diagram for One Process

Let's extend the system so that two processes compete for the 2 units of the single resource type. Again, assume a process may request only 1 unit of the resource at a time (and cannot ask for a cumulative total of more than 2 units, since there are only 2 units in the system). The state diagram in Figure 10.5 needs to be replicated and the two copies combined to describe all the system states (as a combination of the states due to the individual processes). Figure 10.6 represents this combination. The states and transition events have been relabeled to distinguish between the two processes, and s_{ij} refers to the state in which p_0 is in s_i and p_1 is in s_j. Of course, several states from this "cross product" are not feasible. For example, s_{44} would represent the case in which both processes had acquired both units of the resource, which is impossible. Therefore several states from the cross product have been eliminated from the model.

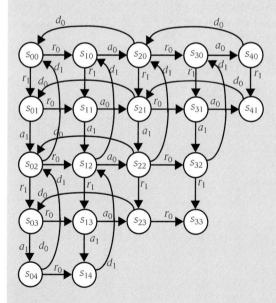

Figure 10.6
State Diagram for Two Processes

State s_{33} is a deadlock state. In s_{33}, both processes are holding 1 unit of the resource and requesting the other. If the system reaches this state, there is no transition out of it. Thus both processes are blocked for all states reachable from s_{33} because there are no other states reachable from s_{33}.

If we extended this example to include more than one resource type, we would have to extend our notation for symbols to represent requests, allocations, and deallocations so that the symbol would represent the event, the process (the subscript), and the resource type (perhaps using a superscript to represent the resource type index).

10.3 ■ Prevention

For a deadlock to occur in a system, all four of the conditions listed in Section 10.1.1—mutual exclusion, hold and wait, circular wait, and no preemption—must hold at the same time. Prevention strategies ensure that at least one of the conditions is always false. The mutual exclusion condition cannot be invalidated, since it ensures that a resource can be used only by one process at a time. For example, if an application program is being executed by a single process and it has requested that a particular tape be mounted on a tape drive, allowing another process to access the tape drive would not make sense. While it may be possible to violate the mutual exclusion condition for some resources, such as UNIX does for a terminal display, it is not possible to do so for every resource type in a conventional system. Prevention strategies must focus on the other three conditions.

10.3.1 ■ Hold and Wait

The hold-and-wait condition precludes a process from holding some resources while requesting others. There are two ways this condition can be violated: (1) a process may be required to request all of its resources when it is created, or (2) the hold-and-wait condition can be violated by requiring the process to release all currently held resources prior to requesting any new ones. This latter approach is extreme, since it requires that a process compete for *all* resources it wants each time it requests any incremental resource.

Batch systems operate on jobs, each of which is implemented by a single process (see Chapter 1). Since a batch job is defined by a "job file" containing all of the system commands to be applied to the job, it is possible to simply require the job control statements to identify all resources needed to execute the job at the outset. When all the resources are available, the job/process can be placed in the ready list and executed on the assumption that it will never request more resources during its execution. This strategy causes a job to acquire resources it may use only for a small phase in a job and to hold them for the duration of the job, thereby making them unavailable to other jobs. Batch jobs often run for hours. Hence, this technique results in poor utilization of resources. A direct effect is that resources become more difficult to obtain, which means that throughput in the system may be dramatically reduced compared to a similar system

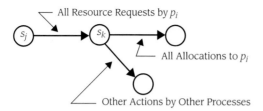

Figure 10.7
Requesting All Resources Before Starting

with no prevention policy. In an extreme case, a job may simply starve due to resource unavailability.

In a state-transition model for this strategy, the nature of the transitions is to have *all* requests take place before any acquisition or deallocation events (see Figure 10.7). If the system is in state s_j and p_i makes any resource requests, then p_i must request all the resources it needs. Thus there is a single transition due to the request by p_i to some new state, s_k. From state s_k, the system may allocate the resources requested by p_i. Or some other processes may cause a transition to a new state before the allocation takes place.

Interactive systems do not require that all commands, or even all processes, be known at the time the interaction begins. Instead, the user may create new processes, delete existing ones, execute commands requesting new processes, and so on at any time during a session. The first hold-and-wait strategy is not plausible in this type of environment. Instead, this second strategy can be used to avoid the hold-and-wait condition: Each time a new resource is required by a process, all of its currently held resources are put into a stable, persistent state and then released. For example, open files are closed, and mounted tapes are rewound and unloaded. Next, the process attempts to reacquire the resources along with any new ones it may need, thereby preventing the hold-and-wait condition from being true. This approach causes a significant amount of overhead in saving the status of held resources in preparation for acquiring new ones. It also will tend to underutilize resources and may encourage starvation.

Also in the generic state-transition model fragment for the second strategy (Figure 10.8), request transitions must occur before any acquisition or deallocation transitions. However, these state diagrams are more complex than those for the batch state, since they must have deallocation transitions leading back to the process's idle state. This is done to capture the scenarios in which a process dynamically determines it needs more resources.

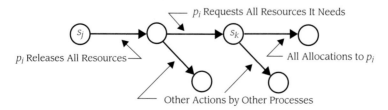

Figure 10.8
Release of All Resources Before Requesting More

10.3.2 ■ Circular Wait

Circular waits occur when there are a set of n processes, $\{p_i\}$, that hold units of a set of n different resources, $\{R_j\}$, such that p_i holds R_j while it requests units of a different resource in the set. In other words, each of the n resources are held by the n processes, but each process then requests unavailable units of one of the resource types held by another process. A circular wait is reflected by the resource-process relationships (represented wholly within a system state), so the state-transition model does not help in the study of this problem.

Suppose we use a new graphical representation to provide a more detailed description of each state and then use this "micro model" of each state to detect a circular wait condition. Let a square represent a resource type, a circle represent a process, an edge (p_i, R_j) denote that p_i has a pending request for units of R_j, and an edge (R_j, p_i) mean that p_i holds units of R_j. Based on this model, Figure 10.9 describes the details of a state in which the circular wait condition is true. The condition is evident by the *cycle* in the graph composed of the nodes representing resources and processes. The graphical representation provides the insight for how to prevent circular waits. The resource allocator must ensure that the system never achieves a state in which the internal graph contains a cycle. (The conditions are actually more complex than simple cycle detection because each resource may have multiple units of a resource. This will become evident when we consider detection algorithms. The cycle condition is sufficient to represent a circular wait only if each resource type has only 1 unit of the resource.)

One technique for preventing the occurrence of a circular wait condition is to establish a *total order* on all resources in a system, for example by using an index number for each of them. The resources are then $R_1, R_2, \ldots R_m$, where $R_i < R_j$ if $i < j$. Suppose we only allow a process to acquire a resource, R_j, if $R_i < R_j$ for all the other resources, R_i, currently held by the process. A process can request units of R_k only if the indices of all R_h are less than the indices of all R_k for the R_h that it holds.

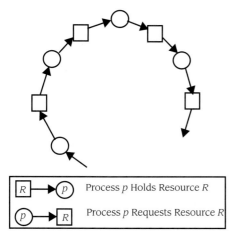

$R \longrightarrow p$	Process p Holds Resource R
$p \longrightarrow R$	Process p Requests Resource R

Figure 10.9
A Model of a State with a Circular Wait

The total order must establish order on all resource units as well as resource types if the units are distinguishable. It must also include consumable resources as well as reusable ones. As in the hold-and-wait situation, if a p_i requires a resource, R_j, such that $R_j < R_k$, for some R_k it currently holds, then the policy will require that p_i release all R_k, acquire R_j, and then reacquire R_k. The effect on the process performance will be negative, since this method can only increase the time that processes have to wait for resources to become available.

Notice that the deadlock that occurs in the dining philosophers problem can be prevented by using this total ordering approach. Suppose we put a total order on all forks (corresponding to their indices). Now philosopher 4 must become a "left-handed philosopher" in the sense that he or she picks up the forks in a different order than the other philosophers (see Figure 10.10). By having philosopher 4 pick up the forks in the opposite order, the circular wait condition is prevented from occurring, and hence a deadlock cannot occur.

Figure 10.10
Dining Philosophers Revisited

```
philosopher(int i){
    while (TRUE) {
        ... /* Thinking */
        P(fork[i]);                 /* Pick up left fork */
        P(fork[(i+1) mod 5]); /* Pick up right fork */
            eat();
        V(fork[(i+1) mod 5]);
        V(fork[i]);
    }
}
philosopher4(){
    while (TRUE) {
        ... /* Thinking */
        P(fork[0]);                 /* Pick up right fork */
        P(fork[4]);                 /* Pick up left fork */
            eat();
        V(fork[4]);
        V(fork[0]);
    }
}
semaphore fork[5] = {1, 1, 1, 1, 1};
fork(philosopher, 1, 0);
fork(philosopher, 1, 1);
fork(philosopher, 1, 2);
fork(philosopher, 1, 3);
fork(philosopher4, 0);
```

10.3.3 ■ Allowing Preemption

Suppose the OS allowed processes to "back out of" a request for a resource if the resource was not available. For example, the system might be implemented so that whenever a process requests a resource, the system responds immediately either by allocating the resource or by indicating that there are insufficient resources to satisfy the request. In cases in which resources are unavailable, the requesting process either polls the resource manager until the desired units become available or does other work. (This approach implicitly assumes that the process has other useful work to do that does not require the specified resource. Use of the strategy requires the programming language and paradigm to support such an approach.)

The state diagram for a system that allows a process to preempt its request—to "back out of a request"—will differ from one not allowing it. Figure 10.11 informally describes how model states change because a process is able to do this. If the system is in state s_i and process p_u makes a request, r_u, then the system transitions into a new state, s_j. Now, since p_u is informed that the resources it requested are not available, it returns the system to state s_i with a new transition, w_u (w means that the request is withdrawn by the process causing the transition). Hence, the system is now back in the state it was in prior to p_u's request. At this point, either p_u may again request the resource (transitioning the system back to s_j again) or a different process, p_v, may cause a system state change out of s_i to a new state s_k—for example by deallocating resources. The new state s_k may be more advantageous for p_u because it allows p_u to obtain the requested resources that were unavailable in s_i. The model represents the case in which p_u continues to poll the resource manager.

This technique cannot be characterized as "full preemption" of resources from processes (as required in a recovery procedure) yet it is sufficient to prevent a deadlock. Unfortunately, there is no guarantee that this technique will be effective, since the system may come to a set of states whereby a community of processes is polling for resources that are held by other processes within the set. While technically the system is not in a deadlock, it will not function properly due to a phenomenon called *livelock,* which means a set of processes causes transitions in the state diagram, but none of the transitions are effective in the long term.

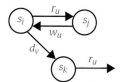

Figure 10.11
State Diagram with Preemption

10.4 ■ Avoidance

Like the prevention strategy, avoidance strategies are a conservative approach to resource allocation. They control state transitions by allowing the system to make a transition only as a result of an allocation when it is certain that a deadlock cannot occur due to subsequent requests. The strategy is to analyze a prospective state—before entering it—to determine if there exists any sequence of transitions out of the state in which every process can still execute.

The avoidance strategy depends on additional information about the long-term resource needs of each process. In particular, when a process is created, it must declare its *maximum claim*—the maximum number of units the process will ever request—to every resource type. The resource manager can honor the request if the resources are available. It can determine that there is some sequence of requests, allocations, and deallocations that enables every process to eventually run to completion even if all of the processes use their maximum number of resources.

With the avoidance approach, the system is always kept in a *safe state*. The analysis performed at the time of a request, then, must consider the allocation status of all resources and the pending additional resources that a process could request up to its maximum claim. It is important to note that the state analysis does not predict that every process will actually request its maximum claim. It merely proceeds under the assumption that *if* every process were to exercise its maximum claim, then there would still be some sequence of allocations and deallocations that would enable the system to satisfy every process's requests. A system state in which this guarantee cannot be made is an unsafe state.

Figure 10.12 is an intuitive description of how a community of processes can operate in a safe state and how the community causes the system to venture into unsafe states. As indicated by the flowchart in the figure, programs normally execute with less than the maximum claim, only occasionally requiring the maximum amount of a

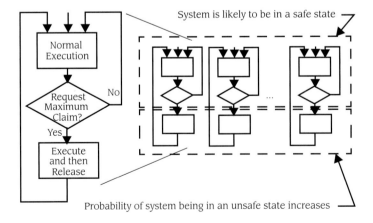

Figure 10.12
Safe State Strategy

resource for a phase of computing. After the resource-intensive phase is completed, the process reverts to operation with a more moderate amount of a resource. This phenomenon is especially true in systems that charge usage fees for resources.

As long as the processes tend to use less than their maximum claim, the system is likely (but not guaranteed) to be in a safe state. However, if a large number of processes happen to have relatively large resource demands (at or near their maximum claim) at the same time, the system resources will tend to be heavily used and the probability of the system state being unsafe is higher.

The avoidance strategy assumes that every process could take the "yes" branch in its respective flowchart at the same time, thus taking the system to a situation in which all processes simultaneously want to exercise their maximum claim. The strategy therefore is to determine that if any pending request is satisfied, and all programs do require their maximum claim, there is still some sequence of allocations and deallocations whereby the requests of all processes can eventually be satisfied.

Clearly this requirement means that the resource manager will block some processes while others use their maximum claim and then will allow the waiting processes to proceed. The strategy does not require that the system have enough resources to simultaneously meet all maximum claims, just that it can eventually service them all in some order. Even though the avoidance analysis assumes this worst case, a system possibly could run in an unsafe state with no guarantee that all maximum claims could be met, yet not enter a deadlock state. This scenario can occur because the resource manager conducts its analysis under the assumption that every process could execute its maximum claim. The system may not be able to guarantee that all maximum claims can be met—the state is unsafe—but some processes may not execute their maximum claim until the system returns to a safe state. Clearly, conservative assumptions on the part of the process can have a substantial effect on the performance of a system.

Recall that if a state is unsafe, it does not mean the system is in a deadlock or even that a deadlock is imminent (see Figure 10.13). It simply means the matter is "out of the hands" of the resource manager and will be determined solely by future actions of the

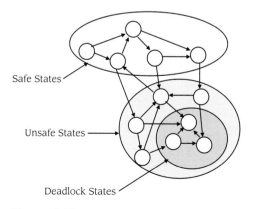

Figure 10.13
Safe, Unsafe, and Deadlock States

processes. The state diagram illustrates that the system can go into unsafe states but then return to safe states, depending on the actions taken by the community of processes. As long as the state is safe, the resource manager can be guaranteed to avoid a deadlock.

The avoidance strategy depends on the analysis of a particular system state to determine whether it is safe. This means we need a more detailed model of each state in the state-transition model so that we can make judgments about safety. The classic model of a state used in the avoidance strategy comes from Dijkstra's [1968] analogy of resource allocation and the way banks work.

10.4.1 ■ The Banker's Algorithm

The banker's algorithm is the best known of the avoidance strategies. The strategy is modeled after the lending policies employed in banking systems. A bank has a limited amount of funds—resources—that can be lent to different borrowers—processes. To accommodate borrowers, the bank may extend a line of credit to a customer. The line of credit is an indication by the bank that it is prepared to lend funds to the customer up to a previously specified limit. Customers agree they will not ask for more than the line of credit without first entering into a new agreement. The line of credit is a maximum claim for resources by the customer.

There is an important tacit assumption in the model. If a customer borrows some portion of the line of credit and then requests additional funds, the first amount borrowed will be paid back to the bank only if the additional funds are loaned. Hence, there is no preemption in the bank's model. The bank's strategy for distributing resources can then be guided by the total lines of credit it has extended to its customers and the total amount of loan funds controlled by the bank. At any moment, the loan department looks at the funds allocated to all customers and the maximum amount that can be requested by each customer. If there is some sequence of activity in which at least one customer's full line of credit can be met, assume that the customer can borrow to the line of credit and then repay the entire loan. After this customer has repaid the loan, the algorithm iterates on the other accounts. If all customers can exercise their lines of credit and repay their loans, then the current state is safe.

Now reconsider the bank example as a set of processes, P, using a set of resources, R. The nature of the current system state, s_k, is determined by the pattern of resources already allocated to processes. The system state can be defined by enumerating the number of units of each resource type held by each process. Let `alloc` be a table in which row i represents process p_i, column j represents R_j, and `alloc[i, j]` is the number of units of resource R_j held by process p_i. Let another table, `maxc`, be the maximum claim on resource R_j by process p_i. The number of available units of R_j can be computed as

```
avail[j] = c_j - Σ_{0≤ i < n} alloc[i, j].
```

It is possible to inspect c_j, the number of units of each resource in the system—`maxc[i, j]` and `alloc[i, j]`—and determine whether the current allocation state is safe simply by enumerating and inspecting all possible sequences of state transitions. The exact algorithm for doing this is shown in Figure 10.14. The algorithm computes the

1. Copy the `alloc[i, j]` table to a table named `alloc'`.

2. Given C, `maxc`, and `alloc'`, compute the `avail` vector. Do this by taking the column sums for `alloc'`, `alloc'[j, *]`. Then compute

   `avail[j] = c`$_j$` - alloc'[*, j]`.

3. Find p_i such that `maxc[i, j]` $-$ `alloc'[i, j]` $\leq$ `avail[j]` for $0 \leq j < m$ and $0 \leq i < n$. If no such p_i exists, then the state is unsafe—halt the algorithm. If `alloc'[i, j]` is 0 for all *i* and *j*, the state is safe—halt the algorithm.

4. Set `alloc'[i, j]` to 0 to indicate that p_i could exercise its maximum claim. Then deallocate all resources to represent that p_i is not permanently blocked in the state that is being analyzed. Go back to Step 2.

Figure 10.14
The Banker's Algorithm

number of units of each resource type that are available in the current state. This gives us a vector of values where `avail[j]` is the number of units of R_j available in this state.

We then consider each process and ask, if a process were suddenly to request resources up to its maximum claim, are there sufficient resources to satisfy the request? If there are, then this process could not be deadlocked in the state, so there is a sequence whereby this process eventually returns all its resources to the operating system. We model this by adding the units of each resource held by this process to the `avail` vector and then reconsider each process to see if any new ones could exercise their maximum claim. If we can determine that eventually every process can execute, we know the state is safe.

➤ IN THE HANGAR

Using the Banker's Algorithm

Suppose a system with four resource types, C = <8, 5, 9, 7>, is supporting five processes that collectively have the maximum claims shown in Figure 10.15. The current system state is represented by the allocation state shown in Figure 10.16. Let's apply the banker's algorithm to determine whether the corresponding state is safe. First, we compute the column sums of the currently allocated resources:

```
alloc'.columnSum = <7, 3, 7, 5>
```

In Step 2, we determine how many units of the resource are currently available:

```
avail[0] = 8 - 7 = 1
avail[1] = 5 - 3 = 2
avail[2] = 9 - 7 = 2
avail[3] = 7 - 5 = 2
```

That is,

```
avail = <1, 2, 2, 2>
```

In Step 3, we search for a process that can have its maximum claim satisfied in the state represented by the `alloc'` table. In this search, we discover the following:

```
maxc[2, 0] - alloc'[2, 0] = 5 - 4 = 1 ≤ 1 = avail[0]
maxc[2, 1] - alloc'[2, 1] = 1 - 0 = 1 ≤ 2 = avail[1]
maxc[2, 2] - alloc'[2, 2] = 0 - 0 = 0 ≤ 2 = avail[2]
maxc[2, 3] - alloc'[2, 3] = 5 - 3 = 2 ≤ 2 = avail[3]
```

This discovery means p_2 could exercise its maximum claim in the current state and then release all its resources, thus causing the following:

```
avail[0] = avail[0] + alloc'[2, 0] = 1 + 4 = 5
avail[1] = avail[1] + alloc'[2, 1] = 2 + 0 = 2
avail[2] = avail[2] + alloc'[2, 2] = 2 + 0 = 2
avail[3] = avail[3] + alloc'[2, 3] = 2 + 3 = 5
```

Next, we determine that p_4 could exercise its maximum claim and then release its resources, thereby resulting in `avail` being set to <6, 2, 5, 5>. In this hypothetical derived state, any of the other three processes could exercise its maximum claim. The state is safe.

PROCESS	R_0	R_1	R_2	R_3
p_0	3	2	1	4
p_1	0	2	5	2
p_2	5	1	0	5
p_3	1	5	3	0
p_4	3	0	3	3

Figure 10.15
A Maximum Claim Table

PROCESS	R_0	R_1	R_2	R_3
p_0	2	0	1	1
p_1	0	1	2	1
p_2	4	0	0	3
p_3	0	2	1	4
p_4	1	0	3	0
Sum	7	3	7	5

Figure 10.16
A Safe Allocation State for a System

The allocation state illustrated in Figure 10.17 is unsafe. This is determined by applying the algorithm and discovering in Step 3 that there is no process that can have its maximum claim exercised (using the maximum claim table in Figure 10.15). However, the state is not a deadlock because even though p_2 can have its maximum claim satisfied, no other process can do so. If p_3 happened to deallocate its single unit of R_0, it is not blocked. The state would be the same as Figure 10.16, so it would again be safe.

PROCESS	R_0	R_1	R_2	R_3
p_0	2	0	1	1
p_1	0	1	2	1
p_2	4	0	0	3
p_3	1	2	1	0
p_4	1	0	3	0

Figure 10.17
An Unsafe Allocation State for a System

10.5 ▪ Detection and Recovery

The detection and recovery strategy allows the resource manager to be far more aggressive about allocation than does the avoidance strategy. Whereas avoidance algorithms avoid unsafe states even if the system might recover from them, detection and recovery algorithms ignore the distinction between safe and unsafe states—the resource managers are allowed to allocate units whenever they are available. If processes seem to be blocked on resources for an inordinately long time, the detection algorithm is executed to determine whether the current state is a deadlock. Detection algorithms make no predictions about states that could be reached from the current state, although they will determine if there is any sequence of transitions in which every process can become unblocked.

Resources have been defined as "anything a process needs to proceed." As pointed out before, this need could be a block of primary memory, a file, or exclusive access to a device. Such resources are called *serially reusable resources* because a process requests the operating system to allocate the resource exclusively to the process and the process will later release the resource for another process to reuse. Individual units of serially reusable resources employ a strict time-multiplexing sharing approach.

Processes also use *consumable resources*. For example, when a process blocks on a read operation that is attempting to read the next character from a keyboard, then the character is needed by the process in order to proceed. However, once the process acquires the character, it will never "release" it. Instances of the two resource classes are treated differently by the resource manager and processes and have different theoretical properties with respect to deadlock analysis. The next several subsections consider serially reusable and consumable resources and then explain how systems containing both classes of resources can be analyzed to detect a deadlock.

10.5.1 ■ Serially Reusable Resources

Serially reusable resources represent traditional hardware resources and their abstractions. For our deadlock analysis, *serially reusable resource, R_j,* has a finite number of identical units such that the following holds:

■ The number of units of the resource, c_j, is constant.

■ Each unit of R_j is either available or allocated to one, and only one, p_i at any time.

■ A unit of R_j can be released only if it was previously acquired.

Next, we define a new family of graph models, which are used to describe each system state for systems containing only serially reusable resources. These graphs are refinements of the one given in Figure 10.9.

10.5.1.1 ■ Reusable Resource Graph Models

A *reusable resource graph* is a micro model that describes the details of a single state in the state-transition model from Section 10.2. It is a directed graph such that the following is true:

■ The $n + m$ nodes represent n processes and m resources.

■ Edges connect processes to resources and resources to processes.

   ■ An edge from process p_i to resource R_j is a *request edge,* which represents a request for 1 unit of R_j by p_i.

   ■ An edge from resource R_j to process p_i is an *assignment edge,* which represents the allocation of 1 unit of R_j to p_i.

■ For each resource type, R_j, there is a count of the number of units of the type, c_j, that is graphically represented by small tokens inside R_j.

■ The number of units of R_j allocated plus the number requested by p_i cannot exceed c_j.

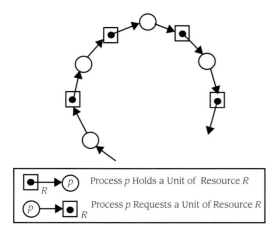

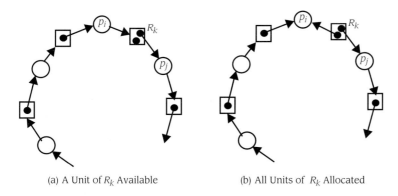

Figure 10.18
A Refinement of the Circular Wait Graph

Figure 10.18 is a refinement of Figure 10.9 showing a reusable resource graph. The refinement represents the number of units of resource configured into each resource type (by "tokens" inside the resource) in addition to the processes, resources, requests, and allocations. For emphasis, we draw the edge representing allocation from a specific unit of a resource to the process.

By our adding the resource count to the graphical model, additional details of the circular wait condition become obvious. In the figure, every available unit of every resource type is allocated, yet each process involved in the circular wait requests a unit of the unavailable resource. The graphical representation is also useful, since it makes it obvious that the cycle in a reusable resource graph is not a sufficient condition for a deadlock. Any resource could have more than 1 unit (for example, as does R_k in Figure 10.19a): hence a single request edge could be satisfied, thus breaking the circular wait.

(a) A Unit of R_k Available   (b) All Units of R_k Allocated

Figure 10.19
Representing a State Transition Using the Reusable Resource Graph

Figure 10.9 was useful for introducing the notion of circular wait. However, it was not complete. It does not allow a detection algorithm to operate on a formal representation of the graphical depiction of the model, since it did not include the unit count.

Each reusable resource graph is a detailed model of an individual state in the system state diagram. In Figure 10.19, part (a) is one system state and (b) is a reusable resource graph for a different state that is reached from the one represented in part (a). In Figure 10.19(b), a transition has occurred in which the idle unit of R_k is allocated to p_i. This example gives us some insight as to how we can use reusable resource graphs to represent states in the system model without actually constructing a state-transition model. That is, we rely on the existence of the model explained in Section 10.2, but there is no need to actually construct it.

A state transition occurs whenever one of three events occurs:

- Any allocated resource is released through the *deallocation* event, d.
- A new resource is requested via the *request* event, r.
- A resource is allocated to a process with the *allocate* event, a.

A specific allocation policy can be represented in an OS by defining the state diagram and transitions more precisely than has been done up to now by describing transformations on the reusable resource graph. For example, one specific widely used policy employs the following resource event semantics:

- *Request:* Assume the system is in s_j. p_i is allowed to request any number, q, of units of any number of resource types R_h ($q \leq c_h$), provided p_i has no outstanding requests for any resources. A request causes a state transition from s_j to s_k, where the reusable resource graph for s_k is derived from the reusable resource graph for s_j by adding q request edges from p_i to R_h (that is, one request edge for each unit requested).
- *Acquisition:* Assume the system is in s_j. p_i is allowed to acquire units of R_h if, and only if, there is a request edge from p_i to R_h in the reusable resource graph representing s_j and all such requests can be satisfied on all resources at one time. An acquisition causes a state transition from s_j to s_k. In this case, where the reusable resource graph for s_k is derived from the reusable resource graph for s_j by changing each request edge to an assignment edge from R_h to p_i.
- *Release:* Assume the system is in s_j. p_i can release units of R_h if, and only if, there is an allocation edge from R_h to p_i and there is no request edge from p_i. A release causes a state transition from s_j to s_k. In this case, the reusable resource graph for s_k is derived from the reusable resource graph for s_j by deleting all assignment edges into p_i from R_h.

This policy, while specific, is still sufficiently generic to apply to many reasonable resource allocation strategies. It is used in the analysis of deadlock detection and recovery in the rest of the chapter.

A simple system was introduced in Section 10.2.1 in which two processes shared two units of a single resource type. The example implicitly assumed the resources were serially reusable. The state diagram for the system was provided in Figure 10.6. We can now consider reusable resource graph models of each state.

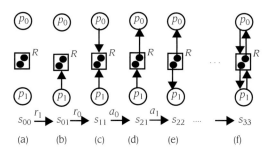

Figure 10.20
Reusable Resource Graph

In Figure 10.20, part (a) represents state s_{00}, where neither process holds or needs a unit of the resource. If p_1 requests a unit of the resource with transition r_1 (only single-unit requests were permitted in this example), the system moves to s_{01}, which has the reusable resource graph shown in (b). If p_0 were then to request a unit of the resource, designated by the r_0 transition, the system would change from state s_{01} to s_{11}, represented by the reusable resource graphs shown in (c). Part (d) represents s_{21} and (e) represents s_{22}, where both processes hold a unit of the resource. When we first considered this example, it was noted that s_{33} is a deadlock state, since there are no transitions out of it, and (f) is the reusable resource graph for the state. Again, note that there is a cycle in the reusable resource graph for s_{33} and that all the resource units are allocated.

10.5.1.2 ■ Analyzing a Reusable Resource Graph

We have a macro model with states and a micro model for representing each state in the macro model in terms of its processes and reusable resources. Using the macro model in Section 10.2, we determined that a state was a deadlock state by analyzing the state diagram in Figure 10.6. Since s_{33} contained no outgoing transitions, it thus had to represent deadlock. This situation would be more complex if the state diagram contained a knot and once the system entered any state in the knot, it could never transition to other states outside the knot. For example, in Figure 10.21 the system could move from state s_j or s_k into the knot, but then it would never be able to change to any of the states outside the knot. This situation complicates the algorithm for checking to see if a process can ever be involved in a transition again—that is, to see if the process is deadlocked.

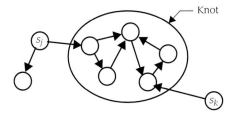

Figure 10.21
A State Diagram with a Knot

The reusable resource graph micro model representing any particular state in the macro model can also be analyzed to determine whether the macro model state is a deadlock. The idea is to consider possible transitions based on the topology in the reusable resource graph. A process is deadlocked in a state if it is blocked in the current state as well as in any state reachable from the current state. According to the semantics associated with request, acquisition, and release events (under the particular policy described previously), the conditions for a process to be blocked can be restated as follows: If there are p_i and R_j such that p_i's requests on R_j exceed the total number of units of R_j in state s_k, then p_i is blocked in s_k.

To detect if s_k is a deadlock state, we must be assured that there is no sequence of transitions unblocking all blocked processes. Rather than exploring the state diagram, we can consider all transformations of the reusable resource graph to determine if there is a new graph reachable by transformations corresponding to the state transitions. If we can find a series of transformations in which p_i is unblocked, the original state is not a deadlock.

A *graph reduction* is a set of transformations representing optimal action by the processes. These transformations are similar to the individual steps testing whether a state is unsafe in the banker's algorithm in the sense that they represent an analysis of a state as opposed to any prediction of future activity by the community of processes. In the banker's algorithm, the intent was to avoid unsafe states; in the detection algorithm, the intent is to decide whether the current state is a deadlock. A serially reusable resource graph can be *reduced* by p_i if the following conditions are met:

- The process is not blocked.
- The process has no request edges.
- There are assignment edges directed into p_i.

The reduction transforms the reusable resource graph by removing all assignment edges to p_i. A reusable resource graph is *irreducible* if it cannot be reduced by any process p. A reusable resource graph is *completely reducible* if there is a sequence of reductions that leads to a graph's having no edges of any kind. It can be proved that given a reusable resource graph representing state s_k, state s_k is a deadlock state if, and only if, the serially reusable resource graph is not completely reducible [Nutt, 1992a].

It would be satisfying if we could correlate deadlock with a static property of the reusable resource graph, such as the presence of a cycle. Unfortunately, there is no static property known. Furthermore, the fact that graph reductions are a necessary and sufficient condition strongly suggests there is no static condition (at least in this model with this resource allocation policy). In the case of cycles, the graph of a deadlock state *must* contain a *cycle;* a cycle in the reusable graph is a *necessary* condition for deadlock. However, it is not a *sufficient* condition for deadlock. This was illustrated in Figure 10.19 and is again illustrated with the simple case in Figure 10.22. Process p_0 holds R_0 and requests R_1, while p_1 holds R_1 and requests R_0, as shown in the graph with a cycle and a deadlock state in part (a) of Figure 10.22. But part (b) is not a deadlock state. Yet it too contains the same cycle.

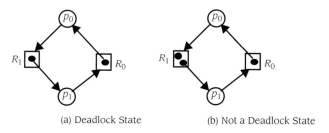

(a) Deadlock State   (b) Not a Deadlock State

Figure 10.22
The Circular Wait (Reconsidered)

For example, suppose a system is in the state represented by the reusable graph shown in Figure 10.23(a). Notice that p_1 and p_2 are both blocked (p_1 on R_0 and p_2 on both R_1 and R_2). However, p_0 is not blocked, so we can reduce the graph by p_0 to show that there is a series of transitions possible from the current state in which p_0 acquires and releases all of its current requests. After reducing by p_0, we obtain the reduced graph shown in Figure 10.23(b). Now the graph can be reduced by p_1, meaning it is possible for the system to move from the state shown in part (b) into the state shown in (c). Finally, we reduce by p_2, resulting in the graph shown in (d)—a completely reduced graph. This graph means the original state is not a deadlock.

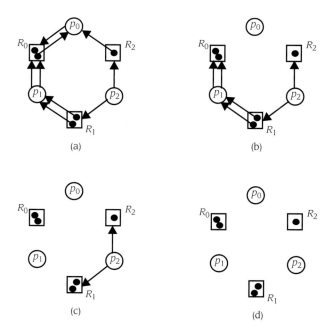

Figure 10.23
Completely Reducible Reusable Resource Graph

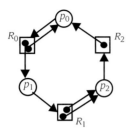

Figure 10.24
Deadlocked Reusable Resource Graph

Figure 10.24 represents an irreducible state and a deadlock. Process p_0 holds 1 unit of R_0 and 1 unit of R_2, while requesting 1 unit of R_0; p_1 holds 1 unit of R_0 and requests 1 unit of R_1; p_2 holds both units of R_1 and requests R_2. No process can proceed.

10.5.2 ■ Consumable Resources

Consumable resources differ from serially reusable resources in that a process may request consumable resources but will never release them. Conversely, a process can release units of a consumable resource without ever acquiring them. A typical consumable resource is a signal, message, or input data. Because such resources may have an unbounded number of units and because allocated units are not released, the model for analyzing serially reusable resources does not apply to consumable resources. However, by our redefining the model for consumable resources, conditions can be found to test a system state for deadlock.

A consumable resource, R_j, has an unbounded number of identical units such that the following holds:

- The number of units of the resource, w_j, varies. (w_j is used instead of c_j to emphasize that the number of available units for a consumable resource differs from the fixed number of units for a serially reusable resource.)
- There is one or more producer processes, p_p, that may increase w_j by releasing units of the resource.
- Consumer processes, p_c, decrease w_j for R_j by acquiring units of the resource.

Just as we used a reusable resource graph as a micro model to consider the properties of a serially reusable resource, we use a consumable resource graph to define a micro model for analyzing the properties of consumable resources.

10.5.2.1 ■ Consumable Resource Graph Model

A *consumable resource graph* is a directed graph such that the following is true:

- The $n + m$ nodes represent n processes and m resources.
- Edges connect processes to resources and resources to processes.
  - An edge from process p_i to resource R_j is a *request* edge, which represents a request for 1 unit of R_j by p_i.

■ An edge from resource R_j to process p_i is a *producer* edge, which identifies p_i as a producer of R_j. Each resource must have at least one producer.

■ The number of units of R_j is w_j, which is graphically represented by tokens inside R_j.

Again, we can specify a specific resource management policy in order to study systems that have consumable resources, just as we did with serially reusable resources. This policy conforms to the usual usage of consumable resources, although we could redefine it to fit the requirements of any particular resource manager. The policy is determined by the following actions:

■ *Request:* Assume the system is in state s_j. p_i is allowed to request any number of units of any number of resource types R_h, provided p_i has no outstanding requests for resources. A request causes a state transition from s_j to s_k, where the consumable resource graph for s_k is derived from the consumable resource graph for s_j by adding a request edge from p_i to R_h for each unit requested.

■ *Acquisition:* Assume the system is in s_j. p_i is allowed to acquire units of R_h if, and only if, there is a request edge from p_i to R_h in the consumable resource graph representing s_j and all such requests can be satisfied at one time. An acquisition causes a state transition from s_j to s_k, where the consumable resource graph for s_k is derived from the graph for s_j by deleting each edge from p_i to R_h and by decrementing w_h once for each edge deleted.

■ *Release:* Assume the system is in s_j. p_i can release units of R_h if, and only if, there is a producer edge from R_h to p_i and there is no request edge from p_i to R_g in the consumable resource graph representing s_j. A release causes a state transition from s_j to s_k, where the graph for s_k is derived from the consumable resource graph for s_j by incrementing w_h once for each unit of the resource produced.

Figure 10.25 shows a series of state transitions for a simple consumable resource system. Processes p_0 and p_1 share a single consumable resource. The first state in part (a) shows that p_1 is a producer of the resource, there are currently no units of the resource available, and there are no pending requests for the resource. The system state changes in part (b) when p_1 releases 1 unit of the resource and again in part (c) when p_0 requests 2 units of the resource. At this point, p_0 is blocked but p_1 continues to run. Part (d) shows that p_1 releases an additional 3 units of the resource. In part (e), the final state,

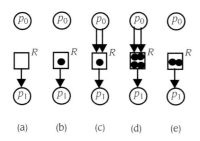

(a) (b) (c) (d) (e)

Figure 10.25
State Transitions in a Consumable Resource Graph

p_0 has obtained 2 units of the resource, thus leaving 2 units available. No process is blocked, so no process is deadlocked.

10.5.2.2 ■ Analyzing a Consumable Resource Graph

Consumable resource systems behave differently from serially reusable resource systems, since there are potentially an unbounded number of units of the resource available. This difference means the analyses used for reusable resource systems cannot be expected to work for consumable resource systems. We can see how this could be true by observing that if a process is blocked on a consumable resource, we can only speculate whether the process will be unblocked if the resource's producer is currently blocked. Hence, if we expect to determine whether a blocked process is deadlocked, the analysis must inspect the producers of resources that are causing other processes to be blocked.

How, exactly, can we determine if a state is a deadlock? As with all types of resources, a process is deadlocked in a state if it is blocked in the current state and in any state reachable from the current state. Thus, to detect deadlock, we again consider transformations in the consumable resource graph corresponding to state transitions. A consumable resource graph can be *reduced* by p_i if the process is not blocked. The reduction causes w_j to be decremented once for each unit of an outstanding request on R_j by p_i, and by deleting the request edges from the graph. If there are producer edges from a resource R_k to p_i, the reduction releases an unbounded number of units of R_k and deletes the producer edge, (R_k, p_i), from the graph.

As with reusable graphs, reduction is the basic tool for testing whether a process is permanently blocked. In Figure 10.26, p_0 is a producer for R_0 and p_1 is a producer for R_1. In part (a), p_0 is blocked on R_1 and p_1 is blocked on R_0; because of the producer relationships, this is clearly a deadlock state. However, if either R_0 or R_1 has an available unit, as in part (b), there is no deadlock. Process p_0 can be allocated the unit of R_1; it then will no longer be blocked. In the analysis technique, p_0 could release an arbitrary number of units of R_0, since it is not blocked. Of course, the system may not take this sequence, but we are attempting to determine whether the state is a deadlock, so we observe that p_0 could release as many units of the resource as will be needed to unblock other processes needing units of the resource it produces.

Figure 10.27 shows a consumable resource graph that represents a state in which p_i is the producer for R_i. There are three requests for R_1 by p_1, and $w_1 = 2$. Since p_0, the

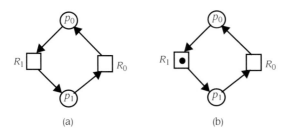

(a)   (b)

Figure 10.26
Deadlock in a Consumable Resource Graph

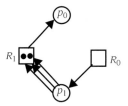

Figure 10.27
Consumable Resource Graph

producer of R_1, is not blocked, it may release (produce) units of R_1 to satisfy the request by p_1. Thus the state is not a deadlock.

Figure 10.28 illustrates, however, that we cannot rely on complete reduction to test for absence of a deadlock when consumable resources are involved. In this figure, p_0 and p_1 each have requests for R_0 and R_1. p_0 is a producer of R_2, 1 unit of which is needed by p_2, which is a producer of R_1. Similarly, p_1 is a producer of R_3, 1 unit of which is needed by p_3, which is a producer of R_0. In the state represented by the graph, no process is deadlocked, since we can reduce by either p_0 or p_1. There is a transition to a state in which p_0 is not blocked and a transition to a state in which p_1 is not blocked. Once we reduce by one of the processes, we cannot reduce by the other.

For example, if we reduce by p_0 we can reduce by p_2. This leaves a situation in which we cannot reduce by p_1 and p_3 because the single unit of R_0 cannot be replenished by p_3, since it is blocked. Similarly, a reduction by p_1 will leave a situation in which we cannot reduce by either p_0 or p_2. The analysis will not characterize the state shown in Figure 10.28 as a deadlock state, since it is not a deadlock state. It is of no consequence that any state reachable from the state shown in the diagram happens to be a deadlock. It can be proved that in a consumable resource graph representing state s_j, process p_i is not deadlocked in s_j, if, and only if, there is a sequence of reductions that leave a state in which p_i is not blocked [Nutt, 1992a].

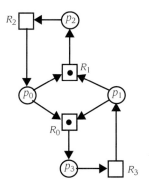

Figure 10.28
A Complex Situation in a Consumable Resource Graph

10.5.3 ▪ General Resource Systems

Real systems incorporate a combination of reusable and consumable resources. Deadlock detection strategies need to combine the consumable and reusable resource analyses techniques. While the formal definition of *general resource graphs* and the analyses for detecting deadlock are not included here, such a system has a set of resources determined by the union of consumable and reusable resources. The necessary and sufficient conditions for a deadlock in a general resource graph are a combination of the conditions for consumable and reusable resource graphs, where the rules applying to each class are applied to the corresponding subsets of resources in a general resource graph. The detection analysis is conducted by using reusable resource graph reductions on all reusable resources and consumable resource graph reductions on consumable resources. For a state to be deadlock free, the reusable resources must be completely isolated by reductions. However, the consumable resource graph must have a sequence in which each process can be demonstrated to not be blocked on any consumable resource.

For example, suppose we have a general resource graph as shown in Figure 10.29(a). Let R_0 and R_2 be reusable resources and R_1 be a consumable resource. p_0 and p_2 are both producers for R_1. Part (b) shows the graph after a reduction by p_3. All request and acquisition edges are removed from p_3, thus leaving all 3 units of R_0 available. In part (c), we have reduced by p_0, a producer of the consumable resource R_1. The request edges from p_0 are removed to indicate it could acquire and release 2 units of R_0. When the producer edge is removed from R_1 to p_0, the available units of R_1 are increased to an arbitrarily large number that can satisfy all future needs for R_1. Although we do not show the reductions in Figure 10.29, we could next reduce by p_1 and then finally by p_2. The state shown in Figure 10.29(a) is not a deadlock.

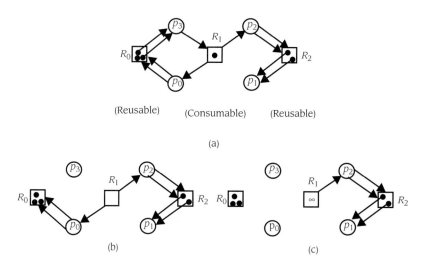

(a)

(b)   (c)

Figure 10.29
A General Resource Graph

10.5.4 ■ Recovery

Once deadlock has been detected in a system, the system will have to be recovered by changing it to a state in which there are no deadlocked processes. Of course, this means that one or more processes will have to be preempted, thus releasing their resources so that the other deadlocked processes can become unblocked. In some cases, the recovery mechanism may use the general resource graph to select processes to destroy. More typically, the operator simply begins destroying processes until the system appears to be operational again. The brute force approach is to reboot the entire machine, thus destroying all processes, even though only the processes involved in the deadlock need to release their resources.

As already said, when resources are preempted from a process, the process normally is simply destroyed. However, sometimes the process can be removed without destroying all of the work it has already performed. This is accomplished by incorporating a *checkpoint/rollback* mechanism into the system by which a process periodically takes a snapshot of its current state—called a *checkpoint*. The OS saves the checkpoint for the process, and the process then continues its activity. If the OS determines that a process is involved in a deadlock, it destroys the process, thereby releasing its resources for other processes to use. Next, it reestablishes the victim process's state (including reallocating resources and rewriting files to their former state) based on the checkpoint information and then restarts the process from the last checkpoint. This method is called "rolling the process back to the checkpoint." It has been widely used in database management systems for many years, so it has become relatively sophisticated.

After a process is destroyed, the deadlock detection algorithm is invoked again to see if the recovery was successful. If it was, the system continues normal operation. If it was not, then another process is preempted. The recovery algorithm will eventually remove the deadlocked processes, potentially by restarting all but one of the processes involved in the deadlock. Then the system continues normal operation.

10.6 ■ Summary

Deadlock creates a situation in which one or more processes will never run to completion without recovery. It can be prevented by designing resource managers so that they violate at least one of the four necessary conditions for deadlock: mutual exclusion, hold and wait, circular wait, and no preemption. Prevention can be effective on batch systems but is usually not practical in timesharing or other interactive systems.

The process-resource state model provides a framework for defining deadlock independent of the strategy chosen to address deadlock. The model allows the precise definition of deadlock in terms of the state diagram. It is used heavily in the subsequent discussions of avoidance and detection and recovery.

Deadlock can be avoided by using additional information, such as each process's maximum claim on each resource type, so as to not put the system into an unsafe state. The banker's algorithm is the classic avoidance algorithm. It is intuitively similar to the operation of a bank's offering lines of credit to its borrowers, even when the sum of the lines of credit exceeds the bank's total resources. Similarly, the banker's algorithm uses the maximum claim to determine if an allocation operation will lead to a state in which the resource manager cannot guarantee that deadlock will not occur. The banker's algorithm effectively performs the same operations used in a detection algorithm's graph reduction algorithm. Avoidance is overly conservative and not often used in contemporary operating systems.

Detection and recovery strategies differentiate between reusable and consumable resources in a system. Detection algorithms use graph reductions to explore state transitions that could occur from the state that is being analyzed. The details of a step in graph reduction depend on whether the reduction is applied to a consumable or reusable resource. Once a state has been determined to be a deadlock, the operating system will invoke a recovery algorithm to remove processes involved in the deadlock until the condition no longer exists.

This chapter completes the discussion of process management. The next chapter covers memory management.

10.7 ▪ Exercises

1. Identify safe, unsafe, and deadlock states in the state diagram shown in Figure 10.6.

2. Assume a system with four resource types, C = <6, 4, 4, 2>, and the maximum claim table shown in Figure 10.30. The resource allocator is considering allocating resources according to the table shown in Figure 10.31. Is this state safe? Why or why not?

3. Reconsider the process-resource model in Figure 10.6. Describe, in words or with a diagram, a similar state diagram for a system with three process and a

PROCESS	R_0	R_1	R_2	R_3
p_0	3	2	1	1
p_1	1	2	0	2
p_2	1	1	2	0
p_3	3	2	1	0
p_4	2	1	0	1

Figure 10.30
Maximum Claim Table

PROCESS	R_0	R_1	R_2	R_3
p_0	2	0	1	1
p_1	1	1	0	0
p_2	1	1	0	0
p_3	1	0	1	0
p_4	0	1	0	1

Figure 10.31
Current Allocation Table

single resource type with 2 units of the resource. How many deadlock states are in the graph?

4. Based on what you studied in this chapter, explain how to change the code fragment in Figure 8.5 so that a deadlock cannot occur.

5. Using the prevention strategy for invalidating the circular wait (Section 10.3), suggest a heuristic for avoiding the nested monitor call problem explained in Section 9.2.

6. A system is composed of four processes, $\{p_1, p_2, p_3, p_4\}$, and three types of serially reusable resources, $\{R_1, R_2, R_3\}$. The number of units of the resources are $C = <3, 2, 2>$.

 ■ Process p_1 holds 1 unit of R_1 and requests 1 unit of R_2.
 ■ p_2 holds 2 units of R_2 and requests 1 unit each of R_1 and R_3.
 ■ p_3 holds 1 unit of R_1 and requests 1 unit of R_2.
 ■ p_4 holds 2 units of R_3 and requests 1 unit of R_1.

 Show the reusable resource graph to represent this system state. Show the reduced form of the graph. Which, if any, of the processes are deadlocked in this state?

7. A system is composed of four process, $\{p_1, p_2, p_3, p_4\}$, and three types of consumable resources, $\{R_1, R_2, R_3\}$. There is 1 unit each of R_1 and R_3 available.

 ■ p_1 requests a unit of R_1 and a unit of R_3.
 ■ p_2 produces R_1 and R_3 and requests 1 unit of R_2.
 ■ p_3 requests 1 unit each of R_1 and R_3.
 ■ p_4 produces R_2 and requests a unit of R_3.

 Show the consumable resource graph to represent this system state. Which, if any, of the processes are deadlocked in this state?

8. A system is composed of four processes, $\{p_1, p_2, p_3, p_4\}$, two types of serially reusable resources, $\{S_1, S_2\}$, and two types of consumable resources, $\{C_1, C_2\}$. S_1 has 2 units and S_2 has 3 units. C_1 and C_2 each have 1 available unit.

 ■ p_1 produces C_1 and is requesting 2 units of S_2.
 ■ p_2 holds 2 units of S_1 and 1 unit of S_2 while it requests 2 units of C_2.
 ■ p_3 holds 1 unit of S_2 and requests 1 unit of C_1.
 ■ p_4 produces C_2 and requests 1 unit each of C_1 and S_1.

 Show the general resource graph to represent this system state. Which, if any, of the processes are deadlocked in this state?

11

Memory Management

H ow to cope with ... wait ... it's right on the tip of my tongue.

—Dave Barry, *Dave Barry Turns 40* ■

CHAPTER OBJECTIVES

The memory system includes all parts of the computer used for storing information. Secondary memory is long-term persistent memory that is held in storage devices such as disk drives. Primary memory holds information while it is being referenced by the CPU. Primary memory has faster access times than secondary memory does, although it is a more volatile form of storage. One challenge in application programming is to keep programs and information in primary memory only while they are being used by the CPU and to write the information back to secondary memory soon after it has been used or updated. If the challenge is met, the process uses a reduced amount of time to execute. Also, the danger of losing processed information due to crash or inconsistency is also reduced.

The memory manager is responsible for allocating primary memory to processes and for assisting the programmer in loading and storing the contents of the primary memory. Managing the sharing of primary memory and minimizing memory access time are the basic goals of the memory manager.

This chapter first considers the basic issues in memory manager design. Then it focuses on the memory manager's storage allocation task. Contemporary memory managers help the application programmer to meet the memory management challenge by dynamically binding and loading parts of the address space into primary memory, and this chapter discusses the key aspect of how they do this: deferred address binding. The last section of the chapter describes the basic strategies that modern memory managers employ: swapping, virtual memory, and caching.

11.1 ■ The Basics

The von Neumann computer incorporates a primary memory unit to hold data and programs when they are about to be used by a process that is executing in the CPU. The primary memory unit is part of the *executable memory* (and is sometimes called the executable memory), since the CPU's control unit can only fetch instructions from this memory. Data can be loaded into ALU registers from primary memory or stored from the registers into the primary memory. The von Neumann computer also incorporates various devices, including storage devices. When data and programs are to be executed, they are loaded in primary memory; otherwise, they are saved in secondary memory (on a storage device).

The purpose of the memory manager is to administer the use of the primary memory, including the automatic movement of programs and data back-and-forth between the primary and secondary memories. This section discusses several basic issues that direct and constrain memory manager design and function. It considers base requirements, the emergence of memory hierarchies, and the classic procedure for creating the address space and mapping it into the allocated primary memory. After studying this section, students should be ready to look at space allocation in the memory manager, which is covered in the next section.

11.1.1 ■ Requirements on Primary Memory

Primary memory and CPU are the fundamental resources used by every process. Without memory, the process has no place in which to execute programs and data. Chapters 6 through 10 focused on how an OS implements processes, with emphasis on CPU management in Chapter 7. This and the next chapters look at the design of primary memory managers.

There are three basic requirements that drive memory designs:

- The primary memory access time must be as small as possible. This need influences both software and hardware design.

- The primary memory must be as large as possible. Using virtual memory, software and hardware can make the memory *appear* to be larger than it actually is.

- The primary memory must be cost-effective. The cost cannot be more than a small percentage of the total cost of the computer.

It is always possible to build memory that can be accessed at CPU speeds. Registers are such a memory. However, these memories are very expensive to build, so modern CPUs typically contain fewer than 100 registers. In today's technology, access times for the primary memory unit are 1.5 to 4 times longer than the time to reference a CPU register. However, a primary memory unit may have over 100MB of memory—roughly a million times more executable memory than CPU registers have. Even though these numbers change rapidly (driven by memory technology and commercial factors), the speed and size ratios tend to stay relatively constant.

Memory managers have evolved with operating systems and hardware technology. However, today's process model uses essentially the same memory interface that was used in 1960. A process is provided with an address space that has the part of the pri-

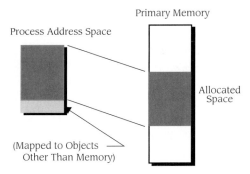

Primary Memory

Process Address Space

Allocated
Space

(Mapped to Objects
Other Than Memory)

Figure 11.1
The Relationship Between the Address Space and Primary Memory

mary memory allocated to the process mapped into the address space (see Figure 11.1). The memory manager must perform three functions:

- Allocate primary memory space to processes.
- Map the process address space into the allocated portion of the primary memory.
- Minimize access times using a cost-effective amount of primary memory.

The problem of implementing large, efficient memory involves both hardware and software technology. As hardware has evolved to have smaller access times for large units, the memory management strategy has changed to take advantage of these improvements. Conversely, as memory management strategies have evolved, they have driven the hardware to incorporate specialized functions. The continuing development of memory management strategies in contemporary computers requires that the designer have a deep understanding of software and hardware.

11.1.2 ■ Mapping the Address Space to Primary Memory

A programmer views a system in terms of the programming language and runtime interface. Chapter 6 explained how a program is translated from source code into an absolute program in an abstract address space, ready to be loaded and executed. In a compiled-program environment, the source program is translated at *compile time* to produce a relocatable object module. A collection of relocatable modules is combined using a linkage editor at *link time* to produce an absolute (or load) module, thus defining the part of the address space for the instructions, data, and stack. When the absolute module is prepared, the linkage editor determines the internal organization of the address space. Generally however, it does not know the location in the primary memory where the address space will be loaded, so it cannot bind the addresses in the instruction to physical memory addresses. The absolute module is constructed as if it were to be loaded and executed at memory location 0. The loader modifies the addresses in the load module at *load time* to produce the executable image stored in primary memory. In building an understanding of the fundamentals of memory management, you need to consider the management of addresses during various phases of the translation process.

Using Memory Hierarchies to Reduce Access Time

Von Neumann computer systems employ three or more levels of memory, arranged in a hierarchy. The highest level is CPU register memory, the middle level is primary (executable) memory, and the lowest level is secondary memory. The primary and secondary memory levels can be refined into levels by employing specific memory technologies. Within the hierarchy, high-level memory tends to be very fast but limited in size. Memory

near the bottom is very large, while access speed is a secondary consideration. At the bottom of the hierarchy, very large amounts of information (for example, terrabytes) are stored for long periods of times (for example, years). At this lowest level, the cost of the storage medium dominates, so magnetic tape is still widely used, even though its access speed is slow and its capacity per tape is limited compared to optical and magnetic disks.

Chapter 4 introduced the hierarchy by describing the three basic levels: processor registers, primary memory, and secondary memory. Contemporary machines have many more levels, including cache memory, and various forms of secondary memory including rotating magnetic memory, optical memory, and sequentially accessed memory (see Figure 11.2).

Computers access information stored in the executable memory part of the

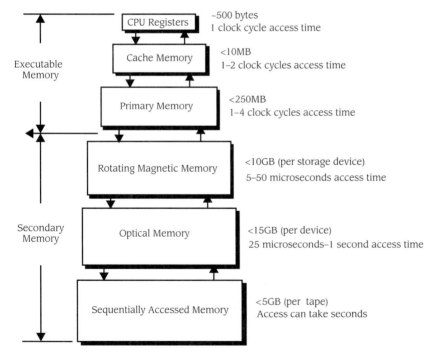

Figure 11.2
Memory Hierarchies

PERFORMANCE TUNING

Using Memory Hierarchies *(continued)*

hierarchy by using different mechanisms than those used to access information in the secondary memory. A process can access executable memory with a single load or store instruction in a few clock cycles. Secondary memory is implemented in the storage devices, so access involves action by a driver and a physical device. Hence, secondary memory takes at least three orders of magnitude more time to access than does executable memory.

The memory manager is required to allocate portions of executable memory and to provide mechanisms to manually move data across the hierarchy. A virtual memory system automates the movement of information between the secondary and primary memories and between cache and primary memories. The file manager provides mechanisms to administer secondary memory according to the user's needs. This chapter discusses the basic memory manager. The next two discuss virtual memory and file management. The first step in memory management is binding the process's address space to storage locations, discussed in next In the Hangar section.

11.1.2.1 ■ Compile Time

Consider a static variable in a source program. A *static variable* is a variable that retains the last value stored in it even when it goes out of scope. At compile time, the translator generates code to allocate storage for the variable and then uses the address of the allocated storage wherever the code references the variable. Since the variable is static, its space is in the program data segment. If it were a C automatic variable, it would be on the runtime stack. The organization of the data segment for the whole program will not be known until the relocatable module is combined with others at link time, so the compiler binds the variable address into a set of contiguous addresses beginning at 0. This set will be combined with other like sets by the linkage editor to make up the data segment.

Next, consider a procedure entry point. In general, the compiler will not be able to determine the address for the entry point, since the target procedure may be in a different relocatable module. For example, if the target is a library routine, such as `printf`, it will have been compiled when the system software was built. Since the target address is unknown at compile time, it cannot be bound at compile time. It instead will be handled at link time. The compiler will annotate each such reference to an external address so that the linkage editor can place the correct address in the code.

11.1.2.2 ■ Link Time

At link time, the various data segments generated by the translators and written to the relocatable module are combined to form a single data segment. The linkage editor then *relocates* the addresses in the instructions that reference the data segment and the external entry points by changing all references so that they point to the correct location in the absolute module.

11.1.2.3 ■ Load Time

At load time, the addresses must be adjusted once again. For simplicity, all addresses in an absolute module are adjusted as if the module were to be loaded at physical location 0. However, the module may eventually be loaded anywhere in the executable memory, depending on the state of the memory and the strategy employed by the memory manager. Once the loader determines the actual location where the program image is to be loaded, it binds the addresses in the program to physical memory locations that contain the respective variables or instructions.

➤ IN THE HANGAR

The Address Binding Procedure

The traditional translation and loading process requires a logical memory cell's address to be treated as a relocatable address at compile time, to be converted to an address in the absolute module at link time, and finally to be bound to a physical memory location at load time. For example, suppose we have the code segment shown in Figure 11.3.

Figure 11.3
A Sample Code Segment

```
static int gVar;
. . .
int proc_a(int arg){
        . . .
        gVar = 7;
        put_record(gVar);
        . . .
}
```

The compiler will allocate space for the variable named gVar in the relocatable object module for proc_a. However, the procedure named put_record is located in a different relocatable object module, so the compiler must leave the reference unresolved. The compiler will generate a relocatable object module similar to the example shown in Figure 11.4. The compiler reserves space for the variable named gVar at the relative address 0036 and records the value in its symbol table. (Figure 11.4 shows an optional symbol table at relative address location 0600 in the relocatable object module.) The external references and definitions also appear in the relocatable object module. The assignment statement is translated into a pair of instructions to load "7" into a register and then to store it into the memory cell associated with gVar. Relative address 0220 contains the load instruction that places the immediate operand, 7, into register R1. Relative address 0224 contains the store instruction that copies the contents of R1 into relative memory location 0036—the memory location bound to the variable gVar by the compiler. When the compiler translates the function call, it first pushes the parameter values onto the stack with the instruction in location 0228. Then, at relative address 0232, it generates an instruction to perform a function call to the externally defined entry point.

Figure 11.4
The Relocatable Object module

Relative Address	Generated Code	
0000	. . .	
. . .		
0008	entry	proc_a
. . .		
0036	[Space for gVar variable]	
. . .		
0220	load	=7, R1
0224	store	R1, 0036
0228	push	0036
0232	call	'put_record'
. . .		
0400	External reference table	
. . .		
0404	'put_record' 0232	
. . .		
0500	External definition table	
. . .		
0540	'proc_a'	0008
. . .		
0600	(optional symbol table)	
. . .		
0799	(last location in the module)	

Since the compiler does not have enough information to bind the address of the entry point to the symbol put_record, it annotates the operand address field for the linkage editor to complete the binding operation at link time and makes an entry in the *reference table,* or ref table, to be processed by the linkage editor. It also makes an entry in the *definition table,* or def table, for each external symbol, such as an entry point, that it is able to define. The example relocatable module is 800 memory cells, including the code, data, and tables.

The linkage editor combines the relocatable object module shown in Figure 11.4 with other such modules, including the one containing the put_record procedure. The result is an absolute module of the form shown in Figure 11.5. The combination is achieved by effectively concatenating all relevant relocatable object modules and then adjusting the relocatable addresses so that they reference the appropriate memory locations. If the programmer directs the compiler to leave the symbols in the absolute program (with a compiler argument), the absolute module may contain a composite symbol table. However, the external references and definitions will have been matched up by the link editor when it combined relocatable modules. In the figure, the relocatable module is relocated to location 1000, meaning the first location in the relocatable module compiled at location 0 is bound to location 1000. This adjustment causes other relative addresses in the module to be rebound at link time. For example, the address for the gVar is changed from 0036 to 1036, so the operand reference to 0036 in the store statement must be changed to store R1 in 1036 rather than in 0036. The linkage editor must change all relocatable addresses to reflect the new binding for the load module. By convention, the absolute module will be created so that its first address is memory location 0000.

Figure 11.5
The Absolute Program

Relative Address	Generated Code
0000	(Other modules)
. . .	
1008	entry proc_a
. . .	
1036	[Space for gVar variable]
. . .	
1220	load =7, R1
1224	store R1, 1036
1228	push 1036
1232	call 2334
. . .	
1399	(End of proc_a)
. . .	(Other modules)
2334	entry put_record
. . .	
2670	(optional symbol table)
. . .	
2999	(last location in the module)

At load time, the absolute module will again have its addresses adjusted so that they reference the memory locations containing the generated images. If the load module were to be placed, for example, in primary memory starting at location 4000 (see Figure 11.6), the program image would have to be rebound. The addresses for gVar and put_record would be rebound to new physical memory locations, and the places in the program referencing those locations would be adjusted at load time. Now gVar would be stored at primary memory location 1036 + 4000 = 5036, and the put_record entry point would be at 2334 + 4000 = 6334. The instruction operand addresses would be bound one final time before the program was executed.

Figure 11.6
The Program Loaded at Location 4000

Relative Address	Generated Code
0000	(Other process's programs)
4000	(Other modules)
. . .	
5008	entry proc_a
. . .	
5036	[Space for gVar variable]
. . .	
5220	load =7, R1
5224	store R1, 5036
5228	push 5036
5232	call 6334
. . .	
5399	(End of proc_a)
. . .	(Other modules)
6334	entry put_record
. . .	
6670	(optional symbol table)
. . .	
6999	(last location in the module)
7000	(Other process's programs)

11.1.3 ■ Dynamic Memory for Data Structures

Programming languages often define a facility to allow a program to manage part of its own data space, although the language does not define how memory allocation and binding should be handled. From the programmer's viewpoint, this facility is used to support dynamic requests for space to store data structures (to implement lists, trees, strings, and so on). Since this facility is usually your first introduction to dynamic memory allocation, it is natural for you to expect that this is a general interface to the memory manager. However, these runtime dynamic memory allocators do not cause memory to be allocated to the process at all. Instead, they allow the programmer to manually bind unused parts of the process's address space to dynamic data structures. The UNIX model is representative of how this type of dynamic memory is handled by the system.

The UNIX runtime system provides a library routine, `malloc`, for requesting memory space for dynamic data structures. The programmer requests more space by writing a code sequence such as

```
struct ListNode *node;
. . .
node = (struct ListNode *) malloc(sizeof(struct ListNode));
. . .
```

When the `malloc` call returns, node points to a memory block large enough to hold an instance of the `struct ListNode` data structure.

In most library implementations, `malloc` does not perform a system call. Instead, the linkage editor anticipates the use of this form of dynamic memory allocation and creates a memory layout to accommodate such requests in the same part of the process's address space that is used by the stack (see Figure 11.7). The maximum size of the stack and of heap storage is not known prior to runtime, so the translation system reserves a single block of storage for both. It then allows them to "grow" toward one another as the process executes. If the stack contains many temporary variables and call frames, it will use a large amount of the space. Similarly, if the program allocates a large amount of space using `malloc`, the stack will be limited in its size.

What happens when this preallocated heap storage is exhausted? `malloc` detects that the heap is completely allocated, so it calls the kernel memory manager (using the `sbrk` system call) to request that the process be allocated more space. When a frame is added to the stack, a similar reallocation may be required. When new space is allocated to the process, the address space may have to be rebound to the primary memory space allocated to the process so that memory references in the program will still reference the various parts of the program, stack, heap, and data areas. How this is accomplished depends on how the memory manager is implemented in the particular version of UNIX; it is discussed further in Section 11.3.

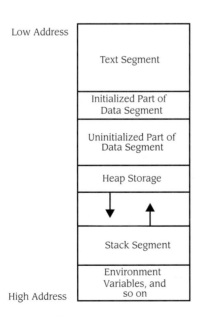

Figure 11.7
UNIX-Style Memory Layout

11.2 ■ Memory Allocation

Once the absolute module has been created by the language translation system, primary memory must be allocated to the process. The address space can then be bound to the block of primary memory allocated to the process and the executable image can be stored in it. Thus address binding cannot be completed until physical memory space has been allocated to the process. The memory manager for a multiprogrammed OS handles primary memory allocation based on space-multiplexed sharing. When a process is staged to run, it requests primary memory space from the memory manager, prepares its program (address space) for execution, and then stores it in the memory. The program preparation may include the compilation and linking of source code or just the loading and execution of previously linked programs.

Suppose the OS supports four-way multiprogramming. The memory manager partitions memory into four blocks and then allocates each block to a process. Figure 11.8 illustrates a diagram of primary memory in which the four processes have been allocated various parts of the memory. Since the OS must have its own memory space for code and tables, there are five different memory blocks in the figure. The OS is using the memory from location 0 to A, the memory between location A and B is not allocated, Process 1 has been allocated memory locations B to C, Process 3 has been allocated locations C to D, locations D to E are not allocated to a process, and so on.

Many different strategies could be used to allocate the memory. These strategies are generally separated into those that divide primary memory into a fixed-number of fixed-size blocks at the time the operating system is configured and those that use dynamically determined, variable-sized blocks. The basic problem to be overcome in memory allocation is fragmentation. Ideally, the memory manager could allocate every

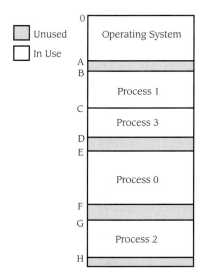

Figure 11.8
Multiprogramming Memory Support

single byte of memory to a process if any process needs memory. In practical terms, parts of the memory cannot be used at any given time because the memory manager is unable to allocate these parts in an efficient manner. How fragmentation occurs is covered in the discussion of the two basic strategies.

11.2.1 ▪ Fixed-partition Memory Strategies

Suppose the primary memory is statically divided into N fixed-size regions or partitions, where region R_i has N_i units of memory. Typically $N_i \neq N_j$ (the regions are different sizes), so processes with small address spaces use small partitions and processes with large address spaces use large partitions. Memory allocation in a fixed-partition system requires that a process's address space size correlate with a partition of adequate size. For example, if a process requires n_k units of memory, it can be loaded into any R_i, where $N_i \geq n_k$. Upon allocation of R_i to the process, $N_i - n_k$ units of the primary memory are unused during the time the process is loaded, since the space is allocated to the process but not mapped into its address space. This phenomenon is called *internal fragmentation*. This form of fragmentation is the loss of the use of part of the memory due to the allocation of N_i memory locations when the process needed only n_k units.

If the memory diagram shown in Figure 11.8 were based on fixed partitions, R_0 might extend from location 0 to location B, R_1 from B to C, R_2 from C to E, R_3 from E to G, and R_4 from G to the last address of the memory. Thus the memory from location A to location B is an unused internal fragment in R_0, the memory from location D to location E is an internal fragment in R_2, and so on. In the example, there is no loss due to internal fragmentation for R_1.

How should memory allocation work for fixed-partition memories? Suppose each memory region has its own queue of processes competing for the partition. When a process requests n_k units of memory, the allocator places the process into the queue for some R_i, where $N_i \geq n_k$. Normally, the allocator would select the R_i that has the *best fit* to n_k, meaning it would select the R_i where $N_i - n_k$ is minimized. Sometimes the allocator may not use a best-fit strategy if some region's queue is becoming oversubscribed. Instead, it might choose any region large enough to hold the process. However, doing this would incur more internal fragmentation than the best-fit approach in order to relieve the competition for the partition with a better fit. Another alternative is for the allocator to keep a single queue of all processes, then to allocate according to utilization.

Once a process is allocated a region and it begins to run a program, the loader binds the absolute program to produce an executable program with addresses determined by the region's physical location in the primary memory. Even if the memory manager chooses to remove the process from memory, it can save the primary memory image on the secondary memory and then reload it in the same partition later without readjusting the addresses.

Fixed-partition memory managers were widely used in batch multiprogramming systems, but they are generally not suitable for use in any system in which n_k is not known ahead of time (for example, in timesharing systems). The memory demands of interactive users vary wildly, depending on the activity at any particular user's interactive terminal. For example, the user may be logged onto the machine but not use the terminal for an hour or two. Hence, the process effectively needs almost no memory until the user returns to the terminal and begins interacting with the system again. At other times, the user may be compiling a program or formatting a text document. These programs require relatively large amounts of memory compared with the memory requirements of a text editor or mail system. Essentially, timesharing systems forced operating systems away from fixed-partition strategies toward dynamic environments that better use memory.

11.2.2 ■ Variable-partition Memory Strategies

Internal fragmentation losses are aggravated by timesharing usage due to the wild variation in a process's memory needs during a login session. The obvious way to address this loss is to redesign the memory manager so that it allocates regions according to the space needs of a process at any given time. This approach effectively removes the possibility of internal fragmentation. (Note that the memory manager will allocate only on multiword boundaries such as 64-byte blocks. If a process requests an amount of memory in an increment different from a multiple of the minimum size, small amounts of internal fragmentation will result. These losses are inconsequential compared with the size of internal fragments in fixed-partition memory schemes.)

11.2.2.1 ■ The Basic Strategy

The new challenge for the memory manager is to keep track of variable-sized blocks of memory and allocate them efficiently. When the system is initialized, the primary memory is configured as a single large block of N_0 units of memory (see Figure 11.9a). The

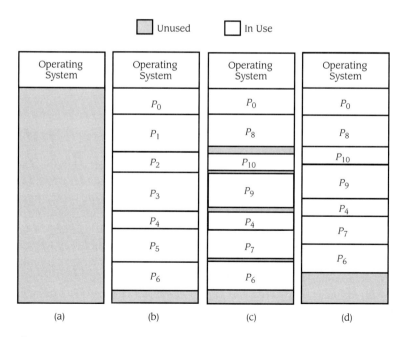

Figure 11.9
Dynamic Memory Allocation in Variable-partition Memory

scheduler allocates memory, n_i units to process p_i, as long as

$$\sum_{i=0}^{k} n_i \leq N_0$$

(see Figure 11.9b). A small amount of memory at the end of the memory space will be lost to external fragmentation—the part of the memory not marked as allocated to the OS or to any p_i. When no more processes can be allocated memory, the memory manager waits for processes to release memory.

In Figure 11.9(c), p_5 has released its memory and p_7 has been allocated $n_7 \leq n_5$ units of memory. The memory manager selected a process "fitting" into the n_5 unit "hole" in memory that resulted from p_5 releasing its memory. Because of varying memory needs, it is possible that $n_7 < n_5$, thus resulting in the creation of a small block of unused memory between the space allocated to p_7 and p_6. This unused block is another instance of external fragmentation.

When p_6 releases its memory, n_5 units of memory are freed adjacent to the unallocated space that follows p_6. The memory manager must keep track of holes so that when two contiguous holes appear, they can be merged into one larger block of unallocated memory. In Figure 11.9(c), p_8 has been allocated to the block previously allocated to p_1, p_{10} to the block previously occupied by p_2, p_9 to the block previously allocated to p_3, and p_7 to p_5's block. This new allocation has created several external fragments similar to the original external fragment at the end of memory in Figure 11.9(b).

As the system continues to run, the chances of external fragmentation increase. This situation occurs because a process can fit into a hole that is only at least as big as its memory requirements. The extra memory creates a small fragment. Furthermore, as the memory becomes increasingly fragmented, the memory manager will tend to favor processes that have smaller memory demands, thus causing the fragments, in turn, to become smaller and smaller. Eventually, the system will reach a state whereby only the smallest memory requests can be satisfied, even when there is sufficient aggregate memory to meet the requirements of larger requests. At this point, the operating system will have to compact the memory by moving all loaded processes so that they use contiguous space in the memory, thus creating one large free block (see Figure 11.9d).

11.2.2.2 ■ Dynamic Allocation

There is another scenario that must be considered in variable-partition memory. The system could allow a process to change the amount of memory allocated to it while it is executing, depending on its phase of computation. This scenario means that sometimes the process will request *more* memory than can fit in its current space plus any adjacent holes. For example, in Figure 11.9(c), suppose p_9 requests additional memory in an amount that exceeds its current space plus the space available in the holes above and below it. How can the request be honored? The memory manager could block p_9 until more adjacent space became available. But this strategy is not favored by interactive users, since they might incur very long waits for service. Alternatively, the scheduler could find a larger hole in memory and move the process to the new hole, thus releasing the old space. However (as in the case of compaction), the system would then require some means of adjusting the program's addresses when it moves the address space. How this is done is discussed in Section 11.3 (see also the Performance Tuning box on the cost of moving programs).

In an environment that supports dynamic memory allocation, the memory manager must keep a record of the usage of each allocatable block of memory. This record could be kept by using almost any data structure that implements linked lists. An obvious implementation is to define a *free list* of block descriptors, with each descriptor containing a pointer to the next descriptor, a pointer to the block, and the length of the block (see Figure 11.10). The memory manager keeps a free list pointer and inserts entries into the list in some order conducive to its allocation strategy; the figure simply orders the blocks in order of increasing primary memory address. Memory is ordinarily allocated in multiword blocks, with 64 or more words per block. A block of free memory is unused, meaning its contents are not used by any process. Therefore memory allocation strategies typically use the first few words in every free block to implement the linked list shown in Figure 11.10. The free list pointer in the scheduler points to the first location of the first free block.

A number of different strategies are used to allocate space to the processes that are competing for memory. Here is a brief explanation of a few of the most popular ones:

- *Best fit:* The memory manager places a process in the smallest block of unallocated memory in which it will fit. For example, suppose a process requests 12KB of memory and the memory manager currently has a list of unallocated blocks of 6KB, 14KB, 19KB, 11KB, and 13KB blocks. The best-fit strategy will allocate the 13KB block to the process.

- *Worst fit:* The memory manager places a process in the largest block of unallocated memory available. The idea is that this placement will create the largest hole after the allocations, thus increasing the possibility that, compared to best fit, another process can use the hole created as a result of external fragmentation. If the list of unallocated blocks consists of 6KB, 14KB, 19KB, 11KB, and 13KB blocks and a process

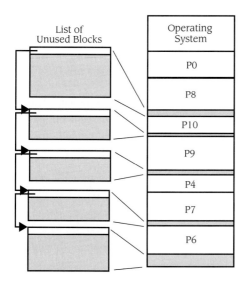

Figure 11.10
Managing Free Memory Blocks

requests a 12KB block, then worst fit will split the 19KB block into a 12KB block to allocate to the process, leaving a 7KB block for future use.

■ *First fit:* If there are many holes in the memory, the scheduler, in order to reduce the amount of time it spends analyzing the free list, begins traversing the list from the beginning and allocates memory from the first hole it encounters large enough to satisfy the request. If the list of unallocated blocks consists of 6KB, 14KB, 19KB, 11KB, and 13KB blocks and a process requests a 12KB block, first fit will allocate the 14KB block to the process.

■ *Next fit:* The first-fit approach tends to fragment the blocks near the beginning of the list without considering blocks further down the list. Next fit is a variant of the first-fit strategy. It converts the list into a circular list, with the last block pointing to the first free one. When a process requests a block, it begins its search where the free pointer indicates. As soon as it finds a block to allocate, it allocates the space and then adjusts the free pointer to address the new fragment or if there is no fragment, to the block that follows the allocated block. Referring to the running example in this section, if the list of unallocated blocks consists of 6KB, 14KB, 19KB, 11KB, and 13KB blocks and the memory manager had last allocated a block from the list between the 19KB block and the 11KB block, then when a process requests a 12KB block, next fit will allocate the 13KB block to the process.

The classic exposition of these (and other) strategies appears in Knuth [1973, vol. 1].

11.2.3 ■ Contemporary Allocation Strategies

Modern memory managers all use some form of variable partitioning. However, memory is usually allocated in fixed-sized blocks (called "pages," as you will see when virtual memory is introduced in Section 11.4), thus greatly simplifying the management of the free list. In this case, all allocatable units are the same size, so the free list management is trivial. In older systems, such as DOS and Version 7 UNIX, the memory manager deals with variable-sized blocks of memory. When a process is created, the memory manager uses a strategy such as best fit to assign an initial amount of memory. As the process executes, it requests and releases memory according to its needs for any particular phase of execution.

The part of the address space that is likely to change is that containing data. This is because once the part of the address space that contains the program has been loaded into memory, it will not ordinarily change size (a change in size would mean the program had been changed). Nevertheless, suppose the part of the address space that contains the program does grow (or shrink). Then either part of the program is being unloaded from memory or the program is somehow growing. In languages like C, this is not normally possible, although it can occur in languages like Lisp. We have already determined that it is critical for the system to provide some better means than conventional static binding for changing the address space binding as the program executes. Otherwise, each time a program grows or shrinks, the loader must rebind each address in the program to the new primary memory location. (This also happens each time a program is moved—for example, by compaction or by unloading and reloading an address space from/to primary memory.)

The Cost of Moving Programs

Compaction requires that a program be moved from one block of memory to another. This in turn requires the program to be relocated, since the address bindings that the loader used when the program was loaded in the first location will no longer be valid when it is loaded into a different location. Unfortunately, the loader is able to relocate only absolute images, not executable images. This happens because the absolute image (for example, as in Figure 11.5) is formatted so that the loader can easily identify addresses by flags left in the code by the compiler and the linkage editor. These flags are removed by the absolute loader when it creates an executable image, since the image is to be interpreted by the control unit as it is decoded and executed (as discussed in Chapter 4). Hence, when the program is moved, the loader must begin with the absolute image created by the linkage editor rather than using the executable image loaded in primary memory (see Figure 11.11). Any changes the process may have made to the data before the address space was moved will be lost unless they have been saved in secondary memory.

There is a better solution to the problem: Have the system change the way it binds addresses to primary memory locations. This approach is explained in Section 11.3 after the description of how unused memory is managed.

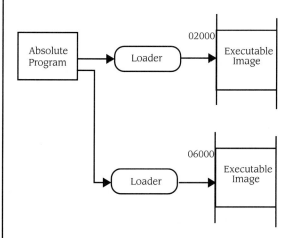

Figure 11.11
Moving an Executable Image

Section 11.1.2 considered how to handle growth and shrinkage of the part of the address space that contains the data. In this case, the memory manager accepts the request for more memory from the process—for example, as an `sbrk` system call in BSD UNIX [McKusick et al., 1996]. It then allocates the memory from the free list as it does with the original request when the process was started. Adjusting the binding of addresses for data can be handled more easily than for programs, since the data does not need to have address relocation. For example, in the UNIX `sbrk` system call memory is added to the address space at the *break address*—the point in the address space between the stack and the heap (see Figure 11.7). In this case, no memory addresses need be adjusted.

In conjunction with variable-sized memory allocation, modern operating systems, program translation systems, and hardware combine to provide a new approach to address space binding. The goal is to provide an alternative to using the loader to rebind addressees.

11.3 ▪ Dynamic Address Relocation

Traditionally, symbols in a source program are first bound to relative addresses in a relocatable module at compile time, then to addresses in an absolute module at link time, and finally to memory addresses at load time. All addresses are bound to memory locations prior to *runtime*. As described in Section 11.1, programming language runtime systems provide one facility for runtime binding, with dynamic memory allocation facilities to support dynamic data structures. In the UNIX `malloc` call, a programmer manually binds addresses using the pointer facilities of the programming language. For example, when a process executes a code fragment such as

```
struct ListNode *node;
...
node = (struct ListNode *) malloc(sizeof(struct ListNode();
...
```

the program uses the node pointer to reference the base address of the memory block and the `ListNode` data structure to reference individual fields in the data structure—for example, by writing variable names such as `node->left`. Recall from the discussion of the implementation of this approach (Section 11.1.3) that this form of dynamic allocation is accomplished by binding unallocated heap space into the address space rather than actually allocating new memory to the process.

If there were a more general tool for binding absolute program addresses at runtime, the memory manager would have the freedom to move the program around in the memory without requiring the programmer to take any special action to compensate for the relocation. This would also enable a general approach for memory managers using variable-partitioning strategies. With these strategies, they could easily change the memory allocated to a process without worrying about relocating the process address space that is using the memory. This approach is called *dynamic relocation*.

Consider the algorithm the loader uses to adjust addresses in the absolute module so that they match the physical addresses. Since the absolute module is built as if it were to be loaded at memory location 0, addresses depending on this fact are said to be relative to the beginning of the module. (Programs can have "addresses" other than relative addresses compiled into operand fields. For example, an immediate operand should not change when a module is relocated. Some instruction sets include an offset address, meaning the operand is an offset from the current PC contents. This offset enables a program to branch forward or backward the number of addresses specified by the operand. Such operands are common in machines that use 16-bit address operands.) When the loader determines the actual address of the first location in the module, it can adjust any relative address by adding the value of the first location to it. In Figure 11.6, each relative address from the absolute module in Figure 11.5 had 4000 added to it because the module was loaded at location 4000.

Hardware can easily be incorporated into the processor design to perform this relocation on each reference to memory. Using hardware allows the last phase of relocation to be deferred until runtime. Suppose the CPU were to ignore relocation and simply begin executing the program. Each address to be relocated would be issued to the memory as if it were a memory address. The hardware would intercept each such address and add a relocation value to it before sending it on to the memory (see Figure 11.12). The *relocation register* is part of the process's state, so it would be changed each time a different process was allocated the CPU. This ability causes an executable image to be produced at load time, but with the assumption that every address sent to the primary memory will have the relocation register content added to it. This *hardware dynamic*

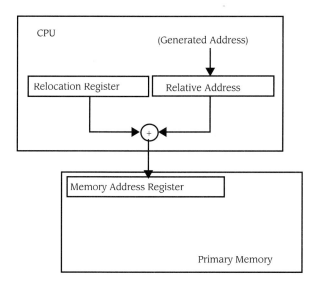

Figure 11.12
Hardware Address Relocation

relocation is commonly used in contemporary processors, independent of any additional memory management strategies. It gives the OS tremendous freedom concerning the location at which executable images are loaded in primary memory whenever the memory manager needs to move programs in the middle of their execution.

Contemporary compilers take advantage of hardware relocation. They are designed to generate data and code into distinct segments within a relocatable object module. For example, provided that the hardware supports multiple segments, C programs are compiled into a text segment that contains the code, a stack segment that contains temporary variables, and a data segment that contains static variables. The UNIX process model (as described in Chapter 2) is modeled after this program modularization. To provide explicit support for such language models, the CPU is designed with at least three relocation registers to manage the code, stack, and data segments as separate relocatable modules. The CPU contains a code segment relocation register, a stack segment relocation register, and a data segment relocation register (see Figure 11.13). The code segment register relocates all addresses during the processor's fetch cycle, the stack segment register relocates addresses for stack instruction execution, and the data segment register relocates all other addresses during the execute cycle.

Could segment register administration be handled "automatically" by the OS? Suppose the compiler generates normal 16-bit addresses when it translates a source module and leaves external references to be handled by the linkage editor. Further suppose that no individual module has a code or data segment larger than 64KB, although the resulting absolute program may be much larger than 64KB. Hence, all generated

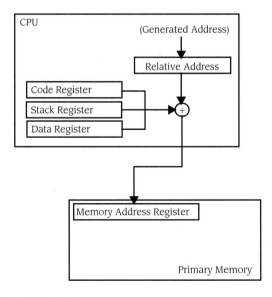

Figure 11.13
Multiple Segment Relocation Registers

code will be 16-bit relative addresses in the code or data segment for the relocatable module. When any function is executed in a module, the initialization code at the entry point loads the code and data segment registers to point to the part of the absolute image corresponding to the relocatable module. The address used by the prologue must be provided by the linkage editor. Now, when control flow moves from one module to another, the calling function will reference an external symbol that will later be resolved by the linkage editor. The compiler recognizes this fact and generates code to adjust the code segment register to call the externally defined function before the instruction is executed (see Figure 11.14). Every call across modules causes the code segment register to change. Since data references outside the 64KB block must also be defined as external references in the source code, the compiler can recognize each of these references and generate code to change the data segment register. Every reference to an external variable causes the data segment register to change. This technique relies on the compiler and the linkage editor to provide a large enough address space through manipulation of the segment register. The approach fails for assembly language programs, for any program that inadvertently changes a segment register value, or in cases in which a source module generates a code or data segment larger than 64KB.

This technique also relies on an unusual `call` instruction in the machine language. What will happen if the compiler generates an instruction to set the code register in the instruction just before the call instruction? The next instruction fetched will not be the one in the location following the segment register load instruction. Rather, it will be one in a corresponding location in another 64KB segment. For this

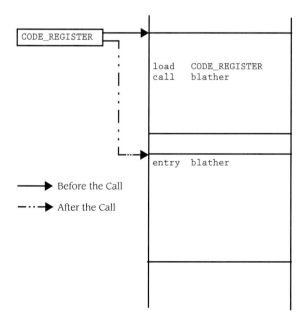

Figure 11.14
Adjusting the Code Register

approach to work, it must be possible to load the segment register and execute the `call` before the segment register is updated rather than just execute the `call` in an instruction.

Machines with privileged instructions can take a slightly more sophisticated approach. Such a machine does not allow the segment registers to be changed except via a privileged instruction. The compiler generates a trap instruction wherever the segment register needs to be adjusted. At runtime, the trap instruction interrupts the program execution and starts the operating system. The trap is recognized as a segment trap and is passed to the memory manager. The memory manager determines the target address and then adjusts the program counter and segment register to reference the distant target address. This technique, too, requires an instruction to be able to set the program counter and the segment register before another instruction is fetched from memory.

11.3.1 ■ Runtime Bound Checking

The relocation register has proved to be a fundamental addition to computer systems, since it enables dynamic address binding. Once such a mechanism has been incorporated into the hardware, it is easy to make small additions to substantially increase the ability of the system to support memory protection. Suppose each relocation register has a companion *limit register* that is loaded with the length of the memory segment addressed by the relocation register. Whenever the CPU sends an address to primary memory, the relocation register is added to the address at the same time it is compared with the contents of the limit register (see Figure 11.15). If the address is less than the

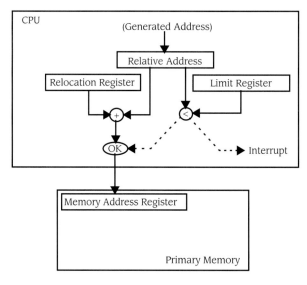

Figure 11.15
Bound Checking with a Limit Register

value in the limit register, the address refers to a location within the memory segment. If the address is larger than the limit register value, it refers to a part of primary memory not allocated to the process that is currently using the CPU. An *out-of-bounds reference*—also called a *segment violation*—will generate an interrupt, thus producing a fatal execution error.

➤ IN THE HANGAR

Expanding Small Address Spaces

Microprocessors take advantage of the relocation registers to solve a different problem. Sixteen-bit microprocessors typically have an instruction format that accommodates a 16-bit address. For example, Intel 8086 instructions employ 16-bit addresses that use four relocation (or *segment*) registers: (1) code segment, (2) data segment, (3) stack segment, and (4) extra segment. With the basic instruction format, a process can reference only 65,536 different bytes (64 KB). In the 8086, the contents of the code segment register are shifted left, then added to the value of any address generated during the CPU fetch cycle to produce a twenty-bit address. Thus the code segment can be located at any block of 64KB. Similarly, the data segment register is loaded having a different value to address the base of the data segment (used during ordinary instruction execution) and the stack segment register addresses the base of the stack segment (used during stack instruction execution). Now the CPU can use $3 \times 64KB = 192KB$ memory locations even though it has only 16-bit addresses. If it also uses the extra segment register, it can have $4 \times 64KB = 256KB$ memory locations.

Memory technology caused microprocessor memory (RAM) to become relatively inexpensive, thus encouraging people to configure 16-bit microprocessors with more than 256KB of memory. How can the "16-bit software" use this memory? The compiler can manage the segment registers contents so that their values change as the program runs. The compiler builds the text and data segments at the time it translates the source program. If the programmer believes either segment will exceed 64KB in the absolute module, the compiler is directed to generate code to reset the code segment register prior to a branch to a location outside the current 64KB block. A similar approach is used for referencing memory in the data segment. Normally, this segment register manipulation is done only if the programmer specifies it should be. The compiler must generate the code to manage the segment relocation registers. However, it would not usually be able to detect that the absolute module will exceed 64KB unless the source module being compiled generates a relocatable module greater than 64KB. This uncertainty means the compiler must load the segment registers for almost all branches and data references, thereby generating relatively inefficient code to be executed at runtime.

11.4 ▪ Memory Manager Strategies

Virtual memory is the dominant memory management strategy in modern operating systems, followed by swapping in lower functionality operating systems and on computers with moderate mapping hardware. Swapping technology was the first to take advantage of dynamic relocation hardware. It has influenced the way virtual memory has evolved. So we study swapping as the basis for understanding virtual memory. Virtual memory is introduced in this section and covered extensively in Chapter 12.

Multiple-partition memory strategies are the basis of multiprogramming. By dividing the memory into regions and allocating those regions to a set of processes, the scheduler can multiplex the CPU across these processes at a high rate of speed. If one assumes that there are always processes ready to execute, then primary memory can become the bottleneck to performance. Suppose N processes are loaded into the primary memory and an additional K processes could run if they had memory allocated to them. Then whenever any of the N processes is blocked on I/O, a semaphore, or other condition, the memory it holds is not being used for any useful purpose. Neither the other $N - 1$ loaded processes nor the K waiting processes can use the memory because it is allocated to the blocked process. Virtual memory and swapping attack this problem by deallocating the memory from blocked processes to enable some of the K waiting processes to use it while the process is blocked.

11.4.1 ▪ Swapping

Swapping memory managers attempt to optimize system performance by removing a process from primary memory when it is blocked, deallocating the memory, allocating it to other processes, and then reacquiring and reloading the swapped-out process when the process returns to the ready state. For example, when process p_i requests an I/O operation, it becomes blocked and will not return to the ready state for a relatively long period of time. When the process manager places p_i into a blocked state, it notifies the memory manager so that it can decide whether to swap the process's primary memory image to secondary memory (see Figure 11.16). When the process manager moves a blocked process, p_j, to the ready state, if p_j is swapped out, the process manager will inform the memory manager so that it can swap the address space back into primary

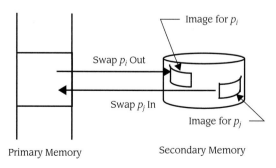

Figure 11.16
Swapping

memory, either immediately if primary memory is available or at least as soon as it becomes available.

When a process is swapped out, its executable image is copied to secondary memory—code, data, and stack. When it is swapped back into available primary memory, the executable image that was swapped out is copied into the new block allocated by the memory manager. Without relocation hardware, swapping would be very difficult to achieve due to the address binding problem. With relocation hardware, the executable image is simply copied into the newly allocated region of memory.

Swapping is especially well-suited to timesharing systems, since such systems often have times when a user logs onto the machine (and hence is using some resources) but is inactive for relatively long time periods (and hence not using the CPU). A swapping memory manager accommodates the timesharing scenario by allocating memory to a process while the user is requesting service at a relatively high rate, but deallocating memory during those phases when the user makes requests for service at a low rate. That is, in a timesharing system, the memory manager may decide to swap a process out of memory even if it is ready, depending on the total load on the machine.

The key observation about a swapping system is that if a process is not going to use the CPU for a relatively long time, it should release the memory allocated. This allows other processes to use the memory and the CPU. Timesharing memory managers often turn this observation around by adopting a strategy to address the case in which there are many more requests for memory and CPU than there are memory resources available. The memory manager selects some processes that are to give up memory (and the CPU) so that other processes have an opportunity to use them. The selected processes are blocked (on a memory request) by the memory manager and then their memory is deallocated. They immediately begin competing with other processes to reacquire memory. Contemporary timesharing systems (such as many versions of UNIX) use swapping to provide equitable service to an oversubscribed timesharing system. When the number of active users surpasses a system-defined threshold, the memory manager will begin swapping processes.

Some form of swapping policy is almost always required with any multiprogramming, interactive system environment, even ones with very large amounts of physical memory. Since the overall load on the machine is determined by continuous and unpredictable human activity, there are large periods of time when a process is holding memory but is dormant. As long as there are no other processes being blocked by the memory manager, there is no need to swap. However, once the memory request queue begins to grow, the memory manager begins swapping processes out of memory whenever they have a period of inactivity that exceeds a threshold amount. As the memory request queue grows, the threshold may decrease. The effect of swapping is easily perceived by the user, since it can result in a noticeable increase in response time.

The decision about whether to swap out a process may depend on either the time the process is expected to be blocked, or the need to swap out a process in an effort to equitably share memory and the CPU. Observe that performance increases gained through swapping are never to the process's advantage, since the process will have to compete to reacquire primary memory. The performance gain is a system-wide gain evidenced, for example, by a reduction in the average turnaround/response time for a process.

What is the cost of swapping out a process? If the process holds S units of primary memory, then we can compute the overhead time required to copy the executable image to a storage device and the time to copy it back into the primary memory when it is swapped in. If a disk block is D units of primary memory, then the memory manager will need to write at least $R = S/D$ (R is rounded to the next highest integer) disk blocks in order to save the executable image. It will need to perform the same number of read operations in order to swap the address space back into primary memory. The cost to the process is the time the process spends competing to regain primary memory after it enters the ready state while being swapped out. So wherever the memory manager arbitrarily decides to swap out a process, the delay in time—the swap time, $2R$, and the time to reacquire memory—is all overhead.

Suppose the process manager changes the state of a process holding S units of the memory to blocked and it remains blocked for T units of time. The space-time product, $S \times T$, represents the amount of resource waste due to the process's being blocked while holding memory. If S is small, then the memory manager will gain only a small amount of memory to be used by other processes if it swaps the process. If T is small, then the process will shortly begin competing for primary memory. If $T < R$, then the process will logically begin requesting memory before it has even been completely swapped out. For swapping to be effective, T must be considerably greater than $2R$ for every process the memory manager chooses to swap out, and S must be large enough that it enables other processes to execute.

The memory manager knows S for every process, but it can only predict the value of T when a process becomes blocked. If the process becomes blocked because it requests an I/O operation on a slow device, then the memory manager can estimate a lower bound on T and hence on $S \times T$. When a process becomes blocked due to an arbitrary resource request (for example a P operation on a semaphore or a request for a serially reusable resource), the memory manager cannot estimate T. In a conservative swapping strategy, a process will not be swapped by such requests. But in an optimistic strategy, the process may be swapped on almost any request operation.

If the memory manager decides to swap out a process due to severe competition for memory, it can compute a different space-time product, $S \times T'$, where T' is the amount of time the process has held S units of memory. If $S \times T'$ is large for some p_i and other processes are waiting to be swapped in, then the process has held the memory for a relatively long time. In the interest of equitable sharing, the memory manager policy may be to swap p_i out and to swap in some other process into the space previously used by p_i.

11.4.2 ■ Virtual Memory

Virtual memory strategies allow a process to use the CPU when only part of its address space is loaded in the primary memory. In this approach, each process's address space is partitioned into parts that can be loaded into primary memory when they are needed and written back to secondary memory otherwise (see Figure 11.17). Programs are written to naturally have implicit partitions. Address space partitions have been used for the code, data, and stack identified by the compiler and by the relocation hardware.

The code segment usually has a more subtle set of partitions relating to the phases of computation defined by the program. For example, almost all programs have a phase for initializing data structures, another for reading input data, one or more for the actual computation (depending on the algorithm), others for error recovery and reporting, and

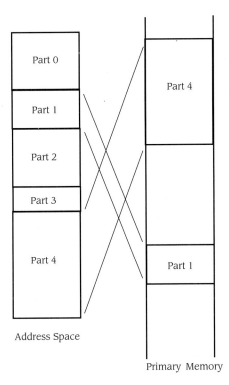

Figure 11.17
Virtual and Physical Memory

one for output. Similar implicit partitions usually exist in the data segment. This characteristic of programs—called *spatial reference locality*—is very important to the strategy used by virtual memory systems. When a program is executing in one part of its address space, its spatial locality is the set of addresses used during that phase of the computation. As the computation moves to a different phase (referencing different parts of the address space for the program and/or the data), it changes locality.

In Figure 11.17, the address space is divided into five parts. However, only parts 1 and 4 span the part of the address space that the program is using at the instant the memory state is observed; therefore only parts 1 and 4 are loaded in the primary memory. Different parts of the program will be loaded at different times, depending on the process's locality. The virtual memory manager's task is to infer the program's locality and to keep the corresponding part of the address space loaded in the primary memory while the process is using it.

A virtual memory manager allocates portions of primary memory that are the same size as the partitions in the address space and then loads the executable image for the corresponding part of the address space into the allocated primary memory. The effect is that the process uses much less primary memory, thus greatly increasing the memory available to other processes. Suppose the virtual memory manager could be designed "perfectly." That is, it always knew the exact set of addresses in the program's locality and always kept exactly those parts of the address space loaded in primary memory before they were referenced (and unloaded when they are no longer part of the locality). Then even the process could not detect that it did not have a primary memory allocation as large as its address space.

What barriers must be overcome to implement virtual memory? The memory manager must be able to treat the address space in parts that correspond to the various localities that will exist during the program's execution. The system must be able to load a part anywhere in the physical memory and dynamically bind the addresses in the part to the physical location in which they are loaded. The amount of memory allocated to the process may vary, so many parts, or only the bare minimum, may be loaded at once. The next chapter addresses these issues.

Virtual memory began to appear in high-end commercial machines in the late 1970s. At that time, primary memory costs were high, so the amount of memory on the machine limited its use. Virtual memory offered a way for processes to execute using a primary memory space that was smaller than its address space. This allowed system designers to use relatively small memory regions with higher degrees of multiprogramming. For example, a machine with 256KB of memory might support eight-way multiprogramming with virtual memory but only four-way multiprogramming using other variable-sized regions. The motivation for virtual memory was to overcome memory size limitations with cost-effective memory configurations. Contemporary virtual memory managers also attempt to use memory hierarchies in conjunction with virtual memory techniques in order to reduce a process's execution time by reducing the memory access time delays. Whereas the original justification was motivated by memory costs, the motivation in modern operating systems is a combination of cost and performance.

11.4.3 ■ Shared-memory Multiprocessors

Multiprocessors have been studied for several decades, but in the 1980s, they matured as viable commercial computers. A few multiprocessors depart from the von Neumann architecture in an effort to increase fundamental processing speeds, but most adapt the basic von Neumann architecture for each processor in the multiprocessor. Two general classes of multiprocessors have evolved: distributed-memory machines and shared-memory machines [Hwang and Briggs, 1984]. Naturally, computer architecture continues to evolve, with newer multiprocessors combining aspects of Hwang and Briggs characterizations. Students of computer architecture are encouraged to consult the current literature, such as the computer architecture conference proceedings [IEEE] or the IEEE/ACM annual ASPLOS conference [IEEE/ACM], to see these new and exciting developments. The discussion here is limited to distributed-memory and shared-memory organizations, since these illustrate the extensions to memory management necessary for this class of machines.

Distributed-memory machines are logically equivalent to networks in that they rely on message-passing to share information across processors. Memory management in these machines, and in networks of machines, is currently a research topic in the study

Using Cache Memory

As discussed in Section 11.1, contemporary computers frequently employ a cache memory to increase a computer's performance. A cache memory is high-speed memory placed on the data path between the processor and the interconnection network (see Figure 11.18). In part (a), when a processor references a primary memory unit the CPU must compete with all the devices for the use of the bus. This often causes the CPU to wait while a device finishes its access. Using the principles of virtual memory, manufacturers can design hardware to incorporate a cache memory between the CPU and the system bus.

In this approach, whenever the CPU accesses the memory, a copy of the accessed information is placed in the cache memory. The next time the processor references the same memory location, the value can be found in the cache memory, so the processor need not use the bus to reference the copy kept in memory.

Just as parts are copied from secondary memory to primary memory in a virtual memory system, in a system with caching, *cache lines* are copied from primary memory into the cache. Most of the cache strategy is implemented in hardware rather than being evenly divided between the hardware and the software, as with general virtual memory. The memory manager for an operating system makes a few compensations for the presence of caching.

The use of a cache memory can affect performance profoundly, depending on the nature of the CPU's memory access patterns and the strategy used in the cache manager. In the worst case, its use brings no improvement, since the cost of the overhead dominates the access time. In the best case, the effective memory access time can be reduced by a factor of two or three.

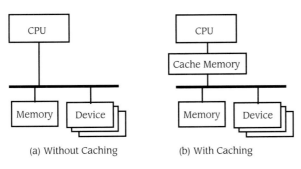

(a) Without Caching   (b) With Caching

Figure 11.18
Cache Memory

of operating systems. Suffice it to say that despite the fact that information can physically be moved between memories only by using some form of message-passing, operating systems for these machines may go to great lengths to provide a shared-memory interface to the application software (see Section 17.4).

This section focuses on shared-memory multiprocessors. A shared-memory machine takes the general form depicted in Figure 11.19. Several processors share an interconnection network (often, just a bus) to access a set of shared-memory modules. The hardware-addressing mechanism allows software on any processor to access any memory location in any memory unit on the interconnection network. The trend in shared-memory multiprocessors is to employ an off-the-shelf microprocessor as the processor engine, to incorporate a sophisticated interconnection network—this component is the performance bottleneck in shared memory machines—and to use industry-standard memory units and devices. Most operating systems for shared-memory machines are adaptations of UNIX, where the changes provide a system call interface extension to manipulate memory addresses so that the corresponding memory locations can be shared.

The goal of a shared-memory multiprocessor is to use processes or threads to implement units of computation whereby information is shared via common primary memory locations. The translation software creates a barrier by providing each process with its own isolated address space (see Figure 11.20). The address space in Process 1 has been laid out so that the last "block" in the address space is to be mapped into shared primary memory. In Process 2, the first block, which is the same size as the last block in Process 1's address space, is to be mapped into the same primary memory location. Now, when the programs are loaded at the same time, the parts of the two independent address spaces map to common memory locations. When Process 1 writes a variable in the memory, Process 2 can read its value. This technique results in very high performance.

In Figure 11.21, multiple relocation-limit register pairs are used to support block sharing. The address space is split into a private part and a shared part. One register pair points at the private part, and one pair points at the shared part. Processes 1 and 2 have their relocation-limit pair for the shared block point to the same physical memory locations. The OS extension must then incorporate a means for the program to identify a block as being shared and provide system calls, thereby causing the shared segments to be bound to a common memory location.

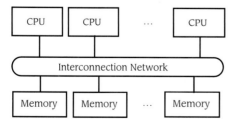

Figure 11.19
A Shared-memory Architecture

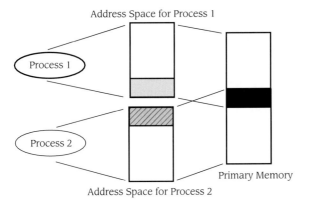

Figure 11.20
Sharing a Portion of the Address Space

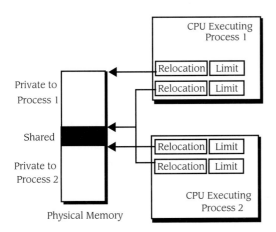

Figure 11.21
Multiple Segments

The interconnection network—the key hardware component of a shared-memory multiprocessor—is used by every CPU for every access of memory. Experience with these CPUs shows that if the network is implemented as a shared bus, the bus will saturate with as few as four CPUs. More sophisticated interconnection networks can be built. But a specialized use of cache memories is used in all shared-memory multiprocessors in order to decrease the load on the interconnection network and to increase each process's performance.

Cache memories can substantially enhance a computer's performance (even a uniprocessor's) by keeping frequently used information in the high-speed cache. This allows the processor to load the information from the cache—a much faster memory than the normal primary memory—without having to use the bus. In a multiprocessor, all CPUs may be trying to use the common bus at the same time. Thus contention for the bus effectively limits the number of processors that can be configured into the multiprocessor.

Incorporating a cache memory for each processor has proved to be quite effective because it enables shared-memory machines to provide performance scaling almost linearly with the number of processors up to about 20 (depending on the nature of the programs executing on the machine). For shared-memory multiprocessors to scale to an even larger numbers of processors, caching can be combined with more-complex interconnection networks.

Using caches in shared-memory multiprocessors introduces a new problem. Suppose some data structure, D, is shared by processes 1 and 2 on processors X and Y, respectively. When process 1 reads D, it is copied from the memory into X's cache. If process 2 were then to read D, it would be copied into Y's cache, thus resulting in three copies of D existing in the memory hierarchy: the original in the memory, one copy in X's cache, and another copy in Y's cache. Suppose process 1 writes to the D data structure. The three copies are now said to be *incoherent,* since they contain different values.

This situation is a serious problem in a shared-memory system, since it means the programs for the two processes are written as if they shared memory, but each process perceives different values in the same memory cell.

There are several approaches to handling the problem. The first is simply to not allow shared information (code or data) to be cached. The result is a performance penalty from interconnection network contention. The second approach is to not guarantee memory consistency for shared memories. If there were no cache, the memory model is said to have strongly consistent semantics. If a cached memory system is *strongly consistent,* the shared-memory implementation has the same semantics it would have if it were not cached. A *weakly consistent* memory allows each of two copies to have different values for short time periods. A weakly consistent memory, then, must incorporate a scheme for making the memory coherent "soon" after any of the copies have been changed with a write operation. Applications in a weakly consistent memory system must be written to have knowledge of the memory semantics, and with explicit synchronization, in order for the programs to behave properly. Therefore a weakly consistent memory system must guarantee that synchronization primitives can be implemented so that they behave properly independent of the memory type.

The mechanism to ensure coherency in all caches and the memory can be difficult to construct, since it must be able to detect a write to any shared memory copy the instant it happens on any processor. This ability suggests that coherency must be implemented by the interconnection network and/or caching hardware in each machine. When a shared-memory location is written, the caching mechanism must immediately inform other caching mechanisms and/or a centralized facility in all other machines that have copies of the memory contents. All copies, except the most recently written copy, are then invalidated until they can be updated with the new value. When shared memory becomes incoherent, the coherency mechanism can update the copy and the original memory immediately by writing the new data into the memory when it writes into the cache. This approach is called a *write-through* strategy. Alternatively, the mechanism may not update the cache immediately but defer updating memory until sometime in the near future. This strategy is called a *write-back* strategy.

11.5 ■ Summary

The memory manager is required to administer the executable memory, allocating it to different processes as needed. It also provides mechanisms that allow information to migrate up and down the memory hierarchy. Address binding is a fundamental barrier to data movement. This is because the traditional program translation environment causes points in a program's address space to be bound to physical memory locations before the program begins to execute. Static binding inhibits the manager's ability to move an address space around in the memory.

The underlying mechanism for deferring binding from load time to runtime is the hardware relocation register. This mechanism allows the memory manager to easily move address spaces around because addresses are bound as an offset from the contents of the relocation register on each memory reference. The limit register complements the relocation register and, at a small cost in complexity, allows the hardware to provide a robust isolation mechanism. With relocation and limit registers, the process can reference only the part of primary memory allocated to it.

Swapping strategies allow memory to be shared among more active processes than can be loaded in the memory at once. Virtual memory extends the swapping technology by loading only parts of a process's address space at once. Contemporary memory managers have evolved (or are evolving) to virtual memory designs.

Armed with a background in memory management provided in this chapter, you are now ready to move to the next chapter, which discusses virtual memory systems in more detail.

11.6 ■ Exercises

1. A memory manager for a variable-sized region strategy has a free list of blocks of size 600, 400, 1000, 2200, 1600, and 1050 bytes.

   a. What block will be selected to honor a request for 1603 bytes using the best-fit policy?

   b. What block will be selected to honor a request for 949 bytes using the best-fit policy?

   c. What block will be selected to honor a request for 1603 bytes using the worst-fit policy?

   d. What block will be selected to honor a request for 349 bytes using the worst-fit policy?

   e. Assume the free list is ordered as the blocks are listed in the problem statement. What block will be selected to honor a request for 1603 bytes using the first-fit policy?

    f. Assume the free list is ordered as the blocks are listed in the problem statement. What block will be selected to honor a request for 1049 bytes using the first-fit policy?

2. A memory manager can sort the free list according to any criteria it chooses.

    a. How would the free list be organized for the best-fit policy?
    b. How would the free list be organized for the worst-fit policy?
    c. How would the free list be organized for the first-fit policy?
    d. How would the free list be organized for the next-fit policy?

3. Suppose a variant of UNIX provides a system call that returns a pointer to a block of memory in the system address space capable of being read from and written to by any process. Explain how a UNIX user process could use such a facility to define a block of sharable memory to be used by two or more of its children. Assume the children have already been execed at the time the block is set up by the parent.

4. If the operating system kept swap images—direct images of the program as it is stored in primary memory for execution—the images would have to be relocated when they were loaded back into primary memory at a different location than the one from which they were retrieved from. Explain why an analysis program could not, in general, be written to read an executable image on secondary memory and be guaranteed to find every address in the executable image, thus allowing the addresses to be relocated when the image was moved.

5. If a computer system does not have relocation hardware yet it implements swapping, then the memory manager will have to use a loader to recompute the executable image from the absolute image. Would it be possible for the swapping system to reload the data and stack segments? Explain how such a system might work, or why it would be impossible.

6. Consider the code sequence shown in Figure 11.22 for a machine with the arrangement of segment relocation registers shown in Figure 11.13. Assuming the code segment register is loaded with 0100 when the instruction in relative address 0100 is executed, from what address will the control unit fetch the next instruction?

Figure 11.22
A Sample Code Segment

Relative
Address   **Contents**

```
. . .
0100        load    =1000, code_segment_register
0104        call    2000
. . .
```

7. Figure 6.6 is the simplified process state diagram with running, ready, and blocked states. Modify the diagram so that it includes new states to represent a new state or states for when a process is swapped out. Show the transitions to represent when the process is swapped due to its becoming blocked and when the memory manager simply decides to deallocate the memory and use it for another process.

8. Suppose a system has a disk with 2KB disk blocks and the average access time on a block is 20 milliseconds. A process holding 40KB of memory transitions from running to blocked due to a resource request. How long must the process remain blocked to justify swapping out the process?

9. [This problem appears in Chapter 9, where the solution used pipes.] Construct a C/C++ program for a UNIX environment to use the trapezoidal rule to approximate the integral of

$$f(x) = 1/(x + 1)$$

for the interval [0, 2]. Construct your solution so that you compute the areas of n small trapezoids by N individual slave processes. The master process should spawn N slave processes using the `fork` and `exec` UNIX system calls. Use the `shmem` facility to implement synchronization and information sharing. Whenever a slave process is ready to compute the area for another trapezoid, it synchronizes with the master using a shared variable and gets new work via shared memory. When the master process receives all the sums from the slave processes, it should sum them and print the answer, along with the amount of time required to obtain the solution. It should ignore the time to set up the shared memory. Experiment with various values of N between 1 and 8 for $n = 64$ trapezoids. Use a `getTime()` routine (see the exercises in Chapter 1) to instrument your program so that you can measure the amount of time spent processing your code. Include a suitably large `for` loop in your procedure to evaluate the area of a trapezoid so that you can measure the time to accomplish the computation. Plot the amount of time versus the number of trapezoids used in the approximation.

   If you have a shared-memory multiprocessor available to use, solve this problem using the shared-memory kernel extensions provided by the machine.

10. [This problem appears in Chapter 9, where the solution used pipes.] Successive overrelaxation (SOR) is a method to solve linear $n \times n$ systems of equations,

$$Ax = b.$$

Given the coefficient matrix A, the right-side vector b, and an initial estimated solution vector x, the algorithm recomputes each x_i based on the x_j $(i \neq j)$, A, and b. Notice that the n equations can be written as follows:

$$a_{11}x_1 + a_{12}x_2 + \ldots + a_{1n}x_n = b_1$$
$$a_{21}x_1 + a_{22}x_2 + \ldots + a_{2n}x_n = b_2$$
$$\ldots$$
$$a_{n1}x_1 + a_{n2}x_2 + \ldots + a_{nn}x_n = b_n$$

Arbitrarily use the ith equation to solve for x_i, yielding

$$x_i = (b_i - a_{i1}x_1 - a_{i2}x_2 - \ldots - a_{in}x_n) / a_{ii}.$$

Now you can implement SOR on an n-process system by having the ith process compute x_i.

Implement an SOR solution using UNIX shared memory. If you have a shared-memory multiprocessor available to use, solve this problem using the shared-memory kernel extensions provided by the machine.

12

Virtual Memory

The possible uses of the [virtual memory] have turned out to be so extensive that the task of utilizing such a large computer effectively without it seems by comparison to be almost impossible.

—T. Kilburn, R. B. Payne, and D. J. Howarth (1961),
Proceedings of the 1961 Eastern Joint
Computer Conference ■

CHAPTER OBJECTIVES

Virtual memory managers provide an abstraction of the physical memory by creating a virtual address space in secondary memory and then "automatically" determining the part of the address space to be loaded into primary memory at any given time. The system handles the transfer of address space blocks back and forth between primary and secondary memories without manual intervention. The abstraction presented to application programmers is that they have a very large address space in which to write programs, even though only part of the address space will be loaded in the primary memory at any given time.

The virtual address space corresponds to the address space created during static program translation. Virtual addresses are bound to physical memory addresses, device addresses, resources, mailboxes, and so on at runtime rather than at the time the program is translated. Virtual memory systems allow programs to use very large address spaces but to execute using a much smaller amount of physical memory. While declining memory costs could make virtual memory less attractive, contemporary systems take advantage of large physical memory space and even larger virtual address spaces; process address spaces seem to grow even faster than physical memory.

The first objective of this chapter is to generalize the binding mechanism from the last chapter so that it applies to virtual address spaces. Another objective is to explain the static paging algorithms that dominated designs in the 1980s and then to discuss contemporary dynamic paging algorithms. The chapter concludes with a discussion of segmented virtual memory as an alternative to paging.

12.1 ▪ Address Translation

Swapping systems make little distinction between the address space in the absolute module and the space in primary memory where the program will be executed, since both spaces are the same size (differing only by relocation values). Virtual memory systems distinguish among symbolic name, virtual address, and physical address spaces. Maps are provided from symbolic names to virtual addresses and from virtual addresses to physical addresses. There are two basic approaches to establishing the virtual-physical mapping: segmentation and paging. This section first considers how address mapping works in general and then discusses how segmentation and paging are the same and how they differ.

12.1.1 ▪ Address Space Mapping

The components of a source program are represented using symbolic identifiers, labels, and variables; these entities are elements of the name space. Each symbolic name in the name space is translated into a virtual address when the program is translated into an absolute image by the compiler and link editor (see Section 11.1). Each virtual address is converted to a physical address in the primary memory when the absolute image is translated into an executable image by the loader. Figure 12.1 summarizes this process. A programmer writes a program using symbolic variable names, labels, and identifiers from the name space. The language translation system converts each name space element into a virtual address; that is, it translates (or *binds*) each symbolic name to a virtual address. The virtual memory system then dynamically binds each virtual address to a physical address when the program is executed. That is, the process's *physical address space* is a set of physical memory locations in the primary memory. The essence of virtual memory systems is in developing efficient techniques for dynamic loading—binding virtual addresses to physical addresses at runtime.

Programs are translated to an executable form when they are loaded into the primary memory; their entities are then referenced using physical addresses. For a program to be in a form suitable for execution, the OS must be able to map each virtual address in the program image to a corresponding physical address, depending on which part of the virtual address space is loaded into the physical address space at any given

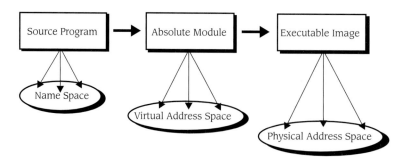

Figure 12.1
Names, Virtual Addresses, and Physical Addresses

time. To be precise, the *virtual address translation map,* Ψ_t, is a time-varying map of a program's virtual address space to a physical address space at time t:

$$\Psi_t: \text{virtual address space} \rightarrow \text{physical address space} \cup \{\Omega\},$$

where t is a nonnegative integer *virtual time* for the process and Ω is a distinguished symbol referring to the null address. In a particular computer, the address translation map implementation can be any technique that satisfies this mathematical definition. (That is why the problem is described as a mathematical abstraction; hence, any mechanism that implements the abstraction is acceptable.)

When an element, i, of the virtual address space is loaded in the primary memory, $\Psi_t(i)$ is the physical address where the corresponding virtual address, i, is loaded. If i is not loaded in the primary memory, then $\Psi_t(i) = \Omega$. If $\Psi_t(i) = \Omega$ at virtual time t and the process references location i, the system takes the following actions:

1. The virtual memory manager will stop the execution of the process.
2. The referenced information is retrieved from secondary memory and loaded into some primary memory location, k.
3. The manager then changes $\Psi_t(i) = k$.
4. The manager finally lets the program continue execution.

Notice that the referenced element from the virtual address space was determined to be missing from primary memory after an instruction started execution, but before it was able to complete. Noticing the missing element caused a series of events to load the element and redefine the map. Once the element has been loaded, the instruction that was in execution when the missing element was detected can be reexecuted at virtual time t. Hence virtual memory systems require the CPU to be able to "back out" of an instruction execution and reexecute the instruction after the address translation map has been redefined. (Again, notice that the mathematical notation precisely defines how a missing page is identified and thus any mechanism that implements the abstraction is acceptable.)

In virtual memory systems, the size of the virtual address space is greater than the size of the physical address space allocated to the process; that is, the process uses more virtual than physical addresses. Recall from the discussion of classic memory management in Chapter 11 that when a process was loaded, its entire address space was loaded at once. In a multiprogramming system, many processes could have their entire address spaces loaded at the same time. This meant that the system implicitly restricted the address space to be relatively small compared to the physical address space in the machine (the size of primary memory). If one of these classic systems was configured with 1MB of primary memory (considered to be a generous amount of memory in 1985) and if the system supported four memory partitions, each process would be allocated about 256KB. Thus the average size of the address space used by a process would be 256K. In today's virtual memory systems, it is not unusual for a process's address space to be a few gigabytes (Windows NT processes have a 4GB virtual address space).

12.1.2 ■ Segmentation and Paging

There are two general approaches to implementing virtual memory: segmentation and paging. Each approach is introduced here and then discussed in more detail in subsequent sections.

Segmentation is an extension of the ideas suggested by the use of relocation-limit registers for relocating and bound checking blocks of memory. The program parts to be loaded or unloaded are defined by the programmer as variable-sized segments, like those described in Chapter 11. Segments may be defined explicitly by language directives or implicitly by program semantics such as the text, data, and stack segments created by the UNIX C compiler. Memory contents are referenced using a two-component virtual address,

    <segmentNumber, offset>

as shown in Figure 12.2. The `segmentNumber` identifies the particular logical block of memory, and the offset is a linear `offset` from the beginning of the segment. In pure segmentation systems, the virtual memory system transfers whole segments back and forth between the primary and secondary memories. Thus a segment is the unit of virtual memory transferred between the two memories in this technique.

Paging uses single-component addresses, like those used to address cells within any particular segment. In paging, the virtual address space is a linear sequence of virtual addresses, a format that differs from the hierarchical segmentation address space. In a paging system, the programmer has no specific mechanism for informing the virtual memory system about logical units of the virtual address space, as is done in segmentation. Instead, the virtual memory manager is completely responsible for defining the fixed-size unit of transfer—the page—to be moved back and forth between the primary and secondary memories. The programmer need not be aware of the units of virtual address space loaded into or unloaded from the physical memory. In fact, the page size is transparent to the process.

Segmentation provides more programmer control over the units of transfer in the memory system than does paging. This control implies that a segmentation system

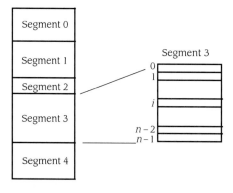

Figure 12.2
Segment Name Space Organization

requires more effort to use than does a paging system, unless the segments are automatically generated, say, by the compiler. Segments can be more efficient than paging, since the programmer can specify the set of virtual address locations to be used at about the same time in the execution, such as "pass 2 of the compiler." However, the virtual memory system will have more difficulty placing segments in primary memory because they are variable-sized and cause the same kind of external fragmentation problems that variable-sized memory partition systems have. In the final analysis, segmentation is probably better suited to the behavior of a process than is paging, although it may be harder to use, and it is definitely harder to implement. Paging is discussed next, followed by a return to segmentation.

12.2 ■ Paging

The allocation strategy in a paging system is to reduce external fragmentation by transferring a fixed-size unit of the virtual address space—a *page*—whenever a virtual address in it is needed to execute the program. Every process's virtual address space is logically divided into pages, with each page having the same number of locations, as shown in Figure 12.3. Only a small amount of fragmentation results at the end of the logical address space if it is not an exact multiple of the page size.

The program translation facilities take no special action to prepare the absolute module for operation, even though the absolute module for a paging system contains virtual addresses rather than flagged relative addresses. The program translation image is constructed to fit in a set of G contiguous memory locations, with virtual addresses ranging between 0 and $G - 1$. When the process executes, it is allocated enough primary memory to store the contents of H memory locations, where $H < G$ (that is, the process has fewer physical memory locations than virtual addresses).

In a binary computer, the paging system maps the virtual addresses in the absolute module (0 to $G - 1$) into a set of $n = 2^g$ pages, each of size $c = 2^h$ (see again Figure

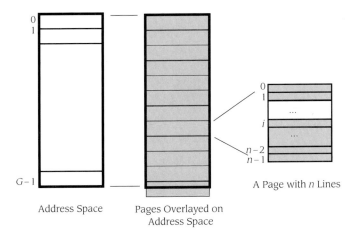

Address Space   Pages Overlayed on   A Page with n Lines
                     Address Space

Figure 12.3
The Address Space and Pages

12.3). If G is not an integer multiple of the page size, then part of the last page will be lost to internal fragmentation; the paging system will adjust G upward to hold the entire virtual address space.

The physical address space is the portion of the primary memory allocated to the process. The units of allocation are *page frames,* a block of primary memory the same size as a page. The page frames allocated to the process need not be contiguous, since the page map, Ψ_t, can map each individual page in the virtual address space to a specific page frame in the memory (or to Ω if the page is not loaded in a page frame). More precisely, the physical address space can be thought of as a set of $m = 2^j$ page frames, each of size $c = 2^h$, so the amount of primary memory allocated to the process is $H = 2^{h+j}$. Figure 12.4 summarizes the relationship between pages and page frames.

Because of the reference locality behavior of programs (see Section 11.4), the process needs to use only a subset of all the pages for execution at any given time. The goal of the paging system is to identify the set of pages needed for the process's current locality and then to load *only those pages* into page frames in primary memory. As the program changes phases—it leaves one locality and enters another—the pages holding the code for the old locality will be unloaded from page frames. The pages containing the code for the new locality then will be loaded into these page frames. The same phenomenon takes place for different parts of the data being used by the program.

The paging system must be able to translate each virtual address (an address between 0 and $G - 1$) into a physical address, a $\langle$pageFrameNumber, offset$\rangle$ for each memory reference. Furthermore, it must be able to dynamically bind pages to page frames as part of the address translation and page-loading process. This task is the first design challenge of a paging system.

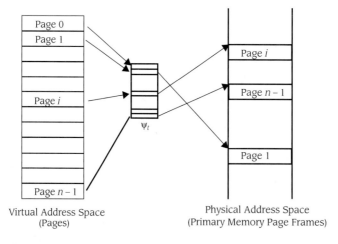

Virtual Address Space
(Pages)

Physical Address Space
(Primary Memory Page Frames)

Figure 12.4
The Page Map

12.2.1 ■ Virtual Address Translation

In the interest of providing a precise, abstract description of virtual address translation, we continue to use mathematical descriptions of address translation. Let

$$N = \{d_0, d_1, \ldots, d_{n-1}\}$$

be the set of pages in the virtual address space, and let

$$M = \{b_0, b_1, \ldots, b_{m-1}\}$$

be the set of page frames allocated to the process from primary memory. A virtual address is a nonnegative integer, i, where

$$0 \leq i < G = 2^{g+h},$$

since there are $n = 2^g$ pages each of size 2^h words. A physical address, k, is a memory address,

$$k = U2^h + V \,(0 \leq V < 2^h),$$

where U is a page frame number. Hence, $U2^h$ is the primary address of the first address in the page frame—the page frame's offset from physical address 0—and V is the offset within the page frame. Since 2^j page frames are allocated to the process, it will have $H = 2^{j+h}$ physical locations allocated for use. The virtual to physical address map has the form

$$\Psi_i\colon [0{:}G - 1] \rightarrow <U, V> \cup \{\Omega\}.$$

Since every page has the same size, $c = 2^h$, the virtual address, i, can be converted into a *page number* and an offset within the page, also called the *line number,* as follows:

$$\text{page number} = \lfloor i/c \rfloor$$

($\lfloor i/c \rfloor$ means the integer part of the result when you divide i by c—a conventional integer divide operation) and

$$\text{line number} = i \bmod c.$$

In binary machines, it is judicious for c to be a power of 2, since a page number can be extracted from the virtual address by shifting the virtual address right h bits and masking out the g least significant bits of the result. This shift operation is equivalent to an integer divide operation by the page size. The offset can be obtained by masking out the h least significant bits of the virtual address before shifting.

Since the page could be loaded in any page frame in the primary memory allocated to the process, the virtual address of the page must be bound to the physical address of the page frame that contains the page. This is done by extracting the page number from the virtual address, mapping it to a page frame base address where the page is loaded (using Ψ_t), and then adding the offset to the page frame starting address.

Fortunately, this type of address translation can be done entirely in hardware. Since the mid–1980s, popular microprocessor chips have a companion memory management chip (often called a memory management unit or MMU) that is used to implement the Ψ_t map. Without the wide availability of such hardware, paging would not be feasible, since it must be performed for each memory reference as a part of the instruction execution. Figure 12.5 represents a simple hardware address translation mechanism implemented in an MMU (this aspect of virtual memory continues to evolve). The g most significant bits of the virtual address are passed to the page map, Ψ_t. The result of the mapping operation is a *missing page fault* if page p_i is not currently loaded, $\Psi_t(p_i) = \Omega$, or a page frame number, b_j, if the page is currently loaded there ($\Psi_t(p_i) = b_j$). If a page fault occurs, the memory management chip halts the microprocessor chip so that the operating system can perform the following steps:

1. The process requesting the missing page is suspended.

2. The memory manager locates the missing page in secondary memory.

3. The page is loaded into primary memory, usually causing another page to be unloaded.

4. The page table in the memory manager is adjusted to reflect the new state of the memory.

5. The process resumes at the point it was executing when it was suspended.

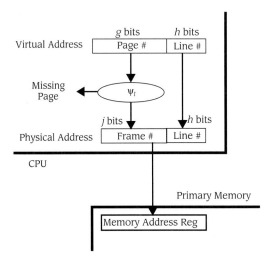

Figure 12.5
Address Translation with Paging

If the translation results in a page frame number rather than a missing page trap, the page frame's base address is loaded into the most significant part of the physical address and the line number is loaded into the least significant part of the physical address. The resulting physical address is passed to the MAR (memory address register) for the primary memory. The sizes of the virtual and physical addresses may differ, depending on the relationship of the sizes of the page and page frame registers.

Ψ_t maps page numbers to page frame base addresses. The map changes each time a page is loaded into primary memory. One mechanism to implement Ψ_t is a table such as that given in Figure 12.6. Logically, the table contains n rows—one for each page number—and one column (the row number in Figure 12.6 is the same as the page number). The entry in row i is $\Psi_t(i)$—the base address of b_j if page i is loaded in page frame b_j—and Ω otherwise. For example, in Figure 12.6, page 0 maps to page frame 3, page 1 is not loaded, page 2 maps to page frame 7, and so on.

Consider a specific example of the mathematical abstraction of address translation. Suppose 3257 is a virtual address in a system with $c = 100$. (c would normally be some power of 2 in a binary machine, but 100 is used in this example, in order to simplify the arithmetic.) The page number is computed as

$$p = \lfloor i/c \rfloor = \lfloor 3257/100 \rfloor = 32$$

and the offset is

$$\text{line number} = 3257 \bmod 100 = 57.$$

Next, the system will use Ψ_t to bind p to a page frame b_j if p is loaded. So $\Psi_t(p) = b_j$ if p is loaded in page frame b_j; $\Psi_t(p) = \Omega$ otherwise. After the page frame containing the page has been found, the offset is added to the page frame base address to determine the physical address corresponding to x:

$$\text{physical address} = \Psi_t(\lfloor i/c \rfloor) + (i \bmod c).$$

PAGE NUMBER	PAGE FRAME NUMBER
0	3
1	Ω
2	7
...	...
$G - 1$	9

Figure 12.6
The Conceptual Page Table

Page Table Implementations

I n general, a page table of the form shown in Figure 12.6 is sparse; that is, most of the entries map to Ω, since most pages need not be loaded at any given time (due to the locality). Hardware can be designed to take advantage of this situation. An *associative,* or *content-addressable,* memory implements the page map as an *inverted page table.* Each cell in an associative memory contains a key field and a data field. The entry is addressed by the key content rather than by cell address. As a bonus, the key search is implemented as a parallel pattern match, meaning associative memory access is very fast. Small associative memories (less than 1K entries) have been feasible since the early 1980s. The Atlas computer used a form of associative memory for its page table in the late 1950s [Kilburn et al., 1962]. In that computer, the associative memory was actually implemented as a bank of "page address registers" for the 32-page frames of the primary memory.

The page table of Figure 12.6 could be implemented with an associative memory as suggested by Figure 12.7.

The resulting inverted page table has only as many entries as there are page frames allocated to the process, since unmapped pages do not appear in this type of table. If a page does not appear in the associative memory, the access will fail and cause a missing page fault. As in systems with page tables implemented using conventional memory technology, the page fault causes the memory manager to load the missing page.

PAGE NUMBER	PAGE FRAME NUMBER
0	3
2	7
...	...
$G-1$	9

Figure 12.7
An Associative Memory Page Table

The scheme suggested here must be modified to avoid having to save the associative memory's contents on each context switch (for example, a process might use only part of the associative memory). The associative memory could contain one entry for each page frame in primary memory (rather than just for page frames

allocated to a process). Next, the key field is expanded to include some form of process identification so that a match on the key field occurs only for a particular page in a particular process's virtual address space. Unfortunately, primary memory sizes have grown more rapidly than the growth of cost-effective associative memories. Thus this technique is fast and effective but very expensive.

In conventional machines, yet another approach is widely used. The system includes a special cache memory called a *translation-lookaside buffer* (*TLB*) used with the address translation hardware. The full-page table is kept in primary memory. When a page is first translated to a page frame, the map is read from primary memory into the TLB. The TLB entry, then, contains the page number, the physical address of the page frame, and various protection bits. On subsequent references to the page, the map entry will be read from the TLB rather than from primary memory. Hennessey and Patterson [1990] provide more details about associative memories and TLBs.

In the example, loading page 32 in page frame 19 at address 1900 would produce

$$\text{physical address} = \Psi_t(\lfloor 3257/100 \rfloor) + (3257 \bmod 100) = \Psi_t(32) + 57 = $$
$$1900 + 57 = 1957.$$

If the page is not loaded, Ψ_t will evaluate to Ω to indicate the missing page condition to the page translation system.

12.3 ■ Static Paging Algorithms

There are two basic types of paging algorithms: static allocation and dynamic allocation. This section focuses on static algorithms; the next section deals with dynamic algorithms. A static paging algorithm allocates a fixed number of page frames to a process when it is created. The paging policy then defines how these page frames will be loaded and unloaded by the virtual memory system. There are three basic policies in defining any paging algorithm:

- The *fetch policy* decides when a page should be loaded into primary memory.
- The *replacement policy* determines which page should be removed from primary memory if all page frames are full.
- The *placement policy* determines where the fetched page should be loaded in primary memory.

Since the number of page frames is fixed in static paging algorithms, the page frame holding the new page is always the one vacated by the page picked for replacement. Therefore, in static page frame allocation algorithms, the placement policy is fixed. The fetch and replacement policies differentiate among well-known static paging algorithms. The placement policy becomes meaningful only in the dynamic paging algorithms described in Section 12.4.

In the interest of precision, we can use another simple mathematical model to consider various policies. Suppose N is the set of pages in the virtual address space, as before. The *page reference* stream, ω, is the sequence of page numbers from N,

$$\omega = r_1, r_2, r_3, \ldots, r_i, \ldots,$$

referenced by the process during its execution. The virtual time of a process is the index of the page reference stream. Thus, if ω is a page reference stream for some process at time i, the process will reference page $r_i \in N$. The virtual time represents the progress the process makes as it executes.

Let the *initial state* of the m page frames in the physical address space allocated to the process, $S_0(m) = \varnothing$, represent the state in which no pages are loaded in the m primary memory page frames allocated to the process. $S_t(m)$ is the set of pages loaded in the m page frames at virtual time t:

$$S_t(m) = S_{t-1}(m) \cup X_t - Y_t,$$

where X_t is the set of pages *fetched* at time t and Y_t is the set of pages *replaced* at time t.

12.3.1 ■ The Fetch Policy

The fetch policy determines when a page should be brought into primary memory. The paging mechanism will not ordinarily have prior knowledge about the page reference stream for programs executing on the machine. So it is difficult to construct paging mechanisms using a *prefetch* policy whereby pages are fetched into the memory prior to the time they are referenced. Instead, the majority of general-purpose paging mechanisms use a *demand* fetch policy whereby a page is loaded into primary memory only when the process references it (that is, when the page reference stream calls for the page). In other words, in demand paging one of the following conditions applies at virtual time t when page r_t appears in the reference stream:

■ If r_t was loaded at virtual time $t - 1$, then nothing is removed from primary memory and nothing is added to it.

■ If r_t was not loaded at virtual time $t - 1$ but there are empty page frames allocated to the process, then the missing page is placed in one of the empty page frames ($X_t = \{r_i\}$).

■ If r_t was not loaded at virtual time $t - 1$ and all allocated page frames contain a page, then the content of some page frame loaded with a different page, y, has its contents replaced by page r_t. (In the general expression for determining the memory state at time t, $S_t(m)$, the set of replaced pages is $Y_t = \{y\}$.)

The discussion of specific paging algorithms begins with a discussion of only those algorithms using static page frame allocation and demand paging. When a process begins to run, it requests a fixed number of page frames; it does not change the allocation during its lifetime. Since the fetch and placement policies have been established, a demand paging policy can be described by specifying its replacement policy. The performance of any particular paging algorithm depends on the page reference stream.

12.3.2 ■ Demand Paging Algorithms

Now we can consider some static demand paging algorithms by focusing on their replacement policies. Given some primary memory state sequence, $\{S_i(m)\}$, and a page reference stream

$$\omega = r_1, r_2, \ldots, r_i, \ldots$$

we let y_t designate the individual page replaced under a given demand paging algorithm when the physical address space is in state $S_{t-1}(m)$ and the process references page r_t. Assume the m page frames allocated to the process are full, but r_t is not in $S_{t-1}(m)$. Then the memory state at time t is defined in terms of the memory state at time $t - 1$ by

$$S_t(m) = S_{t-1}(m) \cup \{r_t\} - \{y_t\}.$$

Thus, by identifying y_t, we will have uniquely identified the replacement strategy, since $S_{t-1}(m)$ and $\{r_t\}$ are defined at the time the page fault occurs.

12.3.2.1 ■ Random Replacement

In the random-replacement policy, the replaced page is chosen at random. That is, the memory manager randomly chooses any loaded page, y, with probability $1/m$, then replaces page $y_t = y$. Because this policy calls for selecting the page to be replaced by choosing the page in any page frame with equal probability, it uses no knowledge of the reference stream (or the locality) when it selects the page frame to replace.

In general, random replacement does not perform well. On most reference streams, it causes more missing page faults than the other algorithms discussed in this section. After early exploration with random replacement in the 1960s, system designers quickly recognized that several other policies would produce fewer missing page faults.

Suppose a process has four page frames allocated (say frame 0 with page 5, frame 1 with page 7, frame 2 with page 6, and frame 3 with page 9), and the process is in a phase in which it uses only two pages (say pages 7 and 9). The random-replacement strategy is equally likely to select frame 0, 1, 2, or 3 for replacement despite the fact that frame 0 or 2 should be selected in order to avoid unloading pages that are heavily used.

12.3.2.2 ■ Belady's Optimal Algorithm

At the other extreme from random replacement is the replacement policy having "perfect knowledge" of the page reference stream; thus it always chooses an optimal page to be removed from the memory. Let the *forward distance* of a page r at time t, $FWD_t(r)$, be the distance from the current point in the reference stream to the next place in the stream where the same page is referenced again. The forward distance is always greater than 0 and is infinite if the page is never referenced again. In the optimal algorithm, the replaced page, y_t, is one that has maximal forward distance:

$$y_t = \max_{x \in S_{t-1}(m)} FWD_t(x).$$

Since more than one page is loaded at time t, there may be more than one page that never appears again in the reference stream—that is, there may be more than one loaded page with maximal forward distance. In this case, Belady's optimal algorithm chooses an arbitrary loaded page with maximal forward distance.

The optimal algorithm can be implemented only if the full page reference stream is known in advance. Since it is rare for the system to have such knowledge, the algorithm is not generally realizable. Instead, its theoretical behavior is used to compare the performance of realizable algorithms with the optimal performance.

In a few special cases (such as a program to predict the weather), large programs are used enough to merit careful analysis of their paging behavior. Although it is usually not possible to exactly predict the page reference stream, one can sometimes predict the next page with high probability that the prediction will be correct. For example, the conditional branch instruction at the end of a loop almost always branches back to the beginning of the loop rather than exiting it. Such predictions are based on static analysis

TABLE 12.1 Belady's Optimal Algorithm Behavior

Frame	0	1	2	3	0	1	2	3	0	1	2	3	4	5	6	7
0	0*	0	0	0	0	0	0	0	0	1*	1	1	4*	4	4	7*
1		1*	1	1	1	1	2*	2	2	2	2	2	2	5*	5	5
2			2*	3*	3	3	3	3	3	3	3	3	3	3	6*	6

of the source code or on observations of dynamic behavior of the program. This analysis can produce enough information to incorporate replacement "hints" in the source code, although the process is labor-intensive and only worthwhile on programs that are long running and frequently executed. The compiler and paging systems can then be designed to use these hints to predict the future behavior of the page reference stream.

As an example of Belady's optimal algorithm, suppose

$$\omega = 0\ 1\ 2\ 3\ 0\ 1\ 2\ 3\ 0\ 1\ 2\ 3\ 4\ 5\ 6\ 7$$

with $m = 3$ page frames. Table 12.1 has a row for each of the three page frames and a column for each reference in the page stream. A table entry at row i, column j shows the page loaded at page frame i after r_j has been referenced. The column headings are the pages in the reference stream. If the entry is marked with an *, the page shown in the entry was loaded as a result of the missing page fault. The optimal algorithm will behave as shown in Table 12.1, which incurs 10 page faults.

12.3.2.3 ▪ Least Recently Used

The least-recently-used (LRU) algorithm is designed to take advantage of "normal" program behavior. Programs are written to contain loops, which cause the main line of the code to execute repeatedly, with special-case code rarely being executed. This means that in the code part of the address space, the control unit will repeatedly access the set of pages containing these loops. This set of pages that contains the code is called the *code locality* of the process. If the loop or loops that are executed are stored in a small number of pages, then the program has a small code locality. In many programs, there is a similar *data locality* or *stack locality* whereby the process tends to repeatedly read from and write to a subset of the data when it executes the program. For example, a program that is solving a system of equations will tend to repeatedly reference the part of the address space that contains the coefficient matrix for the system of equations. While almost all programs have relatively small code localities, several classes of programs have no particularly useful data locality. (For example, a transaction processing system usually has "poor data locality," meaning that there is no relationship between sequential data transactions.)

The LRU replacement algorithm is explicitly designed to take advantage of locality by assuming that if a page has been referenced recently, it is likely to be referenced again soon. The *backward distance* of page r at time t, $BKWD_t(r)$, is the distance (in the reference stream) from r to the last occurrence of the page in the preceding part of the

TABLE 12.2 LRU Behavior

Frame	0	1	2	3	0	1	2	3	0	1	2	3	4	5	6	7
0	0*	0	0	3*	3	3	2*	2	2	1*	1	1	4*	4	4	7*
1		1*	1	1	0*	0	0	3*	3	3	2*	2	2	5*	5	5
2			2*	2	2	1*	1	1	0*	0	0	3*	3	3	6*	6

reference stream. The backward distance is always greater than 0 and is infinite if the page has not been referenced previously. LRU selects a page, y_t, for replacement with the maximum backward distance:

$$y_t = \max_{x \in St-1(m)}(BKWD_t(x)).$$

The assumption is that because of locality, the backward distance is a good estimator of the forward distance of any page. If more than one page has maximal backward distance, LRU may choose an arbitrary page with maximal backward distance for replacement.

Suppose $\omega = 0\ 1\ 2\ 3\ 0\ 1\ 2\ 3\ 0\ 1\ 2\ 3\ 4\ 5\ 6\ 7$ with $m = 3$. The LRU algorithm will produce the behavior shown in Table 12.2, incurring 16 page faults.

12.3.2.4 ■ Least Frequently Used

The least-frequently-used (LFU) replacement algorithm selects a page for replacement if the page has not been used often in the past. Let $FREQ_t (r_t)$ be the number of references to r_t in r_1 through r_{t-1}. Then

$$y_t = \min_{x \in St-1(m)}(FREQ_t(x)).$$

There may be more than one page that satisfies the criteria for replacement, so any of the qualifying pages can be selected for replacement.

LFU tends to react slowly to changes in locality. If a program changes the set of pages it is currently using, the frequency counts will tend to cause the pages in the new locality to be replaced even though they are currently being used. As the process proceeds, this "inertia" will eventually be overcome and the policy will select the appropriate pages.

Another problem with LFU is that it uses frequency counts from the beginning of the page reference stream. For example, initialization code can influence the replacement policy long after the process has moved into the main part of the code. A more popular variant of pure LFU uses frequency counts of a page since it was last loaded rather than from the beginning of the page reference stream. The frequency counter is reset each time a page is loaded rather than being allowed to monotonically increase throughout the execution of the program. The policy will still tend to load pages slowly when the program changes locality, but the effects of phases in the distant past will not influence the behavior.

TABLE 12.3 LFU Behavior

Frame	0	1	2	3	0	1	2	3	0	1	2	3	4	5	6	7
0	0*	0	0	0	0	0	0	0	0	0	0	3*	3	3	3	3
1		1*	1	1	1	1	1	3*	3	1*	1	1	1	1	1	1
2			2*	3*	3	3	2*	2	2	2	2	2	4*	5*	6*	7*

Suppose we use a random rule for selecting among pages having the same frequency of use. The example reference stream results in 12 page faults, as shown in Table 12.3.

12.3.2.5 ■ First-In, First-Out

The first-in, first-out (FIFO) replacement algorithm replaces the page that has been in memory longest. Let $AGE_t(r)$ be the current time less the time at which page r in $S_i(m)$ was last loaded. The replaced page is selected by

$$y_t = \max_{x \in St-1(m)}(AGE_t(x)).$$

FIFO focuses on the length of time a page has been in memory rather than how much the page is being used. FIFO's main asset is that it is simple to implement. Its behavior is not particularly well suited to the behavior of most programs, however, (it is completely independent of the locality), so few systems use it.

This example incurs 16 page faults under FIFO, as shown in Table 12.4.

12.3.3 ■ Stack Algorithms

Certain demand algorithms are more "well behaved" than others. For example, consider the page reference stream

$$\omega = 0\ 1\ 2\ 3\ 0\ 1\ 4\ 0\ 1\ 2\ 3\ 4$$

as it is processed by FIFO with $m = 3$ (see Table 12.5). There are nine page faults, each marked with an *. Now suppose we increase the physical address space to $m = 4$ page frames and process the same page reference stream with the same algorithm (see Table 12.6).

TABLE 12.4 FIFO Behavior

Frame	0	1	2	3	0	1	2	3	0	1	2	3	4	5	6	7
0	0*	0	0	3*	3	3	2*	2	2	1*	1	1	4*	4	4	7*
1		1*	1	1	0*	0	0	3*	3	3	2*	2	2	5*	5	5
2			2*	2	2	1*	1	1	0*	0	0	3*	3	3	6*	6

TABLE 12.5 FIFO Algorithm with Three Page Frames

Frame	0	1	2	3	0	1	4	0	1	2	3	4
0	0*	0	0	3*	3	3	4*	4	4	4	4	4
1		1*	1	1	0*	0	0	0	0	2*	2	2
2			2*	2	2	1*	1	1	1	1	3*	3

In the allocation with four page frames there are ten page faults, one more page fault than in the allocation with three page frames; even though the process has one more page frame it also has more page faults. This is an example of *Belady's anomaly.* The paging algorithm has worse performance when the amount of primary memory allocated to the process is increased. It is natural to be concerned about the class of replacement algorithms susceptible to Belady's anomaly, since such algorithms cannot be relied on to improve performance by increasing the amount of memory allocated to the process. Is there a characterization of algorithms susceptible to Belady's anomaly?

The problem arises because the set of pages loaded with a memory allocation of 3 is not necessarily also loaded with a memory allocation of 4. For example, when page 4 is first referenced, page 0 is left in memory in the example with $m = 3$ but is chosen for replacement in the case with $m = 4$. Once this replacement occurs, the behavior over the rest of the page reference stream can diverge quickly. There are a set of paging algorithms whereby the set of pages loaded with an allocation of m is always a subset of the set of pages that has a page frame allocation of $m + 1$ (this property is called the *inclusion property*). These algorithms are also called *stack algorithms*. Algorithms that satisfy the inclusion property are not subject to Belady's anomaly [Nutt, 1992a]. In the example illustrating the anomaly, notice that after page 4 is referenced (as the seventh reference), in the allocation with $m = 3$, $S_7(3) = \{4, 0, 1\}$. However, when $m = 4$, $S_7(4) = \{4, 1, 2, 3\}$, so FIFO does not satisfy the inclusion property and is not a stack algorithm. However, LRU and LFU can be shown to be stack algorithms.

Stack algorithms display behavior important to the system designer. One needs to be assured that if more resources are allocated to a process, performance will not degrade—that is, that the algorithm will be "well behaved." The correlation of memory use with the number of page faults holds for stack algorithms but not for other algorithms. Stack algorithms also are more easily analyzed than many nonstack algorithms. For example, one can calculate the cost of page fetches with a single pass over the reference stream for a stack algorithm, since it is possible to predict the number of page

TABLE 12.6 FIFO Algorithm with Four Page Frames

Frame	0	1	2	3	0	1	4	0	1	2	3	4
0	0*	0	0	0	0	0	4*	4	4	4	3*	3
1		1*	1	1	1	1	1	0*	0	0	0	4*
2			2*	2	2	2	2	2	1*	1	1	1
3				3*	3	3	3	3	3	2*	2	2

faults by analyzing the memory state. Also, the memory state can be used to predict performance improvement obtained by increasing a process's memory allocation for stack algorithms. This performance improvement is not possible for other algorithms.

12.3.4 ■ Implementing LRU

Over time, LRU has become the most widely used of the static replacement algorithms because it is a reasonable predictor for program behavior and produces good performance on a wide variety of page references streams. However, to implement LRU an accounting of the use of each page frame must be kept. This accounting essentially requires that the page table incorporate another field to reflect the time of the last reference, where the "time" is the virtual time of the process execution. This record is costly to implement, since it introduces another page table memory write and requires virtual time maintenance. Also, the replacement algorithm must search the entire page table to find the loaded page that has the maximum backward distance. The sheer amount of information required to implement the exact behavior of LRU is difficult to implement in hardware. However, it is possible to *approximate* the behavior of the pure LRU algorithm with relatively simple hardware.

Suppose the page table incorporated a single *reference bit* for each page table entry. Also assume the reference bit for each page is periodically set to 0. The address translation hardware can be designed to set the reference bit to 1 each time the corresponding page is read from or written to. Whenever a page fault occurs, it is easy to determine which pages have been referenced since all the reference bits were last cleared. This is done by inspecting their reference bits. Pages with their reference bits set have been referenced since the bits were all last cleared, whereas the pages with their reference bits still 0 have not. The least recently used page is one of those with its reference bit cleared, so the paging system arbitrarily chooses one of those pages to replace. The reference bits are then all cleared once again. Thus reference bits are set if the page has been referenced since the last page fault and are cleared otherwise.

How can we extend the idea of a reference bit to keep more information about the recent usage of a page? Suppose each entry's reference bit is replaced by a shift register in which the most significant bit is treated just like the reference bit; that is, this bit is set when the corresponding page is referenced. Now, suppose the register contents are shifted to the right periodically. When a missing page fault occurs, the shift register contains more information about how recently the page was referenced; hence, a better approximation to LRU can be obtained (see Exercise 11 at the end of this chapter). The precision of the history depends on the length of the period between shift operations and the number of bits in the shift register.

For example, the page table in part (a) in Table 12.7 illustrates the case in which the reference bits have all been cleared. Memory references in

$$\omega = \ldots 4\ 14\ 4\ 28\ 5\ 14\ 4\ 29\ 6\ \ldots$$

are processed until the reference to page 6 causes a page fault. The table in part (b) in the same figure indicates that pages 4, 5, 14, 28, and 29 have all been referenced since their reference bit was set. When the page fault occurs, one of pages 0, 9, or 19 is the least-recently-used page, so the mechanism will randomly select one of these pages for replacement. If all pages have been referenced since the last time the reference bit was

TABLE 12.7   Approximating LRU

Page	Reference	Frame		Page	Reference	Frame
0	0	103		0	0	103
4	0	78		4	1	78
5	0	99		5	1	99
9	0	24		9	0	24
14	0	65		14	1	65
19	0	40		19	0	40
28	0	42		28	1	42
29	0	33		29	1	33

(a) Reference Bits Clear   (b) Some Reference Bits Set

cleared, then of course the selection of the page is purely random. Provided that this latter case rarely occurs, this approach is an inexpensive approximation of LRU.

A significant part of the cost of a page fault is the task of writing a page from primary memory into secondary memory. The page table also can incorporate a *dirty bit,* to be cleared when a page is loaded and set when there is a write to the page. If the page is selected for replacement and if the dirty bit is clear, the page has not been written to since it was loaded. Therefore the copy to secondary memory can be avoided because the page frame image is the same as the page image in secondary storage.

PERFORMANCE TUNING

Paging Performance

Since the process will be delayed when a page fault occurs, it can not normally be expected to execute in the same amount of time in a paging system as it could in a system that allocates enough memory to load the whole address space at execution time. The paging system economizes on the amount of memory a process uses in exchange for a longer time to execute the process.

The value of paging is in a favorable tradeoff between the amount of space saved versus the cost in time to execute the process. For example, it might be considered to be a good tradeoff if a process reduced its memory requirement at runtime by 50 percent but required only a 10 percent increase in execution time. Because of the subjectivity involved in this tradeoff, performance an-

alysis of paging algorithms is usually conducted by comparing the effect of different memory allocations, different page sizes, different page transfer rates, or different replacement strategies.

The dominant cost of paging is the I/O time for replacement. Disk I/O operations are several orders of magnitude slower than primary memory reference times. Even a small difference in the number of

Paging Performance *(continued)*

page faults can dramatically change the execution time for a process. The simple examples given in this section demonstrate that a mismatch between the process's locality and the size of the physical address space can be disastrous because it causes the primary memory to be loaded after every few instructions. This phenomenon, called *thrashing,* can substantially increase the number of page faults and thus slow down the process's execution time by several orders of magnitude (depending on the disk I/O speed).

Each page fault will introduce considerable overhead, say R units of time. The time for page fault processing is added to the total execution time: If $|\omega| = t$ and there are f page faults, the total execution time can be written as

$$T_{exec} = t + f R$$

Normalizing the cost of page replacement across all instructions obtains the average amount of overhead per instruction:

$$\text{average overhead} = T_{exec}/t$$
$$= (t + f R)/t$$
$$= 1 + (f/t) R$$

f/t, called the *fault rate,* is the fraction of page references resulting in a page fault. If the fraction and R are small, the cost of page faults will be absorbed over the full execution without much degradation. As either grows, paging becomes ineffective, since the overhead time dominates the process's total runtime.

The value of f/t depends on the amount of memory allocated to the process, the page reference stream, and the replacement algorithm. The value of R depends on numerous factors, including the nature of the secondary storage, the page size, and the replacement policy overhead. However, the transfer time between primary and secondary storage will tend to dominate R for most implementations, since the transfer ordinarily involves mechanical movement in the storage device. Thus the disk transfer rate is very important to the paging system's performance. Sometimes it even justifies the incorporation of a high-speed disk just to hold executable memory images for the paging system.

Over the years, considerable empirical data have been gathered concerning the performance of various paging algorithms and implementations. While these observations do not provide bounds on performance, they do characterize the performance of various replacement strategies for various processes. Investigators observed that for all page reference streams and all algorithms, thrashing will typically occur for memory allocations of less than half the virtual address space size [Coffman and Denning, 1973]. Conversely, as the memory allocation approaches the virtual address space size, the performance of all algorithms converges to Belady's optimal algorithm. The amount of memory allocated to the process has been observed to be at least as important as the replacement algorithm. Systems unable to allocate enough memory to processes will cause significant performance degradation. This observation also leads to the consideration of better ways of matching the primary memory needs of a process to the allocation than are used in static memory allocation techniques.

12.4 ▪ Dynamic Paging Algorithms

The paging algorithms considered so far all assume that a process is allocated a fixed amount of primary memory when it is started and the amount does not change during the computation. Static algorithms do not adjust the allocation, even if the process passes through phases in which it requires a large physical address space or its memory requirements are modest.

A program's execution produces different fault rates as the amount of memory allocation varies. For stack algorithms, as the memory size is decreased using any particular algorithm, the fault rate will increase. Different paging algorithms will also have different fault rates with any specific memory size. An accurate plot for a particular program will usually have a small region around a point, m', where the derivative of the curve changes rapidly (this is sometimes called a *hysteresis point*). If the amount of memory allocated to the process is less than m', the process will thrash. However, memory allocation that exceeds m' does not substantially reduce the fault rate for the process. This value m' is the ideal memory allocation for the process with the given replacement algorithm.

The explanation for this phenomenon is that a process changes locality as it executes. When the locality changes, not only do the identities of the pages change but also the *number* of pages in the locality is likely to change. Sometimes the process needs only a few page frames to hold the pages it is using, while at other times it needs many page frames. It could be argued that the value of the ideal memory allocation, m', is highly dynamic, depending on the process's behavior at each point in the execution. Therefore, as computations change phases, the locality changes and, in turn, the number of page frames allocated to the process should change. Dynamic paging algorithms adjust the memory allocation to match the process's needs as they change. The working set algorithm is the first well-known dynamic paging algorithm and has led to the paging algorithms used in modern operating systems.

12.4.1 ▪ The Working Set Algorithm

The working set algorithm uses the current memory requirements to determine the number of page frames to allocate to the process. Before describing the algorithm, let's consider how page frames can be allocated dynamically.

Suppose there are k processes sharing the primary memory. Let $m_i(t)$ be the amount of memory allocated to process i at its virtual time t. So $m_i(0) = 0$ and

$$\Sigma_{i=1}^{k} m_i(t) \leq |\text{primary memory}|$$

at time t.

Now, if we substitute $m_i(t)$ for m in the notation from the last section, $S_t(m_i(t))$ is the set of pages loaded in process p_i's memory at virtual time t. This notation is a bit unwieldy, and t is redundantly specified in the expression, so we just use the simplified form $S(m_i(t))$ to represent the set of pages allocated to process i at time t.

Given that $S(m_i(0)) = \emptyset$, the memory state for process i at time $t > 0$ can be derived from the memory state at time $t - 1$ using a parameter, τ:

$$S(m_i(t)) = S(m_i(t - 1)) \cup X_t - Y_t,$$

where X_t is the set of pages placed in primary memory at time t. Y_t is the set of pages removed from the memory at time t. More specifically, if r_t was loaded at time $t - 1$, it remains in memory; if r_t was not loaded at time $t - 1$, $X_t = \{r_t\}$. Independently, page y is unloaded if the backward distance from r_t is greater than or equal to a constant value, τ (that is $BKWD_t(y) = \tau$). Page replacement and placement are decoupled in this algorithm; the τ parameter is the size of a logical *window* on the reference stream, one that is used to bound the set of previous references used with an LRU variant. Since X_t and Y_t have been specified, the memory allocation, $m_i(t)$, is adjusted to allocate exactly the number of page frames needed to hold the pages in $S(m_i(t))$:

- $X_t \neq \emptyset$ and $Y_t = \emptyset \Rightarrow m_i(t) = m_i(t - 1) + 1$ (allocate a page frame)
- $X_t = \emptyset$ and $Y_t = \emptyset \Rightarrow m_i(t) = m_i(t - 1)$
- $X_t = \emptyset$ and $Y_t \neq \emptyset \Rightarrow m_i(t) = m_i(t - 1) - 1$ (deallocate a page frame)

The resulting $S(m_i(t))$ is called the *working set* for process i at time t with window size τ (the window size, τ, determines when a page frame should be deallocated in the backward distance comparison). Notice the similarity between the working set approach and the LRU approach used with static allocation algorithms: Both rely on the backward distance computation to determine the page replacement, but the working set bounds the backward distances being considered with the window size.

Figure 12.8 is an illustration of the way the window is used to determine the working set and the page frame allocation. The segment of the reference stream shows that the current page being referenced, r_t, is to page 1, and that (including the current page) the working set window should consider the most recent $\tau = 3$ page references—pages 1, 0, and 1. These three references only use two pages—pages 0 and 2. Therefore the working set for a window size of $\tau = 3$ is two, meaning that the working set can be loaded into the primary memory if the process is allocated two page frames.

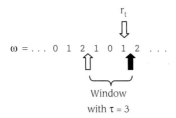

Working set = {0, 1} ⇒ Need 2 page frames

Figure 12.8
The Working Set Window

Intuitively, the working set corresponds to the set of pages in a process's locality. For example, if a process uses only three pages at a time for 10,000 references, it should have only three page frames allocated to it. If it systematically uses 20 pages at a time in the last 10,000 references, it should have 20 page frames in its physical address space.

The original working-set theory used the window size, τ, to estimate the working set [Coffman and Denning, 1973]. However, there are other measures that could be used to estimate the membership of the working set; for example, the page fault frequency algorithm monitors the rate at which a process incurs page faults in order to determine membership. If the rate is above a predetermined threshold value, then the page frame allocation is too small, so it is increased to accommodate the process's working set. On the other hand, if the page fault frequency falls below a different threshold, the algorithm assumes there are more page frames allocated than necessary to hold the working set, so it releases some page frames.

The *working set principle* states that a process i should be loaded and active only if it can be allocated enough page frames to hold its entire working set. Otherwise, the process should be blocked. Working set implementations all depend on an estimator (such as the window size τ or the page fault frequency threshold values) in an attempt to accurately determine the working set.

The performance of the working set algorithm relies both on locality and on a suitable choice of τ (which is related to the locality).

The working set algorithm defines the basis of most contemporary paging systems, although it is rarely (if ever) used in its theoretical form (see the In the Hangar section that follows). While it relies on knowledge of the backward distance to determine membership in the window, it captures the idea of locality and minimum memory required to run the process. The independent variable in the working set is the window size and is determined by the characteristics of the process.

The examples show that the working set algorithm is susceptible to thrashing if τ is too small. It is possible to measure the rate at which page faults occur and then either to adjust τ so that it is larger if the page fault rate surpasses a threshold or to reduce τ if the rate falls below a minimum threshold. Essentially, this approach attempts to adjust τ for the locality based on the observed fault rate. Increases in τ will tend to increase the amount of memory allocated to a process, while decreases in τ will tend to have the opposite effect.

➤ IN THE HANGAR

Working Set Algorithm Example

Suppose the reference stream used to illustrate static allocation algorithms was processed with the working set algorithm with $\tau = 3$. Then the algorithm would experience 16 page faults, as shown in Table 12.8.

TABLE 12.8   Working Set with $\tau = 3$

Frame	0	1	2	3	0	1	2	3	0	1	2	3	4	5	6	7
0	0*	0	0	3*	3	3	2*	2	2	1*	1	1	4*	4	4	7*
1		1*	1	1	0*	0	0	3*	3	3	2*	2	2	5*	5	5
2			2*	2	2	1*	1	1	0*	0	0	3*	3	3	6*	6
Allocation	1	2	3	3	3	3	3	3	3	3	3	3	3	3	3	3

Notice that the number of page frames allocated varies from 0 when the process begins to a maximum of $\tau = 3$ page frames. The performance of the working set algorithm could be increased considerably by adjusting the window size to $\tau = 4$, which is just large enough to satisfy the needs of the locality for this reference stream (see Table 12.9). This window size results in eight page faults, the minimum since there are eight distinct pages in the reference stream and each must be loaded at least once.

TABLE 12.9   Working Set with $\tau = 4$

Frame	0	1	2	3	0	1	2	3	0	1	2	3	4	5	6	7
0	0*	0	0	0	0	0	0	0	0	0	0	0	4*	4	4	4
1		1*	1	1	1	1	1	1	1	1	1	1	1	5*	5	5
2			2*	2	2	2	2	2	2	2	2	2	2	2	6*	6
3				3*	3	3	3	3	3	3	3	3	3	3	3	7*
Allocation	1	2	3	4	4	4	4	4	4	4	4	4	4	4	4	4

In both of these examples, the maximum page frame allocation is τ. For window sizes exceeding the locality sizes, the page frame allocation will be less than τ. For example, suppose $\tau = 9$ (see Table 12.10). While this configuration uses more memory, it does not reduce the number of page faults, since it was already at the minimum.

TABLE 12.10 Working Set with $\tau = 9$

Frame	0	1	2	3	0	1	2	3	0	1	2	3	4	5	6	7
0	0*	0	0	0	0	0	0	0	0	0	0	0	0	0	0	0
1		1*	1	1	1	1	1	1	1	1	1	1	1	1	1	1
2			2*	2	2	2	2	2	2	2	2	2	2	2	2	2
3				3*	3	3	3	3	3	3	3	3	3	3	3	3*
4													4*	4	4	4
5														5*	5	5
6															6*	6
7																7*
Allocation	1	2	3	4	4	4	4	4	4	4	4	4	5	6	7	8

To see an example in which the page frame allocation decreases during execution, we have to consider a different reference stream (in Table 12.11, assume $\tau = 4$):

TABLE 12.11 Another Example with $\tau = 4$

Frame	0	1	2	3	0	1	0	1	2	3	2	3	4	5	6	7
0	0*	0	0	0	0	0	0	0	0	0			4*	4	4	4
1		1*	1	1	1	1	1	1	1	1	1			5*	5	5
2			2*	2	2	2			2*	2	2	2	2	2	6*	6
3				3*	3	3	3			3*	3	3	3	3	3	7*
Allocation	1	2	3	4	4	4	3	2	3	4	3	2	3	4	4	4

12.4.2 ■ Implementing the Working Set Algorithm

The working set algorithm is even more difficult to implement than the LRU algorithm (which could only be implemented cost effectively using approximate implementations). Clock algorithms were introduced as a way to approximate a pure implementation of the working set algorithm. They provide similar fault rate performance but allow for a simpler implementation than, for example, keeping the window contents for each process. The WSClock algorithm is an early implementation of the working set based on a clock algorithm and represents the basic technique used in contemporary implementations.

In *clock algorithms,* the idea is to think of the page frames of all processes as being arranged in a single circular list, like the numerals on the face of a clock. A single pointer addresses one page frame in the list. When the replacement algorithm requires that a page be replaced, the pointer is advanced to the next page frame and this frame is considered for replacement. Each page frame contains a reference bit (as in the LRU implementation for static algorithms), which is set when the page is referenced. At the time a page is considered for replacement, the algorithm checks the bit. If the reference bit is set, then the pointer moves to the next frame; otherwise, the page is replaced and all bits are cleared. Such an interpretation causes the clock algorithm to behave like a *global LRU* algorithm for all pages held by all processes. That is, it is similar to the implementation of LRU for an individual process (discussed in Section 12.3), yet it applies to the pages held by all processes at once.

Suppose process 3 incurs a page fault, and the memory manager decides it needs to load the page. Table 12.12 represents the data structure for the clock algorithm (note the similarity between Table 12.12 and Table 12.7 for the LRU approximation). The table identifies all page frames, a reference bit, and the process to which the page frame belongs. The three columns on the left represent the data structure after the reference bits have been cleared and with the clock hand pointing at page frame 4. When it is necessary to replace a page (the right side of Table 12.12), the memory manager examines page frame 53 and determines that it has been recently referenced, then it examines page frame 9, and so on. Page frame 34 has a cleared reference bit, so it will be

TABLE 12.12 Approximating Global LRU

Frame	Ref	Process	Frame	Ref	Process
10	0	3	10	0	3
⇒ 4	0	7	4	1	7
53	0	9	53	1	9
9	0	3	9	1	3
34	0	2	⇒ 34	0	2
19	0	4	19	0	4
48	0	4	48	1	4
29	0	3	29	1	3

replaced. This means that a page frame 34 will be deallocated from process 2 and added to process 3.

The basic clock algorithm can be extended to the *WSClock algorithm* by approximating the window size using the global LRU mechanism. Suppose the clock algorithm keeps an additional variable named `lastRef` for each page frame. When the reference bit is set, `lastRef[frame]` is set to the current virtual time for the process using it, $T_{process\ i}$. When a page fault occurs, the algorithm begins inspecting records as it does in the usual clock algorithm. When it finds a page frame whose reference bit is not set, it then checks to see if the page frame should have slipped out of its process's window. It does this by comparing

$$T_{process\ i} - \texttt{lastRef[frame]} > \tau,$$

where $T_{process\ i}$ is the current virtual time for process i and `lastRef[frame]` is the time the page was last referenced. Although `lastRef` is the virtual time of last reference for the appropriate process rather than the actual time, it allows the global LRU clock strategy to capture the basic behavior of the working set with window size τ. Variants of WSClock are used in most contemporary paging computer systems.

For example, suppose three processes, p_0, p_1, and p_2, share 15 page frames in primary memory. Assume that p_0 has executed to virtual time 55, p_1 to virtual time 75, and p_2 to virtual time 80 so that $T_{p0} = 55$, $T_{p1} = 75$, and $T_{p2} = 80$. Table 12.13 gives the clock variable settings (where page frame 0 is considered by the algorithms after they have considered page frame 14). The clock pointer addresses page frame number 6. If a page

TABLE 12.13 WSClock Behavior

Page Frame	0	1	2	3	4	5	6	7	8	9	10	11	12	13	14
Ref. Bit	0	1	0	1	1	0	1	0	1	1	0	0	0	0	0
Process #	0	0	1	2	2	1	1	0	2	0	1	2	0	1	2
lastRef	15	51	69	65	80	15	75	33	70	54	23	25	45	25	47
nextPtr							⇑								

fault has just occurred on behalf of p_0, then the basic clock algorithm would inspect the reference bit for frame 6, determine that the page had been used since the last page fault, and then move the pointer to page frame 7. The reference bit is not set here, and the page is allocated to p_0; the missing page replaces the page loaded in page frame 7.

Suppose the page fault had occurred on behalf of p_2. Again, the algorithm would have selected page frame 7 for the replacement, but it would have had to deallocate page frame 7 from p_0 and allocate it to p_2 prior to loading it with the missing page.

Now consider the behavior using WSClock with $\tau = 25$. If a page fault has just occurred on behalf of p_0, then WSClock will inspect the reference bit for page 6, detect that the bit was set, and move on to page frame 7 (as it would with the basic clock algorithm). $T_{p0} = 55$, so

$$T_{p0} - \texttt{lastRef[7]} = 55 - 33 = 22 < \tau.$$

Since the expression is less than τ, the algorithm will go to page frame 8, detect that the reference bit is set, and go on to page frame 9. The reference bit for page frame 9 is also set, so WSClock will next look at page frame 10 (allocated to p_1) and compute

$$T_{p1} - \texttt{lastRef[10]} = 75 - 23 = 52 > 25 = \tau.$$

Page frame 10 will be deallocated from p_1, allocated to p_2, and then loaded with the missing page.

Taking Advantage of Pages with IPC

Paging systems provide an opportunity for a significant performance improvement in any situation in which information is copied from the address space of one process to another, as in message-passing IPC mechanisms. Suppose the information to be copied is loaded into a buffer that is exactly the size of a page. If the buffer is in the sender's address space, the message can be moved from the sender's to the receiver's address space. This is done by deleting the page table pointer to the page that contains the message in the sender's page table and adding it to (or replacing an existing pointer in) the receiver's page table. The information remains in the same physical page frame, but the page frame is deallocated from the sender's address space and added to the receiver's address space.

The deferred copy semantics described in Section 9.3 also can be applied to the IPC mechanism to further increase performance (as is done in the Mach operating system). When a message is sent, its page is mapped into the receiver's space, while remaining mapped into the sender's space. As long as neither process writes to the page, it can be shared without harm to either process (provided the memory manager is instructed not to remove the page from either process's page table). If/when either process writes to the page, the copies are made and the pages are subsequently handled like any other pages in terms of selection for replacement.

12.5 ■ Segmentation

Segmentation is another form of virtual memory where programs use two-component addresses of the form

```
<segmentNumber, offset>
```

An indirect reference to a base location at which the segment is loaded is indicated by `segmentNumber`, and `offset` is the offset of the target cell within the segment. A simple form of segmentation was described in Chapter 11. In that form, processors such as the Intel 80x86 family incorporate four relocation registers called segment registers to dynamically bind instruction fetches. This is done using the "code segment" register, references to static data using the "data segment" register, and references to the process's stack using the "stack segment" register. A fourth data segment register, the "extra segment" register, binds a fourth segment, if needed. The Intel 80x86 address translation hardware does not check for out-of-segment references.

Virtual memory segment registers also use the idea of dynamic hardware relocation through relocation registers. The system is designed to support a comparatively large number of segments at a given time. For example, Multics processes can have 64K different segments. Addresses within a segment can be very general; for example, they may allow the OS to bind offset addresses within a segment at runtime. Full segmentation systems use a logical limit register for each segment, so references intended to be within a segment cannot inadvertently reference information stored in a different segment. Segmented virtual memory systems also employ protection mechanisms in the address translation to prevent unauthorized access to segments. Segment-based virtual memory systems provide a means for processes to share some segments while keeping access to others private.

The rest of this section describes how addresses are translated at runtime from symbolic segments and offset addresses to runtime locations in primary memory. It also covers the Multics segmentation system, since that system is the most general of these systems.

12.5.1 ■ Address Translation

Because address translation is the fundamental concept of virtual memory, the discussion of segmentation begins by considering the nature of the mapping mechanism. The segment name space is a two-component space, so the virtual-physical address map has the form

$$\Psi_i: \text{segment space} \times \text{offset space} \rightarrow \text{primary memory space} \cup \{\Omega\}$$

Any individual name space reference has the form

$$\Psi_i(i, j) = k,$$

where i is a segment number, j is an offset within the segment, and k is the primary memory location where the segment is loaded (Ω if the information is not loaded).

Segment names are typically symbolic names, like filenames, which are bound at runtime. This allows a process to use programs containing symbolic references to other segments without binding the symbolic name to a specific segment unless/until the process makes a reference to it. Segments containing error codes need never be bound to the process (and thus not loaded) unless an error occurs and the process needs to handle it. (This is not an issue in paging because the programmer never makes a symbolic reference to a page.) This generality introduces the requirement for another level of translation:

$$\sigma: \texttt{segment names} \rightarrow \text{segment addresses}.$$

Thus the full address map has the refined form of

$$\Psi_t(\sigma(\texttt{segmentName}), j) = k,$$

where $\texttt{segmentName}$ is a symbolic name of the target segment compiled into the executable image. In the most sophisticated segmentation systems, the offset within the segment is also bound at runtime, thus requiring a third translation operation at runtime:

$$\lambda: \texttt{offset names} \rightarrow \text{offset addresses}.$$

Postponing the binding of the offset in a virtual address to a target offset in a destination segment means the source process need not know the offset in the destination segment at compile/link time. The destination segment offset can be defined by the compiler and linker with no concern for distributing this information to processes that might need to use the segment. The binding will be done at the first reference to the offset at runtime.

Thus the address map could be as complex as

$$\Psi_t(\sigma(\texttt{segmentName}), \lambda(\texttt{offsetName})) = k,$$

where $\texttt{segmentName}$ is a symbolic segment name and $\texttt{offsetName}$ is the symbolic label, such as an entry point name, within the segment.

The task of designing a fully functional segmentation system to handle such general address translation is very challenging. Each memory reference is theoretically a pair of symbols to be translated when the reference occurs. As a further complication, the mappings are time-varying, meaning the segment could be located anywhere in primary and/or secondary memory.

Some implementations make a number of simplifying assumptions about the address translation—for example, they disallow runtime binding of segment and offset names. More comprehensive systems support late-bound segment, and offset names are designed so that the full translation happens only on the first reference to the segment. Subsequent references to a previously loaded segment use the binding established on the first reference. Even though the segment may be unloaded after the first reference, the binding of the symbolic name to a segment number can be reused.

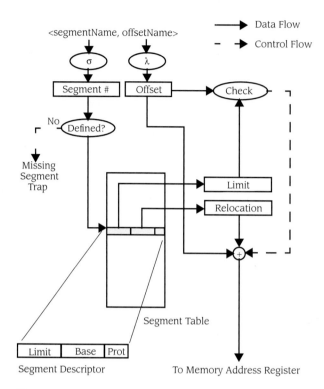

Figure 12.9
Address Translation in Segmentation

Figure 12.9 shows a conceptual implementation of the segment address translation facility. The operating system maintains a *segment table* for each process. The segment table is ordinarily a segment itself. It is usually stored in primary memory as a segment that is not to be unloaded as long as the process can run. It is a set of entries, each called a *segment descriptor.* Each descriptor contains fields to support relocation, specifically *base, limit,* and *protection* register contents for the segment (as described in Chapter 11). The base field contains the segment relocation register for the target segment (if it is loaded), the limit field contains the length of the segment, and the protection field describes allowable forms of access to the segment. If the segment is not loaded, the segment descriptor contents will be marked to indicate this.

When the process makes its first reference to a particular segment, the σ-map translates the segment name into a segment number by using a system-specific form of σ. The result, σ(segmentName), is an offset into the segment table that addresses the correct segment descriptor for the target segment. After the σ-map has bound a particular reference to a segment descriptor, it must make provision for bypassing the σ-map operation on subsequent executions of the program statement. The most primitive way to do this is to rewrite the operand in the instruction so that it contains a segment number rather than a segment name. Note that this does not require that the code segment be changed. However, it does require that an indirect reference table be used if the code is not to be changed. The next subsection gives a specific example of how this can be implemented.

In some systems, the offset must also be bound to a location within a loaded segment. This binding might occur if the compiler generating the segment reference did not have a load map of the target segment. Hence, it would have no way of generating the correct numeric offset. Therefore, on the first reference to the offset, the λ-map must bind the symbolic offset to the location within the segment. Again, the system will make provisions to avoid rebinding the symbol on subsequent references.

Within the segment descriptor, the base field points to the primary memory location where the segment is loaded. The offset is added to the base to obtain the address of the specific primary memory location. Thus the segment base and limit values are used to relocate and bound check the reference at runtime, just as the relocation and limit registers are used for hardware dynamic relocation.

12.5.2 ■ Implementation

There are many ways to implement a segmentation system. However, most implementations make simplifying assumptions about the system, so they do not implement the full address translation model described previously. For example, the hardware dynamic relocation registers are a fundamental hardware mechanism used to address segments of memory, but they do not implement any form of memory protection.

Suppose the hardware incorporates a special set of registers that are loaded when a process is loaded onto the CPU (see Figure 12.10). The segment table register, STR, points to the location of the segment table itself. The hardware now can use three

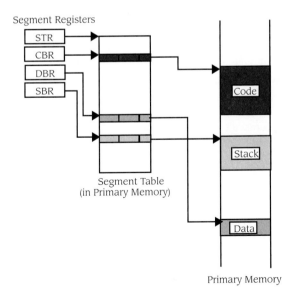

Figure 12.10
Segmentation Address Translation Implementation

additional registers to manage address translation. The code segment base value is kept in the code base register (CBR), also called the procedure base register (PBR) in some machines. A data base register (DBR) is used to dynamically relocate static data references, and a stack base register (SBR) points to a segment containing the process's stack. The implication is that successive instruction references to the segment indirectly addressed by the CBR can be executed very rapidly because no binding is required. The architecture also suggests that the successive data references are to the same segment, while successive stack references are to the same segment.

The figure suggests that the hardware is able to perform an indirect addressing operation on the memory when it forms the target primary memory address. So, when an instruction fetch is in progress for offset location j, the contents of the base field in the segment descriptor pointed to by the CBR are used as the base address of the target segment. A performance penalty results because each memory reference must perform two memory accesses: The first access obtains the segment base address, and the second accesses the target memory location. As long as the process references the same code, data, and stack segments for some period of virtual time, the CBR, DBR, and SBR will not change. If the hardware also incorporates dynamic relocation hardware for the code, data, and stack registers (base and limit registers), those registers can be loaded by the hardware each time the corresponding STR base register is changed. The extreme memory access time overhead is limited to cases in which the process changes the context—code, data, or stack segment—in which it is executing.

The hardware depicted in Figure 12.10 does not provide any particular assistance for dynamic binding. The σ-map must be evaluated in software, and the result can then be stored in the appropriate base register. If the code, data, or stack segment changes, either the σ-map must be reevaluated (if the inter segment reference is to a segment not previously bound into the process's physical address space). Or the CBR/DBR/SBR can be adjusted to point to the segment descriptor of a previously bound segment.

The programming language and compiler must be designed to make effective use of the segmentation hardware. The language must provide some mechanism by which the programmer can specify symbolic segment names. In assembly language programs, this specification is typically accomplished by a pseudo operation—for example, the using pseudo operation. In Figure 12.11, the assembler will initially generate code for segmentA in its own segment. The reference to lab1 is a simple call instruction within the current segment. The CBR will not change when the instruction is executed. However, the call to [segmentC, lab20] will assemble to include instructions to load the CBR with a value determined by the segment name. The CBR load operand will be an external symbolic reference for segmentC, which is bound by σ at runtime. The call instruction will follow the CBR load instruction and is of the same form as the previous call, with an operand of lab20. For the current discussion, assume the value of lab20 is resolved before runtime.

The using pseudo operation causes the assembler, linkage editor, and loader to generate separate execution images for segmentB and segmentC. It is the task of the memory manager to dynamically link the segments at runtime. When segmentA is to be executed, it is loaded through a standard OS command. When the process encounters

Figure 12.11
Inter Segment Referer.

```
        using   seg. entA
        . . .
        call    lab1
        . . .
        call    [segmentC, lab20]
        . . .
lab1:   . . .
        . . .
        using   segmentB
        . . .
        using   segmentC
        . . .
lab20:  . . .
        . . .
```

the symbolic segment reference to segmentC, the symbolic address must be bound to an address in primary memory.

The CBR load instruction must cause a trap to the OS. The normal instruction sequence will be interrupted, and control will be given to the OS just as if an interrupt had occurred. The OS will obtain the symbolic reference and use it to search the file system for the executable image of segmentC. Once found, the image is loaded into primary memory and an entry is made in the segment table to record that segmentC is now present. The CBR load instruction is modified, possibly using indirect links to avoid actual modifications to code, to point to the newly created segment descriptor. Finally, the CBR is loaded with the segment descriptor offset, and the instruction is restarted. On the second execution, the CBR load will encounter a segment descriptor offset. This offset will be loaded into the CBR, thus enabling the rest of the address translation to occur as if segmentC had been present on the first execution of the instruction.

➤ *IN THE HANGAR*

The Multics Segmentation System

The Multics operating system was designed to support a very general form of segmentation with dynamic segment and offset binding. No contemporary machine has anything near the sophistication of this intricate combination of software and hardware to implement a virtual memory system. Multics was several decades before its time, and the trend in memory management likely will lead back to this form of segmentation.

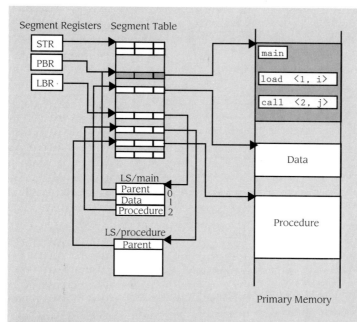

Figure 12.12
Multics Segmentation Mechanism

The hardware that supports Multics, such as the Honeywell/GE 645 computer, has three segment registers (Figure 12.12):

- The usual STR to point at the segment table.

- A PBR that serves the same purpose as the CBR in the general discussion.

- A linkage base register (LBR) that replaces the SBR and DBR, since Multics makes no distinction between the static and dynamic data segments.

As before, the PBR points to the segment descriptor for the code currently being executed. However, to accommodate segment sharing the compiler produces a template for another level of indirection during address formation through a *linkage segment*. Whenever the segment is "made known" (bound into the address space the first time), a unique linkage segment is constructed from a compiler-generated template for the process that is invoking the shared segment. In Figure 12.12, the shared segment is called "main" and the linkage segment is called "LS/main." The linkage segment is pointed to by the segment table, and the LBR is set to point at the segment descriptor for the current linkage segment. Since the linkage segment is created from a compile-time template, it is correlated with the segment indices that are compiled into the shared segment. For example, the references to segments 1 and 2 refer to offsets in the linkage segment, not in the segment table.

Assume the linkage segment pointers have been set. When the load [1, i] instruction is executed, the hardware uses the LBR to find the linkage segment and the "1" to identify an entry in the linkage segment. Entry "1" in the linkage segment, in turn, points to a segment descriptor in the segment table for the data reference. The linkage segment has provided a one-level indirect addressing mechanism for the data reference.

The procedure call instruction causes the PBR and the LBR to change, since the process is moving to a different segment for continued execution. The `call [2, j]` instruction causes the hardware to use the LBR to find the linkage segment entry and the pointer to a new segment descriptor. When the link is traversed, the system will change the LBR to point to the segment pointed to by `LS/main`. By convention, the first entry in the linkage segment points to the procedure segment to which it belongs. Thus the system will follow the first pointer in the linkage segment to the segment descriptor for the called procedure segment, and the PBR will be set to address the new procedure segment descriptor, which points to the new procedure segment.

Linkage segments and procedure segments are constructed to allow runtime binding of symbolic segment names (see Figure 12.13). When the compiler encounters an inter segment call of the form

```
call [segmentName, offsetName]
```

it first creates an entry in an out symbol table containing the symbolic reference, `segmentName`. (The out symbol table is the Multics name for an external reference table that is not to be resolved by the linkage editor but rather is to contain symbols to be defined at runtime.) Next, the compiler adds an entry to the linkage segment at entry k that contains a pointer to the out symbol table entry. The entry also contains a fault flag that is initialized to cause a fault the first time the out symbol is referenced. Finally, the compiler generates code of the form

```
call [(*linkageSegment, k), offset]
```

Now, when the call instruction is executed, it will branch indirectly to the kth entry in the linkage segment. On the first execution of the instruction, the fault flag will be

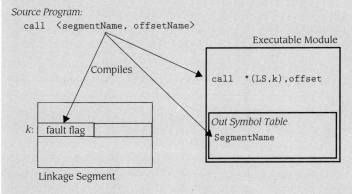

Figure 12.13
Multics Binding Mechanism

set to cause a trap to the OS. The trap handler will follow the pointer in the linkage segment to the entry in the calling procedure's out symbol table. The system can then retrieve the symbolic segment name from the out symbol table, retrieve the segment from secondary storage, enter a descriptor into the segment table, and modify the linkage segment so that it points to the appropriate segment descriptor. The fault flag is cleared to prevent subsequent missing segment faults. The symbolic offset can be handled similarly.

The Multics segmentation system is very complex, although the functionality it provides is more general than that of contemporary virtual memory systems. While it appears the complexity of the solution might severely impact performance, the hardware was designed to specifically support the segment mechanism and was very fast. Also, most of the mechanism was used only when there was an inter segment reference.

12.6 ▪ Summary

Virtual memory systems are an abstraction of the primary memory in a von Neumann computer. Even in a time of decreasing physical memory costs, contemporary computers devote considerable resources to supporting virtual address spaces that are much larger than the physical memory allocated to a process. Contemporary software relies heavily on virtual memory to support applications such as image management with huge memory requirements.

The virtual memory abstraction is built on the idea of runtime address binding. The compiler and the linkage editor create an absolute module that the loader traditionally binds to physical addresses before the program executes. Hardware facilities enable a memory manager to automatically load portions of a virtual address space into primary memory, while the rest of the address space is left in secondary memory.

Paging systems transfer fixed-sized blocks of information between primary and secondary memories. Because of the fixed page size and page frame size, the translation from a binary virtual address to a corresponding physical address is relatively simple, provided the system has an efficient table lookup mechanism. Paging systems use associative memories to implement page translation tables.

A paging system can be characterized by specifying its fetch, placement, and replacement policies. Demand paging algorithms use a fetch policy whereby a page is loaded only when it is referenced. In contrast, a prefetch policy may load several pages when it detects any particular page missing. Most paging algorithms use the demand fetch rule.

The placement policy identifies the page frame in which to store a page when it is to be loaded. In static algorithms, the placement policy is to use the page frame of the page to be replaced if all frames are full. There are several different replacement strategies, including the random, Belady's optimal, LRU, LFU, and FIFO algorithms.

LRU and LFU are stack algorithms, while FIFO and random are not. LRU has been the dominant static demand algorithm in commercial computers, but it is difficult to implement precisely because of the need to keep an inordinately large amount of information about the reference stream. The page translation table can use reference bits to approximate the LRU strategy; the more reference bits, the better the approximation.

Dynamic allocation paging attempts to adjust the number of page frames allocated to a process according to its needs. This can be done by considering an LRU strategy on a window on the reference stream, as done in the working set algorithm.

Segmentation is an alternative to paging. It differs from paging in that the unit of transfer between primary and secondary memories varies. The size of the segments are also explicitly known by the programmer. Translating a segment virtual address to a physical address is more complex than translating a paging virtual address. The segment and offset may both have to be translated at runtime. Multics, although over 25 years old, remains the most comprehensive segmentation system that is implemented commercially.

Segmentation makes the relationship between the primary and secondary memories depend on the existence of a file system, since segments are stored on the storage devices as files. The details of the file manager are covered in the next chapter.

12.7 ▪ Exercises

1. Why are the page size, the number of pages in the virtual address space, and the number of page frames in the physical address space all a power of 2 in binary machines?

2. Suppose a paging system has 2^{g+h} virtual addresses and uses 2^{h+k} locations in primary memory for integers g, h, and k. What is the page size of the system that is implied by the virtual and physical address sizes? How many bits are required to store a virtual address?

3. Suppose the page size in a computing environment is 1KB. What is the page number and the offset for the following:

    a. 899 (a decimal number)
    b. 23456 (a decimal number)
    c. 0x3F244 (a hexadecimal number)
    d. 0x0017C (a hexadecimal number)

4. Contemporary computers often have more than 100MB of physical memory. Suppose the page size is 2KB. How many entries would an associative memory need in order to implement a page table for the memory?

5. Use an example to explain the different representations of a reference to a variable in the name space, the virtual address space, and the physical address space. Using your example, show how the virtual address is derived from the name and how the physical address is derived from the virtual address.

6. What factors could influence the size of the virtual address space in a modern computer system. In your answer, consider the memory mapping unit, compiler technology, and instruction format.

7. What factors could influence the size of the physical address space in a modern computer system (consider various parts of the hardware).

8. Suppose ω = 2 3 4 3 2 4 3 2 4 5 6 7 5 6 7 4 5 6 7 2 1 is a page reference stream.

   a. Given a page frame allocation of 3 and assuming the primary memory is initially unloaded, how many page faults will the given reference stream incur under Belady's optimal algorithm?

   b. Given a page frame allocation of 3 and assuming the primary memory is initially unloaded, how many page faults will the given reference stream incur under LRU?

   c. Given a page frame allocation of 3 and assuming the primary memory is initially unloaded, how many page faults will the given reference stream incur under FIFO?

   d. Given a window size of 6 and assuming the primary memory is initially unloaded, how many page faults will the given reference stream incur under the working-set algorithm?

   e. Given a window size of 6 and assuming the primary memory is initially unloaded, what is the working-set size under the given reference stream after the entire stream has been processed?

9. Let ω = 0 3 0 4 0 5 0 6 1 5 2 6 7 5 0 0 0 6 6 6 6 be a page reference stream. Answer parts a–e for Problem 8 for this reference stream.

10. Describe a program that could be expected to have the following:

    a. A small code locality and a small data locality
    b. A small code locality and a large data locality
    c. A large code locality and a small data locality
    d. A large code locality and a large data locality

11. Suppose hardware were designed to incorporate 3 reference bits rather than the single bit used in the LRU implementation described in Section 12.3.4. Explain how a better approximation to LRU could be achieved using the 3-bit field than can be achieved using the single reference bit.

12. What is the advantage of the page fault frequency algorithm over the estimation of the working set using the window size t? What is its disadvantage?

13. Construct a sample reference stream illustrating Belady's anomaly for frame allocations of 3 and 4.

14. In a paging system, page boundaries are transparent to the programmer. Explain how a loop might cause thrashing in a static allocation paging system when the memory allocation is too small.

15. Why is locality not an issue in a segmentation system?

16. Suppose two processes share a main program segment but each has its own private implementation of a procedure called from the main segment and private data segments. Draw a figure similar to Figure 12.12 to illustrate how the segment registers and segments might be set up to accommodate this situation.

13

File Management

They have the directory, but the problem with the directory is even if you figure out where you are, and where you want to go, you still don't really know which way to walk because it's an upright map.

—Jerry Seinfeld, *SeinLanguage* ■

CHAPTER OBJECTIVES

Files are the mechanism by which users save information from one session to another. They also are used as containers for archiving information for long periods of time. The language translation system uses the file system to store relocatable, absolute, and executable programs. Virtual memory managers that use segmentation rely on the file system to store the segments. Programmers rely on the file system to simplify the use of storage devices to hold sets of data. An individual e-mail message is delivered as a file. An HTML web page is a file.

The objectives of this chapter are to discuss the concepts that guide file management design, including a description of the types of files the system might support, followed by descriptions of low-level and high-level file system implementations. Finally, the chapter discusses how the directory capability is added to allow users to manage their files.

13.1 ■ Files

From the programmer's perspective, files are the fundamental abstraction of secondary storage devices (such as magnetic tapes or disk drives), although the system software may also provide other higher-level abstractions such as virtual memory. Each file is a named collection of data stored in a device. The file manager implements this abstraction and provides directories for organizing files. It also provides a spectrum of commands to read and write the contents of a file, to set the file read/write position, to set and use the protection mechanism, to change the ownership, to list files in a directory, and to remove a file.

The vast majority of all application programs read information from one or more files, process the data, and then write the result to one or more other files. For example, an accounts payable program reads one file containing invoices and another containing purchase orders, correlates the data, and then prints a check and writes a file to describe the expenditures. A compiler reads a source program file, translates the program into machine code, and then writes a relocatable file and an error report file. An optimization program reads a description of the space to be analyzed from a file, searches the space for global minima and/or maxima, and then writes the result to an output file.

This model of operation is so prevalent that it can easily be built into the process model. For example, when a process is created in UNIX, it automatically has access to three files:

- `stdin` as a file abstraction of the input device
- `stdout` as an abstraction of the normal output device
- `stderr` as an error log file

(In UNIX systems, the default is for `stdin`, `stdout`, and `stderr` to reference communication devices rather than storage devices, although the corresponding devices are referenced using the file interface, as explained in Chapter 5.) The extreme of this view of computing is that programs are simply a means of defining filters for reading a file, transforming the data into some other form, and then writing the result to another file.

A file is a container for a collection of information. The file manager provides a protection mechanism to allow machine users to administer how processes executing on behalf of different users can access the information in a file. File protection is a fundamental property of files because it allows different people to store their information on a shared computer, with the confidence that the information can be kept confidential.

How is the functionality provided by the file manager related to virtual memory? The goal of a virtual memory implementation is to support a very large address space in executable memory. A process's full address space image is created and maintained in the secondary memory, and then parts of it are loaded into primary memory as needed. Virtual memory managers provide one abstraction of secondary memory, and files provide another; in Windows NT, memory-mapped files straddle these notions of file and virtual memory (see Section 13.5). The file abstraction predates virtual memory technology by several years. It had become well entrenched by the time virtual memory could be used to reference large address spaces in secondary memory. Programmers were, and still are, accustomed to using files to save information for indefinite periods of time, while virtual memory contents stored in secondary memory are temporary images (lasting as long as the related process exists). Another difference is that the file-names of all files in secondary memory are accessible from any address space, while virtual memory contents are available only to the process associated with them. As a result, modern operating systems employ both paging and file systems as separate inter-faces to secondary memory.

When applications operate on data, they rely on the presence of *structure* in the data, represented as collections of *records* that contain typed *fields* of information (see Figure 13.1). For example, an invoice is an individual record in a file; the invoice record has different fields for names, addresses, the invoice amount, and so on. There is application domain-specific structure on the data in the files to reflect numerical data, images, and audio information.

Unfortunately, as explained in Chapter 5, storage devices are capable of storing only linearly addressed blocks of bytes. The file system provides an abstraction from storage blocks to data structures suitable for use by application programs. At a mini-mum, the file system provides an abstraction that links blocks of the storage system together to form a logical collection of information—called *stream-block translation* in Figure 13.1. Conceptually, such a translation allows one to store and retrieve an arbi-trary stream of linearly addressed bytes on the block-oriented storage system.

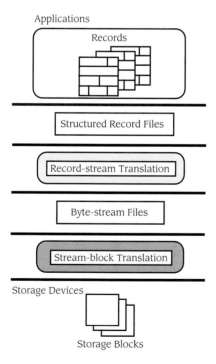

Figure 13.1
Information Structure

When an application's data structure is written to a storage device, it will have to be "flattened" into a byte stream by a record-stream translation procedure, as shown in Figure 13.1. Then the stream can be stored as a set of blocks. Later when the data is retrieved, it will be read block-by-block, converted into a stream of bytes, and then converted back into the application-level data structure. Should the record-stream conversion facilities be provided by the file system? Or does it make more sense for the file system to provide only a minimum structuring facility, with the expectation that programmers will impose their own structure on data? Commercial business-oriented systems have traditionally provided extensive file facilities to support data structuring, while systems such as Windows and UNIX leave structuring to the application. The Apple Macintosh system software provides less-general facilities for structuring data than does an IBM mainframe operating system, but more functionality than do Windows NT and UNIX. If an OS provides only the stream-block translation facilities, it is said to provide a *low-level* file system. If the file system provides the record-stream translation, it is a *structured* (or *high-level*) file system. Windows NT and UNIX provide low-level file systems, while IBM MVS provides a structured file system. Since the Macintosh provides some record-stream translation facilities, it is arbitrarily called a high-level file system.

Structured file systems must provide a specialized language to define data structures used by the record-stream translator. The facility may be simple, allowing the programmer to define a record length and a key field for identifying each record. Or it may be sophisticated enough to allow storage and retrieval of records based on arbitrary fields. The most functional and flexible systems are database management systems. While a database management system is a logical extension of the storage devices, the OS may provide a low-level interface used by application programs to implement the database management system.

Storage systems that support multimedia documents are growing in importance. Contemporary applications require the OS to be able to handle information containers that represent, for example, numerical data, typeset textual data, graphics, images, and audio information. Ordinary low-level file systems are not designed to accommodate these multimedia documents because different media types potentially require different access and modification strategies for efficient I/O. For example, the technique for efficient access of an image differs from one for accessing a floating-point number. More and more application domains are requiring the OS to provide flexible, high-performance access methods suitable for use with multimedia data, where the methods are defined by the programmer.

13.1.1 ■ Low-level Files

A *byte-stream file system* implements the block-stream translation in Figure 13.2. A byte-stream file is a named sequence of bytes indexed by the nonnegative integers. Each byte in the stream of bytes has an index: The first byte has index 0, the second has index 1, and so on. The *file position* is used to reference bytes in the file. At any given moment after the file has been opened, the file pointer references the index of the next byte in the file to be read from or written to.

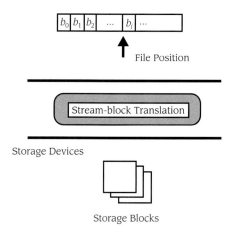

Figure 13.2
Block-stream Translation

The file system keeps a data structure called a *file descriptor* in which it stores detailed information about each file. Different file managers store different information, although most maintain (or are able to derive on request) the following:

- *External name:* A character string name for the file, used at the command line or from an application program. This is the symbolic name that users associate with the file.

- *Current state:* The state of the file; this can be *archived,* meaning that it has been written to a very low level of the storage hierarchy and cannot be opened for use without a significant delay. If the state is *closed,* the file resides in an online storage device and can be opened for use within milliseconds. The file can be *open for reading,* meaning that the file is allocated to a process reading the file; it can also be *open for writing,* meaning that the file is allocated to a process writing to the file, or *open for execution, open for appending,* and so on.

- *Sharable:* A field in which multiple processes can have the file open at once. This field identifies the file as *read sharable, execution sharable, write sharable,* and so on.

- *Owner:* The identifier associated with the user whose process created the file. In some cases, ownership may be assigned by some other policy. The file system may allow a process to pass ownership to another user.

- *User:* The list of processes currently having the file open. If the file is not sharable, this entry is always null or only a single process.

- *Locks:* A process that allows a file system to *lock* a file when it is opened. Locks can be *read locks,* meaning the file is currently opened for reading. If the file is sharable, other processes can open it only for reading. A *write lock* indicates a process has opened the file for writing. Unless the file is write sharable, only one process can use the file at a time.

- *Protection settings:* The protection characterization (different operating systems have different characterizations). The minimum modes of protection are *read* and *write.* The protection settings indicate whether the owner is able to read from or write to the file without overriding the protection. A second protection field specifies whether other processes can read from or write to the file. File protection settings are discussed in Chapter 14.

- *Length:* The number of bytes contained in the file.

- *Time of creation:* The system time at which the file was created.

- *Time of last modification:* The system time at which the file was last written to.

- *Time of last access:* The system time at which the file was last read from or executed or had any other operation performed on it.

- *Reference count:* The count of the number of directories in which the file appears if the directory system allows a file to appear in more than one directory. It is used to detect when the file is deleted from all directories so that its space can be released.

- *Storage device details:* The field that contains the details of how the blocks in the file can be accessed. The details depend heavily on the storage device block management strategy that the file manager uses.

When the file is opened, the file manager will keep additional information to record the state of the session (between the process and the file). Hence, there is a file descriptor kept with the file on the secondary storage system and an extended internal form of the file descriptor with a copy of the information from the external file descriptor along with dynamic information (see Section 13.1.2). For example, the file position value will appear in the open-file description, but it is not included in the secondary storage descriptor.

The following are typical operations on a byte-stream file:

- `open(fileName)`: The `fileName` is a character string that uniquely identifies a file. The operation prepares the file for reading or writing. The `open` operation causes information in the file descriptor to reflect that the file is being put into use. It also may cause additional descriptors to be opened to manage the open file. (For example, if the system supports shared files, then a process-specific descriptor will be opened to keep the file position setting for this process.) The operation sets the file position to 0, and returns a file identifier used as an argument to the other file operations. If the file manager supports file modes (such as "open for reading, but not writing" or "open for reading and writing"), then the appropriate mode will also be a parameter to `open`.

- `close(fileID)`: This operation releases the internal descriptors created when the file was opened along with any other resources used by the file system to manage the byte-stream I/O.

- `read(fileID, buffer, length)`: This operation copies a block of `length` (or fewer) bytes beginning at the current file position into the buffer for the specified file identifier, `fileID`. If the file position is L bytes from the end of the stream and $L <$ `length`, then only L bytes will be copied to the buffer. The operation increments the file position by the number of bytes read and returns that number. If the file is positioned at the end of the stream when `read` is invoked, an end-of-file condition is returned.

- `write(fileID, buffer, length)`: This operation writes `length` bytes of the information from the buffer to the current file position and then increments the file position by `length`.

- `seek(fileID, filePosition)`: This operation changes the value of the file position to the value of the parameter, `filePosition`. Subsequent read/write operations reference the data whose index corresponds to the new value of the file position.

The file manager maps a filename to a collection of physical blocks on the storage devices. It uses device drivers to read and write blocks on storage devices, but it provides information to the application program on a variable-sized block basis. To implement `write` operations, it must be able to allocate unused blocks to the file as needed. If a `delete` operation is provided, it must also be able to deallocate blocks from the file. File manager implementation strategies are discussed in Section 13.2 after a review of how structured files differ from these byte-stream files. This description of the file interface is consistent with the user's view of the UNIX file interface introduced in Chapter 2.

The UNIX file descriptor is called an *inode* (an abbreviation for *index node*). The inode for a file is kept on the storage device that contains the corresponding file. The BSD UNIX inode file descriptor contains the information shown in Table 13.1. The inode is augmented with other information when the file is opened.

TABLE 13.1 UNIX File Descriptor

Field	Description
Mode	Specification of access permissions for the owner and other users.
UID	ID of the user creating the file.
Group ID	ID associated with the file to identify a collection of users having group-access rights to the file.
Length in bytes	Number of bytes in the file.
Length in blocks	Number of blocks used to implement the file.
Last modification	Time the file was last written to.
Last access	Time the file was last read.
Last inode modification	Time the inode was last changed.
Reference count	Number of directories in which the file appears; this field is used to detect when the file is deleted from all directories so that its space can be released.
Block references	Pointers and indirect pointers to blocks in the file.

13.1.2 ■ Structured Files

An application that wants to treat the byte stream as a sequence of records must convert the "raw" bytes into a stream of records with application-specific data structures, as shown in Figure 13.3. Since the programmer uses data structures to define application functionality, when information is referenced in a file some part of the software must handle conversions back-and-forth between the data structure record format used by the program and the stream of bytes.

The use of character files in UNIX illustrates how a community of applications can provide this translation through convention and through the use of a library of support functions: UNIX files are byte-stream files, although various classes of UNIX applications impose additional structure on the byte stream with no explicit support from the OS. The classic example is ASCII character files. Over the years, a set of different programs has been written to process byte stream (text) files known to contain characters. Application software makes two assumptions about these text files. First, the byte stream contains only "printable" ASCII characters, and, second, the characters are arranged into "lines," with each line terminated by the NEWLINE character. The kernel does not distinguish text files from other byte streams, though several commands (including UNIX system software and library routines) do make the distinction. For example, the word count program, wc, reads a file, counts the number of NEWLINE characters, the number of "words" in the file as determined by the placement of punctuation and "whitespace" in the file, and the number of characters in the file as determined by the number of bytes in the file. Then it prints these counts with the name of the file. Of course, a user can apply wc to any file, such as a relocatable object file. wc will assume the file is a text file and count the number of lines, words, and characters appearing in the file—producing results that have no useful meaning. Various other programs have been written explicitly to process text files and have been added to the command library. For example grep, diff, and vi operate on text files. This nonkernel extension

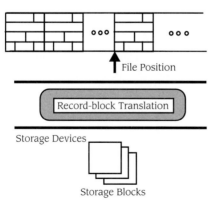

Figure 13.3
Block-record Translation

provides a substantial utility to the system, while the OS implements only the essentials of the byte stream.

The UNIX character file example highlights the fact that if the file system does not support data structures, then the applications must provide that capability. A generic structured file can be used to hold any kind of information, including absolute program images, relocatable object programs, libraries, numeric data organized according to the needs of some set of applications, textual data such as source programs, word processing documents, and information ready to print. Ultimately, structured files are represented on the storage medium as a collection of blocks. Structured file descriptors must contain the same kinds of information that are kept for a low-level file, as well as additional fields to support data structures as follows:

- *Type:* A tag describing the type of the file. For example, the type field might distinguish relocatable object files from absolute object files or PostScript files.

- *Access methods:* A composite of functions to be used to read from, write to, append to, update, or otherwise access the file. Since sophisticated structured files take on the character of an abstract data type, this part of the descriptor identifies the function interface for the abstract data type.

- *Other:* Specific structured file types may have other fields to represent the relationship of this file to related files, the minimum version number of the file manager handling this file type, and so on.

13.1.2.1 ■ Record-oriented Sequential Files

Many applications need to store and access a set of records as a list. For example, an electronic mail system stores messages and folders of messages. A mail message could be processed by many different programs—such as an editor, a mail transport program, a mail receipt program, a mail posting program, and a mail browsing program. Hence, it is convenient to incorporate general information about electronic mail in well-defined parts of the file. This is done by formatting each message as a record, with the various parts of a message being fields of the record. A mail folder is often implemented as a file containing several such records. Each mail program uses this record structure in a consistent manner. This can be accomplished by building on top of a byte-stream file an abstract machine that has knowledge of a mail message structure, or by implementing an alternative file system handling collections of records directly on the device drivers (see again Figure 13.3). Like text files applications, UNIX mail programs provide the data abstraction on top of the UNIX byte-stream files.

A *structured sequential file* is a named sequence of logical records (as contrasted with bytes), indexed by the nonnegative integers. As with byte-stream files, access to the file is defined by a file position, but in this case the position indexes records in the file instead of bytes. Operations on the file are as follows:

- `open(fileName)`: Performs the same function as the `open` for byte-stream files on the given `fileName` and returns a file identifier used in the other operations.

- `close(fileID)`: Performs the same function as the `close` for byte-stream files on the given file identifier, `fileID`.

- ■ getRecord(fileID, record): Returns the record addressed by file position.

- ■ putRecord(fileID, record): Writes the designated record at the current position.

- ■ seek(fileID, position): Moves the file position to point at the designated record.

These operations are equivalent to the operations for the byte-stream file, except the data are stored in records instead of bytes.

What is the format of a record in the file? One approach is to allocate k bytes to contain each record, with an additional H bytes for record descriptor information (see Figure 13.4). The getRecord and putRecord operations read and write $H + k$ bytes at a time from the storage block. The application is responsible for properly interpreting the fields in each record, for example in C, by casting a structure pointer to an I/O buffer that contains the record.

Some applications require very large records—for example, to hold a bitmap image. Others require only very small records—for example, to hold a name or address. With a file system that supports only fixed-sized record containers, either small records will waste large amounts of space when they are written to the storage system or large records will have to be manually fragmented before they are written to the file. Neither constraint is acceptable in a general-purpose system. An alternative is for the file system to be enhanced to include a function to define the record size for a file. The operation, setRecordSize(fileID, size), establishes the size, in bytes, of records to be written into the file. The record size is encoded into the record header.

Suppose records are of different sizes—perhaps some holding an address and others holding a bitmap image. Then there must be a set of block-record translation functions to be applied for the different types of records. This can be accomplished by

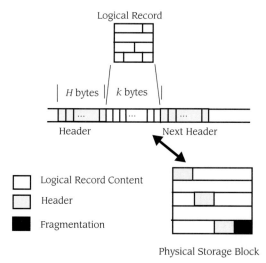

Figure 13.4
A Logical-Physical Record Encoding

prespecifying the set of record types or by using runtime decoding. In traditional record-oriented file structures, the record types are built into the file system itself. In these cases, the *access functions* are operations designed and implemented at the time the file system is designed and implemented. For example, a file system may support strings of characters, where a record is a string. Now, a putRecord operation will write a variable-length array of bytes corresponding to a stream to the storage device. A more general file system might support programmer-defined abstract data types. The application programmer would define the format for logical records and the access routines for reading and writing the records. The file system invokes the programmer-supplied access routines when reading from and writing to the file. As the abstract data types become more sophisticated, the file system increasingly resembles a database system.

For example, an electronic message is often defined as a structured sequential file having the form shown in Figure 13.5. A mailbox is a collection of such records as defined by the struct declaration. The putRecord operation appends a mail message to the end of the mailbox file, and the getRecord routine retrieves the message "under" the file position. Figure 13.5 also shows examples of customized access rou-

Figure 13.5
Electronic Mail Example

```
struct message {
/* The mail message */
    address to;
    address from;
    line subject;
    address cc;
    string body;
};

struct message *getRecord(void) {
    struct message *msg;
    msg = allocate(sizeof(message));
    msg->to = getAddress(...);
    msg->from = getAddress(...);
    msg->cc = getAddress(...);
    msg->subject = getLine();
    msg->body = getString();
    return(msg);
}

putRecord(struct message *msg) {
    putAddress(msg->to);
    putAddress(msg->from);
    putAddress(msg->cc);
    putLine(msg->subject);
    putString(msg->body);
}
```

tines for the message record type. Assume the `get` and `put` operations can be written in terms of the read and write operations.

A structured file manager allows the programmer to export information (such as that shown in the figure) into the file manager. This can be accomplished by having the file manager rely on the existence of a fixed set of access operation names and then having the application program write definitions for each of those names. When the application instructs the file manager to read a record, the file manager uses the application-supplied access operation to define the specific format of the information to be read. The file manager provides all the infrastructure for manipulating the file (such as interacting with the device driver), and the application writer provides only the information that is specific to the record format.

13.1.2.2 ■ Indexed Sequential Files

Sequentially accessed information is not useful in some applications. For example, in an interactive query system, such as an automatic teller system, any particular work done by the program will be concerned only with a specific record rather than with every record in the file. The file system must then be able to read from or write to a specific record independent of the record's location in the file. Indexed sequential files provide this capability, while retaining the ability to access the records sequentially. Each record header includes an integer *index field*. The interface to an indexed sequential file system uses a more general read/write interface than do pure sequential files:

- `getRecord(fileID, index)`: Returns the record with an `index` field set to the index value.

- `putRecord(fileID, record)`: As an access operation, writes the designated `record` into the file at a position chosen by the file system and then returns the value of the `index` field as a result.

- `deleteRecord(fileID, index)`: Removes the `record` with the `index` field set to the index value.

Indexed sequential files force the program to manage the indices so that they can access desired records. For example, suppose a customer wants to know the balance of an account. The customer can supply an account number but not the index value. Therefore an automatic teller machine application would have to keep a table to translate account numbers into record indices (see Figure 13.6).

Suppose the programmer could specify the index for a record when it is written. Then the lookup table could be eliminated by using, for example, the `account#` field as the index field for each record. This would require the `putRecord` operation to be changed to `putRecord(fileID, record, index)`. This access operation writes the designated record into the file at a position chosen by the file system and assigns the index parameter value as the value of the index field. If there is already another record with the specified value, the operation returns a value of `False`; otherwise, it returns `True`.

Indexed sequential files are widely used in business computing for files that have very large numbers of records, particularly if the records are often referenced in a non-sequential manner. An indexed sequential file can also be accessed sequentially if the application intends to systematically process every record in the file.

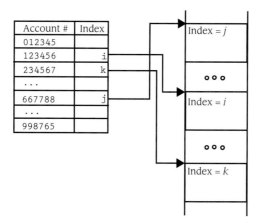

Figure 13.6
An Indexed Sequential File with a Lookup Table

13.1.2.3 ■ Inverted Files

There are many applications in which the index field must be searched by the application before a record can be retrieved. For example, suppose the program were to allow accounts to be retrieved by using the customer's name, but a customer might have more than one account. To find the correct account, all records matching the customer's name would have to be read and then each inspected to access the desired record. In general, each record access would cause a storage I/O operation, since the records would not usually be stored in the same physical block. The number of operations could be substantially reduced by extracting the index field from each record and placing it in an *index table*. This table has the conceptual form shown in Figure 13.6, but it is maintained by the file system, not the application. However, the application program can search the table without incurring excessive storage device I/O operations.

The case in which the application needs to search with different criteria, such as name or account number, suggests that each record might have two or more index fields. One field links the records together by names and the other by account numbers. This can be implemented by including links for each linked list in each record or by preparing one index table with names and another with account numbers. Searches take place on the appropriate table, and the record is then accessed on the storage device.

The external index table can be generalized so that an entry points to various records or fields in the file. When a record is placed in the file, keywords in the record are extracted and placed in the index table with a pointer back into the record to where the keyword appears. This is called an *inverted file,* since records are accessed based on their appearance in the table rather than their logical location or address.

Inverted files can also be generalized to support multiple index fields, each with its own index into the records. The table storage requirements are increased. The overhead to manage the indices increases, since record deletions can cause dangling pointers in an index. However, access times can be substantially reduced by using such files.

13.1.3 ■ Database Management Systems

Database management systems (DBMSs) constitute an entire area of computer science, so the remarks here are superficial, intended only to point out the relationship between DBMSs and operating systems. A database is a very highly structured set of information, typically stored across several files and with the organization optimized to minimize access time. The DBMS enables the programmer to define complex data types in terms of data *schema*. These schema specifications are then used by the database administrator to organize the way information is to be stored in files so the data can be accessed rapidly. Once data have been stored in the database, they can be retrieved by querying the database, changed, and then written back into the database.

The data definition and manipulation languages and their processors are complex entities not considered to be part of an OS. Some DBMSs use the normal files provided by the OS for generic use. Obviously, a low-level file system will be better suited to DBMS support than will a structured file system. This is because the low-level system does not presume any particular structure on files; it expects the application—the DBMS—to do this.

While conceptually every DBMS uses the file system to implement its functions, in many cases it has its own storage device block organization and access routines; hence, it completely bypasses the file system in order to work directly with devices. This enables the DBMS to be more efficient in the way it accesses the storage devices. However, it precludes information stored in the database from being accessible using the file manager's interface to the storage device.

13.1.4 ■ Multimedia Storage

Multimedia documents are highly structured files (or sets of files) designed to contain information represented as numbers, characters, formatted text, executable programs, graphics, images, audio representations, and so on. The storage requirements of multimedia documents (containing images) are five or more orders of magnitude higher than those for traditional alphanumeric information. For example, a page of formatted text characters might require 0.5 to 1KB to save the information, but a similar-sized color image might require 10MB of storage.

This diversity in storage requirements between components of a multimedia document naturally encourages variable-sized records. This in turn requires either of the following: (1) there must be considerable translation functionality in applications that use the multimedia document, or (2) the file manager must provide a means for the application to export very comprehensive access routines (for example, specifying data transfer strategies in addition to formats) to be used by the file manager when managing the multimedia file. Application environments have been constructed in which compound document files can be constructed as elaborate abstract data types or classes. Each abstract data type definition encodes functions able to perform "standard" operations on the information such as reading and printing along with the information. The environment is more complex than conventional file systems. This is because it must not only store the data but also store enough of the abstract data type description for the appropriate manipulation functions to be invoked when the data is to be used.

These very large information containers also cause operating system designers to rethink the mechanisms for storing files and for how the information is copied from the storage device to memory (and back). This topic is revisited in the discussion of implementation in the next section.

13.2 ■ Low-level File Implementations

The byte stream file system provides a minimal mechanism to enable a process to read from and write to information on storage devices. This section considers the implementation of this simplest system. The next section generalizes the necessary parts of the file manager to handle record-oriented file systems.

The storage device may be a sequentially accessed device, such as a magnetic tape, or a randomly accessed device, such as a magnetic disk (see Figure 13.7). A tape realization of the low-level file abstraction requires the logical byte stream to be mapped to logical blocks, which are mapped onto the physical records on a tape. The contiguous bytes are grouped into logical records and then are stored in physical records. Bytes 0 through $k - 1$ are stored in logical record 0, which is stored in physical record 0, where k is the number of bytes in a tape physical record. The order of logical blocks on the byte stream maps to contiguous physical blocks in a magnetic tape realization of the low-level file. So for k-byte physical blocks on the tape, bytes b_0 to b_{k-1} are stored in physical block 0 of the tape, bytes b_k to b_{2k-1} are stored in physical block 1 on the tape, and so on.

A disk realization also maps logical blocks of contiguous bytes from the byte stream, but the mapping of logical to physical blocks will not normally be contiguous on the disk. The disk realization of the low-level file system must provide a mechanism for managing a collection of blocks to store the bytes of a particular file so that they can be accessed as if they were stored as a contiguous byte stream.

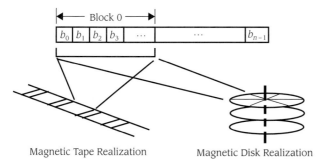

Magnetic Tape Realization   Magnetic Disk Realization

Figure 13.7
Low-level File System Architecture

13.2.1 ■ `open` and `close` **Operations**

The `open` operation instructs the file manager to initialize the internal data structures needed to manage the I/O. Specifically, it performs the following steps:

1. Locates the file descriptor in the file system.
2. Extracts information regarding the file from the file descriptor and information regarding the process from the process descriptor.
3. Authenticates that the process is permitted access to the file.
4. Creates an entry in a *file status table* to keep track of the state of the process's interaction with the file.
5. Allocates resources needed to sustain file usage, such as I/O buffers.

Locating the file in the file system is a directory operation, so discussion of this step is deferred until directories are covered in Section 13.5. When the file has been located on the storage device, the file manager obtains the information from the external file descriptor to finish the steps in making the file ready to use.

Authentication involves checking the protection flags from the external file descriptor for the file versus the protection keys held by the user/process. If the process attempts to open a file for which it does not have the appropriate rights, the authentication procedure will disallow the `open` operation. Independently of protection authentication, the file manager also will need to check other constraints on the `open` operation. For example, it will also check the read/write locks on the file to see if access can be granted.

The file status table stores all information necessary to administer the byte stream while the file is open. This includes information from the external file descriptor, the value of the file position for this process's operation on the file, and the status of physical blocks loaded to achieve the `read` and `write` operations.

The `open` command completes when the authentication and data structure allocation and initialization have been completed. The process's file position will address the first byte in the file, and the process can begin to read from or write to the file, depending on the way the permissions were used to open the file.

The `close` operation causes the file manager to complete all pending operations (for example, to flush output buffers residing in memory), to release I/O buffers, to release locks the process may hold on the file, to update the external file descriptor, and to deallocate the file status table entry.

➤ *IN THE HANGAR*

UNIX `open` **and** `close`

The kernel `open` call for BSD UNIX is of the form

```
int open(char *path, int flags [, int mode ])
```

The first parameters to the kernel call specify the path name for the file to be opened. The `flags` parameter is a bitmap in which each position in the word sets a switch.

For example, the O_RDONLY, O_WRONLY, and O_RDWR values set bits in the flags parameter to indicate that the file should be opened only for reading, only for writing, or for reading and writing, respectively. The man page for each system's open describes all flag values. If the flags parameter sets O_CREAT, a file is to be created on the open call if it does not exist. In this case, the optional mode parameter specifies the protection settings for the new file.

When a file is opened, the file manager searches the storage system for the specified path name. This can be an extended procedure, since it is necessary to open each directory in the path name (starting at the highest-named directory in the path), to search the path for the next file or directory in the path name, to open that directory or file, and so on. This is described in more detail in Section 13.5.

Next, open creates an entry in a process-specific *descriptor table* (see Figure 13.8). The entry is identified by a small integer value returned by the call and is used for all subsequent references to the file. When the process is created, stdin has an entry identifier of 0, stdout has a value of 1, and stderr has a value of 2. The next successful open or pipe call will create an entry in the descriptor table at location 3. (This example is patterned after BSD UNIX; see McKusick et al. [1996, ch. 2.])

When a file is closed, its identifier becomes available; the next open call uses the lowest-numbered available identifier. Thus a close immediately followed by an open will cause an identifier to be reused. For example, in the code sequence

```
close(stdout);
. . .
fid = open("newOut", flags);
```

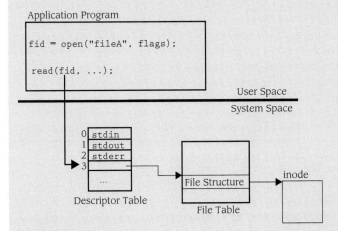

Figure 13.8
Opening a UNIX File

the variable, `fid`, will have value 1 because `stdout` uses identifier 1. This fact is used in implementing I/O redirection (see the Laboratory Exercise in Chapter 9).

The entry in the descriptor table points to an entry in the open file table called a *file structure*. The file structure entry keeps status information specific to the process that opened the file for the process. For example, the value of the file position for this process's use is in the file structure entry; if two different processes have the file open, then each will have their own copy of the file position. The file structure entry references a copy of the inode after it has been loaded into primary memory.

Changes to the in-memory version of the inode are not propagated to the inode on the storage device the moment the file manager makes the changes. Instead, the in-memory version of the inode is copied back to secondary memory periodically, when the file is closed, or when the application issues a `sync` command. If the machine halts while a file is open, the inode on the disk may differ from the one in primary memory if there have been any changes to the in-memory copy of the inode. The result will be an inconsistent file system, since the copy of the inode in secondary memory is saved, but the most recent information about the file is lost when the in-memory copy is destroyed. For example, if the block pointers in the in-memory inode have changed, with corresponding changes to disk blocks, then the disk may have an inode that is inconsistent with pointers in various storage blocks on the disk.

The `fsck` utility is designed to recover from such errors. Briefly, `fsck` reads every file in the file system, then it reads every block on the disk and attempts to correlate the status of each block with the file pointers. If the two views differ, `fsck` knows there is an error, although it cannot necessarily correct it.

The system tables and pointers created on opening a file are summarized in Figure 13.8. Actual implementations incorporate additional tables to handle file system buffering.

➤ IN THE HANGAR

Windows NT `CreateFile` and `CloseHandle`

Windows NT uses objects as the OS mechanism to represent file descriptors (and all other resources it manages). Creating a file will cause a file object to be created and a handle descriptor to be placed in the creating process's handle table. File objects are used to represent various other system resources, particularly devices—including some that are simply abstractions of hardware or OS resources. The rationale for this design decision is that the I/O model for all these devices and abstractions is intended to look as much like ordinary file I/O as possible.

The essential elements of the Windows NT file abstraction are that a "file" is a named byte stream of characters that can be accessed by sequentially accessing bytes one after the other. There is a 64-bit file pointer associated with each instance of an open file. When a file is opened, the file pointer is set to zero. When an I/O operation reads or writes K bytes, then the file pointer is advanced by K. File objects (and the `CreateFile` function call) are used with files, directories, disk drives, serial and parallel ports, pipes, sockets, and the system console.

A file (object) is created with the function

```
HANDLE CreateFile(
    LPCTSTR lpFileName,    // pointer to name of the file
    DWORD dwDesiredAccess, // access (read-write) mode
    DWORD dwShareMode,     // share mode
    LPSECURITY_ATTRIBUTES lpSecurityAttributes,
                          // pointer to security attributes
    DWORD dwCreationDistribution,  // how to create
    DWORD dwFlagsAndAttributes,    // file attributes
    HANDLE hTemplateFile
            // handle to file with attributes to copy
);
```

The `lpFileName` specifies the name of the file to be created or opened. The `dwDesiredAccess` parameter defines the mode in which the file is to be opened: `0`, `GENERIC_READ`, and `GENERIC_WRITE`. `0` means no access is desired, so it is used only when `CreateFile` is querying the file object to determine its current state. `GENERIC_READ` and `GENERIC_WRITE` can be combined by ORing the values (`GENERIC_READ | GENERIC_WRITE`) if the file is to be read and written. The `dwShareMode` can have the value `0` (no sharing), `FILE_SHARE_DELETE` (subsequent open operations will succeed only if they request delete access), `FILE_SHARE_READ` (future open operations must be for reading), or `FILE_SHARE_WRITE` (subsequent open operations must be for writing). Again, the flags can be combined with a logical OR operation. The `lpSecurityAttributes` parameter is treated the same as for other objects. The `dwCreationDistribution` parameter describes what the function should do if the file already exists at the time the create function is called; there are values to indicate that the call should fail if the file exists, to overwrite an existing file, and to just open the existing file (`OPEN_ALWAYS`). The `dwFlagsAndAttributes` parameter is used to pass various file-specific options to the file manager, with `FILE_ATTRIBUTE_NORMAL` being the simplest form of `open`. Finally, the `hTemplateFile` parameter can be used to pass a handle to a different file that contains extended file attributes.

A file is closed by releasing access to the kernel file object using the `CloseHandle(fileObjectHandle)` function. (The parameter is the reference to the kernel file object that was returned by the `CreateFile` system call.)

13.2.2 ■ Block Management

Block management is the most significant part of the file manager for random storage devices. Because storage devices have fixed-size blocks, we assume that all blocks, B_i and B_j, contain k bytes, so the ith byte, b_i, is stored in B_j, where $j = \lfloor i/k \rfloor$. Thus a file with m bytes requires at least m/k blocks on the device (plus one more if m is not a multiple of the block size). The physical storage blocks can be managed in at least three different ways:

■ As a contiguous set of blocks on the secondary storage device

■ As a list of blocks interconnected with links

■ As a collection of blocks interconnected by a file index

The file descriptor will take a different format for each of the block allocation strategies.

13.2.2.1 ■ Contiguous Allocation

The contiguous-allocation strategy maps the N logical blocks in the file into N contiguously addressed physical blocks. This strategy makes the randomly accessed storage device behave like a sequentially accessed device. It allows the driver to read from or write to an entire file in a short amount of time. This is because the file system will pass disk requests to the driver at a very high rate, thus allowing the driver to access blocks adjacent to one another in a short amount of time. The requests will cause minimal head movement on the device. A typical file status entry for contiguously allocated blocks contains the information given in Figure 13.9.

Contiguous allocation does not provide for dynamic file sizes, since it maps the logical structure directly to the physical structure. If a file is stored in some contiguous set of blocks and data is added to the end of the file, then either the next contiguous physical block on the storage device must be made available or the entire file must be copied to a larger group of unallocated contiguous blocks. Whenever the file system intends to allocate N blocks to a file, it must find N contiguous physical blocks on the file system. Presuming space is available on the storage device, it must choose some set of $r \geq N$ unallocated blocks.

Several substrategies are used in this case, the most popular being best fit, first fit, and worst fit (see Chapter 11). It is sufficient for our purposes to recognize that the best-fit algorithm chooses the set of contiguous blocks where $r - N$ is minimal. The first-fit

HEAD POSITION	234
...	...
First block	2035
Number of blocks	7

Figure 13.9
File Status Entry for Contiguous Blocks

algorithm chooses the "first" collection in a linear search of the collections where $r \geq N$. The worst-fit algorithm selects the largest collection that contains N blocks and then partitions it into two parts containing N blocks for the file and a new collection of $r - N$ unallocated blocks.

Contiguous-allocation strategies will tend to externally fragment the physical disk space into small sets of contiguous blocks that are too small to contain most files (although the disk can be compacted to eliminate the fragmentation). Contiguous allocation does have the benefit of very fast access times for whole file transfers, since all blocks in the file are in close proximity on the disk (thus reducing disk head movement when the entire file is copied).

13.2.2.2 ■ Linked Lists

Linked lists of blocks use explicit pointers among an arbitrary set of physical blocks making up the file. Logical block $i + 1$ need not be physically located near logical block i, since i will contain a header with a link that addresses the physical block that contains logical block $i + 1$. The file status table entry for a file will include a copy of the file position and a pointer to the first device block used in the file (see Figure 13.10). The entry may also contain other data used to manage the open file.

Each block in the file contains overhead fields used by the file manager. In the example, two fields in a block are used to hold the next-block pointer and a count of the number of bytes actually stored in the block. The length field enables the file manager to store variable numbers of bytes in each block, thus potentially enabling the file manager to reduce the number of block allocations and deallocations in a dynamic file.

In linked-list block allocation, random access of bytes in the stream will be slow, especially as the file size grows. The seek operation is the basis of random access, since it repositions the file prior to a data transfer operation. Each seek will be costly in this block allocation scheme, since the scheme requires list traversal. This in turn requires each block in the list to be read so that the link field can be obtained and the next block can be referenced. Doubly linked lists (Figure 13.11) can be used to enhance performance during seek operations. When a seek is issued, the file manager calculates whether to move forward on the list, move backward on the list, or go to the front or back of the list to begin searching for the target block.

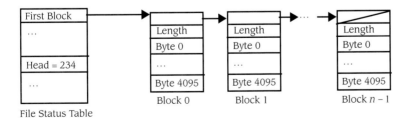

File Status Table

Figure 13.10
File Status Entry for Linked Lists

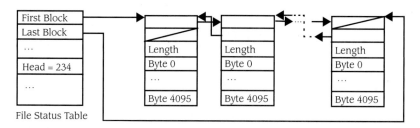

Figure 13.11
Doubly Linked Blocks

13.2.2.3 ■ Indexed Allocation

One criticism of the linked-list strategy is that seeks are I/O intensive (even using the doubly linked list optimization). This criticism can be addressed by extracting the link field from each data block and putting it into a separate index block with N entries. Indexed allocation uses a unique block in the file as an index for all the other blocks used to store data (see Figure 13.12). The block length field is shown in the index block along with the block pointer. This simplifies file position placement because this value can be used when the file manager uses the pointers in the index block for seeking. Files may require more or fewer than the N blocks referenced from the table. If the file requires much fewer than N, the space in the index table will be wasted. If most files are less than N, then the accumulation of wasted space may be significant. This loss of space, called *table fragmentation,* can be serious if the mismatch in sizes is significant or if there are many small files.

If a file requires more than N blocks, the index must be extended by adding one or more blocks to contain additional index pointers. This can be done, for example, by using a linked-list scheme for the index blocks. It also can be accomplished by using multiple levels of indirect tables, where a "super" index block points to other index blocks, which point to storage device blocks.

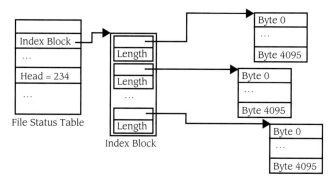

Figure 13.12
File Status Entry for Indexed Allocation

➤ *IN THE HANGAR*

UNIX File Structure

The UNIX file structure uses a variant of the indexed allocation scheme. The storage device detail part of the inode contains pointers to 15 different storage blocks of 4KB each (see Figure 13.13). The first 12 blocks of the file are indexed directly from the first 12 of 15 pointers in the inode. The last three pointers are used for indirect pointers through *index blocks.* If the file manager is configured with 4KB blocks, the 12 direct pointers in the inode accommodate files up to 48KB. Experience indicates this is an efficient mechanism for addressing the blocks (see [Ousterhout et al. 1985]). If a file requires more than 12 blocks, the file system

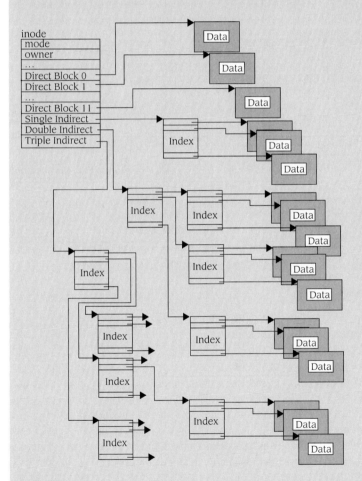

Figure 13.13
UNIX File Structure

allocates an index block and links it into the *single indirect* (thirteenth) pointer of the inode. Hence, blocks 13 to k are indirectly addressed from the inode via the indirect block identified by the thirteenth pointer in the inode. Similarly, larger files use the fourteenth pointer to address a *double indirect* block, and the largest files use the fifteenth pointer to point at a *triple indirect block.*

How big can UNIX files be? This depends on the size of the blocks and the size of the disk addresses used in the system. To simplify the arithmetic, suppose an indirect block can store 1000 disk addresses. Then the single indirect block will provide pointers to an additional 1000 disk blocks. Blocks 0 through 11 are accessed via the direct pointers in the inode, but blocks 12 through 1011 are accessed indirectly through the single indirect block. The fourteenth block pointer in the inode is the double indirect pointer. It points to a block that contains pointers to blocks of the type referenced from the single indirect field. The double indirect pointer addresses a block pointing to 1000 indirect blocks, so blocks 1012 to 1,001,011 are accessed through the double indirect list. The fifteenth block pointer is the triple indirect pointer. It points to a block that contains double indirect pointers. Again, if each block can store 1000 block addresses, then the triple indirect pointer indirectly addresses blocks 1,001,012 to the maximum-sized file (under these assumptions) of 1,001,001,011 blocks.

With this block allocation strategy, very large files are possible, even though as files grow larger, the access times are greater due to the indirection. There are other considerations that prevent a file from reaching this maximum size designed into the inode structure. For example, with the block sizes given previously, a file using the triple indirect index would require that there be a device capable of storing 4000 GB. Current versions of BSD UNIX do not use the triple indirect pointer, partly because of incompatibility of file sizes with storage device technology and partly because the 32-bit addresses used in the file system preclude file sizes larger than 2GB.

13.2.2.4 ■ Unallocated Blocks

When a file is being written, new storage blocks must be allocated to the file as it expands. Another major task of the file manager is to administer the unallocated blocks on the random storage device so that they can be used as needed. When the file system is created, it must know which blocks on the disk can be allocated to files. One obvious way to handle the collection of unused blocks is to initialize them into a dummy link-allocated or indexed file called the *free list.* The free list has the same format as a conventional file, except there is no information stored in any of the blocks. Whenever a block is needed for some real file, it is detached from the free list and allocated to the file needing the block. In the linked-list allocation, either end of the free list file can be allocated. If the free list is implemented using indexed allocation, then blocks will probably be allocated from the end of the last index block.

The free list will tend to be very large, since it contains every unallocated block on the disk. This tends to make the indexed implementation impractical for the free list.

Instead, the linked-list strategy is preferred to the indexed allocation strategy. However, the linked-list strategy makes it difficult to allocate disk blocks in the same physical vicinity on the disk, since the block allocator must traverse the list to search for blocks physically close to the adjacent blocks in the file. Instead, the file manager can keep a *block status map* (also called a *disk bitmap*) of the disk blocks on the file. The ith entry in the map is set if the ith block is allocated and reset otherwise.

A 1GB disk with 4KB blocks will require 256K entries in the block status map. If each entry is a single bit, then the table uses 32 KB of space. This is a reasonable price to pay for a mechanism that provides a quick snapshot of the unallocated blocks on the disk. As a result, the block status map can be kept in primary memory. When there is a requirement for a block to be allocated to a file, the block status map is read in order to quickly locate a storage block, possibly one that is physically near the other blocks in the file. The file manager then assigns the block to the file by adding it to the index block or linking it into the list of allocated blocks and sets the corresponding entry in the block status map. When a block is released, the block status map entry is reset and the file pointers are adjusted correspondingly.

Another advantage of the block status map approach is that it can be used to check a disk to see if the collective pointers in all files address exactly the set of blocks allocated, no block is allocated to more than one file, and the blocks marked as unallocated do not appear in any file's list of blocks.

13.2.2.5 ■ Adding Blocks to the File

If the application program were to perform a single-byte `write` with the file descriptor in the state shown in Figures 13.9, 13.11, or 13.12, then the contents of byte 234 would be overwritten. To accomplish this, the file system reads the block containing byte 234, overwrites the byte, and then rewrites the block to the disk. This requires two calls to the disk driver and two disk I/O operations. The file manager may delay the write-back operation until it is absolutely necessary (for example, because the file manager is running out of buffer space or the file is being closed). Then if the next operation were an operation on any byte in the loaded block—for example, byte 235 if the file were being accessed sequentially—the physical block would already be loaded into the file system's memory. In this way, a disk `read` operation could be avoided and the `write` operation could be amortized over several byte operations. If the file pointer is positioned at the end of the file when a `write` operation is requested, a new block must be obtained and added to the logical end of the list of blocks.

13.2.3 ■ Reading and Writing the Byte Stream

Storage devices read from or write to a fixed-sized block of bytes on any individual operation. Sequential storage devices typically use removable media, such as a tape or tape cassette, so each medium ordinarily holds one file. (Of course, the file can be a composite file of other files such as a UNIX tar file. This enables the effective use of the medium by combining files with an external tool and then writing the resulting information onto a single byte stream.) As explained at the beginning of this section, the order of logical blocks in the file is the same as the order of physical blocks on a sequential storage device. As already explained, randomly accessed storage devices incorporate an additional mechanism to produce the equivalent of a sequentially accessed set of blocks.

In low-level file systems, then, there is a module that focuses on implementing a byte stream, $b_0, b_1, b_2, \ldots$ on top of a contiguous set of blocks, $B_0, B_1, B_2, \ldots$. There are two stages to a `read` or `write` operation:

- Reading bytes into or writing bytes out of the memory copy of a block
- Reading the physical blocks into or writing them out of memory from/to storage devices

13.2.3.1 ■ Packing and Unpacking Blocks with Single Bytes

When a file system read operation occurs, a string of bytes is read from the storage device. The string is obtained from the point in the byte stream that is addressed by the file position for the file. When the file is opened for reading, the first block in the file is copied into memory and the file position points to the first byte in the stream (the first byte in the first block). The prescribed number of bytes is copied out of the in-memory copy of the block into the buffer for the command. If the number of bytes to be read is larger than the number remaining in the in-memory block, then the file manager reads the next block in the file. This *unpacking* procedure is the basis of converting secondary storage blocks into a byte stream.

Write operations *pack* strings of bytes into copies of storage device blocks that are loaded in the memory and then write the blocks to the device when they become full. When the file is opened for writing, the first block of the file is copied into memory so that the string will be overwritten on the existing data. When the write operations cause the file position to move out of the first block and into the second, the first block is written back to the storage device and the second block is copied into memory to be altered by output operations.

Seek operations potentially cause a series of storage device block read operations. If the application calls for a seek to position i, then the file manager must determine which block contains position i. Assume all blocks contain the same number, k, of bytes (except the last block in the file). The simplest implementation for input (based on the read interface) allows the determination j by computing $\lfloor i/k \rfloor$. The file manager then can read block B_j in preparation for subsequent I/O commands.

Suppose the file interface allows insertion (as opposed to overwriting information at the file position). This means the file manager must be able to allocate new blocks and add them to the interior of the block data structure and to deallocate a block from any point in the block structure. This follows because an insert at any position other than at the end of the byte stream will require a block to be allocated just to hold the incremental information. In Figure 13.14(a), a single new byte is to be added between b_i and b_{i+1}. In this example, b_i is in a block of bytes that begins with b_k. Since there is no space in block j for the new byte, a new block, $j+1$, is added to the file and the bytes originally stored in positions $i+1$ to $k+r$ are written into the new block with new indices $i+2$ to $k+r+1$.

If the file interface also allows the deletion of information at the file pointer, the file manager may deallocate a block and return it to the free list. With deletion, the blocks

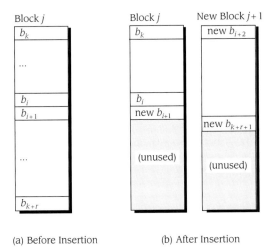

(a) Before Insertion   (b) After Insertion

Figure 13.14
Adding a Byte to a Byte Stream File

will, over time, suffer from internal fragmentation as illustrated in Figure 13.14(b). If inserts and deletes take place at arbitrary parts of the file, the internal fragmentation will eventually cause the amount of wasted space to surpass some threshold established by the file manager, or for the file to surpass its quota of free blocks. In this case, the file can be compacted so that each block is rewritten to be dense. File compaction can also be caused by an explicit operation on the file manager interface.

Suppose the file system maintains partially full blocks. Then characters can easily be added at any point in the file by simply adding them to existing blocks. If a block must be added, it is obtained from the free list and added to the collection of blocks that constitute the file. Then the system may adjust the location of a small number of bytes between the newly allocated block and its neighbors. In indexed files, this implies the index itself must be rewritten. Because of fragmentation, the byte-stream file system with insertions and deletions tends to use more physical space than does the pure byte-stream file system. Whenever bytes are inserted or deleted from the interior of a file, there will be unused space in blocks.

13.2.3.2 ■ Block I/O

Once the file position has been determined in a byte stream file, the file manager can read from or write to the appropriate storage device block. Recall from the introductory remarks in this subsection that storage devices are read/written as needed. Modern operating systems recognize that for files of sequential information, such as a byte stream, performance can be substantially enhanced by overlapping CPU and device operation through buffering.

As discussed in Chapter 5, significant performance increases can be obtained in an OS that overlaps device I/O operation with CPU activity. Block buffering offers the main opportunity to exploit this overlap. A file is an organization of entities that are sequentially accessed by processes. This means that when a process opens a file for reading, the file manager knows there is a high probability that the process will read the information in the file from the beginning to the end. Therefore it can read ahead on the file, depending on the amount of buffer space that it can allocate to the open file and the availability of the storage device. Similarly, files open for writing can overlap CPU and device operation by buffering information destined for a storage device, and then writing the buffered information to the storage device whenever it becomes available.

Studies such as the one by Ousterhout et al. [1985] have shown that file buffering has an enormous effect on the overall performance of the system. The cited study emphasizes another benefit of buffering that might not generally be predicted about file usage. That is, most of the references to information in a file are to a small part of the file that is read from and written to multiple times. This means that if the information is copied into a buffer on first reference, then the second and subsequent references will not even incur a disk operation.

Aside from the phenomenon of multiple accesses to a subset of the information in a file, the performance increase due to buffering is related to the number of blocks read from and written to by a process. If the total block I/O operation for a process requires $T_{I/O}$ units of time and the process has computation time of T_{CPU}, then the time to execute will be no greater than $T_{CPU} + T_{I/O}$ and no less than a maximum $(T_{CPU}, T_{I/O})$. The minimum execution time occurs when the next desired storage device block has already been read whenever it is needed. Obviously, this is more difficult to achieve if the program does frequent seek operations to extremes of the byte stream when the file organization is a linked list.

13.3 ▪ Supporting Other Storage Abstractions

The low-level file systems attempt to avoid encoding record-level functionality into the file manager. If the applications will typically use very large or very small records, a generic file manager cannot be written to take advantage of that fact; this would not be a general-purpose solution. On the other hand, any strategy that is widely used by applications can usually be implemented to be more efficient if it is implemented in the operating system. The trend in modern, open operating systems has been toward low-level file systems. In contrast, proprietary operating systems for machines aimed at particular application domains (such as transaction processing) will usually provide a higher-layer file system. This section surveys some of the classic approaches for supporting storage abstractions.

13.3.1 ▪ Structured Sequential Files

Structured sequential files contain collections of logical records. Records are referenced using an index as in byte-stream files. The two types of files differ in that structured sequential files cause a full record to be read from or written to. The implementation of a structured sequential file manager is logically the same as a byte-stream file manager. If the structured sequential file provides an option of inserting a record at an arbitrary point in the file, then the manager must be designed with the same issues in mind as for the `insertByte` operation.

13.3.2 ■ Indexed Sequential Files

In indexed sequential files, each record contains an index field used to select it from the file. An application program provides an index value with each `read` or `write` operation. The file manager implements a mechanism to search the storage device to find the physical block that contains the record. The implementation may use the same file structure as structured sequential files. The record index ordinarily determines the order in which the records are stored in the file: Record 0 is stored as the first record in the first block, record 1 is the second record in the first block, and so on, until the first block is full. The next record is stored in the second block and so on. The first new task for the file manager is to manage the mapping of records to blocks. Record insertion and deletion may occur at any logical location in the file. Hence, internal fragmentation and compaction issues arise in indexed sequential files.

The file manager may be implemented with a mechanism for direct access of records. Rather than the records being kept in a sequentially accessed data structure, they can be placed in different blocks and then referenced from an index for the file. This requires that the file manager keep a table for each open file and map the index to the block number that contains the record. This direct access implementation can substantially reduce the access times for records in the file. The cost is primarily the space cost of the index, since the complexity of the approach is not substantial compared to the sequential approach. The read and write operations are far more complex for indexed sequential files than for stream-oriented files, since the file manager must access records according to the index value. Further, buffering is not likely to be of any particular value, since the point of having the index field is to enable the application programmer to arbitrarily select the order in which records are accessed.

13.3.3 ■ Database Management Systems

As mentioned earlier, database management systems (DBMSs) constitute an entire area of computer science itself, so the discussion here only briefly mentions the part of the secondary storage management provided to the DBMS designer. DBMSs are built on a fundamental *storage manager,* which replaces the file manager. The storage manager interface is at a relatively low level so as to enable the DBMS designer to directly manipulate storage devices. This avoids performance penalties associated with generalized operation in favor of specialized strategies for databases. DBMS technology depends on the ability of the database administrator to choose the organization of records across and within files. Relational databases require that there be a means for very efficient search of records, while object-oriented databases require that the access methods be defined by application code. Conventional file system interfaces cannot support either of these functions; they require the storage manager to replace the file manager in order to accommodate them. By using a storage manager in place of a file manager, a system that supports a DBMS and a file system usually cannot allow data to be stored in a database yet still be accessed via the file interface.

13.3.4 ■ Multimedia Documents

Multimedia files make demands on the storage system that are similar to those of databases (object-oriented databases are often justified by the need to support multimedia documents). In particular, because multimedia documents tend to be implemented using abstract data types, it is desirable to use application-defined access methods to reference different parts of the document. This argues for a specialized storage manager interface to the secondary storage devices, the same that is used in database implementation.

The need for high bandwidth throughput is at odds with the basic operation of contemporary file managers. If a multimedia document contains a 10MB record (with an image) and a disk block is 4KB, then a read operation will span over 2400 blocks. The block allocation strategy will have a major impact on the rate at which the image can be transferred. The contiguous-allocation strategy would perform the best in terms of transfer time, although the associated fragmentation problem is a costly tradeoff. Similarly, other parts of the file manager are normally designed under the assumption that no application will request multiple blocks at a time, so the multimedia document transfers are not provided with high-performance service.

Operating systems technology is evolving to meet the performance requirements of multimedia files and documents. As of this writing, there are no widely accepted operating systems that provide high-performance support for multimedia files.

13.4 ■ Memory-mapped Files

Some file systems provide a function to map a file's contents directly into the virtual address space so that the file can be read from or written to by referencing the corresponding virtual addresses. The file manager essentially defers all `read` and `write` operations to the virtual memory manager. After the file has been mapped to a virtual address, X, then any access of byte b_i in the file results in an access of the physical memory location corresponding to virtual address $X + i$. When parts of the file are referenced, they are copied into memory on a page-by-page basis, just as other pages are handled by the paging system.

Memory-mapped files are especially useful when a file is shared. In this case, the file contents are bound to virtual addresses in the two or more address spaces of processes. If two or more processes have the file opened at the same time, the OS recognizes this and manages both processes's page table pointers so that they reference one copy of the disk block in memory. For example, suppose p_i and p_j have opened a memory-mapped file. As shown in Figure 13.15, blocks i to $i + 3$ have been cached into memory. p_i is using blocks $i + 2$ and $i + 3$ while p_j is using blocks i, $i + 1$, and $i + 2$. When either process changes a file block, the other process immediately sees the change, since the change is captured in the cached-in storage blocks. The memory-mapped pages could be paged out at any time. However, performance will be best if the pages being used by either process remain in memory.

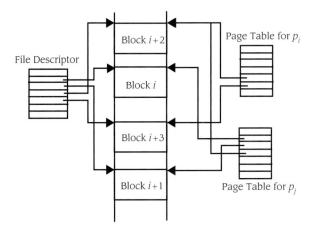

Figure 13.15
Memory-mapped Files

➤ IN THE HANGAR

Memory-mapped files in Windows NT

In Windows NT, a thread running in one address space is ordinarily prevented from reading or writing another's address space. However, the two address spaces can effectively be shared by using memory-mapped files. Furthermore, in Windows NT memory-mapped files are implemented at a low layer of the OS, so they have been made to be very efficient. In Windows NT, they are the preferred mechanism for sharing information among address spaces for processes on a single machine.

Each memory-mapped file essentially defines its own address space as a linear sequence of bytes. A program can be written so that it opens a file as a memory-mapped file, thus introducing the file's address space to the system. Next, the two sharing processes each map a portion of the locations in the file stream to a set of contiguous addresses in their own address spaces. Then each process can read and write the file simply by reading and writing the addresses to which the bytes in the file are mapped. For example, if process A opens a 64K file and maps it into addresses 0x20000000 to 0x2000FFFF, then it can read or write the first byte in the file by reading or writing memory address 0x20000000 or it can reference the sixteenth byte by referencing 0x2000000F. If process B then opens the file and maps it into its address space at 0x30000000 to 0x3000FFFF, then it can read or write the first byte in the file by reading or writing memory address 0x30000000 or it can reference the sixteenth byte by referencing 0x3000000F. Now process B could "transmit" information to process A by writing information at, say, location 0x30001234 and then having process A read the information from its virtual address 0x20001234. Windows NT ensures that both processes can see memory write operations when they occur.

> To use a memory-mapped file, a thread in a process must do the following:
>
> 1. Obtain a handle to the file by creating or opening it.
> 2. Reserve virtual addresses for the file.
> 3. Establish a mapping between the file and the virtual address space.
> 4. Release the mapping when it is no longer being used.
>
> The whole file can be mapped into the address space or only a subset of it—called a *view* of the file.
>
> File *coherence* refers to the situation in which every process that has the file open sees the same information in the file. The difficulty in ensuring coherence arises when there are copies of the information allocated in different parts of the system. If one copy is changed, there is a lag time until the other copies can be updated. Two processes can be designed to use a common mapping mechanism, then Windows NT assures that both processes always see the same file content.

13.5 ▪ Directories

It is not unusual for a computer to be configured with more than 10GB of secondary memory. Empirical studies indicate that most files on a 4.2 BSD UNIX system are less than 10KB in length [Ousterhout et al., 1985]. If an average length of 10KB is assumed, the system could have more than 1,000,000 files, provided the disk were filled to capacity. (As explained in Chapter 16, contemporary machines have access to many more files via the network.) If there were 500 users for such a machine, each could have an average of 2,000 files of their own. Throughout the 1990s, the amount of disk space configured into machines has continued to increase rapidly. It also appears that the number of files on the system increases linearly with the amount of disk space.

A *directory* is a set of logically associated files and other directories of files. Directories are the mechanism by which humans organize the set of files in the entire system. A directory is a logical container of a set of files and, possibly, nested directories. The file manager provides users with a set of commands to administer a directory, including these:

- `enumerate`: Returns a list of all of the files and nested directories referenced by the identified directory. Directory enumeration commands are also used to return the contents of a file's descriptor to the user interface or to a program.
- `copy`: Creates a new duplicate of an existing file.
- `rename`: Changes the symbolic name of an existing file.
- `delete`: Removes the identified file from the directory and then destroys it by releasing all of the blocks in the file, including the file descriptor.
- `traverse`: The majority of directories in contemporary machines are hierarchically structured—that is, directories contain subdirectories. The traversal operation

enables a user to explore the hierarchy by navigating from one directory to another in the hierarchy.

Files are distinguished by their symbolic name—a set of printable characters, such as ASCII characters. Since directories are provided for the benefit of humans to organize their files, the symbolic name is used as an argument for most directory operations.

13.5.1 ■ Directory Structures

The directory is a data structure that lists files and subdirectories in a collection. There are several alternatives for choosing the data structure to represent the table of contents. For example, the data structure may be a linear list of filenames, sorted by name, by size, by last access time, or by some other criterion. A directory that references every file is said to support a *flat name space* (see Figure 13.16a).

A *hierarchical name space* uses a graph structure for organizing the file descriptors (Figure 13.16b). In hierarchical file systems, a *root directory* points to other directories and files. A directory is allowed to reference a "file descriptor" for a subdirectory. The subdirectory in turn points to lower-layered subdirectories or to files.

The simplest form of hierarchical directory is a tree data structure. Every directory or file is pointed to by exactly one superdirectory (except the root directory, which has no predecessor). Tree-structured hierarchical directories are widely used in different operating systems, since they allow the recursive partitioning of files into collections. Such partitions correspond to directories for individual users, for particular systems applications, and for other users. Once the file system has been partitioned to support individual users, users can use the tree-structuring mechanism to partition their own collection of files.

Suppose two users, each with their own directory and subdirectories, want to share a file (or subtree of files through some directory). It is convenient to allow the directories of the two users to both point to the shared subdirectory. However, the resulting structure is no longer a tree; it is a graph (Figure 13.16c). Whenever sharing is allowed, the file

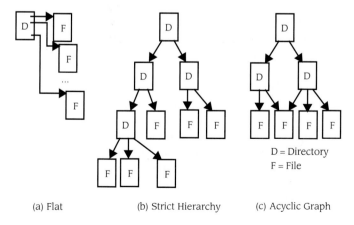

(a) Flat   (b) Strict Hierarchy   (c) Acyclic Graph

D = Directory
F = File

Figure 13.16
Directory Structures

system must be designed to ensure files are deallocated when all references to them have been deleted. This is commonly accomplished by including reference counts for all directories that point to a particular subdirectory or file. Graphs may be *cyclic*—they contain paths that lead from one node back to that same node—or they may be *acyclic*. Directory structures based on acyclic graphs will share many properties with the more constrained tree. For example, a recursive search for a file in a subdirectory tree will terminate in an acyclic directory structure but may not terminate in a cyclic directory structure. Many hierarchical file systems support acyclic structures, but few support cyclic structures.

> ## ➣ IN THE HANGAR

Some Directory Examples

The Apple Macintosh Finder

The *Finder* (or *Multifinder*) is the directory manager part of the Macintosh file manager. It is implemented as a user program in the Macintosh. The Finder employs a user interface that emphasizes the graphical point-and-select paradigm of the machine's overall human-computer interface. Files are organized into a tree-structured hierarchy with the "desktop" as the root. It can contain several different devices (such as hard drives and floppy drives), each of which is the root of a subdirectory hierarchy. Each directory of a subdirectory is represented externally as a "folder" whose contents are viewed in a window by opening the folder. The graphical display implicitly enumerates all files in the folder by being visible, possibly after scrolling, in a window that corresponds to the directory. Files are copied and deleted by explicit commands. A file can be deleted by moving it to the "trash can" directory. A file can be copied across devices by point-and-select "drag" operations. Renaming is an editing operation in the directory window. Traversal is done by opening and closing folders. The Finder provides all the basic directory manipulation operations using a graphical user interface. The Microsoft Windows family implements a directory system with similar syntax and semantics to the Apple Finder, although, legally, the two have been shown to be distinct.

MS-DOS Directories

The DOS directory manipulation interface is text-oriented, being invoked from the DOS shell command line interpreter. As with the Macintosh, each device on the machine has its own root directory; thus the list of devices can be construed as a root directory of the files (see Figure 13.17). DOS makes provisions for the user to reference a file anywhere in the storage system by using relative and absolute path names. The simplest form of a relative path name is just the filename within a directory, such as AUTOEXEC.BAT. More complex forms can be used to reference a file in a subdirectory of the directory where the name is being used. For example, if the current directory contains a subdirectory named BIN and BIN contains a file

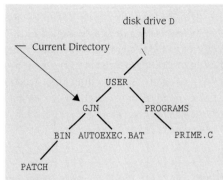

Figure 13.17
DOS File Directory

named PATCH, then a user can refer to the file using the relative path name BIN\PATCH. The path operator, "\", can be used to identify any file in any part of the hierarchy below the current directory. The special file name ".." refers to the parent directory, so it is possible to reference files located at any point in the file system by using ".." in conjunction with "\". For example, if there is a directory with the same parent as the current directory and it contains a directory named PROGRAMS, which contains a program named PRIME.C, then a relative path name for the file is ..\PROGRAMS\PRIME.C.

Absolute path names begin the directory traversal at a root directory. A path name of the form \USER\GJN\BIN\PATCH uniquely identifies a file named PATCH that appears in the directory named BIN, in the directory named GJN, in the directory named USER on the default storage device. Similarly, the absolute path name for the PRIME.C file is \USER\GJN\PROGRAMS\PRIME.C. A variant of the absolute path name allows the device on which the named file appears to be specified. For example, if the PATCH file is on the D disk drive, its absolute path name is D:\USER\GJN\BIN\PATCH.

Directory operations are invoked from the shell. For example, the DIR command lists the directory contents, the RENAME command renames a file, and the ERASE command deletes a file. The Windows Explorer user interface provides a point-and-select interface to this functionality, and Windows 95/98/NT provide file managers consistent with the DOS logical directory structure.

UNIX Directories

UNIX directories are acyclic graphs. That is, they allow a file to appear in more than one directory. UNIX also uses relative and absolute path names, although the operator for traversal is "/" rather than the "\" used in DOS. So UNIX filenames beginning with a "/" are absolute filenames describing the names of directories along a path from the root to the desired file. But UNIX does not allow the specification of device names in a filename in the sense that DOS does. (However, the machine's operator can mount other disks onto the current as described in Section 13.6.) An absolute filename such as

/usr/gjn/books/opsys/chap13 indicates that the root directory contains an entry that describes a directory named usr, which contains a directory named gjn, and so on through the books and opsys directories to the file named chap13. If the base directory were /usr/gjn, then the same file could be referenced using the relative path name books/opsys/chap13. Or if the current directory were /usr/gjn/books, then a file named prime.c in a sibling directory to books named programs could be referenced by the string ../programs/prime.c.

13.6 ■ Directory Implementation

Directories establish a logical file system organization that is independent of the device organization. The first challenge in the directory design is to map the logical file organization to the storage devices. This is done by partitioning the organization and assigning the partitions to devices (see Figure 13.18). Each device keeps a directory of the part of the file system that it implements.

13.6.1 ■ Device Directories

The device directory is an index of the files stored on the device. The simplest structure of the device directory is a sorted linear list with elements of the form

        <fileName, fileDescriptorLocation>

fileName is the relative name of the file, and fileDescriptorLocation is the address where the file descriptor is stored on the device. This information is used by the file manager for the open command.

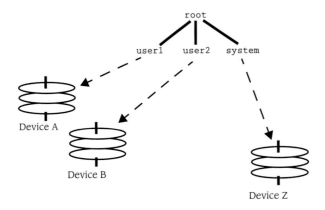

Figure 13.18
Partitioning the File System

As disk sizes increase, it is useful to divide the physical disk into two or more logical disks. Administrators find this useful because it simplifies the mechanical process of archiving the disk's contents—only a portion of the disk needs to be dumped at a time.

In some cases, the disk hardware may be shared among different operating systems that have different file managers. For example, a personal computer may have a Windows NT disk partition and a separate UNIX partition. This environment could be simplified if the disk could be logically partitioned at the device driver level. These concerns have encouraged file manager designers to create the notion of a virtual disk device. The virtual disk is a logical device that has its own device directory, independent of other virtual disks implemented on the same physical disk. Only device driver software is able to read and write information on different disk partitions. On personal computers, disk partitions are used to accommodate different operating systems. In UNIX, they are used to define smaller *file systems* that are treated much like a set of files on a separate device.

13.6.2 ■ File Directory

A general directory is implemented as a structured file in which each record is an abbreviated version of a file descriptor. For example, the record might contain the name, owner, protection state, length, and a disk address for the file descriptor. Depending on the file implementation, the complete file description may be distributed between a file descriptor kept with the file and the record in the directory.

13.6.3 ■ Opening a File in a Hierarchical Directory

When a file is opened in a hierarchical directory, a descriptor for the file must be obtained using the directory that contains the file. In the UNIX absolute path name /usr/gjn/books/opsys/chap13 example, before chap13 could be opened for reading or writing, the system would need to find the file descriptor in /usr/gjn/books/opsys. But before the entry can be found in opsys, its directory descriptor must be found in /usr/gjn/books, and so on. Hence, when the file is opened using an absolute filename, the open routine must first search the root directory to find the entry for the first-level directory—usr in the example. As a result, the first-level directory in the path name is opened and searched for the second-level directory, and so on.

Typical implementations of file systems allow each directory to be implemented using the same basic storage facilities as found on an ordinary file. The information stored in the directory is saved in a list of blocks managed through a file descriptor. As a result, the open procedure requires at least one disk read operation for each directory that appears in the path name. (If the open operation allocates buffers and begins filling them, the open can cause multiple disk reads for each directory in the path name.) Opening a file requires time and effort proportional to the length of the path name, independent of whether the path is relative to a base directory or an absolute name.

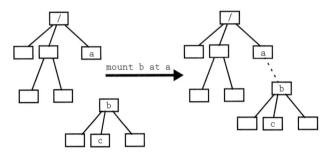

Figure 13.19
The UNIX mount Command

13.6.4 ■ Mounting Removable File Systems

Computers with storage devices that have removable media (such as tape drives and floppy disk drives) must be able to change the system's file structure each time a medium is placed in or removed from a device. The model used by UNIX for mounting and dismounting removable media is common to most file managers, so this description is used to represent all such operations.

The UNIX file manager incorporates a mechanism to allow file systems to be combined into one directory hierarchy. This is especially useful for adding a set of files that are on a removable medium onto an existing file system on a fixed disk. The mount command appends a file system into an existing directory hierarchy. It does this by replacing a directory in the permanent file system by the root of the mountable file system when the corresponding replaceable medium is placed on the system.

For example, suppose a system contains an optical disk reader for removable optical disks. When a particular optical disk is placed on the reader, the mount operation informs the file manager that the disk is mounted. The device root can be used as a directory in the permanent file system hierarchy (see Figure 13.19). In the example, the file named "c" has an absolute path name of /a/c since directories "a" and "b" are combined at the mount point. After the temporary file system has been mounted, it can be accessed through all normal directory operations, including relative and absolute path names and directory traversal operations. When the file system is to be removed, an unmount command is sent to the file manager. This command prevents access attempts to a part of the file hierarchy that no longer exists.

13.7 ■ Summary

Files are the main means of managing and storing large amounts of data on a computer system. The files supported by an operating system can be simple streams of bytes, streams of records, or more complex organizations of records. Byte-stream files have the advantage of being a generic data structure logically used like primary memory to access the data. Their disadvantage is that most application software needs to add structure to the data for it to be well-suited to the application programming domain. Different operating systems take different approaches regarding the amount of support they provide for structuring the data. At one end of the spectrum are UNIX and DOS/Windows, which provide minimal support and expect system software to add data structuring mechanisms and high-level file systems at the opposite end.

File implementations translate byte streams or structured records into physical block images saved on storage devices. Sequential storage devices provide a natural mapping between the records and the physical blocks, since the sequentiality of the file is mapped to the sequentiality of the device. Mapping records to random device blocks is more challenging because the mapping can be arbitrarily complex. Block management, then, becomes a major task for the file system when it is implemented on randomly accessed storage devices.

Directories provide a road map for human users. The storage devices in a system may contain literally thousands of files. A directory provides a systematic way to name and locate those files. The directory management part of the file manager provides facilities to allow a user to navigate in the directory structure; to copy, rename, and erase files; and to administer the file organization across devices, including devices with removable media.

13.8 ▪ Exercises

1. Write a program to determine how a UNIX kernel `write` operation treats bytes that are interior to a byte stream. Does the `write` operation insert a block of characters, over-write a block of characters, or use some other strategy?

2. Explain what the `O_APPEND` flag is used for in UNIX file I/O.

3. Provide an example application or application domain in which sequentially accessed files are well suited to the problem. Your domain should illustrate that in some cases the information must be randomly accessed, yet at other times it must be sequentially accessed.

4. Suppose a disk free space list indicates that the following blocks of storage are available: 13 blocks, 11 blocks, 18 blocks, 9 blocks, and 20 blocks. There is a request to allocate 10 contiguous blocks to a file.

   a. Using the first-fit allocation strategy, which block would be allocated to the file?
   b. Using the best-fit allocation strategy, which block would be allocated to the file?
   c. Using the worst-fit allocation strategy, which block would be allocated to the file?

5. How many device operations (for example, disk sector `reads` and `writes`) are required to add a released node to a free list, where the free list is implemented with the linked-list approach? Do two-way linked lists decrease the number of device operations?

6. How many device operations are required to add a released node to a free list when the block status map approach is used to implement the free list?

7. Explain why a file system that supports indexed sequential files cannot be expected to have the same performance level as pure sequentially accessed files.

8. Suppose a file system is based on the indexed allocation strategy for managing blocks. Assume each file has a directory entry giving the filename, first index

block, and the length of the file. The first index block points in turn to 249 file blocks and to the next index block. If the file is currently positioned at logical block 2010 and the next operation is to access logical block 308, how many physical blocks must be read from the disk? Explain your answer.

9. Suppose a UNIX disk block will hold 2048 disk addresses. What is the maximum-sized file using only the direct pointers? Single-indirection capability? Double-indirection capability? Triple-indirection capability?

10. Early versions of the DOS file system had a limitation of 32MB of addressable space on a disk drive. Based on the description of the directory and files in the chapter, provide some conjectures for the limitation.

11. Suppose a file system is organized like the DOS file system and the device index contains 64K pointers. Explain how the file manager could be designed to use the 64K pointers to reference every 512-byte block on a 512MB disk.

12. File system checkers often take advantage of the block status map used to identify unallocated disk blocks. The basic idea is for the map to be copied into the checker's address space, with each entry in the map enlarged to capture more possibilities for the block's state (for example, allocated, not allocated, duplicate allocation, already checked, etc.). Devise an algorithm to use the block status table to check a disk to see if every block on the disk appears in one, and only one, file or on the free list.

13. Inspect the source code on your laboratory machine to see the details of the inode used in your version of UNIX. You will find the inode C structure in a header file. Its exact location will depend on the version of UNIX you are using. Write a table listing every field in the structure and its type. Also write a 25-word (or less) description of the purpose for the field.

14. Use a text editor to inspect a mail file on the computer on which you keep your electronic mail. Assuming it is similar to the Berkeley mail system, you should be able to recognize message boundaries as well as the message sender, receiver, subject line, and so on. Write an access method to read such a mail file and to print an index with one line per mail message. The line should print the sequence number of the message, the sender, the time and date the message was sent, and the first 20 characters of the subject field.

15. Implement two UNIX functions to read from and write to variable-sized records from a byte stream, where the user of the routines specifies the way information is to be formatted and unformatted when it is read. Use the following function prototypes:

```
int readRecord(int fid, char *record, char *specifier)
int writeRecord(int fid, char *record, char *specifier);
```

(This is intended to be a simple exercise using the stdio library to explore a trivial way to export application-specific record formats to the file manager.)

16. Read the man page for dup on your system and then construct two programs whereby stdout of the first program is redirected to be stdin of the second program. To accomplish this I/O redirection, you will need to use dup (or dup2), open, and close.

Laboratory Exercise: A Simple File Manager

The file manager usually is the largest part of an OS, even though it does not have the most complex algorithms or data structures. Normally, the critical parts of the file manager—at least those parts described as being low-level in this chapter—are implemented in the OS. It is difficult to experiment with a real file manager (because of its size and the fact that it is supervisor mode software). This exercise is designed to give you some experience with file manager technology by having you write a simple file manager that uses a disk simulator (instead of a real disk) and runs in user space.

The file manager is required to implement the API shown in Figure 13.20, using the disk interface shown in Figure 13.21. You may also add a few more routines to the API—for example, if you wish to initialize the file manager prior to using it the first time. Although it is not necessary, you can add a `fcntl/ioctl` command if you need one.

Because a production-level file manager is so complex, you will need to make a number of simplifying assumptions in designing and implementing your file manager:

- Your on-disk file descriptor will fit into one disk block. The on-disk file descriptor need contain only minimal information: (1) a file name of six or fewer characters and (2) at most four disk blocks per file (you can use 2-byte block addresses).

- The disk blocks will be very small—say, 50 bytes per block. (You can choose the final value after you have designed your on-disk file descriptor.)

Figure 13.20
The File Manager API

```
void mkdir(char *name);
void ls();
int cd(char *name);
int fopen(char *name);
void fclose(int fileID);
int fRead(int fileID, char *buffer, int length);
int fWrite(int fileID, char *buffer, int length);
int lseek(int fileID, int position);
```

Figure 13.21
The Disk Interface

```
#define NUM_BLOCKS   100
#define BLOCK_SIZE   50

void initDisk();
int dRead(int addr, char *buf);
int dWrite(int addr, char *buf);
```

■ Directories need contain only minimal information describing the file—just enough to get your file manager working.

  You will also need to remember the following:

■ Do not implement file sharing—no locks.

■ Do not implement file modes such as read, write, or execute.

■ Do not include any protection or authentication in your file system.

■ Do not implement path names, just filenames within the current directory.

■ Do not implement buffering.

BACKGROUND

Much of the design of your file manager is straight-forward. However, this background section provides you with some useful applied information about how to organize your file system.

Disk Layout

The storage device—"the disk"—provides a basic format for the way files will be stored on the disk. When a disk is formatted, it is prepared so that certain fixed locations will contain information expected by a particular file manager. Formatting a disk for Linux does not necessarily mean that it will be formatted for other versions of UNIX, and certainly not for the Microsoft operating systems.

  Modern operating systems usually allow a physical disk to be partitioned into separate logical disks. Normally, a disk driver interoperates with a logical disk rather than the actual physical disk. (Of course we ignore the distinction in the abstract disk interface used for this exercise.) The first few sectors on the disk—starting at surface 0, track 0, sector 0—ordinarily contain the basic information for booting the OS and for establishing a table of contents for the logical disks. Each logical disk may have its own *boot sector* (also called a *boot block*) along with information about the root of the file system that is stored on that (logical) disk. UNIX systems have a *superblock* following the boot block and the collection of all inodes (external file descriptors) for all the files that are stored on that logical disk. The data blocks are placed on the remainder of the disk. The superblock describes the file system that is kept on the logical disk—for example, it specifies the block size for the logical disk.

  The amount of space reserved for the inodes is defined at the time the disk is formatted. According to McKusick et al. [1996], a 150MB files system will typically have 4MB of space reserved for inodes and the remaining 146MB for data. When a file system is mounted, the inode for the root directory is copied from the disk into primary memory (which also results in some updating of the superblock). When a file is opened, its inode location is found in the directory in which the file appears, and the file's inode can then be loaded into memory. As long as the file is open, the inode is loaded in primary memory where all changes are made. The updated inode is written back to memory when the file is closed.

DOS/Windows incorporates a root for each physical disk device in the system. At any given moment, DOS is intended to operate from a default drive. All filenames are assumed to be located in the device directory on the default drive. If a file is to be referenced on a different device, then an absolute filename can include a drive specifier to reference the file system on another device. The DOS directory is a collection of device directories, each prefaced by the name of the device and a colon.

Each device (or floppy diskette) contains a file allocation table (FAT), which is an index to disk blocks that are assigned to any particular file. There is one entry per disk block on the device. The entry is a pointer to the disk block that contains the next logical record in the file. The root directory for the device is located at a fixed disk address. A directory contains a set of entries—one per file—with the basic information for that file. That is, there is no separate file descriptor like an inode in a FAT file system. The directory entry contains a pointer to the first block in the file. The corresponding FAT entry points to the next block in the file (or to null if this is the last block). Lab exercises 10–12 in Nutt [1999a] provide an extended discussion of the details for building a file manager for FAT systems.

File Descriptors

The file descriptor is simply a data structure; its design is determined by the file manager designer at the time the file manager algorithms are designed. If you have Linux source code available, you can look at `struct inode` in the file named `.../src/linux/include/linux/fs.h` for the exact definition for Linux inodes. (You may also find it helpful to see Beck et al. [1998, ch. 6].)

When the external file descriptor is loaded into primary memory, the file manager copies all the information from the disk representation, then adds other information that it needs to manage the open file. For example, the external version of the file descriptor does not indicate which user and process currently has the file open or what the current location is for the file pointer; this information makes sense only for an open file.

The In the Hangar section (p. 372), particularly Figure 13.8, describes the UNIX data structures to handle open files. To summarize: when the file is opened, the file manager looks up the file in the directory to obtain the inode. The inode is copied into a memory-resident set of inodes. The file manager then creates an entry in the file table that will contain new dynamic information needed by the process when the file is open (see the `struct file` definition in `.../src/linux/include/linux/fs.h`). The file table entry references the inode. Finally, the file manager creates an entry in the process's file descriptor table; this entry establishes the "file identification number" returned by the open command, and points to the file table entry.

Directories

Hierarchical file systems are widely used in contemporary operating systems. In a hierarchical file system, each directory contains entries for files and for other directories. Hierarchical file systems are relatively easy to support when, as is usually the case, directories are implemented using ordinary files. The part of the file manager responsible for directory manipulation just uses the normal file open, read, and write system calls. In general, the directory is treated as a file for which the internal structure and semantics are defined by the procedures that use it.

A directory entry must contain enough information to allow the file manager to match a character string filename with the entry's name and to find the external file descriptor on the disk if the names match. For example, in a UNIX system, the directory entry is required to have only the name and the inode number for the file; all information related to the file is kept in the inode. To list the files in a directory, the file manager would traverse the directory contents, printing the name from each entry, then retrieving any other information to be included in the listing directly from the inode. DOS directory entries are 32-byte entries containing the filename and extension, file attributes, creation time and date, size, and the location of the first block in the file [Nutt 1999a].

ATTACKING THE PROBLEM

The concepts needed to solve this exercise are not especially complex, but there are a number of details that must be handled to arrive at a suitable solution. The most significant design challenge will be for you to create your disk layout and file descriptor formats. You are given a disk interface and required to provide an API.

Disk Interface

The disk used in this exercise is merely implemented as blocks of primary memory. Use the following code to implement your virtual disk:

```
#include <stdio.h>

#define NUM_BLOCKS  100
#define BLOCK_SIZE  50

#define RELIABILITY 0.95
#define PERIOD      2147483647.0
#define ERROR       0
#define NO_ERROR    1
#define NULL        0

static int    threshold;
static char  *bList[NUM_BLOCKS];

void initDisk() {
    int i;

    for(i=0; i<NUM_BLOCKS; i++) bList[i] = NULL;
    threshold = (int) (RELIABILITY*PERIOD);
    sleep(3);
}
```

```
int dRead(int addr, char *buf) {
    int i;
    char *bufPtr;

    if(addr >= NUM_BLOCKS) return ERROR;
    if(rand() > threshold) return ERROR;
    if(bList[addr] != NULL) {
        bufPtr = bList[addr];
        for(i=0; i<BLOCK_SIZE; i++) buf[i] = *bufPtr++;
    }
    else
        for(i=0; i<BLOCK_SIZE; i++) buf[i] = 0;
    return NO_ERROR;
}

int dWrite(int addr, char *buf) {
    int i;
    char *bufPtr;

    if(addr >= NUM_BLOCKS) return ERROR;
    if(rand() > threshold) return ERROR;
    if(bList[addr] == NULL)
        bList[addr] = (char *) malloc(BLOCK_SIZE);
    bufPtr = bList[addr];
    for(i=0; i<BLOCK_SIZE; i++)
        *bufPtr++ = buf[i];
    return NO_ERROR;
}
```

This virtual disk is very simple. It statically allocates 100 blocks of 50-bytes each, then reads and writes those with the possibility of I/O failure. Use this code to implement your own virtual disk; change the block size as needed. You can also experiment with different reliability values if you like.

Disk Layout

The virtual disk simulation code simply initializes a set of blocks but does not format the disk. The first step in your solution should be to design your low-level disk format (of course, you need not provide a bootstrap area, but you may need to have information regarding the disk layout, and you will certainly need information regarding the root directory). If you use a version of inodes, you will need to decide how this should be laid out on your disk.

File System Design

The next step is to design your directories. A directory entry need not be complex—it should be just enough to allow you to associate a name and a file descriptor. After you have designed the directory entry, you can implement the root directory. You may wish to postpone adding subdirectories until you get more of the solution working properly. At this point you will almost certainly find it worthwhile to build a tool that creates a simple file system with a root directory and a few files. You will also find it worthwhile to build a tool that dumps the virtual disk contents so you can analyze it as you design and debug the rest of the system.

After your directory is designed and your root directory is implemented, you should implement your first version of the `ls` command—a version that works only on the file system root directory. After you have implemented subdirectories, you can finish implementing `ls`.

Now you are ready to design and implement the file descriptor and the open-file data structure(s). You may find it easiest to use either a FAT-style approach or an inode approach using only direct pointers to the data blocks.

Finally, you will be ready to implement the commands on the API. It will be easier to get the whole system working if you first design and implement the directory commands—only those that read the directory but do not change it, followed by commands that write the directory (such as opening a new file). After you have finished this phase, you can implement file operations—commands that open/close and read/write a file. Again, first implement commands that do not write the directory entries or file descriptors (for example `fRead`). After you get this code working, you can implement the `fWrite`, which will require that you do block allocation.

The final step is to implement subdirectories. In theory, all your previous code should work just with subdirectories, though in practice you will probably find some errors in your original code. Last, you should implement `mkdir` and `cd`.

You will have to write a simple test program to check that each of your commands works. It will be natural to develop this program as you debug each command. Here is a sample driver program (written by Ann Root in 1998):

```
#include <stdlib.h>
#include <stdio.h>
#include <malloc.h>
#include <assert.h>

#include "block.h"
#include "hw8.h"

char* two_block_buf = "This is a long buffer to test. This
will take up two blocks in a file. Length is 98
characters.\n";

char* one_block_buf = "This will test files of one block
length.\n";

main(){
    int i, fileptr;
    char* buf, buf2, buf3;

/* Initialize the disk */
    initDisk();
```

```
/* Test fOpen, fWrite, and fClose */
    fileptr = fOpen("File1");
    if(fWrite(fileptr,
            two_block_buf, strlen(two_block_buf)) == -1)
                printf("Error in write");
    fClose(fileptr);


/* Test mkdir and cd */
    mkdir("Dir1");
    if(cd("Dir1") == -1)
        exit(0);


/* Test fWrite with single block */
    fileptr = fOpen("Test1");
    if(fileptr == -1)
        printf("Error in opening Test1");
    if(fWrite(fileptr,
            one_block_buf, strlen(one_block_buf)) == -1)
                printf("Error in write to file Test1");
    fClose(fileptr);


/* Test fWrite with two-block write */
    fileptr = fOpen("test2");
    if(fWrite(fileptr,
            two_block_buf, strlen(two_block_buf)) == -1)
                printf("Error in write");
    fClose(fileptr);


/* Test ls, fRead */
    ls();
    if(cd("..") == -1)
        printf("Can't cd to ..\n");
    ls();
    fileptr = fOpen("File1");
    if(fileptr == -1)
        printf("Can't open File1");
    buf = (char*)malloc(400*sizeof(char));
    assert(buf);
    if(fRead(fileptr, buf, 20) == -1)
    printf("Can't read from First_file\n");
    printf("buf = %s \n", buf);
    fClose(fileptr);

    mkdir("temp");
    cd("temp");
    fileptr = fOpen("temp1");
    if(fileptr == -1)
        printf("Can't open temp/temp1\n");
    for(i = 0; i < 100; i++)
        buf[i] = 'A';
```

```
      if(fWrite(fileptr, buf, strlen(buf)) == -1)
          printf("Can't write to temp1\n");

/* Test lseek */
   lseek(fileptr,0);
   if(fRead(fileptr, buf, strlen(buf)) == -1)
       printf("Can't read from temp\n");
   printf("temp1 = %s \n", buf);

   if(lseek(fileptr, 40) == -1)
       printf("Error in f_lseek\n");
   for(i = 0; i < 20; i++)
       buf[i] = 'B';
   /*write only the B's in buf to the file*/
   if(fWrite(fileptr, buf, 20) == -1)
       printf("Can't write to temp\n");

   lseek(fileptr,0);
   if(fRead(fileptr, buf, strlen(buf)) == -1)
       printf("Can't read from temp\n");
   printf("temp1 = %s \n", buf);
   fClose(fileptr);

/* Test various other cases */
   fileptr = fOpen("temp2");
   if(fileptr == -1)
       printf("Can't open temp2\n");
   free(buf);
   buf2 = (char* )malloc(100*sizeof(char));

   assert(buf2);
   if(fRead(fileptr, buf2,sizeof(buf2)) == -1)
       printf("Can't read from temp2\n");
   printf("Buf2 = %s \n", buf2);
   fClose(fileptr);

   buf3 = (char* ) malloc(200*sizeof(char));
   assert(buf3);
   fileptr = fOpen("temp1");
   fRead(fileptr, buf3, 200);
   fClose(fileptr);
   printf("File temp1 contains:\n%s\n", buf3);

/* Test cd upward */
   ls();
   cd("..");
   ls();
} /* end main*/
```

14

Protection and Security

Ｎone of the protection systems that exist today ... are completely fail-safe. The best we can do is make it as difficult as possible for somebody to break a security device or get inside.

—Bill Gates, *The Road Ahead* ■

CHAPTER OBJECTIVES

All files are stored on a computer's shared devices. This means there is the potential for a file owned by one user to be read from or written to by a different user. Sometimes this is exactly what is intended; information stored in files is to be shared among the users. At other times, a user may want information to be private. How can the OS establish an environment in which a user can selectively either keep information private or share it with other users? That is the task of the protection and security functions in the OS. Keeping information private is even more difficult when the computer is connected to a network that is in turn connected to other computers.

   Throughout the discussion of the OS managers, various ways to protect resources from unauthorized access have been mentioned—protection and security are pervasive in the OS. This chapter focuses on the strategies and tools by which the various parts of the OS can achieve security according to the organization's requirements. The specific objectives of the chapter are to distinguish between external and internal security and to describe relevant protection mechanisms to implement internal security policies. The classic model for internal protection is also discussed, followed by implementation issues. Since encryption and external authorization are not integral to operating system functionality, less time is spent on these aspects of the problem than on the internal mechanisms.

14.1 ■ Fundamentals

Modern computer systems support many users, either through time- and space-multi-plexing of a single computer or through access of computers using a network. Organizations rely on computers to store all kinds of information, such as that describing the state of their operation and assisting them in administering their organization, as well as their proprietary and confidential information. The computers themselves also represent a significant resource of the organization, so the very use of these machines is an associated expense of operating the organization. Hence, the organization must protect both its information and computers from unauthorized use just as it needs to protect all of its other resources such as buildings, equipment, and financial funds.

The flexibility of software creates a difficult situation with regard to protecting against unauthorized access of resources. Within theoretical computing bounds, the functionality of software is limited by the intellectual effort invested in that software. This means that it is possible to write complex software that might violate any given protection scheme incorporated in the OS. The challenge for the OS designer is to create a protection scheme that cannot be bypassed by any software that might be created in the future. In general, this cannot be done without special assistance from hardware.

Computer networks aggravate the problem because they allow many people to access computers without being in the same physical location as the computer. Physical protection mechanisms such as locked rooms do not present any barrier to network access of a computer.

Consider the problem of protecting a computer and its information in the context of modern system configurations. In Figure 14.1, users *A, B, C,* and *D* employ the resources in Machine *X*. User *D* accesses Machine *X* over a network from Machine *Y*. Users *A* and *B* have private resources storing private data and share other resources and information. Machine *X* also has some resources and information that are accessible to any local user, such as *C*, or remote users of Machine *Y* (such as *D*). The protection system must support this kind of environment by enforcing the desired resource access according to the organization's specific administrative policy.

14.1.1 ■ Policy and Mechanism

An organization's *security policy* defines the rules for authorizing access to its computer and information resources. For example, the organization may allow only employees in its accounting department to use computers that store accounting information. How can an organization's security policy be specified and enforced in a contemporary computer system? The computer's *protection mechanisms* are tools for implementing the organization's security policy. Computers of the same type (with the same OS) can employ distinct security policies even though they use the same protection mechanism. What are the protection mechanisms the system might incorporate to support policies? What is a reasonable way to define the problem so that it can be addressed within the domain of computer software and hardware? These are examples of the protection and security issues that concern computer systems.

The differences between mechanisms and policies have been stressed throughout this book. A *mechanism* is a set of components used to implement any one of different

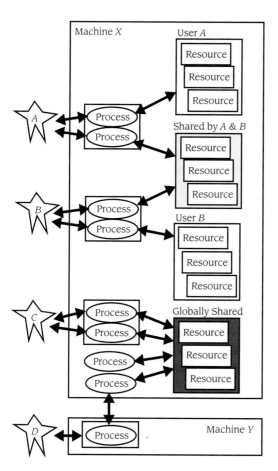

Figure 14.1
Processes Accessing Resources

sets of strategies. A *policy* is a particular strategy that dictates the way a mechanism is used to achieve specific goals. For example, a particular communications policy might be for no two processes to be allowed to share resources except by exchanging messages. A communications mechanism to support the policy would be required to support message passing, perhaps by copying messages from the address space of one process to another. In another example, a demand paging mechanism may support different replacement algorithm policies. A system's security policy specifies the way resources should be shared among members of the organization and with members external to the organization. The mechanism is the specific steps and tools provided by the system to enforce the policy.

As an example, an academic computer science department might have a policy whereby computers in an undergraduate laboratory can be used only by students registered for undergraduate computer science classes. A mechanism to support the policy might require the user's student identification and the department's class lists to implement the policy. This mechanism might have to be supplemented with others to support authentication, physical presence in the computer laboratory, and so on. Establishing a precise policy is difficult, since it requires that a precise set of software requirements be specified in addition to a set of "laws" without loopholes to control the actions of the human users.

14.1.2 ■ Implementing Policy and Mechanism

As a rule of thumb (independent of performance considerations), mechanisms are implemented in the OS when it is necessary to *guarantee* that they perform the function they were intended to do. If mechanisms cannot be guaranteed to behave as defined, then they cannot be depended on to implement a policy. In contemporary operating systems, safe protection mechanisms can be implemented only in the OS.

Policies are selected by the computer's administrators, usually long after the OS and its protection mechanisms have been designed and implemented. In theory, the security policy can be determined by defining it in the user space, although many operating systems layer the functionality. A very small part of the OS implements the mechanism, while other parts of the OS, system software, or user software determine the policy. As a result, a general study of protection and security first depends on the design of the OS protection mechanisms and then on the security policies chosen by the designers and administrators.

Protection mechanisms implement authentication functions to allow the policy to determine that an entity—a user or a remote computer—is who it claims to be. The authentication mechanism also is used to check that an entity has authorization to access resources.

14.1.3 ■ Authentication Mechanisms

Authentication mechanisms are the basis of most protection mechanisms. There are two types of authentication: external and internal. External authentication is concerned with determining whether a user is the person claimed to be. For example, if a person logs into a system with a particular account name, then the basic external authentication mechanism will check to ensure that the person logging in is actually the person who is supposed to be using the account. The simplest form of external authentication is to associate a *password* with each account. The account name then can be widely known—for example, it can be used as an electronic mail address—while the password remains confidential to the person using the account. The password is a static entity and can be changed only by the user or the system administrator. The OS mechanism supporting this type of authentication ensures that it is not possible to bypass the authentication mechanism through a series of surreptitious actions.

Internal authentication must ensure that a process cannot appear to be a process other than itself. Without internal authentication, a user could create a process that appears to be a process that belongs to another user. Then even the most effective external authentication mechanism could easily be bypassed by having one user's process behave as if it were another user's process.

Consider how difficult it can be to create a safe authentication mechanism in a network of UNIX workstations. Originally, timesharing machines were physically located in secure computer rooms. Users logged into the machine over telecommunications lines but had no physical contact with the machine or its operator's console. As workstations began to incorporate UNIX, the scenario changed. Today workstations are physically placed in the workspace of the user. The operator's console is a window on the physical display rather than a separate terminal in a secure area. The physical security of early timesharing systems is not generally present in UNIX workstation environments.

Networks of workstations are generally administered by a central organization, with the workstation's "owner" being an ordinary user. The owner logs into the machine using the logical operator's console with no special administrative privilege. By providing administrators with the root login, the system can be administered remotely without allowing the local owner to alter system files.

However, suppose the user turns off the power to the machine and then turns it back on. In this case, UNIX workstations were classically designed to boot up in single-user mode with the operator's console in root mode (see Chapter 6). Hence, any person wishing to have root permission could power cycle the machine to put it in single-user mode, alter permissions as desired, and then start the OS in multiuser mode. This flaw was quickly recognized and remedied by having the machine boot up in multiuser mode. However, this example illustrates how one cannot depend on simple assumptions such as "the operating system has been proved to be secure, so the system is secure."

14.1.4 ■ Authorization Mechanisms

Authorization mechanisms ensure that users or processes are allowed to use entities in the computer (such as resources) only if the policy permits such use. The authorization mechanism depends on the presence of a safe authentication mechanism. Figure 14.2 shows the classic points at which a computer system authorizes access. When a user attempts to access the computer, an *external access authorization* mechanism first authenticates the user's identity and then checks to see if that user is authorized to access the computer.

The customary approach for interactive computers is for the system to keep a record of login accounts for all authorized users. A user who can authenticate his or her identity is authorized to use the computer. As shown in Figure 14.2, users logging into one machine and then attempting to log into a remote machine must first be authorized to use the local machine. Another form of the authorization process for the remote machine may be used.

Once a user has been authorized to use a machine, the machine's OS will assign a process to perform actions on behalf of the user (in UNIX, this is the user's login process). After the login authorization is complete, the user is free to direct the command line interpreter (shell) process to attempt access to arbitrary resources. For example, a user could attempt to edit the system's password file. As shown in Figure 14.2, each access by a process must be authorized by the system's *internal access authorization* mechanism for the target resource. The external and internal access authorization mechanisms differ. The external mechanism authorizes users to access computers, while the internal mechanism authorizes processes to access resources. The external mechanism is exercised only when an interactive session begins. However, the internal mechanism is potentially invoked each time the user enters a command into the machine. This is because most commands are stored in files and when a command is executed, it often reads from or writes to files. The details of authentication are covered in Section 14.2, followed by internal access authorization in Sections 14.3 and 14.4.

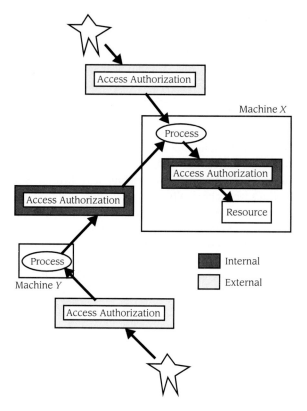

Figure 14.2
Access Authorization Points

14.1.5 ■ Encryption

Encryption is a technique for encoding information into a form where its meaning is obscured as ciphered text. Encryption is rapidly growing in importance in modern computer systems. In networked computer systems, it is difficult to provide a mechanism whereby information is inaccessible. Therefore the information is encrypted into a form in which its information content is indiscernible without decrypting it. The key aspect of encryption is to be able to efficiently create encryptions that essentially cannot be decrypted by unauthorized users. Section 14.5 provides a description of contemporary encryption technology.

14.2 ■ Authentication

Computer security is a complex issue. It involves administrative policies, moral issues, and physical security external to the design of the OS. Because of the nature of computer security threats, the way the system is protected may be even more comprehensive than the other software and hardware of the computer system.

A protection mechanism may rely on physical isolation of the computer or on logical isolation that prevents remote users from accessing the computer with telecommunication networks. In general, this book does not address physical security issues, except to presume that unauthorized users are able to establish some kind of logical access to the computer system by interacting with a device connected directly or indirectly to the system. Note that it is difficult to solve the problem in an uncontrolled external environment. In these cases, security violators are not subject to any particular "rules of the game."

14.2.1 ■ User Authentication

The OS is the software agent with which users interact when they initiate a session with the system. The OS needs to verify that users are who they claim to be. This aspect of protection is known as *user authentication.* If a system could be unequivocally correct in its authentication of users, many aspects of protection would already be solved, although no commercial systems are designed with this assumption. If this were possible, any action caused by a user would be known to be the full responsibility of that user, and not some other user masquerading as the intended user. In general, unequivocal authentication is not possible.

The combination of user identification and password is widely used in operating systems for user authentication. The OS can take additional measures to ensure itself that the human user is the person claimed to be. Such authentication might involve techniques similar to those used by a bank to allow a person to transfer funds by telephone. The user may be asked to provide additional information besides the password, depending on the policy for authenticating a user. Contemporary protection systems may even resort to methods such as fingerprint or eye scan identification.

In the simplest case in which masquerading occurs, a legitimate user identification and password are shared among different human users. Now the system cannot distinguish among the different humans masquerading as the same human, so it cannot provide security among them. A more serious form of masquerade may occur if an authorized user leaves an identification and password in a public place or when the user's identification is well known and the password is easily guessed by other users.

Once a login name for a remote system is known, one computer could possibly be used to initiate a session with another and to simulate a legitimate remote login session to the second on behalf of the login name. The masquerading computer establishes a connection to the authentication process and rapidly and systematically tries many different passwords for the known user identification. The authentication process may detect the penetration attempt when it observes repeated failure to supply a password. That process can then terminate the connection if some threshold of failure to provide the correct password is surpassed. However, the masquerading machine can reestablish the connection later and continue searching for the password associated with the login name.

14.2.2 ■ Authentication in Networks

File transfer mechanisms such as those used to transport electronic mail connections also can be used to penetrate a machine. File transfer requires one computer to be able to transfer information into another system's file space. The transmitting computer must be able to gain access to the receiving computer before it can cause the file to be stored, and the receiving machine must be prepared to accept an arbitrary file to be placed in its file system. The file transfer input port normally incorporates an authorization mechanism to verify that the transmitting computer has the right to store the file. However, in many systems this authentication mechanism is not very sophisticated, since extensive authentication increases the overhead involved in file transfer.

Today network authentication mechanisms are especially necessary to detect incoming files that may contain a virus or a worm. The two differ in how they react once they have been placed in a machine. A *virus* is a software module hidden inside another module. The virus may become established in a file system by replacing some existing module as a bug fix or as an upgrade. It may also be loaded along with a free game or other software. The clandestine file will perform the task it was advertised to do. But it also will perform some unobserved function, such as leaving undetected loopholes for the penetrator to use at some later time or planting a program to destroy system resources. In recent years, viruses have become a significant part of the software industry, particularly because of the evolution of two aspects of computing. First, floppy disks are widely circulated among personal computer users. A floppy disk is an ideal carrier for a virus, particularly since the recipient mounts the disk and runs its programs. Second, the Internet is a prolific breeding ground for viruses, particularly because it offers a broad variety of mail, newsgroups, Web pages, and free software. Today, there are various products explicitly intended to detect the presence of viruses and (if possible) to remove them.

A *worm* is distinguished from a virus because it is an active penetrating entity. The worm may enter the machine as a file, but it then will begin execution on its own. Once a file containing a worm has been placed in the file system, the worm finds a loophole in the process manager in order to execute itself. For example, one well-known worm program, "Morris's worm," was constructed to penetrate UNIX systems by taking advantage of the `finger` command (see the special section on the Internet worm in *Communications of the ACM* [1989] and Stoll [1988]).

In UNIX systems, the `finger name@host` command prints a standard set of information about a user identified by the argument. The name part of the argument can be any part of the user name found in the password file, so if one has the user's real name it is easy to find a user's login name. The `host` part of the argument allows `finger` to connect to remote machines to execute `finger` in search of information about a user. The `finger` command also prints other information found in standard files, such as the `.plan` file. Users commonly put personalized information in the `.plan` file as a courtesy to other users, but the file might also be used as the basis from which to guess passwords. While the `finger` command is an invaluable tool for locating login names to use with electronic mail programs, it is also an example of a tool that is used to gather information to penetrate another system.

Morris's worm executed `finger` on a remote host machine with a name too large for the string array in the `finger` program. This destroyed the runtime stack of the `finger` daemon so that when the daemon completed the command, it did not return to the program it was executing before servicing the incoming `finger` call. Instead, the daemon branched to a small block of code invoking a remote shell for the worm. The worm then had control of a process on the penetrated machine, thus enabling it to cause considerable damage by using various resources to debilitate the penetrated machine. Despite the presence of viruses, worms, and other clandestine modules, commercial systems still use the basic account name and password method to implement external authentication. The system administration policy can be strengthened to watch carefully for behavior suggesting an attempt to start a worm, to guess a password, and so on. Unfortunately, these external authentication mechanisms must take all possible penetration patterns into account and then check for each—a daunting computational task. Also, an audit trail of login attempts can be used to detect penetration attempts *a posteriori,* although this may occur too late to prevent damage.

➤ *IN THE HANGAR*

Kerberos Network Authentication

Kerberos is a set of network protocols that can be used to authenticate access to one computer by a user at a different computer using an unsecure network. That is, Kerberos assumes that information flowing over the network could be tampered with during transmission. Furthermore, Kerberos does not assume that the operating systems on the two machines are necessarily secure. The technique was developed at M.I.T. in the 1980s and is widely used today. The Internet Draft recommendation for Kerberos provides the most recent details of the authentication system [Kohl and Neuman, 1992].

In Kerberos, it is assumed that a process on one computer (the client) wishes to employ the services of a process on another computer (the server) using the network for communication. Kerberos provides an *authentication server* and protocol to allow the client and server to transmit authenticated messages to the companion process in a specific session. The following steps are observed in the protocol (diagrammed in Figure 14.3):

1. The client asks the authentication server for the *credentials* of the server process.

2. The authentication server returns the credentials as a *ticket* and a *session key* with the latter encrypted using the client's key. Section 14.5 explains more details of encryption, but for now observe that the (composite) ticket and session key can be read only by the client. The ticket has fields containing the client's identification and a copy of the session key encrypted using the server's key. This means that the only process that can interpret the ticket's fields is the server.

3. After the client obtains the credentials, it decrypts the ticket and session key, keeping a copy of the session key so that it can authenticate information from the server.

4. The client then sends a copy of the ticket with the encrypted fields intact to the server.

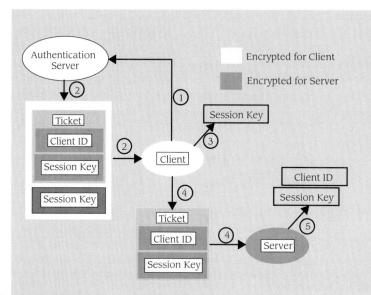

Figure 14.3
Kerberos Session Key Distribution

5. The server decrypts the copy of the ticket so that it can obtain a secure copy of the client's identification and of the session key.

The authentication server must be trusted in this protocol. This is because it has a secure copy of the client's identification, knows how to encrypt information that only the client can decrypt, knows how to encrypt information that only the server can decrypt, and can create a unique session key to represent a logical conversation between the client and the server. Since the authentication server can encrypt information for the client and the server, it can give the client a "container"—the ticket—that contains information that the client cannot read but which it can pass on to the server. This is analogous to having a credit card with an account number encoded on a magnetic strip on the back of it. You (the client) cannot actually read what is on the strip, but when you present the card to an automatic teller machine (the server), that machine reads your account number from the strip. The credit card is a "ticket" with an encrypted account number (although it has no session number).

After Steps 1 through 5 have been completed, the client and server processes both have a copy of the session key that they received as information encrypted by the trusted authentication server. An intruder on the network could not read the encrypted information without knowing how to decrypt it. Nor could it change the information to produce meaningful fraudulent certification. In addition, the server has a trusted copy of the client's identification so that when the client sends a message to the server, the server can authenticate the client ID and session key.

14.3 ▪ Internal Access Authorization

Internal authorization is part of the task of managing resource sharing. Here the concern is to protect one process's resources from the actions of other processes. Suppose process A has resources W, X, Y, and Z, as shown in Figure 14.4. Some of these resources are to be shared with other processes. For example, process B has read access rights to W, while process C has write access rights to W; B has write access to Y, while C has no access to Y; C has read access to X, and B has no access to X; and A has private access to Z. Researchers have characterized several different classes of protection problems, listed next, in this environment and have attempted to design policies and mechanisms to address them.

- *Sharing parameters:* A process's resource policy may be violated if other processes can indiscriminately change parameter values within its address space. For example, suppose a process calls a procedure in some other process's address space and the callee's procedure modifies parameters passed into the procedure so that when the caller regains control, variables in its address space have been changed by the called procedure.

- *Confinement:* Confinement is a generalization of the problem of sharing parameters. Suppose a process wishes to limit the dispersion of information to some particular environment. The challenge is to contain all rights to resources so that they do not propagate outside some chosen set of processes.

- *Allocating rights:* A protection system may allow a process to provide another process with specific rights to use its resources. In some cases, the first process needs to be able to revoke those rights at any time. Rights should be only temporarily allocated by one process to another. A subtle problem may occur if a process provides rights to another process and then the receiving process passes the rights on to other processes without the knowledge or permission of the resource owner. Some protection systems disallow this rights propagation without the explicit permission of the resource owner.

- *Trojan horse:* The Trojan horse problem is a special case of the problem of allocating rights—a service program being used by a client process using its own rights. If the

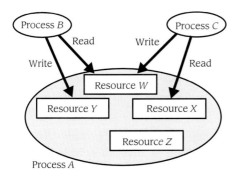

Figure 14.4
Controlled Resource Sharing

server program takes advantage of the client process's rights to access resources on its own behalf, it is called a Trojan horse.

14.3.1 ■ A Model for Resource Protection

In general, a system has *active* parts and *passive* parts. Its active parts, such as processes or threads, act on behalf of users. Its passive parts, corresponding to resources, are called *objects* in the protection literature. (The "protection objects" described here are different from "object-oriented programming objects." The term "object" is used here because it is prevalent in the protection literature [Graham and Denning, 1972].) In the protection model described next, processes access objects according to the *rights* that the process has to do so.

In modern operating systems, a process has different rights to an object at different times, depending on what task it is currently doing. For example, a process that is executing a system call (see again Section 3.3.3) has the access rights of an OS; it would normally have the rights associated with its user. For example, the UNIX file system uses the setUID bit in a binary file to allow a process executing the file to temporarily assume supervisory rights while accessing system tables or otherwise manipulating system resources. The particular set of rights a process has at any given time is referred to as its *protection domain*. So any decision about the access a process should have to objects must include consideration of the protection domain in which the process is executing. A *subject* is a process executing in a specific protection domain. Subject X might be process P executing as an application, and Subject Y might be the same process P executing a system call.

The notion of "access" is generalized to include how one process controls another one; therefore subjects are also objects. This means that the set of objects includes all the passive elements of the system plus all the subjects. Now the basic protection model can be described in terms of the system, subjects, objects, and mechanisms to specify the dynamic relationship among the subjects and objects.

A *protection system* is composed of a set of objects, a set of subjects, and a set of rules specifying the protection policy. It represents the accessibility of objects by subjects as defined by the system's *protection state*. The system guarantees that the protection state is checked for each access of an object, X, by a subject, S (Figure 14.5). The internal protection state can be changed only according to a set of rules that implement an external security policy.

The protection state can be conceptualized as an *access matrix*. The access matrix, A, has one row for each subject and one column for each object. Every subject is also an object, since processes need to be able to exercise control over other processes. Each entry in $A[S, X]$ is a set that describes the access rights held by subject S to object X.

Each access involves the following steps (see Figure 14.6):

1. Subject S initiates type α access to object X.

2. The protection system authenticates S and generates (S, α, X) on behalf of S. The subject cannot forge a subject identity, since the system supplies the identity.

3. The monitor for the object X interrogates $A[S, X]$. If $\alpha \in A[S, X]$, the access is valid. If $\alpha \notin A[S, X]$, the access is invalid.

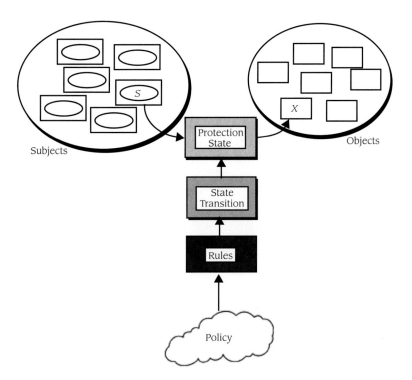

Figure 14.5
A Protection System

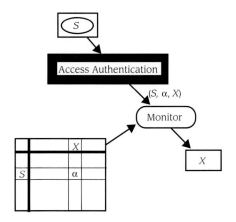

Figure 14.6
Representing the Protection State

An access matrix protection mechanism can be used to implement many different security policies. For example, suppose a simple system is composed as follows:

$$\text{subjects} = \{S_1, S_2, S_3\}$$
$$\text{objects} = \text{subjects} \cup \{F_1, F_2, D_1, D_2\}$$

where F_1 and F_2 are files and D_1 and D_2 are devices. Figure 14.7 is an access matrix that represents an example protection state for the system. Each subject has `control` privilege to itself. S_1 has `block`, `wakeup`, and `owner` privileges over S_2 and `control` and `owner` privileges to S_3. File F_1 can be accessed by S_1 with `read*` or `write*` access. S_2 is F_1's owner, and S_3 has `delete` access.

If, for example, S_2 attempts update access to F_2, then it initiates the access, thereby causing the protection system to create a record of the form $(S_2, \text{update}, F_2)$. The record is given to the monitor for F_2, which interrogates $A[S_2, F_2]$. Since update is in $A[S_2, F_2]$, the access is valid and the subject is allowed to update the file object. If S_2 attempts `execute` access to F_2, then it initiates the access, thereby causing the protection system to create a record of the form $(S_2, \text{execute}, F_2)$. The record is given to the monitor for F_2, which interrogates $A[S_2, F_2]$. Since `execute` is not in $A[S_2, F_2]$, the access is invalid and the violation is reported to the OS.

14.3.2 ■ Changing the Protection State

The protection system uses *policy rules* to control the means by which it alters the protection state. Therefore, a policy can be specified by choosing the type of accesses appearing in the matrix and by specifying a set of rules for protection state transitions. An example set of rules from [Graham and Denning, 1972] is used here to illustrate how rights can be passed among subjects.

For example, the rules shown in Figure 14.8 implement a particular protection policy. They are defined using the access types shown in Figure 14.7. In the figure, S_0 attempts to change the protection state by executing the command to change entry $A[S, X]$ in the access matrix. For example, S_0 might attempt to `grant` read access to S_3

	S_1	S_2	S_3	F_1	F_2	D_1	D_2
S_1	control	block wakeup owner	control owner	read* write*		seek	owner
S_2		control	stop control	owner delete	update execute owner	owner	seek*
S_3					owner		

Figure 14.7
A Protection State

RULE	COMMAND BY S_0	AUTHORIZATION	EFFECT
1	transfer{α|α*} to (S, X)	α* ∈ A[S_0, X]	A[S, X] = A[S, X] ∪ {α|α*}
2	grant{α|α*} to (S, X)	owner ∈ A[S_0, X]	A[S, X] = A[S, X] ∪ {α|α*}
3	delete α from (S, X)	control ∈ A[S_0, S] or owner ∈ A[S_0, X]	A[S, X] = A[S, X] – {α}

Figure 14.8
Policy Rules

for D_2. The command can be executed only if owner belongs to $A[S_0, X]$, thus causing read access to be added to $A[S_3, D_2]$. The goal of the example security policy is to address the problems of masquerading, sharing parameters, and confinement.

In the policy rules, the * is called a *copy flag*. A process, S_0, can transfer an access right, α, to object X to another process, S, if S_0 has an access to X and the copy flag is set for the α access to X. In Figure 14.7, S_1 can change the protection state by transferring read or read* access to S_2 or S_3 for F_1 because S_1 has the copy flag set on the read access. According to Rule 2, a subject, S_0, can grant any access to an object X—with or without the copy flag set—provided S_0 owns the X.

The copy flag and the rules are designed to prevent indiscriminate propagation of access rights among subjects. A right can be propagated only when the owner passes the copy flag to another subject. The copy flag can be transferred from one subject to another, or the right can be transferred to a subject with the copy flag cleared. The transfer rule is a nondestructive copy rule. Another policy might require the transfer to be destructive, meaning that when a nonowner subject transfers an access to another subject, the first subject loses its own access. Such a policy might be useful to closely guard the dissemination of rights by the owner subjects. The delete rule is used to revoke a right for an object from another subject. Before a subject can delete an object, it must either have control over the subject that loses the access or be the owner of the object. According to the policy implied by this set of rules, if a subject is the owner of another subject, it also has control over the subject.

This example illustrates the basic complexity of the problem of determining if the mechanism is sufficient to implement a broad class of policies and if the mechanism and policy combined actually implement an acceptable solution. However, it also shows how rules can be used to build up a desired policy.

Graham and Denning [1972] show that the rules shown in Figure 14.8 (along with a few others) define a protection system that can be used to address several of the protection problems mentioned at the beginning of this section:

- *Masquerading:* The model requires that implementations prevent one subject from masquerading as another. The authentication module can be as complex as any security policy requires. After the module authenticates the subject, it generates an unforgeable signature for S to perform an α-access to X, (S, α, X) and then passes it to X's monitor. This prevents masquerading.

■ *Confinement and allocating rights:* For the model and rules to address the confinement problem, they must provide a mechanism by which rights can be restricted to some designated set of subjects. The copy flag restricts rights propagation through the access transfer, and ownership is required to grant rights. There is a more subtle problem to consider, however. It is desirable to be able to restrict subjects' ability to propagate rights and information. Because `read` access provides the ability to copy information, it is difficult to allow an untrusted subsystem to provide service while ensuring it does not retain rights nor information. In general, this requires that the suspicious subject be guaranteed to be *memoryless*—that is *confined* with respect to its ability to retain information or to leak it to other subjects. This means that the confinement problem can be fully solved only by considering the behavior of programs. If the untrusted subject cannot be shown to be memoryless, the confinement problem cannot be solved.

■ *Sharing of parameters:* Sharing of parameters can be closely monitored by allowing only indirect access to objects by untrusted subjects. An owner subject can create a *gatekeeper* subject to protect an object from unwanted accesses by untrusted subjects. Essentially, this amounts to the owner's delegating access control to the gatekeeper. The ultimate owner need have only owner access over the gatekeeper subject, thereby obtaining implicit ownership of the object. The owner can revoke the untrusted subsystem's access to the gatekeeper subject at any time, and the gatekeeper can authenticate each access from the untrusted subject.

■ *Trojan horse:* The Trojan horse problem arises because a process assumes the rights of another process while executing on its behalf. The model distinguishes between two processes using the same rights as different subjects. The model could make it possible for this problem to be solved with an appropriate set of rules—different ones than those used in the example. However, many rule sets may solve the problem for specific policies but do not guarantee a solution independent of the policy. (Contrast this with the solution of, for example, masquerading, where the problem is guaranteed to be solved by the choice of rules, independent of the policy.)

14.3.3 ■ The Cost of Protection Mechanisms

It is worthwhile pointing out that protection mechanisms introduce administrative overhead that can severely impact system performance. The basic protection model requires that each resource access be passed through a monitor before it can be allowed to take place. This may introduce a substantial performance cost. The OS designer must decide if the cost in performance is justified for the presence of the protection mechanism. In environments in which information must be secure (for example, information about a corporation's financial position or concerning the national defense), the performance cost may not be an issue. The information must be protected; otherwise, the computer system provides no useful benefit.

Nevertheless, a challenge for OS designers is to design the most efficient mechanisms possible. This challenge is considered next.

14.4 ■ Implementing Internal Authorization

The protection model in Section 14.3 describes a logical set of components that can be used to solve various protection problems. What implementations are cost effective for the model? How can an access matrix be implemented efficiently? As in virtual memory systems, implementing a system that behaves exactly like the theoretical model is very costly, so implementations approximate the behavior specified by the model. This section considers implementation strategies.

The generalized protection mechanism is based on a means to save the protection state, to query the state to validate ongoing access, and to change the state. There are several issues to consider in implementing the mechanism:

- The access matrix is not the only possible representation of the protection state, but it is the basis of most implementations.

- The access matrix must be represented in some secure storage medium, only to be read and written by selected processes.

- The goal of the design is to route all accesses through the protection monitor. Such routing will ensure that the current protection state will be used to validate each access.

- The protection system should be able to authenticate the source of each request by a subject, rather than being passed the subject's identity as a parameter through a procedure call.

- The monitor must be a protected process to implement the rules. It must not be possible for other subjects to compromise the monitor and state transition mechanism—for example, by sharing its resources.

The next sections describe how processes can take on different access rights in different domains, in addition to the implementation of the protection monitor and access matrix.

14.4.1 ■ Protection Domains

Figure 14.9 is a visualization of two protection domains. The inner domain represents programs executed in the supervisor mode—in the context of protection, the process is said to execute in the *supervisor domain*. Programs operating in the supervisor domain have additional access rights compared to programs operating in the user domain—for example, rights to memory as well as the right to execute the extended instruction set. If p is a process, then subject $S_1 = (p, \text{user\_mode})$ has fewer rights than does $S_2 = (p,$

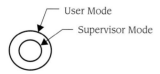

Figure 14.9
A Two-level Domain Architecture

supervisor_mode). Information in each domain is ordinarily stored in files or segments, where the file descriptor describes the domain in which the contents are either executed or used.

The generalization of the two-level domain is a set of N concentric rings called a domain *ring architecture* for protection (see Figure 14.10). The ring architecture is described by generalizing the Multics architecture in which it first appeared [Organick, 1972]. Suppose the protection system is organized as N rings of protection in which rings R_0 through R_S support the operating system domain and rings R_{S+1} through R_{N-1} are used by applications. Thus $i < j$ means that R_i has more rights than R_j. The most critical part of the kernel (in terms of protection) executes in ring R_0. The next more secure level of the OS executes in R_1, and so on. The most secure level of user programs executes in ring R_{S+1}, with successively less secure software executing in outer rings. In this model, the hardware supervisor mode would ordinarily be used when software is executing in the lowest-numbered rings, perhaps only in R_0 (as was the case in Multics). This part of the OS is the most carefully designed and implemented and is presumably proved to be correct.

Software that executes in a ring resides in a file assigned to that ring. The protection mechanism provides a means by which a process can safely change domains—that is, cross rings. If a file in R_i is being executed, then the process can call any procedure in R_j ($j \geq i$) without special permission, since that call represents a call to a domain with less protection. However, when a process calls an outer ring, the OS mechanism must ensure that the return and parameter references, which will be an inner ring reference, will be allowed. Inner ring calls can be accomplished only by having the outer ring software enter an inner ring through a ring gatekeeper—a monitored procedure entry point. Each attempted crossing of an inner ring causes an internal authorization mechanism to validate the call, for example, by trapping to a part of R_0, which then invokes the gatekeeper for the destination ring.

Whenever a process makes an inward call, it changes domains; that is, it becomes a different subject. Implicitly, when a process calls a process in an inner ring, the target function is in a distinct file kept in the inner ring. An alternative view is that the OS has temporarily *amplified* the rights of the process as long as the process executes proce-

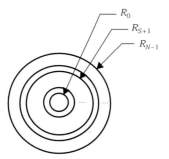

Figure 14.10
The Ring Architecture

dures in the inner ring domain. When the process returns to the outer ring, it will again change domains and resume its previous set of rights.

The generalized ring structure does not need to support inner ring data accesses, only procedure calls. Data kept in inner rings can be accessed using a corresponding inner ring access procedure, much like an abstract data type allows references to its fields only through public interfaces.

Ring structures are used in contemporary computer architectures. For example, the Intel 80386 microprocessor incorporated a four-level structure that has some similarities to the one described here. In the Intel case, there were three levels of instruction sets. Level 2 and 3 instructions were the normal application program instruction sets, although noncritical portions of the OS code were assumed to execute at level 2. Level 1 instructions included I/O instructions. Level 0 instructions manipulated segmented memory using a system global descriptor table and performed context switching. The architecture and its successors (the 80486 and Pentium microprocessors) are intended to support memory segment manipulation at level 0, while I/O operations operate at a lower security level—that is, a higher ring number. The main body of the OS operates at level 2, where its segments are protected by the ring structure.

14.4.2 ■ Implementing the Access Matrix

The access matrix can be implemented in any of several ways. For most collections of subjects and objects, the matrix will be sparse, since most objects will be accessible only by a few subjects and most subjects will access only a few objects. This suggests that efficient implementations might use lists of entries rather than storing the matrix in a rectangular array. For example, the list can contain entries of the form $(S_i, X_j, \{\alpha\})$ if $\{\alpha\}$ is the set of strings logically stored in $A[S_i, X_j]$. The tradeoff is the usual one for sparse matrices. That is, the length of the list is proportional to the number of entries in the matrix—dense matrices yield unwieldy lists.

Alternatively, the matrix could be partitioned into column vectors, with each vector stored as a list of rights to the object it is protecting. Now the monitor for the object can easily search the list whenever S_i attempts an access to the object. The vector is called an *access control list* (*ACL*) for the given object.

Similarly, compressed rows of the access matrix can be associated with the subjects. Whenever the subject initiates an access, the protection system checks the list to see if the subject has the right—the *capability*—to access the designated object. Thus access rights are allocated to the subject much like tickets to an event. If the subject does not possess a capability in its list, then it may not even know the name of the object. When the access matrix is stored in this manner, it is called a *capability list*. Access control lists and capabilities are considered in more detail next. Kerberos tickets are an example of capabilities.

Early systems attempted to provide a protection mechanism using locks and keys. This approach is described in the next subsection. It is a simple mechanism that has some of the properties of ACLs and some of capability lists. Before looking more closely at these full implementations of access matrices, we briefly review the lock and key approach.

14.4.2.1 ■ Memory Locks and Keys

Since the 1970s, considerable effort has gone into incorporating protection monitors for memory objects. Early protection monitors did not support the full generality of the access matrix. Instead, they used a weak form of an ACL.

An allocatable unit of memory may be a word, a partition, a page frame, or a segment. In the 1960s, machines sometimes used memory locks on each allocatable block of h bytes. Suppose each block can be assigned a k-bit *lock* value and each process descriptor includes a k-bit *key* setting (see Figure 14.11). When a block of memory is allocated to a process, the lock is set to be the same as the process's key. Process key and memory locks can be set only while the system is in supervisor mode. The access is checked by hardware on each memory access by keeping the key value in a CPU register and by incorporating a lock register on the memory. Thus these memory locks can be thought of as access control lists. The lock register is loaded with the lock whenever a word in its block is referenced. If the lock and key are the same, the access is allowed; otherwise, the access attempt results in a trap to the operating system. In computers of the 1960s, $h = 16$ and $k = 4$. This meant either the degree of multiprogramming was limited to 16, or locks and keys were reused so that one process's key might coincidentally open a lock on memory held by another process.

This approach is simple to implement and is also efficient at runtime. However, it does not discriminate among different types of access, and it disallows sharing with the OS or among user processes, since the key and lock must match exactly. The sharing problem can be remedied by reserving patterns for special usage; for example, one key pattern might be a "master key" for any subject that has supervisor rights. The corresponding lock pattern may mean "unprotected" memory accessible by any subject. Supervisor access and sharing can then be implemented, although the sharing mechanism is weak.

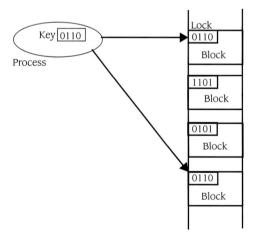

Figure 14.11
Memory Locks

14.4.2.2 ■ Access Control Lists

Access control lists have been used in more general forms for many years. In this approach, the resource manager incorporates an ACL for each resource. In most applications, the subject is authenticated only when it opens or is otherwise allocated the resource (rather than on each access). If the subject and its access type are not in the ACL, then the allocation or open operation fails.

The UNIX file protection mechanism is a well-known application of the ACL approach. Every UNIX user is identified by a user identification, a UID. Each user also can belong to various groups of users, noted by the group identification, the GID. The UID and GID for a process are part of the process's descriptor, which means they are easily checked by any system program when the process attempts to access a file.

Figure 14.12 is the result of executing

```
ls -lg
```

in a directory containing two directories (`Tools` and `bin`) and three files (`Makefile`, `bangfix`, and `cover.tex`). The directory listing shows that each file is owned by the user with login `gjn`. `Makefile` and `bin` have a group ID of `rtsg`, `Tools` is in `ctrg`, and the others are in `faculty`. The first 10 characters in each line describe the permissions required to access the corresponding file or directory. The "d" in the first character position means the entry is a directory and the "-" means the entry is a file. The next nine characters are interpreted in three-character groups, with the first describing the permissions that the file owner, `gjn`, has to the entry. The second group describes the permissions that members of the named group have to the file. The third group describes the permissions that all other users have—called "world" permission bits. If a triplet has an "r" in the first position, the corresponding user has read permission on the file or directory; a "-" means the user does not have read permission. The second position in the triplet represents write permission, "w," and the third position represents execute permission, "x." File `Makefile` is set so that `gjn` and any member of `rtsg` have read permission to the file. Any user process can read the `cover.tex` file, but only members of `faculty` and `gjn` can write to the file.

Each file also has the setUID flag bit that can be used to temporarily increase a process's rights when the process is executing a trusted software module. When a process

```
-r--r-----  1 gjn     rtsg        2335 Apr 11  1996 Makefile
drwxr-xr-x  2 gjn     ctrg         512 Feb  5 10:27 Tools
---x--x---  1 gjn     faculty    37846 Feb  4 12:42 bangfix
drwxr-xr-x  3 gjn     rtsg         512 Feb  5 11:36 bin
-rw-rw-r--  1 gjn     faculty      853 Jan  6  1996 cover.tex
```

Figure 14.12
UNIX File Protection Mask

executes the program that is loaded in a file with its setUID bit enabled, it assumes the UID of the process that owns the file as long as it is executing the program stored in the file.

The lowest level of the Windows NT kernel supports secure operation by including a full ACL mechanism [Solomon, 1998]. The main part of the kernel checks each object's access according to a protection policy specified by user-space components. Whenever any thread makes a system call to access a kernel object, the part of the kernel that handles the access passes a description of the attempted access to the authentication mechanism. The object contains a security descriptor identifying the object's owner, and an ACL of processes that are permitted access to the object. The authentication mechanism determines the thread's identity and access type, then verifies that the thread is allowed to access the object (according to the information in the ACL).

14.4.2.3 ■ Capabilities

A *capability* is a unique, global name for an access right to an object in a system. Thus a capability might be a Kerberos ticket, as well as "read access to sector i on disk k" and "write access to virtual address i in process j's address space." In the context of the protection model, a row in the access matrix is a list of capabilities each of the form (object, α-access) held by subject S. Capabilities are used in contemporary operating systems to implement a protection mechanism and to span address spaces among subjects. Chapter 18 describes how some operating systems use capabilities as a fundamental reference mechanism for all entities.

A capability serves two purposes. First, it provides an address for a resource in a very large address space. Second, possession of the capability represents the authorization of the subject to the described object. The latter is a key aspect of capability-based systems (recall the Kerberos example). That is, when a subject obtains a capability, authentication occurs. Once the capability has been issued, it is not necessary for a runtime monitor and access matrix to check each access.

The use of capabilities suggest certain properties, as follows:

■ The values taken on by a capability must be derived from a large name space. This is because a system using capabilities will need many different instances of a capability in order to represent all accesses to all objects by all subjects.

■ Capabilities must be unique and not reused once they have been assigned. This prevents a "recycled" capability from inadvertently providing a subject with access to an object left over from its original use.

■ Capabilities need to be distinguishable from spurious names. For example, the system must not confuse ordinary integers or pointers with capabilities.

There are two basic approaches to implementing capabilities. Either they may be wholly implemented within the operating system's address space, or the hardware may incorporate specialized support for capabilities. As a practical approach, capabilities are sometimes implemented by providing a very large space and then issuing capabilities randomly from it. This approach, however, does not guarantee absolute protection; capabilities are not guaranteed to be unique although there is high probability that they will be.

A capability can be represented in the OS as a typed scalar value. It is conceptually a record of the form

```
struct capability{
   type tag;
   long addr;
}
```

If c is a capability, then its tag field, c.tag, is set to have the value capability; then the address field, c.addr, is the global address that the capability references. A subject can access an object only if it has a capability whereby c.addr addresses an "entry point" to the resource that corresponds to the type of the access. If an object monitor is included at all, it need only verify that c.tag is set to have the capability value in order to be assured that the access is valid.

Each subject needs to be able to obtain and use capabilities, but none can be allowed to generate them. If the subject's capabilities are all maintained in the operating system's space, the subject is unable to create a data structure resembling a capability without the intervention of the OS. However, the subject can use its capabilities for accessing objects with no special handling by the OS. In the case that capabilities are exclusively managed by the OS, the tag field in the data structure can be eliminated, since the type is implied by the use of the capability. For example, in a segmented virtual-memory system, all capabilities are stored in a subject's capability segment.

Tags can be implemented in hardware by associating a tag field with each unit of memory. For example, early Burroughs computer architectures used hardware capabilities. The tag field in the word can be set to capability or other by a supervisor mode instruction. The tag field can be read only by a supervisor mode instruction in the object's protection monitor.

The Mach OS provides kernel-level capabilities. Mach is the successor of the Rochester Intelligent Gateway (RIG) and Accent operating systems. All three used capabilities in various ways. The use of capabilities in the IPC mechanism is a good illustration of how capabilities are used in many contemporary operating systems [Accetta, et al., 1986].

Mach IPC is based on messages and ports. A message is a data structure, and a port is a communication channel that is implemented in the kernel and used to receive messages from other threads. Each port accepts messages of a particular type. If one thread wishes to suspend another, it sends a suspend message to the target's thread port. Hence, if one thread knows the location and type of another thread's ports, then it has a capability with which it can control the second thread.

Ports are protected kernel objects that must be requested and allocated before they can be used. If a thread knows a port, then it has the authority to send messages to the port, and the receiver will honor those messages. The kernel must allocate a port before it can be used. Ports are equivalent to capabilities. If a thread has the capability, it can send messages to the port; if it does not, it cannot send messages to the port. Section 18.7 elaborates on this example.

14.5 ▪ Cryptography

It is inevitable that even in a secure OS, crucial information will sometimes be temporarily unprotected; for example, when information such as an access matrix entry or a capability is transferred from one part of the system to another. An example of this was given in the Kerberos authentication strategy. Cryptographic techniques can be used to convert *clear text* (or plain text) to *ciphered text* to protect the text whenever it is exposed on an unprotected medium. An encryption function, `encrypt`, and a decryption function, `decrypt` (where `decrypt` is an inverse function of `encrypt`), are defined, where

```
decrypt(key', encrypt(key, clearText)) = clearText
```

`encrypt` with a key, encodes the clear text into ciphered text. A different key, `key'`, is used by `decrypt` to translate the ciphered text back into clear text.

There are two strategies for constructing encryption and decryption mechanisms. One is to build a design in which details of `encrypt` and `decrypt` are unknown so that part of the mechanism is in the secrecy of the implementation. Another is to build a design in which the mechanism is public but the keys are secret and difficult to forge. In the first case, `encrypt` and `decrypt` are complex, thus making it difficult to guess how the translation is accomplished. In the second case, the keys are complex, thus making it difficult to guess a key.

There is a class of symmetric encryption techniques in which the encryption key is the same as the decryption key. This form of encryption is useful if a trusted subsystem performs both the encryption and decryption of information. For example, an OS user authentication system might use this technique for saving passwords. When the user declares a password, the OS uses its private key for encrypting the data and storing it in a password object. At authentication time, the OS uses its key to decode the entry in the password object to compare it to the password supplied by the user. UNIX takes this approach to protect passwords.

Asymmetric encryption and decryption are required in cases in which different subjects perform the encryption and decryption. Each may then have its own private key, suitable for encrypting or decrypting, depending on the rights of the subject. This form of cryptography is required in general protection policies.

Public key cryptography is an instance of the class of asymmetric algorithms whereby one key, K_s is public, but the other key, K_p, is kept secret. If the clear text is encrypted using K_s, it can then be decrypted by K_p, and vice versa. Though the K_s key is kept secure by one user, the K_p key is published to anyone with whom the user wishes to communicate. Then anyone knowing K_p can send secure information to the person holding K_s by encrypting it using K_p. (If the mechanism is correct, then no one other than the holder of K_p can decrypt a message that has been encrypted using K_s.)

In this approach, the holder of the K_s can also create information that any one else can test for authenticity. The creator uses K_s to encrypt the information. Then anyone else can use K_p to see if it decrypts the information. If it does, the information is authentic.

A user can generate authenticated, private communications as follows:

1. The information is signed by the sender and then encrypted with the signature K_s.

2. The encrypted signature and information are encrypted with the receiver's public key.

Pretty good privacy (PGP) is a popular public key cryptography system developed by Zimmerman [1994]. In PGP, public keys include the owner's electronic mail address, the time the key was created, and key characters. Secure keys include the identification and creation time, along with private key characters and a password. A key is kept in a *key certificate,* which includes the owner ID, the time the key-pair was generated, and the material defining the key. A public key certificate contains the public key material, and secure key certificates contain the secret key material. A user can keep several such public key and secure key certificates on public and secure key rings.

A *message digest* is a 128-bit "cryptographically strong one-way hash function" of a message that is to be transmitted in an unsecure network [Zimmerman, 1994]. In general, it is impossible to counterfeit a message digest. Once the message digest has been computed, a signature for the message is derived by encrypting the message digest using the secure key. A secret document is signed by producing a header that contains an internal 64-bit key ID, a signature, and a timestamp of when the signature was created. The recipient uses the key ID either to retrieve the sender's public key (from the receiver's own public key ring), if it is authenticating the message, or to retrieve its own secure key from its secure key ring, if it is decrypting a message.

PGP is widely used for distributing information in networks, since the software is distributed without cost and (unlike Kerberos) it does not require the presence of an authentication server.

14.6 ■ Summary

Protection mechanisms are implemented in operating systems to support various security policies. The goal of the security system is to authenticate subjects and to authorize their access to any object. If the subject is a user, the mechanism verifies that the user is as claimed to be, with the set of predetermined rights set by the system policy maker.

Internal authorization is concerned with verifying that a subject, corresponding to a process executing in a protection domain, has the right to access an object according to the current protection state. The idealized protection model calls for authenticating each access operation according to the current protection state. The security policy must specify how the protection state can change. This is accomplished by specifying a set of rules that represent the policy for changing protection states.

Implementations of the idealized model make assumptions about the model so that the system can be built cost-effectively. The key components of the implementation are the subject authentication module, the resource monitor, and the representation of the protection state (using an access matrix). The innovation in protection system implementation is in the state and resource monitor designs.

Protection domains are extensions of the hardware supervisor mode ability. The ring model generalizes the domains established by the mode flag so that the operating system may support a variety of domains. The access matrix may be implemented as a list of entries in a row saved with the subject, called a capability list. It may also be implemented as an access control list—a list of entries in a column stored with the object.

Cryptography is often used to protect information in cases in which it cannot always be kept in a secure medium; as the Internet usage increases, the importance of cryptography increases. The information to be protected is encrypted while it is not being processed, including while it is in the file system and while it is being transmitted from one computer to another on a network.

14.7 ■ Exercises

1. Assume that a timesharing computer provides a mechanism by which a file can be read by any user but can be written by only one. Informally describe a security policy for administering student transcripts on the computer system (limit your description to a half of one typed page). Students should be able to read their grades but not change them. The Registrar's office must be able to change the grade files.

2. Describe a mechanism—hardware and software—for authenticating users based on their fingerprints. This is an open-ended question in which you are to think about innovative designs based on your imagination (perhaps as it is influenced by movies, science fiction, and so on). Very high-security installations do use such mechanisms.

3. Dynamic relocation hardware is usually considered to be a basic memory protection mechanism. What is the protection state in relocation hardware? How does the operating system ensure that the protection state is not changed indiscriminately?

4. Explain the exact steps a client and server take in Kerberos to authenticate that a message is from the party it claims to be. (You may find it useful to consult the information on the Web regarding Kerberos.)

5. Given the protection state shown in Figure 14.7 and the rules shown in Figure 14.8, do the following.

   a. Explain how S_3 can cause the protection state to be changed so that it has write access to F_2.
   b. Specify two different ways by which S_3 can obtain read permission to F_1.
   c. Explain whether S_3 can obtain seek permission to D_1 from S_1. Why or why not?

6. Use a text editor to read a UNIX system's password file, /etc/passwd. You should be able to find a single-line entry in the ASCII file for your own login. Speculate how your password is saved in /etc/passwd. What user is the owner of /etc/passwd? Do you have write permission for /etc/passwd?

7. Consider a variant of the k-bit key and lock scheme described for memory protection whereby a process can access memory blocks for which every bit position set to 1 within the lock is also set to 1 in the process's key.

   a. How many unique locks are in the system?
   b. Characterize all keys that access a memory block with the lock 01100110 for $k = 8$.
   c. Show how this mechanism can be used to allow a process B to keep some memory blocks private, to share some with process A, and to share others with process C (but for which A and C do not share any memory blocks).

8. Suppose a UNIX system has been set up so that each student and the instructor have their own ID and all are in the same group (with no other users). The files used by the course are on a timesharing system used by other courses.

   a. What permissions should a student have on a file that contains a homework solution?
   b. What permissions should the instructor have on a file that contains course grades?
   c. What permissions should be assigned to a file (owned by the instructor) that is readable and writable by the instructor, executable by a student in the course, and inaccessible to any other student?
   d. Suppose the instructor wants a directory in which each student can write a solution file, but only the instructor can read the files. What permission should the directory have?

9. Explain how the UNIX file protection mechanism could be used to allow any process to read and modify a system file by using special commands named `getSpecial` and `putSpecial`.

10. Argue for conditions under which the access control method is superior to the capability list approach for implementing the access matrix.

15

Networks

The Network SouthEast area offers a wide choice of destinations, for visits to castles, country homes and museums, to seaside resorts, ports and harbours, to picturesque villages, to cathedrals and churches, and to large towns and cities for shopping and tourism.

—Paul Atterbury, *Daytrips from London by Train* ■

CHAPTER OBJECTIVES

Networks are a composition of hardware, system software, and application software. A network device in and of itself provides no significant value to a computer. However, the combination of network devices on multiple machines and a multidrop communication subnetwork creates a communications environment in which diverse processes can communicate with one another across machine boundaries. Because of the spectrum of functions required to make a network useful, the ISO Open Systems Interconnection (OSI) architecture model provides a framework for implementing these functions.

This chapter discusses how today's networks have evolved from traditional computer communications using serial ports and modems to specialized networks with elaborate software support. After describing the ISO OSI model, it reviews the characteristics of network hardware. It then focuses on the parts of the network that are implemented in the OS. Finally, it describes naming and the client-server model of computation in order to illustrate how these important application requirements drive OS support of the network.

15.1 ▪ From Computer Communications to Networks

Contemporary networks are based on telecommunications technology. A serial port (see Chapter 5) can transmit and receive bytes to/from an external device. Computer-to-computer communications take advantage of the serial port technology by connecting a *modem* (MOdulator-DEModulator) to the serial port (see Figure 15.1). The modem converts digital signals sent from a serial port controller into analog signals that can be transmitted over a conventional telephone network. Another modem attached to a remote computer can receive the analog signals produced by the modem and convert them back into the digital signals sent by the first controller. The receiving modem passes the digital signal to its controller. Then the data can be received by the driver software on the remote computer.

This point-to-point, character-oriented communications technology is the basis of modern networks. Any computer with a modem and telephone connection can be programmed to establish a connection with another computer having a modem and a telephone connection. Once the telephone connection has been established, the two computers exchange information using a previously agreed upon *network communication protocol* (or simply *protocol*) to establish the syntax and semantics of the exchange.

Contemporary network controllers incorporate protocols to apply a structure to the stream of characters written to or read from the I/O device. Today, most network protocols send and receive blocks of information called *packets* over a serial network. As shown in Figure 15.2, computer network technology replaces the modem, telephone connection, and telephone switching system with specialized *data communication subnetworks* that contain their own means for allowing a sender to transmit a packet to any other machine on the communication subnetwork.

Like the other devices described in Chapter 5, the hardware/software interface to the network controller is implemented between the device driver and the controller hardware. However, the controller is attached to a communication subnetwork rather

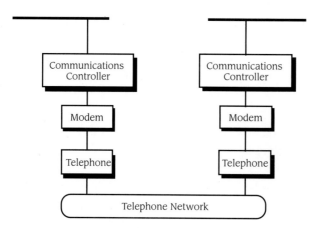

Figure 15.1
Connecting Computers Using the Telephone Network

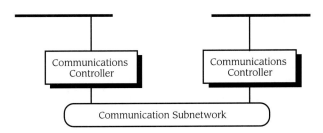

Figure 15.2
Data Networks

than to a local device such as a storage device or terminal. The need for protocols to coordinate the behavior of the sender and the receiver covers a broad spectrum of functions, from determining how one machine detects a signal from another machine to agreement about the format of a floating-point number. Just as some of the functions in managing structure in files can be implemented as part of the applications software, so can some of the network protocol function. Also, just as the basic part of the file system must be implemented in the storage devices and OS, so must part of the network be implemented in the hardware and OS. This chapter and the next two focus on the part of the network that must be handled by the OS.

15.1.1 ■ Communication Subnetworks

The communication subnetwork is a logical medium by which one host computer attached to the network transmits a block of bytes, informally called a *packet,* to any other host computer attached to the network. A process on a host system transmits information by preparing a logical packet with an address and then writing the packet to the communication subnetwork. A process at the destination host computer reads the information by reading the packet of bytes from the subnetwork. Such a communication subnetwork is called a *multidrop packet network.*

In a multidrop packet network, the goal is to provide a cost-effective means to provide faster and cheaper packet networks than can be achieved using the telephone network. The various functions provided by a multidrop packet communication subnetwork include these:

■ Design and implement the most cost-effective "switch fabric"—the medium to carry signals among the host machines connected to the network.

■ Convert a packet into a form to transmit it over the physical medium.

■ Reconstruct incoming transmitted information to form a packet.

■ Direct packets to a destination host, called packet addressing.

The Xerox *Ethernet* network is a widely used multidrop packet network in which bits are transmitted serially over a shared communications medium. When the Ethernet was first implemented in 1980, the physical medium was required to be a coaxial cable, similar to the kind of cable used for cable TV and CB radio antennae. Now the Ethernet can also use twisted pairs of wires, similar to the kind used by a telephone or modem.

Software uses the Ethernet by reading and writing variable-sized packets from/to the Ethernet controller. In a write operation, the network controller receives a copy of the packet to hold in a buffer while the network device transmits the contents bit-by-bit. It is beyond the scope of this book to explain the exact technique used by the device to obtain control of the network and for transmitting information, although those techniques were so economical that they created a breakthrough for the use of data networks in the early 1980s. Today's Ethernet can transmit up to 1 Gbps among a set of hosts connected by a cable up to 1 kilometer in length.

15.1.2 ■ Network Communication Protocols

In the late 1960s, researchers and developers began to experiment with networks. It soon became apparent that different applications required different functions in the communication subnetwork, implying that the subnetwork had to support many more functions than first expected. Also apparent was that there were many additional functions that could substantially improve the way the basic signaling mechanism was used. For example, these additional functions would allow the network to do the following:

- Control information delivery rates.
- Provide a means for a host on one network to communicate with a host on a different network.
- Allow a stream of packets to contain a stream of bytes analogous to a byte stream file (or UNIX pipe).
- Ensure reliable transmission in cases in which information might occasionally be lost in the network.
- Provide security features.
- Provide a standard pattern of behavior for processes involved in IPC across the network.
- Be used to transfer files.
- Be used to allow a user on one machine to log in to a different machine.
- Simulate a procedure call from a process on one machine to a procedure on another.
- Translate information among machine-dependent representations (since different machines often use different representations for multibyte words).

Furthermore, it became clear that some applications required many of these generic functions, while others required only a few. This led to the idea of implementing the functions in a layered architecture, similar to that used in operating systems, as described in Chapter 18. Such an approach requires that the functions be divided into sets and that there be a partial order among the sets so that any operation in a more abstract set (layer) can use any of the functions in its supporting layer. In networks, the functionality implemented in any layer defines a network communication protocol by which the software written to use that level can communicate with other software using the same level. Applications can be built to use either a subset of the functions at a layer or only layers 0 through K in an N-layer organization ($K < N$).

The idea of protocols is not new to networks. Programmers routinely use protocols to allow one part of their program to communicate with other parts. For example, a function call protocol specifies that the calling part of the program will identify another part of the program it wishes to communicate with by using a function name. In ANSI C, the function prototype explicitly specifies the protocol for how parameters will be passed—the number and type of each argument.

As mentioned in the previous subsection, protocols are also used in reading from and writing to files. When a process writes to a structured file, it follows a protocol for formatting the information so that any other process can use the protocol to read the information from the file.

Network communication depends on two autonomous processes existing at the same time and on their agreeing to communicate. Cooperative communication can succeed only if the two processes agree on the precise syntax and semantics of the information to be exchanged. For example, if process p_1 intends to send a file to process p_2, both processes must first synchronize according to the mechanisms described in Chapter 8. Hence, p_2 should be prepared to read the network to accept the file when p_1 transmits it. What should the units of data transfer be? Is there a useful common model for the data? Should there be more than one model? If the machines have different representations for floating-point numbers, how should the processes ensure conversion is done appropriately? To address these and a myriad of other questions, the programs for the two processes must agree on a protocol defining all the syntactic and semantic aspects of the communication.

File transfer is only one kind of communication. The processes may wish to exchange messages, to request remote services, and so on. So there are many different network protocols used to address the range of communications applications. This has all led to an evolutionary path in network development that is guided by an international standard, called the ISO Open Systems Interconnection (OSI) architecture. The model specifies general aspects of protocols, in some cases including highly specific details of the protocols. The ISO OSI architecture is described next.

15.2 ■ The ISO OSI Network Architecture Model

The ISO OSI architecture model is the dominant model for defining network protocols in contemporary networks. The model is a standard architecture that has been adopted by a wide class of developers and users (though details within the architecture may vary). It is helpful to consider the evolution of the model to understand why it has the form it does.

15.2.1 ■ The Evolution of Network Protocols

In the late 1960s, network technology evolved to the point that distributed computing began to be cost effective for a few application domains. By 1975, the Department of Defense *ARPAnet* had been established as a working long-haul network to support a broad spectrum of defense applications in the United States. Meanwhile, in Europe, the X.25 network, which supported commercial applications, had become a viable technology.

In the late 1970s, the ISO was circulating its first draft documents on the OSI architecture model for network communication. The drafts reflected a strong influence by the X.25 network. Zimmerman [1980] wrote one of the first technical papers describing the ISO OSI model in detail. However, in the United States, the ARPAnet had already become the dominant force in network development.

By 1980, the Ethernet had irrefutably demonstrated the viability of the *local area network* (*LAN*) in a commercial domain [Metcalfe and Boggs, 1976]. Whereas X.25 and the ARPAnet were both directed at communications over distances measured in miles or hundreds of miles, the Ethernet was used to connect a set of machines located within a few hundred feet of one another (technically, up to 1 kilometer apart). X.25 and the ARPAnet transmitted information at variable rates of speed (in the range of 1Kbps to 1Mbps), depending on the part of the network being used. The research Ethernet transmitted information at a rate of 3 Mbps throughout its local area and the commercial counterpart at 10 Mbps. Today, the Ethernet can transmit signals at a rate of 100 Mbps.

The IBM System Network Architecture (SNA) also had a major impact on commercial computing installations during the 1970s. Whereas ARPAnet, X.25, and Ethernet protocols were openly available to anyone, the SNA protocols were proprietary. The importance of SNA was in establishing data networks as a viable technology. By 1980, SNA had introduced the Token Ring LAN as an alternative to the Ethernet to be used in open environments.

In 1980, DEC, Xerox, and Intel jointly announced the commercial Ethernet LAN. They adapted the midlayer ARPAnet protocols for use with their low-layer LAN. At roughly the same time, IBM announced its Token Ring LAN. An IEEE standards committee studied the Ethernet and the Token Ring in an attempt to arrive at a commercially viable standard LAN that complied with the ISO OSI model. A draft standard, IEEE 802, was published and used as the basis of LANs in the 1980s. In the IEEE 802 standard, both the Ethernet and Token Ring were accepted as alternatives, though it is not possible to directly connect an Ethernet and a Token Ring. This is an example of how the standard architecture model (IEEE 802 in this case) can be used for two different actual implementations. An IEEE 802 network can be built with an Ethernet implementation and another with a Token Ring implementation, yet the two cannot be directly connected. In the early 1990s, the IEEE 802 draft became the ISO 8802 standard for LAN communication.

Thus there were three major thrusts in network technology in the 1980s (see Figure 15.3). The ISO OSI model established the basis of standardized network protocols. They essentially came from the X.25 networks but were certainly influenced by the ARPAnet. Today, this model is the dominant general protocol architecture in networks. With the adaptation of key ARPAnet midlayer protocols by the Ethernet (specifically, TCP, UDP, and IP), the Ethernet rapidly became a success. When Ethernet was introduced as an IEEE draft standard, the Token Ring was its main competitor (along with another approach called the Token Bus). After several years of debate, the IEEE 802 committee adopted the Ethernet approach (IEEE 802.3), the Token Bus approach (IEEE 802.4), and the Token Ring approach (IEEE 802.5) within a single draft standard. The ISO 8802 is the international version of IEEE 802.

Unfortunately, the TCP/UDP/IP protocols do not strictly comply with the ISO OSI model details. However, with the commercial success of the Ethernet and Token Ring

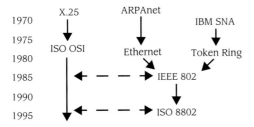

Figure 15.3
Network Evolution

LANs, considerable effort has been made either to change IEEE 802 or to modify ISO OSI so that the IEEE 802 networks would have some measure of compliance with the international standard. The dashed lines in Figure 15.3 indicate that the developers attempted to make this effort converge. Today, there is a continuing strong desire by end-user organizations to embrace the *framework* of the ISO OSI model, yet to use TCP/UDP/IP as an integral part of their implementation, since so many successful network products (including X windows and various file servers) use the ARPAnet protocols. Technically, TCP/UDP/IP organizations do not comply with the ISO OSI model, although they are often used as part of a networking strategy that is guided by that model. How this can be accomplished is shown after further explanation of the model.

15.2.2 ■ The ISO OSI Model

The ISO OSI architecture model defines a general set of functions found to be useful for all network communications. It then organizes those functions into a layered architecture. Any specific use of the network, such as a file transfer capability, uses a specific set of protocols, called a *protocol stack,* to specify the network protocol to be used for a particular network session. ISO OSI-compliant networks define a family of protocol stacks that have functions implemented in seven layers, as follows according to the architectural model:

- *Physical layer:* The lowest layer in the model. A specific protocol complying with the ISO OSI physical layer defines how bytes are to be encoded and transmitted to another machine. The RS–232 asynchronous serial communication protocol used to connect terminals, modems, and printers to computers resembles a physical layer protocol, although it is not normally considered to be a network protocol. The Ethernet carrier sensing and collision detection are good examples of a physical layer network protocol (see Section 15.3).

- *Data link layer:* Built on top of the physical layer and, in the case of Ethernet and Token Ring networks, implemented in hardware in conjunction with the physical layer. (However, in the case of SLIP and PPP the data link layer is a software implementation using an RS–232 physical layer; see Stevens [1994, ch. 2].) The data link layer defines a protocol that establishes the *frame*—the data link name for a packet. Frames of information incorporate a header, a block of data, and a trailer. A user of the data link layer can exchange frames with another host machine on a network. The data link layer is discussed in Section 15.3.

■ *Network layer:* Creates a very large address space of communication "endpoints" called an *internet address space.* This facility encouraged the development of networks of networks, called *internets,* in which each node in the internet is itself a network. Information is transmitted across the internet as *packets.* The network layer is usually implemented as a part of the OS. It is discussed in Section 15.4.

■ *Transport layer:* Uses the network to provide various application interfaces to the services implemented by the network layer, including block, byte stream, and record stream communication. It is usually implemented, at least in part, by the OS (with the rest of the implementation being system software). It is discussed in detail in Section 15.5.

■ *Session layer:* Extends the transport layer functionality by applying specific interprocess communication strategies. For example, a network message protocol or a remote procedure protocol would be implemented at the session layer. The session layer is typically implemented as application libraries. It is introduced in Chapter 17.

■ *Presentation layer:* Defines data abstraction and representation protocols and is also implemented as library code. It is summarized in Chapter 17.

■ *Application layer:* Implements application software for the distributed computation in the ISO OSI model. There are no standards for the application layer, since it is intended to apply to any domain. It exists in the model to illustrate where application programs fit into the layered architecture.

The layers in the ISO OSI model define a family of layered abstractions of communications functions. Each process uses a particular protocol stack, with selected members of the family to implement its own network. Figure 15.4 illustrates the relationship between the abstractions for two communications processes in terms of the ISO OSI model. The physical layer of the sending process is the only layer that actually transmits information to the physical layer of the receiving process. The data link layer of the sending process *logically* transmits a frame to the data link layer of the receiver. It does this by *physically* translating the frame into the form used by the physical layer and then passing the information to the physical layer so that it can transmit the information. The physical layer transmits the information that makes up the data link frame to the physical layer on the receiving machine, where it is abstracted into a frame in the receiver's data link layer. Thus there is a *peer-to-peer layer communication* between the two data link layers. In Figure 15.4, the heavy, solid line is used to emphasize that information between two machines is only physically transmitted at the physical layer, yet (as indicated by the lighter lines with different patterns) there is logical communication between the peers at each corresponding level of the network.

At the network layer, packets are exchanged between peer layers by translating a network packet into a data link frame and then into the physical layer format. The physical layer transmits the information to the receiving machine, where the information is translated into a data link frame and then into a network packet. The same technique is used for peer-to-peer communication at the transport, session, presentation, and appli-

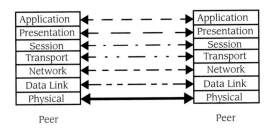

Figure 15.4
Peer-to-peer Communication

cation layers. The application layer uses a highly abstracted communications mechanism provided by the presentation layer interface; for example, a remote file server interface, a remote print server interface, or a remote procedure call interface.

The ISO OSI architecture model is a general model that reflects the agreement among various manufacturers that produce networks and host machines using the networks. While the general form of the model has been accepted for several years, the detailed protocols are still evolving. For example, the ARPAnet IP protocol is the dominant implementation used with the ISO OSI network layer, even though it is not part of the standard. With the de facto adaptation of TCP (and UDP) at the transport layer and IP at the network layer, the interfaces at the transport layer and below are relatively stable.

Any contemporary OS must provide support for various data link and physical layer network controllers, as well as an implementation of the network and transport layers. The next section summarizes the trends in data link and physical layer implementations and then talks about the midlayer protocols. Since the high-layer protocols are not well formed in modern systems, only the factors influencing the designers at these levels are described in Chapters 16 and 17. Discussion of the remote procedure call protocols is deferred to Chapter 17, after the rationale for its design and use is discussed. There are several excellent books describing the ISO OSI model in detail; for example, see Piscitello and Chapin [1993].

It should now be apparent how the ARPAnet protocols can be used with an ISO OSI protocol stack. TCP and UDP are equivalent to transport layer protocols, and IP is equivalent to a network layer protocol. The ISO OSI Transport Layer Interface (TLI) provides many of the same functions as does TCP (Transmission Control Protocol). Thus the pure ISO OSI protocol stack shown in Figure 15.5(a) may be implemented to use an ISO OSI session layer protocol, implemented on top of TCP, implemented on top of IP, or implemented on top of Ethernet (see Figure 15.5b). A user of the ISO OSI session layer in either implementation will receive the same service, independent of the protocol stack implementation. Of course, an implementation on an Ethernet data link layer cannot communicate directly with an X.25 data link layer implementation, but the network layer software written to use the Ethernet version can be used with no change on the pure protocol stack.

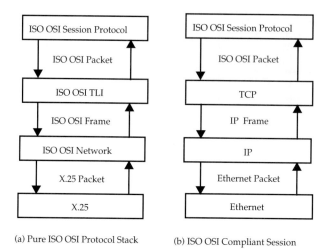

(a) Pure ISO OSI Protocol Stack   (b) ISO OSI Compliant Session

Figure 15.5
Using TCP/IP in an ISO OSI Protocol Stack

15.3 ■ Low-level Protocols

The low-level protocols used to construct communication subnetworks have considerably influenced the design of modern operating systems by providing a challenging, new hardware resource for them to manage. Traditionally, communications were handled by the device management portion of the OS. As network functionality increased to support more general distributed computing, networks also began to influence file management design. They are now impacting the design of memory and process managers.

First, the emergence of the 10 Mbps commercial LANs enabled organizations to interconnect computers with a shared medium. Organizations began to replace serial lines that operated at speeds lower than 10 Kbps with LANs. LAN bandwidth has increased by an order of magnitude over the 1980s technology, operating in the 100 Mbps range by the mid 1990s, and is now available in the gigabit (1 billion bits) per second range. Besides the substantially increased speed of operation of these LANs, their physical range has also systematically increased to the point at which the LAN technology is sometimes difficult to distinguish from wide-area network (WAN) technology.

At the time of this writing, it is still too early to characterize the full impact of these new high-speed networks on operating systems. However, it is clear that this kind of raw speed for the network will allow processes to have address spaces that span machines, as well as enabling the scheduler to execute processes on any of a set of different computers rather than on a local CPU. This situation requires a fundamental rethinking of the design of process and memory managers.

The change in operating systems and networks is also prompting the development of a new breed of applications in which larger amounts of data are transmitted among machines as files, continuous streams (usually of audio and video information), or typed information such as images or audio. For example, emerging networks have sufficient bandwidth to distribute multimedia information among machines on a network.

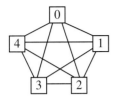

Figure 15.6
Fully Connected Network Topology

This bandwidth requires that the OS be able to manage high-speed data transfers between the network device and the application program.

This rapid growth in the total technology is led by changes at the physical and data link layers of the network. While it is beyond the scope of this book to focus on these technologies, this section describes their basic behavior so that the student can better understand the influence they have on the evolution of operating systems.

15.3.1 ■ The Physical Layer

The multidrop requirement was a barrier to networking technology until it was broken in the early 1980s by the Ethernet and Token Ring networks. The barrier resulted from the need for the network to be scalable. A multidrop network must allow every host node in the network to be able to send and receive information to/from all other nodes in the network. This requirement means there must be a (logical) transmission path between every pair of nodes in the network. If this full connectivity is implemented by directly mapping logical connections to physical connections, each computer will have a point-to-point connection to all other computers. If there are n host machines, then each host must have $n - 1$ communication ports (see Figure 15.6). There will be

$$n(n - 1)/2$$

connections in the resulting network. Such fully connected networks do not scale very easily, however, because the number of connections in the network increases as the square of the number of hosts. For large networks to be built, different topologies need to be employed at the physical layer.

Multiaccess bus physical layer topologies, such as that used in the Ethernet, broke the cost barrier for communications networks (see Figure 15.7). Multiaccess buses employ a common signaling medium, allocating the data transmission capability of the bus to different senders at different times. Information is transmitted from one host to

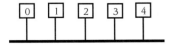

Figure 15.7
Multiaccess Bus Network Topology

another by placing it on the shared medium, along with an address designator. Each receiver scans the shared medium and retrieves information addressed to it. In this topology, much of the physical layer protocol will address issues such as synchronous versus asynchronous operation and centralized versus decentralized allocation of the shared medium. Reliability and contention are the major issues for the multiaccess bus topology. Reliability is handled at a higher level of the architecture model, while contention is handled by the controller.

PERFORMANCE TUNING

Fast Physical Layers

The signaling technique used in an Ethernet transmits information 1 bit at a time in a manner similar to the way an RS–232 serial port transfers information (see Chapter 5). The speed at which electric signals can traverse physical wires is limited to roughly 77 percent the speed of light. However, even though signals can be transmitted at that rate, mechanisms that can distinguish different voltage levels cannot perform this task at this maximum rate. The 10 Mbps signaling rate for the Ethernet is bounded by the rate at which the voltage level can be recognized by a receiver. How can a physical layer network be made to be faster than an Ethernet? There are three techniques: (1) make a better voltage sensing mechanism, (2) transmit multiple bits at a time, or (3) use a different signaling medium. The 100 Mbps Ethernet improves

on the performance of the 10 Mbps Ethernet by using a better mechanism to sense voltage levels.

In bit-parallel communications, multiple bits (such as a byte) are transmitted at a single time. For example, a parallel communication port transmits all 8 bits of a byte at the same time, while a serial communication port transmits the 8 bits one after another. Networks can be designed with multiple physical paths—for example, the fastest Ethernets actually use multiple physical wires [Schulzrinne, 1999]. The network can also employ another technique to achieve the same effect as transmitting bits in parallel. Rather than using only 3 voltage levels (no signal, transmitting 0, and transmitting 1), they can use $N = 2^k + 1$ voltage levels. For example, if 5 levels are used, the voltage levels could represent no signal, 00, 01,

10, or 11. This technique is used in the 1000BaseT network [Schulzrinne, 1999].

Fiber optic media might be assumed to be faster than copper wire media. However, the signal propagation rate in fiber optic is about 65 percent the speed of light (compared with 77 percent the speed of light in copper wire) [Schulzrinne, 1999]. When digital information is to be transmitted on a fiber optic medium, it is converted to a distinguishable light signal and transmitted over a fiber optic cable. Fiber optic can potentially provide higher effective transmission rates by using more cost-effective signal level transmitters and receivers than can be used with copper wire. Fiber optic cable can currently achieve gigabit per second transmission rates when used in contemporary high-speed physical layers.

15.3.2 ■ The Data Link Layer

Data link layer protocols partition a stream of bytes at the physical layer into a group of bytes called a *frame*. A frame has a header and a trailer together specifying various information about the frame, such as the destination of the frame, the transmitter of the frame, the type of the frame, the number of data bytes, and a checksum.

Above the data link layer the network allows a Host *i* to send a typed frame to Host *j*. The data link network also supports flow control and error control. Flow control is used to determine the rate at which packets flow between any pair of host machines. The data link layer supports the idea of frames flowing from one host to another. Therefore, by implication, a receiver host must be able to accept frames when they are transmitted. There are several reasons why a host may not be able to accept incoming frames:

■ The frame may have been sent to a nonexistent host or to one currently powered down.

■ The receiving host network device driver may be interrupt-driven. If the interrupts are disabled, incoming frames will be lost.

■ The network device driver accepts frames ultimately intended for a process located at the host. Accepting a frame requires the driver to contain its own buffer space to hold incoming frames until the receiver process requests them from the local OS. If the buffer space is full, the receiver machine will be unable to accept a frame without overwriting frame buffer storage.

The receiver needs to be able to control the rate at which frames are transmitted to it, particularly from some single transmitter. The simplest protocol for accomplishing flow control is the *stop-and-wait* protocol, summarized in Figure 15.8. The stop-and-wait protocol corresponds to a synchronous send IPC operation. The synchronization is accomplished with the special type of packet, ACK, that has no data field. The timeout

Figure 15.8
Stop-and-Wait Flow Control

```
    Sender transmits a frame;
    Sender sets a time-out on the transmission;
    Sender waits for an ACKnowledgment;
    ...
    if (Sender receives ACKnowledgment) continue;
    if (frame times-out)
        Retransmit timed-out frame;
```

(a) Transmitter

```
    Receiver accepts the frame;
    Receiver transmits the ACKnowledgment;
```

(b) Receiver

is used to prevent the sender from waiting forever if the outgoing data frame or the incoming ACK frame is lost. If the sender does not receive an ACK before the time-out expires, the sender assumes that the transmission has failed. The data link layer does not assume that frames can be transmitted reliably.

The *sliding-window protocol* is a generalization of the stop-and-wait protocol that allows a transmitter to have up to N frames in transit before it receives an ACK. Whenever the data link layer intends to transmit some number, N, of frames to another machine, it may be slowed down by the physical layer or by a slow receiver. There is no way for the transmitter to distinguish between the two. If the transmitter advances N frames beyond ACKs from the receiver, it will quit transmitting until it either times out on old transmissions or until acknowledgments are received. When frames are rejected on the receiver end, the transmission will eventually time out, thus causing frame retransmission.

Error control is intended to ensure that the contents of a frame are delivered in the same state as they were transmitted. This checking is accomplished by taking a checksum of the header and data and writing it in the trailer of the frame. The receiver computes the corresponding checksum upon receipt of the frame. If the computed checksum value differs from the transmitted checksum, the frame is assumed to have not been received properly. The frame is rejected by treating it as if it were never transmitted at all. This error detection and frame rejection is one of the sources of unreliability in the communication subnetwork.

15.3.3 ■ Contemporary Networks

A small number of low-level network technologies dominate in contemporary computer systems in the United States, including the Ethernet, the Token Ring, and various fiber optic technologies such as FDDI and ATM. This section touches on the highlights of Ethernet, Token Ring, and ATM networks.

15.3.3.1 ■ The Ethernet

Having exerted a profound impact on network technology, the Ethernet implements physical and data link layer protocols for a LAN. Information is delivered in packets (equivalent to data link frames) with a sustained signaling rate of 10 Mbps. Newer versions of the standard transmit information at 100 Mbps.

As mentioned earlier in the chapter, the physical topology is a multiaccess bus. Packets are placed on the bus by the sender. One or more receivers can retrieve the packets by reading the bus. The Ethernet is logically a broadcast medium, similar to the radio broadcast used in the predecessor Aloha net.

The unique aspect of the Ethernet is its incorporation of decentralized control of the shared bus; it uses carrier sense, multiple access protocol with collision detection (CSMA/CD). The LAN is not guaranteed to be reliable, meaning the physical and data link layer protocols may drop packets—for example, because of congestion on the network. The Ethernet makes a "best effort" to deliver, but the delivery may fail if successive attempts to transmit, perhaps a dozen, fail.

Whenever a sender wishes to transmit a packet, it first listens to the multiaccess bus. If another host is currently transmitting, the sender waits for a clear carrier on which to transport the packet. When the bus is idle—the clear carrier is sensed—the sender begins to transmit the packet, reading the shared medium as it writes it.

There is a race condition among senders. Suppose senders at physical extremes of the shared bus simultaneously begin to transmit. Each will sense the carrier and begin to send. Eventually, the signals will interfere with one another, thus causing a *collision* among the signals. Each sender will eventually detect this occurrence, since each is reading each bit as it places it on the cable. This approach implements decentralized collision detection, which means that contention on the network is determined by every node that is using the network at the time the collision occurs (rather than by a single centralized arbiter).

The time frame in which the race can occur is the amount of time required for a signal to propagate from one end of the shared medium to the other end and back again. This time frame is called the *slot time*. If a sender attempts to transmit a packet, it must monitor the transmission for at least the slot time in order to guarantee that the race condition does not occur and the packet will not experience a collision.

At this point, the individual sender recognizes if the shared medium has been inadvertently allocated to two senders, and at least one of the senders needs to defer to the other. The idea is to resolve this competition for the shared medium using a decentralized algorithm. Each sender will *backoff* for some interval of time and attempt to obtain the shared medium again later. To prevent the reoccurrence of the collision after the backoff time has passed, each sender chooses a random amount of time for its own backoff. Hence, if two senders collide one will backoff for X time units and the other will backoff for Y time units, where X and Y are likely to be different, since they were chosen randomly. It is clear the time units should be integer multiples of the slot time, since these are the lowest time units in which one can detect collisions.

As contention for the shared medium increases, the chances of collisions increase. Furthermore, the longer the net remains in a saturated condition, the higher the chance that two or more senders will choose the same backoff time. Ethernet uses a *binary exponential backoff* algorithm to address this problem. On the first collision, a sender backs off 0 or 1 slots. On its second collision, it backs off 0, 1, 2, or 3 slots. And on the ith successive collision, it backs off between 0 and $2^i - 1$ slots. The more often a sender fails due to collision, the longer the time it likely will defer before attempting to retransmit.

The Ethernet LAN stimulated network configurations and distributed computing. It is widely used in distributed systems, since it is relatively fast and economical. However, it is beginning to be displaced by higher-speed networks operating over larger geographical areas. It does not address higher-layer protocols, but it does provide a sound data link layer on which one can implement other protocols.

15.3.3.2 ■ The Token Ring

The Token Ring LAN evolved from an IBM SNA variant. At the physical layer, this LAN operates at signaling rates of up to 16 Mbps. At the data link layer, each host is assigned a logical address from a set of N nonnegative numbers. Host i can receive packets from Host $i - 1$ (modulo N) and send packets to Host $i + 1$ (modulo N). The placement of the host on the physical layer medium is independent of this logical address assigned to a host. Thus the data link layer implements a logical ring topology on a somewhat arbitrary medium.

The logical network contains a single, specialized packet called the *token*. When the token packet arrives at Host i, if the token is "available," Host i can attach information for Host j to the packet and send the token packet on to Host $i + 1$. If the token packet already contains information, Host i must wait for the token to return as an empty packet. When the token packet arrives at Host j, that host receives the information from Host i and marks the token packet as "in transit" from Host i. At Host i, the packet is again marked "available" and sent to Host $i + 1$.

The Token Ring also employs decentralized control, although in a more regimented manner than in the Ethernet. While the Ethernet allows any host to obtain the shared medium as often as it likes, the Token Ring enforces fairness by passing the token around the ring. When the Ethernet detects a collision, it must recover from the situation. Collisions do not occur in Token Rings.

However, the Token Ring depends on each host's behaving properly. If Host i crashes, the ring must be reconfigured so that Host $i - 1$ will send tokens directly to Host $i + 1$, and Host $i + 1$ must accept such packets.

15.3.3.3 ■ ATM Networks

Some researchers speculate that *asynchronous transfer mode (ATM)* will have the same kind of impact on computing in the next 15 years that the Ethernet had in the previous 15. ATM technology has evolved from a combination of the telecommunications and computer industries rather than just the computer industry, as with the Ethernet and Token Ring. Two results of this heritage are the incorporation of reliable transmission at the low layers of the network abstraction and the potential of the network to cover relatively large geographical areas.

An ATM network employs a fiber optic physical layer that transmits data in 53-byte packets called *cells*. The lower layers of an ATM network ensure that cells will be delivered reliably. Furthermore, the network can guarantee various levels of service quality with respect to communication bandwidth and variation. This guarantee is invaluable for communications tasks that support continuous streams of data, such as an audio or video stream, particularly when the streams must be synchronized, as in multimedia applications.

The rapidly evolving ATM technology of today relies on relatively expensive switches, which are currently incapable of operating at the speeds planned for ATMs in the next few years. Today, ATMs transmit signals at less than 500 Mbps, but it is expected they will operate in the gigabit per second range in the next few years.

15.4 ■ The Network Layer

The network layer allows a host computer on one network, such as Host X on Network A in Figure 15.9, to send information to a host located on a different network, such as Host Y on Network C. This implies that there is a path that interconnects networks with intermediate host machines. For example, in Figure 15.9 information can be *routed* from Host X to Host R over Network A, then from Host R to Host S on Network B, and finally from Host S to Host Y on Network C. The network layer provides the functionality to enable such communication scenarios.

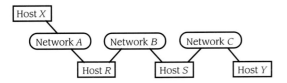

Figure 15.9
Routing in an Internet

The network layer transmits information in *packets,* each one addressed to a receiver using an address that identifies the receiver's network as well as the host machine. Thus a network layer address must contain more information than a data link layer frame. For example, Host *X* on Network *A* does not have a frame address for Host *Y* on Network *C,* so when the information is transmitted by Host *X,* the packet address references Host *Y* on Network *C,* but the frame address causes the frame to be sent from Host *X* to Host *R.*

The network level provides not only the expanded address space for packet delivery but also facilities for routing packets over a set of partially connected networks of hosts, as shown in Figure 15.9. A specific network layer transmission may consist of several *hops* across individual networks. Each hop corresponds to a data link layer frame transmission. The details of the data link layer transmission—for example, the number of hops involved—are transparent above the network layer interface.

The network configuration in Figure 15.9 is called an *internetwork,* or *internet.* An internet is literally a network of networks. Normally one thinks of a network as some set of nodes interconnected by edges. In a LAN, the nodes in the network are host machines and the edges in the logical network are the communication subnetwork. In an internet, the nodes are a complete network and the edges correspond to the host machines that are connected to two or more networks and are capable of routing packets from one network to the other. For example, Host *R* is connected to both Networks *A* and *B,* and Host *S* is connected to both Networks *B* and *C.* Provided that Hosts *R* and *S* are willing to route packets, they correspond to edges in the internet, while Networks *A, B,* and *C* correspond to nodes in the internet. A host machine connected to two or more networks (and that is willing to route packets) is called a *gateway machine.*

At the network layer, a process on Host *X* on Network *A* transmits information to a process on Host *Y* on Network *C* by passing information to the network layer with an internet address identifying the network and host, such as (`Network_C`, `Host_Y`). The host implementing the first hop in the internet copies the network packet intended for (`Network_C`, `Host_Y`) into a data link layer frame and then transmits it to Host *R* on the attached network. When Host *R* receives the data link layer frame from Host *X* on Network *A,* it retrieves the packet from the frame, determines the destination of the next hop, and then copies the packet into a frame to be transmitted to Host *S* on Network *B.* When Host *S* receives the packet, it follows the same algorithm. However, because the destination is on the network to which it is attached, it performs a normal data link layer delivery. Hence, the network layer packet is encapsulated inside of a different data link layer frame for each hop through the internet (see Figure 15.10). Packet addresses are completely transparent to the data link layer, since they appear only in the packet header

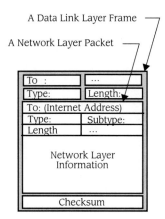

Figure 15.10
Example Network Layer Packet

in the data field of the frame. When a gateway retrieves the packet from inside a frame, it uses the internet address to determine the next hop through the internet.

15.4.1 ■ Addressing

The prevalent internet address model is adopted from the ARPAnet *Internet Protocol* (IP). In fact, much of today's knowledge about network layer architecture is a direct result of experience with the ARPAnet. IP addresses are 32-bit addresses that specify a host and network. (The new IPV6—IP Version 6—protocol has 128-bit addresses.) Today, an IP address may have any of four different formats, depending on how system administrators have configured their portion of an internet. For example, an internet may have a small number of networks, each with a large number of host machines. Or it may have a large number of networks, each with a small number of host machines. IP Class A addresses are used for the first configuration; IP Class C addresses are used for the second.

Every host machine in an internet has two or more addresses: its physical network address used by the data link layer and one or more internet addresses, depending on the number of networks to which it is attached. In Figure 15.11, the software to send a data

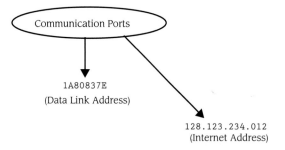

Figure 15.11
Using Data Link and Network Layer Addresses

link frame must use the data link address, `1A80837E` in the example, to deliver the frame to a destination host or an intermediate gateway machine. Once the frame has been delivered, higher-layer software can use the internet address. If the network layer packet is to be delivered to a machine on another network, the network layer software will use the internet address, `128.123.234.012` in the example, independent of the frame address used at the data link layer. (The form of the 32-bit address in the figure uses the "dotted decimal notation," where each of the four decimal numbers represents a byte in the address.)

All software above the network layer references other machines on its own network and on its internet by using an internet address. The internet address space enables the same software to be used to address host machines on its own LAN and on an internet. However, the network layer (routing) software at each host must be able to determine the appropriate data link address to which a frame (carrying a packet) must be sent for any given internet address.

15.4.2 ■ Routing

Routing technology has evolved directly from the original ARPAnet. Figure 15.12(a) illustrates the configuration style of the original ARPAnet. It was a set of large host machines, each with a special interface message processor (IMP) network frontend machine. The IMP performed store-and-forward routing without intervention from the host machine. At the time the ARPAnet was built, an IMP was the equivalent of a high-end channel processor. Today, it is possible to implement its function in a device controller or, more commonly, in a device controller and network software that are executing as part of the OS. In Figure 15.12(a), the IMPs are interconnected using point-to-point communication lines using IP. As LAN technology evolved, ARPAnet host machines began to be replaced by a LAN that interconnected a set of smaller host machines with the IMP. This has evolved into the contemporary configuration of the

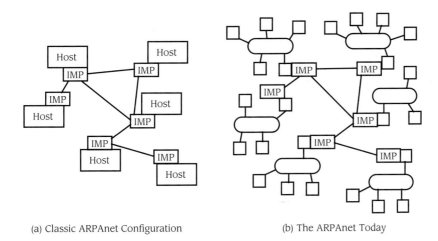

(a) Classic ARPAnet Configuration   (b) The ARPAnet Today

Figure 15.12
Routing in the ARPAnet

ARPAnet and internets (see Figure 15.12b). The routing technology used in the original WAN-based ARPAnet evolved into the version of IP used in contemporary internets of the form shown in Figure 15.12(b). Gateways perform the routing function of the original ARPAnet IMPs.

Figure 15.13 represents the evolution from the IMP-based ARPAnet technology to contemporary internets with gateway machines. Since the function of the original IMP can now be packaged as a device with network layer software, the networks in an internet can generally be thought of as being connected by a collection of gateways instead of communication lines. Since many of the individual networks are separated by great distances (measured in miles or hundreds of miles), an internet will contain many pairs of half gateways. A half gateway machine is a machine that is connected to a network on one side and to an ARPAnet-style long-haul, point-to-point communication line on the other side. A pair of *half-gateways* interconnected with a point-to-point line provides the functionality of a full gateway, where information moves between the two halves across the communication line.

The primary task of the network layer is to handle routing. The particular style of routing depends on the style of the internet, but the basic tasks remain the same:

■ The sending host uses a local routing table to select a destination for the first hop in the route to the ultimate receiver.

■ The sender encapsulates the packet into a frame and then transmits it to the intermediary.

■ The intermediary decapsulates the packet and determines whether the packet should be routed to another intermediary, using its routing table, or the packet has reached its destination.

■ The intermediary encapsulates the packet into the frame for the outgoing network or local host and forwards the frame.

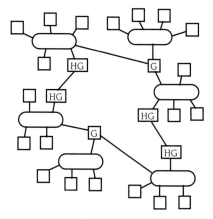

Figure 15.13
A LAN Internet

An internet can become large, which suggests that routing tables can also become large. If each host keeps a routing table to indicate how to reach all other hosts on the internet, the size requirement may make it impossible for a host to be part of the internet. Of course, any one host is not likely to need to communicate with all other hosts on a very large network. (The internationally shared Internet has thousands of networks and host machines throughout the world; see the next subsection) The host could keep a subset of the destination hosts in its routing tables, provided there is some mechanism by which a host can add new entries to its local routing table as they are needed. Can the same strategy be applied to a gateway machine? Is it possible for a gateway machine to perform internet routing when it has only an incomplete routing table? The answer is yes, provided all the topology of the network appears in some collection of gateways reachable from any host (see Stevens [1994, ch. 3]). The gateways also must provide a protocol among themselves for ensuring that all information is maintained and can be shared on demand.

15.4.3 ■ Using the Network Layer

The LAN-based internet topology common in the commercial world stimulated the creation of one large, globally accessible internet, commonly referred to as the *Internet*. (Internet is capitalized to distinguish the global internet from others that use the same technology.) Using the Internet, a process running on a host machine in Boulder, Colorado, can exchange packets with a process on another machine located in Paris, France, by using the same programs it uses to exchange packets with a process on a machine in the same laboratory. Network layer technology also allows users to interconnect different types of LANs—for example, an Ethernet and a Token Ring. Since each gateway acts as a host for two or more LANs, it must include physical and data link layer protocols for the respective LANs. This function is referred to as media translation done by the gateway. When a packet from one LAN is passed to another LAN by the gateway, the packet may have to be reformatted or otherwise converted to match the destination LAN protocols. Such gateway machines are said to perform *protocol translation* in addition to the normal media translation.

In theory, it is possible to use the features and functions of the network layer as the basis of application programs. In practice, IP is usually accessible only to programs with supervisor permission, since the implementation interface contains many protection loopholes. The transport layer UDP (described in the next section) provides an interface similar to IP, although its interface is better suited for use by application programs. Applications implemented on the network layer view the network as an unreliable packet network making its best effort to deliver packets. Users of this unreliable packet network must compensate for situations in which packets might be lost at some lower layer—for example, due to checksum failure in the data link layer or collisions in the physical layer. The application programs must also compensate for the possibility that a stream of packets will be delivered out of order because the packets were routed through the internet on different paths. The transport layer provides functions to address reliability using standardized facilities.

15.5 ■ The Transport Layer

The transport layer provides a reliable, end-to-end mechanism for transmitting information from one host to another. Programmers using the transport layer need not be concerned with packets or internet details. The transport layer creates a new abstraction of network communication that includes a spectrum of services:

■ The address space is extended beyond internet addresses so that the transmitting process can reference a specific *port* on a remote host on a remote network. The port might be an application process mailbox, a UNIX pipe end, or other OS-specific entity used to provide a means by which a process can communicate with other processes.

■ The transport layer provides various data types to the application program, including datagrams, network messages, and byte streams. The ISO OSI *Transport Layer Interface (TLI)* is not a significant factor in commercial systems due to the popularity of the ARPAnet *User Datagram Protocol (UDP)* and the *Transmission Control Protocol (TCP)*. Although technically the ARPAnet protocols do not comply with the ISO OSI transport layer standard, they provide the same functions as do compliant transport layer protocols. They can be made consistent with the ISO OSI model by adapting TCP and UDP to work with an ISO-compliant data link layer.

■ Reliable communication (in the face of unreliable network layer operation) is provided at the transport layer.

15.5.1 ■ Communication Ports

The network must allow a process to identify an explicit location in a network where a process can have information delivered from other processes. This is analogous to a street address, a post office box, a telephone number, or a voice mailbox. The internet address can be used for the delivery of a packet to a machine but not to locations *within* the machine. Multiuser and multiprocess machines require a number of individual communication addresses within each machine, so the transport layer provides communication ports to extend the internet address.

Figure 15.14 shows host machine *X* with its unique `<net, host>` address used at the network layer and with a number of communication ports, *p*, within the machine.

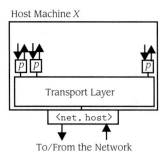

Figure 15.14
Extending the Address Space with Ports

Ports are managed by the transport layer, usually as an OS resource. If a process wants to use a port, it must request the use of a port just as it would any other serially reusable resource. Once a port has been allocated, it can be used to send and receive network packets via the transport layer.

Outgoing transport layer communications require the sender to know the `<net, host, port>` for the destination. This means that a receiver's port number must somehow be made known to any process that wants to send information to that receiver. Section 15.6 explains the general technique for supporting this requirement. For now, observe that before a process can receive information from the network, it must have both a port allocated for this purpose and the port number must be known by processes that will send information. In general, port *creation* and *binding* to an internet address are separate operations. The Laboratory Exercise at the end of this chapter illustrates how Berkeley UNIX sockets are used to create a socket and bind it to an internet address.

15.5.2 ■ Data Types

The transport layer supports two main data types: datagrams and byte streams. Datagrams are similar to network layer packets, except they use the three-component transport layer addresses. Byte streams allow processes on two different machines to exchange information by transmitting and receiving contiguous bytes of information, similar to how a UNIX pipe works. Because of the wide use of message-passing for interprocess communication, the transport layer can also implement a protocol that supports messages, similar to the message-passing extension to byte streams on a UNIX file or pipe (see Chapter 9).

15.5.2.1 ■ UDP Datagrams

UDP delivers blocks of information at the transport level. A UDP datagram is a block of information that may be fragmented and transmitted in one or more network packets (which implies there is another level of encapsulation at the network layer). The network layer delivers individual datagrams to arbitrary hosts on the internet without ensuring reliable delivery. That is, UDP does not guarantee that any packet will be delivered to its destination. However, it does guarantee that if any part of the datagram is delivered, then all of the datagram will be delivered.

Datagram services provide a level of abstraction of the network similar to the block I/O abstraction for storage devices. If the programmer decides that the underlying implementations of the network and lower layers are sufficiently reliable for the application, then the application software can be written to use datagrams with a protocol such as UDP. However, unlike local storage device operation, network layer communication may lose information. For example, the network may lose a frame at the data link layer or a packet may be lost at the network level. UDP makes no provision to notify or correct for the loss. Reliability is the full responsibility of the application program. As a result, UDP is not used for applications where reliable transmission is required, as in the case of most applications. It can, however, be used for transmitting audio or video information, since the application program would normally interpolate the information it received prior to using it.

The incremental OS support (beyond network layer functions) of datagram service is small—namely, the management of the port component of the address—since most of the functionality is logically part of the underlying network layer.

15.5.2.2 ■ Byte Streams

ARPAnet TCP implements byte streams among processes on different hosts on an internet. (These byte streams are sometimes called *connections* and sometimes *virtual circuits.*) Before two processes can establish a byte stream between them, both must be willing to communicate. The two processes take on different roles in establishing the byte stream. The active process establishes a byte stream by requesting a connection with a passive receiver process prior to exchanging information. If the passive receiver accepts the request, a connection (or virtual circuit) is established between the two processes. Once the connection has been established, a sender writes variable-sized blocks to the byte stream and the receiver reads variable-sized blocks from the connection to obtain the information. In TCP, the size of the blocks read do not have to correspond to the size of the blocks that are written. Since the byte stream is created between a pair of processes, it is unnecessary to include the destination of each piece of information transmitted over the connection.

15.5.3 ■ Reliable Communication

Datagrams are analogous to telegrams in the sense that each is separately addressed and sent to the receiver. Byte streams implicitly assume reliable packet delivery. Reliability can be achieved by using a communication model that bears more resemblance to telephony than to telegraphy. The telephone system uses the notion of a connection (or circuit) for communication. A caller establishes a connection by placing a call to the callee prior to exchanging information. Once the connection has been established, the caller need not include addressing information, since the connection already specifies the communication ports for both the caller and the callee.

The telephone analogy is used by the TCP to implement the connections (or virtual circuits) introduced in the previous subsection. If two processes agree to establish a virtual circuit between them, then either can transmit a byte stream across the virtual circuit without being concerned about packet boundaries. Furthermore, TCP *guarantees* that all packets used to hold the byte stream will be delivered in the order they were sent. This is accomplished by attaching sequence numbers to each packet used by the byte stream. The transport layer then uses a peer-to-peer protocol to generate and test sequence numbers to ensure that no packet is lost or delivered out of order.

Opening a virtual circuit requires that the sender and the receiver agree to exchange information. As described previously, any process intending to communicate with other processes must establish a port so that other processes have an endpoint on which to connect the virtual circuit. After both processes have created a port, one of them—the active one—must establish the virtual circuit by setting up its own endpoint. The active process then requests the remote end—the passive process—to accept the request to connect the virtual circuit to the specified communication port on behalf of the receiver.

Transport layer connections use handshaking protocols for flow control on the byte stream. Such protocols help ensure that packets do not get dropped, since lost packets will cause retransmission. When a flow control protocol such as the sliding-window protocol is used at the transport layer, it manages a stream of packets between ports, rather than the flow of frames between host machines, as is done at the data link layer. Thus a sliding-window protocol could conceivably be used at the data link level and again at the transport level. When a pair of processes have completed their use of the virtual circuit, they must "tear it down," since network resources are required to keep the virtual circuit intact.

TCP is the prevailing transport layer implementation in contemporary networks. It provides virtual circuit capabilities that enable a sending process to establish a virtual circuit to a remote machine and to exchange information bidirectionally over the connection. Communication using TCP is reliable, so TCP has become the workhorse protocol for contemporary network applications. It is used in window systems (including the X windows system), remote file systems, and mail systems.

PERFORMANCE TUNING

Datagrams and Virtual Circuits

Because TCP provides reliable delivery of information and implements a byte stream, why would a programmer ever choose to use UDP? The answer to this question is, better performance.

When a block of information is sent using TCP, the block must be flattened into a byte stream, then fragmented to fit into network layer packets with sequence numbers, and finally transmitted over the network layer. The sequence numbers are used to acknowledge the receipt of each packet and to ensure that they arrive in order. As a result, each packet that is sent must (nominally) have an acknowledgment packet transmitted back to the sender (the sliding-window protocol can eliminate some of these acknowledgments).

The overhead for ensuring reliable delivery of information is very significant. In Stevens [1990, ch. 17], the various studies cited show that when a 10 Mbps Ethernet is used that has only a sending and a receiving host using the internet, 4.2BSD TCP had a maximum throughput of about 90 Kbps, while UDP had a maximum throughput of about 185 Kbps. However, Stevens also reports that various optimiza-tions of the software can increase the throughput of TCP to 890 Kbps using a Sun 3/60 on a 10 Mbps Ethernet. (With the normal overhead in an Ethernet, the theoretical maximum throughput for TCP for 1K packets is 1192 packets per second, or 1,203,920 bytes per second.) Stevens does not provide corresponding speed-up figures for UDP. This data suggests that TCP can be made to be almost as fast as UDP. Unfortunately, not all implementations incorporate the optimizations, so the trade off between UDP and TCP remains clearly one of performance versus reliability.

15.6 ▪ Using the Transport Layer

Section 15.5 described the fundamentals that must be implemented by the OS. How the transport layer is used by applications is considered more fully here. The required support for name management and the client-server paradigm also influence the OS design.

15.6.1 ▪ Naming

The transport layer three-component addresses represent the set of names in a global *name space,* which is accessible to any process using the transport layer. The process can bind an internal address or name to a global name, thus enabling other processes on other machines to reference the internal address. Hence, references to the global name are associated with the name in the process's local name space. The Laboratory Exercise explains how a BSD UNIX process can create a local name and then bind the global name, `<netNo, hostNo, port>`, to the local name.

An analogy for names in a process's local name space is the set of telephone extensions for the various telephones within a corporation. Similar to names in a process's local name space, telephone extensions refer to various kinds of entities. Some numbers refer to people, while others refer to answering machines, FAX machines, computer modems, or a telephone in a conference room. The extension numbers, usually three-, four-, or five-digit numbers, are used to call within the PBX system. If a telephone subscriber intends to reference a name outside the corporation's local name space, a different set of names, from a global name space, must be used.

Processes can share information only by sharing names from a common global name space. For example, suppose processes A and B both have their own name space (consisting of a set of names, represented as boxes in Figure 15.15). Both desire B to be able to use name X in A's name space. Suppose process A is located on machine number 88 on network number `3456` and it has bound a local communication entity such as a BSD

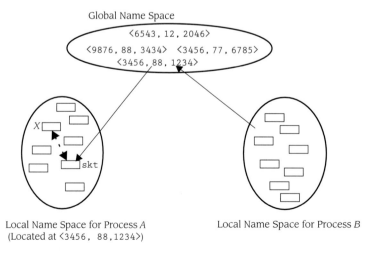

Local Name Space for Process A
(Located at `<3456, 88,1234>`)   Local Name Space for Process B

Figure 15.15
Sharing Names

UNIX socket, `skt`, to port number `1234`. Now a reference to the name `<3456,   88,   1234>` in the global name space will be associated with the socket variable name in process *A*. If process *B* wishes to establish a connection with process *A* at `skt` or to send a datagram to process *A* via `skt`, it will use the transport layer address `<3456,   88,   1234>`. The variable named *X* in process *A*'s name space is referenced like any other variable by software in *A*'s name space. When *B* references *X*, it communicates with *A* via the name it knows—`skt`—whereupon *A* will perform the reference to *X* on *B*' s behalf.

The following is a summary of the set of name spaces that are to be managed at the transport layer and below in order to provide orderly communication among a set of processes (see Figure 15.16). Each process exists in a local name space established by the language translation system and the OS. Communication ports are added at the transport layer to identify individual endpoints that are within the host machine but external to the process's local name space. The communication endpoints are bound to a data link layer host address, independent of the internet address. The tuple of the internet address is taken from the internet address of the subject host, `<3456,   88>` in the figure. This tuple is then combined with the port number to produce a 3-tuple in the global name space used by the transport layer. The 3-tuple is converted to a 32-bit internet address used at the network layer.

For a process to use a global name, a *name registry* must be available to it. The name registry allows a process to use informal key names to look up global names in a directory. For example, the name registry might allow a process to obtain the address `<3456, 88>` using the keyword "mail service" or "`gjn@cs.colorado.edu`." In the telephone system analogy, if one subscriber intends to place a call to a different subscriber, the initiator must know the telephone number of the recipient of the call. In some cases, the calling subscriber knows the name of the recipient, but often the subscriber must use the directory assistance name registry to bind the key name—the receiver's name—to the proper global name—that is, to the receiver's telephone number.

A name registry is essentially a database accessed by the key name. It provides value by allowing several key names to map to a global name and possibly several global names to match a single key name. The database can be implemented as a remote

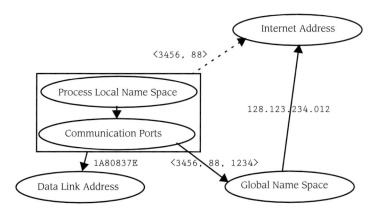

Figure 15.16
Naming Domains

name service located at a particular address in the internet or as a fully decentralized set of duplicate tables, whereby every process contains a copy of the full registry. Telephone directory assistance corresponds to the remote service approach, while distributing copies of telephone books to subscribers is an example of decentralized distribution of duplicates. The former approach relies on the presence of a centralized service. The latter approach is difficult to maintain and tends not to scale well in a network environment. A middle approach is to distribute copies of the database across a network, either by partitioning or by replication. If the copies are distributed, then the name service internals will provide a consistency mechanism to ensure all copies are relatively up-to-date.

The name registry is a network service, so it has its own transport address. This is an example of a *well-known global name,* since its address will usually not change and will be hardcoded into applications. The well-known global name is analogous to the universal telephone number for calling directory assistance. Subscribers remember this number, since they call it to get other numbers.

There are a number of different name registries, or directory services, used in contemporary networks. The X.500 directory service is the official ISO OSI directory service. (For a discussion of the OSI directory service, see Piscitello and Chapin [1993, ch. 7]). The Domain Name System (DNS) is a specialized directory service for use with Internet names.

➤ IN THE HANGAR

The Domain Name System

The Domain Name System (DNS) is widely used with TCP/IP to map text strings into internet addresses (see Stevens [1994, ch. 14]). The DNS presumes that there is only one name hierarchy for all names used in the global Internet. The hierarchy has an unnamed root with top-level names of `arpa`, `com`, `edu`, `gov`, `int`, `mil`, `net`, `org`, and a set of two-character country names (specified by ISO 3166) referring to countries (such as `us` for United States, `fr` for France, and `ca` for Canada). No single organization manages the entire name space, but there is an entity to manage each top-level name by registering any children of that name. Each of the top-level names can have a large number of second-level names. For example, the top-level name `edu` has a second-level name of `colorado`. The `colorado` domain is managed by an entity interested in establishing names within the domain of internet names of educational institutions at the University of Colorado at Boulder. The full name of the domain is `colorado.edu`. Within the `colorado` domain is another domain called `cs`, which is managed by the Computer Science Department at the University of Colorado. This domain's name is `cs.colorado.edu`. Similarly, other names in the DNS domain have the same form; for example, `cs.arizona.edu`, `compuserve.com`, `nsf.note.gov`, and `inf.enst.fr`.

A *resolver* in each user machine keeps a copy of part of the hierarchy for reference and has the ability to contact a DNS name server for help with DNS names for which it does not know the Internet address. The `gethostbyname` call in the BSD socket library invokes the client port of the resolver to determine the Internet address of the machine whose DNS name is passed as an argument. The client port of the resolver is implemented as library code, so it is linked into the calling process's address space. The server port of the resolver is a network service that is contacted by the resolver library code.

15.6.2 ■ The Client-server Model

The *client-server model* of computation is a general distributed computation paradigm that relies on the transport layer facilities, including the name service. According to the model, one process, the server, is a passive process that provides a specified service to any active process, a client, desiring the service.

Several contemporary products employ the client-server model, including file servers, print servers, database servers, and window servers. As suggested by the name, the client-server model has asymmetric behavior. The server always exists in the network, passively waiting for requests for service, while autonomous client processes decide when to utilize the server. A server is a worker process soliciting work, while a client is a supervisory process requiring services.

The server is initiated as an autonomous process in a network of machines. The schematic structure of a server process is shown in Figure 15.17. The structure suggests a datagram interface, since the server is able to accept requests from any particular client, service the request, and then accept a request from a different client.

Suppose a client requests a server to send it a copy of a file. The client might be in the process of obtaining a service for a relatively long time, since the server could incur substantial I/O time to read the file from its local disk before transmitting it over the network. In this case, a client might monopolize a server's time even though it is not using all of the service potential of the server. Often the machine implementing the

Figure 15.17
Server Structure

```
int serverSkt; /* The socket used to receive requests */
struct request_type *request; /* Details of a request */

serverSkt = initialize(); /* Create a socket and bind it
                           * Register server with the registry
                           * Initialize data structures, etc
                           */
while(TRUE) { /* Service requests until the process dies */
   request = waitForRequest(); /* Get a request */
   serviceTheRequest(request); /* Then service it */
};
```

server would be able to support more than one request for service at a time, through multiprogramming, provided the services did not interfere with one another. The client-server model can be expanded to allow this multiprogramming. Suppose the server is initiated with a special *listener* process whose only job is to accept service requests and to delegate them to other processes, which perform the actual service. Now the server processes takes the form shown in Figure 15.18.

The listener process is the persistent process (or thread) at the server's transport layer address. It accepts the initial service request from each client, authenticates it if necessary, and then spawns a server process (or thread) for each request for service. Each client can exchange information with its copy of the server without blocking other clients from using the service. In this model, a machine is likely to have several processes executing identical procedures on a shared data structure—the data structure describing the state of the shared service. Context switches among the server processes can become the dominant processing task on the server machine. Thus this application is a natural fit for thread-based processing.

In Figure 15.19, the client process requests service by sending a message to a `wellKnownSocket` address in the transport layer. The client program is required to know the name to initiate a service request. Since the address is "well known," it either is hard-coded into the procedure or obtained from a user. If the address is compiled into the procedure, the service cannot move around the network. The processes executing the procedure will not be able to obtain service from alternative sources. How could the user know the address? Probably by looking up the address of the service in a well-known name service. If the address is stored in a name service, the binding of service name to service address can be delayed until the moment the service is required. The user can look up the service address in the name service and specify the address at the time the request is made. If the server is unavailable, the directory can be changed to reflect an alternative address from which similar service may be obtained.

The client process can automate this action by using a name server located at a well-known port. When the client process intends to request a service, it uses the name

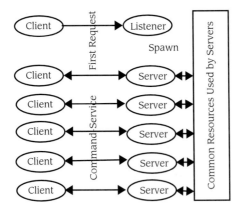

Figure 15.18
A Concurrent Server

Figure 15.19
Refined Server Structure

```
/* The Listener/Server Processes */
int main(int argc, char *argv[]) {
    void runServer(int);
    char serverHostName[HOSTNAMELEN];
    int on = 1, port, clientLen, newSkt, skt, run = TRUE;
    struct sockaddr *client, listener;
    struct hostent *host;

    initialize(); /* Get the server host name and port number */
                  * Set up a socket for listening
                  * Fill-in the internet info
                  * Bind the listener's name
                  * Set the backlog */
/* Wait for client requests */
    clientLen = sizeof(client);
    while(TRUE) {
    /* waitForRequest() */
        newSkt = accept(skt, &client, &clientLen);
/* Start a server to serveTheRequest, use a TCP connection*/
    if (fork() == 0) {
    /* Only the server child executes this code */
        close(skt); /* Server doesn't need the listener skt */
        runServerCommand(newSkt);
        close(newSkt); /* Server done ... terminate */
        exit(0);
    }
    close(newSkt); /* Listener doesn't need the server skt */
    }
}
```

service to map the service name into an address from which the service might be obtained. The name server keeps a current directory of services in which it can look up mappings.

The client-server model is the most widely used paradigm for organizing distributed computations. OS designers use the model heavily in implementing the OS; for example, the remote file systems described in the next chapter are all designed around the client-server model. The model also highlights the need for efficient process management and encourages OS support of the thread model.

15.7 ■ Summary

Modern computer systems use the ISO OSI architectural model extensively as the framework for defining network protocols. The model is a layered architecture composed of these layers: physical, data link, network, transport, session, presentation, and application. This chapter described the low-level protocols, since they are hardware resources to be managed by the OS, and the network and transport layers, since they are usually implemented in the OS.

The low-level protocols define the physical signaling protocol and the structuring of bit streams into data link frames. The network layer implements the internet—a network of networks because it uses gateways to connect independent networks. Most network-level implementations are based on the ARPAnet Internet Protocol, IP.

The transport layer implements multiple data structure types and, most important, reliable network communication over the unreliable lower layers of the ISO OSI model. Addresses at the transport level differ from those at the network level through the use of the port specification to distinguish among communication endpoints on a specific `<net, host>` location. Transport layer addresses have the form `<net, host, port>`.

TCP is the dominant protocol at the OSI transport layer. It provides a virtual circuit function that enables programmers to open a virtual circuit and to read and write bidirectional byte streams over the virtual circuit.

How do applications use the network protocols to support distributed computation? Remote files are the most widely used application of the transport layer network. The next chapter explains how remote files use the transport layer to allow a process on one machine to use the files loaded on another machine.

15.8 ■ Exercises

1. Suppose a 10 Mbps network transmits 1024-byte packets containing a 128-byte header and a 4-byte checksum. If a workstation on the LAN is guaranteed to be able to transmit at least one packet every X time units (since the network is shared with other workstations), what maximum amount of time, as a function of X, should be required (based only on these factors) to transfer a 3 MB file from a server to a workstation? What is the effective transfer rate from the server to the workstation?

2. A 10 Mbps Ethernet has a minimum gap between packets of 12 bytes, a 22-byte header, and a 4-byte trailer. Assume a user data field of 1464 bytes in a frame, with a minimum gap between each frame.

   a. What is the maximum theoretical rate at which user data can be transmitted on the Ethernet?
   b. IP packet headers are 20 bytes, and UDP packet headers are 8 bytes. What is the maximum theoretical rate at which user data can be transmitted using UDP on the Ethernet?
   c. IP packet headers are 20 bytes, and TCP packet headers are 20 bytes. What is the maximum theoretical rate at which user data can be transmitted using TCP on the Ethernet? (Ignore the cost of ACKs.)

3. Suppose an internet has the organization shown in Figure 15.20, with software using the given transport layer addresses and machines using the given data link layer addresses:

   a. List the network layer address for each machine.

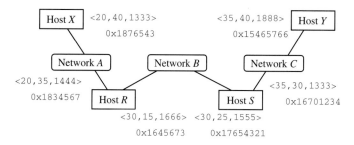

Figure 15.20
An Internet Configuration

b. Describe the frames used to send a UDP packet from <20, 40, 1333> to <30, 40, 1888>.

4. Consider the scheme for employing only partially complete routing tables in each node and gateway of the ARPAnet. If the union of all the information in the partial routing tables is complete, consistent, and stable, explain why routing will operate correctly. There are many details in the actual ARPAnet that constrain their solution, details not covered in this text. So you will need to state all assumptions you make about gateway behavior.

5. The Berkeley UNIX `connect` system call has a time-out interval of about 1 minute, but the `accept` call has no time-out interval. Explain why these functions might have been designed in this manner.

6. Write a pseudo C code definition of the `waitForRequest` function referenced in Figure 15.17. (*Hint:* You may find it useful to look at Figures 15.22 and 15.23 in the Laboratory Exercise.)

Laboratory Exercise: Using TCP/IP

UNIX systems provide a facility called `talk` that enables two different users logged into the same computer to have a real-time dialogue. One user invokes `talk` with another user's login name to request a `talk` session, and the "connection" between the two is completed when the second user accepts the request. This lab exercise asks you to implement a skeletal `talk` facility between two different processes on two different machines. As a simplification, assume that the facility is asymmetric in the sense that one of the processes acts as an *initiator* and the other as a *receiver*. The initiator begins the `talk` session by requesting a virtual circuit with the receiver. Use the BSD socket communication mechanism with the internet address domain as the IPC mechanism. Each process should provide a single console window for both sending and receiving (UNIX `talk` splits the screen into two windows). Precede outgoing messages with a > symbol and incoming messages with a < symbol. It is acceptable for your solution to allow an incoming line from the remote user to interrupt the local user if he or she is currently typing a line.

BACKGROUND

To solve this lab exercise, you will need to learn how to create a BSD socket with IP addresses, how to create a virtual circuit, and how to implement nonblocking read operations.

Berkeley UNIX Sockets

The BSD socket mechanism is a kernel mechanism that implements transport layer services. Earlier in the chapter you learned how the transport layer protocol can use datagrams or virtual circuits, and that both require that a communication endpoint be established within a process's address space before that process can use the transport layer mechanism. In the BSD socket package, a *socket* is that endpoint. A socket is an OS entity that is allocated to the process through a system call having a prototype of the form

```
int socket(int addressFamily, int socketType, int
protocolNo);
```

The `addressFamily` parameter specifies a name domain and protocol family that will be used with the socket. The supported domains depend on the particular version of UNIX (for example, the Sun Release 4.1 supports a UNIX internal domain, the ARPA internet protocols, and the ARPA IMP domain [Sun, 1990]). The `socketType` parameter defines the data type that will be used on the socket. In the Sun Release 4.1, the data types are byte streams, datagrams, raw internet packets, and sequenced packets; later releases also support Xerox Network System addresses and protocols. The `protocolNo` parameter identifies a protocol to be used on the given data type with the given address family.

The `addressFamily` parameter indicates which name space will be used by the socket if it is mapped to an external name space. Internet addresses will be used with the socket if `addressFamily` is set to `AF_INET`. In most implementations, TCP is used with the virtual circuit type and UDP is used with the datagram data type. This means that if the socket is created with a `socketType` of `SOCK_DGRAM`, then the default `protocolNo` refers to UDP. Similarly, if the `socketType` is `SOCK_STREAM`, the default `protocolNo` will be the TCP protocol. (The default protocol will be chosen if the `socketType` is defined and `protocolNo` is passed as zero.) For example, to specify that the socket is to use internet addresses and datagrams, the call would have the form

```
int socket(AF_INET, SOCK_DGRAM, 0);
```

Even though it is necessary to specify the address family for a socket, a socket can be used to *send* information over an internet without ever being associated with an internet address. However, before information can be sent to any specific location on the internet, the *receiving* socket must have been bound to an internet address of the form <net, host, port>. Otherwise, a sender would not be able to identify the socket using a <net, host, port> internet address. The rationale for the `socket` system call design is that the system must know how a socket will be used—the kind of addresses and the protocol to use when sending or receiving information. However, there is no requirement that it have an associated internet address just to send information through the socket.

In sockets that use internet addresses (those where `addressFamily` is set to `AF_INET`), a global (internet) name of the form <net, host, socket> can be associated with a socket—one says the internet address is *bound* to the socket—with an explicit system call. If one process wants to use the socket to transmit information over the internet to a remote site, then the local process can only reference the socket in the remote process by using the internet address that was previously bound to that remote socket. Therefore, if a process wants other processes to be able to send information to its own socket, it must create a socket in its own address space, then bind the socket to an internet address.

In BSD UNIX, *port* numbers are used to identify internet delivery points within a particular host machine. Port numbers 0 to 1023 are reserved for well-known services (for example, port number 21 is used by the FTP application). BSD UNIX will select a port number automatically, or the programmer can specify a specific port number (assuming it is not already bound at the time of the binding call). The `bind` system call has the form

```
int bind(int skt, struct sockaddr *addr, int addrLen);
```

The `skt` parameter is the socket identifier returned by the `socket` call. `addr` is a structure holding the internet address (for sockets using the `AF_INET` name domain).

Figure 15.21
Binding a Socket to an Internet Address

```
skt = socket(AF_INET, SOCK_STREAM, 0); /* Create the socket */
host = gethostbyname(serverHostName);   /* Get <host, net> */

/* Create a structure containing my internet address */
bzero(&addr, sizeof(addr));
addr.sin_family = host->h_addrtype;
addr.sin_port = htons(1234);
bcopy(host->h_addr, &addr.sin_addr, host->h_length);

/* Bind the internet address to my socket */
if(bind(skt, &addr, sizeof(addr))) {
        printf("Bind error ... restart\n");
```

The `sockaddr` type is used for any domain, but the `sockaddr_in` type refers to the `AF_INET` domain. The `addrLen` parameter is the length of the `addr` data structure.

The code segment shown in Figure 15.21 creates a socket in the UNIX process's address space and then binds it to an internet address at port 1234, where `netNo` and `hostNo` are the internet addresses of the machine executing the code and 1234 is the port number chosen by the programmer.

Opening a Connection in Berkeley UNIX

For two processes to successfully create a virtual circuit (or connection), one of them must play the role of an active process and the other a passive process. In a telephone analogy, the active process is the entity that requests the connection ("places the call") and the passive process accepts it ("answers"). Figure 15.22 is a code segment representing the behavior of an active process for opening a TCP connection, Figure 15.23 is a code segment representing the passive process.

Both code fragments create a socket using the internet domain and TCP. The active process then creates a data structure with the internet address of the passive process in `struct sockaddr passive` so that it can initiate the connection operation. The `connect` call specifies the socket of the active process and the `<net, host, port>` of the passive process. The active process blocks on calling `connect` until either the passive process accepts the connection request or the OS for the active process decides the call will fail and thus returns with an error code. The error return can result from various conditions, including a timer expiration (that is, the passive process does not accept the connection request in some preestablished time interval—for example, 1 minute).

The passive process creates a socket to use for accepting a connection request from an active process. Since it will receive information on this socket, it must bind the socket before the active process attempts to connect to it. The `listen` call passes information to the OS to tell it the maximum number of connection requests it should queue up for the passive process; in this case, a constant of `BACKLOG`

Figure 15.22
The Active Process in Opening a Connection

```c
#include <sys/types.h>
#include <sys/socket.h>
#include <netinet/in.h>
#include <netdb.h>

/* The active (client) process */
int main (int argc, char *argv[]) {
    int skt, port;
    char serverHostName[HOSTNAMELEN];
    struct hostent *host;
    struct sockaddr passive;
    struct protoent *protocol;

/* Get server name, serverHostName */
/* Get the port number, port */
    . . .
/* Set up a socket & address to talk to the server */
    protocol = getprotobyname("tcp");
    skt = socket(AF_UNIX, SOCK_STREAM, protocol->p_proto);
    host = gethostbyname(serverHostName);
    bzero(&passive, sizeof(passive));
    passive.sin_family = host->h_addrtype;
    passive.sin_port = htons(port);
    bcopy(host->h_addr, &passive.sin_addr, host->h_length);
    if(connect(skt, &passive, sizeof(passive))) {
                printf("Connect error ... restart\n");
                printf("(Must start Server end first)\n");
                exit(1);
    };

/* The connection is ready for use ... */
    . . .
/* All done — tear down the circuit */
    close(skt);
}
```

requests. The `accept` call is passed the connection request on `skt`, but it creates another socket, `newSkt`, and then causes the connection to be established on the `newSkt`. The passive process blocks on the `accept` call until either the process is killed or a connection request arrives on the socket (there is no time-out period for an accept operation). After the connection has been completed, the original socket, `skt`, is no longer needed, since the connection is established on `newSkt`. Both processes use a normal `close` operation to release the connection and the sockets.

Figure 15.24 provides a BSD UNIX code fragment to implement the listener and server processes. The code fragment reuses much of the code in Figure 15.23. A con-

Figure 15.23
The Passive Process in Opening a Connection

```
/* The passive (server) process */
int main(int argc, char *argv[]) {
    char serverHostName[HOSTNAMELEN];
    int port, activeLen, newSkt, skt;
    struct sockaddr *active, passive;
    struct hostent *host;

/* Get the server host name, serverHostName */
/* Get the port number, port */
    . . .
/* Set up a socket for listening */
    skt = socket(AF_INET, SOCK_STREAM, 0);
    host = gethostbyname(serverHostName);
    bzero(&passive, sizeof(passive));
    passive.sin_family = host->h_addrtype;
    passive.sin_port = htons(port);
    bcopy(host->h_addr, &passive.sin_addr, host->h_length);
/* Bind the listener's name */
    if(bind(skt, &passive, sizeof(passive))) {
        printf("Bind error ... restart\n");
        exit(1);
    }

/* Now begin waiting for a request */
    listen(skt, BACKLOG);
/* Wait for client requests */
    activeLen = sizeof(active);
    newSkt = accept(skt, &active, &activeLen);
    close(skt); /* Release extra socket */
/* Use newSkt for the connection */
    . . .
/* Disconnect */
    close(newSkt);
}
```

current BSD server (Figure 15.24) can be used by a client that has the form shown in Figure 15.25.

Reading Multiple Input Streams

The talk program will need to be able to receive input from stdin (the keyboard), and from the socket. However, if it performs a read on stdin and input arrives on the socket, the talk process will not see the network data until after the user enters data at stdin. Conversely, if the process blocks on a socket read, then if the user types information at the keyboard, that input will be ignored until after information

Figure 15.24
Server with a Listener Process

```
/* The Listener/Server Processes */
int main(int argc, char *argv[]) {
    void runServerCommand(int);
    int clientLen, newSkt, skt;
    struct sockaddr *client, listener;

    initialize(); /* Get the server host name and port number */
                   * Set up a socket for listening
                   * Fill-in the internet info
                   * Bind the listener's name
                   * Set the backlog */
/* Wait for client requests */
    clientLen = sizeof(client);
    while (TRUE) {
    /* waitForRequest() */
        newSkt = accept(skt, &client, &clientLen);
    /* Start a server to serveTheRequest, use a TCP connection*/
        if (fork() == 0) {
    /* Only the server child executes this code */
            close(skt); /* Server doesn't need the listener skt */
            runServerCommand(newSkt);
            close(newSkt); /* Server done ... terminate */
            exit(0);
        }
        close(newSkt); /* Listener doesn't need the server skt */
    }
}
```

arrives on the socket. This situation can be addressed in two different ways: by using a nonblocking (also called an asynchronous) read instead of the normal blocking read used with the stdio library, or by using the select command.

As with any file, the read end of a pipe, a file descriptor, or a socket can be configured to use nonblocking semantics with an ioctl call. After the call has been issued on the descriptor, a read on the stream returns immediately with the error code set to EWOULDBLOCK in 4.3 BSD (or EAGAIN in POSIX). Also, the read will return a value of 0, thereby indicating it did not read any information into the buffer. Alternatively, the program can check the length value to see if it is nonzero and if the read succeeded. Figure 15.26 illustrates the use of the ioctl to switch the read end of a pipe from its default blocking behavior to nonblocking behavior. You can apply this technique to a socket or stdin.

The select command allows a process to poll all its open input streams to determine which of them have data. After calling select a process can determine which input streams have data; it can then execute a normal blocking read operation on any stream that contains data. Use the man page to find out more about select if you decide to use this approach in your solution.

Figure 15.25
The Generic Client Process Schema

```
int main (int argc, char *argv[]) {
/* Data structure declarations */
/* Get server name and port number */
/* Set up a socket, s, to talk to the server */
/* Run the client application code */
    while(TRUE) {
    /* Other processing */
    /* Request service from the server */
        write(s, outBuf, BUFLEN);
        if((len = read(s, inBuf, BUFLEN)) > 0)
            inBuf[len] = '\0';
        if(inBuf[0] == TERMINATION CONDITION) break;
    }

/* All done — tear down the circuit */
        close(skt);
        exit(0);
}
```

Figure 15.26
Nonblocking read Example

```
#include <sys/ioctl.h>
int errno; /* For nonblocking read flag */
...
main() {
  int pipeID[2];
  ...
  pipe(pipeID);
/* Switch the read end of the pipe to the nonblocking mode */
  ioctl(pipeID[0], FIONBIO, &on);
  ...
  while( ...) {
  /* Poll the read end of the pipe */
    read(pipeID[0], buffer, BUFLEN);
    if (errno !=EWOULDBLOCK){
    /* Incoming info available from the pipe—process it */
        ...
    } else {
    /* Check the pipe for input again later—do other things */
        ...
    }
  }
  ...
}
```

ATTACKING THE PROBLEM

Your solution framework should be based on a client and a server process, where the client will initiate the `talk` session using an `open` system call and the server will `accept` it. Thus the server process should be started so that it will be in a state where it can accept a connection request when the client issues it.

The client and server roles are important at the time the `talk` session is started, but once the session has been established then either process can temporarily assume the role of client (that sends information to the other process). If you have used `talk` on a single machine, then you are aware that the UNIX `talk` program makes no distinction about which process is the client: If the two users begin to type at the same time, the order in which information is transmitted is arbitrary. You do not need to be concerned about solving such "unorderly" communication between two people, as that part of their protocol is not addressed by `talk`.

Your solution will thus require that you employ a client-server architecture for establishing the `talk` session but you must then have peer processes communicating with one another using byte streams over a network after the connection has been established.

Here are some suggestions for how you might go about constructing your solution:

- Write only one `talk` application program that can be used by your client and by your server after a connection has been established.

- Focus on getting a TCP connection working first. Start by making the connection work between two processes on one machine. Let the server's system choose a port number, and then specify the port number for the client at runtime. After you get that to work, be sure your code works across an internet between two machines.

- In this phase of the work, let your connection client also be the process that sends a few bytes to the connection server. That is, you will temporarily let your connection client be the data source, and have your connection server block on a read on the socket after the connection has been established.

- Add code so that the `talk` program reads `stdin` (using a blocking `read`) then transmits the information to the other program. That is, design and debug so that each process alternately reads one line of code from `stdin` then from the socket.

- Generalize your `talk` program so that it uses nonblocking read operations or the `select` system call so that it never blocks on an input stream.

16

Remote Files

> ...but what you really need is something just a little bit different
> than all the Blue-Winged Olives that the rainbow has already seen.
>
> —John Gierach, *Sex, Death,*
> *and Fly-Fishing* ∎

CHAPTER OBJECTIVES

Network technology is the principal enabling technology for distributed computation. In a network of computers, processes can communicate with one another at bandwidths three or more orders of magnitude higher than with traditional serial communication devices. The fastest networks may eventually approach the speeds of communication across the bus within an individual machine. How can software take advantage of the additional bandwidth?

This chapter uses the file abstraction of memory to consider how the OS takes advantage of networks to reference secondary storage devices located on machines across the network. Its objectives are to help the student gain a perspective of the computational model for network-based computing and to consider various OS strategies for distributing the file system across machines on the network so that an application program's use of the remotely located files is the same as the use of files stored on the local machine. The first strategy allows the file manager to use storage devices located on remote machines. The second strategy calls for the file manager functionality to be distributed between the local and the remote machines. The third strategy is for the OS to transparently copy files from remote machines, to keep multiple copies consistent, and to restore the copy to its original machine when the file is closed. This remote file technology is the foundation support for distributed computing provided by the OS, so it is covered before the more abstract support described in Chapter 17.

16.1 ■ Sharing Information Across the Network

The most obvious application of network technology is to have the OS enable a process on one machine to use the primary and/or secondary memory on another machine. Just as the OS abstracts the secondary memory's use so that the memory can be referenced using a virtual memory model, contemporary operating systems should allow processes to read from and write to the memory on remote machines that are accessible via the network.

Von Neumann computers distinguish between primary and secondary memories by providing explicit, distinct interfaces to each (see Figure 16.1). The *primary memory interface* is defined by the computer architecture itself (see Chapter 4) and extended through the address space organization described in Chapter 11. Virtual memory systems use the primary memory interface to provide access to secondary memory storage devices by loading information into the physical primary memory when it is needed.

There are two secondary storage interfaces, one implemented by storage devices and the other implemented by the file system. The storage device interface is not widely used except as a layer in the file system architecture. The file system interface is used by application programmers to reference secondary memory (see Chapter 13).

How should the process interact with remote primary and secondary memories? Even in the basic von Neumann architecture, a process must use separate interfaces to reference primary and secondary memories. Under these circumstances, the natural goal in a network environment is for a process to reference remote primary memory using the local primary memory interface and the remote secondary memory using the local secondary memory interface. Ideally, a process should be able to write a memory address to the primary memory interface, thus causing the address to be stored in a related primary memory location on another machine. It should also be able to read a remote file as if the file were stored in the local file system.

Soon after the ARPAnet had become a viable network, software was developed to implement rudimentary forms of remote file reference. The earliest system facilities allowed a user to copy files over the network from one host to another by using explicit commands. Remote file technology evolved so that today it is possible to reference

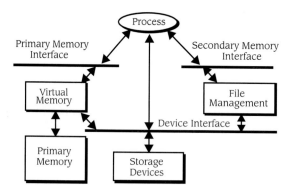

Figure 16.1
Traditional Memory Interfaces

remote files using the local file management interface. By 1990, operating systems researchers had begun working hard to use the primary memory interface to implement various kinds of remote primary memory. Following this evolutionary path in OS support for network-accessible memory, this chapter focuses on OS technology to support remote file access. Chapter 17 considers the exploratory work in distributed memory technology along with other contemporary network protocols to support distributed computation.

16.1.1 ■ Explicit File Copying Systems

Files are the classic unit of sharing among processes. Information can be created by one process, written to a file, and then used by another process. Information also can be shared across machines by explicitly copying files from one machine to another across the communication network. In classic WAN communications systems, such as the ARPAnet, explicit file copy operations were the most common mechanism available to accomplish sharing across machines. When a process on a local machine needed information from a process on a remote machine, the remote process wrote the information to a file and then the user explicitly copied the file from the remote machine to the local machine.

Explicit operations are used in a conventional file manager to copy files from one location to another in a system's directory using a simple shell command. The earliest network system software provided a facility to allow a user to copy a file out of one machine's file system into another. This can be accomplished by using either the operating system's point-to-point communications functions or transport layer software to "connect" with a remote machine and then having a surrogate process on the remote machine retrieve a copy of the target file and write it to the connection. After the local end of the connection passes the information requesting the file copy operation, it waits on the connection for the surrogate to begin sending a copy of the file over the connection. The local end accepts the copy and stores it in the local file system for subsequent use. The ARPAnet `ftp` and UNIX `uucp` commands (see below) represent examples using the network and communications facilities, respectively.

There are other manual file transfer packages used across heterogeneous networks. (A heterogeneous network is a network that has different kinds of host machines.) The ISO OSI File Transfer, Access and Management (FTAM) protocol is the standard ISO OSI mechanism for manual file transfer; `telnet` and `ftp` are widely used for the same purpose in contemporary computer networks.

16.1.1.1 ■ The ARPAnet File Transfer Protocol

The File Transfer Protocol (FTP) can be invoked from a user interface—for example, the `ftp` program in UNIX systems—to explicitly copy files between host machines on a network using TCP/IP. The `ftp` program is a user interface to FTP. Each host that supports FTP starts a server process to accept service requests. When an application process intends to use FTP, it executes `ftp` client code on the local machine.

FTP uses a control connection and a data connection for file transfer. The server expects the initial service request to arrive on well-known port 21, so when a client wishes to use FTP, its TCP connection request is directed at `<net, host, 21>`. When the connection has been opened, the client and server use the control connection to exchange subsequent commands and control responses.

Data is transferred between the client and server when a file is copied (either way) and when the client obtains a listing of the files in a directory. Each time the client issues a command causing this kind of data transfer, a data connection is opened to accommodate the transfer. During an FTP session, the data connection may be opened and closed more than once, depending on the nature of the commands.

Otherwise, FTP is a relatively straight-forward client-server program and is well documented in a number of places, including in Stevens [1994, ch. 27].

16.1.1.2 ■ The UNIX UUCP Command

UUCP (Unix to Unix CoPy) is a UNIX program that exchanges files using serial communication devices and dial-up modems; the user interface program for UUCP is `uucp`. UUCP uses a routing table defined by the machine's system administrator to call up a UUCP program on another computer and copy files back and forth.

The UNIX `uucp` command has the same appearance as the local `cp` command, except that one source or destination of the copy is a path name to, and inside of, a remote machine. The remote filename has the form

```
system_name_1!system_name_2!... system_name_N!n_pathname
```

where each `system_name` is the name of a UNIX machine stored in the UUCP routing table. If there is more than one `system_name` in the remote file name, they define a path through `system_name_1` to `system_name_2` and so on to `system_name_N`, where `n_pathname` defines a location for the file in the file system for machine `system_name_N`. Authentication applies to UUCP operations at each system; thus UUCP is normally used to read a file from a remote host. If the intent is to write a file to a remote host, then the protection settings may allow the user only to log in to the remote machine and to perform a `uucp` back to the original local machine.

UUCP has been supplanted by newer commands that operate in more modern network environments, including `rcp` and `rdist`. In these commands, the file is referenced by providing a DNS host name to reference the remote host and an absolute path name on that host.

16.1.2 ■ Implicit File Sharing

Explicit file transfer of the type described in the previous subsection requires yet another interface, or at least an extension to the normal file interface as illustrated in both the FTP and UUCP examples. Implicit file sharing makes better use of existing file and secondary memory interfaces.

The separate primary and secondary memory interfaces, and the implied separate address spaces, reflect the vast difference in memory access times for secondary and primary memories. Secondary memory access times are normally several orders of magnitude slower than primary memory access times. Of course, if the primary memory implementation incorporates virtual memory, the differences in access times for information only loaded on the storage device will be about the same through either interface. However, the virtual memory implementation will handle the details for retrieving and restoring information to/from the storage devices and will tend to keep information being referenced in the primary memory. The Multics-style memory interface (see Figure 16.2) enables a programmer to reference all primary and secondary memories using an extended primary memory interface. Since a primary memory address employs a segment and offset, the segment names can be mapped to filenames. The memory manager in the OS automatically loads segments on reference and then binds physical addresses to the resulting two-component address in the primary memory interface. All information stored on the storage devices can be referenced as segments and offsets. (These systems also supply a file interface to reference secondary storage, so the file and device interfaces are illustrated as redundant interfaces in the figure.)

Ideally, when information stored at a remote site is to be accessed by a process, the corresponding program could use one of the two customary memory interfaces. Using existing interfaces is the main feature of remote files, since this approach uses the secondary memory interface to reference files stored on remote machines. Figure 16.3 represents the general design strategies for reusing the secondary storage interface with a remote server: The server can be a *remote disk* facility to provide a virtual disk driver (to a physical disk located on a remote machine) with an interface similar to that of a local disk driver. Alternatively, the remote server could be a *remote file* extension to the local file system and use a new, internal remote file interface. Both alternatives are used in contemporary computers. Section 16.2 describes the remote disk approach, and Sections 16.3 and 16.4 address two different remote file approaches. Before considering the details, this section discusses the general criteria for choosing one approach over the other.

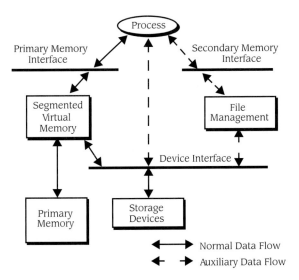

Figure 16.2
The Multics Segmented Memory Interface

16.1.3 ■ The Remote Storage Interface

Recall from the discussion of device management in Chapter 5, supplemented by the new information regarding security in Chapter 14, that the device driver interface is used primarily by system software rather than application software. In terms of Figure 16.3, this means application program access to local storage devices occurs over the local file interface. In the interest of consistency, the remote disk and remote file interfaces also use the local file interface with little or no change for remote storage access. They do this by reimplementing the local file manager so that it can either reference local files in the normal way or reference remote storage using the remote service interface.

Low-level file system interfaces are substantially easier to implement with remote file services than are file systems that have more sophisticated functions at the interface. In this book, the file system interface is assumed to be similar to the one described in Section 13.1.1. The file is represented as a byte stream accessed by a logical read/write head. The file organization and status is maintained in the file's descriptor. The essential operations on the file are open, close, read, write, and seek.

Because the low-level file interface is used for manipulating both local and remote files, access to a remote file is said to be *transparent*. However, there is one caveat concerning transparency: While the file manipulation commands are the same for local and remote files, the *names* of the files identify them as being either local or remote. Hence, the transparency applies to the functions on the interface but not to the actual path names of files available to an application. By taking advantage of the UNIX-style mount operation, remote filenames can even be made to appear to be local filenames. This means the file location is completely transparent to the programmer and user, although the system administration will have to handle the problem with appropriate mount commands. How this is done is described in Section 16.5.

Remote disks always provide location transparency (except to system administrators), meaning that the access to the remote storage device containing the file is handled

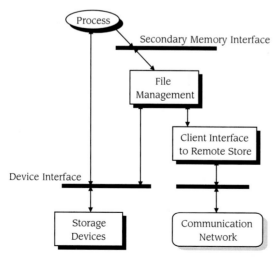

Figure 16.3
Using the Secondary Memory Interface for Remote Memory

entirely by the file system. From the application program's perspective, references to remote disks are the same as references to a local disk, since both use the local file interface. In the extreme, the local machine may not even be configured with a disk, meaning every file (and disk) access is to a remote machine.

For example, whenever an interactive user runs a program, it is loaded from the remote machine's disk. When the compiler translates a program, the source program is read from the remote machine's disk and the relocatable modules are written to the remote machine's disk. The remote disk location is determined by the system administrator, so the remote access is logically transparent to the user, even with respect to the name. The primary place where remote disk access could be perceived by the user is in the time required to access a file implemented on a remote disk, although this too may be transparent depending on the relative speeds of a local disk and the remote disk and network.

16.1.4 ■ Distributing the Work

Implicit file sharing that is using the local file interface assumes that the system implements the logic illustrated in Figure 16.3. The figure identifies a local server interface that is implementing functionality to the remote machine using the network controller and protocols. Figure 16.4 is an elaboration of the block diagram shown in Figure 16.3. Specifically, the architecture is a client-server architecture, with the application program executing on the client machine and the remote file facility acting as a server. The client machine OS implements part of the function for implementing remote files within the "remote access" module. In fact, this local part of the remote server may be a significant part of the remote file service. The approach is to keep the local file manager

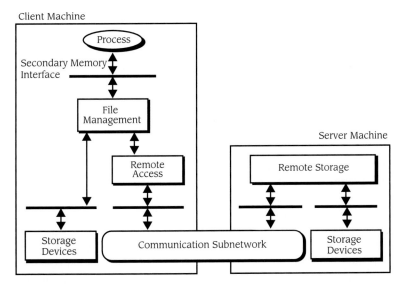

Figure 16.4
The Application Client and the Remote Server

as similar as possible to one with no remote file capability. This means that a configuration that does not use remote files need not absorb performance or space costs associated with remote access. Hence, the "remote access" module is the part of the OS that is responsible for implementing the remote file operations, network interactions, transparency, and other features required when using remote files. However, it allows an application process to simply invoke the client part of the file server without knowing the details of the remote access.

The "remote storage" module in the server machine accepts storage commands from the client remote access module, performs the operation on its storage devices, and then returns results to the client remote access module. The main question in this organization is how should the normal file system functionality be divided between the remote access module in the client machine and the remote storage module on the server machine? Once a strategy is determined for partitioning the functionality, then several other questions must be answered in the design, including these. What network protocols are best suited to this distributed file manager? Can a distributed file manager provide an acceptable level of performance? How can network and server reliability be assured in such a configuration? These questions characterize the fundamental design issues in remote file systems.

In the last 15 years, three basic strategies for partitioning the file system functionality have been widely used:

■ Have the server implement remote disk functionality, meaning the client-server interface is similar to the interface that a local file system has with a local disk driver. In this case, a client machine reads and writes disk blocks from and to a disk server. Very little of the overall file system functionality is implemented in the server. For example, the disk server does not know what a file is, or even what blocks are in a file. This approach is described in Section 16.2.

■ Distribute a larger portion of functionality to the server so that, for example, the remote file server can service file requests on the basis of information in a file's descriptor. The client-server interface is an internal interface that differs from any interface used in a normal local file system. This difference results because a conventional file manager essentially is split into two modules, with one implemented in the client remote access module and the other in the server remote storage. This approach is described in Section 16.3.

■ Replicate cooperating file managers in the client and server so that files are implicitly copied. A remote access operation obtains a local copy of the file from the remote storage when the file is opened. In this file caching approach, the file server is a complete file system that provides service at the level of full file operations, such as copying and deleting a file. File caching systems must explicitly keep track of the location of various copies that are made for clients and manage the copies so that their contents are always consistent with one another. The idea of information caching and the consistency problem was introduced in Section 11.4. This is an equivalent problem, although consistency is ensured for an entire file rather than a block of information. Because of this dramatic difference in information container characteristics, the techniques used to ensure consistency in file caching must be different from those used for block caching. This approach is described in Section 16.4.

16.2 ■ Remote Disk Systems

In the 1980s, the cost of disk drives was a dominant cost of the hardware in a workstation. Today, disk drive costs have decreased so that they are no longer an issue in constructing cost-effective workstations. Disk drives of the 1980s also produced heat and noise, sometimes causing them to be an annoyance when directly attached to a workstation in an office environment. Both rationales encouraged the development of OS support for remote disks. Workstations were configured with a network connection but with no local disk. Within the network, one or more server machines were configured with one or more large, fast disk drives. The diskless workstations used the disks on the server machine as their secondary storage. While the diskless workstation is no longer a cost-effective solution (having been replaced by diskless *X* terminals, interacting with a server using the *X* protocol), it provided an important step in the evolution of distributed computation technology. However, the recent trend to network computers (with a Web browser and virtual machine interpreter) signal a return to diskless workstations. Remote disk servers illustrate many important aspects of a popular class of client-server applications that must be supported by modern operating systems. While remote disk technology is less widely used today than it was in 1990, it is important to understand the rationale and design of these systems prior to studying remote file systems.

Figure 16.5 illustrates the organization of function between a client workstation and the remote disk server. Rather than a new remote file manager having to be provided, the client machine incorporates a local *virtual disk driver* (*VDD*) to replace the conventional local disk driver for remote accesses. The VDD software interface serves the same purpose as a local disk driver in the sense that it allows the file system (and other client software) to reference an abstract storage device—the *remote disk application* (*RDA*). The abstract disk can be read from or written to as if it were a local disk, but other low-level disk operations such as formatting, partitioning, and reading boot

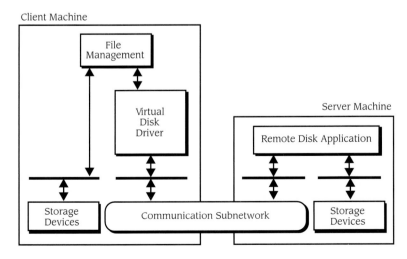

Figure 16.5
A Shared Remote Disk Server

records from a disk cannot normally be done from the client machine. The remote disk application accepts commands from the VDD, applies them to the server's disk driver, and returns the result to the client VDD. Notice that the file manager must distinguish between local and remote disk accesses. Thus it must contain local disk addresses for normal local file accesses and virtual disk addresses for remote file accesses.

Just as a physical disk has a device address and a set of logical block addresses, the remote disk has a transport layer address, <net, host, port>, and a set of logical block addresses. Hence, the VDD must reference the server that is using the network's naming facilities. This is accomplished by using the transport layer facilities to bind the server's address into a name registry in a network name server when the disk server begins operation. The system administrator will have configured the client machine so that it can use an easily determined name to retrieve the disk server transport layer address from a name server. The VDD can then begin communicating directly with the disk server, as is done in the FTP example.

16.2.1 ■ The Remote Disk Operation

The VDD encapsulates each disk command into a network packet and then transmits it to the surrogate RDA on the disk server machine (see Figure 16.6). The RDA unpacks the disk command from the network packet and generates a request to its local disk, based on the command it received. For example, a read command includes the command and a virtual disk address. The RDA translates the virtual disk address to a local disk address and issues a local disk read operation. Similarly, a write command packet includes the command, a virtual disk block, and the virtual disk address. When the disk server's local disk operation completes, the RDA encapsulates the result of the operation—a write completion notification, or, in the case of a read, a disk block—and sends it to the VDD on the client machine. The client VDD unpacks the result and returns it to the local application, which is ordinarily the client file system.

Figure 16.6
Client-Server Machine Interaction for Remote Disks

Client System	Server System
. . .	(waiting for a request)
file_mgr: diskRequest(details);	. . .
VDD: Pack parameters;	. . .
VDD: Send request;	(waiting for a request);
(waiting for a reply)	RDA: Unpack parameters;
. . .	RDA: Generate local disk op;
. . .	(Local disk op in progress)
. . .	RDA: Disk op complete;
. . .	RDA: Generate reply;
(waiting for a reply)	RDA: Send reply;
VDD: Receive reply;	(waiting for a request);
VDD: Unpack reply parameters;	. . .
VDD: Return to file_mgr;	. . .
. . .	. . .

Recall the nature of the interface to a disk driver described in Chapter 5. Since disks are block-oriented devices, units of transfer are disk sectors. Suppose a sector fits wholly within a single network packet, with a small amount of extra space for the command and address. Then it would be possible to transmit a disk sector between the client machine and the server machine by using a single packet. This observation supports the use of a datagram level service, especially since the service delivers a higher level of performance than do connection-based protocols.

The remote disk architecture is simple, but it potentially suffers from reliability problems. Assuming that LANs have considerably lower reliability than do computer buses, are they sufficiently reliable to carry disk access requests and responses, especially using network-level protocols? Is a client machine permanently blocked, or does it lose data stored on a disk if the disk server crashes while being used by the client? These issues are discussed next.

16.2.2 ■ Performance Considerations

Performance is an important criterion for remote disk servers. For a remote disk server to be competitive with local disk access times, the client must be able to transmit a command to it and have it perform an I/O operation on its disk drive. The server then must return the result of the operation to the client over the network and return the result to the application in an amount of time similar to the local disk access time. This scenario clearly depends on there being a significant difference in the access times of an inexpensive disk that might be configured into a client machine and of a high-end disk that might be configured into a shared server. In today's highly competitive disk drive market, the difference in access times for inexpensive and expensive disk drives is only a factor of three or four, whereas in 1980 it was a factor of ten or more.

When is a remote disk server sufficiently fast? If we were to compare transfer rates of a local floppy disk and those of a high-speed hard disk on a server, remote disk access is likely to be much faster than the local disk access. The rotational delay and seek times in a floppy disk are so slow compared to hard disk technology that the network overhead is easily overcome in comparison.

If the client machine has a slow hard disk and the server has a fast hard disk, empirical evidence suggests that the access times of remote disk servers are still close enough to justify their use for most computing environments. For example, in a remote disk server of the late 1970s local disk operations required about 60 milliseconds to transfer a block, while a fast disk required about 25 milliseconds. In an experiment reported in the literature at that time, a client machine connected to a server machine configured with a high-speed disk of the era required about 48 milliseconds per block transfer, provided that only a single client was using the server [Swinehart et al., 1979]. (In these experiments, the client and server were connected with a prototype Ethernet operating at 3 Mbps.) However, when two clients were using the server, the access time increased to 76 milliseconds and when three clients shared the disk server, to 100 milliseconds. These measurement experiments suggested that the bottleneck in performance is with the server rather than the network.

In another measurement study, researchers showed that remote disk servers were still cost effective [Lazowska et al., 1986]. The experiments reported in this paper again pointed to the server, rather than the network, as the source of the performance bottleneck.

TCP provides reliable communication at the expense of explicit packet acknowledgments transmitted at the network level. UDP is faster than TCP because it does not incorporate any mechanism to ensure reliable delivery. For performance reasons, remote disk servers are designed to use datagrams or, in some cases, raw network layer packets. This approach explicitly relies on the ability of the client and server to handle reliability through specific higher-level mechanisms.

In a remote disk environment, a network transmission cannot be permitted to wander around in the internet due to routing. Therefore remote disk systems require the disk server and client to be attached to a common LAN. This means the network need not use the routing functionality at all. Instead, a highly specialized protocol for client-server interaction can be implemented directly on the data link layer. Hence the datagram/packet/frame performance can begin to approach the threshold of performance possible in the physical network.

In local file systems, block caching is used to overlap the disk I/O time with the CPU time. In a remote disk server, the client can cache blocks by reading ahead, but the server cannot do this because it has no knowledge of the file organization. Client-side caching is widely used as a performance enhancement in remote disk systems.

16.2.3 ■ Reliability

Suppose a virtual disk sector, ordinarily the same size as a physical disk sector on the server, fits wholly within a packet. Then the reliability is related to two issues. The first is ensuring that a disk command eventually gets executed by the server. The second is synchronizing the operations of the client and the server should one or the other crash during a disk request.

The network layer guarantees reliable delivery of the contents of a maximum-sized packet. This guarantee is independent of the underlying data link layer frame size. This means the network packet may be fragmented and reconstituted within the sender and receiver network layers. However, the entire packet may be lost. (In an internet configuration, packets could be delivered in a different order than they were transmitted if they were to pass through a series of gateways. However, for performance reasons the configuration has already been restricted so that the client and server must be on the same LAN.) The focus for reliability is ensuring that the system works properly even if a packet is lost.

16.2.3.1 ■ Reliable Command Execution

Local disk commands are restricted to a small number of operations: block `read` and `write`, track `seek`, status commands, and a few more obscure disk commands—for example, to start or stop the drive motor. The very low-level commands, such as drive motor control, are not implemented across the remote disk interface, since only the server should have this level of control over the physical disk. Similarly, support of most other obscure disk commands is not needed. Thus the VDD is really required only to transmit `read`, `write`, and `seek` commands.

In normal operation, the client issues a `read` or `write` command and then waits for the server to respond, either with an acknowledgment of completion of a `write` or with the return of a disk block to complete a `read`. Suppose a client issued a `read` command and either the packet containing the command was lost before it was delivered to the server or the result was lost after the server had completed the `read` operation. From the client's perspective, the command was unsuccessful in both cases. What should the client do? The customary protocol is for the VDD to start a countdown timer running when it issues the command. If the result is returned before the timer expires, the timer is disabled. If the timer expires before the result is returned, the VDD assumes the `read` command failed and reissues it to the server.

There are three cases to consider when the timer expires:

■ If the first command never reached the server, ignoring the command is the correct thing to do.

■ Suppose the first operation had reached the server, but the result was lost in the network. The second `read` operation does not affect the correct operation of the server, but it allows the client to recover from the lost packet. In this case, the `read` operation is said to be *idempotent*. This means it can be executed repeatedly, producing the same result as if it had been applied only one time (provided we do not consider higher-level problems such as a different client writing the block between the first `read` and the second `read`).

■ Suppose the server was oversubscribed so that after the client timed out and reissued the command, the server responded to the first `read` operation and then sometime later to the second operation. In this case, the second `read` did no logical harm, although it contributed to the work of an already overworked server. The client end of the protocol must be prepared to throw away such late-arriving results from a command.

There are two key points in these cases. First, idempotent operations can be issued with impunity to the server. Second, only the client might be harmed if it cannot handle multiple responses to repeated requests. (However, it can count how many times it repeated a command and thus be prepared to handle a bounded number of responses.)

A disk `write` command is also idempotent. If the command packet is lost before it is delivered to the server, the VDD will time out and reissue the command. If the command was delivered to the server and the information was written to the disk but the acknowledgment was lost, a second `write` command will cause the RDA to overwrite the disk sector with the same information. Multiple writes will cause multiple acknowledgments to be issued to the client. These acknowledgments are easy to handle.

A command to step the read/write head to the next higher-numbered track is not idempotent. Suppose the head is at track 50. Then on execution, the head will move to track 51, while a second execution will move it to track 52.

Suppose the client-server interface is designed so that all commands issued by the client are idempotent commands and all have acknowledgments. Then, assuming the network will eventually deliver a matching pair of command and acknowledgment packets, the system can ensure that commands will be executed. The key issue in achieving this level of reliability is the idempotent nature of the commands. If any command is not idempotent, then the approach will not work.

With respect to acknowledgments, certain heuristics can be applied to reduce the number of explicit communications for them. In the case of a `write` command, the acknowledgment must be explicit. But in the case of a `read`, the acknowledgment is implied by the client's receiving the result of the `read`.

This approach, like many other client-server protocols, relies on the client's using a countdown timer to reissue the command if an acknowledgment is not received in a reasonable amount of time.

16.2.3.2 ■ Recovering the Disk after a Server Crash

Suppose the server crashes during some session of `read` and `write` operations on the disk—for example, after the VDD opened a file on the client machine. If the server never recovers from the crash, the client machine will be unable to complete its work. In modern systems, the disk server will eventually recover and attempt to respond to any requests it had not serviced prior to its recovery. Because of the timeout strategy employed in the client, the client will continue to reissue commands to the server after it crashes. (Some designs count the number of consecutive failed commands and abandon the command after the number reaches some threshold. In principle, the client can continue to reissue commands for an indefinite period of time—until the server recovers from its crash.) How will the server know what commands it had received prior to crashing but which it had not serviced? How will the server know how to recover from the command it was executing when it crashed? What will happen to files opened by the client but stored on the server? Will their contents be destroyed by inconsistent file descriptors or disk block pointers?

With the approach that remote disk servers take, most of these difficult questions can be ignored. The approach is based on the idea of a *stateless server.* A remote disk server need not keep any state related to any file, just as a physical disk need not keep any state related to the files stored on it. The disk server simply reads and writes blocks with no knowledge of any links encoded into blocks. The file descriptor is interpreted entirely by the file system in the client system. Hence, when a file is opened, its file descriptor is read from the disk server through one or more block read operations. The server does not need to know that the client has retrieved a file descriptor. When the file system traverses the block list for the file, it issues block read/write operations according to the client software interpretation of the file descriptor. Again, the disk server is unable to even traverse a list of file blocks.

When blocks are added to or deleted from the file, the file system in the client reads the appropriate blocks from the disk server and then manipulates them. Later, the client writes the blocks back to the disk server according to its caching strategy. As a result, if the server crashes while a file is open, then when it recovers, there is no state for it to recover in order to be consistent with operations pending prior to its recovery. The server does not need to know what commands were issued prior to its recovery, since the respective clients will eventually timeout and reissue the commands after the recovery.

The main issue regarding recovery that the disk server must handle relates to the operation it was processing when it crashed. If the disk sector involved in the operation was to be written, then if the server started the physical write operation to the disk, it must complete it before crashing. Otherwise, the disk sector would contain some old and some new information. Of course, this is a requirement for local disk operations as well. If the local disk fails during a write operation, then in general the information in that sector is lost for either a local or remote disk write. If the server had not started the actual disk write operation, then the server command can be repeated by the client with no harm. In order for the client to know whether the operation completed, the server must acknowledge each operation. If no acknowledgment is received by the client within a prespecified time interval, the client simply reissues the command.

16.2.4 ■ The Future of Remote Disks

Remote disk servers are attractive because it is easy to design a server to recover from network and server crashes. However, such servers have performance penalties due to the nature of the work partition. Consider an operation such as file positioning in a system in which the blocks are combined using a linked list. As noted in Chapter 13, even in a local disk system this can be a time-consuming operation, since it requires the file manager to read every disk block from the head of the file (or current position) to the disk block containing the destination. In a remote disk system, each block read also causes a network transfer from the server to the client. If the server were to be designed so that it had knowledge of the file descriptor, then substantial network traffic—and delay—could be eliminated by issuing the seek command to the server to have it locate the block that contains the target. This would be done without its interacting with the client. However, this approach changes the character of the disk server to be that of a file server.

Disk technology has essentially eliminated remote disks as a viable commercial product. As of this writing, a 20 GB disk drive with 10-milliseconds access time can be purchased for a few hundred dollars in retail markets. The economical and performance motivations for diskless workstations no longer exists. Nevertheless, the advantage of keeping a single copy of files on a shared server for different clients to use has become even more important now than it was 15 years ago. This combination of factors has shifted interest from remote disk servers to remote file technologies.

16.3 ■ Remote File Systems

Remote file systems provide the same interface to the application program as local file systems (which could be implemented with a remote disk). They may differ from local file systems in the naming scheme (depending on whether the mount technique is used). Their implementation differs from remote disks in the way the file system functionality is distributed between the client and the server. As indicated previously, file servers can be designed to substantially reduce network delays by reducing the amount and frequency of information flowing between the client and the server. The cost is that the client and server must each contain part of the state of the file system operation and then coordinate their activities correspondingly. A file server is a concrete example of how the OS uses distributed software to provide a network service.

16.3.1 ■ The General Architecture

A local file is implemented on a disk device as a collection of related disk blocks. As discussed in Chapter 13, the relation may be implemented as a linked list, an index table, or some other data structure. The file descriptor provides the "road map" to the disk blocks by pointing to the first block in the list for linked lists, by addressing blocks for indexed allocation, or by indirectly addressing blocks—for example, in UNIX inodes. The goal in file server design is to increase performance over a disk server by having it take advantage of knowledge of the file structure in implementing file manipulation commands.

The remote file system is divided into a client part and a server part, as shown in Figure 16.7. The client part implements the operations required to interact with the server part. Less obviously, the local file manager must be changed to accommodate its existing access to local files and to be able to use the remote file service. A generic file system module replaces the ordinary local file system module. The generic module is used by the application software on the client machine to interact with the local file system and with the remote file system. Based on whether the operation applies to a local or to a remote file, the generic part passes file system requests to its local part or to the client part of the remote file system.

For the sake of discussion—and because it reflects reality in most systems—assume the file system supports low-level byte stream files. This means the operations implemented by the file system correspond to `open`, `close`, `read`, `write`, `seek`, and possibly some form of `ioctl`. Here is a brief summary of I/O in a local file system. The `open` command causes the file descriptor to be loaded into a server's primary memory from the disk, thus preparing the file's byte stream to be read from or written to. A `read` or `write` operation applies to the current read/write file position into the byte stream and may cause blocks to be read or written, depending on past `read`s and `write`s and the contents of the file systems buffers. Part of the operation is for the file system to pack and unpack blocks as needed. The `close` operation causes output-full buffers

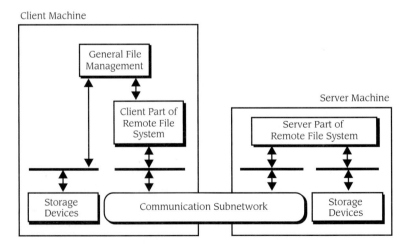

Figure 16.7
Architecture for a Remote File Server

(those that are full and waiting to be written to a device) and the file descriptor to be written back to the disk.

The logical file system functionality could be split in several different places. For example, the server might use the file descriptor to implement block management and buffering. The client would handle read/write head management, packing and unpacking, and additional buffering (see Figure 16.8). This approach is appealing because it causes most of the details of block list management to be encapsulated in the server, while the details of block-to-stream translation are encapsulated in the client. The client must still maintain a current copy of the file descriptor so that it can perform authentication, maintain the part of the current state related to reading and writing the byte stream, and manage locks. Conversely, the server also needs to know where the file position references the byte stream so that it can read/write blocks as required. It further must know where the file's blocks are located. An alternative approach might be to attempt to keep block management in the client but to have the server implement block buffering. This approach also requires that the state of an open file be kept in both the client and the server. In general, the client and server need to share information kept in the file descriptor, since the different parts of a file system use various parts of the file descriptor. When the functionality is distributed, the file descriptor must be replicated in the client and the server.

In all of the remote file server approaches, an open command is passed to the server. The server then retrieves the file descriptor, keeping a copy of it and transmitting another copy to the client part of the file system. Thus redundant copies of the file descriptor exist on the remote disk, in the remote server, and in the client.

Independent of the specific function partitioning, there are two major issues to decide in designing the remote file system:

■ Since both the client and the server may buffer disk blocks, what is the most effective buffering strategy to incorporate into the system? Is there an advantage to buffering in one place or the other, or should buffering be used on both sides?

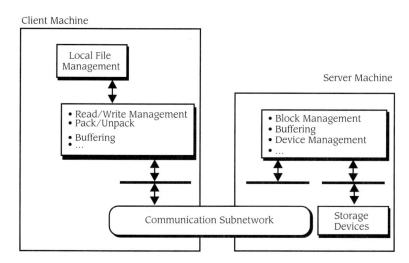

Figure 16.8
One Partition of the File System Functionality

■ Idempotent operations and stateless servers can be used to implement a simple crash recovery policy but at a cost of increased network traffic. Since the file descriptor must be maintained on both the client and the server, how can this strategy be applied to file servers? What is the effect on performance if it is used?

16.3.2 ■ Block Caching

Logically, when a remote file `read` operation is issued to the client part, it is packaged and sent to the server. The server decodes the message, reads the block from its disk, and then returns the block to the client. Recall from the discussion of local file systems that the sequential nature of files strongly encourages buffering to overlap the operation of the device and the CPU. This can result in substantial performance gains (a reduction in run-time for the process). In a remote file server, buffering can be used to overlap the operation of the network transmission as well as the disk access on the server by buffering in both the client and the server (see Figure 16.9). On the read side, the server reads ahead on the disk and buffers blocks for the client to request. When the client is able, it requests read buffers from the server and enqueues them in anticipation of the client application that is requesting them. Buffered write information travels in the opposite direction.

The strict read-ahead, write-behind buffering policy can be made more effective by adding one layer of sophistication to the technique. Data references to a file tend to follow a locality pattern, as was observed in virtual memory studies years ago. That is, when one item in a block is referenced, then the sequential file semantics suggest that the next byte will also be referenced. In many applications, however, data within a block may be referenced repeatedly without following pure sequential patterns; that is, the data references have a locality.

The existence of the locality means that when a block is copied into a memory buffer, it may be referenced repeatedly, just as a page is referenced repeatedly in a virtual memory system. So it is easy to add a replacement policy to the buffering scheme so that it does not remove a buffer once it has been read from or written to by the client unless the replacement policy, such as LRU, specifies that it should be removed. Such a policy replaces the natural read-ahead, write-behind buffer semantics. Once the buffering technique takes a replacement strategy into account, it can also vary the amount of

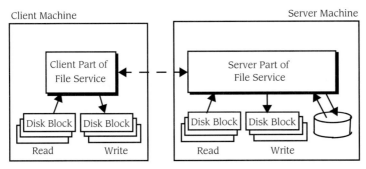

Figure 16.9
Buffering in a Remote File System

information copied into the client by applying the policy to large or small blocks of the file. Large blocks tend to capture the data locality because they keep a large number of bytes in the client buffers. However, when a new block must be loaded, the time to load it also will be high. This technique is distinguished from simple buffering by calling it *block caching*.

Remote file systems allow multiple clients to access the same files, potentially at the same time. In a local file system, if two or more processes open a file for writing at the same time, then each of their individual `write` operations will be written back to the disk shortly after the logical `write` has occurred. In caching, a block may be retained in the client for some time before it is written back to the server's disk. Suppose two processes have opened a single file for writing and each has cached the same block into its client machine. Now, when one writes the block in the client, the result of the `write` will not be perceived by the other client for an arbitrary amount of time. This is known as the block cache consistency problem. It is analogous to the cache consistency problem in shared-memory multiprocessors.

How can the OS address the block cache consistency problem? Some file servers support only *sequential write sharing*. In this approach, multiple clients are precluded from having any file open in which any one of the clients has write permission. If a file is written to as if it were a local disk and then closed, the caches are flushed and any subsequent open will operate on the data created by the `write`. Sequential write sharing ensures that tardy cache blocks from a previously opened file do not interfere with a new open command on the file. The more difficult problem of handling pending write-back blocks from some other client is addressed by forcing the tardy writer to update the server's disk image if an open arrives before the write-back has completed.

Concurrent write sharing is a more flexible approach in which several clients may have the same file open for reading or writing. In this case, newly written data must be propagated to the reader clients in a timely fashion. Concurrent write sharing is handled by simply disabling caching if any client has a shared file open for writing.

The Sprite Network File System—a UNIX-compatible file server implemented at the University of California at Berkeley—uses a more aggressive strategy for caching to achieve high performance. It was designed to take advantage of two empirical observations about UNIX files. First, high-performance local file systems make extensive use of buffering between the user-level process and the disk. Second, the amount of physical memory used for buffering has a large effect on the performance.

Sprite is carefully designed to enhance performance through caching techniques:

■ Since it exploits client caching techniques, it must go to extra effort to ensure coherency among the cached copies of the file.

■ It employs dynamic space allocation for each cache, in which the cache allocation strategy is intertwined with the virtual-memory mechanism.

Sprite uses a *delayed write-back policy* whenever a client writes into its cache. Instead of the clients immediately flushing the cached information to the server and through the server cache onto the disk, `writes` are accommodated when there is "idle" time at the server or after a suitable time interval (about a minute) has elapsed. This allows the client `write` operations to complete without waiting for the server disk `write` to complete. It sometimes economizes in `writes` when data is deleted shortly after it is written. For example, a compiler may create an intermediate file between passes 1 and 2 and then destroy the file when the compilation has completed. Text editors also tend to keep temporary files around for short periods of time. In the delayed write-back approach, the cached information may not yet have been written to the disk. Sprite uses a 30-second delay on write-back operations and then has another 30 seconds in which to actually accomplish the action.

Sprite researchers reported that their experiments with the file system resulted in attractive performance comparisons. Clients using caching had a 10 to 40 percent speedup over clients not using caching. Also, by using caching, diskless clients were less than 12 percent slower than workstations with a similar disk for their benchmark set. Based on the utilizations observed in the experiments, the developers conjectured that for a typical configuration of clients running "average" programs, a server ought to be able to handle up to 50 client machines.

16.3.3 ■ Crash Recovery

In local file systems, buffering carries another danger. That is, if the disk or machine crashes while information is buffered, especially the file descriptor, then information may be lost. The danger is higher in a remote file system, since not only can the disk and machine crash but also information may be lost due to an unreliable network. If the server crashes and then recovers, one must be able to determine the full state of each session that was in effect at the time of the crash. Crash recovery is an important consideration in the design.

Some file server designs are oriented more toward reliable operation at the cost of performance, while others are more performance-oriented, thus requiring the incorporation of complex crash recovery algorithms. Both designs attempt to have high reliability and high performance, but the tradeoffs are balanced differently.

16.3.3.1 ■ Recovery-oriented File Servers

The strategy of designing a server so that it is stateless (to simplify recovery after it crashes) can be extended from the technique used in a disk server for a remote file server. In a stateless file server, the file descriptor is always kept on the client machine and the client always sends a copy of the relevant parts of the descriptor to the server whenever the client requests an operation. As a further hedge, on the execution of an open command the server retrieves the file descriptor and makes a copy of it before passing it to the client. The information in the server's file descriptor is correct at the time the open command is executed. Now assume the server uses only the contents of the file descriptor as a "hint" for all subsequent operations. The copy of the file descriptor in the client keeps the actual state of the file. This means the server can use the file descriptor to perform any operation to enhance performance, such as buffering. However, the server is not allowed to perform any operation in which the correctness of the operation depends on the correctness of its copy of the file descriptor. If the server needs to know the file descriptor state before it performs an operation, such as block management, it must obtain a current copy of the appropriate part of the file descriptor with the request. The client will always cause the server to perform such operations by virtue of a request. Each such request includes the correct values of the file descriptor with the request. The server is never allowed to perform operations whose correctness depends on the file descriptor state without being instructed to do so by the client or without first obtaining permission to perform the operation from the client.

Next, the operations invoked by the client must all be idempotent. For low-level file systems, this is not difficult to ensure, since these operations are `close`, `open`, `read`, `write`, and `seek`. The `read` and `write` semantics are the same as the disk `read` and `write` semantics and can be made to be idempotent. `open` is idempotent because it can be repeated without the file descriptor changing. Similarly, `close` is idempotent because it causes buffers to be flushed to the disk and the file descriptor to be written back to the disk.

This file server design allows the system to use faster network protocols than those that require reliable communication. For example, this style of remote file server could use UDP or a raw packet interface in the network layer of the network.

The Sun Network File System (NFS) is the most well-known crash recovery oriented file system. NFS has enjoyed tremendous popularity since its introduction in the early 1980s [Sandberg et al., 1985]. Sun's goal was to support heterogeneous file systems, even within the client machine, that were capable of reasonable performance and industrial-strength reliability through a simple crash recovery mechanism. NFS became so popular that its basic behavior became a network protocol, also called NFS. Fifteen years after its introduction, it is in Version 3 and is still the dominant commercial remote file service.

NFS has the same general organization as other file servers (see again Figure 16.7), modified as shown in Figure 16.10. The basic UNIX file system interface is replaced by a virtual file system, VFS, interface in the client and server kernels. The VFS implements the standard local UNIX file interface that can be passed through to a conventional UNIX local file manager. It can also be made to translate the UNIX file operations into file operations for a different file manager on the client machine, so VFS could, for example, use a file manager from a different OS. (This was included to allow NFS to be implemented on PCs, specifically so that the VFS could generate DOS file manager commands.) Operations to be applied to remote files are passed to the client part of NFS.

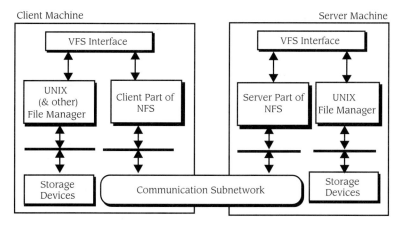

Figure 16.10
Sun NFS Organization

An NFS file hierarchy can be heterogeneous, so different parts of the hierarchy are implemented by different operating systems' file managers. The system is then designed to use the proper file manager for each subtree in the hierarchy. To accomplish this, any local system file interface, such as the UNIX file interface can be implemented on top of VFS. The VFS module can be used to match file manager interfaces to file manager implementations. But more important, it can also route a standard set of commands to a remote server. These commands use an abstract file descriptor called a *vnode* and establish a peer-to-peer protocol, called the NFS protocol, between the client and server. The vnode captures the correspondence between the file manager and the type of a subtree in the file hierarchy.

An NFS server manages a subtree in the network file hierarchy. If a client needs to use files in the subtree, it mounts the subtree into its own hierarchy (see Section 16.5). Then the client and server parts of NFS use the protocol to coordinate the actions at the client's VFS interface with the actions of the NFS server. In the extreme case, a diskless client can mount a server's root file system by using NFS as a remote disk server. Part of the NFS protocol is designed to implement and coordinate file system mounting.

The NFS protocol also handles data transfer between the NFS client and server. It is this part of the protocol that directs the server to manipulate inodes for individual files and directories according to commands from the client application and the client part of NFS. The NFS protocol is intended to allow the server to be stateless, thus greatly simplifying crash recovery. Each server command is atomic and will either run to completion or have no effect on the server's data. This is accomplished by keeping the full file descriptor in the client and a copy of the descriptor in the server; the NFS protocol uses a LOOKUP command rather than an open command to do this. Whenever the client issues a command that requires the state to be correct, it copies the relevant portion of the descriptor into the command message and transmits it to the server along with the command. Consequently, NFS can use datagrams rather than requiring a connected protocol, and either the client or the server can crash without affecting the operation of the other.

The NFS protocol is used between the NFS client and server modules, both implemented in the kernel. The first version of NFS used UDP, although versions 2 and 3 use either UDP or TCP over IP (NFS works across an internet). Additional details about the protocol can be found in Stevens [1994, ch. 29]. Sun Microsystems' documentation describes the implementation.

16.3.3.2 ■ Performance-oriented File Servers

The recovery-oriented approach can be criticized for its need to pass a copy of the file descriptor for many operations. The alternative is to allow the client and server to distribute the file descriptor and then to use other means to ensure that the distributed file state is always consistent and can be reconstructed if either the client or server crashes. The client and server's task can be simplified considerably if the network connecting the two is reliable. Therefore this approach ordinarily uses a transport layer protocol such as TCP.

The client executes file I/O commands as byte stream operations, with the server handling the translation between the byte stream and disk blocks. Hence, the server maintains the file position for the byte stream. For example, the client issues a `write` operation with a block of bytes to be written to the file. The command is not required to fit into a packet, since the block of bytes may be arbitrarily large. Because the client maintains part of the file descriptor and the server the rest, when the client issues the `write` operation, it will do either of the following: (1) it will assume that the server received the command and the data and completed the `write` operation, or (2) it will not put any part of the block onto the byte stream and the command will subsequently fail.

Both the client and the server contain part of the file descriptor, including file and record locks if they are used. Thus if the server crashes while a client has a file open, the server is required to recover the state of each open file descriptor. Otherwise, for instance, the client might believe a file was locked, while the server recovers the descriptor that indicates the file is unlocked. The client must detect when the server crashes. Virtual circuit mechanisms such as TCP will signal the client machine if the server machine crashes. When the client detects a server crash, it saves the state of the file descriptors currently distributed between itself and the server. When the server indicates that it has recovered, the suspended open files are reinstated and the remote file operations continue. Application programs can be notified by the client file manager and can be allowed to do other things, although by default, they will simply block, waiting for the server to recover.

The server is assumed to be volatile, so it is designed with special care to assist in recovery. First, every open file descriptor is saved in *stable storage* so that it can be retrieved if the server crashes while the file is open. When a client requests the server to perform an operation, the state of the file and of the descriptor are saved prior to the server's beginning to execute the operation. If the server crashes during the operation, the original state of the file descriptor and file are used in the recovery. When the server completes an operation, it updates the file descriptor in the stable storage and saves the changes to the file.

Stable storage is difficult to implement so that it never fails [Lampson and Sturgis, 1979]. Most implementations of stable storage are "almost always correct," but they can sometimes fail. The general idea is to create hardware-level critical sections— blocks of physical activity that run to completion even if the machine's power fails—to guarantee that information gets written to a storage device. Next, two copies of the stable storage contents are kept, presumably on different devices, in order to prevent a device failure from destroying the stable storage. When a stable storage write operation occurs, the critical section encapsulates writes to both copies of the stable storage. If the machine fails during the critical section, a recovery process must be able to detect that the machine failed during the critical section. It then compares the two copies. If the first was being written, then it is discarded and the second is used. This corresponds to the case in which the machine failed before the write occurred. If the second was being written, the first is used as the stable storage content. If the crash occurred between writes, the first copy is used.

Few commercial operating systems implement stable storage. They rely instead on power backup systems to allow the machine to run for several milliseconds after a power failure. An interrupt is generated when the power fails; the system then uses battery backup to execute the power failure interrupt. Pending code completes any existing write operations so that the machine does not fail on a write. Such an approach is still susceptible to disk device failure, however, since a disk head crash will destroy the single copy of the stable storage, thereby making recovery impossible.

16.4 ■ File-level Caching

Recall that Section 16.2 considered how a remote disk can support sharing. The topic was expanded in the discussion of remote file servers in Section 16.3. File caching is a logical extreme of caching in file servers. It is the third class of sharing. It allows entire files to be automatically copied from the server to the client and then returned to the server when the client closes the file. Thus client machines are ordinarily expected to include a small disk. File-level caching improves overall performance by eliminating individual disk block or file block updates across the network. All changes are made to the local copy before it is rewritten to the server. File-level caching does not prevent the consistency problem; however, the problem now occurs on a file-by-file basis. The literature in this area characterizes files as being either *immutable* or *mutable*. An immutable file may not be changed by the client after it has been copied to the client's machine. Mutable files may be changed, and the server is required to manage the change.

A radical approach to handling changes in files is to require that all files be immutable. When a client retrieves a copy of a file, it is assumed it will not be changed. This works well for many files, but it does not allow the file to be updated. Changes to files are handled via the support of different *versions* of the file. If a client retrieves a file and then needs to change it, the client creates a new version of the file with the necessary changes included. The updated file can then be written back to the server when it is closed. If no other client has retrieved a copy of the file between the time the first client retrieved its copy, then the new version becomes the default version for the file.

On the other hand, suppose two clients obtained the same version of a file, updated it, and then wrote it back to the server. The server would assign each a unique version number. "Inconsistent" files are allowed to exist on the server as different versions of the same file. Now the server uses different versions for different operations. Note that "operations" has a different meaning in this type of file service than it does in conventional file systems. For example, a file removal operation removes the oldest version of a file, but an open uses the newest version of the file.

The consistency mechanism requires that the client and the server each maintain state about the file system. This forces the server to use a callback each time the file is written at the server location and to incorporate a crash recovery scheme.

➤ *IN THE HANGAR*

The Andrew File System

The Andrew file system project is a distributed computing environment at Carnegie Mellon University [Satyanarayanan 1990]. Vice is the name for the collective servers that implement it. The file system's high-level goal is to incorporate acceptable performance in conjunction with scalability. The Vice file system works on the principle of file-level caching, whereby each client machine is presumed to contain a disk. The motivation for file-level caching is to minimize network traffic and disk head contention at the server. Cached files are not necessarily immutable, so the file system incorporates a mechanism to ensure consistency among the cached copies. While the intention in Sprite and other systems generally is to distribute more of the work of the file system into the server, the Andrew file system is designed with the idea that the server will be shared by many clients. Thus it should do only the minimum necessary to ensure safe sharing.

Early versions of the system cached only files into the client. Later versions also cached directories and symbolic links. Each client machine employs BSD UNIX, so open files are cached onto the client's disk and into the client's memory (at the block level). File changes are sent back to the server only when the file is closed. Directory changes are written through to the server when they occur.

Because the client contains a disk, a closed file may be resident on the disk when it is needed. When the client opens the file, it assumes the local copy is consistent. The server is responsible for notifying the client of inconsistencies for all files cached onto the client's disk by using a callback mechanism. When the server detects a change in a file, it notifies all clients having a copy of the file, whether or not the file is currently open. As a result, the server need not receive open validation requests of locally cached files. If the client machine crashes, the server assumes all its local files are inconsistent. So it generates a cache validation request for each file on its disk.

➤ IN THE HANGAR

The LOCUS File System

Developed by Popek and his colleagues at UCLA in the late 1970s [Walker et al., 1983], LOCUS is an OS that operates on a network of local memory machines. In an effort to provide efficient sharing, LOCUS uses automatic file replication (without immutability), with the OS guaranteeing file coherency. File replication is also used to increase a file's availability whenever the network fails, whereupon it partitions a single network into two or more smaller networks. As long as there is a copy of the file in each partition, the system can continue to operate until the network repairs itself, at which time the various versions of the files are made consistent.

LOCUS extends the UNIX file system model by providing a remote mount facility similar to the one described in Section 16.5. A remote directory is called a *filegroup*. Filegroups can be added to a local directory using remote mounting at local mount points. Once a filegroup has been added to the local directory, the OS has enough information to open the corresponding remote subtree root. The actual location of the remote-mounted filegroup is completely transparent to all applications and users for normal UNIX file operations.

The *using site* contains the information needed by the file manager to reference remote filegroups. When a client opens a file in a remote filegroup, the using site

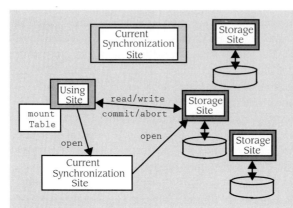

Figure 16.11
LOCUS Using Site, Storage Site, and Current Synchronization Site

portion of the file manager sets up an open file interaction with a server (see Figure 16.11). Once the file has been opened, the using site will read and write pages cached from a separate *storage site*. The storage site supplies pages to the using site according to the read/write operations supplied by the application software. When a file is opened, the using site software contacts the *current synchronization site* (CSS) for the filegroup. The using site determines this CSS location from information in its file descriptions. The CSS may choose to replicate the file at a new storage site, or it may use a copy of the file at some existing storage site, depending on the type of access requested when the file is opened and the relative locations of the using site and the storage site. For example, files opened for reading can be copied with little penalty. LOCUS may also replicate a file to increase its availability, depending on the nature of the file path. For example, since directories are generally accessed in read mode, replicating directories throughout the network is natural, particularly directories located close to the root, since those tend to be updated less often than directories located close to leaf nodes.

Once a file has been added to a storage site, the CSS is responsible for implementing the global synchronization policy for access of the file. For example, CSS may allow only one process to have a file open for writing or it may allow multiple writers under the assumption that they will write to separate parts of the file. The CSS maintains information that specifies which storage sites have a copy of the file and which one has the most current version of the file. It passes version information to a storage site when an open is processed so that the storage site may update to a newer version if necessary. Finally, the CSS notifies the using site where its storage site is located. Subsequent read and write operations will use the storage site directly.

A process at the using site reads and writes pages from the file at its storage site the same as it would a local file. On file read operations, the LOCUS file manager at the using site caches pages from the storage site using the same algorithms as those for caching pages from a local disk. On write operations, the using site writes

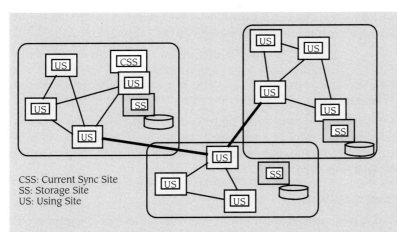

Figure 16.12
File Availability in an Unreliable Network

pages through to the storage site when they are written at the using site. If there are multiple writers for various copies of a file, transactions are used to serialize the updates to the file at all sites. The transaction commands, `commit` and `abort`, are issued by the LOCUS file manager at the using site without the application program's having to know about transactions. The file system includes `commit` and `abort` commands in addition to the usual `read`, `write`, and so on. When a file is opened for writing, the storage server starts a pending version of the file in shadow pages for each set of writes from a using site. When a using site commits a set of write operations or closes the file, the pending version becomes the actual version of the file. If the using site aborts the transaction, the pending version is discarded.

The availability philosophy is illustrated in Figure 16.12. The CSS for a file-group decides when to create more storage sites (SS in the figure) based on the topology of the network. If it can determine places in the network that will enable it to continue service through single-point failures in the network, it will create replicated copies of files. In the figure, the three partitions could result if the thick, network connections were to fail. Files opened prior to a failure of either link could continue to be used, although the CSS would not be available to perform new open commands.

16.5 ■ Directory Systems and Their Implementations

Directory systems typically employ a hierarchical structure because this approach naturally fits with the structuring techniques used by humans in manual filing systems. Remote file systems extend any individual host's hierarchical file organization to fit into a network of hosts. Networks themselves also use hierarchical organizations. For example, a network layer internet address is a three-layer tree with an unnamed root—presumably the name of the particular internet. The children of the root are the networks in the internet, and the children of a network are the host machines attached to the network (see the discussion of the Domain Name Service in Chapter 15). Remote file systems extend each host's hierarchical filename structure for identifying files located at various machines in the network.

16.5.1 ■ Filenames

Files may be referenced on remote servers in two general ways: *superpath names* and *remote mounting*. While superpath names were the first to be used in network file servers, most systems have evolved to the remote mounting technique, since it provides name and location transparency.

16.5.1.1 ■ Superpath Names

Superpath names expand the normal hierarchical path names to include a "level above the root." Names in the super level are machine names taken from a flat space of names. For example, one set of remote file servers identifies files by a superpath name of the form

```
goober:/usr/gjn/book/chap16
```

The machine name is `goober` and the absolute path name of the file on `goober` is

```
/usr/gjn/book/chap16
```

An alternative scheme selects names based on this algorithm: "Start at this machine's root, go up one level, and then follow the path from there." Files in this naming scheme have the form

```
/../goober/usr/gjn/book/chap16
```

Superpath naming causes the application software to distinguish between local files and remote files, since remote filenames have the superpath notation. A remote file system that supports this form of naming will use the machine name and parse it from the absolute path name according to the syntax used on the machine in order to identify the host. It will then use the machine name—for example, `goober`—to look up the network location of the machine that is using a name server. The part of the file server implemented on the client machine will then collaborate with the server process on the remote machine to access the target file.

16.5.1.2 ■ Remote Mounting

The remote mount approach is more widely used because it supports name and location transparency. It has evolved from the UNIX mount operation for removable media disk drives (see Chapter 13). The local mount operation allows an administrator to attach a file system—for example, one on a removable disk—to the file system on the machine. The mounted file system replaces a node in the local file system. Then path names can extend over the two file systems as long as the subtree file system remains mounted.

The `remote mount` command extends the `mount` command by allowing a subtree located at a remote host machine to be mounted on a local file system. Hence, a path name on a local file system can extend across the network to another file system, provided the latter is currently remote mounted.

The `remote mount` command shown in Figure 16.13 mounts directory `s_root` in Machine *S* at mount point `mt_pt` in Machine *R*. Thus

`/usr/gjn/mt_pt/zip`

in Machine *R* refers to the same file as

`/m_sys/s_root/zip`

when referenced in Machine *S*. This approach causes processes on each machine to see a different topography of the network file system, although local and remote filenames have the same form. One result of this different perspective is that absolute path names cannot be passed among processes on different machines without remote mount topography knowledge. For example, if a process, p_i, on Machine *R* passed the network-wide absolute path name in a message to a process p_j on Machine *S*, then p_j would not be able to access the file without changing the absolute path name.

For a file system to be remotely mounted or otherwise referenced from a client machine, the name may need to be advertised in a global name space—for example, by registering the name with a name server. Remote file systems ordinarily operate in a network configuration that includes such a name server. For example, a network domain (or portion of a larger network) includes a central name server to register advertised file systems within the domain. File servers may not support remote file operations that span domains. The client looks up a file system name in the name server and

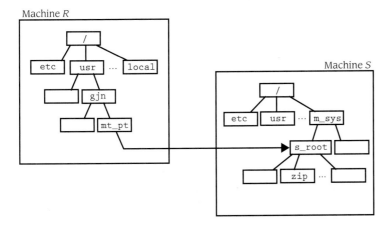

Figure 16.13
A Remotely Mounted File System

then remotely mounts the file system in the client's filename space. Upon completing the first remote mount between a client and a server, a virtual circuit is established between the two machines. Subsequent remote mounts use the existing virtual circuit by time multiplexing the connection.

16.5.2 ■ Opening a File

Recall the steps for opening a file in a tree-structured directory. The path name through the tree specifies a sequence of directories to be searched to find the file descriptor for the target file. As pointed out in Chapter 13, a path traversal can result in the file system reading a significant number of disk blocks, since each directory level will ordinarily involve at least two device `read` operations. When these operations are carried out over the network to a remote disk, the resulting load on the server and the delay for network transmission can become extreme.

As mentioned in the concluding remarks on disk servers in Section 16.2, this is the basic rationale for remote file systems. While remote disks are simple and relatively efficient, there are cases in which a client machine needs to do several reads with a relatively small amount of computation between each read—for example, to look up a pointer in a block. If such operations could be implemented in the server, then an overall increase in efficiency would result, caused by the elimination of network delays. A remote file system differs from a remote disk system in that some of the semantics of the file and directory system are implemented within the server as well as within the client machine. The server provides shared files, which are accessible from each client machine. As part of the file service, the server may provide concurrency control and file protection.

When a process opens a file that is located on a remote file server, this may cause a relatively complex and time-consuming set of steps. In general, the open command causes a serial search of each directory in the path name. At each level of the search, there is the possibility of encountering a remote mount point. When a remote mount point is encountered, the subsequent directory search must be handed off to the file server in the remote machine to complete the open command. For example, in Figure 16.14 a network file system is organized so that directory `s_root` on Machine *S* is remotely mounted at mount point `mt_pt` on Machine *R*. Also, directory `bin` on Machine *T* is remotely mounted at mount point `zip` on Machine *S*. If a process located on Machine *R* opens a file using the pathname

        /usr/gjn/mt_pt/zip/xpres

the open request is first processed in Machine *R* until the traversal encounters the remote mount point `mt_pt`. Machine *R* then passes the path search to Machine *S*, which resumes the search at directory `s_root` until it encounters the remote mount point `zip`. Machine *S* then passes the path traversal to the file system in Machine *T*, beginning at directory `bin`, which opens the file named `xpres`. Absolute path names in remote file systems can potentially result in a significant amount of distributed processing across the various file systems.

In UNIX file systems, a successful file open operation results in the file descriptor being loaded into the client's memory. This is likely also to be required in most systems, since the current state of the file is saved in the descriptor. If two different client processes

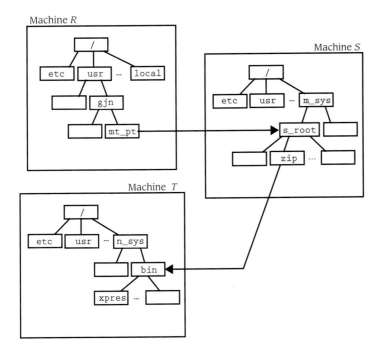

Figure 16.14
Opening Remote Files

open the same file, then each will have a cached version of the open file descriptor. Depending on the OS policy, both systems may be allowed to have the file open for writing at the same time. This is acceptable in, for example, many versions of UNIX. This situation illustrates the necessity for storage locks to control concurrent access to a file that has the potential for multiple open operations. Some remote file systems provide a mechanism for locking. Others—for example, early versions of Sun NFS—do not.

16.6 ■ Summary

Files are the traditional unit of persistent storage for computers and are a natural means for exchanging information among a set of processes. The simplest form of sharing using files is via explicit file-sharing commands such as UNIX's uucp.

Network file services are a logical extension to the file abstraction. They use the normal file management interface, supported by facilities to copy or reference files located on other machines, in conjunction with a distributed file manager. Remote disk servers partition the functionality so that the device driver is implemented on the server, with the entire file manager being implemented on each client machine. Remote file servers partition the file manager so that part of it is implemented on the server and the rest on the clients.

The key issues in remote disk design are performance and recoverability. Performance concerns stem from the introduction of management overhead for implementing remote access to the disk and from the overhead incurred with network transmission. Caching is used to decrease the time to access a file, but it introduces inconsistency as a major subproblem. Recoverability can be divided into issues related to reliable command execution and crash recovery. Reliable command execution is achieved using timeouts on each client call to the server. Recoverability is most easily achieved by designing the server so that it does not contain any state. In this case, if the server crashes and then recovers, it need not recover any state in order to synchronize with its clients, since the clients contain all of the state.

Remote file servers can be characterized as those that cache only parts of files at one time or those that cache entire files at one time. In either case, maintaining coherence among cached information is an important design issue that can be difficult to resolve. In servers that cache only part of a file, performance and recoverability are traded off against one another, although both are important. File servers that cache entire files take the position that files are immutable unless otherwise specified.

All file servers must support hierarchical filenames and directory operations. The predominant naming approach in UNIX systems is to generalize the local system `mount` command to a special `remote mount` command in order to extend directory hierarchies across the network. Remote mounting is widely used, but it can complicate file open operations because of the need for each system's file server to resolve only the part of the path name that passes through its part of the hierarchy.

This chapter early on introduced a model that described the memory interfaces used by a programmer. It also elaborated on the use of the secondary memory interface to support distributed access to information stored in files. The next chapter reconsiders these interfaces to see how primary memory can be used to access information over the network and how new interfaces can be added to the programming environment to support distributed computing.

16.7 ▪ Exercises

1. Suppose a file server supports a command to remove a directory. Is the operation idempotent or not? Explain your answer.

2. Suppose a remote disk server system is configured so that the disk on a server has an average block transfer time of 8 milliseconds, while a local disk for a client has an average block transfer time of 88 milliseconds (this would be a very slow disk by today's standards).

   a. How fast must the throughput be on the network for the remote disk server to have an access time lower than that of a local disk?

   b. What three network protocol parameters/factors would most affect this simple analysis? Why?

3. In 1980, empirical studies indicated that the server was the bottleneck in a remote file system. Assume a stateless file server such as Sun NFS using a packet-level

protocol such as raw IP. Hypothesize where bottlenecks would be for file read and write operations.

4. Given a file server in which the state is distributed between the client and the server, explain why the client and the server must both have copies of file locks for open files.

5. What are some arguments in favor of and against allowing the same directory to be remotely mounted from two different mount points on two different machines?

6. What is the advantage of having a file caching server allow only one client to have a file open for writing at any time?

7. Argue for or against caching files in /bin (on a UNIX system) when they are referenced by a client.

8. Describe an application domain in which immutable files might be the most effective way to handle file caching between clients and servers.

9. Design and implement an elementary file server that is able to save a file, copy a file to a client, and list a set of files that were previously saved in the server. (It is not necessary to implement more general directories or other file management facilities.) When the server receives a save command, it should accept a stream of *n* bytes in subsequent packets and then save the stream as a file in the local file system (using conventional UNIX file commands for the local file management). The copy command should identify a file and then cause the server to write the entire file to the client in a series of datagrams. The list command should cause the server to return a list of filenames to the client.

   The client and server should interact using UDP (rather than TCP). It is not necessary to implement reliable datagrams; that is, you may assume that datagrams are received reliably. You will have to write a simple client to exercise your server. The client should copy a few files to the server, list them, and then retrieve some of them.

17

Distributed Computing

"...Taylor put forth an unorthodox proposal: Why not move beyond timesharing to a connected network of computers, each dedicated to a single user?"

—Douglas K. Smith and Robert C. Alexander,
Fumbling the Future ■

CHAPTER OBJECTIVES

Remote file systems were the first heavily used mechanism to take advantage of high-speed networking. However, files are large-grained information containers originally designed to accommodate the batch processing model of computation. Use of the file manager interface and storage model constrains the form of distributed programs. More recent operating systems consider other ways to support computation, methods that are better suited to the network environment.

The objective of this chapter is to introduce the most important OS technologies that support distributed computing. In general, distributed computing is supported by deriving new, specialized network protocols, so the topic could be approached as the study of high-level protocols. However, as discussed in Chapter 16, file and device support for distributed computing changes the requirements and design of local file managers. In this chapter, the goal is only to introduce distributed operating systems by considering how they affect the process and memory managers. The material is an introduction. The study of operating systems to support distributed computation is the subject of graduate courses, and it usually has the majority of a book devoted to it (for example, see Maekawa et al. [1987], Nutt [1992a], Singhal and Shivaratri [1994], and Tanenbaum [1995]).

The chapter begins by considering characteristics of process management in a distributed environment. It then focuses on how the OS supports message passing in a network environment. Historically, as people gained experience with using messages as the basis of distributed computing, a pattern of use consistently emerged that strongly resembled the logical control flow of procedure call/return. This led to the development of a remote procedure call paradigm that is now widely used in distributed computing. How this procedure call works is explained here. Suppose a process on one machine could use the memory configured into another machine (connected to the same network as the first machine). The chapter concludes with a discussion of current technology that is being explored in distributed-memory management to support this kind of use of network-accessible memory.

17.1 ▪ Distributing Process Management

Contemporary software is evolving rapidly toward distributed and parallel computation. The distribution is supported by shared- and distributed-memory multiprocessors and by networks of individual machines that effectively provide an abstract form of the distributed-memory multiprocessor. An essential goal of any of these "multicomputers" is to provide a simple and efficient environment for designing and executing distributed computations so that the degree of parallelism in an application computation can scale up with reasonable cost and effort. Tremendous progress has been made in the technology, although today's operating system researchers are still concentrating on most of the problems addressed in this chapter.

17.1.1 ▪ Partitioning the Work

A computer in a network of computers can always be used with the traditional sequential process model to accomplish application processing. As shown in previous chapters, the challenge of operating systems is to allow autonomous processes to execute concurrently on a uniprocessor system. The network provides an opportunity for the computation to be partitioned into logical units and then to have the logical units executed simultaneously on different computers in the network. Ideally, this could allow a computation that requires T_1 seconds to run on a uniprocessor to be executed in $T_5 = T_1/5$ seconds in a network with five or more computers on it. Such a computation is said to have a *speedup* of 5 when executed in the network environment. Because of the overhead introduced by administration, synchronization, and communication, it is very rare to achieve a speedup of N in a network of N computers, although this is a good goal toward which to work. The essence of the problem, from the application programmer's viewpoint, is to partition the serial computation into units, where there are N units that all execute simultaneously with a minimum of overhead. If this partition is "perfect," and there is no overhead from administration, synchronization, or communication, then the speedup is N.

Besides having the ability to share files, remote file systems are an attempt, implemented wholly within the OS, to partition the work of file management and to distribute the work across two different machines. Chapter 16 discussed many new problems that are arising as barriers to achieving ideal speedup—among them, overhead for communication and the need for crash recovery. In the case of remote files, the distribution actually *increased* rather than decreased the execution time of the process. The advantage of remote files is entirely in the sharing. None is in performance improvement of the type that motivates application program partitioning. It is natural to ask if it is ever possible to reduce the execution time of a program by partitioning it and executing the

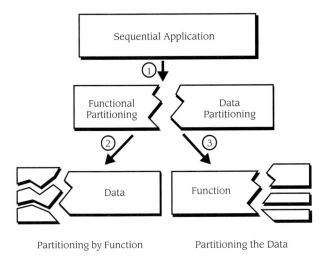

Figure 17.1
Factoring a Sequential Computation

parts in parallel. The answer is an emphatic yes. However, the partitioning must be done carefully. If the degree of the partition is large—remote file systems have only two parts—the speedup is more likely to occur.

How does a programmer go about partitioning a serial application so that it will have significant speedup? The application programmer must know the behavior of the algorithm used in the computation. First the address space is divided into two parts: One part contains software to execute the application function (for example, to compute the roots of an equation), and the other contains the data. This partitioning scheme is illustrated as the first transformation in Figure 17.1.

There are two schools of thought regarding how the computation should be partitioned beyond the first-level function-data partition. Transformation 2 on the left side of Figure 17.1 shows that the data could be held in one address space, while the functionality of the computation could be partitioned and implemented as independent processes on independent processors. This form of partitioning is called *functional partitioning* of the computation. The strategy behind functional partitioning is to divide the function into independent stages and then to pass all the data through the different stages record-by-record. If the computation has conditional control flow, then some data records may follow a different route through the computational parts than will others. In either case, parallelism is achieved by having the function stages operate in parallel as an assembly line, where conceptually the data passes through every phase for computation as required. Distributed objects are an example of a distributed computation based on functional partitioning. The philosophy behind this approach is that data management is much smaller than the function computation, so the function is partitioned into parts that can be executed simultaneously with one another and with the data management.

Transformation 3 on the right side of Figure 17.1 is an alternative to functional partitioning. Called *data partitioning,* it divides the data into independent units so that they can be processed by copies of the full sequential function. The idea here is that the functional computation is replicated on N different machines and then each machine is given a part of the data to be processed. That is, each of the N processes operating on the N different machines is executing in its own address space. Now there can be N different processes executing simultaneously, each with the responsibility for processing only a fraction of the total data. The data for each process is loaded into that process's address space. Notice that data partitioning is sometimes simpler to do than functional partitioning, since (at least conceptually) a full copy of the original sequential program can simply be given to N different processes operating on the N different machines. In practice, this can be difficult to do: If a process needs to have access to data outside its own partition (in another address space) to execute the function, then data partitioning becomes much more complex. For example, to multiply matrix A times matrix B, the product matrix, $C[i, j]$ in the result matrix is computed by taking the dot product of row i in A times column j in B. If a process on Host R in a network were to compute all the values in row i of the result, then it would need to read row i in A repeatedly and to read every column in B. Similarly, if another process on Host S were to be computing all the values in row k of the result, it would need to read row k of A repeatedly and to read every column of B. This imposes an impossible constraint on any data partition (without using copies), since B must appear in the partition used at Host R and the partition used at Host S.

17.1.2 ■ Supporting Partitioned Computation

Can the OS provide generic tools to support data and functional partitioning strategies or must it provide specialized support for each approach? Modern operating systems that support distributed computations generally do not assume either model of computation. Instead, they only provide facilities used in both forms of computation. Future operating systems may be more customized for functional or data partitioning, but there is no particular thrust toward customization in contemporary strategies. Applications specialists from one school or the other sometimes argue that this is a weakness of modern operating systems.

What are the general requirements to support distributed computation? In process management, the following major tasks have been identified:

- *Creation/destruction:* When a computation starts, normally a single process decides at runtime what other processes should be created and used in the computation. The OS must provide facilities to allow the process to create (and destroy) child processes on other machines.

- *Scheduling:* In some distributed environments, the location where a process executes is determined by the scheduler rather than the process. When a process becomes ready in such an environment, the scheduler looks around the network for an appropriate place to execute the program, attempting to automatically overlap execution.

- *Synchronization:* The classic synchronization mechanisms described in Chapters 8 rely on the existence of shared memory to coordinate process activity. In a network, the OS generally has to provide an alternative synchronization mechanism based on messages, rather than to rely on shared memory.

- *Deadlock management:* Deadlock detection algorithms rely on the knowledge of the allocation state of the system's resources to determine whether a deadlock exists. In a network, the set of resources includes all resources on every machine. Furthermore, detecting the status of all machines at any given moment has proved to be very difficult to do. Thus distributed deadlock detection is a difficult issue to resolve in a network environment. The topic is not discussed further in this book. Interested readers are encouraged to see Singhal and Shivaratri [1994, ch. 7].

17.1.3 ■ General Process Management

Sequential operating systems provide a process creation call to invoke a new child process on the same machine as the parent—for example, the UNIX `fork` system call. In the client-server model of computation, there is no explicit system call to dynamically create a process on another machine. Instead, when a distributed program is to be executed, server processes are first started at remote machine locations. Then the client (or clients) are manually started. This represents the state of the art for process creation in commercial operating systems.

There are leading-edge systems, such as Java, that use lighter-weight units of processing (objects or threads) to achieve dynamic execution of components. A user at an arbitrary machine can start an independent application (typically a Web browser containing a Java Virtual Machine in the case of Java) that provides an execution framework for the computation. Now a process on one machine can communicate with the execution framework on the remote machine to execute units of computation (applets in the case of Java) at the remote site. The control usually follows the classic client-server flow in this environment. That is, provided that a server is running on the network, a user can start an execution framework and invoke actions that cause units of computation to be instantiated (again, applets in the case of Java) that will interact with the server to achieve application-specific distributed computing.

This is an area of continuing exploration in contemporary operating systems. Because it has so much influence on the programming model, the research on this topic occurs in operating systems and programming languages.

17.1.4 ■ Scheduling

There are two general types of scheduling used in distributed environments:

- *Explicit scheduling:* The application programmer takes responsibility for determining where the schedulable units' computation should be executed.
- *Transparent scheduling:* The application process begins to execute as a single process on one computer. Then, when new schedulable units of computation are created and made ready to run, the scheduler on the local machine interacts with schedulers on other machines to determine the best place to execute a unit.

The client-server model is an explicit scheduling model. The servers are started on the network at explicit locations (and registered with a name service); the clients start independently at arbitrary places in the network, using the servers. In this case, a client or server unit of computation is treated as an ordinary process within the computer in which it executes. In the default, the computer's multiprogramming scheduling policy is used to provide service to that part of the computation.

User threads, such as C threads and POSIX threads, provide more control to application programmers, allowing them to use the CPU time allocated to the parent process to be scheduled to specific threads as determined by the application program. However, thread scheduling is not usually applicable across machines, except when process/ thread migration is supported by the OS.

In transparent scheduling, the application creates schedulable units of computation to be executed in the distributed environment without considering which machine will actually be used to execute any particular unit. The schedulers on the machines in the network are designed to communicate with one another. In this way, when a schedulable unit of computation is made ready to run, the unit is transferred to a selected machine and then executed in that machine. Normally, once the unit has been assigned to a particular machine, it will complete its execution on that machine. It will share the CPU with other units according to the local multiprogramming scheduler's policy. Transparency is a primary motivating factor for the OS to support network-transparent threads or objects.

Process Migration and Load Balancing

Static scheduling strategies, such as those used with simple client-server computations, do not take dynamic behavior of computational phases into account. There is considerable research and experimental work on dynamic, adaptive techniques to attempt to maximize speedup by determining situations in which a computation (or distributed system) has a load imbalance— where some processors have too much work to do and others are idle. The basic idea is to migrate work from the busy to the idle processors after work has been initially assigned, using a transparent scheduling strategy.

The issues in process migration to achieve a balanced load across the network are primarily performance-related. That is, the impetus to use the technique is to increase performance. Therefore the goal is to overcome the implicit overhead required to achieve load balancing through global performance gain. The key performance barrier is the cost of migration. To move a process from one machine to another, it is necessary to stop the process (or thread or object), save its complete state, transfer the executable image and state to another machine, and then restart the process on its new machine. If this overhead exceeds the benefit of migrating the

process, then apparent gains in performance will be lost.

Researchers have followed a trend of using lighter-weight units of computation in load-balancing approaches. For example, the Emerald system [Jul et al., 1988] and the follow-on PRESTO system [Bershad et al., 1988] migrate objects. This work eventually led to focusing on thread migration strategies [Bershad, 1990]. Although this research reports impressive performance gains, the effectiveness of the approach ultimately relies on the strategy by which the application programmer partitions the computation. The OS work focuses on highly efficient communication mechanisms for the environment.

17.1.5 ■ Coordinating Processes

Once the schedulable units of computation have been created and are executing on different machines, the OS must provide efficient means by which the units can coordinate their execution (when that is necessary). Development in this area follows two general trends:

- *Explicit synchronization:* Units of computation use an OS mechanism to allow the programmer to synchronize the execution at desired points.

- *Transactions and concurrency control:* Critical section accesses are assumed to be handled wholly within a server, so the focus is on achieving the effect of atomic operation on the server, even when the interactions are spread out over several individual client requests.

17.1.5.1 ■ Synchronization

Semaphores and monitors implicitly assume the existence of shared memory in which a lock variable is stored. Processes synchronize by testing and setting the variable with atomic operations. While it is possible to implement a "semaphore server," the overhead time to test and set the semaphore variable on the server using a transport layer protocol would take thousands of times longer than the time to read/write a variable in local memory. Better means of synchronizing must be used in distributed systems.

In network-based distributed systems, synchronization can be achieved through the use of messages to establish an order on the computation. The seminal work in this area took place in the late 1970s. For example, Lamport [1978] describes a theory by which processes executing on different computers can synchronize the operation by using an abstract global clock based on the order in which messages are transmitted in a network. Messages are associated with synchronizing events in each process. Each message is timestamped with the sending computer's local time. The local timestamps are then combined to determine a global order in which events associated with the messages occurred. In this abstraction, if one computer clock is behind another, an event *A* that occurred on the machine with the slow clock may be treated as if it occurred after an event *B* that occurred on a machine with a fast clock even when the actual time that *A* occurred was before the time that *B* occurred. Reed and Kanodia [1979] describe an experimental system to achieve the same synchronization effect as semaphores without using any shared memory.

Both of these techniques are beyond the scope of this book, since they are largely experimental and relatively complex. Singhal and Shivaratri [1994] provide a comprehensive discussion of the techniques used to synchronize processes in a distributed system.

17.1.5.2 ■ Transactions

Transactions can be used to achieve the same effect as synchronization in many cases. Interactions among distributed components can become very complex, resulting either in an exchange of related messages or in a stream of related messages being sent from one component to another. Such a stream of related messages is called a *transaction*—a sequence of commands for which the effect on associated data is as if either all of the commands are executed or none of them are. A transaction causes a specific set of micro actions and interactions between two components to achieve some macrolevel effect. For example, a computerized airplane guidance system may issue a number of microlevel operations to change the direction in which the aircraft is traveling. These operations may be changing individual engine speeds, adjusting the ailerons, and adjusting the attitude of the aircraft. The amount of adjustment depends, for example, on the aircraft's speed, perhaps on its altitude, and on the current state of the controlling surfaces. The macrolevel operation of changing the direction of travel requires that the individual components of the computerized system send relevant information to the guidance system, which can then change other components to produce the overall effect. In this case, it is important that either all of the course change microlevel operations take place in concert or none of them change at all.

As a software system example, suppose a server contains a set of records with N fields that can be updated by any of a set of client processes. The problem arises if two or more clients attempt to update multiple fields in a single record concurrently. Suppose process p_i changes fields 3, 6, 2, and 8 (in that order) in record k at the same time that process p_j attempts to change fields 5, 8, 4, and 6. There would be two sequences of client commands, as shown in Figure 17.2. p_i first sends a message to the server to update field 3 in record k and then sends a message to update field 6 in record k, and so on.

There is a race condition since p_i may update fields 3 and 6, and then have p_j update fields 5, 8, 4, and 6, and then have p_i update fields 2 and 8. Now the server will have the result of p_i's update in field 8 but the result of p_j's update in field 6. In some applications, this may be acceptable. But in others it is disastrous—for example, if field 6 is a person's name and field 8 is the address.

The idea in transactions is that the sequence of operations is recognized as one that must be executed as if the commands were a single command; the transaction will behave correctly if the sequence is performed completely or not at all (until a later time). In the previous example, this would mean that either process p_i or p_j completes its entire transaction before the other begins.

Transactions are widely used in distributed databases, since this is a natural place where multiple-field records are updated in many different operations. They are also useful in systems that are susceptible to crash or in which the consequences of an unfortuitous crash are catastrophic. If the server crashes in the middle of a transaction, the record may have only some of the fields updated before the crash, thus leaving the permanent data in an inconsistent state.

Figure 17.2
Updating a Multiple Field Record

Process p_i

```
. . .
send(server, update, k, 3);
send(server, update, k, 6);
send(server, update, k, 2);
send(server, update, k, 8);
. . .
```

Process p_j

```
. . .
send(server, update, k, 5);
send(server, update, k, 8);
send(server, update, k, 4);
send(server, update, k, 6);
. . .
```

The programmer identifies a transaction using markers for the beginning and for the end of the sequence of instructions. The server detects the transaction-begin marker and then treats all subsequent commands from the client as part of the transaction until it receives a transaction-end marker. If the server begins processing a transaction on behalf of a particular client, then it is the responsibility of the server either to execute all commands until it receives a transaction-end marker or to leave the state of the server as if no command had been executed. When the server encounters the transaction-end marker, it *commits* the effect of the command sequence to change the server information state. If the server determines that it cannot complete the sequence due to conflicts with other transactions, then it may *abort* the transaction. In so doing, it will restore all the information that was changed by commands at the beginning of the sequence to the state they were in before the transaction was begun. A client can also abort the transaction. However, if the transaction is to be aborted, it is ordinarily aborted by the server due to command conflicts.

There are many occasions when operating systems use transactions to coordinate the operation of processes. For example, remote file systems use transactions for most forms of caching at the page level, block level, and file level, since movement of information requires the client and server state to have multiple fields updated at any given time.

Transaction implementation must in effect take a snapshot of the state of the relevant resources when a transaction is begun. The operations within the transaction are then executed on a copy of the resources or on the original resources, provided the snapshot information can be used to restore the resources to the state existing at the checkpoint. If another transaction is started when one is in progress, the state must be saved carefully so that the effect of the first transaction is preserved if it commits. If the transaction is aborted, the resource state is restored on the basis of the checkpoint information. If it is committed, the copy of the changes becomes the master version. The checkpoint information then can be released.

Transactions naturally suggest situations in which a deadlock might occur. Since a server is executing all transactions that might be involved in the deadlock, the server can execute a detection algorithm whenever transactions do not appear to be progressing. Because a server is allowed to abort any transaction due to conditions it detects, it can recover from a deadlock with only a loss in processing time on the behalf of the aborted transaction.

17.1.5.3 ■ Concurrency Control

Concurrency control is a technique by which the system enables a set of processes to interleave a set of transactions on a set of shared resources. This provides the same result as if each process were given exclusive control of all related resources for the duration of a transaction. Thus concurrency control guarantees logical serializability of a set of transactions, even though the operations within the transactions may be interleaved.

Resource locks in a server are the simplest mechanism for implementing concurrency control. When a transaction changes a part of the resource, the server locks the resource for the duration of the transaction. Subsequent processes attempting to alter the locked part of the resource will be unable to do so until the first transaction completes.

The *two-phased locking protocol* ensures that a set of transactions will produce correctly serialized results without incurring a deadlock. During the first phase, the transaction acquires all the locks it needs to complete the transaction and does not release any. During the second phase, it releases locks and does not acquire any. In the degenerate case, all acquisitions take place when the transaction is initialized and all releases take place when the transaction terminates.

Two issues arising from indiscriminate use of locks are related to the size of a "part" of the resource and deadlock:

■ If the resource is a file, then should the lock apply to a disk page, a logical file block, or the entire file? Different researchers make strong arguments for each case. The arguments revolve around the trade-off of the number of locks to manage versus the amount of concurrent access supported across transactions.

■ A deadlock can occur if transactions happen to lock parts of the system's resources while requesting other parts. In cases in which the two-phased locking approach forces each transaction to acquire all of its locks when it is initiated, the concurrency control mechanism must be allowed to explicitly avoid deadlock. Otherwise, it will have to employ one of the techniques described in Chapter 10—for example, enforcing the order in which each transaction acquires locks, detection, or preemption.

Concurrency control revolves around a logically centralized lock manager. If the resources are distributed on a network, the lock manager must be able to obtain state from each of the constituent nodes. Because of the relative speed of network communication compared to that of multiprogramming environments, distributed concurrency control based on locking will encourage the use of locks that control relatively large units of resource. Recall that the earlier discussion of file caching explained how versions can be used to address concurrent file access. A similar approach can be used in concurrency control by placing a timestamp on each transaction and then maintaining copies of versions based on the timestamps. Postprocessing of the versions allows one to determine cases in which there are access conflicts and to determine the order in which the transactions occurred. While this will not resolve all conflicts, it does support many cases.

Another difficulty is the same as in general synchronization. That is, if the transactions originate on different machines, their timestamp values must have been derived from a global rather than a local clock. In general, locks are used to arbitrate conflicts at runtime, while the timestamping approach establishes an a priori order of serialization.

17.2 ■ Message Passing

Message-passing mechanisms are the basis of distributed computing in network environments. High-performance application domains frequently provide an interface to the network message-passing facility directly to the application programmer, even when the interface is also used by the OS to implement other aspects of distributed environment. The programmer, of course, must learn a new interface for sharing information: explicit interprocess communication (IPC) using messages.

Basic IPC operation was discussed in Chapter 9. The purpose in this section is to explain how IPC is mapped onto the underlying network protocols. Briefly, summarizing from Chapter 9, messages are blocks of information sent by one process and received by another. The message serves two purposes:

- It is an explicit mechanism for one process to share information with another.
- It can be used to synchronize the operation of the receiver with the operation of the sender.

A receiver process must have a mailbox to buffer messages that have been sent to, but have not yet been logically accepted by, the receiver. Send operations can be synchronous or asynchronous. In a synchronous operation, the sender waits until the message is safely delivered to the receiver's mailbox. In an asynchronous operation, the sender transmits the message and proceeds without waiting to see if the message was actually placed in a mailbox. Receive operations can be blocking or nonblocking. In the former case, when a receiver reads a mailbox the blocking receive prevents the receiver from proceeding until a message is available. In a nonblocking receive operation, a receiver proceeds in either case.

In a network system, the contents of the information usually must be copied several times in order to cause the information to be placed in another process's address space on a remote machine. Figure 17.3 summarizes the logical copy operations incurred by a send operation over a network. First, the sender generates the information to be transmitted in an internal buffer. The information is then copied into the operating system's address space so that it can be copied into another process's mailbox. Assuming that a network layer protocol is used, the information is copied from the generic message buffer into the packet. The information in the packet must be copied into the data link layer frame, usually a hardware buffer in a controller, and then copied from there to the physical network for transmission. At the receiver machine, a similar set of copy operations must occur. Note that this message transmission requires eight logical copy operations. Also note that it does not use a transport layer protocol and it ignores message box management, which may require yet another copy operation.

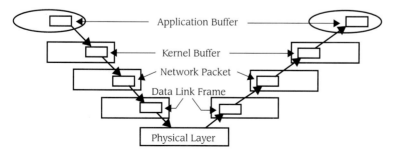

Figure 17.3
Message Copying Operations

Copy operations are usually the limiting factor in network-based message-passing performance. The challenge to the OS designer is to minimize the number of such operations. Contemporary operating systems strive to provide implementations of the message-passing mechanism that eliminate unnecessary copy operations. This suggests that the OS must first provide an application-level message-passing interface, one that might be used by application programmers directly and that is used by system software. The OS then can optimize the implementation of that interface according to its design strategy and the type of network protocols being used for communication. We next consider network message-passing interfaces.

17.2.1 ■ Message-passing Interfaces

There is a large and evolving body of application software that uses message-passing interfaces to the transport layer protocols. Application programming experts often assail system designers for providing only a "low-level send-receive" mechanism to support distributed computing because this places all the responsibility for distributing information on the application programmer. Furthermore, the application programmer must use these send-receive operations to synchronize the operation of the parts of the computation. While some programmers in this camp advocate the use of higher-level distribution paradigms—usually some form of distributed memory—others have embraced application-oriented message-passing interface libraries in order to obtain all the performance they can.

PVM—parallel virtual machine—is one example of a widely used message-passing interface [Geist and Sunderam, 1992]. It has the significant advantage of being a portable, easy to use message-passing environment that can be implemented on many different kinds of machines. Thus the programmer can install PVM on a set of heterogeneous machines connected to a common network and then use the underlying TCP/UDP implementations to support interoperating PVM library routines. An application can then be written to distribute computation across machines built by different manufacturers without having to address any of the details of each machine's transport layer protocols.

PVM is usually implemented not in an OS but rather as a library of user-level routines that make extensive use of TCP and UDP to support the notion of a PVM message. However, some organizations (such as Control Data Corporation) have implemented PVM in the OS to avoid the performance overhead suggested by Figure 17.3.

PVM provides minimum process management facilities to create and manage PVM processes. A PVM *task* is a schedulable unit of computation that uses a parallel virtual machine—PVM—to execute. The `pvm_mytid` call must be executed by each PVM task so as to associate the task with a parallel virtual machine; the call returns a task identifier. The task identifier for other tasks using the virtual machine are obtained with the `pvm_gettid` call. A task can create another task using `pvm_spawn` and can destroy itself with `pvm_exit`. A set of tasks can be identified as siblings by joining a logical group with the `pvm_joingroup` call; a task can abandon the group using `pvm_lvgroup`.

PVM contains synchronization calls, including conventional signal (V) and wait (P) calls. The portable PVM library implements the equivalent of a semaphore using TCP/IP protocols, as if there were a shared memory with a semaphore.

PVM messages contain sets of typed data. A sending task initializes a message buffer with the pvm_initsend call. Typed data is placed into a message buffer using packing routines; in the example below, pvm_pkint is used to place an integer into a message. The receiver uses pvm_upkint to retrieve the data from the message buffer. Once a sending task has filled its message buffer, it sends the buffer to another task using the task identification with the pvm_send, pvm_multicast, or pvm_broadcast operations. Messages are accepted with the pvm_recv operation, thus causing the message to be placed in a buffer where data is unpacked using the unpack command set and the values placed in local variables.

The examples shown in Figure 17.4 and Figure 17.5 are abstracted from an example in the PVM 3.3 documentation [Geist et al., 1994]. SPMD is a distributed computation paradigm, meaning several processes execute the same procedure ("SP") on multiple data streams ("MD"). It is an example of the data partitioning strategy described in Section 17.1.1. Each host machine in a set of PVM hosts executes the code shown in the figures to pass a token from one host to another.

Figure 17.4
The SPMD Computation in the PVM Main Program

```
#define NPROC 4
#include <sys/types.h>
#include "pvm3.h"
main() {
    int mytid;              /* my task id */
    int tids[NPROC];        /* array of task id */
    int me;                 /* my process number */
    int i;

    mytid = pvm_mytid(); /* enroll in pvm */
/* Join a group; if first in the group, create other tasks */
    me = pvm_joingroup("foo");
    if(me == 0)
        pvm_spawn("spmd", (char**)0, 0, "", NPROC-1, &tids[1]);
/* Wait for everyone to startup before proceeding. */
    pvm_barrier("foo", NPROC);
/*--------------------------------------------------------------*/
    dowork(me, NPROC);
/* program finished leave group and exit pvm */
    pvm_lvgroup("foo");
    pvm_exit();
    exit(1);
}
```

Figure 17.5
The SPMD dowork Function in PVM

```
dowork(int me, int nproc) {
    int token;
    int src, dest;
    int count = 1;
    int stride = 1;
    int msgtag = 4;

    /* Determine neighbors in the ring */
    src = pvm_gettid("foo", me−1);
    dest= pvm_gettid("foo", me+1);
    if(me == 0) src = pvm_gettid("foo", NPROC−1);
    if(me == NPROC−1) dest = pvm_gettid("foo", 0);
    if(me == 0) {
        token = dest;
        pvm_initsend(PvmDataDefault);
        pvm_pkint(&token, count, stride);
        pvm_send(dest, msgtag);
        pvm_recv(src, msgtag);
        printf("token ring done\n");
    } else {
        pvm_recv(src, msgtag);
        pvm_upkint(&token, count, stride);
        pvm_initsend(PvmDataDefault);
        pvm_pkint(&token, count, stride);
        pvm_send(dest, msgtag);
    }
}
```

17.2.2 ■ Computing Paradigms

The client-server model describes a paradigm, or pattern of organization, for a distributed computation. Any particular application can use the paradigm by dividing a computation into one set of passive servers and another set of active clients. Clients perform computations according to the application input data and then invoke the server when service is needed.

The PVM example describes a more refined paradigm in which there is a single program executing on multiple data streams. These patterns of organization are an important part of distributed application programming. After a decade of networks being used in application programming, it became clear that a prevalent paradigm had emerged in which a client process sends a message to a server and then blocks until the server responds with a message indicating the service has been performed. For example, in a remote disk system the client performs a read request and then blocks until the result of the read is returned from the disk server. On the server side, the server process blocks until it receives a request for service. When such a request arrives, it processes the request and returns the result (or an acknowledgment that the request was completed). The pattern of control flow in the paradigm is the same as the control flow for a local procedure call. That is, a program calls a function, the function executes to completion and returns, and the caller then resumes operation. This repeated use of the paradigm stimulated the idea for providing specialized OS support for the paradigm in the form of the remote procedure call.

17.3 ■ Remote Procedure Call

For several decades, procedures have been used to modularize computation in a sequential program. Today, professional programmers are trained to design software so that modules encapsulate data and function implementations behind public procedural interfaces. Distributed computation introduces a new level of complexity. Modularization in sequential programming hides implementation. However, in distributed programs it also enables location transparency and scheduling. This suggests that programmers need to learn a new environment in which to construct application programs if they wish to take advantage of the underlying distributed hardware. However, no specific distributed programming environment has come to the forefront as the "standard" one. This can be attributed in part to the differences of opinions about the best way to partition a computation and in part to the lack of emergence of a standard distributed computing environment. Today, advocates push for a broad spectrum of different distributed environments, including the Java model, OSF DCE, and the object-based CORBA approach. The remote procedure call (RPC) paradigm is the dominant extension to sequential programming environments that takes advantage of networks. RPC has analogs in Java, DCE, and CORBA.

17.3.1 ■ How Does RPC Work?

RPC is implemented as a set of network protocols that allow one procedure to call another procedure that is loaded on a different machine and pass it copies of parameters to be used for the computation. Hence, an RPC executes in a different address space from the calling procedure. RPC is a specialized pattern of interprocess communication in which the initiating program performs a send operation immediately followed by a blocking `read` operation. The receiving program performs a blocking read until it receives the message sent by the "caller" process. It then provides the service and returns a result by sending it to the original process. From the calling process's point of view, the scheme creates a behavior as if it were a procedure call from one to another.

This control flow/synchronization paradigm is summarized in Figure 17.6. In a conventional procedure call, the main program packs the arguments onto the stack and calls the procedure. The process discontinues execution of the main program and begins executing the procedure. First, the procedure obtains the parameters from the caller by popping them off the stack. Next, it executes the function. Finally, it returns, after placing any return parameters back on the stack.

The RPC crosses address spaces belonging to two different processes, called `theClient` and the `rpcServer` in Figure 17.6b. The process for `theClient` executes the main program in its own address space, and the `rpcServer` process executes the remote procedure in its address space. The call occurs by having the `theClient` package up parameters in a message, appending the name of the procedure to be called, and

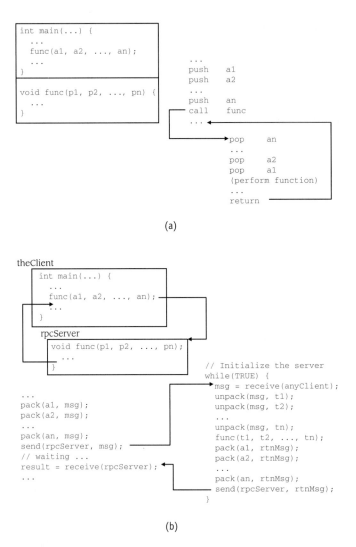

Figure 17.6
Remote Procedure Call Synchronization

then sending the message to the `rpcServer`. After the `theClient` sends the call message, it performs a blocking receive to await the result of the RPC, thus simulating the control flow of the serial call. Hence, the caller is idle while the called procedure executes in both the conventional (Figure 17.6a) and RPC (Figure 17.6b) paradigms. The `rpcServer` process will have performed a blocking receive when it is available to do work. When a call message arrives, it unpacks the arguments; in the conventional case, this is analogous to retrieving the parameters from the stack. It then determines the name of the procedure and calls it. Once the procedure has completed executing, it returns to the main program in `rpcServer`. The main program packages up return parameters and notifies the `theClient` of the call completion.

The RPC mechanism enables two processes to interact with one another using the control flow paradigm from conventional procedure calls. The RPC facility allows a programmer to write calling and called application procedures and then to execute the caller procedure in one process and the called procedure in a remote process on another machine without the programmer's knowing any details of messages or networks. From Figure 17.6, it is apparent that the RPC paradigm is a structured set of message `send`s and `receive`s. Hence, RPC is normally thought of as a high-layer network protocol.

17.3.2 ■ Implementing RPC

There are several issues to be addressed by an RPC implementation:

■ The syntax of the RPC should have the same syntactic appearance as a local procedure call in the high-level programming language.

■ While it may be difficult for the semantics of the call to be exactly the same in the remote and local cases, they should be as similar as possible. One example of when it is difficult to implement local procedure call semantics in the RPC is in the treatment of call-by-reference parameters. Call-by-reference allows the procedure to change variables in the caller's program. In the RPC case, this would require an assignment to a call-by-reference parameter to generate a `send` by the `rpcServer` and a `receive` by `theClient`, thereby resulting in `theClient` changing the value of a variable in its address space. Most RPC implementations do not support call-by-reference.

■ The recipient of the RPC should execute in an environment similar to the one in which the call was made. Hence, in a conventional environment a procedure can reference and change global variables. To provide the same semantic behavior, such changes would again require specialized communication between `theClient` and `rpcServer`. In general, it is usually not possible to create the caller's dynamic stack in the called procedure's address space.

17.3.2.1 ■ General Organization

RPC implementations take the general form shown in Figure 17.7. The client machine executes the `theClient` process, which consists of the client application code, a *client stub,* and the transport mechanism. The server machine implements the `rpcServer` process with a transport mechanism, a *server stub* main program, and the server implementation of the remote procedures. The client stub translates local procedure calls into actions for the client side of the RPC protocol, and the server stub implements the server side of the RPC protocol. As shown in the figure, the `theClient` process RPC invokes the client stub code. The client stub locates the machine executing the `rpcServer` process using a name server. Before the name server can respond to the lookup request, the `rpcServer` process must have previously registered the global name used for the remote procedure, `remoteF` in the example. The lookup need only take place on the first call, after which the client and server will have established a connection between themselves. Subsequent calls use the existing connection. Next, the

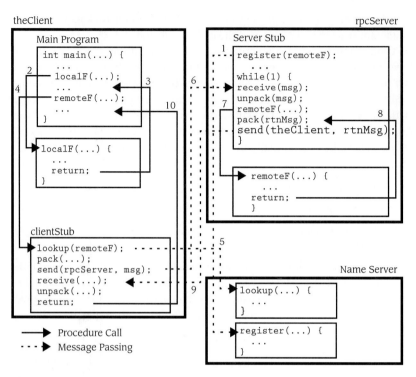

Figure 17.7
Remote Procedure Call Implementations

client stub packs the parameters in a message and transmits the message to the server stub in the `rpcServer` process. Since this server stub may service several different remote procedures, it will use the incoming message to select a remote procedure. The server stub performs the call and then packs the result parameters and returns them to the `theClient` process. Meanwhile, the `theClient` process will have been blocked waiting for the completion of the call. When it gets the return message, it unpacks the return parameters and passes them to the main program.

17.3.2.2 ■ Modeling Remote Calls After Local Calls

What mechanism will be used to distinguish between local and remote procedures? How and when will the remote procedure server be made known to the caller? It must be possible to write the client software so that the RPC has the same syntax as a local call. If the procedure is to be remote, then the RPC mechanism might force the programmer to distinguish between RPCs and local procedure calls at compile time, link edit time, or runtime. If this distinction is made at compile time, the programmer will need to use a different interface for an RPC than for a local procedure call. For example, a remote procedure might take the form:

```
callRemote(remoteF, a1, a2, ..., aN, ...);
```

where `callRemote` is a local procedure to be linked into the calling program's address space. The parameters specify the name of the remote procedure, `remoteF`, as well as the arguments for the procedure call.

However, suppose a programmer chooses for the distinction between local and remote procedures to be made at link time; then the system employs the same format for both local and remote procedure calls. The compiler will not distinguish between the two and will automatically call the client stub for remote procedures. The linkage editor will be required to satisfy all external references. Thus for it to resolve the external reference, it will need information analogous to library linking information so as to specify which procedures are local and which are remote. The minimum information required by the linkage editor is an indication that the corresponding symbol reference is to a remote procedure.

Runtime specification of remote procedures is the most general approach and effectively requires the same kind of dynamic binding support used for dynamic segment binding. The compiler and/or linkage editor will be unable to resolve the external reference, so the reference will be assumed to be bound at runtime. This late binding requires the static binding mechanism to leave sufficient information in the compiled code to enable the runtime system to resolve the external reference.

17.3.2.3 ■ Locating Remote Procedures

Independent of the means by which remote procedures are identified, the calling routine must be able to locate the server that is to execute the remote procedure. Again, this information can be specified at compile time, link edit time, or runtime. Regardless of the approach used, the calling routine must generate an address in the calling process's address space mapping to the `<net, host, remoteProcedurePort>` where the remote procedure is to be executed. If the location is determined at compile time, then the fact that it is an RPC will, of course, also be known at compile time. Hence, the RPC shown previously will have additional parameters to specify the location of the remote procedure server. One is

```
callRemote(remoteF, a1, a2, ..., aN, ...,
           internetLocation);
```

where `internetLocation` is a name, such as `<net, host, remoteProcedurePort>` where the remote procedure's server process is executing.

Link time location specification is meaningful only if the identification of a remote procedure is specified at compile time or link edit time. Again, this form of static binding is conceptually the same as compile time binding. In link time specification, the remote procedure server is specified with external symbol definition information but is static for the execution of the program.

Dynamic binding of the remote procedure network location is the most useful and most widely used approach. It is shown in Figure 17.7. The client stub is the intermediary and is statically linked into the calling program. However, as mentioned earlier in the chapter, the client stub uses runtime information to look up the RPC server's location and then establishes a connection to it. When the RPC is performed the first time, the client stub queries the naming facility to determine where the remote procedure server is located. On subsequent calls, it will already know the location.

In dynamic binding, the client stub for a remote procedure must be generated when the procedure is compiled. Once the calling process has confirmed that the procedure is a remote procedure, it will bind itself to the client stub. For example, client stubs can easily be statically bound to the calling program at link time when local procedures are bound, but with the location determined dynamically.

17.3.2.4 ■ Stub Generation

How can the client stub be generated automatically? Contemporary programming languages employ procedure interface modules that define the calling sequences of all procedures. A function prototype in ANSI C or C++ is an example of an interface specification for a procedure. A module implementing a procedure is said to *export* it; a module using a procedure is said to *import* it. The interface module provides sufficient information to generate the client stub, since it identifies the symbolic procedure name and parameters. A stub compiler can use the interface module to generate calls to the local transport mechanism so as to accomplish the interchange of calls and returns and to package the parameters into appropriate network messages. At runtime, the client stub will use a name server to locate the server and then will exchange messages with the server as required. When the remote procedure is called and the location of the server has been bound into the address space, the client stub can begin simulating the local call by using messages to call and return. It packages parameters and sends them to the server stub. The client stub, and hence the client process, waits for the RPC to complete before resuming operation.

17.3.2.5 ■ Network Support

The transport mechanism implements network message passing. While the requirements are for reliability, actual implementations tend to use a datagram protocol with a special-purpose RPC protocol. OS designers justify this approach by noting that the RPC protocol does not require the full generality of virtual circuits as provided by TCP. A customized protocol is relatively easy to construct when the sender and receiver are always client and server stubs with known behavior.

On the server side, each module that exports a procedure must be prepared to accept remote calls. This requires the server to contain a surrogate calling process—the server stub—to accept call requests from the client stub and to make the local call. The server stub is generated by using interface modules and the export directives in procedures implemented in its address space. In the general case, the server registers each procedure with the name server, thereby enabling the client stub to locate the procedure at call time. Registration includes adding the name to the name server and mapping internal identifiers to the procedure.

At call time, the client stub packs the calling parameters into a message and sends it to the network port specified by the name server. The transport part of the server then delivers the message to the server stub, which unpacks the parameters, identifies the procedure to be called, and calls it. When the procedure returns, the server stub packs the results and returns them to the client stub. The client stub unpacks the results and returns to the caller.

Parameters passed as call-by-value are easy to handle with this mechanism. Parameters passed by name or reference are difficult to handle because their use suggests that the client and server stubs should be required to evaluate parameters passed to the server. Different remote procedure packages use different approaches to this latter problem. However, each will require network traffic between the client stub and the server stub.

RPCs are useful for distributing processing across different machines, but they do not encourage parallel computation. When a caller invokes a remote procedure, it blocks during the procedure's execution. Performance is always a major runtime issue when considering an RPC implementation. While RPC provides late binding, its performance penalty must be made as small as possible. Even so, remote procedures are widely used in contemporary distributed applications because they implement a traditional programming model while requiring little knowledge of distribution mechanisms and strategies.

17.4 ■ Distributed-memory Management

Figure 17.8 expands on Figure 16.1, which describes the normal interfaces a process has to the memory system, including OS support for remote disks and remote files. OS designers use several different models for handling remote memory: A new interface may be added to allow programs to explicitly reference primary memory allocated at remote hosts (see Figure 17.9). In Figure 17.10, distributed objects are a special case of distributed shared memory; some OS designers use a single local object interface (as in

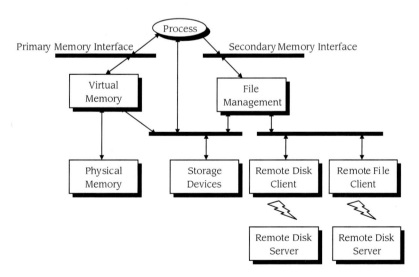

Figure 17.8
Normal Interfaces to the Memory System

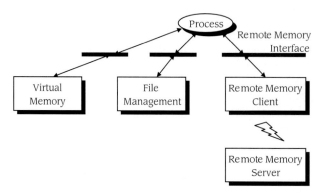

Figure 17.9
A New Interface to Remote Memory

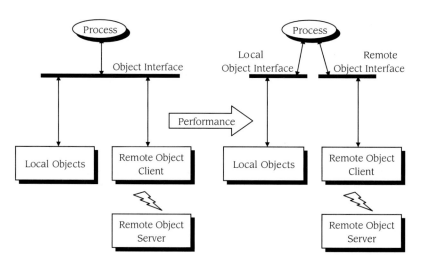

Figure 17.10
Distributed Objects

CORBA) while others provide both a local and remote object interface so that local object references will not be "slowed down" by having to use a general protocol that can reference local and remote objects. Figure 17.11 indicates how distributed virtual memory extends a local system's paging system across the network. A page server manages secondary memory so that the missing page can be retrieved from the server rather than from the local disk when a page fault occurs.

The figures provide several alternatives for representing a remote address space. What is the best way to represent the distributed-memory address space to the programmer? The distributed memory is shared memory, since it is used by two or more processes executing on two or more machines. Hence, any design must accommodate sharing as well as provide remote access. Contrasted with a file-oriented interface, a

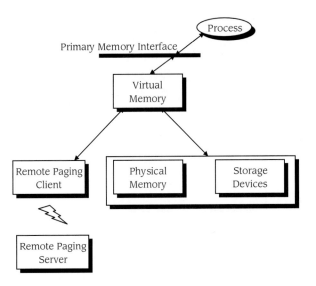

Figure 17.11
Distributed Virtual Memory

distributed memory typically appears as a collection of blocks of primary memory. The block specifications are derived from the programming language, so they may be objects, derived data structures, or dynamically allocated memory. The operating systems on the relevant machines allocate the memory space and map the shared blocks into the address spaces of the application processes.

There are two classes of architecture to implement distributed memory:

■ *Multicomputer:* Many multiprocessors are built as a "multicomputer" with several different processors having access to the entire memory of the machine. Many of these machines are nonuniform memory access (NUMA) machines because access times for various memory locations are biased toward a particular processor. While these machines are interesting in their own right, their distributed memory designs are not described in this book. Instead, the focus is on network environments.

■ *Network of machines:* Another class of distributed-memory designs provides a logical shared-memory interface using the packet-based network to support access to the memory blocks.

Figure 17.12 illustrates two general approaches to distributed-memory design. In Figure 17.12a, the operating system for machine S allocates a block of memory, M, to be shared by processes 1 and 2 executing on machines R and S, respectively. When process 1 references the distributed memory, the reference is translated to a server request in machine S. The communication between the distributed memory client in R and the server in S uses a suitable network protocol.

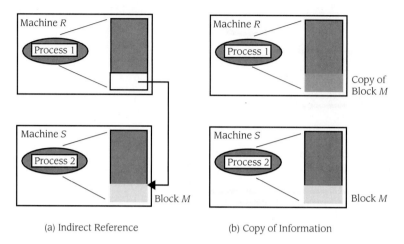

(a) Indirect Reference   (b) Copy of Information

Figure 17.12
Sharing a Block of Memory

Figure 17.12b illustrates an alternative approach. Here, machine R makes a copy of block M in the address space of process 1. Now, each reference by process 2 to block M is local in machine S and each reference by process 1 to block M is local in machine R. As in all other cases in which copies are created, the problem arises when process 1 writes into block M. The copies in machine R and machine S are inconsistent. The distributed-memory system must provide a mechanism to ensure memory coherence if blocks are cached.

Several fundamental issues must be considered when designing distributed-memory systems:

■ *Memory interface:* Should the model employ a distinct interface for referencing network memory, or can it reuse the existing primary memory interface to reference remote memory?

■ *Location transparency:* How much knowledge should the process have about the location of the remote part of the address space?

■ *Unit of sharing:* What should the unit of sharing be in the address space? The unit could be data structures, pages, segments, or some other unit.

■ *Name management:* Information will have to be imported and exported by naming the unit to be shared. How should this be handled?

■ *Implementation efficiency:* Assume the two processes and their address spaces are on different machines. What are efficient implementations of the remotely stored shared memory?

There is no general agreement as to the best way to resolve these issues. As with most other topics in this chapter, research in distributed-memory approaches is very active.

The rest of this section describes three approaches to implementing distributed memory: remote memory, distributed virtual memory, and distributed objects.

17.4.1 ■ Remote Memory

Remote memory refers to any of a broad spectrum of approaches in which the distributed memory is accessed using an interface that differs from the normal primary-memory interface and from the file interface. The remote-memory interface specifically extends the conventional programming model suggested by von Neumann machines. For example, the programmer explicitly identifies parts of the program to be mapped to the corresponding process's shared memory, while all other parts are mapped to its private local memory. This suggests that the programming language is extended and that the programmer must identify shared data structures at compile time—for example, by declaring a data structure and marking it as shared.

17.4.1.1 ■ The Memory Interface

Two critical issues are involved in designing the memory interface:

■ How is memory declared to be remote? That is, how can remote memory be mapped into a process's address space?

■ How is the memory read from and written to once it has been declared?

Memory interface design is an evolving area. It requires the development and general acceptance of a new programming paradigm for using the remote memory. There is no dominant approach in today's operating systems. Two examples are given here to illustrate the breadth of well-known approaches: the POSIX system call extension for shared memory and the Linda programming language extension.

> ➤ *IN THE HANGAR*

Examples of Distributed Memory

The POSIX Shared-memory Interface

The POSIX system call interface defines a shared-memory extension that is intended to be used by processes on a multiprogrammed machine to share access to the machine's memory. Nevertheless, it is similar to the memory interface used on commercial shared-memory multiprocessors and conceptually could be used on a network of machines that support remote memory.

A shared-memory segment is created by the shmget system call. The call returns an integer variable that can be used by any process to reference the segment. Once the segment has been created, it can be attached by other processes that use the shmat system call, with the integer identifier returned through the shmget call. A process can remove the shared segment by detaching it with a `shmdt` call. With the general usage of shared-memory segments, there is no special provision for passing the integer identifier among processes. (Both System V and BSD UNIX variants make special provisions to allow a segment to be shared without using the integer name.) The `shmctl` system call is a general-purpose call for passing specific commands to the kernel. For example, a process can manipulate certain fields in the shared-memory segment descriptor with `shmctl`, lock or unlock the segment, and destroy the segment.

This style of interface addresses the memory interface design issues using a style inspired by the time-honored `malloc` usage. Memory is introduced into a process's address space using the integer "global name" returned by `shmget`. The `shmat` call returns a typeless ("`void`") pointer that addresses the first address in the shared-memory segment. Thus the memory is referenced using pointers, just as memory obtained by `malloc` is referenced in a C program.

The POSIX system call interface characterizes an approach for adding an explicit remote-memory interface.

The Linda Programming Language

The Linda programming language [Carriero and Gelernter, 1986] represents an extreme opposite to the POSIX-style interface. It was explicitly intended to be used with remote memory by using a radical extension to conventional programming models. In Linda, data are stored remotely as tuples, which are referenced by associating access keys with field contents in the tuple. Rather than using conventional `read` and `write` operations to manipulate the memory, Linda provides a paradigm whereby tuples can be read from, added to, and removed from the tuple space. Information in the tuple space is changed by removing a tuple, updating it, and then replacing it in the space.

For example, an integer named `studentCount` with a key named `course` could be updated with a code segment of the general form

```
tmp = read(course=3753);
++tmp.studentCount;
write(tmp, course=3753);
```

While this approach may seem awkward (compared to an assignment statement), the approach provides an application programming interface that is easily compiled into memory references over the network.

In addition, coordinated reading and writing of data can be explicitly managed by managing tuple updates. It could be argued that these memory interface extensions are independent of the programming language, just as a file interface is independent of the language. However, Carriero and Gelernter take the position that Linda defines a programming language rather than an OS. In particular, Linda can be used to extend a wide class of serial programming languages into parallel programming languages.

17.4.1.2 ■ Memory Unit Sizes

Since remote memory is "manually defined" by explicit programming directives, it is natural for the size of the units to be defined explicitly by the programmer rather than by the system. For example, the tuple is defined to be the unit of sharing in Linda and is the sharable unit size.

17.4.1.3 ■ Location Transparency

Remote memory can be placed at any network location, so some part of the system must be able to locate the remote memory referenced from within an address space. Pure location transparency implies that there is a global address space completely hiding the physical location of any address appearing in it. A process references the remote memory by using a name from its local address space that maps to a global address. The global address is statically or dynamically bound to the correct network address.

For example, if the remote memory is allocated at the transport address `<net, host, port>`, the process must be able to reference the block and offset at the given server address. Assuming the server manages more than one block, a simple address in the local name space corresponds to an address of the form

```
<<net, host, port>, block, offset>
```

The Linda approach addresses this problem by using associative reference operations for the shared global address space. A program can write a tuple to the global tuple space without knowing anything about the network location of the memory.

Alternatively, the system could be designed so that the binding takes place at compile time, load time, or runtime. Compile time binding essentially requires that the location be completely visible and "hardwired" into the software. As a consequence, few systems take this approach. With load time binding, the network location is defined by the linkage editor at the time it resolves external references. This means the user provides the remote memory's location at the time the program is linked and loaded. Few systems use this approach because runtime binding is more flexible. With runtime binding, the program is compiled with enough information to use a name server to bind the remote memory location when the memory is referenced the first time. Subsequent references reuse the first-reference binding. Runtime binding requires the system to provide a mechanism equivalent to the one used to map a segment name to a segment number, as discussed in Chapter 12.

Because the implementation of the shared memory is explicit, it is possible to apply special semantics to data stored in the shared memory. Data consistency can be "defined away" by explicitly not guaranteeing that data stored in the shared memory is coherent. Coherency then becomes the responsibility of the programmer rather than the system. The programmer must add a synchronizing mechanism where it is needed. Lamport describes how these alternative memory consistency models can be used in distributed environments in [Lamport, 1979].

It is also possible to introduce new abstract data type semantics that conform to specific application domain needs. For example, the environment can supply a specialized mechanism for computational paradigms with a single producer of data and N different consumers. The producer writes information into the shared memory, and N copies must be consumed, thus causing the data to be logically removed from the memory.

The criticisms of general remote-memory systems primarily concern the level of transparency at the interface. The distribution of the memory is specific, hence providing the programmer with maximum flexibility in tuning the access. However, as a result the remote memory must be treated differently from local memory. Distributed virtual memory addresses this concern by using the virtual-memory interface to provide an interface with no special syntax and few special semantics.

17.4.2 ■ Distributed Virtual Memory

Shared remote memory inherently has an aspect of additional abstraction to it. This is because it is treated as if it were local memory even though it is physically allocated on a remote machine and accessed using network protocols. Virtual memory incorporates its own memory-mapping mechanism as an inherent part of its operation. The technique uses this mechanism to implement distributed memory.

Virtual-memory references differ from physical memory references because each virtual address is mapped to a physical address prior to being referenced within the physical memory module. In distributed virtual memory, distributed virtual addresses are mapped into a shared virtual address space. The shared unit address identifies the location of the target memory location if it is loaded in the local machine's primary memory, or its location on a global secondary memory, as indicated in Figure 17.13.

When a page from the private part of a process's address space is loaded, it is obtained from the process's local secondary memory image. When a page that is mapped to the shared part of the virtual address space is loaded, it is obtained from a shared, global secondary memory location that is accessible by more than one process. Figure 17.13 shows the shared, global secondary memory as residing on a separate machine. However, the critical aspect is that the shared page is referenced via a server process—on the local machine or on a remote machine.

Distributed virtual memory is very attractive from the programmer's viewpoint. It can be allocated and referenced in the same manner as local virtual memory. From the memory manager's perspective, the mechanism for constructing the virtual address space needs to address the usual network naming and transparency issues.

The global secondary memory server must register its service with an appropriate name server so that clients can bind to the server at runtime. There are several ways to invoke the server name binding. The simplest is for the programmer to call an initialization routine, identifying the key name of the appropriate page server. The initialization procedure looks up the page server's transport layer address, <net, host, port>, establishes a connection to it, and then allows the process to begin executing. When the local memory manager detects a missing page fault, it determines if the page is in the distributed memory or local virtual memory. If it is local, the fault is handled as described in Chapter 12. If it is distributed, the fault handler uses the connection to the page server to retrieve the missing page and place it in the local primary memory.

How can the various copies of pages in local primary memories be made consistent with the page image on the global pager server? Both centralized and distributed algorithms exist to do this. A paging cache coherence solution must take the *page syn-*

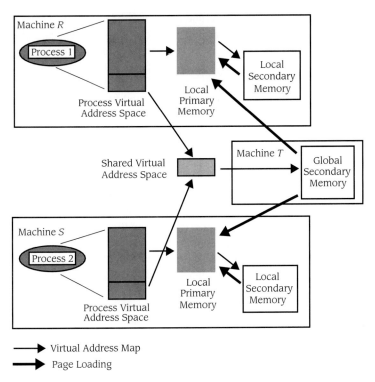

Figure 17.13
Distributed Virtual Memory

chronization and the *page ownership* strategies into account when providing a solution. Page synchronization uses an invalidation approach to ensure that when a process writes to a cached page, coherency is maintained across all other processes using the page. Each page has one "owner" processor for a writable page. The "owner" contains the last process to write to the page. A write fault causes all cached copies of the page to be invalidated and the processor causing the fault to change its access to the page copy to write. Now the processor "owns" the page and proceeds with the write operation.

Dynamic ownership can be implemented using a centralized or a distributed-memory manager. The centralized-memory manager approach relies on there being a single copy of the memory manager on a particular processor in the network. The manager keeps global information as to the current access rights, ownership, and locks existing in the network. As with other centralized approaches, this manager is relatively simple to implement; however, it tends to be a bottleneck and a crucial single point in the network.

A distributed-memory manager uses a strategy whereby the set of shared pages is statically partitioned and allocated to different managers. The client machine is responsible for using the correct server to satisfy placement and replacement requests. Alternatively, rather than the client having to know the location of its server, the client can use a broadcast protocol to determine ownership.

Distributed virtual memory approaches continue to be researched, but even experimental implementations are providing encouraging performances. It appears this approach may dominate in distributed storage designs as applications move to tighter coupling and away from traditional I/O models. You can read more about contemporary distributed virtual memory by first reading Li and Hudak [1989] and then by exploring current operating system research literature (such as the most recent proceedings of the ACM Symposium on Operating Systems Principles).

17.4.3 ■ Distributed Objects

Object-oriented programming has become a popular model for defining computations because it inherently relies on messages as the exclusive means of interaction among components. The model's primary advantage is that it is based on explicit message-passing (see Figure 17.10). Programmers choosing to write applications in an object-oriented language have already accepted the responsibility for encapsulating data in objects and for defining the interactions in terms of messages. The model's disadvantage has been the tendency of object-oriented language semantics to undermine distributed implementations through reliance on sequential operation within a single address space. For example, C++ semantics rely heavily on single-thread, single-address space behavior in defining how parameters are passed to member functions.

Software systems have been built to extend the semantics to define an object-oriented language better suited to distributed computation (see Bennett [1987] for an early example). In these systems, each object maintains its own address space, with the union of all objects constituting the computation's address space. Hence, the object names provide the visible names for the shared name space. Provided object names can be managed across a network, the object model is a viable means for transparently representing distributed computations with inherently distributed memory.

Objects are difficult for an OS to manage efficiently because they can be as small as an integer or as large as a bitmap image. With distributed memory, the difficulty is moving objects around on the network so that when an object is being heavily used by another object, the two are loaded on the same machine. Thus object mobility is a key issue in implementing distributed objects. While similar to load balancing, object mobility differs in the sense that only portions of address spaces are moved, with the object names being maintained in a global address space.

Emerald is an example of a distributed object system. It is a combination language and system to support object mobility (see Jul et al. [1988]). While the Emerald designers accept the idea that the implementation of small and large objects differs, they believe these implementation differences should not be apparent at the object interface (see Figure 17.10). As a result, Emerald provides a single object interface for local and remote objects. The compiler distinguishes between the two implementations and generates code that allows large objects to be migrated at runtime. The Emerald implementation distinguishes global objects from local objects and generates an object descriptor capable of incorporating a global name. If the object is remote, the descriptor will contain enough information for a local message to be forwarded to the object. Since objects migrate and are dynamic, the descriptor must also keep reference counts so that the descriptor space can be recovered when objects are deallocated. Global object forwarding addresses may potentially exist on several machines, depending on the system's ability to track the object's movement.

17.5 ■ Summary

This chapter introduced ways for operating systems to support distributed computation. The OS must provide basic tools to allow process management to occur in the network environment. Synchronization must be handled as an explicit extension to local OS functionality. This has led to the use of transactions and the incorporation of mechanisms to establish an order on event occurrences across the network, rather than relying on the traditional shared-memory synchronization mechanisms.

Messages are the traditional means for supporting computing based on distributed functionality. Unfortunately, message-based programming is not widely dispersed in programming communities. In the last few years, there has been a strong movement in the scientific programming community to use messages to support high-speed computation and a movement toward packages such as PVM. While many domain experts argue for better approaches than message-passing, contemporary high-speed computation uses it extensively.

The RPC approach has become the workhorse mechanism to support client-server computing. Contemporary remote file servers such as the Sun NFS, window systems such as X windows, and many other distributed services are implemented using RPC. Commercial systems have offered RPC programming facilities since the beginning of the decade, so there is also a rapidly emerging set of commercial applications that use RPC. Today RPC is the most widely used tool for implementing distributed software.

The emerging trend is for the OS to provide some form of distributed memory. Distributed memory can be added to a computing environment by creating a new remote-memory interface to be used by application programmers or by implementing distributed virtual memory under the primary memory interface. While the distributed virtual-memory approach has the most attractive interface to the application programmer, it is the more experimental of the two. Remote-memory implementations are more prevalent because they are easier to design and implement, they give the programmer more control over data placement, and they have a larger following in various application domains. In the long run, distributed virtual memory will almost certainly dominate because of its simplified programming interface.

17.6 ■ Exercises

1. In a certain program, the N elements of the A array are computed in parallel using the same program by the code fragment

```
for(i=1; i<=N; i++) {
    A[i] = A[i-1] * B[i];
    <Other computation>;
}
```

Either recommend a data partitioning scheme to achieve good speedup for the computation or argue why it cannot be done.

2. These questions are associated with the ideas of data versus functional partitions of computations:

   a. Does the trapezoidal rule quadrature program in the exercises for Chapter 9 use the data or functional partitioning strategy? Explain your rationale.
   b. Does the SOR program in the exercises for Chapter 9 use the data strategy or functional partitioning strategy? Explain your rationale.

3. State the type of workstation you use to do your programming assignments, including its memory access time. What would you expect the ratio of remote-memory references versus local-memory references to be if the remote-memory server were connected to your machine with a 10 Mbps Ethernet. ATM networks will soon have a bandwidth of about 1 Gbps. How do you think this will change the ratio of local-memory to remote-memory references? Besides the raw network speed, what other factors are likely to influence the performance?

4. Could a remote page server for a distributed virtual-memory system be designed to be faster than a conventional remote file server? Argue why or why not.

5. Write pseudocode definitions of a client stub and a server stub for RPC. Assume that the remote procedure is bound to the client stub at link time but that the server is not known until runtime.

6. Using PVM or other publicly available message-passing package such as MPI, implement the quadrature program from Chapter 9.

7. Using PVM or other publicly available message-passing package, implement the SOR program from Chapter 9.

8. Using an RPC package, implement the quadrature program from Chapter 9.

9. Using an RPC package, implement the SOR program from Chapter 9.

10. Using an RPC package, write a program generating data and three remote procedures in a common module on a remote machine. The first remote procedure should open a UNIX file for writing, the second should store the data in an open file, and the third should close the specified file. The main program must generate a structure—for example, a record containing a field of type `timeval` [see the man page for `gettimeofday(2)`] and a `char[N]` (for some small, fixed *N*). An example record might look like this:

```
{
    {
        123454678;
        9012345;
    };
    "This is record 1"
}
```

The first remote procedure should have a string argument naming the file to be opened. The third remote procedure should have an argument specifying which file is to be closed. The program should call the "store" remote procedure once for each record it generates and pass the record as a parameter. The remote procedure should then store the record at the end of the specified file.

18

Strategies and Examples

Any sufficiently advanced technology is indistinguishable from magic.

—Arthur C. Clarke ■

Operating systems provide an environment in which a programmer can easily and conveniently direct computer facilities to solve information-processing problems. At the highest level, domain-specific application programs are written to solve the problems using an abstract machine environment created by system software. User space system software, in turn, uses the OS interface. The OS abstracts hardware behavior to create a programming environment with processes and resources.

This book has considered the details of individual parts of the operating system—process and resource management, device management, memory management, and file management. Chapters 15 through 17 described how processes and resources can be abstracted for networks of computers. The objective of this chapter is to complete the study of operating systems. The chapter incorporates information about design issues that were covered in earlier chapters into a discussion about how a few operating systems apply the strategies introduced in Chapter 1.

The hardware provides processors, memory, and devices. Processes are abstractions of processor execution defined by the specification of a program. Resources are an abstraction of anything a process requests in order to proceed; for example, resources are generalizations of memory and devices. Economic pressures to share resources and, later, user pressure to share information, have resulted in operating systems being required to support multiple users at the same time. Doing this introduces complexity in the OS. This is because the OS must isolate resources used by independent processes; yet it must also provide for orderly sharing when processes cooperate with one another.

18.1 ▪ OS Components and Relationships

Traditionally, the heart of the OS is process and resource management. Devices and memory are specific instances of resources to be managed by the OS, and files are an abstraction of storage devices. OS technology has evolved around the four tasks of process and resource management, device management, memory management, and file management (see Figure 18.1). The discussion of OS topics in this book has reflected this modularization. However, organization of the OS implementation does not necessarily conform to this idealized functional organization, so the book also considers software approaches traditionally used in OS design.

A significant design problem for operating systems is how to implement the logical managers in comprehensive, efficient software. For example, while it is useful to discuss the theory of operation of the virtual-memory system as an isolated topic, the device manager must influence the page replacement policy if it is performing I/O on a page. Similarly, the scheduler interacts with the device manager and the memory manager, the file manager depends on the device manager, and so on. Figure 18.2 summarizes the functions described in previous chapters and illustrates some of the interactions and relationships among these functions. In the figure, the file, device, memory, and resource managers are explicit. Note that the process manager functionality is further subdivided into a core process manager, scheduler, IPC, and synchronization modules. Protection, deadlock, and interrupt handlers are distributed across different modules according to the system design.

The challenge in designing a modern OS (for an individual uniprocessor) is to decide how the software should be organized so as to implement these functions according to some set of external requirements. Modular design principles suggest that the functions should be packaged in order to minimize interactions among the modules. Principles of correctness suggest that the overall functionality should be partitioned so

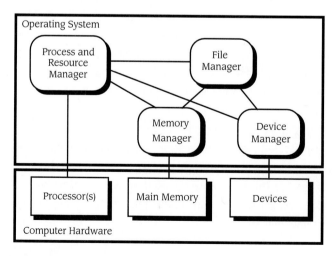

Figure 18.1
OS Function Organization

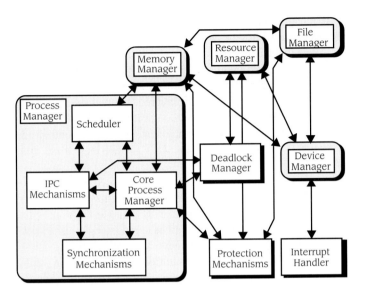

Figure 18.2
Function Interactions

that any module is not too complex. The basic problem of OS organization is to define modules that meet the principles of not only correctness but also performance, maintainability, and flexibility. Designers do not agree on how this is best achieved, since the detailed design issues may dramatically influence the modularization strategy. For example, a prevention strategy to deadlock is implemented entirely within the set of all resource managers, but a detection and recovery strategy interacts with the core process manager, memory manager, and so on. The rest of this chapter considers the basic approaches to operating systems organization. It then looks briefly at several different operating systems to see how they are organized.

18.2 ■ General Organizational Issues

An OS is a collection of software modules. Each module encapsulates information that it uses to fulfill its task and exports an interface for other modules to use to obtain services from the module. The task of determining the correct internal operation of a module is proportional to the size of the module: Large modules are difficult to prove correct and to maintain, while small modules are easier to design and maintain on the basis of correctness. Since modules communicate only through the exported interfaces, the form and style of intermodule communication is related to the complexity of the interface. As the number of individual interfaces on the module increases, the task of determining the correct external operation of the module increases. At the same time, the module potentially becomes more complex to use. However, a smaller number of interface components restricts the style and efficiency by which two internal parts of different modules are able to communicate. Suppose the module interface is implemented with procedure calls. When component R in module A wants to know the value of a variable *X* in module *B*, it cannot just read *X* as it would a local variable. Instead *R* must call *S* on *B*'s interface to request *B* to read *X* and return its value to *R*.

The job of any software designer is to consider how to design modules to implement functions so that they satisfy maintainability/correctness requirements as well as performance requirements. In operating systems, four general approaches are taken: (1) monolithic, (2) modular, (3) extensible nucleus, and (4) layered. In practice, an OS will be designed primarily with one of these approaches, although it is rare that the system uses only one style throughout its design. Most operating systems use elements of the other styles within the general framework. Section 18.2.1 describes these four approaches in more detail.

Hardware technology evolution into distributed systems has posed a dilemma for OS designers. Should the distributed hardware be controlled by a centralized OS, by a loose-knit community of centralized operating systems, or by a single OS that is distributed over the hardware? In network systems, the idea of using a single, central OS on one machine to control all other computers on the network has never been feasible, although this approach can sometimes be applied to multiprocessors. Section 18.2.2 considers the distinction between the loose-knit and distributed approaches. Then the chapter considers how a few prominent operating systems use the software modularization strategies for centralized and distributed system environments.

18.2.1 ▪ Software Organization

Figure 18.3 represents the software style for monolithic, modular, extensible nucleus, and layered organizations. Realistically, modern operating systems are divided into parts that execute "in user space" and "in system space." That is, the *kernel* (or *nucleus*) is the part of the OS that executes when the CPU is in supervisor mode, while the rest of the OS executes in user mode like any other system software or application program. This discussion focuses on the implementation of the OS kernel (although in the microkernel approach, this distinction is blurred).

Once an OS has been implemented and released, the OS functions that execute outside the kernel or nucleus cannot generally distinguish among the implementation techniques. Other system software is even more remote from the implementation of the supervisor mode, and application software is completely independent of the OS implementation technique (except when the OS interface has been violated by the application software). For example, today the UNIX system call interface is implemented by kernels using monolithic organizations (see Section 18.3) and extensible nucleus organizations (see Sections 18.7 and 18.8).

18.2.1.1 ▪ Monolithic Organization

In a *monolithic organization*, all software and data structures are placed in one logical module, with no explicit interfaces between any parts of the OS software. OS organizations (Figure 18.3a) are classic because they require the least amount of analysis prior to implementation and they tend to be very efficient if well implemented. However, they are difficult to understand and maintain and, hence, are difficult to prove correct. Classic program partitioning is based on data structures. The OS data structures include resource queues, process descriptors, file descriptors, device descriptors, semaphores,

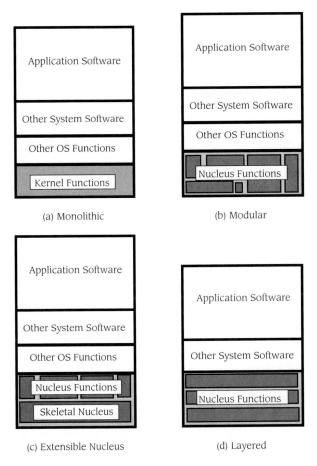

Figure 18.3
Software Organization

deadlock information, virtual-memory tables, and the like. Thus each concept discussed so far requires some form of data structure to track the state of the system. The OS must keep the cumulative data structures in a safe place so that it can implement its algorithms on correct status information.

Partitioning the program on the basis of the use of data structures can be very difficult. For example, it is tempting to encapsulate scheduling information in a module that allocates the CPU to waiting jobs. However, the scheduler will also need to know the swapping state of a process before it can make an intelligent scheduling decision. Similarly, the swapper must know about pending I/O operations involving memory buffers before it can decide to swap out a process. While one can find partitions that minimize the amount of interpartition communication, the minimum may be unacceptable. For example, a partitioned OS might be too inefficient for a hardware with limited computing or information transfer bandwidth. The performance factor overwhelms the software engineering design aspects of the solution. The result is to implement the OS as a single monolith. The AT&T System V and BSD UNIX kernels (Section 18.3) are the most prominent examples of a monolithic kernel organization, possibly with the exception of MS-DOS.

MS-DOS was a monolithic kernel (although it did not use supervisor mode in the CPU) that supported a single task. The basic OS kernel was wholly implemented in the read-only memory (ROM) resident Basic Input/Output System (BIOS) routines, and two executable files named IO.SYS and MSDOS.SYS [Chappell, 1994]. When a computer was booted up to run DOS, the CMOS memory and processor were queried to obtain various parameters for running it. Next, a 512-byte bootstrap loader was retrieved from the startup disk and then executed to begin loading IO.SYS. After loading the first few sectors in IO.SYS, the bootstrap loader jumped to IO.SYS to finish the loading process. IO.SYS subsequently loaded MSDOS.SYS and then read the user-defined CONFIG.SYS and AUTOEXEC.BAT to determine if OS extensions, called *drivers,* should be added to the kernel. These drivers could range from loadable device drivers of the type described in Chapter 5 to memory management extensions (for example, see HIMEM.SYS). Perhaps the most interesting of these device drivers was one named EMM386.EXE; the original Intel 8086 CPU did not have a mode bit, but the 80386 did. This particular driver constructed a supervisor mode environment in which the rest of DOS executed as a single user-mode task, thus allowing supervisor mode tasks to be executed separately from the ordinary DOS task.

18.2.1.2 ■ Modular Organization

A *modular program* is one in which the functionality is partitioned among logically independent components with well-defined interfaces among the related modules. In contrast to monolithic designs, a modular OS is implemented with distinct program modules and/or processes (see Figure 18.3b). Here, the engineering tradeoff of function encapsulation versus performance swings toward functional encapsulation. As with all such software architectures, the modular nucleus is considerably easier to maintain and modify than is the software in the monolithic approach. Data abstraction allows modules to hide implementations of data structures so they can be modified without changing the interface. The cost of modularization, compared to monolithic implementations, is potential performance degradation. Hence, it is potentially difficult to design an organization that provides an acceptable compromise between performance and modularity requirements. A side benefit of modularization is that the system can be implemented as abstract data types or objects.

There are no leading-edge commercial operating systems that use a pure modular organization, although one could argue that the extensible nucleus is a special case of the modular organization (and it is currently heavily used). An excellent example of a research OS using a modular approach is the object-oriented Choices operating system described in Section 18.4.

18.2.1.3 ■ Extensible Nucleus, or Microkernel, Organization

The *extensible nucleus* organization is a modular organization intended to implement real-time systems, timesharing systems, and the like, by using a common set of skeletal facilities (Figure 18.3c). The approach is to define two types of modules for any particular OS: policy-specific modules and the skeletal policy-independent modules. The policy-independent modules implement the extensible nucleus, or *microkernel*. It is not intended to provide complete functionality. Rather, it is supposed to create an environment in which policy-specific operating systems can be constructed to meet the needs of an application domain. The skeletal component is a general-purpose foundation for policy-specific parts of the architecture.

The philosophy behind this approach is that the OS can be implemented in two parts: (1) a mechanism-dependent, hardware-dependent part and (2) a policy-dependent, hardware-independent part. The first part provides a low-level virtual machine with some form of memory and process management, usually with only the bare essentials for device management. The second part reflects the requirements of the specific OS.

This architecture supports two new directions in operating systems. It allows policy-dependent variants of an OS to be built on a single hardware platform, as shown in Figure 18.4(a). The RC 4000 nucleus (see Section 18.5) was the first OS to make the architecture work in a commercial environment. This was followed by the tremendous success of the IBM VM system. Both of these systems were driven by the requirement to support multiple OS policy implementations. Neither nucleus is capable of performing the functions expected of an OS by itself. However, both establish a virtual machine interface used to implement policy-specific extensions that complement the nucleus and form a full operating system.

The microkernel operating systems, such as Mach (Section 18.7) and CHORUS (Section 18.8), are logically equivalent to the extensible nucleus strategies used in the

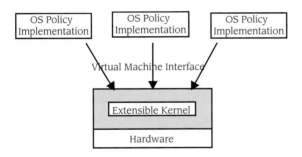

(a) Multiple-Policy Organization

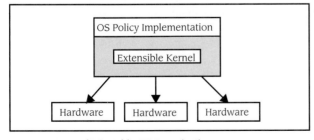

(b) Portable OS Organization

Figure 18.4
Using an Extensible Nucleus

RC 4000 and VM. However, the details of the approach differ from those of these earlier systems. The microkernel provides skeletal, policy-independent functions that are extended with specialized servers to implement a policy. For example, both Mach and CHORUS have a UNIX server that works with the microkernel to implement the UNIX system call interface. In addition, this architecture allows a specific policy-dependent part of the OS to be portable (see Figure 18.4b). The IBM VM system was used in this way to allow any version of an OS product to be used with any product within a broad family of products.

18.2.1.4 ■ Layered Organizations

A *layered organization* partitions the functionality into an abstract machine hierarchy in which the functions in layer i are implemented in terms of the functions provided by layer $i - 1$ (see Figure 18.3d). The layered architecture is a classic technique for dividing complex software systems into manageable parts. For example, layered architectures are the means by which ISO OSI network protocols are defined (see Chapter 15). They are used as a guiding principle in many OS architectures, but no prominent systems are pure in their use of it.

The intellectual challenge regarding layered architectures is in determining the order and content of the layers. How can the operating system's functions be partitioned into layers so that functions in layer i cannot use the facilities in layer $i + k$? This suggests that one could possibly draw a figure of the functions as an acyclic graph, with no circular dependencies among the modules. One variant to pure layering is for the kernel to use layers in which there are two types of processes—ordinary processes and system tasks. This provides the opportunity to use one form of task to implement general processes and another for applications. While this variant tends to proliferate levels, its general applicability is irrefutable. However, few if any contemporary operating systems are actually able to adhere to it.

The classic example of a layered OS is Dijkstra's THE system, developed in the 1960s at the Technische Hogeschool Eindhoven (THE), hence the unusual English name [Dijkstra, 1968]. The goal of THE was to design and implement a *provably correct* OS (people still argue today whether the study met its goal). The layering approach provides a model for isolating various aspects of the OS, proving properties about a level of the system, implementing the level, and then using the level to implement more-abstract levels of the system. The THE layering is summarized in Figure 18.5. Level 1 implements processes, scheduling, and the synchronization mechanism among these processes. This allows the memory management system to use processes in its

Level 5   User Programs
Level 4   Input/Output Management
Level 3   Operator Console
Level 2   Memory Management
Level 1   CPU Scheduling and Semaphores
Level 0   Hardware

Figure 18.5
Dijkstra's THE Layered Architecture

implementation. However, it disallows the possibility of the scheduler's using information about memory management in making its decisions. So, for example, the scheduler could potentially dispatch processes that are swapped out of memory. The higher levels of THE had more relevance to machines in the 1960s than to contemporary machines. For example, the traditional operator console did not use the normal I/O buffering and device driver mechanisms. Instead, it provided its own. However, in the THE architecture, I/O management and the operator console can use virtual memory.

THE is an important OS because it illustrates how to build an OS that can be proved to be correct [Dijkstra, 1968]. As a modern OS, the layered architecture is overly restrictive. It requires the designer to establish an ordering on all of the functions, a strategy in stark contrast to the monolithic kernel or microkernel approaches. However, layering is a goal toward which most operating systems strive at one level of abstraction or another.

18.2.2 ■ Managing Distributed Hardware

The emergence of inexpensive networks of computers has stimulated a new direction in the organization of operating systems. Distributed hardware introduces a new set of requirements that encourage operating systems to be designed with a new set of modules (but still using the basic software organizations described in Section 18.2.1). Network operating systems have evolved from conventional single-machine operating systems. Distributed operating systems take a revolutionary approach in an attempt to create an abstract environment in which machine boundaries are transparent to the programmer. These two classes of operating systems are summarized next.

18.2.2.1 ■ Network Operating Systems

A *network operating system* is generally a single-machine operating system adapted for use in a network environment (see Figure 18.6). The modifications can be modest, providing high-speed communications facilities, such as file transfer, and terminal interconnection, such as remote login. Or they can be ambitious, providing IPC, remote file systems, and RPC. Many of the more ambitious efforts could be argued to be distributed operating systems rather than network operating systems because they make several aspects of the physical distribution transparent to the application programmer.

The limitations of network operating systems are generally architectural limitations in which the original OS was designed specifically for a uniprocessor environment, yet it is being used to manage the resources in a multiprocessor or network environment. Because of the wide use of UNIX on individual timesharing machines and its evolution as a workstation OS, it is usually the base OS for a network extension.

Network operating systems do not necessarily attempt to make the location of a file transparent at the operating systems interface, although, as discussed in Chapter 16, the `remote mount` operation can provide application programmers with transparent access to files on a network. In older network operating systems, the lack of transparency required a user to copy a file from a remote machine to the local machine before accessing it.

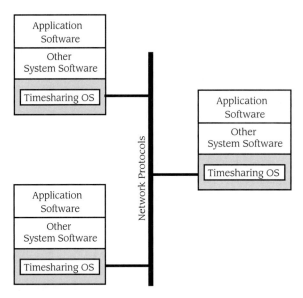

Figure 18.6
Network OS Environment

Executing a program at a remote location requires overt action by the user. For example, the user may have to use a remote login facility to create a session with a shell program at the remote site and then cause the shell to execute the program.

4.3 BSD is an excellent example of a network OS. It evolved from the pure time-sharing Version 6 UNIX. The fundamental change to the kernel to enable it to support network computing is the socket interface. (AT&T System V, Release 3, was also extended from a timesharing operating system to be a network OS. This was done through the addition of I/O streams; see Section 18.6.4.2 to see how Windows NT uses the I/O stream concept.) One feature of sockets is a mechanism by which a process can reference network addresses outside its own address space. Without sockets, there is no adequate naming facility to enable a process to reference other unrelated processes. Nor is there a mechanism for sending and receiving messages across the network. The socket mechanism is also the platform on which Sun builds its RPC mechanism.

18.2.2.2 ■ Distributed Operating Systems

The state-of-the-art effort in OS research is in the design and development of *distributed operating systems.* Most contemporary OS research papers focus on one aspect or another of distributed operating systems. While several significant systems have been built, none enjoy wide commercial success. Tanenbaum and van Renesse [1985] identify five issues that distinguish distributed operating systems from network operating systems:

■ *Communication primitives:* The need is to find alternatives to shared-memory synchronization primitives such as semaphores and monitors.

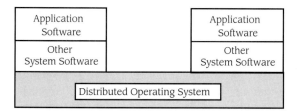

Figure 18.7
Distributed Operating Systems

- *Naming and protection:* These are related to the problem of a process on one machine identifying and communicating with processes on a remote machine.
- *Network-wide resource management:* This is concerned with issues such as scheduling, load balancing, and distributed deadlock detection.
- *Fault tolerance:* This is related to the robustness of a system under isolated failure.
- *Services to provide:* These are related to the design and use of file servers, print servers, remote execution facilities, and miscellaneous other facilities.

A distributed OS abstracts the set of distinct computer systems in a network so that an application process perceives the computing environment as a single, transparent system rather than a collection of individual computers interconnected with a network (see Figure 18.7). Sometimes the distinction between a network OS and a distributed OS is somewhat arbitrary, since the network OS will allow some aspects of the hardware environment to be location transparent, while others will be apparent. For example, in 4.3 BSD UNIX, file services may be location transparent, although `telnet`, `ftp`, `rlogin`, `rsh`, `finger`, and other commands make the machine boundaries explicit.

Mach (Section 18.7) is usually thought of as a distributed OS, although it is sometimes described as a network OS. CHORUS (Section 18.8) is another microkernel-based OS, similar in many respects to Mach, and is generally considered to be a distributed OS.

18.3 ▪ The Traditional UNIX Kernel

Today's most widely known example of a monolithic OS is the traditional Version 6 UNIX kernel [Ritchie and Thompson, 1974]. In recognition of the negative aspects of monolithic software, the UNIX philosophy has been to keep the kernel functionality as limited as possible, while requiring the other system software to implement as many normal OS functions as possible. The file system approach exemplifies this approach. The kernel implements byte stream files; the `stdio` library is used to format the byte stream.

UNIX was popularized as an interactive, timesharing OS for the 16-bit DEC PDP–11 minicomputer family. The designers of UNIX had participated in the Multics project, so their design decisions in UNIX were made with a full awareness of robust

OS support and its requirement for special purpose hardware to implement segmentation and protection (as was done in Multics). UNIX takes a more modest approach than Multics in recognizing the limitations of inexpensive, slow hardware. For example, Version 6 UNIX and its predecessors used swapping rather than virtual memory. When Version 7 UNIX was introduced to the public in 1973, it was recognized as a departure from the extant trend in operating systems. It was unique in its simple file system, pipes, clean user interface—the shell—and extensible design.

18.3.1 ■ The Kernel

The UNIX kernel was intended to provide basic machine resource management, with the ability to easily extend the OS to create specific computational environments. UNIX had limited goals with respect to services for application programs; it was assumed that the application programmers for the system would be the OS developers themselves. It was also recognized that the kernel would need to be reconfigured often to accommodate new devices. Therefore, in light of limited bandwidth from the hardware platform, the best engineering tradeoff would be to build the kernel as a monolithic software module able to implement process management, memory management, and a minimal file system (see Figure 18.8).

The early kernel had two significant interfaces. The first was between user space programs—such as applications, libraries, and commands—and the kernel. The second was between the main part of the kernel and the device drivers. The driver-kernel interface relied on device drivers' having entry points with standard names, but whose locations could be determined from information in special files in the /dev directory. The kernel used device numbers to search /dev and then to bind addresses (obtained from

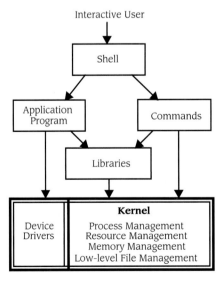

Figure 18.8
The UNIX Architecture

the corresponding special files) to the fixed entry point names. This allowed any part of the device driver to be called using a standard, dynamically bound name. As described in Chapter 5, the interrupt handler provided the second part of the interface between the device and the kernel.

The kernel-user space interface was originally small and simple. This was consistent with the kernel design philosophy—namely, that the kernel should be a minimal OS to implement critical functions, while the bulk of the functionality should be implemented in user space as library routines. Today's UNIX systems tend to betray the original design philosophy so that they can better address increasing functionality requirements.

The original UNIX process model is described in Chapter 2. It remains nearly the same in contemporary UNIX implementations. In summary, the process model divides the process into text, data, and stack segments. The process manager maintains a process descriptor that contains the current status of the process. Process administration is based on the `fork`, `exec`, and `wait` system calls. Early versions of UNIX support only interprocess communication using pipes. The kernel implemented scheduling, pipes, interrupts, and the process-spawning mechanism. Memory management was accomplished using the three-segment (text, data, and stack) model in conjunction with a swapping strategy. The swapping strategy was intimately intertwined with the scheduling subsystem, thus encouraging the monolithic design. Modern versions of UNIX incorporate virtual memory—specifically, paging—implemented within the monolithic kernel. The kernel file system provided disk block management, including free-list and inode management. The actual `read/write` operations were implemented in device drivers.

18.3.2 ■ The Monolithic Organization

The original UNIX kernel was small, efficient, and monolithic. Designing the kernel as a monolith made sense because of the constraints and goals for the original system. Since the kernel was to have a minimum of functionality, a partitioned approach was not necessary. In particular, it was feared the target hardware would not be fast enough to support a modular implementation. UNIX is still widely used today, often for relatively large systems. It has been expanded, ported, and reimplemented many times since its inception, always retaining the monolithic structure; even Linux retains the monolithic structure. By the 1980s, almost all UNIX implementations had moved from swapping systems to paging systems. Process management has been upgraded to address multiprocessor and distributed hardware configurations.

Network and graphics device support proved too difficult for the monolithic approach. The network protocols must interact with the memory manager, and sometimes with the process manager, so as to provide efficient implementations. Similarly, bitmap graphics devices employ a memory to define a device screen appearance, but it must be manipulated by an application program. How could these kinds of functions be implemented efficiently? The first attempts incorporated much of the device functionality in the driver, as intended with earlier devices. However, the device-kernel interface was not designed to support devices in this manner so some kernel implementations incorporated network and graphics device functions directly in the kernel. In contemporary UNIX systems, including AT&T System V and BSD variants, bitmapped devices are handled largely in user space and the system call interface is expanded explicitly to address networks.

18.3.3 ■ Conclusion

Today's commercial UNIX kernel is huge and complex. Most implementations are difficult to modify due to the close coupling of various parts of the kernel. Many of the reasons for using a modular approach rather than a monolithic approach now exist in UNIX environments. Only a few of the reasons justifying the monolithic approach still dominate in these machines.

However, the UNIX application program interface has become well entrenched, to the point of becoming the basis of the POSIX.1 open systems standard. There are two alternative paths taken to support the traditional UNIX system call interface: the BSD UNIX 4.x approach and a complete redesign of the kernel, such as the Mach 2 extensible kernel and the newer Mach 3 microkernel approach (see Section 18.7).

UNIX has had a profound influence on the evolution of commercial operating systems without ever dominating commercial computers. Manufacturers were forced by their users in the 1980s to address open systems concerns. While UNIX provided one avenue for doing this, the POSIX.1 interface implemented on a proprietary OS provided another alternative approach. Today, there is a trend back toward proprietary operating systems.

UNIX has been the system call interface of choice in research organizations and universities for over two decades. As a result, much of the new system technology continues to be developed in a UNIX environment.

18.4 ■ Choices: An Object-oriented OS

Choices is an experimental research OS built with an object-oriented language and design, thus making it a prime example of a modular OS. The goals of the Choices system include being able to experiment with various approaches through rapid prototyping and to easily port the base design to new hardware. Choices demonstrates how object-oriented technology can be used in OS design and implementation. This section explains how Choices uses type hierarchies in its design environment.

18.4.1 ■ Frameworks

Choices makes heavy use of object frameworks to define the basic structure of the OS. It then uses type hierarchies to specify particular characteristics for the prototyping testbed and for any particular hardware target. The framework explicitly identifies the modules in the OS as a set of base classes and then establishes generic interactions and relations among the base classes. When Choices is to be implemented on a new hardware platform, the module functions, interfaces, and interactions are already defined. The implementation of a module is inherited from the base class and then refined to define the implementation for the target hardware.

In Choices, objects model the application interface, resources, mechanisms, policies, and hardware interface. All applications are expected to be object-oriented programs that manipulate other objects and use inheritance and polymorphism to define their behavior. Computational units are *kernel objects* with a related *ObjectProxy* executing in user space. An OS "call" occurs when an object of type `ObjectProxy` sends a message to the corresponding kernel object.

The structure of the OS is captured in the framework hierarchy. A framework describes a set of subframeworks used as base classes for the parts of the OS. The base framework creates a generalized environment in which Choices's processes, address spaces, and memory objects execute as objects of, respectively, type `Process`, `Domain`, and `MemoryObject`. Subframeworks describe how the memory manager, the process manager, the file manager, and the message-passing system interoperate to support processes, address spaces, and memory objects.

18.4.2 ■ Using a Framework for the Memory Manager

For example, Figure 18.9, inspired by a similar figure in Campbell et al. [1993], illustrates the abstract control flow diagram for the memory manager; the numbers represent the sequence of messages. The rectangles represent the main components of the memory manager, and the arrows represent the control flow among them. Alternative diagrams represent data flow, synchronization, and other relationships that exist among the components as required. The memory manager subframework inherits the `Domain` and

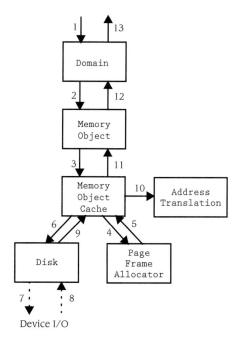

Figure 18.9
The Choices Memory Manager Subframework

MemoryObject components from the base framework. However, their behavior, in terms of control flow, is elaborated in the subframework. A MemoryObject is an encapsulation of pages inside an object. A process operates in a Domain object in the process's address space. The Domain translates the references into a MemoryObject reference, which is passed to the Memory Object Cache. Memory Object Cache then copies the relevant pages from secondary storage into primary memory. The details of the caching operation control flow are for the Memory Object Cache to interact with the Page Frame Allocator to adjust the amount of primary memory allocated to the process if required. Once the primary memory allocation has been adjusted, the Memory Object Cache directs the Disk object to read its disk. The Disk object is an interface to the disk hardware that encapsulates the device driver and interrupt. When the MemoryObject has been cached, the Address Translation component of the framework adjusts the page table. Hence, the Address Translation component is an object wrapper for the memory management hardware on the target computer.

The subframework is used as the basis of an actual implementation of the Choices memory manager in the prototyping testbed—called *Virtual Choices*—or on target hardware. The Virtual Choices facility is used to develop, modify, and test the design in a simulator environment. Figure 18.10, also inspired by a similar figure in Campbell et al. [1993], shows the Sun SparcStation implementation of the Choices memory manager. Every component in the generic subframework, and in the Virtual Choices implementation, has a component in the inherited implementation. Although the SparcStation

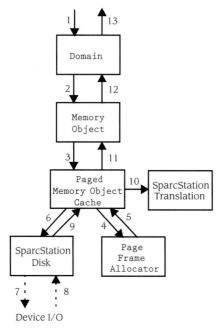

Figure 18.10
The Choices SparcStation Memory Manager

component implementations will differ from the generic implementations, the control flow will be the same. In Choices, the arrows in the control flow diagram can also represent hierarchical relationships. For example, the generic diagram can be annotated with virtual function names to be provided by the derived classes in the implementation.

18.4.3 ■ Conclusion

Work on Choices began in 1987, and its design has since then evolved through several different concrete implementations. Implementers are often concerned about the performance of object-oriented implementations due to the tendency for C++ implementations to proliferate small functions. In 1993, the Choices designers argued that the performance for system call, context switching, and message passing were all competitive, although still not as fast as the fastest operating systems on the same hardware.

Choices remains a research OS; it has no commercial counterpart. As object-oriented technologies continue to grow in commercial importance, the experience from Choices will help to guide operating systems designs that use the technology. For comparison, see Section 18.6 to see how Windows NT uses objects.

18.5 ■ The RC 4000 Nucleus

The RC 4000 and the IBM VM were among the first operating systems to use the extensible nucleus approach. Both were intended to create an extensible nucleus to support different versions of timesharing and batch operating systems for different application domains in the commercial marketplace. Today, the extensible machine ideas have been extended to microkernel architectures. VM is described in system documentation and in a number of books (for example, see Deitel [1990, ch. 21]). A brief description of the RC 4000 is given next.

18.5.1 ■ The Nucleus

The RC 4000 was a multiprogrammed computer manufactured in the late 1960s by A/S Regnecentralen [Brinch Hansen, 1973]. It was intended to be useful for a variety of different applications ranging from timesharing to real-time process control support. To help accomplish this goal, an abstract machine called the *monitor* or the *nucleus* was built to manage resources in the machine but not to implement any particular OS policy. The nucleus was not useful for supporting application programs unless the rest of the OS was built as a higher-level abstract machine that used the nucleus.

The nucleus implements preemptive scheduling, initiation and control of processes, IPC, and initiation of device I/O operations. It has no inherent strategy for resource allocation or for process management policy—those policies implemented above the nucleus. The nucleus mechanism assumes that process creation implies a process hierarchy, as described in Section 6.6. An OS built on top of the nucleus is like any other child process in terms of resource management. The child receives resources when it is created, and any processes it creates are its children. The OS is responsible for the resources held by the processes within its hierarchy. Not only are the resource and process policies deferred to OS applications, but also any application process can be created or destroyed during the nucleus's normal operation, thus allowing operating systems to be dynamically created and destroyed.

18.5.2 ■ Interprocess Communication

The IPC facilities illustrate the principles behind the nucleus design philosophy. The nucleus defines messages, queues, and four primitives to `send message`, `wait message`, `send answer`, and `wait answer`. As illustrated in Figure 18.11, each process is allocated a fixed number of message buffers from the parent's own buffer pool by the parent when it is created. The `send message` primitive copies a message into a particular buffer and delivers it to the queue of the specified receiver. If the receiver has performed a `wait message`, it will be blocked as it awaits the incoming message. The sender proceeds after the message is delivered to the queue, whether or not the receiver was waiting. When the receiver succeeds with the `wait message` call, it is provided with the name of the sender, the contents of the message, and the address of the buffer. The buffer is used to return an answer to the sender. The sender proceeds asynchronously until it needs the answer, at which time it calls `wait answer`. If no answer has been delivered to the sender's queue, it blocks until one arrives. When the answer arrives, the data is copied into the sender's address space and the buffer is released to the sender's free pool.

18.5.3 ■ Conclusion

The RC 4000 nucleus is an early example of a virtual machine OS. It supports many different higher-level operating systems by focusing on primitive resource management mechanisms and leaving the policy to the higher-level portion of the OS. Because the OS was used only on the RC 4000 computer, it never enjoyed the commercial success of IBM VM. Nevertheless, it established the extensible nucleus idea as a fundamental

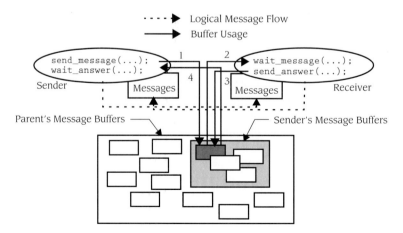

Figure 18.11
RC 4000 IPC

technique for designing operating systems. Because of the demonstration of the approach in the RC 4000, OS designers have factored the intent of extensible nuclei into operating systems since the 1970s, culminating in the microkernels of the 1990s.

18.6 ■ Microsoft Windows NT

NT is a commercial OS, first released for public use in July 1993 (Solomon, 1998; Nutt, 1999a).[1] Microsoft operating systems, particularly Windows 95, Windows 98, and Windows NT, are among the most widely used commercial systems available today. Windows NT uses a computational model based on processes and threads (rather than just processes). It also has a pervasive underlying object model. Even so, Windows NT carries on the MS-DOS legacy, meaning it supports 16-bit application programs written for MS-DOS.

18.6.1 ■ General Architecture

The product goals for Windows NT were that it should be an *extensible, portable, reliable,* and *secure* OS for contemporary computers, including symmetric multiprocessors (Solomon, 1998). These terms can mean many things, so they warrant some discussion to see how they influenced the Windows NT design.

18.6.1.1 ■ Extensibility

There are at least two dimensions to the extensibility aspect. The first relates to OS configurations. A Windows NT machine can be configured for a workstation or a server. In either configuration, the OS uses the same source code, but different components are incorporated into each at compile time. This allows Windows NT to be optimized to perform best according to the way the machine will be used—as a workstation or as a server—without building two different operating systems.

The second, and perhaps a more significant, aspect of extensibility is in the way the OS software is structured. Windows NT is designed using the extensible nucleus software model (see Section 18.2). In this approach, only the most essential OS functions are implemented in a small nucleus of code (analogous to a microkernel). Additional mechanisms are then implemented on top of the nucleus to define policy as needed. This approach has the advantage that key mechanisms (such as protection mechanisms) can be carefully designed and tested as one trusted subassembly that can then be used to implement many different policies. This is a basic approach to support the goals of good security and reliable operation. The *NT Kernel* provides these essential low-level mechanisms as a layer of abstraction from the hardware (see Figure 18.12). The *NT Executive* is designed as a layer of abstraction of the NT Kernel. It provides specific mechanisms (and many policies) for general object and memory management, process management, file management, and device management. Together, the NT Kernel and

---

[1]The discussion of Windows NT in this section is abstracted from Part 1 of Nutt [1999a, part 1].

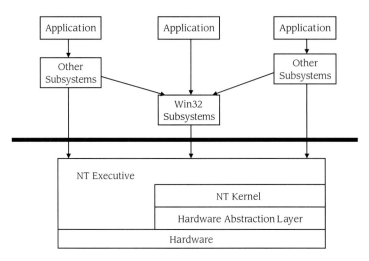

Figure 18.12
Windows NT Organization

the NT Executive provide the essential elements of an OS, though this nucleus is extended yet again by the subsystems (as explained below).

Although the NT Kernel and the NT Executive are designed and implemented as distinct software modules, they are combined into a single executable image when they are translated into machine code (Solomon, 1998). This image also invokes additional dynamically linked libraries (DLLs) whenever they are needed. Thus the logical view of Windows NT—that of a modular nucleus—is quite different from the way the OS code actually appears in memory—as a monolithic block of code.

The next layer of abstraction of Windows NT is the subsystem layer. Subsystems provide application *portability* for Windows NT software. An *NT Subsystem* is a software module that uses the services (mechanisms) implemented in the NT Kernel and the NT Executive to implement more abstract "services," especially the services offered by some target OS. For example, Version 4.0 has a POSIX subsystem that executes on top of the Kernel and the Executive that makes Windows NT look like POSIX; such subsystems are called *environment subsystems,* or *personality modules.* Other subsystems implement specialized services such as the security subsystem. All subsystems (and all application programs that use the subsystems) execute when the processor is in user mode. Subsystems are the key component in allowing Microsoft to support various computational models, such as the MS-DOS and Win16 program models (personalities). Application programs written to run on MS-DOS use the MS-DOS subsystem interface. This subsystem provides the same API to the application as does MS-DOS, thereby allowing old MS-DOS programs to run on an NT system.

18.6.1.2 ■ Portability

The portability aspect of the Windows NT overlaps its extensibility. Subsystems allow Windows NT to be extended to meet various application support requirements, and they are also a cornerstone of portability (since a subsystem allows application programs written for other operating systems to be easily ported to Windows NT). Microsoft has built various subsystems to implement OS personalities of interest to their customers. Besides the MS-DOS subsystem, there are subsystems to support Win16 applications and POSIX programs, as well as a new Win32 subsystem. In general, it is possible for software developers to implement any subsystem to satisfy their general requirements for OS service; such a subsystem uses the Executive/Kernel interface. Even so, the Win32 subsystem takes a special role in Windows NT because it implements various extensions of the NT Executive that are needed by all other subsystems; every subsystem relies on the presence of the Win32 subsystem. While it is possible to add new environment subsystems to Windows NT, and to omit most of them, the Win32 subsystem must always be present.

Another aspect of portability that has driven the design of Windows NT is the ability to port Windows NT itself across different hardware platforms. Microsoft's goal was to be able to reuse the NT Kernel, NT Executive, and Subsystems on new microprocessors as they became available without having to rewrite the Kernel (or Executive, and so on). The goal was for Windows NT itself to be written to be portable. Windows NT's designers carefully identified the things that were common across a wide set of microprocessors and the things that were different. This allowed them to create a *hardware abstraction layer* (*HAL*) software module to isolate the NT Kernel (and the rest of the OS) from hardware differences. The HAL is responsible for mapping various low-level, processor-specific operations into a fixed interface that is used by the NT Kernel and Executive. The HAL also executes with the processor in supervisor mode.

The HAL, NT Kernel, and NT Executive are supervisor-mode software that collectively export an API that is used by subsystem designers (but not by application programmers). Environment subsystem designers choose a target API (such as the Win16, POSIX, or OS/2 API) and then build a subsystem to implement the API using the supervisor portion of Windows NT. Microsoft has even chosen its own preferred API—the Win32 API—which is also the API for the Win32 subsystem. NT application programs are written to work on the Win32 API rather than on the interface to the kernel. The remaining subsections consider these components in a little more detail (starting at the HAL in Section 18.6.2 and working up to the subsystem level in Section 18.6.5).

18.6.1.3 ■ Reliability and Security

Both the reliability and security requirements for Windows NT are reflected in the details of how the NT Kernel and Executive are designed and implemented (rather than in their overall organization). Reliability is supported by separating the HAL, Kernel, Executive, and subsystem functionality from one another, thus eliminating unnecessary interactions. It is further supported through the software design techniques used in implementing Windows NT.

It is easier to identify how security has influenced Windows NT's design. Windows NT is designed to meet standard requirements for trusted operating systems. Much of the security mechanism is implemented in a Security Subsystem, which depends on the Security Reference Manager in the Executive (Section 18.6.4). Note that even though the presence of these mechanisms makes it possible to create very secure systems, if the application software does not use the security mechanisms, the overall system will not be especially secure (most production software does not use the protection mechanism).

18.6.2 ■ The Hardware Abstraction Layer

The hardware abstraction layer (HAL) is a low-level software module that translates critical hardware behaviors into a standardized set of behaviors. The HAL functions are exported through a kernel-mode DLL. The OS calls functions in this DLL when it needs to determine the way the host hardware behaves. This allows the Windows NT code to call a HAL function (rather than just using a hardwired address) everywhere a hardware-specific address is needed. For example, device interrupts usually have addresses determined by the microprocessor architecture, and they differ from one microprocessor to another. The HAL interface allows Windows NT to reference the interrupt addresses via functions rather than by using the hardware addresses directly.

The HAL implementation for any specific microprocessor provides the appropriate hardware-specific information via the corresponding function on the HAL API. This means that it is possible to use the same source code on a Digital Equipment Alpha processor as is used on an Intel Pentium processor. It also means that it is possible to create device drivers for Windows NT that will also work without change in Windows 95/98.

The use of the HAL is transparent above the NT Executive/Kernel interface. Subsystem and application programmers are generally unconcerned with the type of processor chip in the computer. Windows NT provides a fixed set of services independent of the hardware platform type.

18.6.3 ■ The NT Kernel

The NT Kernel creates the basic unit of computation and provides the foundation for multitasking support. It does so without committing to any particular policy/strategy for process management, memory management, file management, or device management. To appreciate the level of support the NT Kernel provides, think of the NT Kernel as offering a collection of building components such as wheels, pistons, lights, and so on, that could be used to build a sports car, a sedan, a sports utility vehicle, or a truck. Similarly, the NT Kernel's clients can combine the components to build a compound component that defines a policy for how the low-level components are used.

The Kernel provides objects and threads (computational abstractions) on top of the HAL and the hardware. Software that uses the NT Kernel can be defined using objects and threads as primitives—that is, these abstractions appear to NT Kernel client software as natural parts of the hardware. To implement objects and threads, the Kernel must manage the hardware interrupts and exceptions, perform processor scheduling, and handle multiprocessor synchronization.

18.6.3.1 ■ Objects

The NT Kernel defines a set of built-in *object types* (usually called *classes* in object-oriented languages). Some kernel object types are instantiated by the NT Kernel itself to form other parts of the overall OS execution image. These objects collectively save and manipulate the Kernel's state. Other objects are instantiated and used by the Executive, subsystems, and application code as the foundation of their computational model. That is, Windows NT and all of its applications are managed at the NT Kernel level as objects.

Kernel objects are intended to be fast. They run in supervisor mode in a trusted context, so there is no security and only limited error checking for Kernel objects, in contrast to normal objects, which incorporate these features. However, Kernel objects cannot be manipulated directly by user-mode programs, only through function calls. Kernel objects are characterized as being either control objects or dispatcher objects. Control objects implement mechanisms to control the hardware and other Kernel resources. Dispatcher objects are used to implement threads along with their scheduling and synchronization operations. Each dispatcher object has built-in characteristics that are used to support user-level synchronization (see the In the Hangar section in Chapter 9, p. 236).

18.6.3.2 ■ Threads

As mentioned in the discussion of objects, a thread is an abstraction of a computation. An NT process object defines an address space in which one or more threads can execute, and each thread object represents one execution within the process. In the normal UNIX environment, there is only one thread executing in each address space. In the NT environment it is common to have more than one thread—a logical path traversal through the code in an address space—executing in a process. The separation of the thread concept from the rest of the process concept has been done so that it is natural to think of several different "threads of execution" within a single address space, all sharing the same resources.

The Windows NT thread scheduler is a timesliced, priority-based, preemptive scheduler. The basic unit of processor allocation is a time quantum computed as a multiple of the number of clock interrupts (for example, a time quantum might be three ticks of the host system's clock). On most Windows NT machines, the time quantum ranges from about 20 to 200 milliseconds (ms). Servers are configured to have time quanta that are six times longer than for a workstation with the same processor type.

The scheduler supports 32 different scheduling queues. As in all multiple-level queue schedulers, as long as there are threads in the highest-priority queue, then only those threads will be allocated the processor. If there are no threads in that queue, then the scheduler will service the threads in the second highest-priority queue. If there are no threads ready to run (that is, no runnable threads) in the second highest-priority queue, the scheduler will service the third highest-priority queue, and so on.

There are three levels of queues:

- *Real-time level,* consisting of the 16 highest-priority queues
- *Variable-level,* consisting of the next 15 higher-priority queues
- *System-level,* consisting of the lowest-priority queue

The scheduler attempts to limit the number of threads that are entered into the real-time queues, thereby increasing the probability that there will be little competition among threads that execute at these high-priority levels. (There is a model used for real-time scheduling on the Win32 API. It requires that a thread be authorized as a real-time thread before it is placed in a real-time level queue.) However, Windows NT is not a real-time system and cannot *guarantee* that threads running at high priority will receive the processor before any fixed deadline. The highest-level queue processing continues through the variable-level queues, down to the system-level queue. The system-level queue contains a single "zero page thread" to represent an idle system. That is, when there are no runnable threads in the entire system, it executes the zero page thread until an interrupt occurs and another thread becomes runnable. The zero page thread is the single lowest-priority thread in the system, so it runs whenever there are no other runnable threads.

The thread scheduler is also fully preemptive. This means that whenever a thread becomes ready to run, it is placed in a run queue at a level corresponding to its current priority. If there is another thread in execution at that time and that thread has a lower priority, then the lower-priority thread is interrupted (it is not allowed to finish its time quantum) and the new, higher-priority thread is assigned the processor. In a single-processor system, this would mean that a thread could cause itself to be removed from the processor by enabling a higher-priority thread. In a multiprocessor system, the situation can be more subtle. Suppose that in a two-processor system, one processor is running a thread at level 10 and the other is running a thread at level 4. If the level 10 thread performs some action that causes a previously blocked thread to suddenly become runnable at level 6, then the level 4 thread will be halted and the new level 6 thread will begin to use the processor that the level 4 thread was using.

18.6.3.3 ■ Multiprocess Synchronization

Single-processor systems can support synchronization by disabling interrupts (see Chapter 8). However, Windows NT is designed to support multiprocessors, so the NT Kernel provides an alternative mechanism to ensure that a thread executing on one processor does not violate a critical section of a thread on another. As is traditional in multiprocessor operating systems, the NT Kernel employs spinlocks, by which a thread on one process can wait for a critical section by actively testing an NT Kernel lock variable to determine when it can enter the critical section. If the hardware supports the test-and-set instruction (or other machine instruction that is logically equivalent to test-and-set), spinlocks are implemented using the hardware. Spinlock synchronization is used only within the NT Kernel and Executive. User-mode programs use abstractions that are implemented by the Executive.

18.6.4 ■ The NT Executive

The NT Executive builds on the NT Kernel to implement the full set of Windows NT policies and services, including process management, memory management, file management, and device management. Since Windows NT uses object-oriented technology, its modularization does not strictly follow the classic separation of OS functionality as described in a textbook. Instead, the NT Executive is designed and implemented at the source code level as a modularized set of elements (Solomon, 1998; Nagar, 1997):

- *Object Manager:* Defines Executive-level objects that can be used directly by user mode software. An Executive object exists in supervisor space, though it can be referenced by user threads. This is accomplished by having the Object Manager provide a *handle* for each Executive object. Whenever a thread needs a new Executive object, it calls an Object Manager function to create the object (in supervisor space), to create a handle to the object (in the process's address space), and then to return the handle to the calling thread.

- *Process and Thread Manager:* This is the part of the OS responsible for the following:

  - Creating and destroying processes and threads

  - Overseeing resource allocation

  - Providing synchronization primitives

  - Controlling process and thread state changes

  - Keeping track of most of the information that the OS knows about each process and thread

  In short, it manages all aspects of threads and processes that are not managed by some other specialized element (such as object-specific characteristics and the file characteristics).

- *Virtual Memory Manager:* Described in Section 18.6.4.1.

- *Security Reference Manager:* This is an Executive-level mechanism to implement the critical parts of certifiable security policies. It is constructed to check object access according to any given protection policy (specified within subsystem components that manage the specific access that a process is trying to perform). The kernel mechanism works with a user space subsystem component, the *Local Security Authority (LSA) server,* to represent the desired security policy. The LSA uses its own policy database, stored in the machine's Registry, to hold the details of the particular machine's policy. (The policy for the particular machine can be changed by editing the policy database.) The authentication mechanism the LSA server uses to compare access requests with the database contents can also be provided on an installation-by-installation basis, though a default mechanism is provided with Windows NT. The Security Reference Manager authenticates access to Executive objects. Whenever any thread makes a system call to access an Executive object, the manager checks an access control list of processes that are permitted access to the object.

- I/O Manager: Described in Section 18.6.4.2.

- *Cache Manager:* The Cache Manager works with the Virtual Memory Manager and the I/O Manager to perform read-ahead and write-behind on virtual files. The idea is a classic OS idea. That is, since files are usually accessed sequentially, whenever a thread reads byte *i,* it is likely to read byte $i + 1$ soon thereafter. Therefore, on a read-ahead strategy, when the thread requests that byte *i* be read from the device, the Cache Manager asks the Virtual Memory Manager to prepare a buffer to hold $K + 1$ bytes of information from the virtual file and instructs the

I/O Manager to read byte i and the next K bytes into the buffer. Then when the thread requests byte $i + 1, i + 2, \ldots, i + K$, those bytes will have already been read, so the thread need not wait for a device operation to complete. The write-behind strategy works similarly.

18.6.4.1 ■ Virtual Memory Manager

Windows NT is a *paging virtual memory system.* When a process is created, it is given 4 GB of virtual addresses, though none of the addresses are actually allocated at that time. When the process needs space, it first *reserves* as much of the address space as it needs at that moment; reserved addresses do not cause any actual space to be allocated; rather virtual addresses are reserved for later use. When the process needs to use the virtual addresses to store information, it *commits* the address space, meaning that some system storage space is then allocated to the process to hold information. Ordinarily, a commit operation causes space on the disk (in the process's *page file*) to be allocated to the process; the information is stored on the disk until it is actually referenced by a thread.

Like all paging virtual memory mechanisms, when an executing thread references a virtual address, the Virtual Memory Manager ensures that the page containing that virtual address is read from the page file and placed at some system-defined location in the physical executable memory. The Virtual Memory Manager *maps* the virtual address referenced by the thread into the physical memory address where the information is loaded.

The Virtual Memory Manager has been designed so that a large portion of each process's address space (usually half of it, though different configurations of Windows NT use different fractions) is mapped to the information used by the system when it is in supervisor mode (see Figure 18.13). There are a few important implications of this decision, as follows:

- A process can directly reference (but not necessarily access) every location in the system space.

- Every process shares the same view of the system's space.

- Such a large, shared virtual address space makes memory-mapped files feasible.

In Figure 18.13, when a thread references an address in the user space, the virtual memory system loads the target location into the physical memory prior to its use so that the thread can read or write the virtual memory address by referencing a physical memory address. The same mapping takes place for OS memory references, though these references are protected, and every process's OS addresses map to the OS memory rather than to the application-specific part of the address space.

18.6.4.2 ■ I/O Manager

The I/O Manager is responsible for handling all the input/output operations to every device in the system. Its operation can be quite complex (Solomon, 1998).

- The I/O Manager creates an abstraction of all device I/O operations on the system so that the system's clients can perform operations on a common data structure.

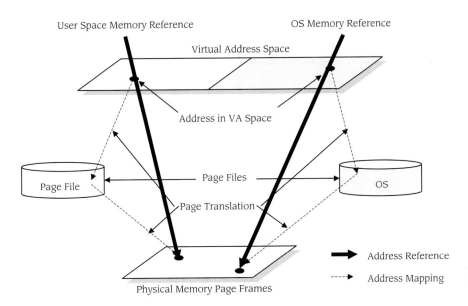

Figure 18.13
Virtual Memory

- The client can perform synchronous and asynchronous I/O.
- The client can invoke the Security Reference Monitor whenever security is an issue.
- The I/O Manager must accommodate device drivers written in a high-level language by third parties. Those drivers must be able to execute in supervisor mode. Installation and removal of a device driver must be dynamic.
- The I/O Manager can accommodate alternative file systems on the system's disks. This means that some file systems might use the MS-DOS format, others might use an industry standard CD-ROM format, and yet others might use Windows NT's own file system (NTFS).
- I/O Manager extensions—device drivers and/or file systems—must be consistent with the memory-mapped file mechanism implemented in the Virtual Memory Manager, so extension designs are constrained by the facilities provided by the manager.

The I/O Manager is made up of the following components, as shown in Figure 18.14 (Nagar, 1997).

- *Device drivers* are at the lowest level. They manipulate the physical I/O devices. These drivers are described generically in Chapter 5.
- *Intermediate drivers* are software modules that work with a low-level device driver to provide enhanced service. For example, a low-level device driver might simply pass an error condition "upward" when it detects it, while an intermediate driver might receive the error and decide to issue a retry operation to the lower-level driver.

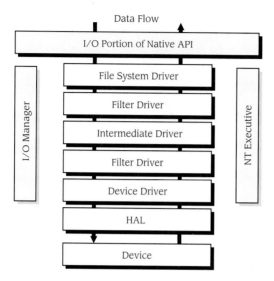

Figure 18.14
The I/O Manager

- *File system drivers* extend the functionality of the lower-level drivers (such as intermediate and device drivers) to implement the target file system.

- A *filter driver* can be inserted between a device driver and an intermediate driver, between an intermediate driver and a file system driver, or between the file system driver and the I/O Manager API to perform any kind of function that might be desired. For example, a network redirector filter driver can intercept file commands intended for remote files and redirect them to remote file servers.

Drivers are the single component that can be added to the NT Executive to run in supervisor mode. The OS has not been designed to support third-party software, other than drivers, that want to add supervisor mode functionality.

The Windows NT I/O Manager defines the framework in which device drivers, intermediate drivers, file system drivers, and filter drivers are dynamically added to and removed from the system and are made to work together. The basic idea of a stream of modules between the API and device was first used in the AT&T System V UNIX I/O streams (Ritchie, 1984). The dynamic stream design allows one to easily configure complex I/O systems; the System V streams were the basis of the network protocol implementations.

Also similar to System V streams, the I/O Manager directs modules by issuing *I/O request packets* (IRPs) into a stream. If the IRP is intended for a particular module, that module responds to the IRP; otherwise, it passes the IRP to the next module in the stream. Each driver in the stream has the responsibility of accepting IRPs, either reacting to the IRP if it is directed at the driver or passing it on to the next module if it is not.

All information read from or written to the device is managed as a stream of bytes called a *virtual file*. Every driver is written to read and/or write a virtual file. Low-level device drivers transform information read from the device into a stream and transform stream information into a device-dependent format before writing it.

18.6.4.3 ■ The Native API

While the NT Executive and Kernel are designed and programmed as separate modules, they are combined with the `kernel` executable when Windows NT is built. The combined NT Executive and Kernel module (with the underlying HAL) implements the full NT OS. In Version 5.0, the `kernel` exports about 240 functions (Russinovich, 1998), most of which are *undocumented,* meaning that only subsystem developers should base their software on the functions.

18.6.5 ■ NT Subsystems

The Windows NT system software is constructed as a layered architecture. Layer i is constructed using the services provided by layer $i - 1$ ("at the layer $i - 1$ interface"), creating its own services and exporting them through its own (layer i) interface. In the Windows NT architecture, *subsystems* provide a layer of service above the Native API. There can be many different subsystems, some related, but others independent of one another, as functionality is added to the computer system. For example, a typical Windows NT system includes the following:

- The Win32 subsystem
- The WinLogon service (to authenticate users, using the LSA server and Secure Reference Monitor described in the NT Executive section, when they begin to use the system)
- A remote procedure call service

It may also include a Win16 subsystem. If the Windows NT machine were required to support POSIX application programs, a POSIX subsystem could be added as a component in the subsystem layer.

Each subsystem uses the Native API to provide the services it implements. The *environment subsystems* behave as a traditional interior layer. In the layered architecture approach, they use the Native API, add functionality and services, and then export their own API. In the Microsoft strategy, subsystem APIs are documented APIs, meaning that a programmer can write new software at the next higher-level layer and be assured that the API will be unchanged when implementations at a lower-level layer in the architecture are changed.

Figure 18.15 shows how this layering works in Windows NT. The *Win32 subsystem* exports a documented interface, the *Win32 API,* as a set of about 2000 functions. The Win32 API is a documented interface. An application programmer can write software above the Win32 subsystem that calls the API functions to accomplish an application-specific task.

The Win32 subsystem also provides one other type of service: It implements a user interface management system, since the NT Executive/Kernel does not have one of these. This is primarily a matter of practicality—when the system begins to run, some part of the system software needs to read the keyboard and mouse and manage the display. Rather than have each environment subsystem provide its own user interface, the

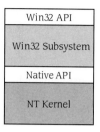

Figure 18.15
The Win32 API

Win32 subsystem implements the common window manager for all subsystems. This means that there is a single human-computer interaction model implemented in a single subsystem but used by all other subsystems.

A subsystem's design can be simple or complex. In the simplest case, each function or service that the subsystem exports is implemented wholly within the subsystem itself. For example, the subsystem might keep a data structure filled with information it extracts from information obtained through the Native API. When a program queries the subsystem, it simply reads the data structure and returns a result without ever interacting with the OS.

A slightly more complex case occurs when a subsystem function requires that the subsystem implementation interact with the OS via the Native API. For example, the Win32 API function `CreateProcess` causes the Win32 subsystem to call the Native API functions `NtCreateProcess` and `NtCreateThread`.

18.6.6 ■ Win32 API: The Programmer's View of NT

The Win32 API is the "official OS interface" to all Microsoft operating systems: Windows NT, Windows 95, Windows 98, and Windows CE. The rationale for having a single OS API relates to portability. That is, if all Microsoft operating systems can export the same API, then an application writer can produce application software that will work on all OS versions. (This is the same strategy that UNIX implementers have used for many years; different kernel implementations provide a standard system call interface for all UNIX applications. The Berkeley Software Distribution (BSD) UNIX and POSIX system call APIs have many different implementations.) Furthermore, enhancements to any of the OS products still provide the same services (presumably of a better quality) via the same, fixed interface. The cost of adopting this strategy is the need for a subsystem between the OS's native API and the API used by the application programmers.

MS-DOS created a set of fundamental OS services on which application programmers came to depend. Unfortunately, the original MS-DOS API is very old (MS-DOS first came out in the early 1980s). As a result, it had many built-in dependencies on 16-bit address spaces, single thread of execution, and so on. The MS-DOS API was upgraded to a Windows interface, now generally regarded as the Win16 API (implemented by the Win16 NT subsystem). Yet that still was not adequate to allow program-

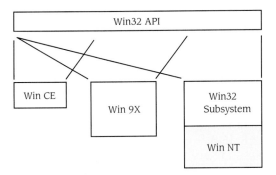

Figure 18.16
The Microsoft OS Family

mers to use the full power of Windows NT, Windows 95/98, and CE. As shown in Figure 18.16, all of Microsoft's current OS family implement some variant of the Win32 API. Whenever an application programmer writes code for a Microsoft OS, the only documented interfaces available are the Win32 API versions for each OS. There are few differences between the Windows 95/98 and Windows NT implementations of Win32 API. Since Windows CE is aimed at such hardware as palmtop computers and television set-top boxes, its variant of the Win32 API is distinctly different from the "mainstream" API.

18.7 ■ The Mach Operating System

A fundamental motivation for the Mach OS design was to investigate OS organizations that support efficient message-passing [Accetta et al., 1986]. The emphasis on message-passing could have substantial payoff in hardware environments that do not support shared memory, since IPC would ultimately have to use some form of messages. So an explicit related motivation for Mach was to support communities of processes in a multiprocessor environment in which communication might be possible only by using messages. Other goals for Mach include investigating new virtual memory designs having large, sparse address spaces and experimenting with new computational models more well suited to fine-grained shared-memory multiprocessors than are the classic processes. Others are to exploit capabilities to support more secure communication and network transparency, as explained above, and to explore the practical implications of implementing systems with an extensible nucleus.

Like the earlier work on UNIX at the University of California at Berkeley, Mach was selected as a research project by the Department of Defense Advanced Research Projects Agency (ARPA). ARPA was especially interested in the research and development of operating systems capable of controlling multiprocessors. Because of the common funding source and the wide acceptance of BSD UNIX in research organizations, it was natural for Mach to be designed to be binary-compatible with BSD applications.

Therefore all versions of Mach have supported the BSD 4.3 UNIX system call interface. Another factor in the success of Mach is its adaptation as the basis of the Open System Foundation standard operating system, OSF/1.

All versions of Mach have been intended to be extensible nuclei, meaning one could define certain features of the OS as user space programs. However, Version 3.0 and newer versions of Mach are explicitly designed with a microkernel to support function extensibility. Since the kernel was intended to support the BSD system call interface, versions prior to 3.0 used portions of the BSD 4.3 kernel in the kernel. Legally, this reuse required anyone acquiring the Mach source code to have a source code license for UNIX from AT&T and another for BSD 4.3 from UC-Berkeley. This encouraged the Mach design team to construct the kernel so that they could use the code independently of their possession of UNIX licenses. Interestingly, then, a primary rationale for deriving the microkernel version of Mach was driven by regulations as much as it was by technical requirements.

Today, the Mach microkernel is intended to establish a common set of critical functions used to support different operating systems that have different policies (see Figure 18.17). As explained in the previous paragraph, BSD 4.3 is the default OS supported by the microkernel. Figure 18.17 illustrates other extensions of the microkernel, including the OSF/1 operating system, other UNIX variants, and RT-Mach for real-time domains.

The microkernel provides mechanisms for process management, memory management, and device management. An OS is created by defining a server that uses the microkernel to implement the desired OS interface. The server implements the file manager and various policy modules for mechanisms implemented in the microkernel. The rest of this section describes the process and memory managers, especially including the IPC mechanism, due to its unique nature.

18.7.1 ■ Process Management

Mach supports tasks and threads, where the normal notion of process corresponds to a task with a single thread executing within it. A task is an execution environment with its own address space, port capabilities, and a collection of associated threads. It can be thought of as a static representation of a process, since it is missing the active ingredient that represents the dynamic computation. Each thread is a sequence of instruction executions within a task and shares the task's resources. A combination of one thread

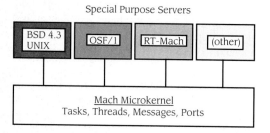

Figure 18.17
Mach Microkernel-based OS

and a task corresponds to the standard notion of a process. Any task may support several threads. If the task is implemented in a multiprocessor environment, the threads use inter-thread synchronization to coordinate access to resources within the task.

Resources are allocated to tasks but are used by the threads in the task. Threads are useful for implementing several different instances of a computation that is operating on a common set of resources. For example, a server might have a set of network-accessible resources and several different clients might wish to use various units of those resources at the same time. In the Mach model, the server resources would be represented by a task and each client would interact with a thread. This means the various threads must synchronize their activity so that their interaction with the task resources is correct. Mach provides a set of thread-specific synchronization mechanisms to support inter-thread synchronization.

The granularity of a distributed computation partition depends in part on the speed of the communication mechanism among the individual parts of the computation. Shared-memory multiprocessors support very high-speed message-passing because the transmission amounts to a memory-to-memory copy. If processes implemented the individual parts of the computation, then the limiting factor to distribution granularity changes from message transmission time to the context switching time for processes. Threads provide a lightweight model for context switching, so thread-based applications can take advantage of the fast message-passing time in a shared-memory multiprocessor.

The Mach process manager provides two levels of primitives, one for managing tasks and another for managing threads. The task-level primitives are used to create, destroy, suspend, and resume tasks. When a task is created, it may or may not inherit the parent's resources, depending on the parameters used in the create call. When a task is active, any thread in the task is schedulable, but when the task is suspended, all threads are blocked. Task suspension calls are counted so that threads in a task cannot run until there is a corresponding resume call for every suspend call.

Mach threads are kernel entities operating within a task. Thread management primitives include `fork`, `join`, `detach`, and `exit`. Since threads are defined to exist within a task, they share a common address space; hence, they have common global variables. The `fork` command is patterned after the UNIX `fork` command, and the `join` command is similar to the `join` command described in Chapter 2. The `detach` command is used to break the parent-child relationship between two threads so that the parent can exit while the child continues to run.

A kernel thread also can be suspended or resumed, provided the task is active. Again, kernel thread suspension calls are counted, so the task, to be runnable, must have received at least as many resumption calls as suspension calls. Since threads may run on single processors, there is a `yield` command to invoke the microkernel thread scheduler at the explicit command of the application.

The microkernel scheduler manages only threads, not tasks. In thread-based computing environments, there will tend to be many more threads than there are processes to schedule. Also, since Mach is intended to address multiprocessors, its scheduler must not assume there is only a single processor to manage. Every processor and every thread is assigned to a *processor set*. The processor set scheduler allocates runnable threads to an available processor in the processor set. The scheduler is a multilevel queue with priorities assigned according to the level of service that the thread is receiving. If the amount of service the thread has recently received is large, its priority is low. The priority is used to assign the thread to the end of one of 32 run queues. Some threads must be executed on a particular processor—for example, threads on I/O devices associated with that processor. Such threads are scheduled in a set of local run queues, while other threads can be scheduled in a global run queue for the process set. When a processor becomes idle, it selects the thread at the head of the highest-priority local run queue and dispatches it. If the local run queues are empty, the scheduler proceeds to the global run queue to select a thread. Because the global run queues are shared among the processors in the process set, locks are used to prevent more than one processor from scheduling at a time.

18.7.2 ■ Message Passing

Mach is descended from the Accent OS, which in turn is descended from the Rochester Intelligent Gateway (RIG) system. Each of these systems focuses on an efficient IPC facility to support communities of communicating processes.

18.7.2.1 ■ Messages

RIG was less concerned with the distribution of the processes across a multiprocessor or network of hardware machines than were its two successors. However, it began to focus on flexible and efficient IPC using messages. RIG used the ideas of messages and ports to support IPC, originally within a multiprogramming environment and then on a network of machines. A *message* is a header and data, while a *port* is a queue for typed message data structures associated with a process. A port can be thought of as a mailbox with a write entry point and a read entry point. A port bears a similarity to UNIX pipes by its half-duplex, typed communication, but it differs in its support of typed messages rather than byte streams. If two processes wish to exchange messages, they must each have a port so as to accomplish two-way communication.

The Accent designers found the RIG IPC mechanisms to be insufficient in several ways. First, the protection on ports was not sufficient, since there were no restrictions on which processes could write to a port. Second, the ports did not have adequate failure notification, meaning a port might allow dangling references to failed ports. Since ports were bound to the machine and to the process, it was difficult to move a process. Third, the message sizes were too small for some message-passing applications.

Accent was developed for a network of Spice workstations (also marketed by Three Rivers Computer Company as the PERQ), again using messages and ports. Messages are delivered reliably over the network using connected protocols. Recognizing the shortfalls of RIG, Accent's developers redesigned ports as protected kernel objects that are accessible with capabilities rather than with integer pointers. Thus, for a process to send a message to a port of another process, it must possess a capability to do so. Since the kernel manages capabilities, it knows which processes are able to send messages to any particular port. In particular, if a sender process fails, the kernel can inspect its capability list to determine which other processes depend on the failed process. Thus the kernel knows which processes should receive failure notifications. RIG allows any sender process to know the location of the receiver port by virtue of the address. In Accent, capabilities are network location transparent, thus preventing a sender from depending on the location of a receiver port. This transparency allows Accent to easily move a process from one machine to another with no worry that senders will be unable to locate the transient process.

Part of the message size limitation in RIG can be traced to its lack of support for virtual memory and to the small address spaces supported by the OS. Accent incorporated virtual memory and used it to address the message size limitation. An Accent message is a header followed by a collection of typed data objects. The length of the message is essentially unrestricted, although it must be less than or equal to 2^{32} bytes— the size of a paged address space. Accent virtual memory is built on memory objects. When one process sends a large message to another machine on the same node, the pages in the memory object are written into the receiver's page table so that both page tables reference the single memory object (see Figure 18.18). If the receiver writes to the memory object, then the pages touched by the receiver are copied and remapped prior to performing the `write` operation.

Mach reuses the basic Accent strategy for messages and ports to implement message passing. However, the goal hardware domain is extended to include shared-memory multiprocessors. These multiprocessors provide a raw IPC mechanism that supports finer-grained computation than exists on the networks of local memory machines targeted in the Accent design. As mentioned earlier in the chapter, Mach replaces the Accent notion of process by tasks and threads.

18.7.2.2 ■ Ports

Messages and ports are extended from process-to-process communication to be thread-to-thread communication. Ports are associated with a task and are shared by the threads associated with the task. For example, every thread in a task can read the task's ports and can write to any port for which the task has the capability. A thread uses a port to communicate with other threads within the same task or with threads in tasks on remote machines.

Although ports are kernel data structures, they are created by a thread. Any other thread in the same task has the capabilities of the creator to use the port, since the kernel

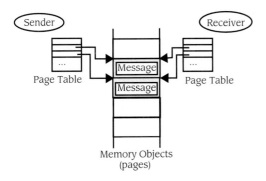

Figure 18.18
Transferring Large Messages in Accent

does not distinguish among threads, only among tasks. If a local thread wants a remote thread (one in a different task) to communicate with it, then the kernel creates a capability in the remote task to allow its threads to send messages to the local task's port.

The communication package provides kernel calls to support all variants of synchronous/asynchronous send and blocking/nonblocking `receive` operations. It also includes an ability to combine a `send` operation with a blocking `receive` to adopt the behavior of the RPC.

Since ports support typed messages and tasks may have specialized threads executing their code, tasks usually have several different ports. This means a thread may have to use a nonblocking read to poll every port to detect incoming messages. Mach provides *port sets* to simplify reading. A blocking read on a port set returns an arbitrary message from one of the ports in the port set if any of the ports contain messages. If no port in the port set contains a message, the thread blocks on the `read`.

18.7.2.3 ■ Network Messages

The Mach kernel does not support message transfer across the network. Instead, it provides for a user space server program to handle network-related communication. A *network message server* interacts with the kernel to address network transparency issues, including locating remote tasks and using the appropriate network protocols to transmit and receive messages. Since the network message server is not part of the kernel, it can be redefined as required by registering a new server with the kernel.

Each node in the network contains a network message server to route and receive traffic to/from the network. The abstract message network implemented by the collective network message servers creates a new name space with global *network ports* to be used by threads. When a task on a host obtains a capability to access a port on another machine, the network port is defined and the network message server maps the network port to the host location that contains the port. Now a send operation results in a series of actions in the sending and receiving machines. First, the kernel detects that the message is for a remote port, so it forwards the message to the local network message server. The local network message server uses the network port to determine the network location of the destination port. It then forwards the message to the network message server on the destination host. The remote network message server maps the network port to a local port on its own machine and then passes the message to its kernel for placement in the port queue.

Network message servers are more complex than this simple scenario suggests due to various additional tasks and complications. For example, since the network message server is a user space task it must have an appropriate set of capabilities to various ports along the message flow path. It also must manage capabilities on behalf of the senders and receivers so that they are not compromised by the network or by the server's implementation. Besides these Mach-specific tasks, several network-oriented tasks must be performed by a server, such as supporting, naming, detecting and maintaining the location of all remote hosts, performing data type conversion when needed, and conforming to authentication requirements.

While the approach of user space servers for message management has been shown to be valuable, it also can be slow. The inefficiency comes from context switching among threads/tasks and distributing work between the kernel and the server. Mach 3.0 provides a kernel space implementation of the network message server for configurations of multicomputers with "no remote memory access," called NORMA multiprocessors. The presence of the kernel space implementation does not preclude the presence of a user space network message server. If both mechanisms are present, the kernel will route traffic in the NORMA multicomputer to the kernel server and all other traffic to the user space server.

18.7.3 ■ Memory Management

The microkernel provides a means for the policy of managing memory objects to be implemented in a server [Rashid et al., 1988]. The basic memory manager mechanism, implemented in the microkernel, encapsulates the memory-mapping hardware much as the Choices Address Translation component encapsulates mapping hardware (see Figure 18.19). When the hardware detects a missing page fault, it must run another part of the memory manager to check the reference, change the protected page maps, and perform other secure housekeeping. This, too, must be microkernel code, although it is independent of the details of the memory-mapping hardware. Another part of the memory manager implements a specific, hardware-independent, secure memory management policy to keep track of disk and remote network addresses for pages, to identify replaced pages, and so on. As shown in Figure 18.19(a), this part of the memory manager is traditionally implemented in the kernel. However, Mach is designed to allow it to be executed in user space as an application program (Figure 18.19b). This requires the interface between the microkernel portion of the memory manager and the user space portion of the memory manager to have a well-defined interface so that either can use the services of the other.

A memory object is the unit of memory management in Mach. A memory object may be a page, a set of pages, a stack, or even a file. Memory objects can be associated with a region in the virtual address space used by a process—a 2^{31}-byte address space. Memory objects are loaded into the virtual address space at a particular address if desired or at an unallocated address if the application does not care where the memory object is to appear. Each memory object has a port and can react to messages.

Each task, including the kernel, has its own 2^{31}-byte paged address space managed by the kernel. When a "large" memory object is to be moved from one place in the virtual address space to another, the pages storing the memory object are logically transferred to the receiver task via its port. The microkernel copies the page table entry for the memory object from the sending process's page table to the kernel's page table while the message is queued in the port. When the destination process executes a receive for the message, the memory object's pages are mapped into the receiving process's page table. This design is exploited in *out-of-line* transfers of large amounts of data within a single node on the network.

In some cases, information in a message may exist in the part of the address space currently being used by more than one process. Therefore Mach implements a *copy-on-write* strategy so that two page tables can reference a common message body until one or the other of the two processes writes into its own logical copy. This write operation

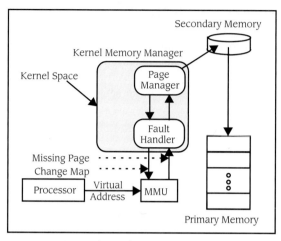

(a) Kernel-Based Memory Manager

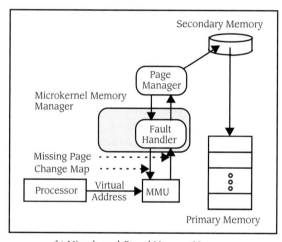

(b) Microkernel-Based Memory Manager

Figure 18.19
Mach Memory Management

causes actual copies of the specific pages containing the references to be created so that each process has its own version.

When a memory object is sent to a port on another machine, the kernel marks its pages as *copy-on-reference,* meaning they are not to be physically transmitted to the remote machine until that machine is referenced by the receiving process. However, the page table for the remote process will be updated to indicate that the memory object has been logically delivered. Mach can support very general policies to accomplish the binding. This is because the memory object is bound to a physical memory location on reference and the reference can be resolved by the memory object manager of the user space if they are "missing."

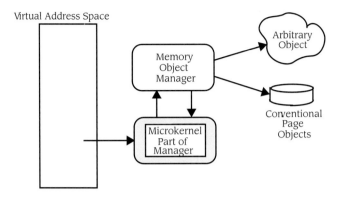

Figure 18.20
Binding Memory Objects

For example, in Figure 18.20, the sender's OS copies the memory object that contains the message from its kernel to the remote system kernel so that it can be mapped into the receiver's address space. However, the remote machine's Mach traps the reference and provides the sending process with the opportunity to bind information to the memory object when it is referenced, thus allowing the virtual address to be bound to an arbitrary object. This means the sending process maps virtual memory pages when they are referenced, even if they are referenced by a process on a remote machine.

18.7.4 ■ Conclusion

The Mach operating system is the major challenger to UNIX technology in network-oriented operating systems. The Open Systems Foundation OSF/1 OS is based on the Mach 2 technology. Mach is also available on a number of different machines.

The prevailing criticism of Mach is its performance. Mach implementations are typically unable to achieve the performance of monolithic UNIX kernels. This is because of the generality of the policy-mechanism separation that allows various parts of the operating system to execute in user space servers. Another limiting factor is the general message-passing mechanism. Microkernel performance in general, and Mach performance in particular, is the subject of much contemporary applied operating systems research and development.

18.8 ■ The CHORUS Operating System

CHORUS started as a research project in distributed systems at the French national computer science research institute (INRIA) in the early 1980s. By the late 1980s, it had evolved into a commercial OS supported by Chorus Systèmes. It is currently available on various hardware platforms [Rozier et al., 1988].

In CHORUS-V3, the goals of the microkernel are to provide efficient support for an OS with the System V Interface Definition, real-time operating systems, an object-oriented operating system (COOL), in an open, distributed hardware environment. Like

Mach, CHORUS evolved from earlier work on a microkernel architecture. The Version 3 microkernel, called the *nucleus,* supports heavyweight units of computation called actors, lightweight units called threads, and IPC based on messages and ports. The microkernel supports subsystems to host system servers to implement specific OS policies (see Figure 18.21).

An OS is implemented as a set of system servers within a subsystem built on top of the microkernel. The microkernel itself is modularized into a machine-dependent supervisor and machine-independent process manager, memory manager, and IPC manager. The process and memory management are local tasks, and the IPC manager is used to implement global services. These components of the microkernel implement six basic abstractions:

- *Actors:* A unit of computation analogous to a Mach task. It has resources, ports, and a paged address space divided into regions, but it is a passive entity with respect to computation.

- *Thread:* The active unit of serial computation. A thread executes in an actor, using its resources and address space. Threads in the same actor share the actor's resources. The thread's state is represented by a PC, registers, and a stack.

- *Message:* A byte stream used to exchange information among address spaces. Messages are the explicit means for threads to communicate across machine boundaries.

- *Port:* A mailbox holding messages sent to an actor. A port can be thought of as an address for a service. A port can belong to a *port group* in order to enable multicasting to several ports using the port group.

- *Unique Identifier (UI):* A 64-bit global name intended to be unique throughout the life of the operating system, including across reboot operations.

- *Region:* A smaller block of contiguous addresses managed by the memory manager. The actor's address space is large, for example 2^{32} addresses. Pages implement regions.

Actors in subsystems and the microkernel jointly manage three other abstractions:

- *Segment:* A unit of data encapsulation defined by the application and referenced by a capability.

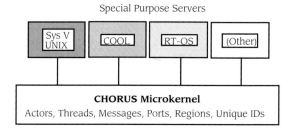

Figure 18.21
The CHORUS Microkernel and Servers

- *Capability:* A 128-bit key that uniquely references resources in the distributed system. Half of the capability is a Unique ID managed by the microkernel; the other half is defined by the subsystem.

- *Protection identifier:* An identifier appended to all messages by the microkernel and used by subsystems to authenticate the message.

A machine configuration consists of a set of *sites* interconnected by a *network*. A site may be a workstation or a CPU board in a multiprocessor, and a network may be a packet network or an internal bus. Each site has physical resources and is managed by a copy of the microkernel. An actor's address space is split into a user portion and a system portion, with all actors at the same site sharing the system portion of the address space.

The microkernel architecture is summarized in Figure 18.22. The supervisor implements the low-level handlers for external events such as interrupts and traps; hence, it is a machine-dependent module. The real-time executive implements thread-multiplexing and synchronization. It uses the supervisor for several different services, including interrupts for priority scheduling, although it is machine-independent. The VM manager implements a paged virtual memory, including page frame allocation and virtual address management. It is largely machine-independent, except for the interactions with the memory-mapping unit hardware. The VM manager is visible at the microkernel interface to allow a user space system server to participate in memory management. The supervisor, real-time executive, and VM manager provide local services. Global services are supported by the IPC manager through its message mechanism. The IPC manager implements a machine address space and location transparency and also provides higher-level mechanisms for RPCs and multicasting.

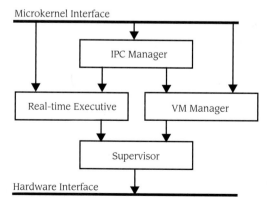

Figure 18.22
CHORUS Microkernel Architecture

18.8.1 ■ Process Management

The process management function addresses actors and threads. An actor bears a strong resemblance to Mach tasks, and a thread resembles a Mach thread. Threads use the actor's ports to receive communications from other actors. The port is identified by a capability. An actor has a default port used by other threads to reference the actor.

Threads are scheduled by the real-time executive using preemptive priority scheduling. Priorities of each thread are adjusted by the microkernel according to fairness and response criteria. Thread synchronization is accomplished using the common memory available to all threads in an actor.

18.8.2 ■ Interprocess Communication

The communication mechanism relies on the UI to implement location transparency for ports. Each port is referenced using a capability, and each capability contains a UI. Hence, when a task uses a capability to send a message to a port, it need not be concerned with the location of the actor that owns the port. Instead, the IPC manager is responsible for translating the UI into a network address, using the naming scheme in the supporting network. To avoid encoding any such scheme, such as internet addresses, into the microkernel, the IPC manager interacts with a subsystem component that is able to translate UIs to internet addresses.

In CHORUS, messages are simply byte streams rather than structured messages. The IPC manager copies the byte stream from the sender's address space into the port of the receiver's address space. Large messages use the same copy-on-write approach used in Accent.

A port group is a set of port UIs assigned to another UI. The port group UI is analogous to a multicast address in an Ethernet. When a message is sent to the port group, the IPC manager delivers a copy of the message to every port in the port group. Multicasting is used by many different subsystems to implement reliability algorithms on a network. It is also useful to implement designs in which a client "broadcasts" a request to a group of servers without knowing exactly which server it should use. The correct server responds to the multicast message, while all the others ignore it. CHORUS designers refer to this use as dynamic binding to a service, since the client need not be associated with any particular server until it needs to use it.

18.8.3 ■ Memory Management

A segment is a logical block of information, such as a files or swap area. Segments are mapped into a region in an actor's address space by a system actor executing in a subsystem, called a segment server, or *mapper*. Whereas the segment has a UI, the region has a virtual address and protection. Each region is mapped into page frames by the microkernel VM manager using demand paging. Hence, a reference to a segment is mapped to a region by a user space mapper. The region is mapped to a page frame by the nucleus and then referenced by the executing thread. A missing page fault is first handled by the supervisor and then passed to the VM manager. The VM manager informs the relevant mapper that it needs a page, and the mapper retrieves the target page from an arbitrary location according to its design principles. As in Mach, CHORUS implements the low-level paging mechanism in the microkernel and allows the page replacement policy to be implemented in the user space.

18.8.4 ■ Conclusion

The discussion in this section provides an overview of the organization of the CHORUS microkernel. Rozier et al. [1988] provide a complete discussion of the organization, behavior, and design rationale for CHORUS. Like Mach, CHORUS provides a commercial alternative to UNIX for network and multiprocessor environments. Just as Mach has enjoyed limited commercial success in the United States, CHORUS has enjoyed limited commercial success in the European Community.

18.9 ■ Summary

Operating systems include a diversity of functionality that spans process and resource management, memory management, file management, and device management. As was illustrated in Figure 18.2, the interactions among the various functions is logically complex, thus making it difficult to modularize the functions to minimize traffic among them. Over the last 40 years, designers have continued to experiment with software architectures to implement all of these functions in an efficient, flexible, and maintainable way. Until the 1980s, monolithic architectures were the dominant form of operating systems, including classic UNIX implementations. In the late 1960s and 1970s, researchers experimented with layered architectures and extensible nucleus approaches. Dijkstra's THE and Brinch Hansen's RC 4000 nucleus were important operating systems for their technology. IBM embraced the extensible nucleus machine with its VM nucleus in the 1970s. Economic considerations drove IBM to the VM approach, since the company marketed many different computers for which customers desired a single operating system interface. Conversely, some installations required that different operating systems be used on a single IBM machine. VM has proved to be a valuable component in IBM's operating system strategy.

Choices is a research OS based on the modular nucleus approach. It demonstrates the value of reuse in OS experimentation and continues to be valuable in its designer's OS and software engineering research. Objects, as opposed to full object-oriented technology, are used in many operating systems (including Windows NT). They allow the system to be designed to use capabilities to reference functions in distributed parts of the system, as is done in Mach, CHORUS, and others.

Today, microkernel-based operating systems are the emerging architecture. This chapter described how Mach and CHORUS use this technology to implement UNIX servers as well as real-time operating systems. Both are distributed message-passing operating systems with only the critical parts of the OS implemented in the microkernel. In this class of operating systems, the file system and parts of the process manager, resource managers, and memory managers are implemented in user space.

18.10 ■ Exercises

1. Many UNIX designers also participated in the Multics project. It is often stated that UNIX was designed to be a simple OS using many concepts and ideas from Multics. Draw some comparisons between UNIX and Multics.

2. Mach, CHORUS, and other operating systems use capabilities extensively. Explain how capabilities enable these systems to implement location transparency of entities in a distributed system. How do the capabilities used in CHORUS differ from the capabilities discussed in Chapter 14?

3. Can a Mach thread read a message it wrote to a task's port? Why or why not?

4. Regarding schedulable units of computation:

   a. Distinguish between a task and a thread in Mach.
   b. Distinguish between an actor and a thread in CHORUS.
   c. Distinguish between a process with two threads and two processes that each have one thread.

5. What is the distinction between a port set in Mach and a port group in CHORUS?

6. Both Mach and Chorus are implemented as groups of threads in the microkernel, yet they implement a UNIX system call interface. Speculate about how a procedure call interface can be implemented in the UNIX server, yet be implemented with threads.

7. What prevents the entire page replacement algorithm from being implemented in user space in Mach and CHORUS?

8. Choose a contemporary OS other than one discussed in this chapter and write a paper summarizing how the system addresses device management, file management, process management, and memory management. You do not need to provide a critical analysis of the papers describing the OS or of the OS itself. Part of the purpose of this exercise is for you to explore the technical literature. Do not use another textbook as the primary source of your information.

9. Which OS organization is used to implement Linux?

10. What is the unit of computation supported in Linux? Is there kernel-level thread support in Linux?

Glossary

absolute loader. See **loader.**

absolute program. A form of a program derived by the linkage editor when it combines relocatable object modules with library functions. The absolute program contains a representation of all object code in the program, although it will usually be translated into a new form by the absolute loader prior to execution.

abstract machine. See **virtual machine.**

access control list. A list of all subjects and their access rights kept by an object in a protection system.

ACL. See **access control list.**

ALU (arithmetical-logic unit). The unit that performs all arithmetical and logical instructions.

API (application programming interface). Defines a programming interface to a software module, in particular, to system software modules. Databases, window systems, and the APIs of other modules describe the data types and functions that are used to procure services from the module.

application. A program or process that is specific to a problem domain rather than generic across problem domains. For example, a processor scheduler is generic, but a classroom scheduler for a university is a domain-specific application.

application programming interface. See **API.**

arithmetical-logic unit. See **ALU.**

associative memory. Memory that addresses cells by using the contents of a key field on each cell rather than an explicit address. Associative memories are used to implement page tables.

avoidance, deadlock. A strategy for addressing deadlock in which the resource allocator decides if an allocation request can be honored, while guaranteeing that there is some feasible execution sequence that honors all outstanding requests.

batch system. A batch operating system services a collection of jobs, called a *batch*, by reading the jobs into the machine and then executing the programs for each job in the batch.

baud rate. Signaling rate for a communications device, in signals per second.

block status map. An in-memory map describing the allocation status of each block on a disk. It is common for the map entry to use one bit to represent each block's status.

busy-wait. A situation in which a process is blocked on a resource (or semaphore) but does not yield the processor.

byte-stream file. A low-level file in which information in the file is organized as a linear sequence of bytes. Byte i is accessed by first accessing byte $i - 1$.

C

---

c list. See **capability list.**

cache line. A unit information transfer into and out of a cache memory. Typically, a cache line is 16 to 128 bytes.

cache memory. A high-speed memory on the data path between the processor and the primary memory. When the processor reads a memory cell, the contents are copied to the cache, thus enabling subsequent reads to use the value in the cache.

capability. A unique, global name for an access right to an object in a system, originally used only as a right held by an subject to access an object.

capability list. A row in an access matrix in a protection mechanism. A capability list identifies the set of access rights to various objects in a system. Each access right is a capability.

channel. See **I/O processor.**

checkpoint. A snapshot of a process's complete status that can be used to restart a process at the point at which the checkpoint was taken.

circular wait. A situation in which process p_1 holds resource R_1 while it requests resource R_2, and process p_2 holds R_2 while it requests resource R_1. There may be more than two processes involved in the circular wait.

client process. A proactive process interacting with a reactive process—a server process—to obtain service.

client stub. System software residing in the client machine to prepare a remote procedure call, to issue the call to the server, to accept the result back from the server, and to return it to the calling program.

command line interpreter. A program that reads operating system commands from a job stream or interactive terminal and then executes them.

concurrent processing. Concurrent operation across a set of processes refers to the case in which the processes logically appear to be executing in parallel although they may be physically executing serially on a uniprocessor. Multiprogramming systems support concurrent processing in a sequential processor environment.

condition variable. A structure that may appear within a monitor, global to all procedures within the monitor, that can have its value manipulated by the wait, signal, and queue operations.

consumable resource. Any resource that is allocated to process but is never deallocated. Instead, the process consumes it. Each consumable resource must also have at least one producer process.

control unit. The part of the computer hardware that decodes instructions and then causes them to be executed.

CPU (central processing unit). See **processor.**

critical section. A segment of code that cannot be executed while some other process is in a corresponding segment of code. For example, a critical section might be code segments in two different programs that write a shared variable.

CSMA/CD (carrier-sense multiple access protocol with collision detection). This is the Ethernet local area network protocol.

D

---

daemon. A UNIX process that operates on behalf of the operating system rather than on behalf of any particular user. For example, the line printer daemon accepts print jobs as files and prints them as the printer becomes available.

datagram. A network transport level packet. Its addresses specify the sending and receiving locations using three-component addresses, `<net, host, port>`. UDP is the most widely used protocol for sending and receiving datagrams.

data link layer. An ISO OSI network architecture layer defining frame-based communication. This layer allows processes to send and receive frames of information across an individual network.

DBMS (database management system). System software that abstracts file operations to provide an interface to the storage system where users and programs can access records by using operations such as queries. This is a major area of computer science; it has entire books devoted to it.

deadlock. A situation that can arise when two or more processes hold resources and request others. Some process holds a resource that another wants while requesting a second resource, and the other process holds the second resource while requesting the first. Hence, neither process can progress.

demand paging. A page is loaded only when it is referenced.

detection and recovery. A deadlock strategy in which an algorithm is run to check the system for a deadlock. If it discovers a deadlock, then it preempts resources to remove it.

determinate. See **nondeterminate.**

device. A unit of a computer that can be used to store information, to transmit and receive information to/from another machine, and to export/import information to/from users.

device management. The part of the operating system that creates device abstractions and provides mechanisms for manipulating and controlling them.

device status table. An operating system table used to hold the pending state of a device operation that is currently in progress.

direct access device. See **random device.**

direct I/O. An I/O operation that is managed by the processor rather than by an auxiliary I/O processor.

direct memory access. See **DMA.**

directory. A set of logically associated files and other directories of files.

dirty bit. A flag used in a page table to indicate if a page has been written into since it was loaded.

disk cylinder. A set of corresponding tracks on a disk drive that incorporates multiple recording surfaces and a ganged read/write head.

disk sector. An angular portion of a track on a rotating disk that contains one block of information within a track that passes through the sector.

disk track. A circular recording area on a rotating storage medium. A disk will have several concentric rings that are divided by disk sectors to form blocks.

distributed memory. A general class of memory management schemes whereby physically separate blocks of memory are implemented on different machines yet are accessible from the address spaces of different processes.

DMA (direct memory access). A technique by which an I/O controller transfers information directly to/from the primary memory without intervention from the processor.

E

entry point. The first location of a program to be executed when the program is to be executed.

executable program. A program image loaded into primary memory in a form in which it is ready to execute.

extensible nucleus organization. A modular operating system organization intended to implement real- time systems, timesharing systems, and so on using a common set of underlying policy-independent modules.

F

fetch policy. A paging policy that decides when a page should be loaded into primary memory.

file. A named abstract resource capable of storing a byte stream for later access or from which a stream of bytes can be read to obtain data.

file descriptor. An OS data structure for keeping the status of a file.

file management. The part of the operating system that creates file abstractions and provides mechanisms for manipulating and controlling them.

free list. A linked list of unallocated blocks, usually in a file system.

frontend machine. A conventional von Neumann computer used to control an unconventional parallel machine.

G

Gantt chart. A two-dimensional chart that plots the activity of a unit on the y-axis versus the time on the x-axis. The chart quickly represents how the activities of the units are serialized or can overlap in their occurrence.

gateway. A service that interconnects two or more different domains, thus providing some form of translation among the domains. In the network context, the gateway interconnects two or more different networks so that packets can be exchanged among hosts attached to separate networks.

H
---

heterogeneous system. A parallel machine with different types of processors or a network of computers of different types.

hold-and-wait condition. A situation in which a process holds one resource at the same time that it requests another one.

homogeneous system. A parallel machine or network of machines that contains all the same type of processors.

horizontal architecture. See **layered organization.**

I
---

idempotent operation. An operation that can be applied repeatedly, producing the same effect as if it had been applied just once. An increment operation is not idempotent, but an assignment operation is. Idempotent operations are used in stateless protocols to make interoperation more reliable.

inclusion property. A property of certain page replacement algorithms whereby every page loaded under a page replacement algorithm with a page allocation of m would also have been loaded for a page allocation of $m + 1$.

indexed addressing. The contents of an index register, added to the address compiled into an address so as to derive the target operand address.

indirect addressing. The address compiled into the instruction word that references a memory cell containing the address of the target operand.

inode. File descriptor in a UNIX system.

input/output processor. See **I/O processor.**

internet. A collection of individual networks configured so that some hosts on each network are connected to other networks. The resulting network of networks can be thought of as a logical graph in which nodes are an entire network and edges are the gateway machines interconnecting the networks.

Internet Protocol. See **IP.**

interprocess communication. See **IPC.**

I/O processor. An autonomous input/output processor capable of operating at the same time as the central processor to direct the operation of one or more I/O devices.

IP (Internet Protocol). A network layer protocol derived from the ARPAnet that provides addresses with network, host, and port components. A protocol implementation also provides routing through the corresponding internet.

IPC (interprocess communication). The class of mechanisms used for two processes to exchange information using messages.

IR (instruction register). A control unit register that contains a copy of the instruction currently being decoded and executed.

instruction register. See **IR.**

interrupt. A signal that causes the control unit to branch to a specific location to execute code to service the occurrence of an external condition.

interrupt handler. An operating system routine that is executed whenever an interrupt occurs. It saves the processor state, then dispatches a device handler to service the device that caused the interrupt.

interval timer. See **programmable interval timer.**

L

LAN (local area network). A communication mechanism that allows multiple computers to exchange information among themselves.

latency time. In disk technology, the rotational delay that occurs once the read/write head is aligned with the target track. In a message-passing context, it is the message transmission delay time.

layered organization. An operating system organization in which the functionality is partitioned into an abstract machine hierarchy in which the functions in layer i are implemented in terms of the functions provided by layer $i - 1$.

least recently used replacement. See **LRU replacement.**

lightweight process. See **thread.**

link editor. A translation tool that combines relocatable object modules with library modules to produce an absolute program that is suitable for loading.

livelock. A phenomenon in which a set of processes are effectively deadlocked, although each can perform operations such as polling.

loader. Also called the *absolute loader.* A tool to retrieve an absolute program module from secondary memory, translate it into a format suitable for execution, and place the resulting executable image into primary memory.

local area network. See **LAN.**

locality. The property of a program in execution causing it to reference pages that it has recently referenced. Locality is caused by loops in code that tend to reference arrays or other data structures by indices.

lock. A flag associated with a resource such as a file or critical section indicating that the resource is in use or available.

long-term scheduler. A device used in batch spooling systems to allocate disk space to a spooled job so that it can begin to compete for memory.

LRU (least recently used) replacement. A page replacement algorithm that selects the loaded page referenced the longest time in the past.

M

MAR (memory address register). A memory unit register that is loaded with the address of a cell for a subsequent **read** or **write** operation to the cell.

maximum claim. A bound on the amount of resources a process will ever request in its session. The maximum claim is used in deadlock avoidance strategies.

MDR (memory data register). A memory unit register that is loaded with the datum to be written to the memory prior to the **write** operation and which contains the result after a **read** operation.

mechanism. An operating system function that can be used to implement many different policies without commitment to any specific policy. See also **policy.**

medium-term scheduler. Manages primary memory allocation.

memory address register. See **MAR.**

memory data register. See **MDR.**

memory hierarchy. A collection of individual memory components in which elements higher in the hierarchy tend to be faster, smaller, and more expensive than elements lower in the hierarchy.

memory management. The task of creating abstractions and providing mechanisms for manipulating and controlling memory abstractions.

memory-mapped I/O. A device organization in which software references various parts of the controller using addresses that have the same appearance as memory addresses.

missing page fault. An indication by the page translation mechanism signaling a failure to map a page into a page frame since the page is not loaded.

modular organization. A software organization in which the functionality is partitioned among logically independent components, with well-defined interfaces among the related modules.

monitor. An abstract data type that can be used by multiple processes. The monitor will allow only one process to use the monitor at a time.

monolithic organization. A software organization that places all software and data structures in one logical module, with no explicit interfaces between any parts of the software.

multidrop network. A network that can switch information between any two nodes in the network.

multiplexing, space. Sharing a resource by dividing it up into smaller units and allocating units to different processes. A process has exclusive control of its allocated units while other processes have exclusive control of other units at any given moment.

multiplexing, time. Sharing a resource by allocating the entire resource to one process for a time segment and then to another process for another time segment. A process has exclusive control of the entire resource at any given moment.

multiprocessing. A computer architecture that incorporates two or more processors.

multiprogramming. A style of process management in which multiple programs are loaded into the memory simultaneously and a short-term scheduler time- multiplexes the processor across the processes executing the programs.

mutual exclusion. Two or more processes cooperating so that only one of the processes has access to a shared resource at a time.

N

---

network layer. An ISO OSI network architecture layer that defines facilities to address host machines on remote networks and provides facilities for routing network packets across a collection of networks to be delivered to a host on a remote network.

nondeterminate. A situation in which there is no assurance that repeated execution of a parallel program will produce the same results. The differences are explainable by the order in which critical sections were executed among the individual processes in the community.

nonpreemptive scheduling. A strategy for time-multiplexing the processor whereby a process does not release the processor until it has completed its work.

nonuniform memory access. See **NUMA.**

NUMA (nonuniform memory access). A computer architectural style that calls for multiple memory modules. Each processor can access every memory module, although the access times vary depending on the relationship of the processor and the memory module to each other.

O

object. An instance of a class definition of an abstract data type. The object reacts to external messages. Each message causes the object to run a method that may issue other methods or execute arbitrary code from the class.

P

packet. The unit of information transmitted on contemporary subcommunication networks. A packet may contain from 1K to 4KB.

page table. A translation mechanism to convert page numbers into page frame addresses.

password. A string of characters that users provide to the computer to authenticate their login identity.

PC. There are two widely used meanings for this abbreviation. Its classic meaning is "program counter" register, which is in the control unit that addresses the memory cell that contains the next instruction to be executed. Its more currently popular, commercial meaning is "personal computer," specifically the IBM PC.

physical layer. The lowest level of the ISO OSI network architecture model for network communications. Defines how a process on a host machine sends and receives a byte of information and how the host machines exchange bytes.

pipe. The UNIX mechanism for passing information as a byte stream from one process to another. Pipes use the file interface.

placement policy. Paging that determines where the fetched page should be loaded in primary memory.

policy. A specific scheme for managing resources, independent of the means for implementing the scheme. See also **mechanism.**

preemptive scheduling. A strategy for time-multiplexing the processor whereby a running process is removed from the processor whenever a higher-priority process becomes ready to execute.

prefetch policy. A page-fetching strategy whereby the system loads pages before they are referenced.

presentation layer. An ISO OSI network architecture layer that provides facilities to translate data from the format of one domain to another.

prevention. A deadlock strategy whereby one of the four necessary conditions for deadlock is guaranteed to be false at all times.

primary memory. Memory for which an individual byte or word can be directly addressed and accessed by the processor.

privileged instruction. An instruction that can be executed only if the processor is in the supervisor mode. I/O instructions and instructions that effect the protection mechanisms are privileged, while all others are ordinary instructions.

process. A serial program in execution on a von Neumann computer.

process management. The task of creating the process abstraction and providing mechanisms to manipulate processes.

process status. The operating system record of the current details of a process's execution.

processor. The computation unit in a computer, consisting of the control unit to fetch and decode the stored program from primary memory and the ALU to execute arithmetic-logical instructions.

program. A list of instructions that can be executed sequentially by a process.

program counter. See **PC.**

program text. The list of instructions of a program in executable format.

programmable interval timer. A hardware device that produces an interrupt after a specified amount of time has elapsed. The time period is determined by software.

protection domain. An execution environment that determines the set of access rights a process has.

R

---

race condition. A condition in which the behavior of two or more processes depends on the relative rate at which each process executes its programs. A race condition can cause a pair of processes to violate a critical section or deadlock.

RAM (random access memory). The memory technology used to implement executable memory.

random device. A storage device in which the drive can access any block independent of the last block it accessed. Contrast with *sequential device.* An example of a random device is a magnetic disk drive.

randomly accessed device. See **random device.**

read-write head. The point of access in a byte-stream file; a mechanism to read from or write to a storage device.

reconfigurable device driver. A strategy for operating system design whereby a driver can be added to an operating system without recompiling or relinking the operating system code.

reference bit. A 1-bit flag in each entry in a page table that is cleared when any page is loaded and set when the particular page is referenced. On replacement, any page with its reference bit set has been referenced since the last page fault.

relocatable object module. A module created by a compiler or other source language translator from a single source program module.

remote memory. A distributed-memory design whereby logical primary memory is shared through a primary memory interface extension over the normal von Neumann interface.

replacement policy. A paging policy that determines which page should be removed from primary memory if all page frames are full.

resource. Any abstract machine environment entity referenced by the program and explicitly allocated to the process so that it can execute the program.

resource descriptor. An operating system data structure used to keep all information known about the status and characteristics of a resource.

resource isolation. The task of the system software that ensures the execution of concurrent programs does not allow individual program executions to interfere with one another.

resource management. The task of creating resource abstractions and providing mechanisms for manipulating and controlling resources.

reusable resource. A resource that can be allocated to a process but which must be released back to the resource manager at some later point. A system is configured with a fixed number of reusable resources.

reusable resource graph. A deadlock detection model that represents the allocation state of a system composed solely of reusable resources.

rights amplification. The case in which a process changes its domain to one that enables it to have more access rights than it had in its original domain.

rollback. The act of restarting a process at an earlier point in its computation—the last checkpoint. The result of a rollback is as if the process did not do any computation beyond the last checkpoint.

ROM (read only memory). A type of memory that has its contents written by a special device prior to being installed in the computer. Once the ROM is installed, the computer can read the memory but not rewrite its contents.

S

SCSI (small computer serial interface). An industry standard interface between devices and their controllers.

secondary memory. Memory that is addressed and accessed as blocks using I/O instructions. For example, disk and tape devices implement secondary memory.

seek time. The time needed to move the read/write heads to the target track in rotating storage devices.

segment descriptor. An entry in a segment table that contains a segment base address, a segment length, and protection bits.

segment table. A table to translate symbolic segment names to segment addresses in primary memory in a segmented virtual-memory system.

semaphore. An abstract data type that contains a nonnegative integer variable with P and V operations that test and set the variable. Semaphores are the fundamental synchronization in modern operating systems (see Chapter 8).

sequential device. A storage device in which blocks are physically stored so that block $i + 1$ can be accessed only after block i has been accessed. Magnetic tape drives are an example of sequential devices.

sequentially accessed device. See **sequential device.**

serially reusable resource. See **reusable resource.**

server process. A reactive process that responds to service requests from a client process.

server stub. The part of a RPC system that implements the called procedure. It accepts the RPC from the client stub, executes the procedure, and then returns the result to the client stub.

service time. The amount of time a process requires in the running state, using the CPU, before it is completed.

session layer. An ISO OSI network architecture layer providing facilities to manage virtual circuits that are implemented at the transport layer. It may also implement alternative forms of communication, such as RPC.

shared-memory multiprocessor. A multiprocessor in which every processor can access every unit of memory via an interconnection network.

shell. See **command line interpreter.**

short-term scheduler. A device that manages processor allocation.

signal, UNIX. A mechanism by which one process can notify another of the occurrence of an event. The sender raises the signal, and the receiver catches it by providing a function associated with the signal occurrence.

speedup. The ratio of time to execute a computation on one processor compared with the time to partition and execute it on N different processors.

spinlock. A shared lock that is implemented using busy-waiting.

stable storage. An algorithmic approach to guarantee that information committed to by an atomic **write** operation will either be saved or completely ignored. It is typically used in servers to assist in crash recovery (see Chapter 16).

stack algorithm. A class of page replacement algorithms whereby increasing the memory allocation is guaranteed not to cause more page faults.

starvation. A phenomenon in many resource allocation strategies in which some sets of processes are perpetually ignored because their priority is not as high as that of other processes. Starvation can occur in CPU scheduling, disk arm optimization, or any other kind of resource allocation scenario.

static variable. A variable that retains the last value stored in it even when it goes out of scope.

surrogate system process. The process associated with each hardware port that is configured to service interactive users.

superuser. A UNIX user mode that has full administrative authority in the machine.

swapping. A memory management technique where a process may periodically have its primary memory space deallocated. This forces the swapped-out process to compete for memory before it can once again compete for the processor.

system call interface. The set of data types and functions implemented by the operating system. These facilities are used by other system software and by application software.

system software. Software that provides an application programming environment on top of the hardware. It is provided to extend the functionality of the hardware so that it can be shared among simultaneous computer users and programmers can direct the hardware with reduced effort.

T

test-and-set instruction. The operation on a memory location that causes the contents of the specified memory location to be loaded into a CPU register (with condition code register contents set to reflect the value of the data) and the memory to be written with a value of TRUE.

thrashing. A phenomenon in paging systems whereby a process repeatedly replaces pages about to be referenced. This happens because the process has not been allocated a sufficient number of page frames.

thread. A unit of computation that contains minimum internal state and resources. It is associated with a normal, heavyweight operating system process.

throughput rate. The rate at which a computer completes requests to perform processing.

timesharing system. A style of multiprogramming operating system that supports interactive users.

transaction. A sequence of commands for which the effect on associated data is as if either all or none of the commands are executed.

transport layer. An ISO OSI network architecture layer that provides virtual circuits to implement byte streams and to ensure reliable delivery of information across an internet.

trap instruction. An instruction that causes the control unit to behave as if an interrupt had occurred. It is normally used to preempt the current process and to start the operating system.

turnaround time. The amount of time between the moment a process first enters the ready state and the moment the process exits the running state for the last time.

V

---

virtual address. An address generated by the program translation system that can be bound to a physical memory location as the program executes.

virtual machine. A design concept in which the programming model is implemented by the operating system rather than by the underlying physical hardware. That is, the operating system provides a simulation of hardware for the programmer's use.

virtual terminal. An operating system entity that presents a programming model similar to the one used with physical terminals, except that the operations are applied to a physical terminal according to user-applied restrictions. See also **window system.**

vnode. An abstract file descriptor, analogous to a UNIX inode, used in the Sun NFS remote file server.

von Neumann architecture. The basic organization for modern computers. The architecture uses a processor composed of an arithmetical-logical and control unit, a primary memory unit, and various I/O devices.

W

---

wait time. The time a process spends waiting in the ready state before its first transition to the running state.

window system. System software that provides a virtualized model of a physical terminal to the application programmer. Screen operations on the window model are applied to a bounded area of the physical screen.

write-back cache. A cache memory strategy where changing a value stored in the cache memory causes the corresponding value in the primary memory to be updated as a background activity.

write-through cache. A cache memory strategy where changing a value stored in the cache memory causes the corresponding value in the primary memory to be updated immediately.

Bibliography

Accetta, M., R. Baron, W. Bolosky, D. Golub, R. Rashid, A. Tevanian, and M. Young. "Mach: A New Kernel Foundation for UNIX Development." *Proceedings of the 1986 Usenix Summer Conference* (1986): 93–112.

ACM. *Proceedings of the ACM Symposium on Operating Systems Principles,* ACM Publications, published biannually.

Beck, Michael, Harald Böhme, Mirko Dziadzka, Ulrich Kunitz, Robert Magnus, and Dirk Verworner. *Linux Kernel Internals.* Reading, MA: Addison-Wesley, 1998.

Bennett, John K. "Distributed Smalltalk: Inheritance and Reactiveness in Distributed Systems." Ph.D. diss., University of Washington, Seattle, 1979.

Bershad, Brian N. "High Performance Cross-Address Space Communication." Ph.D. diss., University of Washington, Seattle, 1990.

Bershad, Brian, Edward D. Lazowska, and Henry M. Levy. "PRESTO: A System for Object-Oriented Parallel Programming." *Software Practice and Experience* 18, No. 8 (August 1988): 713–32.

Brinch Hansen, Per. *Operating System Principles.* Englewood Cliffs, NJ: Prentice Hall, 1973.

Brinch Hansen, Per. *The Architecture of Concurrent Programs.* Englewood Cliffs, NJ: Prentice Hall, 1977.

Brooks, F. P. *The Mythical Man-Month: Essays on Software Engineering* Reading, MA: Addison-Wesley, 1975.

Campbell, Roy H., Nayeem Islam, David Raila, and Peter Madany. "Designing and Implementing Choices: An Object-Oriented System in C++." *Communications of the ACM* 36, No. 9 (September 1993): 117–26.

Carriero, Nicholas, and David Gelernter. "The S/Net's Linda Kernel." *ACM Transactions on Computer Systems* 4, No. 2 (May 1986): 110–29.

Chappell, Geoff. *DOS Internals.* Reading, MA: Addison-Wesley, 1994.

Coffman, E. G., Jr., and Peter J. Denning. *Operating Systems Theory.* Englewood Cliffs, NJ: Prentice Hall, 1973.

Conway, M. "A Multiprocessor System Design." *Proceedings of the AFIPS Fall Joint Computer Conference* (1963): 139–46.

Corbato, M., M. Daggett, and R. C. Daley. "An Experimental Time-Sharing System." *Proceedings of the Spring Joint Computer Conference* 21 (1962): 334–35.

Courtois, P. J., F. Heymans, and D. L. Parnas. "Concurrent Control with 'Readers' and 'Writers'." *Communications of the ACM* 14, No. 10 (October 1971): 667–68.

Deitel, H. M. *Operating Systems,* 2nd ed., Reading, MA: Addison-Wesley, 1990.

Dennis, J. B., and E. C. Van Horne. "Programming Semantics for Multiprogrammed Computations." *Communications of the ACM* 9, No. 3 (March 1966): 117–26.

Dijkstra, E. W. "Co-operating Sequential Processes." in *Programming Languages,* edited by F. Genuys, New York: Academic Press (1968): 43–112.

Dijkstra, E. W. "The Structure of THE Multiprogramming System." *Communications of the ACM* 3, No. 9 (May 1968): 341–46.

Geist, G. A., and V. S. Sunderam. "Experiences with Network-Based Concurrent Computing on the PVM System." *Concurrency: Practice and Experience* 4, No. 4 (June 1992): 293–311.

Geist, Al, Adam Beguelin, Jack Dongarra, Weicheng Jiang, Robert Manchek, and Vaidy Sunderam. "PVM 3 Users' Guide and Reference Manual," Oak Ridge National Laboratories technical report (September 1994).

Graham, G. S., and Peter J. Denning. "Protection—Principles and Practice." *Proceedings of the AFIPS Sprint Joint Computer Conference* (1972): 417–29.

Hamilton, Graham, and Panos Kougiouris. "The Spring Nucleus: A Microkernel for Objects." *Proceedings of the 1993 USENIX Summer Conference* (1993): 147–60.

Hauser, Carl, Christian Jacobi, Marvin Thiemer, Brent Welch, and Mark Weiser. "Using Threads in Interactive Systems: A Case Study." *Proceedings of the Fourteenth ACM Symposium on Operating Systems Principles* (1993): 94–105.

Hennessy, John L., and David A. Patterson. *Computer Architecture: A Quantitative Approach.* San Mateo, CA: Morgan Kaufmann, 1990.

Hoare, C. A. R. "Monitors: An Operating System Structuring Concept." *Communications of the ACM* 17, No. 10 (October 1974): 549–57.

Hwang, K., and F. A. Briggs. *Computer Architecture and Parallel Processing.* New York: McGraw-Hill, 1984.

IEEE. *Proceedings of the International Symposium on Computer Architecture,* IEEE Publications, published annually.

IEEE and ACM. *Proceedings of the Conference on Architectural Support for Programming Languages and Operating Systems,* IEEE Publications and ACM Publications, published annually.

International Standards Organization. "Status of OSI (and Related) Standards." *ACM SIGCOMM Computer Communications Review* 20, No. 3 (July 1990): 83–99.

Jamieson, L. H., D. B. Gannon, and R. J. Douglass, *The Characteristics of Parallel Algorithms.* Cambridge, MA: MIT Press, 1987.

Johnson, Michael A. *The Linux Kernel Hacker's Guide,* Alpha Version 0.6, 1992a. Available from ftp site sunsite.unc.edu.

Johnson, Michael A. "Writing Linux Device Drivers," 1992b. Available from the World Wide Web at http://www.ssc.com/ssc/Employees/johnsonm/devices.

Jul, E., H. Levy, N. Hutchinson, and A. Black. "Fine-Grained Mobility in the Emerald System." *ACM Transactions on Computer Systems* 6, No. 1 (February 1988): 109–33.

Khalidi, Yousef A., and Michael N. Nelson. "An Implementation of UNIX on an Object-Oriented Operating System." *Proceedings of the 1993 USENIX Summer Conference* (1993): 469–80.

Kilburn, T., D. B. G. Edwards, M. J. Lanigan, and F. H. Sumner. "One-Level Storage System." *IRE Transactions,* EC-11, 2 (April 1962): 223–35.

Knuth, Donald E. *The Art of Computer Programming, vol. 1, Fundamental Algorithms,* 2nd ed., Reading, MA: Addison-Wesley, 1973.

Kohl, John, and B. Clifford Neuman. "The Kerberos Network Authentication Service (V5)," Internet draft (September 1992). Available from the World Wide Web at http://mitvma.mit.edu/mit/kerberos.html.

Lamport, Leslie. "Time, Clocks and the Ordering of Events in a Distributed System." *Communications of the ACM* 21, No. 7 (July 1978): 558–65.

Lamport, Leslie. "How to Make a Multiprocessor Computer that Correctly Executes Multiprocess programs." *IEEE Transactions on Computers,* C-28, 9 (September 1979): 241–48.

Lampson, Butler W., and David W. Redell "Experience with Processes and Monitors in Mesa," *Communications of the ACM* 23, No. 2 (February 1980): 105–17.

Lampson, Butler W., and Howard Sturgis. "Crash Recovery in a Distributed Data Storage System." Technical report, Xerox Palo Alto Research Center (April 1979).

Lazowska, Edward D., John Zahorjan, David R. Cheriton, and Willy Zwaenepoel. "File Access Performance of Diskless Workstations." *ACM Transactions on Computer Systems* 4, No. 3 (August 1986): 238–68.

Lewin, Mark. "Windows NT: An Architectural Overview." *USENIX Winter 1994 Conference Tutorial,* 1994.

Li, Kai, and Paul Hudak. "Memory Coherence in Shared Virtual Memory Systems," *ACM Transactions on Computer Systems* 7, No. 4 (November 1989): 321–59.

Linton, Mark A., John M. Vlissides, and Paul R. Calder. "Composing User Interfaces with InterViews." *IEEE Computer* 22, No. 2 (February 1989): 8–22.

Maekawa, Mamoru, Arthur E. Oldehoeft, and Rodney R. Oldehoeft. *Operating Systems Advanced Concepts.* Menlo Park, CA: Benjamin/Cummings, 1987.

McKusick, Marshall Kirk, Keith Bostic, Michael J. Karels, and John S. Quarterman. *The Design and Implementation of the 4.4 BSD UNIX Operating System.* Reading, MA: Addison-Wesley, 1996.

Messmer, Hans-Peter. *The Indispensable PC Hardware Book,* 2nd ed., Reading, MA: Addison-Wesley, 1995.

Metcalfe, Robert M., and David R. Boggs. "Ethernet: Distributed Packet Switching for Local Computer Networks." *Communications of the ACM* 19, No. 7 (July 1976): 395–404.

Nagar, Rajeev. *Windows NT File System Internals: A Developer's Guide,* Sebastapol, CA: O'Reilly & Associates, 1997.

Nemeth, Evi, Garth Snyder, Scott Seebass, and Trent R. Hein. *UNIX System Administration Handbook,* Englewood Cliffs, NJ: Prentice Hall, 1995.

Nutt, Gary J. *Centralized and Distributed Operating Systems.* Englewood Cliffs, NJ: Prentice Hall, 1992a.

Nutt, Gary J. *Open Systems.* Englewood Cliffs, NJ: Prentice Hall, 1992b.

Nutt, Gary. *Operating System Projects for Windows NT.* Reading, MA: Addison-Wesley, 1999a.

Nutt, Gary J. "Windows NT in the OS Curriculum." Department of Computer Science, University of Colorado, Technical Report Number CU-CS-880-99, February, 1999b.

Organick, E. I. *The Multics System: An Examination of Its Structure.* Cambridge, MA: MIT Press, 1972.

Ousterhout, John K., Hervé Da Costa, David Harrison, John A. Kunze, Mike Kupfer, and James G. Thompson. "A Trace-Driven Analysis of the UNIX 4.2 BSD File System." *Proceedings of the Tenth ACM Symposium on Operating Systems Principles* (1985): 15–24.

Peterson, G. L. "Myths About the Mutual Exclusion Problem." *Information Processing Letters.* 12, No. 3 (June 1981): 115–16.

Piscitello, David M., and A. Lyman Chapin. *Open Systems Networking: TCP/IP and OSI.* Reading, MA: Addison-Wesley, 1993.

Rashid, R., A. Tevanian, M. Young, D. Golub, R. Baron, D. Black, W. Bolosky, and J. Chew. "Machine-Independent Virtual Memory Management for Paged Uniprocessor and Multiprocessor Architectures." *IEEE Transactions on Computer Systems* 37, No. 8 (August 1988): 896–907.

Reed, D. P., and K. Kanodia. "Synchronization with Eventcounts and Sequencers," *Communications of the ACM* 22, No. 2 (February 1979): 115–23.

Richter, Jeffrey. *Advanced Windows,* 3rd ed., Redmond, WA: Microsoft Press, 1997.

Ritchie, Dennis M. "A Stream Input-Output System," *AT&T Bell Laboratories Technical Journal* 63, No. 8 (October 1984): 1897–910.

Ritchie, Dennis, and Ken Thompson. "The UNIX Time-Sharing System." *Communications of the ACM* 17, No. 7 (July 1974): 1897–920.

Rozier, M., V. Abrossimov, F. Armand, I. Boule, M. Gien, M. Guillemont, F. Herrmann, C. Kaiser, S. Langlois, P. Léonard, and W. Neuhauser. "CHORUS Distributed Operating Systems," *Computing Systems* 1, No. 4 (Fall 1988): 304–70.

Russinovich, Mark. "Inside the Native API." Technical report (March 1998). Available at www.sysinternals.com.

Sandberg, R., D. Goldberg, S. Kleiman, D. Walsh, and B. Lyon. "Design and Implementation of the Sun Network File System." *USENIX Proceedings* (June 1985): 119–30.

Satyanarayanan, M. "Scalable, Secure, and Highly Available Distributed File Access." *IEEE Computer* 23, No. 5 (May 1990): 9–21.

Schulzrinne, Henning. Personal communication regarding physical and data link layer network characteristics. April 1999.

Silberschatz, Abraham, and Peter B. Galvin. *Operating System Concepts,* 4th ed., Reading, MA: Addison-Wesley, 1994.

Singhal, Mukesh, and Niranjan G. Shivaratri. *Advanced Concepts in Operating Systems.* New York: McGraw-Hill, 1994.

Solomon, David A. *Inside Windows NT,* 2nd ed. Redmond, WA: Microsoft Press, 1998.

"Special Section on the Internet Worm." *Communications of the ACM* 32, No. 6 (June 1989): 677–710.

Stallings, William. *Operating Systems,* 2nd ed., Englewood Cliffs, NJ: Prentice Hall, 1995.

Stevens, W. Richard. *UNIX Network Programming.* Englewood Cliffs, NJ: Prentice Hall Software Series, 1990.

Stevens, W. Richard. *Advanced Programming in the UNIX Environment.* Reading, MA: Addison-Wesley, 1992.

Stevens, W. Richard. *TCP/IP Illustrated,* vol. 1. Reading, MA: Addison-Wesley, 1994.

Stevens, W. Richard, and Gary R. Wright. *TCP/IP Illustrated,* vol. 2. Reading, MA: Addison-Wesley, 1995.

Stoll, C. "Stalking the Wily Hacker." *Communications of the ACM* 31, No. 5 (May 1988): 484–97.

Sturgis, Howard W. *"A Postmortem for a Time Sharing System."* Ph.D. diss., University of California at Berkeley, 1973.

Sun Microsystems. "Networking on the Sun Workstation," Sun Microsystems, Inc., Document Number 800-1345–10 (September 1986).

Sun Microsystems. "Manual Page for the socket System Call," Sun Microsystems, Inc., Release 4.1 (January, 1990).

Swinehart, Daniel, Gene McDaniel, and David Boggs. "WFS: A Simple Shared File System for a Distributed Environment." *Proceedings of the Seventh ACM Symposium on Operating Systems Principles* (1979): 9–17.

Tanenbaum, Andrew S. *Operating Systems: Design and Implementation.* Englewood Cliffs, NJ: Prentice Hall, 1987.

Tanenbaum, Andrew S. *Modern Operating Systems.* Englewood Cliffs, NJ: Prentice Hall, 1992.

Tanenbaum, Andrew S. *Distributed Operating Systems.* Englewood Cliffs, NJ: Prentice Hall, 1995.

Tanenbaum, Andrew S., and R. van Renesse. "Distributed Operating Systems," *ACM Computing Surveys* 17, No. 4 (December 1985): 418–70.

Thacker, C. P., E. M. McCreight, B. W. Lampson, R. F. Sproull, and D. R. Boggs. "Alto: A Personal Computer," in *Computer Structures: Principles and Examples,* 2nd ed., New York: McGraw-Hill, 1981.

Usenix. *Usenix Windows NT Workshop* (August 1997), Seattle, Washington.

Walker, Bruce, Gerald Popek, Robert English, Charles Kline, and Greg Thiel. "The LOCUS Distributed Operating System." *Proceedings of the Ninth ACM Symposium on Operating System Principles* (October 1983): 49–70.

Zimmerman, H. "The ISO Model for Open Systems Interconnection." *IEEE Transactions on Communications,* Com-28, 4 (April 1980): 425–32.

Zimmerman, Philip. "Pretty Good Privacy: Public Key Encryption for the Masses, Version 2.6," 1994. Available at http://www.math.ucla.edu/pgp/PGP_Users_ Guide.html.

Index